THE LIBRARY The Library is operated by UU Bibliotech Ltd, a owned subsidiary company of the University of

University of Ulster at Magee

Due Back (subject to recall)

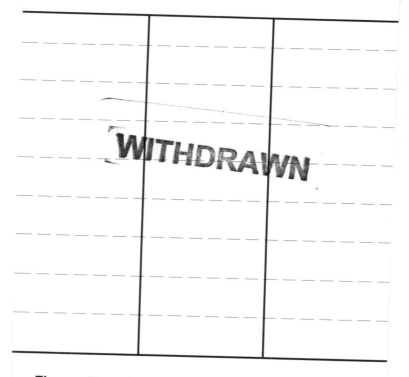
Fines will apply to items returned after due date

We work with leading authors to develop the
strongest educational materials in Law,
bringing cutting-edge thinking and best
learning practice to a global market.

Under a range of well-known imprints, including
Longman, we craft high quality print and
electronic publications which help readers to understand
and apply their content, whether studying or at work.

To find out more about the complete range of our
publishing, please visit us on the World Wide Web at:
www.pearsoneduc.com

Insolvency Law:

Corporate and Personal

by

Andrew R. Keay LLB; MDiv; LLM; PhD
Professor of Corporate and Commercial Law and
Director of the Centre for Business Law and Practice
Department of Law, University of Leeds

Peter Walton LLB
Senior Lecturer in Law,
School of Legal Studies,
University of Wolverhampton

PEARSON
Longman

Harlow, England • London • New York • Boston • San Francisco • Toronto
Sydney • Tokyo • Singapore • Hong Kong • Seoul • Taipei • New Delhi
Cape Town • Madrid • Mexico City • Amsterdam • Munich • Paris • Milan

Pearson Education Limited
Edinburgh Gate
Harlow
Essex CM20 2JE

and Associated Companies throughout the world

Visit us on the World Wide Web at:
www.pearsoneduc.com

ISBN 0582 43719 9

British Library Cataloguing-in-Publication Data
A catalogue record for this book is available from the British Library.

Library of Congress Cataloging-in-Publication Data

Keay, Andrew R.
 Insolvency law: corporate and personal / by Andrew R. Keay and Peter Walton.
  p. cm.
 Includes bibliographical references and index.
 ISBN 0-582-43719-9 (pbk.)
 1. Bankruptcy–England. 2. Bankruptcy–Wales. I. Walton, Peter, 1965– II. Title.

KD2139.K43 2003
346.4207'8–dc21

20003050671

10 9 8 7 6 5 4 3 2 1
06 05 04 03

Typeset in 10/12 pt New Baskerville by 68
Printed in Great Britain by Henry Ling Ltd, at the Dorset Press, Dorchester, Dorset

Contents

Part II Non-Terminal Insolvency   **49**

16   The Players in a Liquidation   253

17   The Liquidator   261

Preface

Insolvency was until recently subsumed under company law and commercial law, but over the past decade it has become a separate discipline within law. And while at undergraduate level corporate insolvency issues are often still tacked on to the end of a company law course and bankruptcy is lucky to find its way into a commercial or business law course, there are quite a number of insolvency law modules taught to both law and business students in England and Wales. Also, insolvency law modules or specialist corporate insolvency modules have become quite popular at LLM level and even as electives in Legal Practice Courses. A reasonably comprehensive and readable text is needed for these modules and this publication endeavours to meet this need. Additionally, it is intended that this book might be of use to legal and accounting practitioners, particularly those who want an exposition of fundamental issues or are coming new to the field. We should point out that the book is, predominantly, a doctrinal study of insolvency law. In places we do refer to theoretical discussions, particularly in Part I, and to the need for reform, but for the most part we limit ourselves to an exposition of the current law given space constraints.

Given the anticipated readership of the book, it is not intended to provide an exhaustive treatment of insolvency. That would be impossible in a volume of this length and kind, unless the treatment was little more than superficial. We have endeavoured to keep the book to a manageable size, so that it is more easily read and it is not too daunting. Some areas that might justify inclusion in a book of insolvency, but are of marginal relevance or are not frequently considered in practice have not been discussed. We have sought to focus on the most critical aspects of insolvency law given the state of the law at the present time and the likely areas of development in the near future. One area that is becoming increasingly important is that of cross-border insolvency. This is a complex area and we do not think that we could do justice to it in a book of this kind. There are separate volumes that deal with the topic. Also, we have refrained from giving long expositions of matters relevant to procedure. While we have mentioned some of the more critical aspects of procedure in some places, we are generally of the view that if the reader wishes to become conversant with most procedural steps either reference to a specialist text or the Insolvency Rules themselves is the best course of action.

Where possible we have inserted citations of cases and statutes in the body of the text for ease of reference. However, in some situations it has been more appropriate to include the citations in footnotes. We have endeavoured to keep footnotes to a minimum, and have only used them, in the main, to deal with issues that are deemed to be worth considering, but which would inhibit the flow of the text if referred to in the body of the book.

A consequence of keeping the book within manageable proportions is that while we have provided some authorities for the propositions stated, we have not included references to all relevant cases. Likewise we have, from time to time, included in the footnotes references to helpful articles and books, but we have not attempted to refer to all relevant materials that are available. But we have included at the end of each Part a list of some of the articles and books that either we have found most helpful or we believe might be of assistance to others. Also, we have not embarked on discussions of a large number of cases as this, again, would not be possible for a book covering such a large range of areas of law. We have refrained, except where necessary, from quoting statutory provisions as we assume that readers will have access to the relevant pieces of legislation.

Essentially, while the book purports to provide an exposition of insolvency law principles that apply in England and Wales, we do discuss in places some interesting contentious issues. However, again because of length, and also so that the book does not become overly complex, we have refrained from dealing with these issues in great detail. More specialist texts such as (in no particular order) I.F. Fletcher, *The Law of Insolvency*, 3rd edn, Sweet & Maxwell (2002), R. Goode, *Principles of Corporate Insolvency Law*, 2nd edn, Sweet & Maxwell (1997), A.R. Keay, *McPherson's Law of Company Liquidation*, Sweet & Maxwell (2001), E. Bailey, H. Groves and C. Smith, *Corporate Insolvency Law and Practice*, 2nd edn, Butterworths (2001), C. Berry E. Bailey and S. Schaw-Miller, *Personal Insolvency Law – Law and Practice*, 3rd edn, Butterworths (2001), R. Pennington, *Pennington's Corporate Insolvency Law*, 2nd edn, Butterworths (1997), G. Lightman and G. Moss, *The Law of Receivers and Administrators of Companies*, 3rd edn, Sweet & Maxwell (2000) and D. Milman and C. Durrant, *Corporate Insolvency: Law and Practice*, 3rd edn, Sweet & Maxwell (1999) might be referred to for more extensive discussion. Reference is made in the book from time to time to some of these and other specialist texts.

As alluded to above, the main purposes of the book are to act: as a text for law and commerce students, at both undergraduate and postgraduate level; as a reference tool for lawyers and insolvency practitioners; and as an introduction to the area for those practitioners who wish to familiarise themselves with the essential principles and issues in insolvency law.

The book is published at an important time for insolvency law in the UK. Recently, Parliament enacted the Enterprise Act, a wide-ranging statute that, *inter alia*, introduced some significant changes to insolvency law. The foremost are probably the overhaul of the administration process, the abolition of administrative receivership in all but a few limited cases, the abolition of the Crown preference and the introduction of a new bankruptcy set-up including the advent of bankruptcy restriction orders. We endeavour to address these innovations and some of the issues that accompany them in the text. However, it must be emphasised that the bankruptcy provisions in the Enterprise Act 2002 are not going to be operative until 2004 and the other insolvency provisions in the legislation were not operative when the book went to press. We have, however, assumed all of the insolvency provisions in the Act, save for the bankruptcy provisions, to be in operation.

While we have discussed matters relevant to all parts of the book, for the most part Andrew Keay was responsible for the writing of Parts I, III, IV, VI, VIII and IX, and Peter Walton was responsible for writing Parts II, V, and VII.

We have endeavoured to use gender neutral language where possible. In the places where we have had to use pronouns, we have attempted to be encompassing by referring to both the masculine and feminine. In situations where the use of both pronouns makes the exposition cumbersome, we have used the masculine pronouns, 'he' and 'his', with the intention of referring to both male and female.

In recent years the Internet has become more and more important for all professionals and students. In places we refer to websites that are either helpful or the source of our commentary. Of particular interest are the following sites:

www.insolvencyservice.gov.uk (the Insolvency Service);
www.dti.gov.uk (the Department of Trade and Industry);
www.companieshouse.gov.uk (Companies House).

We have debts as authors. Andrew Keay would like to thank Rhonda for her usual support and patience when he engages in a writing exercise. Peter Walton would like to thank Debs for her constant support, understanding and crowd control skills.

We have endeavoured to state the law as it was available to us as at 1 January 2003.

Andrew Keay
Peter Walton

Leeds and Wolverhampton

Abbreviations

Abbreviation	Name
AC	Appeal Cases
ACLC	Australian Company Law Cases
ACLR	Australian Company Law Reports
ACSR	Australian Companies and Securites Reports
All ER	All England Law Reports
BCC	British Company Law Cases
BCLC	Butterworths Company Law Cases
BPIR	Bankruptcy and Personal Insolvency Reports
BRO	Bankruptcy Restriction Order
BRU	Bankruptcy Restrictions Undertaking
CA	Court of Appeal
CDDA	Company Directors' Disqualification Act
Ch D	Chancery Division
CLR	Commonwealth Law Reports
CPR	Civil Procedure Rules
CVA	Company Voluntary Arrangement
DPP	Director of Public Prosecutions
DTI	Department of Trade and Industry
EHRR	European Human Rights Reports
EPA	Environmental Protection Act
Eq	Equity
ERA	Employment Rights Act
F & F	Foster and Finlasoin's Nisi Prius Reports
FLR	Family Law Reports

IIR	International Insolvency Review
IL&P	International Law and Practice
INSOL	International Association of International Insolvency Practitioners
IR	Insolvency Rules
IVA	Individual Voluntary Arrangement
KB	Kings Bench
KBD	Kings Bench Divison
LJ Ch	Law Journal Reports, Chancery (1831–1946)
LPA	Law of Property Act
LT	Law Times (1859–1965)
M & W	Meeson and Welsby's Exchequer Reports
Mer	Merivale's Chancery Reports
NPC	New Property Cases
PAYE	Pay As You Earn
QB	Queens Bench
QBD	Queens Bench Division
Qd R	Queensland State Reports (1958-)
SJ	Solicitors Journal (Old)
St R Qd	State Reports (Queensland)
UNCITRAL	United Nations Commission on International Trade Law
VAT	Value Added Tax
VLR	Victorian Law Reports (1875–1956)
WLR	Weekly Law Reports
WR	Weekly Reporter (1853–1906)

Table of Cases

Table of Statutes

Table of Statutory Instruments

Table of International Legislation

Acknowledgements

We are grateful to the folowing for permission to reproduce copyright material:

R3 (The Association of Business Recovery Professionals) for permission to reproduce Clause 7 from their Standard Conditions for Individual Voluntary Arrangements (March 2002) in Chapter 33. This is subject to the following conditions of use:

1. Copyright of the attached Standard Conditions is the property of the Association of Business Recovery Professionals (hereinafter referred to as 'R3').
2. No liability attaches to R3 in respect of the use of the Standard Conditions or any consequence thereof or in respect of any proposed or approved arrangement of which the Standard Conditions form a part.
3. R3 licences all its members to use the Standard Conditions without payment of a fee subject as follows:
    -   the Standard Conditions must be used in their entirety, or alternatively
    -   the proposal of which they form part must draw attention to any ommisions or variations and give reasons for them.
4. Members of R3 may authorise the use of the Standard Conditions by debtors, but subject to the conditions set out in paragraph 3.
5. Other persons wishing to use the Standard Conditions may obtain a licence to do so from R3, for which a fee may be charged. Use of the Standard Conditions by other persons is subject to the conditions set out in paragraph 3.
6. If the Standard Conditions are used in any published work the conditions of use must be made clear.
7. If R3 amends the Standard Conditions users must specify the version they are using.

8. Use the Standard Conditions does not relieve the nominee of the requirement to issue a full copy of the proposal, including the Standard Conditions, to every creditor.
9. Where the Standard Conditions are used they must be fully explained to the debtor.
10. Any variations to the Standard Conditions should not seek to affect statutory rights or obligations.

Association of Business Recovery Professionals
March 2002

In some instances we have been unable to trace the owners of copyright material, and we would appreciate any information that would enable us to do so.

Part I

Introduction

This Part of the book is very much introductory in character. It is designed primarily to lay the foundation for the balance of the book and, more specifically: to introduce the reader to an idea of where insolvency fits in the world in which we live; to provide some historical background; to explain the concept of insolvency and its meaning; to introduce the principles, purposes and theory underpinning insolvency law; to explain the insolvency regime that applies in England and Wales; to set out the options that are generally available to insolvents, both individual and corporate; and finally, to explain the layout of the book.

Except where indicated to the contrary, any reference to 'the Act' or to section numbers will be references to the Insolvency Act 1986. Except where indicated to the contrary, any reference to 'the Rules' or to rule numbers will be references to the Insolvency Rules 1986.

Chapter 1

Introduction

1.1 The context

Putting it simply, insolvency law is concerned with companies and individuals who are debtors and who are unable to repay their debts. Such a law is going to be necessary in a system that employs credit and, of course, life in the UK is very dependent on credit. At one time, not too far in the past (perhaps 15 years ago), it would have been possible to find that most people, not associated with the law and even some associated with it, had either not heard the word 'insolvency' or did not understand what it meant. It is submitted that that is no longer the case. The savage recession of the last days of the 1980s and the early 1990s which saw some high-profile companies (e.g. Maxwell Communication Corporation, Bishopsgate Investment Management Ltd, Bank of Credit and Commerce International) collapse and huge leaps in the number of people entering bankruptcy, together with more and more significant media coverage of corporate collapses at the end of the twentieth century and the beginning of this century, has seen to that.

In recent times we have seen, for instance, the collapse of Enron and the problems of WorldCom in the United States, and the insolvency of HIH Insurance and Ansett Airlines in Australia and Marconi, Railtrack and ITV Digital in the UK, as well as the well-documented struggles experienced by Equitable Life. All of these companies were regarded, not as fly-by-night companies, but as substantial companies that had a significant share of the relevant markets and were worth investing in. The fact that many English professional football clubs, which are household names in England (such as Leicester City, Derby County, Coventry City, Crystal Palace, Bradford City, Hull City, Barnsley),[1] have struggled

---

[1] Even Italian clubs have not been saved the ignominy of being subjected to some form of administration. For example, Fiorentina.

financially, most of which have entered in the past, such as Bradford City, or are, at the time of writing, in administration, such as Leicester City, has further brought home insolvency to the British public in recent years. People have begun to realise that the insolvency of a large company, in particular, can have knock on effects for others. Take for example, the financial woes at the car-maker, Rover. Before a consortium was put together to buy the car-maker from BMW, it looked as if the car factory would be closed and that would throw thousands of people living in the West Midlands out of work. For when a big company like Rover stops production it sends a ripple effect through the local communities.[2] Because the major employer ends its production suppliers and those who rely in turn on the suppliers are often pushed into insolvency. Rather worryingly, we have seen in the UK the continuation of a significant number of individuals becoming bankrupt, despite the fact that since about 1996 the UK has enjoyed good economic conditions – low interest rates, low unemployment and low inflation – and the economic strength to ride out a downturn in the United States' economy in 2000. The bankruptcy figures are most instructive. In 1960 only 2,944 persons became bankrupt. This probably reflected the fact that few people were conversant with the notion of insolvency. But by 1992, when the effect of the recession at the end of the 1980s was really biting, the numbers rose, alarmingly, to 32,106. From 1993–1999 the figures fell, but in 2000 onwards we have seen increases.

The broader perception of insolvency as a not uncommon phenomenon in British life parallels, not surprisingly, the rise of insolvency law as a separate field of law in the UK. Until the late 1980s insolvency law in the UK was rarely the subject of scholarly articles and was often never broached in undergraduate and postgraduate law courses. If it was, it was generally simply tacked onto the end of company law modules, or mentioned briefly in commercial law modules. Now, however, there are journals devoted to insolvency law and general journals even carry articles focusing on relevant insolvency issues. Many universities in their company law modules now include corporate insolvency as a separate topic in the module and a number of university law schools now offer insolvency law as an option, both at undergraduate and postgraduate level. More and more legal practitioners have during the past 15 years specialised in insolvency law and related areas. Many practitioners, both legal and accounting, have come to realise that insolvency law impinges on many other areas of the law, such as company, family, employment, banking, consumer and environmental law, just to mention a few. Certainly while it cannot be said that insolvency has enjoyed significant government focus, since 1986 the British government, as we will shortly

---

[2] See A. Keay, 'Insolvency Law: A Matter of Public Interest?' (2000) 51 NILQ 509.

see, has devoted more resources and time to the issues surrounding insolvency law than ever before. The cynic might say that the government has had to do so due both to the failure of past governments to do anything worthwhile and to make them look good by tackling the financial malaise affecting some businesses. The most recent attentions of the government have, as we will shortly consider, seen the enactment of legislation to lessen the effects of insolvency on individuals and to streamline the procedure to be followed to try to rescue companies that are suffering from insolvency.

The heightened interest in, and focus on, insolvency law in the UK is mirrored in other jurisdictions. Insolvency law, or as it is usually referred to, 'bankruptcy law', in the United States has had a prominent role for many years and particularly since the late 1970s when a form of insolvency administration known as 'Chapter 11 bankruptcy', utilised by many US corporations that are global players, such as Continental Airlines, WorldCom, United Airlines and K-Mart (the retailer), was introduced. The story of the rise in the awareness of insolvency in the UK is very similar to the same development in Australia (whose insolvency law framework is modelled on the English), from where the present form of administration (discussed in detail in Part II) hails. There have been significant discussions on the international stage for some years, but particularly in the last decade, about streamlining the insolvency administration of global enterprises. This is known as cross-border insolvency. It is trite to state that, due to increased globalism, the insolvency of a company in one country can affect companies and people in many more countries than just those in the insolvent's home jurisdiction. This effect can be direct, or it can even be indirect as we saw when Enron collapsed in the United States. This collapse indirectly affected the positions of many companies and the lives of countless people around the world.

Until recently attempts to make it easier for insolvency practitioners to administer insolvent companies that had been trading across borders bore little fruit. INSOL (International Association of International Insolvency Practitioners) had made some headway in the 1980s and early 1990s at getting countries to think a little more internationally when it came to insolvencies. However, it was not until in 1997 that a major step was taken when UNCITRAL (United Nations Commission on International Trade Law) adopted a Model Law on Cross-Border Insolvency which was approved by the General Assembly on 15 December 1997.[3] The General

---

[3] For a discussion of the Model Law, see, for instance, in I.F. Fletcher, *The Law of Insolvency*, 3rd edn, Sweet & Maxwell, London (2002) at 854–62; G. Lightman and G. Moss, *The Law of Receivers and Administrators of Companies*, 3rd edn, Sweet & Maxwell, London (2000) at 552–61.

Assembly of the United Nations established UNCITRAL in order to act as a vehicle for the United Nations to play a greater part in 'reducing the disparities caused by the domestic rules governing international trade'.[4] The Model Law was designed to permit countries to adapt it to their own conditions and needs, so as to gain greater acceptance around the world, although UNCITRAL's recommendation to countries has been that they should make as few changes as possible. It must be added that the Model Law is an attempt to facilitate more beneficial administrations of insolvent estates and does not purport to confer substantive rights, something that is left to individual countries. Following the adoption of the Model Law, a Guide to Enactment of the Model Law was issued by UNCITRAL to aid states that wanted to enact the Model Law by way of their own legislative instruments. The Insolvency Act 2000 made provision for the Model Law to be given effect in the UK by Regulations made by Statutory Instrument.

Also, in May 2000 a European Community (EC) Regulation (No.1346/2000) was adopted and this imposes control over the exercise of jurisdiction to commence insolvency proceedings in any of the states comprising the EU and provides uniform rules for choice of law and the law applying to proceedings. A couple of years was allowed for states to make changes to their laws to accommodate the Regulation and from 31 May 2002 the Regulation applied across the EU.[5]

The UNCITRAL Model Law, together with other promising contacts and commitments, like the EC Regulation on Insolvency Proceedings, will, it is hoped, make insolvency administration easier and will bear more fruit for creditors. We may even see more companies saved from the scrap heap as rescue packages are formulated for implementation across borders as well in national contexts.

Insolvency law is voluminous and growing all of the time. What we have sought to do in the remaining part of the book is to tackle the formal insolvency administrations permitted under law, as well as explaining some of the informal arrangements that do occur and address the primary issues that have to be faced in the course of an insolvency administration.

With the above as background we come to considering the field of insolvency law, no longer the poor relation of commercial law and no longer regarded as peripheral.

---

[4] P. Omar, 'The UNCITRAL Insolvency Initiative: a five-year review' [2002] *Insolvency Lawyer* 228 at 228.

[5] For a discussion of the Regulation, see, for example, I.F. Fletcher, *The Law of Insolvency*, 3rd edn, at 829–52; R. Obank, 'Cross-Border Harmonisation of Insolvency Proceedings and the Quest for Comity Parts 1, 2 & 3' (2002) 17 JIBFL 89; 126; 169; J. Goldring, 'The new European insolvency regulation – a synopsis' (2002) 18 IL&P 52; G. Moss, 'The Impact of the EU Regulation on UK Insolvency Proceedings' (2002) 11 IIR 139.

1.2 Historical background

1.2.1 *General*

It is not intended to provide a detailed discussion and evaluation of the history of insolvency law, but a few comments might be helpful to provide some background for the reader in coming to an understanding as to how insolvency law has developed over the years.[6]

There have been various kinds of laws regulating the relationship between creditors and debtors for a very long time. One commentator has traced such laws as far back as the Hammurabi dynasty, in Babylon, which may have existed in about 2250 B.C.[7] From that time we can see that many different cultures have provided for the situation where a person becomes a debtor and unable to pay his or her debts. As commerce has developed so have the laws regulating the credit relationship. By necessity, these laws have had to deal with the consequences of a person being unable to pay his or her debts. Without doubt, many of the laws and customs which have arisen over the years (particularly those introduced by the Romans) have, directly or indirectly, found their way into the laws of insolvency which we have today.

1.2.2 *Bankruptcy*

The insolvency of companies is a relatively modern phenomenon, because the limited liability company is a rather recent form of legal animal. Individual insolvency, which until recent times usually meant bankruptcy, dominates the early history of insolvency in England and Wales. The law of bankruptcy can be traced back to the law that was applied in a number of Italian city states to merchants during the medieval period.[8] This law had its roots in Roman law.[9] Like the laws of these Italian states, in medieval times the early bankruptcy laws of England were formulated to act as an additional remedy to enable a creditor to attach the property of the debtor.[10]

The beginning of insolvency law in England is usually taken as the enactment of the first bankruptcy statute in 1542,[11] although the

---

[6] Professor Ian Fletcher provides a useful outline of the history in I.F. Fletcher, *The Law of Insolvency*, 3rd edn, at 6–10. A readable account of the history of bankruptcy law is provided in D. Rose, *Lewis' Bankruptcy Law*, 11th edn, Law Book Co, Sydney (2000) at 8–18.

[7] L. Levinthal, 'The Early History of Bankruptcy Law' [1918] *University of Pennsylvania Law Review* 223 at 230.

[8] Jordan and Warren, *Bankruptcy*, Foundation Press (1985) at 17.

[9] Ibid.

[10] A. Keay, 'Balancing Interests in Bankruptcy Law' [2001] *Common Law World Review* 206 at 222.

[11] 34 & 35 Hen 8, c. 4.

common law stretching back to medieval times did make some provision for debtors. The 1542 statute sought to prevent 'crafty debtors' escaping the realm,[12] to ensure that all of the debtor's assets were available for creditors and that these assets were divided equally and rateably among the debtor's creditors. It is safe to say that at this point in time and for some years later, bankruptcy was regarded as quasi-criminal and even criminal by some such as Lord Kenyon who said, in 1798 in *Fowler v Padget*[13] 'Bankruptcy is considered as a crime and a bankrupt in the old laws is called an offender'. This was in line with the general view that bankrupts were fraudsters. Bankruptcy was, during the sixteenth century and all the way until the nineteenth century, restricted to 'traders', which meant that those persons who were not traders could not be bankrupted, leaving them subject to the general debtor laws which were unrealistic and generally unfair, essentially because imprisonment was the main 'remedy' invoked by creditors.[14]

From 1542 until the last one in 1914, there were numerous bankruptcy statutes enacted for England and Wales, many of which were passed to overcome some inefficiency or inequity produced by their precursors. It has been asserted that:

> For the most part the history of bankruptcy law in England manifests a litany of *ad hoc* decision-making, with changes based on pragmatism and not predicated on any policy or attempt to achieve a balance between the stakeholders. Parliament reacted and over-reacted to every problem or perceived problem which arose.[15]

Notwithstanding the volume of legislation, it is possible to pick out, besides the initial bankruptcy statute in 1542, some critical points. Perhaps the first was legislation in 1705[16] which gave the Lord Chancellor the authority to discharge a bankrupt once he or she had a certificate of the bankruptcy commissioners providing that there had been full disclosure and adherence to their directions. Discharge has been, ever since, a marked aspect of Anglo-American law. In 1825 legislation[17] allowed debtors to initiate proceedings for their own bankruptcy. Hitherto, bankruptcy could only occur where a creditor took proceedings. Subsequently, in the Bankruptcy Act 1869,[18] bankruptcy became something that was open to all persons and not just traders.

---

[12] I. Treiman, '*Escaping the Creditor in the Middle Ages*' (1927) 43 LQR 230 at 233–4.

[13] (1798) 7 Term Rep 509; 101 ER 1103.

[14] A. Keay, 'Balancing Interests in Bankruptcy Law' [2001] *Common Law World Review* 206 at 222–5.

[15] Ibid at 225.

[16] 3 Anne, c. 17. The legislation was not in fact passed until 19 March 1706.

[17] 6 Geo IV, c. 16.

[18] 24 and 25 Vict c. 134; section 69.

1.2.3 *Corporate insolvency*

With the growth of joint stock companies during the nineteenth century came legislation to regulate the winding up of such entities.[19] The Joint Stock Companies Act 1844[20] incorporated companies that registered under its provisions. But the first statute enacted to regulate the winding up of companies was the Winding-up Act 1844.[21] Until this latter statute creditors could proceed not only against the company's property but also against the property of shareholders. The Winding-up Act provided for the first time that remedies of creditors of companies only extended to company property. Its purpose was, *inter alia*, to enable companies to be forced into bankruptcy in a like manner to individuals.[22] After this statute there were a few more statutes introduced to govern the winding up of companies in England and Wales,[23] and then from the time of the enactment of the Companies Act 1862,[24] the winding up provisions were incorporated in companies legislation. The similarity between bankruptcy and winding up meant that many of the principles included in bankruptcy legislation were adopted by statutes regulating company windings up. While companies have been, and are, wound up for several reasons other than insolvency, insolvency is easily the most common reason for winding up and is the one on which we focus.[25]

At one time winding up was the only real option available when a company was insolvent, but as companies became more critical to commercial life and legislation developed, provision has been made for forms of insolvency administration other than winding up and this book will discuss the traditional options available. The same can be said in relation to personal insolvency. At one stage there was little option but for a person who was insolvent to let his or her creditors initiate bankruptcy proceedings to send him or her bankrupt, or, since the nineteenth century, to actually commence proceedings himself or herself to become a bankrupt. But in more recent years there are viable options for individual debtors to consider.[26]

1.2.4 *Modern developments*

Notwithstanding the fact that bankruptcy and winding up were very similar, the provisions dealing with them were retained in separate legislation – for the most part the Bankruptcy Act and the Companies Act. Not only that,

---

[19] For a detailed discussion of the development of winding up law, see A. Keay, *McPherson's Law of Company Liquidation*, Sweet & Maxwell, London (2001) at 11–24.

[20] 7 & 8 Vict c. 110.

[21] 7 & 8 Vict c. 111.

[22] Section 1.

[23] A. Keay, *McPherson's Law of Company Liquidation* at 17–21.

[24] 25 & 26 Vict c. 89.

[25] See Part V in particular.

[26] A. Keay and M. Murray, *Insolvency: Personal and Corporate Law and Practice*, 4th edn, Law Book Co, Sydney (2002) at 6–7.

bankruptcy and winding up were administered by separate courts pursuant to different procedural rules. This produced some unusual situations. For example, the law on the avoidance of transactions entered into prior to bankruptcy and contained in the Bankruptcy Act, was incorporated by reference into the Companies Act to cover the avoidance of pre-winding up transactions. The problem was not only that the Companies Act did not contain the relevant substantive provisions, but some of the bankruptcy provisions, such as section 42 of the Bankruptcy Act 1914, were not appropriate for companies. Some of these problems were solved by the enactment of insolvency legislation in the mid-1980s, when, for the first time in English law, one statute covered both personal and corporate insolvency. This process began with the enactment of the Insolvency Act 1985. It provided for the bankruptcy of individuals and partly for the insolvency of companies, but the Companies Act 1985 still governed aspects of corporate insolvency.[27] The Insolvency Act became law on 30 October 1985, but few of its provisions became operative. The government had decided to put forward a fresh Insolvency Bill. This latter Bill, to become the Insolvency Act 1986, was to act as a consolidating statute in relation to most of the Insolvency Act 1985[28] and to the parts of the Companies Act 1985 which covered corporate insolvency,[29] so giving us unified legislation. While personal and corporate insolvency are contained within the four corners of the same statute, that statute does not provide for a unified system *per se*. This is because, in the main, separate procedures and rules are maintained for the two forms of insolvency. As Professor Ian Fletcher has noted:

> [A]lthough a high degree of harmonisation has been achieved between many parallel provisions belonging to the different branches of insolvency law, the traditional distinction survives between corporate and personal insolvency and the pre-existing procedures have retained their respective, and separate features.[30]

There is little cross-over between the provisions dealing with personal insolvency and those dealing with corporate insolvency and vice versa. Truly unified legislation, something that the Americans have and the South Africans are seeking to implement, sees the enactment of legislation which applies equally, as far as possible, to both individuals and corporations.[31]

---

[27] For example, winding up in sections 501–650 and 659–74.

[28] For example, sections 12–14, 16, 18 and Schedule 2 were consolidated into the Company Directors' Disqualification Act 1986.

[29] Sections 467–650 and 659–74.

[30] I.F. Fletcher, *The Law of Insolvency*, 3rd edn, at 20. For example, the Cork Committee had advocated the creation of an Insolvency Court (at paras 1000–1032) but the existing arrangements of having different courts dealing with individual and corporate insolvency continued.

[31] For a discussion of unified legislation, see A. Keay, 'To unify or not to unify insolvency legislation: International Experience and the latest South African Proposals' (1999) 1 *De Jure* 62; A. Keay, 'The Unity of Insolvency Legislation: Time for a Re-think?' (1999) 7 *Insolvency Law Journal* 4.

It was not until the Report of the Insolvency Law Review Committee, *Insolvency Law and Practice* (known as the 'Cork Report')[32] was published that serious thought had been given to the idea of unified legislation, although the Cork Committee's terms of reference had contemplated unification.[33] The Cork Report is a critical development of modern insolvency law in the UK. It involved a comprehensive report on insolvency. The Cork Committee was set up because of concern over the state of insolvency law in the UK. The Report was delivered in 1982 and it recommended a fundamental reform of the law. Many of the recommendations of the Report were implemented, some adapted and quite a number ignored. The Report is referred to frequently by academics, practitioners and judges. The commentary in the Report is highly regarded – and quite rightly given the august body of professionals assembled to sit on the Committee – and is worth consulting when confronted with an insolvency issue.

The Insolvency Act has been amended in a substantial way by the Insolvency Act 1994, the Insolvency Act 2000 and the Enterprise Act 2002. While all of these legislative enactments have been important, the last has probably had the most impact. The legislation was intended to address a number of matters that affect commercial life in today's Britain. Besides dealing with insolvency the Act addresses issues concerning law affecting competition, mergers and consumers. As far as insolvency goes, its main aspects related to the revamping of the administration process for companies, abolishing administrative receivership, abolishing Crown preference on distributions of the assets of insolvents and the regulation of bankrupts. The Enterprise Act received Royal assent on 7 November 2002, but, because of the need to enact secondary legislation, the provisions dealing with administration and administrative receivership have not yet become operational. The provisions covering bankruptcy will not become operational until early in the financial year of 2004.[34]

It is worth mentioning the fact that the Human Rights Act 1998, which came into operation for England and Wales in 2000, has had an impact on insolvency practice and it is likely to have an even greater effect in the years to come. From time to time in the book we make reference to the legislation and how it has impacted, or may impact, on insolvency law.

---

[32] Cmnd 8558, 1982.
[33] At para 197.
[34] 'Enterprise Bill Receives Royal Assent' DTI Press Release, 8 November 2002, P/2002/687.

1.3 Terminology

It is important at the outset of a book of this kind to ensure that readers understand the terminology used. Frequently the term 'bankruptcy' is employed to describe any process which involves dealing with the affairs of an insolvent business or person and commonly people say that a company has become 'bankrupt'. A company that is being wound up is often referred to by the media as being a 'bankrupt company'. This is not accurate as far as the UK is concerned, although it would be in the United States. In the UK (and most Commonwealth countries), only individuals can go bankrupt; and not all insolvents do, as we will see. Insolvent companies, if they are unable to initiate some procedure for their rescue, might enter winding up, or as it is often referred to, 'liquidation'. As discussed earlier, bankruptcy and winding up (liquidation) are equivalents.

Seeing as the struggles of large American corporations are often in the news, it is probably worthwhile mentioning that American corporations can enter what is known as 'Chapter 11 bankruptcy' (the name derives from the part of the American bankruptcy legislation that the corporations rely upon) if they are having difficulties. Many large corporations have done so in the past 20 years, such as Continental Airlines, Texaco, Enron and WorldCom. Doing so provides the corporations with a shelter from their creditors and may enable them to work out an arrangement with their creditors to allow the corporations to recover and to continue to trade.

1.4 The effects of insolvency

Insolvency is not, *per se*, a crime. Also, just because a person or a company is insolvent does not mean that the insolvent will become subject to an insolvency administration of the kind discussed in this book. There might not in fact be any legal consequences for a person or company that is insolvent. There are at any one time many people and companies in the UK that are insolvent but not under some form of insolvency administration. There will be people and companies who will, regularly or from time to time, find that they are unable to pay debts when their creditors legally seek payment. But that does not mean that they will become subject to insolvency administration. Most creditors will give debtors time either to pay from income that they will earn, or to pay from funds obtained from the sale of assets. It is often not worth the while of creditors to take legal action without giving debtors some indulgence and an opportunity to pay.

Some creditors are known as unsecured creditors, which means that they can only rely on a contractual right against the debtor. Conversely, other creditors, known as secured creditors, have not only a contractual right against debtors, but also a proprietary right in relation to some or all of a debtor's property. That is, the creditor might have a mortgage or a charge. A proprietary right usually enables the creditor to sell off the debtor's property and provided the sale of the property produces enough to pay off the creditor, no proceedings will be commenced against the debtor.

Of course, although a person or a company might be able to keep functioning while insolvent and no legal sanctions are imposed, the insolvent's standing in the community will diminish as creditors realise that the insolvent is not a good risk. Eventually, if the state of affairs is not remedied, a creditor will lose patience and take action to initiate some insolvency administration, or the insolvent will have all credit facilities withdrawn and, therefore, will be unable to continue to operate.

It must be emphasised, however, that continuing to operate while insolvent, or for a company even operating when not insolvent but where the directors suspect that insolvent winding up is going to happen, could have some legal consequences for the insolvent or insolvent company's directors.

This book focuses on the legal effects of insolvency, rather than the economic and social effects, although these latter consequences are not ignored. We now move on from a general contextualising of insolvency to consider the meaning of 'insolvency' in the commercial world.

Chapter 2

The Meaning of Insolvency

2.1 Introduction[1]

Determining whether a person or a company is in fact insolvent can be of extraordinarily practical importance. For instance, in most cases court applications to wind up companies (known as 'winding-up petitions') rely upon the insolvency of the company against whom the petition is filed. As mentioned earlier in Chapter 1, insolvency will not, ordinarily, see legal sanctions apply to a person or company – it does not constitute a criminal or civil wrong. If insolvency exists, it may lead to some formal insolvency administration. A court is only able to order the bankruptcy of a person if he or she is insolvent and, while there are various grounds that enable a company to be compulsorily wound up by a court order, the ground of insolvency is by far the most frequently employed. There is provision in the Insolvency Act 1986 for persons and companies to be deemed to be insolvent even though insolvency has not been proved technically, and this state of affairs might lead to the filing of a bankruptcy petition in relation to a person or the filing of a creditor's petition against an insolvent company. But importantly other consequences may be visited on certain persons if insolvency occurs and continues. For instance, a director of a company may be liable pursuant to section 214 of the Insolvency Act if his or her company has gone into insolvent liquidation and, at some time before the commencement of this administration, he or she knew or ought to have concluded that there was no reasonable prospect that the company would avoid insolvent liquidation. This is known as wrongful trading.[2]

---

[1] Some parts of the following discussion are based on, and adapted from, A. Keay and M. Murray, *Insolvency: Personal and Corporate Law and Practice*, 4th edn, Law Book Co, Sydney (2002) at 12–17 and A. Keay, *McPherson's Law of Company Liquidation*, Sweet & Maxwell, London (2001) at 84–91.

[2] For a consideration of this provision, see below at 523.

Below, we first briefly discuss what tests the law sets to determine whether a debtor is in fact insolvent and then we discuss the meaning of those tests.

2.1.1 *The tests for insolvency*

There are two primary tests which are generally employed to determine whether any person or company is solvent. These are known as the 'cash flow' or 'commercial' insolvency test on the one hand and the 'balance sheet' or 'absolute' insolvency test on the other.[3]

Under the former test a person or a company is generally regarded as insolvent when unable to pay debts as they become due.[4] This means that there are insufficient resources available to the debtor to pay creditors. The critical issue is: can the person pay his or her way in carrying on his or her business, or conducting his or her affairs?[5]

The second test holds that a person or company is insolvent if the total liabilities are greater than the value of the assets, with the consequence that the debtor has insufficient assets to discharge the liabilities.[6]

It is quite possible for a business to be insolvent in cash flow terms, but be asset rich and able to be regarded as solvent on the balance sheet test. Similarly, a business may be able to pass the cash flow test, but its liabilities are greater than its assets. Notwithstanding this, in practice, businesses usually tend to fail or pass both tests. Professor Sir Roy Goode makes the point that:

> there is a close link between cash flow insolvency and balance sheet insolvency in that where a company is a going concern and its business can be sold as such with its assets in use in the business, those assets will usually have a substantially higher value than if disposed of on a break-up basis, divorced from their previous business activity. So a company which is commercially solvent has a much greater chance of satisfying the balance sheet test of insolvency than one which is unable to pay its debts as they fall due.[7]

2.1.2 *Shortcomings of the tests for insolvency*

Neither test is perfect. Primarily, the difficulty with the cash flow test is that its meaning is vague and imprecise[8] and, determining whether a person or a company is, on a particular day, insolvent is often difficult.[9]

---

[3] R.M. Goode, *The Principles of Corporate Insolvency Law*, 2nd edn, Sweet & Maxwell, London (1997) at 67–8.
[4] Ibid.
[5] Ibid at 68.
[6] Ibid at 69 and 83.
[7] Ibid at 70.
[8] D. Milman, 'Test of Commercial Insolvency Rejected' (1983) 4 Co Law 231 at 232.
[9] K. Chiah, 'Voidable Preference' (1986) 12 *New Zealand Universities Law Review* 1 at 6.

With the balance sheet test the problem lies with marginal cases, which is often the situation where a company or person is being attacked for the failure to pay debts or claims; the problem is that it is not easy to assess whether the test is satisfied. A critical reason is the fact that assets have to be valued and this:

> is not an exact science but to a considerable extent a matter of judgement as to the amount a willing buyer would pay in the market when dealing with a willing seller.[10]

Establishing the value of some assets, particularly where circumstances can affect them, is not easy. Moreover, it is sometimes difficult to estimate the value of some kinds of liabilities, notably unquantified existing liabilities and contingent liabilities.[11]

2.1.3 *What the legislation says*

Both tests are found in legislation in the UK. Australia, however, while it has used the balance sheet, includes the cash flow test in relevant legislation.[12] Conversely, the United States, while it is cognisant of the cash flow test, uses the balance sheet test.[13] In the UK, for instance, section 122 provides that a company may be wound up if it is 'unable to pay its debts', i.e., it is insolvent. This phrase is explained in section 123 in two ways, using the two tests for insolvency. Section 123(1)(e) provides that a company is unable to pay its debts if it is unable to pay debts as they fall due. Section 123(2) incorporates the balance sheet test and provides that a company is unable to pay its debts if it is proved that the value of the company's assets is less than the amount of its liabilities. The cash flow test is employed in the provisions that allow for the adjustment of pre-winding up transactions entered into by a company, yet in relation to the wrongful trading provision, the balance sheet is relevant.

2.1.4 *What the courts say*

2.1.4.1 *Cash flow insolvency*

Prima facie, the concept of cash flow insolvency seems simple, but in some cases it may be far from easy to determine whether the test is satisfied at any particular point of time – namely, the time at which that person or company

---

[10] R.M. Goode, *The Principles of Corporate Insolvency Law*, 2nd edn, at 69.
[11] Ibid at 95.
[12] Corporations Act 2001, section 95A; Bankruptcy Act 1966, section 5(2)(3).
[13] Bankruptcy Reform Act 1978, section 101(32).

is unable to pay debts. English courts have not tackled some of the issues which the cash flow formulation in section 123(1)(e) raises. For example, how far into the future, if at all, should courts look to see what debts will become payable in the future? Should courts take into account debts which are due but creditors have granted extensions of time to pay? As far as being able to pay, are companies to be limited to the money at hand or can courts have regard to the realisation of assets and the borrowing of funds?[14] Because of the dearth of English law, much of the following discussion relies on the law as it has been laid down by Australian cases, because there has been a quite developed jurisprudence on the subject in that jurisdiction.

The court, in examining whether a company is suffering cash flow insolvency, will consider whether the company is actually paying its debtors. Courts must take into account what current revenue the company has as well as what the company can procure by realising assets within a relatively short time (*Re Capital Annuities Ltd* [1979] 1 WLR 170 at 182, 188). A company can rely upon money which might be obtained from the sale of assets or upon money which might be obtained by a loan on the strength of its assets (*Sandell v Porter* (1966) 115 CLR 666). It is possible that sometimes a debtor might be able to establish solvency by demonstrating that funds can be obtained through an unsecured loan.[15] In considering whether a person or a company is insolvent, the debtor's whole financial position must be studied (*Hymix Concrete Pty Ltd v Garrity* (1976) 13 ALR 321 at 328), and a temporary lack of liquidity does not necessarily mean that the company is insolvent (*Hymix Concrete Pty Ltd v Garrity*; *M & R Jones Shopfitting Co Pty Ltd v National Bank of Australasia Ltd* (1983) 7 ACLR 445).

It is probable that the presence of the words 'as they fall due' means, as far as the debts to be taken into account are concerned, that the courts may look into the future to see what debts will fall due in the future (*Bank of Australia v Hall* (1907) 4 CLR 1514 at 1528; *Kyra Nominees Pty Ltd v National Australia Bank Ltd* (1986) 4 ACLC 400 at 402). To what extent a court is permitted to gaze into the future is not really settled, although what is clear is that it will depend on the debtor and the debtor's circumstances. The issue has not been canvassed in England and Wales. In Australia there is some divergence in the cases as to whether or not 'debts due' includes liabilities not payable because creditors had granted the debtor extended terms of repayment. It seems that the better supported view now is that it is proper to take into account any extensions of time granted to the debtor to pay its creditors and in turn to take into account the dates when it might be reasonably expected that the creditor would receive debts due and owing to it (*Re Newark Pty Ltd (in liq)* [1993] 1 Qd R

---

[14] See A. Keay, *Avoidance Provisions in Insolvency Law*, LBC Information Services, Sydney (1997) at 98–114.
[15] See *Re a Company* [1986] BCLC 261 at 262; *Re RHD Power Services Pty Ltd* (1991) 3 ACSR 261; (1991) 9 ACLC 27.

409, 419–414; (1991) 6 ACSR 255, 259–260; *Pioneer Concrete (Vic) Pty Ltd v Stule* (1996) 14 ACLC 534 at 536).[16]

What is clear in English law is that 'contingent and prospective liabilities' are not to be taken into account in determining a debtor's solvency under the cash flow method because, unlike section 123(2) (dealing with balance sheet solvency), which includes a reference to 'contingent and prospective liabilities', section 123(1)(e) does not. This has led to the following comment:

> But the relative accuracy of modern accounting methods and actuarial predictions moves one to question the wisdom and fairness of such a change to the law [omitting the words 'contingent and prospective liabilities' from section 123(1)(e)]. For, given a reliable balance sheet and the assistance of expert evidence, there seems to be no reason why it should be beyond the court's powers to arrive at a conclusion that the company is insolvent in this sense without becoming involved in speculation about its future business prospects.[17]

At one time courts were rather strict on what they required to be established before they were willing to deem a person or a company insolvent, but in more recent times they have become more liberal as far as creditors are concerned and have held that a debtor is insolvent if a creditor is able to prove that he or she has not been paid an undisputed debt after a demand has been made (*Re Camburn Petroleum Products Ltd* [1979] 3 All ER 297 at 307; *Re Taylor's Industrial Flooring Ltd* [1990] BCC 44 (CA)); and this is the case even if there is other evidence which suggests that the value of assets outweighs liabilities (*Cornhill Insurance plc v Improvement Services Ltd* [1986] 2 BCC 98, 942). In *Cornhill Insurance plc v Improvement Services Ltd* the court was asked to restrain the presentation of a petition against a well-known and apparently profitable company. The court declined to do so and agreed with Vaisey J in *Re a Company* ((1950) 94 Sol Jo 369) that the delay in the discharge of a company's obligations creates some suspicion of financial embarrassment.

Whether a company is cash flow insolvent is principally a question of fact and one which may be established in any number of ways, such as the existence of a large number of outstanding debts and unsatisfied judgments (*Re Tweeds Garages Ltd* [1962] Ch 406), or there is lack of assets on which execution can be levied (*Re Douglas Griggs Engineering Ltd* [1963] Ch 19).

---

[16] For more detailed discussion of this issue see A. Keay, 'The Insolvency Factor in the Avoidance of antecedent Transactions in Corporate Liquidations' (1995) 21 *Monash University Law Review* 305 at 316–22.

[17] A. Keay, *McPherson's Law of Company Liquidation* at 88. But compare the view of Professor Ian Fletcher who says that contingent and prospective liabilities have no part to play in a cash flow evaluation of the affairs of a company: *The Law of Insolvency*, 2nd edn, 1996 at 527. Also see the comment of Professors Len Sealy and David Milman in *Annotated Guide to the Insolvency Legislation*, 5th edn, 1999 at 158.

It has been said that a debtor is not to be regarded as solvent just because if sufficient time were granted the debts could be paid off (*Re Attiwell: Official Receiver v Braithwaite Bros* (1932) 5 ABC 54; *Re Whitgift Nominees Pty Ltd* (1983) 7 ACLR 680; (1983) 1 ACLC 1133).

2.1.4.2 Balance sheet insolvency

This test actually looks at the affairs of the company and is provided for, for example, in section 123(2). In determining whether the assets are outweighed by the liabilities a court is able to take into account contingent and prospective liabilities, but not contingent and prospective assets (*Byblos Bank SAL v Al-Khudhairy* (1986) 2 BCC 99, 549 (CA)). It has been said that 'liabilities' is a broader term compared with 'debts' (*Re A Debtor (No 17 of 1966)* [1967] Ch 590; [1967] 1 All ER 668). 'Liabilities' is defined for the purposes of winding up in rule 13.12(4) to mean 'a liability to pay money or money's worth, including any liability under an enactment, any liability for breach of trust, any liability in contract, tort or bailment and, any liability arising out of an obligation to make restitution'. Then rule 13.12(3) states that it is immaterial whether the liability is present or future, whether it is certain or contingent, or whether its amount is fixed or liquidated, or is capable of being ascertained by fixed rules or as a matter of opinion.

Clearly with this test it is only possible to take into account the assets owned by the company, including the uncalled capital of the company (*Re National Livestock Insurance Co* (1858) 26 Beav 153; 53 ER 855).

In establishing balance sheet insolvency in court a creditor might need to adduce expert evidence from a person such as an experienced accountant.[18]

Having considered what is meant by insolvency, we now turn our attention in the following chapter to studying what underpins the concept of insolvency, that is, what are the theory, principles and purposes of insolvency law.

---

[18] A. Keay, *McPherson's Law of Company Liquidation* at 90.

Chapter 3

Purposes, Principles and Theory

3.1 Introduction

It is critical to an understanding and appreciation of insolvency law, and before embarking on a study of the content of insolvency law, that we identify the principles on which the law is founded and the purposes which it seeks to achieve. This chapter purports to do that in a brief fashion. Also, while this book adopts primarily a doctrinal approach, it is helpful and important to examine, albeit briefly, the theory that has developed in relation to this area of the law. The theory is inextricably linked to principles.

Before moving on to a consideration of the purposes, principles and theory, we must recognise that determining what our insolvency law looks like is far from an easy task. No one wins where there is insolvency, save for:

- those people who improperly received assets of the insolvent at less than their market value;
- those people who improperly received money from the insolvent in exchange for assets they sold to the insolvent at greater than their market value;
- insolvents and officers of insolvents who were able to spirit away assets; and,
- where the relevant office-holder is unable to remedy the improper conduct.

The law has to engage in some hard decision-making, involving the weighing up of who is to lose and what are they to lose. This is never easily done for those who lose and their champions at law will point out the relevant injustices. Most people affected by an insolvency can articulate 'a beef' concerning the way that the law has treated them. The fact of the matter is that any law of insolvency will, probably like most law, never go close to satisfying all. There will always be some people or groups that can point to some malady in the law. Recognition of this should lead us to be ready to give all approaches a hearing. There is no room in insolvency for dogma.

3.2 The purposes

These have never been carefully and systematically articulated in case law or by commentators. To do so here is really not within the intended aim of this book. Purposes depend somewhat on what theory of insolvency law is adopted, an issue which is discussed later in the chapter. The purposes build on the principles set out in the next section of the chapter. For our needs the following purposes may be enumerated:[1]

- to provide an equal, fair and orderly procedure in handling the affairs of insolvents, ensuring that creditors receive an equal and equitable distribution of the assets of the insolvent;
- to provide procedures which ensure that debts are satisfied with as little delay and expense as possible;
- to ensure that administrations are conducted in an honest, independent and competent manner;
- to provide mechanisms which allow for the treatment of the affairs of insolvents before their position is hopeless. This is the idea of rescue and particularly relevant for companies;
- to provide relief and protection for individual insolvents from harassment and at the same time to take into account the rights of creditors and the risks that they might be subject to;
- to provide procedures which enable both debtors and creditors to be involved in the resolution of the insolvency problem and to prevent conflicts between creditors of insolvents;
- to attempt to diminish, as far as possible, the deleterious effects of insolvency on the interests of the public;[2]

---

[1] These are adapted from some of those given by the Report of the Insolvency Law Review Committee, *Insolvency Law & Practice* ('Cork Report'), Cmnd. 8558, London, 1982, at paras 191 and 198, Australian Law Reform Commission, *General Insolvency Inquiry*, Report No. 45, 1988, Canberra (known as 'the Harmer Report'), para. at 33, and referred to in A. Keay and M. Murray, *Insolvency: Personal and Corporate Law and Practice*, 4th edn, Law Book Co, Sydney (2002) at 17.

[2] This might be regarded as somewhat debatable. For more detail, see A. Keay, 'Insolvency Law: A Matter of Public Interest?' (2000) 51 NILQ 509.

- to provide a system that is flexible, but is also well respected;
- to ascertain the reasons for the insolvency and to provide mechanisms which allow for the examination of the conduct of insolvents, their associates and the officers of corporate insolvents. This aim is designed to support the maintenance of commercial morality.

3.3 Principles

It is never easy to compile a list of principles on which an area of law is based, but it does provide some orientation to those seeking to study the area and, hence, we set out perhaps the most essential principles that pervade insolvency law.[3] Some principles are peculiar to individuals, while others are peculiar to insolvent companies.

It is generally asserted that the foremost and most fundamental principle of insolvency law is the *pari passu* principle. The principle, which is discussed later in the book,[4] means that there should be an equal and rateable distribution of the assets of insolvents among the creditors. The idea is that the loss should be spread among the claimants. However, as will be demonstrated later,[5] the principle is subject to so many exceptions that now it is really little more than a default rule.

Insolvent individuals should not regard insolvency as an easy way out of their problems, but conversely they should: be kept from creditor harassment; be entitled to retain some items of property; and be able to start afresh at some point.[6]

Insolvent individuals and the directors of insolvent companies should be held accountable for the state of their or their company's affairs. Following on from this, where there is a formal insolvency process and it is appropriate to do so, then it is a matter of fairness and justice that an insolvent's affairs should be subject to investigation.[7]

Companies should be rehabilitated if at all possible and with an enterprise, such as a large company, which is the lifeblood of a community and the insolvency of which can affect the livelihood and well-being of those dependent on it (creditors, suppliers, employees, community), concern should be had to public interest issues.[8] This is a debatable principle and will be considered in the next section of the chapter.

---

[3] Many of these are adapted from those given by the Cork Report and dealt with in Chapter 4.
[4] See below at 395.
[5] See below at 397.
[6] Cork Report at paras 191–2.
[7] Ibid at para 194.
[8] Ibid at para 204.

Most insolvency administrations, like bankruptcies or liquidations that are initiated, take the form of collective proceedings, that is, the creditors lose their pre-administration right to pursue their claims for repayment of what they are owed by way of separate action, and in exchange they are given the same right to participate in the collected property of the insolvent with all unsecured creditors.

Insolvency practitioners (see Chapter 4) who administer insolvency processes must be persons of integrity and competence and have the confidence of creditors and the public in general.[9]

The possibility of a detailed investigation of the insolvent's affairs is critical to ensuring the retention of commercial morality and public confidence.

Secured creditors are to retain, for the most part, the right to their priority where it was obtained fairly and prior to the advent of insolvency administrations.[10]

Where an insolvent company is a limited liability company, the members are not liable for the company's debts;[11] the corporate entity is liable.[12]

3.4 Theory

Generally speaking there has been little developed comment in the UK (or in the Commonwealth) on the theory underpinning insolvency law, perhaps because of the pragmatic way in which English law has developed.[13] The concentration of academics and practitioners alike has been on statutory developments and the case law, rather than seeking to divine any theoretical framework. A theoretical perspective involves 'academic analysis of the law which requires a degree of abstraction from the principles stated in case law and statute-based law.'[14] The position in England and the Commonwealth is in stark contrast with the United States where there is a voluminous amount of scholarship proposing various approaches. While the American material is very helpful, it must not be forgotten that it addresses a different legal system, namely a federal system that can throw up some peculiarities not relevant

---

[9] Ibid at para 230.

[10] R.M. Goode, *Principles of Corporate Insolvency Law*, 2nd edn, London: Sweet & Maxwell (1997) at 54, 55–6.

[11] In winding up members might be liable to pay what they owe on any partly paid up shares.

[12] Directors might be liable in certain circumstances. See Parts VIII and IX.

[13] R.M. Goode, *Principles of Corporate Insolvency Law*, 2nd edn, at 35.

[14] P.E. Nygh and P. Butt (eds), *Butterworths Australian Legal Dictionary*, Sydney: Butterworths (1997) at 681 and quoted by B. Cheffins, 'Using Legal Theory to Study Law: A Company Law Perpsective' (1999) 58 CLJ 197 at 198.

to the UK. This section can hardly do justice to the positions that have been articulated,[15] but it is appropriate to at least provide some brief discussion of the main views, some of which draw on economics, sociology, politics, philosophy, ethics and theology, that have been put forward. It must be emphasised, by way of disclaimer and apology to the relevant theorists, that this discussion is not exhaustive by a long way and in some respects is rather simplistic. It merely deals with three of the primary approaches and seeks to introduce readers to these theories and the issues that are at the heart of the debate. Perhaps the primary issue is whether insolvency law is only about creditor rights or whether other interests, including the public interest, should be allowed to intrude. But even more important is to recognise that the very centre of the whole debate on theory involves deciding who and what is to be protected by the insolvency regimes.[16]

Some of the arguments propounded do affect what the purposes and principles of insolvency law are. Also, it is notable that some of the theories that have been propounded are clearly in conflict, depending from which perspective their advocates come.

3.4.1 *The creditors' bargain theory*

This theory of insolvency law has, arguably, dominated the field in the past 20 years and continues to have a profound influence despite the fact that its main champion, Professor Thomas Jackson (writing often with co-authors such as Professors Douglas Baird and Robert Scott), no longer writes in the area.

Jackson[17] and his acolytes have argued that the goal of insolvency law is to maximise the amount that creditors receive, because at its core bankruptcy law involves debt collection. The theory is derived from the general principles espoused by contractarian theory and, more especially, influenced markedly by the law and economics movement that was born in the United States in the mid-1970s and which has had a significant impact on scholarship, not only in the United States, but around the world, including the UK.

Jackson asserted that insolvency law is essentially a debt collection device and he has argued that the insolvency system is to reflect the bargain that the creditors would have made (*ex ante*) if they had the chance prior

---

[15] For a helpful and reasonably succinct discussion of the primary theories, albeit focusing only on corporate insolvency, see V. Finch, 'The Measures of Insolvency' (1997) 17 OJLS 227.

[16] K. Gross, 'Taking Community Interests into Account in Bankrutpcy: An Essay' (1994) 72 *Washington University Law Quarterly* 1031 at 1047.

[17] For instance, see *The Logic and Limits of Bankruptcy*, Harvard Press (1986) and 'Bankruptcy, Non-Bankruptcy Entitlements, and the Creditors' Bargain' (1982) 91 Yale LJ 857.

to entering into transactions with the insolvent. As the bargain never occurred, it is referred to as a 'hypothetical bargain'. In line with the efficiency ideals of the law and economics school, Jackson regards the collectivist approach to insolvency law, applied in the Anglo-American jurisdictions, as being attractive to creditors, in that transaction costs are reduced and the asset pool increased. Jackson ignores distributional objectives. He also seeks to keep intact creditors' pre-insolvency ownership rights and resists a post-insolvency redistribution of rights. The learned author is intent on protecting security interests and this is one of the principal aspects of the credit bargain theory.[18] This approach endeavours to make insolvency procedure look like a market process.

As the name of this theory suggests, it is creditor focused and the interests of others who might be affected by the insolvency of the debtor are not the concern of insolvency law.[19] All insolvency law is to be tested by one question: does it enhance the collective benefits of creditors?[20] According to Jackson, insolvency law does not and should not concern itself with the public interest. He takes the view that there is no need to protect non-creditor interests in insolvency law as that should be done outside of insolvency law. Professor Sir Roy Goode's riposte is that certain problems confronting non-creditor claimants only arise in the context of insolvency, so it is appropriate for insolvency law to protect interests other than creditors.[21] Professor Karen Gross categorises this approach as 'bankruptcy Darwinism' in the sense that only the fittest companies will survive financial problems.[22]

While many have accepted the Jackson approach, many others have criticised it. For instance, some have said that the theory is flawed in that it is based on highly questionable assumptions and contradictions.[23] It might also be said that the theory both treats creditors as if they were equal in terms of knowledge, experience and power and focuses on voluntary creditors who were able to bargain freely in their transactions with the insolvent. It fails to take account of the fact that creditors are not uniform, for some are clearly stronger than others and creditors such as tort victims and employees probably would not agree

---

[18] D. G. Baird and T. H. Jackson, 'Corporate Reorganizations and the Treatment of Diverse Ownership Interests: A Comment on Adequate Protection of Secured Creditors in Bankruptcy' (1984) 51 *University of Chicago Law Review* 97.

[19] T. H. Jackson, *The Logic and Limits of Bankruptcy*, Harvard Press (1986) at 17.

[20] D. G. Baird and T. H. Jackson, 'Corporate Reorganizations and the Treatment of Diverse Ownership Interests: A Comment on Adequate Protection of Secured Creditors in Bankruptcy' (1984) 51 *University of Chicago Law Review* 97 at 103.

[21] R.M. Goode, *Principles of Corporate Insolvency Law*, 2nd edn, at 38.

[22] 'Taking Community Interests into Account in Bankruptcy: An Essay' (1994) 72 *Washington University Law Quarterly* 1031 at 1035.

[23] D. G. Carlson, 'Philosophy in Bankruptcy' (1987) 85 *Michigan Law Review* 1341.

to the *ex ante* bargain. The real danger of this theory, according to Vanessa Finch, is that:

> [I]t fails adequately to value the continuation of business relationships that have not been formalized in contracts and may, indeed, omit from consideration those who suffer the greatest hardships in the context of financial stress.[24]

The bottom line is that the theory can be criticised for an attempt at being too clear-cut and glib.

3.4.2 *Communitarian theory*[25]

This theory is in marked contrast with the creditors' bargain theory as this latter theory focuses on private rights while the communitarian theory[26] seeks to consider a range of constituent interests and takes on a more public law focus.[27] Not only are creditors' interests taken into account, but the interests of others, such as employees, suppliers, government, customers, neighbours and the local and wider community are also considered. For instance – this is rather a simplistic summary of the complexities facing Rover and its employees – take the case of the car-maker Rover, situated in the West Midlands. It was suffering financial problems in the late 1990s and its German owners were unsure what to do with it. It had a huge factory and employed many people. Those holding to a creditors' bargain approach would ask, in relation to the problems facing Rover: what is best for the creditors in getting something of what is owed to them? In contrast, the communitarians would have regard for the effects on employees and the West Midlands region as well as the positions of the creditors. Communitarians would say that while the community and the interests of groups like employees should be considered, these interests do not overtake those of the creditors. In defence of this position and in response to allegations that this approach fosters inefficiency, it has been submitted that taking into account the effect on communities is not necessarily non-economic, but rather it indicates a concern for a wider economic

---

24 'The Measures of Insolvency' (1997) 17 OJLS 227 at 234 and referring to D. Korobkin, 'Contractariansim and the Normative Foundations of Bankruptcy Law' (1993) 71 Texas L Rev 541 at 581.

25 This is similar to what Professor Axel Flessner refers to as 'enterprise philosophy' ('Philosophies of Business Bankruptcy Law: An International Overview' in J. Ziegel (ed.), *Current Developments in International and Comparative Corporate Insolvency Law* Oxford: Clarendon Press, (1994) at 24.

26 Founded by the sociologist A. Etzioni: *The Spirit of Community Rights, Responsibilities and the Communitarian Agenda* (1993).

27 Examples of a communitarian approach is found in Professor Karen Gross's monograph, *Failure and Forgiveness: Rebalancing the Bankruptcy System*, New Haven: Yale University Press (1997), and her article, 'Taking Community Interests into Account in Bankruptcy: An Essay' (1994) 72 *Washington University Law Quarterly* 1031, although the learned author does state that she is also influenced by feminist legal theory.

approach.[28] Unlike theories such as the creditors' bargain, which focus on the individual as private and rational decision-makers, communitarianism sees individuals as interdependent on each other and that it is incumbent on them to act in the best interests of their communities, even if doing so prejudices or limits their own individual freedom.[29] While law and economics theories focus on the rights of individuals, the communitarian theory places emphasis on the fact that individuals live in a society and as a concomitant they owe responsibilities.

The Cork Report seemed to implicitly endorse the communitarian approach, from what is said.[30] Rather than ignoring distributional issues, to the communitarians such issues are matters to be evaluated in making decisions in insolvency law.

The problems with this theory, according to some, is that that one cannot lay down parameters because there are so many community interests that could be taken into account[31] and there will, necessarily, be conflicts between those interests that are considered. It might be argued that it is for the courts to undertake a balancing exercise to resolve such conflicts, as that is what they often do in deciding cases.[32] While creditors' bargain theory might be glib, communitarian theory suffers, so the argument goes, from being complex. Although some might say that it is only because insolvency is complex.

3.4.3 *Multiple values approach*[33]

The approach taken by some American scholars[34] – which overlaps in some ways with the communitarian approach – and apparently endorsed by Professor Sir Roy Goode,[35] is that there are other values besides the maximisation of the interests of creditors and efficiency that warrant consideration. Professor Elizabeth Warren has said that:

> I see bankruptcy as an attempt to reckon with a debtor's multiple defaults and to distribute the consequence among a number of different actors.

---

[28] K. Gross, 'Taking Community Interests into Account in Bankruptcy: An Essay' (1994) 72 *Washington University Law Quarterly* 1031 at 1033.

[29] Ibid at 1036.

[30] See para 204.

[31] B. Schermer, 'Response to Professor Gross: Taking the Interests of the Community into Account in Bankruptcy' (1994) 72 *Washington University Law Quarterly* 1049 at 1051.

[32] See A. Keay 'Insolvency Law: A Matter of Public Interest?' (2000) 51 NILQ 509 at 530–3. For a discussion concerning one kind of conflict that can exist, see A. Keay and P. de Prez, 'Insolvency and Environmental Principles: A Case Study in a Conflict of Public Interests' (2001) 3 *Environmental Law Review* 90.

[33] This is the title that Vanessa Finch gives to this approach: 'The Measures of Insolvency' (1997) 17 OJLS 227 at 240.

[34] For instance, Professor Elizabeth Warren in 'Bankruptcy Policy' (1987) 54 *University of Chicago Law Review* 775.

[35] R.M. Goode, *Principles of Corporate Insolvency Law*, 2nd edn, at 37–42.

> Bankruptcy encompasses a number of competing – and sometimes
> conflicting – values in their distribution. As I see it, no one value dominates,
> so that bankruptcy policy becomes a composite of factors that bear on
> a better answer to the question, How shall the losses be distributed?[36]

Unlike the creditors' bargain theory, which provides a unified coherent
system and a single justification for insolvency law, it provides an approach
that is far from clear-cut. It is complex, necessarily because insolvency is
complex. The creditors' bargain theory arrives at conclusions to answer all
questions, while the multiple values approach produces complex questions
and no definitive conclusions.[37] It takes a broader approach than the
creditors' bargain theory, because it asserts that the effects of failure are
wider than just creditor interests. Besides considering creditor interests it is
necessary to take into account such things as priorities in the distribution
process, protection of the investing public, the need for investigations of
insolvents and upholding commercial morality, and the interests of those
who would be involved in the continuation of the business run by the
insolvent. For this approach the judge is central in that he or she will
have to balance a number of values, such as fairness and justice as well as
efficiency, in making a decision. Because there are so many values to take
into account the answer arrived at is not usually going to be complete.

A neat way of summing up some of what this theory embraces is to quote
Professor Elizabeth Warren's comment that:

> I have offered a dirty, complex, elastic, interconnected view of bankruptcy
> [insolvency] from which I can neither predict outcomes nor even necessarily
> fully articulate all the factors relevant to a policy decision.[38]

The problem with this theory, acknowledged by adherents, is that it does
not provide clear and uncomplicated answers to the questions that it
raises. There will be inevitable conflicts between various interests and
there is little or no guidance for courts in deciding how to resolve such
conflicts.

3.4.4 *Other Approaches*

It is not possible to provide an exposition of all of the approaches that have
been put forward over time. Yet it is worthwhile mentioning that other
theorists have attacked the issue of insolvency law philosophy from other
perspectives than the ones discussed above. Jukka Kipli, a philosopher, has
sought to consider bankruptcy from the perspective of a philosopher[39]
and evaluated bankruptcy from an ethical standpoint. He points out some

---

[36] E. Warren, 'Bankruptcy Policy' (1987) 54 *University of Chicago Law Review* 775 at 777–8.
[37] Ibid at 777.
[38] Ibid at 811.
[39] *The Ethics of Bankruptcy*, London: Routledge (1998).

of the ethical dilemmas that face debtors and the legislature in dealing with insolvency. While this does not resolve things clearly, it does mean that policymakers have some issues, other than purely legal ones, to take into account in coming to a decision about how insolvency law should be framed. Professor Philip Shuchman[40] is also concerned about ethics. He takes the view that in the establishing of insolvency laws there is a tendency to eschew any philosophical base and moral issues are ignored. He maintains that many issues must be taken into account in formulating insolvency law: the position of a debtor, the moral worthiness of the debt involved, the size of the creditor and the position of the creditor.

One other approach warrants a brief mention, namely the social justice/ theological approach as advocated by scholars such as Professor Veryl Miles.[41] In a nutshell she advocates that bankruptcy policy be based on Aristotle's concept of justice and Thomas Aquinas's concept of theological justice. In relation to the latter there is an emphasis on the principles of mercy, justice and charity. These principles might be regarded as the rationale for the concept of discharge from bankruptcy for individuals.[42]

There are many others who have taken a different approach and have contributed to the debate, but lack of space dictates that we must move on to other matters.

3.5 Conclusion

Devising principles based on sound theory is critical to insolvency law. However, thus far, the law has developed in an *ad hoc* fashion largely devoid of clear principles.[43] Changes have been made to the law in order to accommodate a particular problem, often not taking into account the broader picture. In circular fashion we have, in English law, examined the statutes and the cases and then determined our principles for insolvency law. In turn that has informed the legislature and the courts. There is a need to devise theory that is separate and distinct from the statute and case law, so that we can break out of the circular, at some stage.

---

[40] 'An Attempt at a Philosophy of Bankruptcy' (1973) 21 UCLA L Rev 403.

[41] 'Assessing Modern Bankruptcy Law: An Example of Justice' (1996) 36 *Santa Clara Law Review* 1025.

[42] It is arguable as to whether the concept of discharge was first introduced in response to these virtues, but its development over the years might well be based, at least partly, on them.

[43] See A. Keay, 'Balancing Interests in Bankruptcy Law' [2001] *Common Law World Review* 206 for a discussion of this state of affairs in bankruptcy.

Chapter 4

The Administration of Insolvency Regimes

4.1 Introduction

There have been many changes to the way that problems with insolvents have been handled over the years. It is probably fair to say governments of all persuasions have from time to time struggled with knowing what is the best way to address insolvency issues. In this chapter we seek to sketch the present mechanisms that exist for addressing insolvency in the community. The bulk of this book is devoted to considering formal insolvency administrations, such as bankruptcy and winding up, and it is necessary that these administrations are regulated in order to protect the interested parties and the public interest.[1]

4.2 The Courts

In many ways the courts are at the apex of the system in that they are able to, either of their own volition or upon applications made by interested parties, direct how an insolvency administration is to be conducted and to decide contentious issues that arise during the course of an insolvency administration. We must hasten to note that courts do not, as a matter of necessity, have to be involved in an insolvency administration, except in cases of bankruptcy and compulsory winding up where the courts must be involved in the initiation of the process. Some administrations such as

---

[1] See A. Keay, 'Insolvency Law: A Matter of Public Interest?' (2000) 51 NILQ 509.

company voluntary arrangements and voluntary winding up can proceed to a satisfactory conclusion without the courts ever being involved. Of course, it is generally to everyone's advantage that the courts are not involved if at all possible, as that reduces costs across the board and will, normally, mean that creditors will be paid more of what they are owed.

It is necessary to talk in general terms. Certain county courts and the High Court have concurrent jurisdiction to hear winding-up cases. In the London Insolvency District jurisdiction resides in the High Court alone for both winding up and bankruptcy (where the debtor has resided in London for the greater part of six months prior to the presentation of the petition – rules 6.9(1)(b) and 6.40(1)(a)) cases (section 374). Bankruptcy applications outside London are to be heard by the relevant designated county court. The jurisdiction of the High Court is exercised by judges who are assigned to the Companies Court, a part of the Chancery Division, in London and at district registries. The Companies Court was a term introduced in the forms made under the Companies Act 1929. There is no entity by that name; it has been used as a convenient term for the Chancery Division when exercising jurisdiction pursuant to the Companies Act (*Re Tasbian Ltd (No2)* [1990] BCC 322 at 324).[2]

4.3 The Insolvency Service

The Department of Trade and Industry has the oversight of the regulation of the administration of insolvencies. The Insolvency Service, which is an executive agency within the Department of Trade and Industry, fulfils a supervisory role in relation to the persons who administer administrations, such as liquidators.[3] The Mission of the Insolvency Service is to 'ensure that financial failure is dealt with fairly and effectively, encouraging enterprise and deterring fraud and misconduct.'[4]

The Inspector General manages the Insolvency Service and is responsible for the work of the official receivers and has oversight of the conduct of all private insolvency practitioners. The official receivers, being appointed by the Secretary of State for Trade and Industry (section 399(2)), are part of the Service, but will be discussed separately.

---

[2] A. Keay, *McPherson's Law of Company Liquidation*, London: Sweet & Maxwell (2001) at 57.
[3] The Insolvency Service has its own informative web site. See www.insolvencyservice.gov.uk.
[4] Strategic Plan 2002–2005, The Insolvency Service Executive Agency. This is accessible on the Insolvency Service's web site.

4.4. Official receivers

The official receivers carry out an important role in relation to many aspects of insolvency law. We will only touch on some of them – others will be more apparent as we discuss the various administrations throughout the course of the book.

All official receivers are attached to either the High Court or a county court that has a jurisdiction to hear insolvency cases and they are authorised to act, as official receiver, in relation to all bankruptcy and winding-up matters coming within the court's jurisdiction (section 399(3)). The Secretary of State may appoint one or more of her officers to act as deputy official receivers in order to assist an official receiver deal with the tasks that he or she has to undertake (section 401(1)). Such deputy official receivers may be given the right to exercise the functions and have the status of an official receiver (section 401(2)).

Before being appointed as official receivers, such persons have usually occupied positions as civil servants within the Department of Trade and Industry, but when appointed as official receivers they cease 'to be civil servants in the proper sense of servants of the Crown employed in the business of government within (in this case) a department of state' (*Re Minotaur Data Systems Ltd* at 72 per Aldous LJ). Because Beldam LJ in *Mond v Hyde* ([1999] 2 WLR 499 at 516; [1998] 2 BCLC 340 at 357) was of the view that the relationship between the Department of Trade and Industry and official receivers was not that of master and servant, each official receiver is entitled to initiate legal proceedings, in his or her own name and is able to have a right of audience before the court to which he or she is attached (*Re Minotaur Data Systems Ltd*).

The Secretary of State is permitted to give directions to official receivers as far as the disposal of their business is concerned (section 399(6)). The Secretary of State may confer on official receivers further functions (section 400(1)). In carrying out the functions of office, official receivers are subject to the directions of the Secretary of State (section 400(2)). Because official receivers have the status of officers of the court in carrying out their functions (section 400(2)), if there is any interference with their work it could constitute a contempt of court.

Significant roles that the official receiver carries out are acting as the first liquidator in compulsory windings up (section 136(2)), and the receiver of a bankrupt estate until the appointment of the first trustee in bankruptcy (section 287). Where no private insolvency practitioner is appointed as liquidator or trustee (often where there are few or no assets owned by the insolvent), the official receiver continues to act as liquidator or becomes the trustee (section 295). If a private practitioner is appointed, official receivers then exercise a general supervisory role in relation to the liquidation or bankruptcy. One of their major functions in this regard is to investigate the causes of failure of insolvents (sections 132

and 295). Some of the other duties of official receivers are: pursuant to
the Company Directors' Disqualification Act 1986 (section 7(3)), to report
to the Secretary of State any director, past or present, of an insolvent
company who appears to be unfit to be concerned in the management of
a company; where necessary, to require certain persons to make out a
statement of affairs where there is a compulsory winding up (section 131);
to take over as the trustee of a bankrupt estate where there is a vacancy
(section 300).

4.5. The Secretary of State for Trade and Industry

The Secretary of State is the political head of the Department of Trade and
Industry and is granted significant powers to initiate and approve insolvency
rules and regulations. For instance, under section 411(1) rules may only be
made in England and Wales by the Lord Chancellor with the agreement of
the Secretary of State. Furthermore, the Secretary of State may, subject to
the Act and the Rules, make regulations with respect to any matter provided
for in the Rules as relates, *inter alia*, to the carrying out of the functions of
office-holders, such as liquidators and trustees with respect to certain
specific matters arising in insolvency administrations, with examples being
the auditing of office-holders' accounts and the manner in which moneys
coming into the hands of liquidators and bankrupts during windings up and
bankruptcies are handled and invested, and the payment of interest on sums
which have been paid into the Insolvency Services Account.

Some of the things that can be done by the Secretary of State are:
appoint a liquidator to a winding up (section 137); exercise the functions
of a liquidation committee where none exists (section 141(4) (5)); and
petition, in the public interest, for the winding up of companies (section
124A).

An important duty of the Secretary of State is to undertake surveillance
of insolvency practitioners, including their records and accounts
(Insolvency Practitioners' Regulations 1990, reg. 18).

The Secretary of State may have matters referred to her by the Director
of Public Prosecutions concerning possible offences committed by
directors of companies that are in voluntary liquidation, and she is to
investigate the matter reported and in undertaking the investigation the
Secretary of State may exercise any of the powers given to inspectors
appointed under sections 431 or 432 of the Companies Act 1985 to
investigate a company (section 218(5)).

The Secretary of State has the right to apply, in the appropriate case, for
the disqualification of directors (Company Directors' Disqualification Act
1986, section 7(1)).

4.6. Qualified insolvency practitioners (office-holders)

The Report of the Insolvency Law Review Committee, *Insolvency Law and Practice* (known as 'the Cork Report')[5] acknowledged that the success of an insolvency regime was heavily dependent on those who administer it, namely the insolvency practitioners in private practice who did the work of liquidators, receivers, trustees and so on.[6] The Report noted that while most practitioners discharged their duties properly there were some who did not.[7] At the time of the Cork Committee's study, insolvency practitioners were not required to have any particular qualifications and this was identified by many as a major shortcoming in the system.[8] There was general recognition in the commercial world that there were some persons who were acting as insolvency practitioners who might be termed 'cowboys'. The Cork Committee agreed with the need for regulation and standards for qualification as an insolvency practitioner and when the Act was passed it included the essential requirement that practitioners should be members of professional bodies that could regulate and discipline its members. The aim is to ensure that there is a qualified, independent and competent insolvency profession that is marked by integrity. The Secretary of State was granted the power to declare bodies to be recognised professional bodies (section 391(1)), membership of which permitted a person to be able to act as an insolvency practitioner within the meaning of the Act. There are seven bodies that have been recognised for the purposes of section 391 as being ones that were professional and able to discipline and regulate members; they include the Law Society of England and Wales and the Institute of Chartered Accountants in England and Wales.[9] Regulation includes setting requirements for eligibility to practise as insolvency practitioners, such as laying down educational and experience requirements on members (section 391(2)). While the professional bodies that are recognised exercise control over their own qualified members, there is governmental monitoring as the Insolvency Service supervises the regulatory process, conducts regular visits to all of the professional bodies and endeavours to ensure that necessary standards are maintained. The professional bodies operate various processes to control and correct those acting improperly, with expulsion from membership of the professional body as the most stringent penalty available. Of course, if a person was expelled then his or her right to act as an office-holder would be revoked automatically.

[5] Cmnd 858 (1982).
[6] At para 732.
[7] At para 735.
[8] Ibid.
[9] Insolvency Practitioners (Recognised Professional Bodies) Order 1986 (SI 1986/1764).

Many practitioners have become members of the Association for Business Recovery Professionals (formerly, the Society for Practitioners of Insolvency) and known as R3 (standing for Rescue, Recovery and Renewal). This Association is involved in training practitioners and also determining ethical issues.

An alternative way, besides being members of recognised professional bodies, to secure the right to be able to act as insolvency practitioners is for persons to apply to the Secretary of State for an authorisation to act (section 393). They may be authorised to act as insolvency practitioners if they are fit and proper persons (Insolvency Practitioners Regulations 1990, regulation 4). If a person is refused an authorisation to act or has his or her authorisation withdrawn, the person may require the matter to be referred to the Insolvency Practitioners Tribunal (section 395).

The Act made it a criminal offence to act as an insolvency practitioner without being qualified under section 391 (section 389). Acting as an insolvency practitioner in England and Wales includes acting, in relation to a company, as a liquidator, provisional liquidator, administrator, administrative receiver, or as a nominee or supervisor of a company voluntary arrangement, and acting, in relation to an individual, as a trustee in bankruptcy, interim receiver or as a nominee or supervisor of an individual voluntary arrangement (section 388(1)(2)). All of this is not relevant to official receivers (sections 388(5) and 389(2)), who are able to carry out these functions by virtue of their office.

Besides having to be qualified under the terms of section 390(2), a person is not able to act as an insolvency practitioner unless he or she provides security (section 390(3)). This is designed to safeguard the positions of creditors where an insolvency practitioner has acted in such as way as to cause loss to creditors. Finally, persons are unable to act as insolvency practitioners if they are undischarged bankrupts, are subject to a disqualification order under the Company Directors' Disqualification Act 1986, are patients under the Mental Health Act 1983 (section 390(4)) or they are, in the future, subject to a bankruptcy restriction order (section 390(5)). It should be noted that only individuals are able to act as insolvency practitioners (section 390(1)), thereby ruling out companies.

People unhappy with the actions of insolvency practitioners who are members of recognised bodies should initially complain to those bodies. If no satisfaction is obtained, the person should then go to the Department of Trade and Industry. The latter action is the appropriate action for anyone who is aggrieved about the conduct of insolvency practitioners not members of recognised bodies, but who were granted authorisation to act as practitioners.

Although solicitors may be qualified to act as insolvency practitioners, very few do so, leaving the bulk of the work to accountants. Those lawyers who specialise in insolvency advise those insolvency practitioners who are not lawyers, as well as clients who have an interest in insolvencies, such as banks.

In this book, for ease of exposition, we use, unless it is indicated to the contrary, the term 'office-holder' as a generic term to refer to qualified insolvency practitioners, carrying out any of the following roles:

- liquidator;
- provisional liquidator;
- administrator;
- administrative receiver;
- a supervisor of a company voluntary arrangement;
- trustee in bankruptcy;
- interim receiver;
- supervisor of an individual voluntary arrangement;
- or official receivers undertaking any of the aforementioned roles that they are entitled, by law, to carry out.

Chapter 5

Options for Insolvents and the Layout of the Book

This chapter does two things briefly. First, it explains in very general terms what options there are for insolvent individuals and companies. Second, it explains how the book is laid out.

5.1 Options for insolvents

If a person is insolvent he or she basically has choices, although, of course, one or more of these might not be appropriate or feasible. The choices for a debtor are:

- Evade the payment of debts. This is questionable morally and, in today's world, it is not going to be as successful as it once was.
- Attempt to re-finance.
- Try to come to some informal arrangement with some or all of the creditors (this is discussed in Part II).
- Seek, where a judgment has been made against the debtor, the making of an administration order by a county court, provided that the debtor's total debt does not exceed £5,000 (this is, again, considered briefly in Part II).
- Put forward a proposal for the debtor to enter, under the Insolvency Act 1986, an individual voluntary arrangement whereby all creditors will be bound by the arrangement if the required vote is obtained from creditors (this too is discussed in Part II).
- Present a debtor's petition seeking one's bankruptcy (this is considered in Part V).
- Wait to see if a creditor presents a bankruptcy petition (this is discussed in Part V).

If a company is insolvent it has a similar range of choices:

- Evade payment of debts. This is probably harder for a company than a person.
- Attempt to re-finance.
- Try to come to some informal arrangement with some or all of the creditors (this is discussed in Part II).
- Enter administration (this is considered in Part II).
- Put forward a proposal for the debtor to enter, under the Insolvency Act 1986, a company voluntary arrangement whereby all creditors will be bound by the arrangement if the required vote is obtained from creditors (this too is discussed in Part II).
- Approach a secured creditor about appointing a receiver where the secured creditor holds a floating charge over the whole, or substantially the whole, of the company's property (receivership is examined in Part II).
- Resolve to enter voluntary liquidation (this is discussed in Part IV).
- Wait to see if a creditor presents a petition for compulsory liquidation (this is also considered in Part IV).

It is worthwhile now to provide a very basic overview of the major insolvency administrations that have been mentioned above and that are discussed in far more detail later in the book.

5.2 Personal insolvency

5.2.1 *Bankruptcy*

Bankruptcy is the process to which an individual may be made subject, where his or her debts are so overwhelming as to be incapable of being paid in full as and when they are due. The process begins with a petition to the court for a bankruptcy order. The person presenting the petition will usually be one or more of the debtor's creditors, or the debtor himself or herself. The procedure and process bears many similarities to the compulsory winding up of companies.

Although bankruptcy tends to be viewed by society in a very negative manner with a social stigma attaching to the bankrupt, it is in fact frequently a beneficial process for the debtor. If a debtor has overwhelming debts, which can never be realistically paid off, the only way the debtor can be released from those debts is by bankruptcy. Bankruptcy is the process by which the debtor in effect hands over whatever assets he or she has, to an official who will usually sell them and distribute the proceeds of sale among the debtor's creditors.

Following the petition, if the court is satisfied that the debtor is insolvent, it will usually make a bankruptcy order. At this point, the debtor is said to be an undischarged bankrupt and, as such, is subject to a number of personal restrictions; for example, an undischarged bankrupt cannot act as a director of a company. As soon as the bankruptcy order is made, the official receiver takes control of the bankrupt's estate and acts to secure the bankrupt's assets. If the estate has enough value in it to pay the fees of a private sector insolvency practitioner to realise the estate and pay off the creditors, such a person will usually be appointed as the trustee in bankruptcy. If the estate is so poor as to be incapable of paying such fees, the official receiver will usually continue in post as trustee in bankruptcy. One feature of bankruptcy is that upon appointment of the trustee, the bankrupt's estate vests automatically in the trustee without the need for any separate conveyance or assignment.

The trustee will act to maximise the assets available to the debtor's creditors. The trustee will then attempt to pay off as many of the creditors who have 'proved' their debts in the bankruptcy. There exists a statutory hierarchy of debts which governs the order in which different classes of debts are paid. Generally, normal unsecured trade creditors come at the bottom of the statutory order of distribution. They frequently receive no payment for their debts in a bankruptcy. The trustee will divide up whatever money is available to pay the creditors and is said to declare a 'dividend.' This is expressed in the form of so many pence in the pound.

Once the estate has been got in, realised and distributed, the trusteeship will come to an end. After a certain period of time has elapsed, the undischarged bankrupt is either automatically discharged or can apply to the court for discharge. The effect of discharge is that the bankrupt is released from virtually all the debts that had been incurred up to the time of the bankruptcy order. This is the great benefit of bankruptcy as it operates to wipe the slate clean. Under the bankruptcy provisions of the Enterprise Act 2002 (estimated to be in force early in the 2004 financial year), a new process will come into force, which will enable discharge automatically after one year. Where the bankrupt is in some way culpable, certain bankruptcy restrictions will stay in place for up to 15 years.

5.2.2 *Individual voluntary arrangement*

As an alternative to bankruptcy, an individual may consider putting to his or her creditors a proposal for an individual voluntary arrangement (an 'IVA'). Such a proposal can even be made after the individual has been made bankrupt. An IVA will take the form of either a compromise of debts or a scheme of arrangement. What this means is that the debtor will admit that he or she cannot pay all his or her debts either in full or immediately they fall due. A composition of debts involves the debtor promising to pay a proportion of the debt owed. A scheme of arrangement typically asks for further time to pay debts. Whatever form the IVA takes, it is crucial that it provides for a better financial deal for the individual's creditors than they could expect under a bankruptcy. An IVA cannot be made binding on secured or preferential creditors unless they consent to it.

An IVA may typically consist of the debtor making monthly payments to a supervisor who will distribute the funds among the creditors according to the terms of the IVA. Such an IVA may run for a number of years. Alternatively, the IVA may not be based upon projected income of the debtor but, instead, may be based upon the distribution of proceeds of sale of capital assets belonging to the debtor. Such IVAs will usually be completed in a shorter period of time.

Where the debtor is not already a bankrupt, he or she may apply to the court for an interim order pending the consideration of the IVA proposal by the creditors. The interim order is designed to create a form of moratorium on creditor actions against the debtor until the creditors have had a chance to consider the proposal. It prevents certain types of creditor 'jumping the gun' by acting swiftly and enforcing their rights against the debtor to the detriment of the collective body of creditors.

An insolvency practitioner, acting as nominee, will consider the terms of the IVA proposal and make a report to the court. As long as the report is positive, the nominee will proceed to call a meeting of creditors to consider the proposal. If a majority in value of greater than 75 per cent of the unsecured creditors, entitled to vote and voting, vote in favour of the IVA, it becomes binding upon all those creditors who were entitled to vote at the creditors' meeting; even those who voted against it or did not attend the meeting. The nominee will usually act as the supervisor of the IVA and give effect to its terms.

5.3 Corporate insolvency

5.3.1 *Liquidation*

This administration is also known as 'winding up' and there is no important distinction to be made in relation to the different terms used. In this book, as is the usual custom in this field, the two labels will be used interchangeably.

Liquidation may take place for a variety of reasons, but the usual reason for it in the overwhelming number of cases is the insolvency of the company. Liquidation bears many similarities to bankruptcy (in the nineteenth century it was sometimes referred to as company bankruptcy) and was based on bankruptcy, adopting many of its rules.

There are two principal forms of liquidation – voluntary winding up and winding up by the court,[1] the latter being commonly known as compulsory winding up. Voluntary liquidation is initiated by the company and occurs as a result of a resolution for winding up passed by the company in general meeting.[2] Voluntary liquidation can either be a members' voluntary (only when the company is solvent) or a creditors' voluntary. We will not deal with the former as it cannot occur where the company is insolvent.[3] While the members must vote in favour of a creditors' voluntary liquidation, the creditors will have input, if they wish, in how the winding up proceeds. Voluntary liquidations may be finalised without any court involvement.

Compulsory winding up is deemed to have commenced with the presentation of a petition, which is the process that commences any winding-up proceedings. In this situation the company is normally, though not necessarily, insolvent. If a court, which has a wide discretion, orders the winding up of a company, the official receiver is appointed as liquidator and will continue to be so unless, as often occurs, he or she is replaced by a private liquidator, who is an office-holder as discussed in Chapter 4.

Liquidation does not end the corporate identity or powers of a company, but it does place the company and those who control its affairs under certain disabilities. Liquidation, other than where there is a 'members' voluntary liquidation', sees a transfer of power to manage the affairs of the company from the directors and members to the liquidator and the creditors' meeting.

The person appointed as the liquidator is the central player in a winding up. When a winding-up order is made the powers of the directors cease and the liquidator assumes the function of managing the company and of collecting, realising and distributing its assets. In voluntary winding up the appointment of the liquidator means that the powers of the directors cease unless they are preserved. Like a director the liquidator acts as an agent of the company and, like a director, owes fiduciary duties to the creditors. The liquidator will take control of all of the assets of the company, which may involve recovering some from other people and to administer them for the benefit of the creditors who, if they provide the liquidator with the necessary proof of the company's liability to them, will receive a distribution after the assets have been sold for as much as possible. This distribution, which will be based on creditors being paid so many pence in the pound (for instance if a creditor was owed £50,000 and the liquidator calculated that he or she could pay 10p in the £, the creditor would receive £5,000), can be small and in some cases consist of nothing at all.

Once a winding up is complete the company is then dissolved, which is equivalent to death, although it is able to be revived in certain limited circumstances.

---

[1] Insolvency Act, section 73(1).
[2] Insolvency Act, section 84(1).
[3] For a discussion of members' voluntary winding up, see A. Keay, *McPherson's Law of Company Liquidation* London: Sweet & Maxwell (2001), Chapter 2.

5.3.2 *Receivership*

Receivership, in an insolvency context, is where a secured creditor of a company enforces the security by appointing a receiver. For centuries it has been possible for a mortgagee, following default under the terms of a mortgage by the mortgagor, to enter into possession of the mortgaged assets and sell them in order to pay off the secured debt. As an alternative to entering into possession, secured creditors of companies have, since the nineteenth century, appointed a receiver to realise the secured assets and pay off the creditor from the proceeds of sale.

It is extremely common for a company to raise trading capital by borrowing money from a bank or other financial institution. The bank will normally want security for its loan. The loan agreement, in this context, is usually referred to as a 'debenture' and will usually charge all the company's present and future property. When the company defaults under the terms of the debenture, for example, by failing to make monthly instalment payments to the bank, the bank will usually have the power to appoint a receiver to realise the charged assets. Where the debenture covers all or substantially all of the company's assets, the receiver is referred to as an 'administrative receiver'.

Although the receiver will be appointed by the debenture holder, the receiver will act as agent of the company and will usurp the powers of management of the directors. The receiver's function is to realise the charged assets and pay off the debenture holder. In carrying out this function, the receiver will usually wish to sell the company's business as a going concern, as this type of sale is likely to demand a higher price than a piecemeal sale of the company's individual assets.

Once the receiver has realised enough assets to pay off the debenture holder, he or she will vacate office. As can be appreciated, if a large proportion of, or even all, the company's assets have been sold, the company itself will be left as an empty shell. In such circumstances the company will usually be wound up immediately and thereby killed off.

The Enterprise Act 2002 effectively abolishes the right to appoint an administrative receiver where the debenture in question is executed after the commencement of the 2002 Act (estimated to be early in the 2004 financial year).

5.3.3 *Administration*

Since the mid-1980s it has been possible for an ailing company to be put into administration. Until very recently, the only way this could be done was by obtaining an administration order from the court. This is still possible, but in addition, following the commencement of the Enterprise Act 2002, it will be possible for an administrator to be appointed out of court either by a debenture holder, or the company itself or its directors. Where an administrator is appointed, he or she takes over the management of the company from the directors and, in common with administrative receivers, has wide powers of management and disposal of company assets.

The most distinguishing characteristic of administration is that it brings about a wide-ranging moratorium on actions against the company. While a company is in administration, virtually all its creditors are prevented from taking any action against the company without the permission of either the court or the administrator. The administrator's function is to take advantage of this freeze on creditor harassment, by putting together a plan to improve the position of the company's creditors. The plan may involve the proposed rescue of the company by way of a company voluntary arrangement or otherwise, or may involve the realisation of the company's assets in a more ordered and beneficial manner than could be achieved in a winding up. Once the purpose of the administration has been achieved, the administrator will vacate office. Depending upon whether or not the administration has been a success, and what form that success takes, the company may thereafter immediately be placed into liquidation or continue to trade as before.

5.3.4 *Company voluntary arrangement*

In the same way that an individual can enter into an IVA, a company can enter into a company voluntary arrangement (a 'CVA'). The procedural and substantive requirements are essentially the same for both types of voluntary arrangement. The main difference is that until recently there was no equivalent of the IVA's interim order for CVAs. In order for a company to have the benefit of a moratorium on creditor actions, while it puts together a CVA proposal, it was necessary for the company first to be put into administration. Following the CVA provisions of the Insolvency Act 2000 (in force 1 January 2003), it is now possible for 'small companies' to obtain a short-term moratorium pending the drafting of a CVA proposal, without the need to put the company into administration. It remains to be seen how often this procedure will be used, as following the commencement of the corporate insolvency provisions of the Enterprise Act 2002 (due to be early in the 2004 financial year) it will be far easier to put a company into administration than it has hitherto been. Administration may be seen as an easier route to achieving a moratorium than the procedure under the 2000 Act.

5.4 The layout of the book

Now moving to the layout of the book. What we assume at the outset is that a person or a company is insolvent according to the meaning set out in Chapter 2. The book is divided up into nine parts in order to facilitate exposition of the law and to enable readers to understand the various procedures and processes that are available under English insolvency law. Following Part I, Part II discusses the options available to insolvents if they do not wish to be wound up (companies) or bankrupted (individuals). We have titled this Part 'Non-Terminal Insolvency' to contrast the procedures discussed with the administrations of bankruptcy and winding up, which might be termed 'Terminal Insolvency'. This is not strictly correct because, although winding up usually leads to the death of a company (dissolution), individuals, of course, are not terminated. But they are subjected to certain limitations that effectively end their control of businesses. The concept of non-terminal insolvency is used to indicate that the purpose behind invoking one of the options discussed in this Part is to enable the insolvent to be kept from the limitations of bankruptcy and the terminal nature of winding up. The hope is that the company or individual might be able to 'get themselves back on their feet', which will produce overall benefits not only for the debtor, but also for the creditors. Part III considers provisional liquidation, which is an administration that might be implemented before a winding up is ordered by the court. This is followed by Part IV which provides a detailed discussion of winding up (liquidation). The final insolvency administration examined is, in Part V, bankruptcy. The last four Parts of the book focus on matters, some of which are relevant to all administrations while others are relevant only to some of the administrations featured in this book. Part VI addresses some of the primary issues that have to be considered by office-holders in the course of administering an insolvent estate. Part VII examines issues affecting creditors as well as the different types of creditors and their particular concerns. Part VIII deals with the legal actions that might be initiated by office-holders in order to swell the amount of funds that will be available to be paid to creditors. Finally, Part IX examines the consequences of misconduct, in particular, of individual insolvents, their associates and officers of corporate insolvents.

References

Baird, D. and Jackson, T., 'Corporate Reorganizations and the Treatment of Diverse Ownership Interests: A Comment on Adequate Protection of Secured Creditors in Bankruptcy' (1984) 51 *University of Chicago Law Review* 97.

Bradley, M., 'Cross-Border Insolvency Reform: A Critical Review' (2001) 4 *Receivers, Administrators and Liquidators Quarterly* 285.

Carlson, D., 'Philosophy in Bankruptcy' (1987) 85 *Michigan Law Review* 1341.

Chiah, K., 'Voidable Preference' (1986) 12 *New Zealand Universities Law Review* 1.

Crystal, M., 'The Approach of the UK Courts to Insolvency: 1986–1994' (1994) 1 *Receivers, Administrators and Liquidators Quarterly* 71.

Dawson, K., 'The UNCITRAL Model Law on Cross-Border Insolvencies: Will it Make a Difference?' (2000) 4 *Receivers, Administrators and Liquidators Quarterly* 147.

Dawson, K., 'The European Regulation on Insolvency Proceedings' (2001) 4 *Receivers, Administrators and Liquidators Quarterly* 345.

Finch, V., 'The Measures of Insolvency' (1997) 17 OJLS 227.

Finch, V., 'Insolvency Practitioners: Regulation and Reform' [1998] JBL 334.

Finch, V., 'Controlling the Insolvency Professional' [1999] *Insolvency Lawyer* 228.

Finch, V., *Corporate Insolvency Law: Perspectives and Principles*, Cambridge: Cambridge University Press (2002).

Flessner, A., 'Philosophies of Business Bankruptcy Law: An International Overview' in J Ziegel (ed), *Current Developments in International and Comparative Corporate Insolvency Law*, Oxford: Clarendon Press (1994).

Fletcher, I.F., 'The Genesis of Modern Insolvency Law – An Odyssey of Law Reform' [1987] JBL 365.

Fletcher, I.F., *The Law of Insolvency*, 3rd edn, London: Sweet & Maxwell (2002).

Gearty, C. and Davies, S., *Insolvency Practice and the Human Rights Act 1998*, Bristol: Jordans (2000).

Goldring, J., 'The new European insolvency regulation – a synopsis' (2002) 18 *Insolvency Law and Practice* 52.

Goode, R.M., *The Principles of Corporate Insolvency Law*, 2nd edn, London: Sweet & Maxwell (1997).

Graham, D., 'A Dark and Neglected Subject: Landmarks in the Reform of English Insolvency Law' (2002) 11 *International Insolvency Review* 97.

Gross, K., 'Taking Community Interests into Account in Bankrutpcy: An Essay' (1994) 72 *Washington University Law Quarterly* 1031.

Gross, K., *Failure and Forgiveness: Rebalancing the Bankruptcy System*, New Haven: Yale University Press (1997).

Jackson, T.H., 'Bankruptcy Non-Bankruptcy Entitlements and the Creditors' Bargain' (1982) 91 Yale LJ 857.

Jackson, T.H., *The Logic and Limits of Bankruptcy*, Harvard Press (1986).

Keay, A., 'The Insolvency Factor in the Avoidance of Antecedent Transactions in Corporate Liquidations' (1995) 21 *Monash University Law Review* 305.

Keay, A., *Avoidance Provisions in Insolvency Law*, Sydney: LBC Information Services (1997).

Keay, A., 'To unify or not to unify insolvency legislation: International Experience and the latest South African Proposals' (1999) 1 *De Jure* 62.

Keay, A., 'The Unity of Insolvency Legislation: Time for a Re-think?' (1999) 7 *Insolvency Law Journal* 4.

Keay, A., 'Insolvency Law: A Matter of Public Interest?' (2000) 51 NILQ 509.

Keay, A., 'Balancing Interests in Bankruptcy Law' [2001] *Common Law World Review* 206.

Keay, A., *McPherson's Law of Company Liquidation*, London: Sweet & Maxwell (2001).

Keay, A. and de Prez, P., 'Insolvency and Environmental Principles: A Case Study in a Conflict of Public Interests' (2001) 3 *Environmental Law Review* 90.

Keay, A. and Murray, M., *Insolvency: Personal and Corporate Law and Practice*, 4th edn, Sydney: Law Book Co (2002).

Kilpi, J., *The Ethics of Bankruptcy*, London: Routledge (1998).

Korobkin, D., 'Contractariansim and the Normative Foundations of Bankruptcy Law' (1993) 71 Texas L Rev 541.

Levinthal, L., 'The Early History of Bankruptcy Law' [1918] *University of Pennsylvania Law Review* 223.

Lightman, G. and Moss, G., *The Law of Receivers and Administrators of Companies*, 3rd edn, London: Sweet & Maxwell (2000).

Miles, V., 'Assessing Modern Bankruptcy Law: An Example of Justice' (1996) 36 *Santa Clara Law Review* 1025.

Milman, D., 'Test of Commercial Insolvency Rejected' (1983) 4 Co Law 231.

Moss, G., 'The Impact of the EU Regulation on UK Insolvency Proceedings' (2002) 11 *International Insolvency Review* 139.

Obank, R., 'Cross-Border Harmonisation of Insolvency Proceedings and the Quest for Comity Parts 1, 2 & 3' (2002) 17 JIBFL 89; 126; 169.

Omar, P., 'The UNCITRAL Insolvency Initiative: a five-year review' [2002] *Insolvency Lawyer* 228.

Pike, N., 'The Human Rights Act 1998 and its Impact on Insolvency Practitioners' [2001] *Insolvency Lawyer* 25.

Rajak, H., 'The Harmonisation of Insolvency Proceedings in the European Union' [2000] *Company Financial and Insolvency Law Review* 180.

Rose, D., *Lewis' Bankruptcy Law*, 11th edn, Sydney: Law Book Co (2000).

Sealy, L. and Milman, D., *Annotated Guide to the Insolvency Legislation*, 5th edn, Bicester: CCH (1999).

Schermer, B., 'Response to Professor Gross: Taking the Interests of the Community into Account in Bankruptcy' (1994) 72 *Washington University Law Quarterly* 1049.

Shuchman, P., 'An Attempt at a Philosophy of Bankruptcy' (1973) 21 UCLA L Rev 403.

Simmons, M. and Smith, T., 'The Human Rights Act 1998: the practical impact on insolvency' (2000) 16 *Insolvency Law and Practice* 167.

Treiman, I., 'Escaping the Creditor in the Middle Ages' (1927) 43 LQR 230.

Trower, W., 'Bringing Human Rights Home to the Insolvency Practioners' (2000) 13 Insolvency Intelligence 41 (Part 1) and (2000) 13 Insolvency Intelligence 52 (Part 2).

Veach, J., 'On Considering the Public Interest in Bankruptcy: Looking to the Railroads for Answers' (1997) 72 *Indiana Law Journal* 1211.

Warren, E., 'Bankruptcy Policy' (1987) 54 *University of Chicago Law Review* 775.

Warren, E., 'The Bankruptcy Crisis' (1998) 73 *Indiana Law Journal* 1079.

Weisberg, R., 'Commercial Morality, the Merchant Character and the History of the Voidable Preference' (1986) 39 *Stanford Law Review* 3.

Part II

Non-Terminal Insolvency

As has been explained in Part I, this Part will consider what we shall refer to as non-terminal insolvency procedures. Until the changes brought about by the recommendations of the Cork Report,[1] there were only very limited options open to an insolvent individual looking to avoid bankruptcy or to a company hoping to avoid the terminal procedure of winding up.

An individual could attempt to come to some arrangement with his or her creditors, either informally or through the formal medium of a deed of arrangement. Either type of arrangement would fail if not supported by all or virtually all of the individual's creditors. The mere fact of entering such an arrangement would usually constitute grounds for the court to make a bankruptcy order against the debtor.

A company trying to avoid winding up could attempt to enter into an informal arrangement with its creditors but the chances of such an agreement being successful was equally as precarious as for an individual. A formal scheme of arrangement has long been possible with the sanction of the court. As we shall see, this type of arrangement may be useful to a company in financial trouble but due to its being procedurally complex and expensive it has only really been available to large undertakings. For smaller enterprises the only option, apart from liquidation, has historically been receivership. The problem with receivership, as we shall see in Chapter 6, is that it is a procedure designed with one thing in mind: paying a secured creditor. It is not intended to turn the company around and is itself usually the precursor to liquidation.

Due to the problems facing insolvent debtors who wanted to avoid bankruptcy or liquidation (as the case may be), the Cork Report recommended the introduction of new mechanisms which have come to be referred to generally as forming part of today's 'rescue culture'. Parliament followed

---

[1] *Insolvency Law and Practice*, Cmnd 8558, 1982.

the Cork recommendations in general terms, in creating administration and voluntary arrangements. The modern law is contained principally within the Insolvency Act 1986.

Administration only applies to companies and was originally intended to provide a breathing space for the company free from hassle from its creditors. The idea was to allow the company a set period of time to try to get its act together and come up with a plan for its rescue or at least a beneficial disposal of its assets. The idea for administration came from the Cork Report's view that, although receivership was by no means a collective process, it often had a positive impact upon the company's ailing business. The introduction of an outside manager, usually an accountant, as receiver of the company, frequently had the consequence that the company was managed in a far more efficient manner than had been the case when under the control of the company's directors. Administration has, as its origins, the idea that the imposition of a professional to manage a company's business can lead to the business being turned around and saved.

As we shall see, the Enterprise Act 2002 has impacted seriously on the ability in the future for receivers to be appointed at all. In the medium term, administration will effectively replace receivership as the most popular non-terminal corporate procedure.

In addition to the benefits of a freeze on creditor action against a company in administration, Cork also recommended the introduction of a procedure whereby either companies or individuals could make a proposal to their creditors. The proposal becomes binding on all unsecured creditors if more than three quarters in value of the unsecured creditors agree to it. Although these voluntary arrangements have, in general, been a success, there have been a number of teething problems with them, necessitating recent statutory amendments.

In this Part, we shall look at receivership, administration, company voluntary arrangements, individual voluntary arrangements and other possible formal or informal types of arrangement. These are the options available to an insolvent debtor short of the 'terminal' procedures of liquidation (for companies) and bankruptcy (for individuals).

Throughout this Part, except where indicated to the contrary, any reference to 'the Act' or to section numbers will be references to the Insolvency Act 1986. Except where indicated to the contrary, any reference to 'the Rules' or to rule numbers will be references to the Insolvency Rules 1986 (SI 1986/1925).

Chapter 6

Receivership

6.1 Introduction

As the name suggests a receiver is a person who receives or controls property on behalf of others and will normally also have power to sell assets and distribute the proceeds. The estates of individuals or partnerships may be subject to receivership but this does not usually occur due to insolvency. For example, a receiver may be appointed under section 39 of the Partnership Act 1890 where a partnership is being dissolved and the partners cannot agree as to their respective entitlements. In contrast, a corporate receiver is almost always appointed over a company which is either insolvent or nearly insolvent.

There is a common misconception that receivership is the same as liquidation. As we shall see, they are fundamentally different procedures with different goals. Essentially, liquidation is the process by which all the affairs of the company are wound up and the company is then dissolved. Receivership is the process by which assets are realised to pay off particular creditors. It may be that after the receivership is over, the company can return to profitable trading. Most commonly a company, which has been in receivership and had all or some of its assets disposed of by the receiver, cannot recover and will end up in liquidation either during the receivership or shortly thereafter. The business may survive relatively intact in the hands of a buyer but the company itself will usually be an empty shell following the sale of the business and will be wound up.

The appointment of a receiver is, in the majority of instances, the favoured action of a secured creditor of a company where the company has breached the loan agreement, usually referred to as a debenture.[1] The breach will usually be failing to keep up with repayments. The lender will

---

[1] Chitty J in *Levy v Abercorris Slate and Slab Co* (1887) 37 Ch D 260 at 264 stated 'a debenture means a document which either creates a debt or acknowledges it'.

usually be a bank or other financial institution. Often a company, which is aware of its own financial problems, will invite the lender to appoint a receiver. The media commonly reports a company as having called in the receivers. In fact, it will be the secured lender who appoints the receiver.

It is important to note that receivership as a remedy for debenture holders has been extremely restricted by the Enterprise Act 2002. For debentures entered into prior to the commencement of this Act it remains an important option. For debentures entered into after this date, the option to appoint a receiver has been seriously restricted. For these newly executed debentures, the lender, in order to enforce its security, will instead usually have to appoint an administrator. This major change will be considered below.

A creditor who lends money without taking any security will only have a bare contractual right to enforce the debt. If the company fails to pay, the creditor will need to take legal proceedings to obtain judgment against the company and then enforce the judgment.[2] If, in the meantime, the company has gone into liquidation, the creditor will usually be at the end of the list of creditors to be paid out and may ultimately receive little or nothing of the debt owed.

Any substantial creditor will wish to avoid this consequence by taking security over the company's assets. If this is done, the creditor has two rights against the company. As with the unsecured creditor it has the contractual right to sue for recovery of the debt. In addition, as a secured creditor, it has the right under the secured loan agreement (or debenture) to look to the assets subject to the security ahead of other creditors. The assets subject to the security will be sold to pay off the secured creditor. The creditor will hope the value of the secured assets is enough to pay off the debt owed. This is commonly not the case, for instance, due to the claims of other creditors or due to depreciation of the property secured.

The type of security taken by the lender (debenture holder) will usually include a fixed charge (or mortgage) on large permanent or semi-permanent items such as land, buildings and machinery and a floating charge over assets which by their nature change day to day, such as stock in trade or book debts.

If security is taken over land, the terms 'mortgage' and 'charge' essentially mean the same thing and can be used interchangeably.[3] Security over personalty is categorised according to common law rules. A mortgage of personalty involves the transfer of property to the lender who re-transfers title to the mortgagor when the loan is paid off or redeemed. A fixed or specific charge over personalty does not involve a transfer of title but the charged assets are subject to the lender's rights prior to other creditors.[4] In

---

[2] For the rights of judgment creditors to execute their judgment against an insolvent debtor see Chapter 32.

[3] See sections 85 and 87 Law of Property Act 1925.

[4] See e.g. Lord Hoffman in *Morris v Agrichemical Ltd* [1997] BCC 965 at 972 and Millett LJ in *Re Cosslett (Contractors) Ltd* [1997] BCC 724 at 733.

terms of the priority afforded to the secured creditor there is little practical difference, if any, between the mortgage and the fixed charge.

Under the terms of a debenture, the secured creditor will usually have the power, upon default by the company, either to enter into possession of the assets and sell them to pay off the secured debt or to appoint a receiver with the power to manage and sell the company's business as a going concern to raise the money.

It has long been accepted by the courts that as soon as a mortgage or fixed charge is executed it freezes the secured assets in the company's hands. The company must acquire the express consent of the debenture holder every time it wishes to deal with any of the secured assets. There is no general licence to deal with the assets in the ordinary course of business and so, for example, a mortgage or fixed charge over stock in trade is not practical as the stock will need to be turned over each minute of each day. It would effectively paralyse the company's business if it needed to obtain consent for each individual dealing. Once default has occurred and the fixed charged assets come to be sold, they can only be sold piecemeal. There is no implied power under a fixed charge to manage the business as an interim measure pending sale, or a power to sell the company's business as a going concern. The consequence of this in practical terms is that any sale by a mortgagee or receiver under a fixed charge would be likely to realise less money on a piecemeal sale than it would if the business could be sold on as a going concern.

A floating charge executed over a company's 'undertaking' assists the position of the company and the debenture holder. By the term 'undertaking', the floating charge covers all the company's property both present and future, including its goodwill and the ability to carry on the business. This is a charge over assets which by their nature change, such as the company's stock in trade, but which the company can use in the ordinary course of business until some event occurs which 'crystallises' the charge and makes it enforceable. A receiver appointed over the undertaking of a company has the power to carry on the business and sell it as a going concern, thus usually maximising the value of the security. Secured creditors usually take a fixed charge over those assets the company does not wish to deal with on a regular basis and a floating charge over the remainder. On the insolvency of a company, a fixed charge has priority over a floating charge.

The secured creditor will not usually wish to enter into possession of the secured assets itself, as it will then become subject to the onerous duties of a mortgagee in possession.[5] The appointment of a receiver puts the enforcement of the security in the hands of a third party who is invariably deemed to be the agent of the company, not of the appointing creditor.

The vast majority of receivers appointed over the assets of insolvent companies are privately appointed receivers as opposed to court

---

[5] For a consideration of the duties of a mortgagee in possession see e.g., *White v City of London Brewery Co* (1889) 42 Ch D 237.

appointed receivers. Receivers are appointed by the court only very rarely and may, for example, be the product of a poorly drafted loan agreement which failed to give the lender the power to appoint a receiver out of court. Court appointed receivers do not provide a particularly attractive option for a creditor seeking to protect his or her rights for a variety of reasons:

- the appointment is expensive and cumbersome;
- the receiver's powers are limited by the court order making the appointment;
- the receiver is under the direct control of the court;
- an applicant for such an order would probably be obliged to provide security for the receiver's costs.

The future for court appointed receivers in an insolvency context looks bleak. Prior to the Enterprise Act 2002 such appointments were rare. Following the Enterprise Act's expansion of the administration order regime, it is likely that court appointed receivers' practical importance will recede further.[6]

The appointment of an out of court receiver has been the favoured remedy of a secured creditor, following default by the chargor company, for well over a century. It is useful at this point, prior to considering the detailed provisions governing receivers, to consider briefly the history of trade financing as it relates to secured creditors. An understanding of the history of secured lending will assist in understanding how receivership and the other non-terminal insolvency procedures operate. In order to grasp how corporate lending rules evolved, it is first necessary to consider in outline the history of unincorporated secured lending.

6.2 History of trade finance[7]

6.2.1 *Unincorporated secured borrowing*

Until the passing of the various Companies Acts in the middle of the nineteenth century, the most common forms of business media were sole traderships or partnerships. From the turn of the fifteenth century onwards a large amount of trade was conducted on credit with the

---

[6] It is outside the purpose of this book to consider court appointed receivers in any detail and the reader is directed to more specialist works such as H. Picarda, *The Law Relating to Receivers, Managers and Administrators*, 3rd edn, London: Butterworths (2000).

[7] See generally R. Gregory and P. Walton, 'Fixed and Floating Charges – A Revelation' [2001] LMCLQ 123.

consequence that security became a significant issue. The practice of mortgaging personalty became commonplace and, just as landowners mortgaged their land, so less wealthy commoners pledged their goods, comprising stock in trade, household chattels and implements of their trade, without parting with actual possession.

Equity had always recognised mortgages over present and future assets. It was therefore possible in equity to mortgage one's changing assets such as a business's stock in trade or the debts which were owed to the business (its book debts). The mortgage (or bill of sale as it was commonly called) was effective as soon as any future item came into the mortgagor's hands satisfying the description of the mortgaged goods, for example, stock in trade. No transfer separate from the original mortgage was required and priority existed as from the moment of acquisition by the mortgagor. The classic example of this principle is *Holroyd v Marshall* ((1862) 10 HLC 191) where a mortgagee of present and future 'machinery implements and things', fixed in or placed about a mill, had an equitable title to after-acquired items which the House of Lords held to prevail over an execution creditor.

In the event of a trader's financial collapse, his or her creditors received nothing from the trader's bankruptcy because the assets were all swept up in the mortgage bill of sale, which was usually a secret document. Thus a large and visible stock, which created the appearance of ownership, wealth and creditworthiness, was, or could be, a delusion. Parliament acted on several occasions to limit the impact of this delusive credit.[8] In 1854 the Bills of Sale Act was passed which made such mortgages subject to public registration.

This Statute covered mortgages of personalty, but equity soon came up with a way to bypass the Act. The equitable charge was invented. Charges were not registrable under the 1854 Act as they were not, and are not, strictly speaking mortgages. A mortgage at common law or in equity requires the transfer of title to the mortgagee who, upon being paid the amount owing, re-transfers the title to the mortgagor. A charge does not involve a transfer of title. It merely gives the chargee the right to have the charged assets realised in order to pay off the debt.

The Bills of Sale Act (1878) Amendment Act 1882 killed off the bill of sale mortgage (or charge) as far as individuals were concerned. The Act provided that no individual or partnership could mortgage or charge their future property. Only property in existence at the date of the security being taken could be subject to it. In a commercial setting this effectively ended the reign of the bill of sale, as it was crucial in practice to be able to give security over present and future stock in trade.

---

[8] These secret mortgages were often struck down as a fraud under the Statute of Elizabeth 1570 (13 Eliz I c. 5). See e.g., *Ex parte Games* (1879) 12 Ch D 314. The Bankruptcy Act 1623 (21 Jac I c. 19 section 11) introduced the order and disposition clause which also frequently invalidated such mortgages. See e.g., *Ryall v Rolle* (1749) 1 Atk 165.

At the same time that Parliament was acting to reduce the incidents of bills of sale, parts of the judiciary were doing something similar to hamstring their effects. While the bankruptcy law was, from its inception in 1542, a statutory process, the judges had developed rules which they engrafted onto it. The concept of a 'fraud on the bankrupt laws' was one such. Its rationale was that bankrupts' property should be distributed rateably to creditors.[9]

In 1852, *Graham v Chapman* ((1852) 12 CB 85) extended the principle of 'fraud on the bankruptcy laws':

> Larke, a Norwich draper being indebted to Chapman, borrowed further from him on a mortgage securing both loans. The mortgage covered all present and future property including stock and debts. Larke carried on trade for six months, defaulted (was dispossessed) and went bankrupt. In an issue between the bankruptcy estate and Chapman, the mortgage was held a fraud on the bankruptcy laws and void in the bankruptcy.

Jervis CJ commented (at 102): '. . . the goods remaining in the trader's keeping gave him a false credit, whereas, in truth, he had legally no power to continue his trade, or to dispose of a single article of his stock, if the deed was good'; and (at 106) '. . . the deed here is not for future advances, but for a present payment and a by-gone debt: it conveys all the trader's property, including the advance, and any property purchased with the advance: it necessarily defeats and delays creditors and is, therefore, an act of bankruptcy.'

The consequence was that the very transaction by which the trader sought to escape from financial difficulty (borrowing on present and future property mortgage) was itself the fatal blow to the business. The rejection of the power to deal was particularly crucial as it prevented a trader from mortgaging assets such as stock in trade and book debts as, under *Graham*, the mortgage tied up these assets from use in the business and was held void in a subsequent bankruptcy.

Graham was an unpopular decision but was accepted as law. The Court of Appeal eventually overruled it in 1883 (in *Ex parte Hauxwell* (1883) 23 Ch D 626). It was too late to save the bill of sale mortgage (or charge) as a useful mechanism for unincorporated businesses to borrow money. Although presently owned personalty could be the subject of a security after the Bills of Sale Act (1878) Amendment Act 1882, it was no longer possible to mortgage or charge assets which, by definition, would change day to day in the ordinary course of business, such as stock in trade. The 1882 Act is the reason why individuals and partnerships cannot execute floating charges. Companies, though, can and do with great regularity.

---

[9] See e.g., *Worseley v Demattos* (1758) 1 Burr 467.

6.2.2 *Secured borrowing by companies*

From the latter half of the eighteenth century the term 'undertaking' was used by draftsmen of private Acts of Parliament which created companies to construct large public utilities such as canals and, later, railways and waterworks. Parliament included a power in these statutes for a company to borrow large sums on mortgages of the company's 'undertaking'. This form of mortgage was eventually standardised in Schedule C of the Companies Clauses Consolidation Act 1845. The courts interpreted such mortgages as being over the business as a going concern. The mortgage did not give any rights to the mortgagee to enforce the security while the company continued its business. The mortgagee had no specific interest in any individual items owned by the company because if it did, and it enforced the mortgage, it would paralyse the company's business. A railway would cease to be an effective railway if all its locomotives were seized and sold by the mortgagee.

The company's undertaking, while it was a going concern would not be allowed to be broken up, as the public good would thereby be harmed. The mortgage of the undertaking could not be enforced for public policy reasons; it was not like an ordinary mortgage.[10]

Draftsmen of securities issued over the assets of companies formed under the Companies Acts (from 1844 onwards) borrowed the term 'undertaking' from the statutory companies.[11] The courts' interpretation of such securities relied partly on the established reasoning in the public utility cases, but did not apply the protection and permanence enjoyed by public utility companies to companies registered under the Companies Act.

Re Panama, New Zealand, and Australian Royal Mail Co ((1870) 5 Ch App 318) is usually cited as the case which first recognised the floating charge. The charge in question was virtually identical to Schedule C of the 1845 Act. An important point to note here is that the debenture was in the form of a charge rather than a mortgage. This avoided any potential questions of validity under the Bills of Sale Act 1854. At this time it was uncertain whether companies were subject to the registration procedures of the 1854 Act. The company relied heavily on the fact that the Schedule C decisions governed the case and that the charge holder could not be allowed to enforce its charge. The Court of Appeal decided that there were no public policy considerations to prevent the charge holder from enforcing the charge against the company once it had entered liquidation and therefore ceased to carry on its business. This, in itself, goes no further than the private Act mortgage cases.

---

[10] See e.g., *Marshall v South Staffordshire Tramways Company* [1895] 2 Ch 36 and also the leading case of *Gardner v London, Chatham and Dover Railway Co* (1867) 2 Ch App 201.

[11] See E. Manson, 'The Growth of the Debenture' (1897) 13 LQR 418.

In the words of Giffard LJ (at 322–3) 'the moment the company comes to be wound up, and the property has to be realized, that moment the rights of these parties, beyond all question, attach. My opinion is, that even if the company had not stopped the debenture holders might have filed a bill to realize their security.' This last sentence is the change from the public utility approach. Either the company being wound up or its entering receivership would lead to the company's inability to carry on its undertaking, which in turn would cause the charge to become enforceable.

Although it is generally heralded as the case that introduced the floating charge to fill a yawning gap in the range of secured lending available to companies, *Panama* did no such thing. It largely followed the reasoning in the Schedule C cases but extended it by lifting the restriction on the enforcement of the charge prior to winding up. This is how the floating charge started.

Re Florence Land and Public Works Co ((1878) 10 Ch D 530) followed *Panama*. The case turned upon the meaning of a charge on the 'estate, property and effects' of a company which was in liquidation.

The main problem facing the court was that section 10 of the Judicature Act 1875 expressly applied bankruptcy law principles to insolvent winding up of companies with regard to 'the respective rights of secured and unsecured creditors'.

In argument (at 535) Jessel MR asks the following question:

> Can a company, any more than an individual, charge its future property? This is not a charge on the 'undertaking' as in other debentures, but on the 'estate, property and effects'. By the Judicature Act 1875 section 10, the administration of the estates of companies in winding up has been assimilated as to the respective rights of secured and unsecured creditors to the administration of estates in bankruptcy. Would it not be contrary to the policy of the bankruptcy laws that a mortgage security should affect after-acquired property?

Jessel MR clearly appreciated the danger that the principle in *Graham* (which destroyed the dealing power in cases of all present and future property security, paralysing the business and necessitating security holder consent to all dealing) might apply to companies through the operation of the Judicature Act.

Jessel MR drew a distinction between the type of charge created on the facts of *Florence Land* (shortly thereafter to become known as a floating charge)and the more conventional specific type of security (at 541):

> It is therefore inconsistent to suppose that the moment you executed a bond or debenture you paralyzed the company and prevented it carrying on its business, for if you read the words to mean a specific charge on the property of the company, then, of course, no practical use could be made of the money borrowed, because that would become the property of the company, and anybody with notice would be liable on that view to repay it to the mortgagee or debenture holder.

The theory that fixed charges, by definition, prevent dealing and cause paralysis of the company's business with regard to the charged assets has this statement as its origin. Jessel MR's dictum is a clear reflection of Jervis CJ's views in *Graham*.

Jessel MR held on the facts (at 540–1) that the charge on the 'estate, property and effects' was to be interpreted as 'a security on the property of the company as a going concern, subject to the powers of the directors to dispose of the property of the company while carrying on its business in the ordinary course.' James LJ (at 546) equated 'estate, property and effects' with 'undertaking'. It is important to note that security over the 'undertaking' was, and is, unknown to the financing of the unincorporated trade sector. It could be used to sidestep any possible problems thrown up by *Graham* as being outside the grasp of the law on individual insolvency.

Jessel MR's views on the paralysing effect of specific security continue up to the present day. The invention of the floating charge allowed the courts to recognise a form of security over changing assets which did not fall foul of *Graham*.

It is also important to note that the Court of Appeal in *Re Standard Manufacturing Co* ([1891] 1 Ch 627) finally settled that floating charges issued by companies were not subject to the Bills of Sale Act (1878) Amendment Act 1882. This decision coupled with that in *Florence Land* helped to create the great popularity of the floating charge. Forming a company under the Companies Acts was the only practical way to borrow money on the security of the business's changing assets.

Subsequent to these two developments, the floating charge became and remains the most commonly used security device for securing loans to businesses.

The classic definition of the floating charge was given by Romer LJ in *Re Yorkshire Woolcombers Association Ltd* ([1903] 2 Ch 284 at 295):

> I certainly think that if a charge has the three characteristics that I am about to mention it is a floating charge: (1) if it is a charge on a class of assets of a company present and future; (2) if that class is one which in the ordinary course of business of the company, would be changing from time to time; and (3) if you find that by the charge it is contemplated that, until some step is taken by or on behalf of those interested in the charge, the company may carry on business in the ordinary way so far as concerns the particular class of assets I am dealing with.

The position today remains the same. A fixed charge over a company's assets prevents the company from dealing with the charged assets without consent first being obtained from the debenture holder for each individual dealing. A floating charge may be taken over changing assets as, by definition, the floating charge permits the company to deal with the charged assets in the ordinary course of business. The floating charge is said to crystallise or become fixed in nature on the occurrence of a number of events, which usually involve the intervention of the debenture holder. These crystallisation events terminate the power in the company to continue to use the assets in the ordinary course of business and usually coincide with the company's business ceasing to be run in the same way as before. The events which cause crystallisation are:

(1) The company enters liquidation.
(2) A receiver is appointed by the debenture holder over the company's assets.
(3) The company's business ceases.
(4) Another creditor enforces its security.
(5) An event specified as causing crystallisation in the debenture itself occurs and causes the charge to crystallise automatically (e.g., the company's overdraft exceeds a specified amount).

The most common crystallisation event has traditionally been the appointment of a receiver by the debenture holder. In the first four events listed something very public is occurring. There is no secrecy as to the state of the company. Under the fifth event there is no publicity of the automatic crystallisation.[12] Partly due to this secrecy there is some uncertainty as to whether automatic crystallisation clauses should be permitted. The main problem identified with such clauses is that the charge could crystallise without either the company, the debenture holder or other creditors being aware of the fact. If the charge crystallises automatically but no one is aware of it, the charge is said to become fixed in nature and will attach straight away to, for example, any goods supplied to the company by unsecured trade suppliers or even goods sold by the company *bona fide* to purchasers without notice for value. The supporters of automatic crystallisation would say that a debenture is a contract between commercial entities and that freedom of contract should be permitted. The parties should be able to put whatever provisions they wish into the debenture.[13]

The principal benefit of using automatic crystallisation clauses was formerly that if the floating charge could be seen to have crystallised prior to the appointment of a receiver under the charge, the charge was said to be fixed prior to the receivership. Prior to 1985 this allowed the charge holder to be treated as holding a fixed charge in the receivership and so was paid

---

[12] Note the provisions of the Companies Act 1989 which would have required such publicity prior to the crystallisation being effective. These provisions have not been brought into effect and will not be. The matter of registration requirements for company charges is currently the subject of consultation by the Law Commission (*Registration of Security Interests: Company Charges and Property other than Land*, Consultation Paper No 164).

[13] See generally J. Farrar, 'The Crystallisation of a Floating Charge' (1976) 40 Conv 397.

out ahead of the preferential creditors.[14] To prevent this benefit, Parliament defined a floating charge for priority purposes as one which as created is a floating charge (see section 251). Whatever the date of crystallisation it no longer makes any difference to priority in the subsequent insolvency of the company. The benefits of automatic crystallisation are thus greatly reduced.

It is the badge of the floating charge that the debenture allows the company to control the assets charged. Even if a charge is drafted as being fixed, if the debenture holder does not retain control over the charged assets, the court will only recognise the debenture as creating a floating charge.

In the event of the company's insolvency the debenture holder will enforce the security. The fixed charge has priority over a floating charge and over nearly all other creditors. A floating charge is subject to the prior claims of preferential creditors and may take subject to the rights of execution creditors and landlords who have levied distress. A fixed charge is the best type of security.

In the past twenty years or so, lenders have made various valiant attempts to draft a debenture which would give them a fixed charge over a company's book debts.[15] The reason for this is that, in practice, the debts owed to a company can be the largest asset the company owns. The quest for the Holy Grail of the secured lending world has largely been in vain.

The Privy Council in *Agnew v Commissioner of Inland Revenue* (*Re Brumark Investments Ltd*) ([2001] 2 AC 710) has recently settled the law on book debt charges. Following *Agnew* the practical problem faced by the lender is that if the company has the power to deal with the book debts without getting individual consent for each separate dealing from the debenture holder, the courts will categorise the charge as floating, even if in its own terms it claims to be a fixed charge. The only way a debenture holder can achieve a fixed charge over a company's book debts is to show that the debenture holder, not the company, controls the realisation of the debts. This can usually only be shown if the debenture requires, and this requirement is acted upon, that the debts when realised are paid into a blocked bank account which the company can only access if it obtains the debenture holder's consent for each drawing. The charge must be drafted as a fixed charge and also conducted as one. The consequence of this reasoning is that a fixed charge on book debts is not likely to be a practical option in most situations due to the expense of properly policing it.

As will been seen later, it is crucial in practice for a receiver, in distributing the charged assets, to be aware which assets are subject to a fixed charge and which assets are subject to a floating charge.

---

[14] Prior to the Enterprise Act 2002, the Crown as a preferential creditor would frequently eat up a company's assets ahead of a floating charge. See generally A. Keay and P. Walton, 'Preferential Debts: An Empirical Study' (1999) 3 *Insolvency Lawyer* 112.

[15] See e.g., *Siebe Gorman & Co Ltd v Barclays Bank Ltd* [1979] LIL Rep 142, *Re Brightlife Ltd* [1987] Ch 200, *Re New Bullas Trading Ltd* [1994] 1 BCLC 485 and *Re Cimex Tissues Ltd* [1994] BCC 626.

6.3 Types of receiver

At common law mortgagees had an implied power to take possession and to sell mortgaged assets upon default by the mortgagor.[16] This power was generally expressly stated in the mortgage deed itself and was usually added to by an express power permitting a receiver to be appointed. The receiver could be appointed out of court as an alternative to the mortgagee exercising the power of sale. The receiver was originally limited to receiving the income from the mortgaged property in order to pay off the secured debt (hence the title 'receiver'). The mortgagee's powers to sell or to appoint a receiver were put on a statutory footing in 1860.[17] Such powers can now be found in section 101 Law of Property Act 1925.

The statutory powers given to a receiver under this provision are limited to receiving the income from the mortgaged property. The mortgage deed may extend or add to these powers and in practice, such receivers are often expressly given the power of sale. This type of receiver is appointed where the secured lender has the benefit of a fixed charge or mortgage over certain premises. The receiver is usually called a fixed charge or Law of Property Act ('LPA') receiver. Such receivers are frequently appointed today.[18] LPA receivers need not be licensed insolvency practitioners[19] and will often be appointed because of their particular profession, for example estate agents may be appointed due to their expertise and knowledge of the local property market. The Enterprise Act 2002 has not made any changes to the appointment or operation of LPA receivers.

Once the floating charge became commonplace, it became usual practice to add to these statutory powers in the actual debenture document, permitting a receiver to be appointed by the debenture holder out of court and to give the receiver powers of management and sale over the charged assets. Although common, it was for many years not universal practice to include such powers or to act upon them.

Consequently, there are many instances at the end of the nineteenth century and well into the twentieth century where debenture holders, following default by the company, brought debenture holders' actions asking the court to appoint a receiver and manager over the company.

---

[16] See e.g., *Re Morritt* (1886) 18 QBD 222.

[17] An Act to give to Trustees, Mortgagees, and other certain Powers now commonly inserted in Settlements, Mortgages, and Wills 23 and 24 Vict c. 145, section 11 (later Conveyancing and Law of Property Act 1881, section 19).

[18] For recent judicial consideration of LPA receivers see *Sargent v Customs and Excise Commissioners* [1995] 2 BCLC 34 and *Phoenix Properties Ltd v Wimpole Street Nominees Ltd* [1992] BCLC 737.

[19] But note section 30 of the Act – companies cannot be appointed as receivers.

Jessel MR explained the distinction between receivers on the one hand and receivers and managers on the other in *Re Manchester & Milford Ry Co* ((1880) 14 Ch D 645 at 653):

> A 'receiver' is a term which was well known in the Court of Chancery, as meaning a person who receives rents or other income paying ascertained outgoings, but who does not, if I may say so, manage the property in the sense of buying or selling or anything of that kind. We were most familiar with the distinction in the case of a partnership. If a receiver was appointed of partnership assets, the trade stopped immediately. He collected all the debts, sold the stock-in-trade and other assets, and then under the order of the court the debts of the concern were liquidated and the balance divided – If it was desired to continue the trade at all it was necessary to appoint a manager, or a receiver and manager as it was generally called. He could buy and sell and carry on the trade.

As time progressed it became ever more common to include the power to appoint a receiver and manager in debentures. Nowadays it is invariably the case that such a receiver will be appointed by the debenture holder out of court. Instances of court appointed receivers in an insolvency context are thus extremely rare today.[20] Out of court receivers can be appointed more speedily and are considered less costly than those appointed by the court. In an insolvency context court appointed receivers have until recently still had a role to play where assets are in jeopardy and the authority of a court order will help to safeguard the assets. This role would seem to be largely superseded by the availability of the appointment of an administrator[21] who can be appointed out of court by a debenture holder but still has the status of an officer of the court.

The most common form of lending to a company today involves the lender taking a fixed and floating charge over all the company's property both present and future including its undertaking. Default by the company will usually lead to the debenture holder appointing a receiver and manager over all the company's assets. This type of receiver and manager has been entitled an 'administrative receiver' since 1985.[22] An administrative receiver is defined in section 29(2) of the Act:

---

[20] For a recent example of a court appointed receiver see *Bank of Credit and Commerce International SA v BRS Kumar Bros Ltd* [1994] BCLC 211. The court's authority to appoint a receiver, originally part of the inherent jurisdiction of the old Court of Chancery, is now found in section 37 of the Supreme Court Act 1981 which allows the court to appoint where it appears 'to be just and convenient to do so'.

[21] See para 14 Schedule B1 of the Act introduced by section 248 and Schedule 16 of the Enterprise Act 2002.

[22] Originally contained within Chapter IV of the Insolvency Act 1985, provisions relating to receivers generally and specific provisions relating to administrative receivers were thereafter consolidated in Part III of the Act. The provisions of the Enterprise Act 2002 greatly impact upon the rights of debenture holders to appoint administrative receivers under debentures entered into after the commencement of the 2002 Act.

(a) a receiver or manager of the whole (or substantially the whole) of a company's property appointed by or on behalf of the holders of any debentures of the company secured by a charge which, as created, was a floating charge, or by such a charge and one or more other securities; or

(b) a person who would be such a receiver or manager but for the appointment of some other person as the receiver[23] of part of the company's property.

An LPA receiver, as appointed under a fixed charge only, will not qualify as an administrative receiver.[24] It is also possible for a receiver and manager to be appointed over only part of a company's undertaking, for example, only one factory where the company owns six factories in all. Such a receiver will not be an administrative receiver as the appointment will not be over the whole or substantially the whole of the company's property. In summary, there may be four types of receiver appointed where the company is insolvent or is likely to become insolvent:

(1) administrative receiver;
(2) LPA receiver;
(3) a receiver (and manager) of only part of the company's property;[25]
(4) a court appointed receiver.

Due to the common form of financing by way of a fixed and floating charge over the whole of a company's undertaking, the vast majority of companies entering receivership will enter administrative receivership. It is important to realise that the Act gives a number of powers to, and imposes a number of duties on, administrative receivers, which do not apply to other types of receivers.[26] These will be discussed below. Although these statutory provisions to some extent regulate how receiverships are conducted, a number of important issues affecting receivers are still governed by the common law.

---

[23] In this context receiver appears to refer to an LPA receiver.

[24] See T. Green, 'Receivership – a comparative summary' (1994) 10 *Insolvency Law and Practice* 143 for a note of the important differences between administrative and LPA receivers.

[25] Other than a receiver or manager who would be a receiver or manager of the whole or substantially the whole of the company's assets but for the appointment of another person as receiver of part (section 29(2)(b) of the Act).

[26] Sections 42–49 of the Act only apply to administrative receivers. Sections 33–38 apply to all receivers or managers appointed out of court (except section 37 which excludes administrative receivers from its operation). Sections 39–41 apply to all receiverships (although section 40 only applies where the receiver is appointed under a debenture containing a floating charge).

6.4 Appointment

6.4.1 *Mode of appointment*

A debenture holder who wishes to appoint a receiver must ensure that the appointment is made consistently with the terms of the debenture. If, for example, the debenture requires the appointment to be made in writing, an oral appointment will not be effective. The debenture will usually list a number of events which constitute default by the company. On the occurrence of any of these events the debenture will frequently state that the default has the consequence that all monies owing by the company to the debenture holder immediately become payable on demand. The debenture holder will then have to serve a demand for all outstanding monies and if that demand is not met (which, assuming the company is insolvent, is highly likely), the receiver can thereafter be appointed.

Common default events listed in the debenture would be:

(1) failure to pay interest owing under the debenture within a period specified;

(2) breach of any covenant by the company under the debenture;

(3) the company suffering a distress from its landlord or execution is commenced against the company property by one of the company's creditors and the distress or execution is not discharged within a specified period;

(4) the company enters liquidation or a petition for a compulsory winding up or administration is presented or a meeting to consider entering voluntary winding up is called;

(5) a prior debenture becomes enforceable or a receiver is appointed over any of the company's property;

(6) the company becomes unable to pay its debt within the meaning of section 123 of the Act;

(7) the company enters or resolves to enter an arrangement or composition with its creditors;

(8) the company ceases to carry on all or a material part of its business;

(9) circumstances arise which in the opinion of the debenture holder adversely affect the company's ability to perform its obligations under the debenture.

As can be seen, these events are generally related to the company's solvency and its ability to continue to make payments under the debenture. The final ground is expressed very widely and certainly gives the debenture holder scope to appoint a receiver if unforeseen events occur which cause it consternation.

If, as is commonly the case, the debenture states that upon an event of default occurring the whole of the money owing, both principal and interest, become payable on demand, the debenture holder must then formally demand payment. If the payment is not made then the receiver may be appointed. It has been held that the debenture holder must allow enough time for the 'mechanics of payment' to be put into operation before going ahead with the appointment. In *Cripps (Pharmaceuticals) Ltd v Wickenden* ([1973] 1 WLR 944 at 955) Goff J commented 'all the creditor has to do is to give the debtor time to get it from some convenient place not to negotiate a deal which he hopes will produce the money.' It seems from this case and *Bank of Baroda Ltd v Panessar* ([1987] Ch 335) that about an hour is the appropriate period which must elapse prior to the appointment, as long as the demand is made during normal working hours. Although this gives a company with financial problems virtually no chance of repaying the money, the test is based upon the premise that there is a convenient place where the money is sitting. Companies heading towards insolvency are unlikely to have recourse to such a convenient place and so almost invariably the receiver will be appointed.

There is no statutory form of appointment which needs to be used. The form used will commonly be a letter of appointment but may need to be by deed depending on the wording of the debenture. It may be prepared in advance[27] and will commonly include the appointor's details and explain that the right to appoint a receiver has arisen under the debenture. It will take effect when it is given to the proposed receiver and the receiver has accepted the appointment.

The appointment of an administrative receiver (or other receiver and manager) is only effective if it is accepted before the end of the business day after that on which the instrument of appointment is received. If accepted the appointment is effective from the moment the instrument of appointment is received (section 33).

6.4.2 *Validity of appointment*

It is important for a receiver to check that the appointment is validly made. If there is a defect in the form of the appointment or relating to the validity of the debenture itself, the appointment may be invalid. Although section 232 of the Act states that the acts of a receiver are valid notwithstanding any defect in appointment, nomination or qualifications, this protection is limited to defects in form or procedure and will not safeguard a receiver appointed under an invalid security or where the power to appoint has not arisen.[28] If the appointment is invalid, the receiver may be liable to the company in trespass. An invalid appointment does not of itself constitute the receiver as agent of the

---

[27] See e.g., *Windsor Refrigerator Co Ltd v Branch Nominees Ltd* [1961] Ch 375.

[28] By analogy with the similar standard form provision applicable to directors under section 285 Companies Act 1985. For a consideration of section 285 see *Morris v Kanssen* [1946] AC 459.

debenture holder (*Bank of Baroda Ltd v Panessar* [1987] Ch 335). If the appointment is found to be invalid, the court may, under section 34, order the debenture holder to indemnify the receiver for any liability which is incurred.

In a bid to avoid any possible action in trespass, a receiver will make a number of enquiries before accepting an appointment. A number of interested parties may wish to challenge the appointment for different reasons. The company itself may wish to challenge it. If successful the directors will retake control of the company assets and the company may sue the receiver in trespass. Generally, it is accepted that if an execution creditor has not completed the execution prior to the appointment of the receiver (an event which causes a floating charge to crystallise), the floating charge will have priority over the execution creditor.[29] The execution creditor stands to benefit if the appointment is seen to be invalid as it may give the execution creditor priority over the floating charge.

In practice, the most likely person who will wish to attack the validity of the appointment will be a liquidator. Whether the liquidator is appointed before or after the receiver, the liquidator will be keen to invalidate the debenture in whole or in part as this will generally mean there will be more assets available to the company's unsecured creditors. A liquidator (and an administrator) has various statutory powers to attack the validity of a debenture including those under sections 239 and 245 of the Act.[30] Under section 239 a liquidator (or administrator) may attack the debenture as a preference. The liquidator will need to show that, within certain time limits, the execution of the debenture was influenced by a desire to put the debenture holder into a preferred position in the event of the company being wound up insolvent. A floating charge may only be invalidated under section 245 if it can be shown, again within certain time limits, that the floating charge was executed at a time when the company was insolvent and was executed to secure pre-existing indebtedness. If a liquidator (or administrator) successfully acts to invalidate the debenture itself or the appointment of the receiver, the appointment will generally be invalidated retrospectively to the date of the purported appointment.

Prior to accepting an appointment, it is crucial for the proposed receiver to obtain a copy of the debenture document and ensure it has been properly executed by the company.[31] It will also be necessary to check that its execution was not *ultra vires* the company, although in practice the provisions of section 35 of the Companies Act 1985 make this an unlikely concern. The terms of the debenture will detail the procedure which should be complied with to appoint the receiver. The receiver needs to be satisfied that this procedure has been followed.

---

[29] See Chapter 31.
[30] See Chapters 37 and 39.
[31] Under section 36A Companies Act 1985.

It will also be necessary to carry out a Companies Search against the company at Companies House. From the details of the Search results, it can be seen if the debenture was correctly registered. If it is not registered within 21 days of its creation (or such longer period as the court has permitted), the debenture will be void against a liquidator, administrator or other creditor of the company (section 395 of the Companies Act 1985). The Search will also show whether or not any prior or other securities have been registered against the secured assets. The Search will also show details of the company's participants and may contain other important information, for example, whether the company is in liquidation. An indemnity for loss occasioned due to an invalid appointment should also be sought from the debenture holder.

6.4.3 *Agency of receivers*

A receiver will be appointed by a debenture holder to realise the assets subject to the security and, if the assets realise sufficient proceeds, to pay off the debenture holder. Administrative receivers are deemed to be agents of the company unless and until the company goes into liquidation (section 44(1)(a)). LPA receivers are also deemed to be agents of the company (section 109(2) of the Law of Property Act 1925). Other types of out of court receivers will usually be expressly stated to be the agents of the company in the charge document.[32]

This agency is unusual as the company, the principal, has no power to dismiss the receiver or, in the absence of breach of duty by the receiver, to interfere in the conduct of the receivership. Also, as we will see, the receiver may be personally liable on certain contracts entered into on behalf of the company. Most importantly perhaps, the receiver's agency differs from a normal agency in that the receiver's primary duty is owed to the debenture holder and not to the company.

Powers of a receiver are usually written into the debenture document but sections 42 and 43, and Schedule 1 in addition, confer wide-ranging powers upon administrative receivers (subject to express variation in the debenture). Once appointed, an administrative receiver takes control of the company replacing the management powers of the directors.[33]

The agency of an administrative receiver is stated to terminate on the appointment of a liquidator under section 44(1)(a). At first sight, this suggests that the administrative receiver cannot continue to act after the company enters liquidation. This is not the case. After liquidation, the administrative receiver can continue to act to enforce the security for the benefit of the debenture holder. This issue is discussed below.

---

[32] See e.g., *Re Vimbos Ltd* [1900] 1 Ch 470.
[33] See e.g., *Moss Steamship Co Ltd v Whinney* [1912] AC 254 and *Re Emmadart* [1979] Ch 540.

6.4.4 *Theoretical basis of appointment*

Although it will be the debenture holder who in fact appoints the receiver, in strict legal terms the debenture holder acts as agent of the company in doing so, subject to the terms of the contract between the debenture holder and the company. The effect is that legally the appointment is made by the company. The receiver is appointed with the task of paying off the debenture holder and once this task is accomplished, the receiver must account to the company as principal for any surplus proceeds (if any). The company cannot dismiss the receiver as it has, for valuable consideration (that is, by entering into the debenture agreement), committed its management to the receiver. Nor can the company interfere with the exercise by the receiver of management powers unless a breach of duty by the receiver can be established.[34] The powers under the company's articles of the directors are in effect delegated to the receiver by the directors authorising the execution of the debenture. The receiver cannot do anything which the directors were unable to do and so, for example, is subject to the *ultra vires* doctrine and any restrictions contained in the articles. An administrative receiver will by definition invariably be appointed under a floating charge over the company's undertaking and consequently will have the power of carrying on the company's business.

6.4.5 *Effect of appointment of an administrative receiver*

The appointment of an administrative receiver has a number of effects on the company's business:

(1) It crystallises any floating charge (this may have occurred already if, for instance, the company is in liquidation or has ceased to carry on its business).
(2) Generally it will prevent the company entering administration. If a debenture holder exists with the power validly to appoint an administrative receiver, any attempt to put the company into administration is effectively subject to the debenture holder's power of veto. If prior to the appointment of an administrator the debenture holder appoints an administrative receiver, the company will generally not be able to enter administration.[35]
(3) It does not generally terminate contracts of employment.[36]

---

[34] See e.g., *Gaskell v Gosling* [1896] 1 QB 669 per Rigby LJ at 692–3.

[35] See paras 15–17, 25 and 39 of Schedule B1 Insolvency Act 1986 introduced by section 248 and Schedule 16 of the Enterprise Act 2002. For the previous regime, still applicable in limited circumstances, see section 9 Insolvency Act 1986. See Also Chapter 7 for more detail as to how this operates.

[36] But see *Re Mack Trucks (Britain) Ltd* [1967] 1 All ER 977 and *Griffiths v Secretary of State for Social Services* [1974] QB 468.

(4) It has no effect generally on contracts of the company with third parties.
(5) The directors' powers of management over the charged assets are suspended. The administrative receiver becomes the managing agent of the company and generally usurps the powers of the directors in this regard (*Re Emmadart* [1979] Ch 540). The directors retain certain residual powers, for instance the power to sue the receiver on behalf of the company for breach of duty.[37]

6.5 Powers of receivers

The powers to manage the company's business and to realise the charged assets will usually be listed extensively in the debenture itself. An administrative receiver, in addition to such express powers, has a number of powers implied under section 42, which are listed in Schedule 1. These powers include:

- Power to take possession of, collect and get in the property of the company and, for that purpose, to take such proceedings as may seem to him expedient.
- Power to sell or otherwise dispose of the property of the company by public auction or private contract.
- Power to raise or borrow money and grant security therefor over the property of the company.
- Power to appoint a solicitor or accountant or other professionally qualified person to assist him in the performance of his functions.
- Power to bring or defend any action or other legal proceedings in the name and on behalf of the company.
- Power to do all acts and to execute in the name and on behalf of the company any deed, receipt or other document.
- Power to appoint any agent to do any business which he is unable to do himself or which can more conveniently be done by an agent and power to employ and dismiss employees.
- Power to do all such things (including the carrying out of works) as may be necessary for the realisation of the property of the company.
- Power to make any payment which is necessary or incidental to the performance of his functions.

---

[37] *Watts v Midland Bank* [1986] BCLC 15. Directors also retain the power/obligation to maintain statutory books, file annual returns and to obtain information from the receiver for such purposes (see *Gomba Holdings UK Ltd v Homan* [1986] 3 All ER 94). Also it seems that directors may have the power to oppose a winding-up petition (see R. Goode, *Principles of Corporate Insolvency Law*, 2nd edn, London: Sweet & Maxwell (1997) at 230).

- Power to carry on the business of the company.
- Power to establish subsidiaries of the company.
- Power to transfer to subsidiaries of the company the whole or any part of the business and property of the company.

6.5.1 *Mechanics of power of sale*

Prior to the company entering winding up, an administrative receiver may sell the assets covered by the debenture in either of two ways:

(1) The receiver sells as agent in the name of the company (*Re Real Meat Co* [1996] BCC 254). The sale takes effect subject to the debenture and other incumbrances. The receiver cannot transfer any greater right than the company has. In order that the purchaser takes free from the debenture under which the receiver was appointed and other incumbrances either a deed of release will be necessary or the debenture holder and the other incumbrancers will need to be made a party to the sale.
(2) The debenture holder can sell as mortgagee and appoint the receiver as its agent for that purpose. This overrides junior incumbrances whose rights attach to any surplus proceeds.

Once the company is in liquidation only (2) above is possible as the administrative receiver will no longer be agent of the company under section 44.

If the receiver decides to sell company assets subject to the charge under which the receiver is appointed, to a person connected to the company, the transaction will, if it is of requisite value, require the consent of the general meeting by ordinary resolution under section 320 Companies Act 1985 otherwise the transaction will be voidable.[38] The transaction will always be of requisite value if the value of the non cash asset is greater than £100,000. It will not be of requisite value if it is for less than £2,000. If the value is between £2,000 and £100,000 it will be of requisite value if it is for an amount which is greater than 10 per cent of the company's net assets (as found in the company's latest set of accounts).

It is possible, under section 43 of the Act, for an administrative receiver to sell assets subject to prior or equal ranking securities, but the approval of the court is necessary. This power may be useful to a receiver who is trying to sell the company's business as a going concern where certain important assets of the company, such as a piece of land or machinery, are subject to a prior security. In order for the court to allow the sale it must be satisfied that it would promote a more advantageous realisation of the company's assets than would otherwise be possible. A condition of the court order will be that the proceeds of sale are used to pay off the

[38] See e.g., *Demite v Protec* [1998] BCC 638.

security holder first. If the disposal does not achieve a sum, which in the court's view should have been possible by a sale in the open market, any shortfall must be made good from the other assets of the company.

6.5.2 *Actions against the debenture holder*

Directors' powers remain exercisable with regard to assets outside the debenture or which the receiver decides to ignore or abandon. A particular example of this type of asset would be a potential action that the company has against the debenture holder who has appointed the receiver. If the directors believe an action lies against the debenture holder they may tell the receiver. The receiver must then decide whether or not to sue the person who has just appointed the receiver. If the receiver chooses not to sue, the directors can, it seems, sue on behalf of the company. The action will be in the name of the company and will be financed by the charged assets. This places the debenture holder in a seemingly impossible position.

   If the debenture holder loses such an action and the debenture is held to be invalid by the court, the debenture holder will lose its security. If the debenture holder successfully defends the action, the debenture will be held to be valid and the court will usually award costs against the company. If this occurs, the debenture holder will lose out indirectly as the costs of the action will be paid out of the company's assets, that is, the assets subject to the debenture holder's security. The consequence will be that even if the debenture holder wins the action the effect will be to diminish the value of the debenture holder's security. In recognition of this problem, the cases of *Newhart v Co-op Bank* ([1978] QB 814) and *Tudor Grange v Citibank* ([1992] Ch 53) suggest that the directors will only be able to bring an action in these circumstances if there is an indemnity for costs from a third party.[39]

6.6 Contractual liability of receivers

The position of an administrative receiver regarding personal liability under contracts entered into by the company in receivership is governed by section 44.[40] Unlike normal agencies, the agency of the receiver is one whereby personal liability may arise. Such liability is essentially limited to new contracts entered into by the company while

---

[39] See R. Goode, *Principles of Corporate Insolvency Law*, 2nd edn, London: Sweet & Maxwell (1997) at 231–2.

[40] For the position of non-administrative receivers see section 37 of the Act.

under the control of the receiver and to contracts of employment of workers of the company which the receiver is deemed to have adopted. It is crucial to read closely the wording of section 44. It was amended by the Insolvency Act 1994. The reasons for this amendment will become apparent. Section 44 states:

(1) The administrative receiver of a company—
   (a) is deemed to be the company's agent, unless and until the company goes into liquidation;
   (b) is personally liable on any contract entered into by him in the carrying out of his functions (except in so far as the contract otherwise provides) and, to the extent of any qualifying liability, on any contract of employment adopted by him in the carrying out of those functions; and
   (c) is entitled in respect of that liability to an indemnity out of the assets of the company.
(2) For the purposes of subsection (1)(b) the administrative receiver is not to be taken to have adopted a contract of employment by reason of anything done or omitted to be done within 14 days after his appointment.
   (2A) For the purposes of subsection (1)(b), a liability under a contract of employment is a qualifying liability if—
      (a) it is a liability to pay a sum by way of wages or salary or contribution to an occupational pension scheme,
      (b) it is incurred while the administrative receiver is in office, and
      (c) it is in respect of services rendered wholly or partly after the adoption of the contract.
   (2B) Where a sum payable in respect of a liability which is a qualifying liability for the purposes of subsection (1)(b) is payable in respect of services rendered partly before and partly after the adoption of the contract, liability under subsection (1)(b) shall only extend to so much of the sum as is payable in respect of services rendered after the adoption of the contract.
   (2C) For the purposes of subsections (2A) and (2B)—
      (a) wages or salary payable in respect of a period of holiday or absence from work through sickness or other good cause are deemed to be wages or (as the case may be) salary in respect of services rendered in that period, and
      (b) a sum payable in lieu of holiday is deemed to be wages or (as the case may be) salary in respect of services rendered in the period by reference to which the holiday entitlement arose.
   (2D) In subsection (2C)(a), the reference to wages or salary payable in respect of a period of holiday includes any sums which, if they had been paid, would have been treated for the purposes of the enactments relating to social security as earnings in respect of that period.
(3) This section does not limit any right to indemnity which the administrative receiver would have apart from it, nor limit his liability on contracts entered into or adopted without authority, nor confer any right to indemnity in respect of that liability.

6.6.1 *New contracts*

Section 44(1)(a) states that an administrative receiver is deemed to be the agent of the company at least until the company goes into liquidation. The effect of liquidation on the receiver will be examined below. As agent of the company, the administrative receiver can commit it to future liabilities by entering into new contracts in the company's name. Note the receiver's personal liability under section 44(1)(b) if contracts are entered on behalf of the company unless the contract provides otherwise. The receiver has the benefit of an indemnity out of the company assets under section 44(1)(c). It is common for a receiver in entering into a contract on behalf of the company to attempt to exclude personal liability under any contract. As the receiver is not a party to the contract but the company is, the receiver's disclaimer is not subject to the Unfair Contract Terms Act 1977.[41]

6.6.2 *Existing contracts*

As the receiver acts as agent of the company, if the company in receivership continues an existing contract, the company remains liable under it. The receiver incurs no personal liability. An example of this principle is *Hay v Swedish and Norwegian Ry Co* ((1892) 8 TLR 775):

> The company in receivership carried on business as a railway. It had previously entered into two hire purchase contracts under which it had hired 300 railway wagons. In the course of the receivership the wagons had been retained by the receiver and to some extent used in the business. The owner of the wagons claimed that the receiver was liable to pay the due instalments under the contract for the period for which the wagons had been used. The court held that the receiver was under no such liability. He could choose to pay the owner in order to keep the use of the wagons but if he chose not to pay he could not be forced to pay. The owner had his rights under the contract to terminate the contract and repossess the wagons. These were rights against the company. The owner had no rights against the receiver personally.

In a receivership, there is no statutory prohibition on creditors enforcing their rights against the company, for example, by repossession, forfeiture or distress. Due to this freedom which the company's creditors enjoy, it is up to them how they deal with the company in receivership. If they are not paid by the receiver, the creditors can generally enforce their legal rights against the company notwithstanding the receivership. If this would involve the loss to the company of assets crucial to an attempted sale of the business as a going concern, the receiver may decide it is better to pay off the creditors in question as a legitimate expense of the receivership.

---

[41] See R. Goode, *Principles of Corporate Insolvency Law*, 2nd edn, London: Sweet & Maxwell (1997) at 245.

6.6.3 *Repudiation of existing contracts*

Again, due to the receiver being an agent of the company, receivers are not liable if they cause the company to repudiate an existing contract in the company's name or to fail or refuse to perform its part of the contract. This remains the case even if the breach is a fundamental breach which leads to the contract thereby being terminated and leaves the company liable in damages for breach. The position of the receiver demands that this should be the situation. The receiver is in post to realise the assets in order to pay off the debenture holder. The continuance of a particular contract, under which the contracting third party is paid all that is owing under the contract, would lead to the third party being paid out ahead of the debenture holder. If such contracts are to be enforceable against the receiver, he or she will be forced into continuing the company's business even if the business is unprofitable and should be closed down. The receiver will have to pay over monies under these contracts, leaving the debenture holder, to whom the receiver owes a primary duty, to lose out at least partly on the secured assets in favour of a (likely unsecured) creditor. For these reasons a receiver incurs no liability if he or she causes the company to repudiate an existing contract. In *Airline Airspares v Handley-Page* ([1970] Ch 193):

> A company had entered into a contract to pay A a commission of £500 for every aircraft the company sold. The company went into receivership and the receiver set up a subsidiary company to hive down the profitable part of the business to permit its sale. As part of this scheme A was informed that the company would no longer honour the contract to pay the commission.
> A attempted to enforce the contract against the company and receiver but was refused. It was necessary, to be fair to all the unsecured creditors that no one unsecured creditor could achieve a preferential position in this way. The receiver must be permitted to repudiate existing contracts in realising the assets in the most beneficial way.

It must be remembered that the contract remains enforceable against the company. If the company enters liquidation either during or shortly after the receivership (as is common), the contracting party will rank in the liquidation only as an unsecured creditor and will frequently only realise a small proportion, if any, of the amount owing under the contract.

Although generally free to ignore contractual rights of third parties, a receiver cannot ignore proprietary rights which have already passed under a contract. For example, in *Freevale v Metrostore Holdings* ([1984] Ch 199):

> The company in receivership had, prior to the receiver's appointment, entered into a binding contract to sell land although completion had not occurred. The receiver claimed that he could repudiate the contract and leave the proposed buyer as an unsecured creditor with a claim in damages only against the company. The court disagreed and ordered specific performance of the contract. The reason for this is that on exchange of

contracts for the sale of land (or other assets where damages would be an inadequate remedy) the seller becomes a constructive trustee for the buyer. The buyer becomes the owner in equity. The buyer has become entitled to a proprietary interest in the land upon exchange. The subsequent appointment of the receiver made no difference to this.

If a proprietary interest has passed to a third party under a contract, the receiver cannot thereafter repudiate the contract. Other examples of this would include a situation where an option had already been assigned in equity (*Telemetrix plc v Modern Engineers of Bristol (Holdings) plc* (1985) 1 BCC 99, 417) or where a lien over goods existed (*Re Diesels & Components Pty Ltd* (1985) 9 ACLR 269).

6.6.4 *Contracts of employment*

The appointment of an out of court receiver did not, and does not, terminate contracts of employment of employees of the company. At common law, a receiver who was expressly appointed as agent of the company had no personal liability on any employment contracts. It is usual for a receiver upon taking office to dismiss some employees but to continue to pay others more crucial to the business for the period of the receivership. This is important if it is intended to sell the business as a going concern. This system seemed to work sensibly in practice. Employees who were kept on during the receivership would normally be paid for services rendered in this period and stood some chance of keeping their jobs if the business were sold on as a going concern. The problem with this system was that there was no obligation on the receiver to pay employees who were kept on. The potential injustice of this can be illustrated by *Nicoll v Cutts* ((1985) 1 BCC 99, 427):

> The company in question was run by N. N suffered a serious car accident which left him in hospital for several months. During his hospital stay a receiver was appointed over the company's undertaking. The receiver discussed the company's business with N while he was in hospital and later gave notice of termination of N's service contract. N was not paid for any services rendered during the receivership. The Court of Appeal agreed with the receiver that the receiver was not obliged to make any payment for this period. Had the receiver made the payments they would have been costs and expenses of the receivership but as the payments had not been made, the debenture holder had priority over N and the receiver was not personally liable to pay.

The mischief of *Nicoll* was thought to have been avoided by section 44(1)(b), as originally drafted, by making administrative receivers personally liable on contracts of employment which they adopted. The original section 44(1)(b) stated that an administrative receiver was personally liable:

. . . on any contract entered into by him in the carrying out of his functions (except in so far as the contract otherwise provides) and on any contract of employment adopted by him in the carrying out of his functions . . .

Section 44(2) adds some light to the meaning of adoption by stating:

For the purposes of subsection (1)(b) the administrative receiver is not to be taken to have adopted a contract of employment by reason of anything done or omitted to be done within 14 days after his appointment.

The problem with the original section 44(1)(b) was the uncertainty as to what adoption of the contract amounted to and whether or not the receiver could get around this provision. In practice, receivers wrote to all employees usually in terms that, although the employees were being kept on, the receiver was not adopting their contracts of employment and was not to be personally liable under the contracts of employment. In doing so receivers were relying on an unreported decision of Harman J in *Re Specialised Mouldings Ltd* (13 February 1987).

The legal effect of these letters was later considered by the High Court and the Court of Appeal in *Powdrill v Watson sub nom Re Paramount Airways Ltd (No 3)* ([1993] BCC 172 affirmed [1994] BCC 172). Although the case involved a company in administration,[42] it centred on the meaning of 'adoption' of employment contracts under section 19 of the Act (which for present purposes contained the same wording as section 44) and considered the effect of '*Specialised Mouldings* letters'. Both at first instance and on appeal it was held that adoption of the employment contracts occurred by the employees being kept on beyond the 14-day period. The letters were of no legal effect. This seems to be an entirely logical decision. On a reading of the original section 44, it can be seen that although receivers had the power to exclude liability under ordinary contracts, such a power was not available for employment contracts.

The panic in the insolvency profession caused by the Court of Appeal decision cannot be underestimated. It had been the common practice of receivers, at least since 1987, to issue '*Specialised Mouldings* letters' to all employees immediately upon being appointed. In the belief that the receivers were avoiding personal liability on the contracts of employment, many employees were kept on for more than 14 days as the receivers tried to find a buyer for the company's business as a going concern. Employees kept on frequently included executive directors with high salaries and long service contracts. Suddenly, the insolvency practitioner profession was facing potentially billions of pounds' worth of claims from former employees of companies which had entered receivership.

Receivers who had adopted contracts of employment were liable for all the liabilities under those contracts, even if they were breached prior to

---

[42] For the rules on adoption of employment contracts in administration see para 99 Schedule B1 of the Act and the discussion in Chapter 7.

the receiver's appointment or later. Adoption meant liability on all the terms of the contract. If an executive director was subsequently dismissed for reasons of redundancy, the director could claim damages for breach of any or all his or her terms of employment even if the breach complained of occurred prior to the receivership. A five-year service contract at £100,000 per annum would be enforceable personally against the receiver, if the director had been kept on for more than 14 days after the receiver's appointment. As well as the financial problems this created for extant and old receiverships, the ruling also in effect blunted any attempt by practitioners to embrace fully the idea of a rescue culture. No sensible receiver could afford to keep the business going in the hope of a going concern sale if it meant opening the receiver up to almost infinite personal liability.

The potential ruin of the insolvency profession and the likely abandonment of the rescue culture were averted by quick legislative action. This was in the form of the Insolvency Act 1994, which solved the problem for future administrative receivers but was not retrospective. Receiverships entered prior to 1994 would still be subject to the courts' interpretation of the original section 44.

The new section 44[43] restricts the rights of employees to 'qualifying liabilities'. This limits claims to, in effect, pay for work actually rendered during the receivership (or administration) after the contract has been adopted. No liability is therefore incurred for services rendered during the first 14 days. If employees are kept on for longer than 14 days the administrative receiver is personally liable for pay (and related claims such as holiday pay) after the 14-day period has elapsed as the receiver is deemed thereafter to have adopted the contracts of employment. The receiver is only liable for services rendered during the receivership. No liability is incurred in relation to periods before the receiver's appointment or after discharge.

These changes reach a reasonable compromise between the employees' rights to be paid for services rendered and the administrative receiver's need to keep the business as a viable economic entity for as long as possible in order to seek out potential purchasers, without the receiver incurring major personal liability. It is interesting to note that the Insolvency Act 1994 made no amendments to section 37 which is the equivalent of section 44 for non-administrative receivers. The potential for financial disaster under *Powdrill* still remains a real risk therefore for LPA receivers who, for example, are appointed over a hotel business and wish to keep the business going pending a sale.

The story does not quite finish there. Almost contemporaneously with the 1994 Act, Lightman J heard together two cases with similar facts to

---

[43] See now para 99 of Schedule B1 of the Act for the equivalent provision in administration. This was formerly section 19 of the Act.

Powdrill involving claims by employees of companies in administrative receivership. In *Re Leyland DAF Ltd (No2); Re Ferranti International plc* ([1994] BCC 658), his Lordship decided that a receiver who had adopted the contract of an employee became personally liable under all the terms of the contract and could therefore be liable for breaches of contract either before, during or after the receivership.

Lightman J's decision was clearly a matter of enormous financial consequence for existing receiverships and receiverships where employees' claims were not yet time barred under the Statute of Limitations (that is, receiverships not covered by the 1994 Act's amendments). As became clear later, employees could and did open up old receiverships to make receivers personally liable on contracts of employment terminated by receivers years earlier. Such claims rumbled on for years.[44] In order to defend such actions receivers in practice claimed that certain employees, usually directors with large claims, had acted in breach of their duty to the company to such an extent as to go to the root of the contract and make it unenforceable. Another get out for receivers has been to claim that certain directors are not in fact employees of the company.[45]

The House of Lords heard together the appeal in *Powdrill* and, using the 'leapfrog' procedure, the appeal directly from the decision in *Leyland DAF* and *Ferranti*. The decision is reported as *Powdrill v Watson sub nom Re Paramount Airways (No3)* ([1995] 2 AC 394). The House of Lords largely followed the lower courts but did limit the width of the judgments in certain respects. Importantly, their Lordships decided that if an employee is kept on for more than 14 days the receiver or administrator has adopted the contract. '*Specialised Mouldings* letters' were of no effect. This meaning of adoption is equally applicable to receiverships beginning after the 1994 Act as before.

Liability of the receiver or administrator to pay out under the contract for pre-1994 Act insolvencies was limited to liabilities incurred during the receivership or administration and did not extend to periods of time before or after. This last point was enormously important for receivers as they could not be held liable, for example, for a dismissal of an employee occurring months or years after the receivership had ended. This was not a concern for administrators as under section 19(6) employees' claims were limited to liabilities incurred during the administrator's tenure.[46]

In conclusion, under section 44 as amended, if an administrative receiver causes an employment contract to remain in force by not acting to terminate it within 14 days of taking office, the administrative receiver will be personally liable to pay out under the contract for services rendered

---

[44] For a recent example of an attempted *Powdrill* claim see *Ramsay Maclaine v Leonard Curtis* [2001] BPIR 389.

[45] See e.g., P. Walton, *Buchan v Secretary of State for Employment* (1997) 3 RALQ 155.

[46] For the current provision in administration see para 99 of Schedule B1 of the Act.

after the contract is deemed to have been adopted. Liability for receiverships entered prior to 1994 are still governed by the House of Lords decision in *Powdrill* and the interpretation of the original section 44.

It should also be noted that for any personal liability incurred by the administrative receiver, the receiver is entitled to an indemnity out of the charged assets under section 44(1)(c). Such liability will rank as an expense of the receivership and will be paid ahead of preferential creditors and the debenture holder.[47]

As well as having the above personal action against the receiver for pay due during the receivership, an employee may also qualify as a preferential creditor under section 40 of the Act for fairly modest payments in respect of services rendered prior to the receivership. The maximum amount that the employee can claim as a preferential creditor is four months' pay with an aggregate maximum of £800. In addition the employee has the right to claim under section 184 of the Employment Rights Act 1996 an amount from the Secretary of State from the National Insurance Fund due to being made redundant by reason of the company becoming insolvent. The rights under this scheme are similarly limited in that the employee is generally limited to arrears of eight weeks' pay (maximum £250 per week SI 2002/10), an amount representing payments in lieu of statutory notice entitlement under section 86 of the 1996 Act and up to six weeks' holiday pay.

In practice, the National Insurance Fund normally pays out before the administrative receiver makes any distribution. In such circumstances, the Secretary of State is subrogated to the right of the employee to be treated as a preferential creditor to the extent that the payments out of the National Insurance Fund overlap with the employee's preferential claim.

6.6.5 *Other creditors*

Other creditors may have priority over the charge under which the receiver is appointed. A landlord who is owed rent by the company may distrain for unpaid rent even after the receiver has taken office. The landlord will usually take priority over the claims of the debenture holder (*Cunliffe Engineering v English Industrial Estates* [1994] BCC 972). A judgment creditor who attempts to enforce judgment against the company must complete the execution prior to the appointment of the receiver otherwise the judgment creditor cannot retain the benefit of the execution (*Evans v Rival Granite Quarries* [1910] KB 979). Execution for these purposes under a writ of *fifa* will only be completed if the sheriff has actually handed over the money to the judgment creditor. Owners under leasing or hire purchase agreements can normally repossess their goods if

---

[47] See e.g., *Re Glyncorrwg Colliery Co Ltd* [1926] Ch 951.

they are not paid (Nicholls LJ in *Re Atlantic Computer Systems plc* [1992] Ch 505 at 524–5 and *Brown v City of London Corpn* [1996] 1 WLR 1070).

Under section 233 of the Insolvency Act 1986, utility suppliers of gas, electricity, water and telecommunications cannot make payment of existing liability a condition for continued supply to the company in receivership (section 233 also benefits liquidators, administrators and supervisors of company voluntary arrangements). The supplier is only able to require the office holder to undertake personal liability for payment of any new supply. This provision prevents suppliers achieving priority over the company's other creditors. It was formally possible for the supplier to force full payment before continuing with the supply. If the company's business was dependent upon on the supply, for example, a frozen food supplier needed electricity to power the freezers where the food was kept, the office holder was left with no choice usually but to pay the utility.

6.7 Duties of receivers at common law and in equity

When considering what duties are owed by receivers it is important to note at the outset that, due to the similarity in function, the law regards mortgagees exercising their power of sale and a receiver appointed by a debenture holder as owing very similar duties.[48] Historically, mortgagees whose mortgagors defaulted under the secured loan agreement would enter into possession of the mortgaged assets. As the mortgagee had title to the assets he or she could then proceed to sell them to pay off the debt, accounting to the mortgagor for any surplus funds. Although this was and remains an effective remedy, mortgagees who take possession are subject to certain duties owed to the mortgagor[49] and to any other person who is interested in the equity of redemption. In order for mortgagees to avoid such potentially onerous duties, certainly when the assets of a business were secured, the practice developed of mortgagees appointing receivers to realise the security instead. The mortgagee could find himself or herself liable for errors in judgment in realising or trying to continue to run what might be quite a sophisticated or complex business, the detail of which the mortgagee would most likely be entirely ignorant.

Initially, receivers in this context were appointed by the court in so called 'debenture holders' actions'.[50] It soon became common practice to draft into debenture documents the power to appoint receivers out of

---

[48] For a recent example of this principle see *Cohen v Smith & Williamson* [2002] BPIR 243.

[49] See e.g., *White v City of London Brewery* (1889) 42 Ch D 437.

[50] See e.g., *Re Joshua Stubbs Limited* [1891] 1 Ch 475.

court[51] and for many years there appears to have been a choice available to the debenture holder whether to appoint out of court or to obtain a court appointment. As we have seen, in modern times the appointment by the court has rarely been relied upon. The receiver appointed out of court was and is appointed as agent of the borrower. The lender chooses who is to act as receiver and the receiver in turn takes control of the secured assets. By the appointment of the receiver as agent of the company, the mortgagee avoids the risks inherent in being a mortgagee in possession.

How receivers carry out their function can have an impact on a wide range of people. If the charged assets are sold for a price greatly less than their true market value or if the business is managed negligently, these things may have consequences for the debenture holder, the company, any guarantors of the company's debts and the unsecured creditors in general. The bank may still be owed money by the company. Any guarantor will have the guarantee called in where perhaps if the business or its sale had been managed more efficiently the guarantor may have escaped all liability. The likelihood is that there will be no assets available to the company's unsecured creditors who come at the bottom of the priority list for distribution of assets in any subsequent liquidation.

A receiver's primary duty is owed to the debenture holder, a secondary duty is owed to the company and to any third parties who can show they are interested in the equity of redemption, for example, guarantors of the company's debts or subsequent chargees. No duty is owed to directors or members of the company nor to unsecured creditors of the company as none of these persons has a direct interest in the charged assets.[52]

Although the duties owed by mortgagees in possession and receivers may not be identical,[53] the case law explaining the duties of receivers has relied upon decisions dealing with mortgagees and vice versa. In order to consider the law relating to receivers it is therefore necessary to consider case law dealing with mortgagees as well.

6.7.1 *Nineteenth-century case law*

Uncertainty has bedevilled this area for nearly two hundred years. There has been some confusion as to whether the duties owed are merely restricted to good faith and acting within one's powers, or whether a wider duty of care is owed. A subsidiary issue in more recent case law has been whether the duties owed are imposed in equity or by the common law. The cause of the initial confusion appears to have been a misinterpretation of Lord Eldon's judgment in *Downes v Grazebrook* ((1817) 3 Mer 200). In that

---

[51] See e.g., *Re Henry Pound, Son & Hutchins* (1889) 42 Ch D 402.
[52] See e.g., *Burgess v Auger* [1998] 2 BCLC 478 and *Medforth v Blake* [1999] BCC 771.
[53] See generally the comments made by Scott V-C in *Medforth v Blake* [1999] BCC 771.

case the court held that the purchaser from a mortgagee held the property on trust for the mortgagor. The facts of *Downes* turned upon self-dealing by the mortgagee through an agent leading to the imposition of a constructive trust. Although the judgment does not justify it, a doubt nevertheless grew from this as to whether or not a mortgagee owed the same duties to the mortgagor as a settlement trustee owed to a beneficiary.

In *Robertson v Norris* ((1859) 1 Giff 421 at 424) Stuart V-C commented that in exercising a power of sale a mortgagee 'shall exercise the power of sale in a provident way with a due regard to the rights and interests of the mortgagor in the surplus money to be produced by the sale'. In *Tomlin v Luce* ((1889) 43 Ch D 191) the Court of Appeal made a mortgagee liable for the loss caused by the negligent sale by auctioneers appointed by the mortgagee which led to a second mortgagee suffering loss. In *McHugh v Union Bank of Canada* ([1913] AC 299) a mortgagee took possession of a herd of horses and failed to take sufficient care of them. The mortgagee was held liable for the loss occasioned by their significant deterioration pending sale. In a typically clear judgment, Jessel MR in *Nash v Eades* ((1880) SJ 95) denied that *Downes* had the effect of constituting the mortgagee as trustee of the power of sale for the mortgagor but also refused to limit the duty owed to one of good faith. According to his Lordship the mortgagee, when exercising the power of sale, 'must conduct the sale properly, and must sell at a fair value' (at 95).

A different line of cases during this period recognised the problems caused by *Downes* but restricted the duties of a mortgagee to good faith. It was explained in *Warner v Jacob* ((1882) 20 Ch D 220) by Kay J by emphasising that the power of sale given to the mortgagee is for his or her own benefit. It enables the mortgagee to realise the assets and pay off the debt. As long as the power is exercised *bona fide*, according to Kay J, the court will not upset the sale even if the price achieved is low. Another case in favour of a very limited duty of good faith only is *Kennedy v de Trafford* ([1897] AC 180) where Lord Herschell stated that once a mortgagee had established a sale was in good faith 'it would be very difficult indeed, if not impossible, to establish that he had been guilty of any breach of duty towards the mortgagor' (at 185).

6.7.2 *Modern case law*

Modern case law on receivers' duties has until recently shown a similar lack of consensus among the judiciary. The case of *Re B Johnson & Co (Builders) Ltd* ([1955] 1 Ch 634) clearly limits the duty owed by receivers as a duty to act in good faith and within their powers. The case was brought under the predecessor of section 212 of the Act which permits a liquidator to bring an action in misfeasance against any former officer of the company including an administrative receiver or administrator. In an echo of *Warner v Jacob* the Court of Appeal explained that a receiver and manager was not under a duty to carry on the company's business nor to preserve its goodwill. The receiver is appointed with powers of management not to act in the best interests of the company but to realise the assets for the debenture holder. The receiver's primary duty is owed to the debenture holder.

The next case of significance, involving a mortgagee exercising its power of sale, is *Cuckmere Brick Co Ltd v Mutual Finance Ltd* ([1971] Ch 949). The Court of Appeal couched the duty owed by the mortgagee in terms of common law negligence. The duty owed was to act in good faith but also to act with reasonable care to obtain the 'proper market value' (or 'best price' or 'proper price') of the mortgaged assets at the moment the mortgagee chooses to exercise the power of sale. There is no duty to wait and only sell at the best possible moment. The mortgagee can choose when to sell, but once a time has been chosen, the mortgagee must act with reasonable care to obtain the proper market value at that time.

Prior to this case, the courts had always formulated the rules owed by mortgagees and receivers as equitable in nature. The use of the neighbour principle and discussion of proximity caused some disquiet at the time, as it was not clear how far these principles could go. For instance, could unsecured creditors be owed a duty? This type of concern never really came to anything although there remains a doubt even today as to whether the duties owed are equitable or common law in nature.

The common law negligence formulation was followed in a number of subsequent cases.[54] In *Standard Chartered Bank v Walker* ([1982] 3 All ER 938):

> A company had entered receivership. There was evidence to suggest that debenture holder may have interfered in the receivership by instructing the receiver to realise the charged assets swiftly. The Walkers, the company's directors, had personally guaranteed the company's secured debt. The sale of the charged assets realised far less than expected and the guarantees were called in. There was evidence that the auction held to dispose of highly specialist equipment was only attended by one overseas buyer and that most of the persons attending were local people even though the market for such machinery was worldwide. Although it was a bitterly cold day, there were few heaters in the auction room and these were so noisy they had to be switched off to allow the auctioneer to be heard. The decrease in temperature occasioned by this caused some prospective bidders to leave. The Court of Appeal held that there was a triable issue as to whether the receiver had breached a duty to take reasonable care to obtain the best possible price in the circumstances. The other triable issue was held to be that the bank could be held liable for the actions of the receiver if it has instructed the receiver on how to act.

In *Palk v Mortgage Services Funding plc* ([1993] 2 All ER 481) the Court of Appeal considered the duties owed by a mortgagee in possession. Sir

---

[54] See e.g., *Standard Chartered Bank Ltd v Walker* [1982] 1 WLR 1410 and *American Express v Hurley* [1986] BCLC 52.

Donald Nicholls V-C characterised such duties as owed both at common law and in equity. If the mortgagee takes possession, he or she cannot leave the property empty and wait for market conditions to improve. He or she is accountable for actual receipts from the property and must account to the mortgagor if he or she defaults in this regard. Reasonable care must be taken to realise a fair rent from the property when letting and to sell at the market value when selling.

The Privy Council decision in *Downsview Nominees v First City Corporation* ([1993] AC 295) stopped the judicial rush to increase the scope of common law negligence. In giving the Board's advice Lord Templeman explained that the duties owed by receivers were equitable in nature and not based in the common law.[55] His lordship confined the *Cuckmere* case as an authority only for the proposition that, if a mortgagee decides to sell, it must take reasonable care to ensure a proper price. A receiver selling assets owes the same duty but apart from that specific duty only owes a duty to act in good faith and not beyond his or her powers. This case was criticised widely[56] and may be seen as a product of its time – a time when the courts were concerned to cut down the seemingly relentless expansion of negligence in the areas of economic loss and professional liability.[57] Nevertheless, it was accepted as authoritative by the Court of Appeal in *Yorkshire Bank plc v Hall* ([1999] 1 All ER 879).

The law has recently been restated by the Court of Appeal in *Medforth v Blake* ([1999] BCC 771) which has in effect rejected the restrictive *Downsview* decision but at the same time not adopted a wide common law neighbour principle approach.

The issue before the Court was whether a receiver and manager appointed by a mortgagee over a pig farm owed any duty of care to the mortgagor in conducting the farming business. The debentures under which the receiver was appointed contained a form of floating charge permitted under the Agricultural Credits Act 1928. This Act permits farmers to charge their farming stock and business in much the same way as a company charges its undertaking. The receiver had run the business for four years. Evidence before the Court showed that pig feed was a major expense in the trading costs of the business and that obtaining discounts on large purchases of pig feed was normal commercial practice. The farmer claimed that the receivers owed him a duty of care in managing the business and had breached that duty by not taking advantage of the freely available discounts. The point was raised as a preliminary point on appeal.

---

[55] His lordship was in effect confirming the comments he had made in the previous Privy Council decision of *China and South Sea Bank Ltd v Tan Soo Gin* [1990] 1 AC 536.

[56] See e.g., A. Berg, 'Duties of a Mortgagee and a Receiver' [1993] JBL 213 and M. Fealy, 'Receivers' Duties: a return to orthodoxy' [1994] NILQ 61.

[57] See also the comments made by Nicholls V-C in *Palk v Mortgage Services Funding plc* [1993] Ch 330 at 338 where his lordship, in expressing some dismay with the state of the law, had difficulty in seeing why the duty of a mortgagee in selling or letting property should be confined to taking reasonable care to achieve the proper market price or rent.

Scott V-C in giving the judgment of the Court looked at the difficult historical development of the case law in this area and concluded that the apparent inconsistencies of approach could be explained by invoking the idea that equity was not inflexible and was capable of evolving. As common law negligence has evolved so had equitable doctrine. There is no difference in the result which the common law would reach from that which equity would reach in assessing what duties are owed by a receiver in managing mortgaged property. His lordship laid down seven propositions:

(1) A receiver managing mortgaged property owes duties to the mortgagor and anyone else with an interest in the equity of redemption.
(2) The duties include, but are not necessarily confined to, a duty of good faith.
(3) The extent and scope of any duty additional to that of good faith will depend on the facts and circumstances of the particular case.
(4) In exercising his powers of management the primary duty of the receiver is to try to bring about a situation in which interest on the secured debt can be paid and the debt itself repaid.
(5) Subject to that primary duty, the receiver owes a duty to manage the property with due diligence.
(6) Due diligence does not oblige the receiver to continue to carry on a business on the mortgaged premises previously carried on by the mortgagor.
(7) If the receiver does carry on a business on the mortgaged premises, due diligence requires reasonable steps to be taken in order to try to do so profitably.

Medforth gives welcome clarification to a difficult area. Scott V-C does not think it matters whether the duties are to be defined as equitable or common law. Traditionalists would prefer the duties to remain labelled as equitable but the current trend appears to be that the distinction between equitable and common law doctrine is being slowly eroded away.[58] The decision does ensure that receivers are to be judged by proper professional standards. It undoes the straightjacket imposed by *Downsview* by applying a duty of reasonable care or 'due diligence' to the management function of receivers, no longer limiting that duty to the actual sale of assets.

The recent case law on this area clears up a number of matters but leaves one very important issue unresolved. Doubts remain as to whether or not receivers owe a duty to cooperate with the chargor in selling property where a business is conducted, in such a way as to protect the business's goodwill. In short, it is unclear whether receivers may owe a duty in certain

---

[58] See e.g., *Henderson v Merrett Syndicates Ltd* [1995] 2 AC 145 and *Bristol and West Building Society v Mothew* [1996] 4 All ER 698.

circumstances to sell a business as a going concern. As the vast majority of administrative receiverships will cover going concern businesses, this remains a matter of some practical significance.[59]

6.8 Formalities of administrative receivership

6.8.1 *Publicity of administrative receivership*

Under section 39, invoices, orders for goods and other business letters must disclose the fact that a receiver has been appointed. Creditors of the company must be notified of an administrative receivership under section 46 and the Registrar of Companies needs to be notified of the appointment under section 405 Companies Act 1985.

6.8.2 *Information gathering and imparting*

Administrative receivers owe a duty under section 47 to obtain a statement of the company's affairs from present or recently departed officers or employees of the company. The statement should contain details of the company's assets, liabilities and details of the company's creditors (both secured and unsecured). Under section 48, within three months of appointment, the administrative receiver must prepare a report which must be filed with the Registrar of Companies and served on all the company's secured creditors (and a liquidator, if one is in office). Unsecured creditors must either be sent a copy of the report or be notified by publication of how they can access the report. Unless the court orders otherwise, the report must be laid before a meeting of unsecured creditors.

The report must contain a summary of the statement of affairs and the administrative receiver's comments upon it, if any. It will also detail the events leading up to the receivership, any disposal or intended disposal of company property by the receiver, any continuance of the company's business, amounts owing to the appointing debenture holder and to preferential creditors and any amount, if any, likely to be available to the other creditors. The administrative receiver need not include any information which would seriously prejudice his or her functions.[60] The meeting of unsecured creditors may, as well as considering the receiver's report, decide to form a Creditors' Committee under section 49. The Committee,

[59] See e.g., *AIB Finance Ltd v Debtors* [1998] 2 All ER 929 and *Hadjipanayi v Yeldon* [2001] BPIR 487.
[60] See e.g., *Gomba Holdings UK Ltd v Homan* [1986] 1 WLR 1301.

if formed, can request information from the administrative receiver. The receiver need only furnish information it is reasonable to hand over. The detail as to who forms the Committee and how its business is conducted is contained in rules 3.16–3.30.[61]

6.9 Ending of administrative receivership

6.9.1 *Effect of winding up*

Although it is technically possible for a company which is in receivership, immediately after the receivership ends, to enter into administration or company voluntary arrangement, such a turn of events is unlikely. What is far more common is for the company to enter liquidation either before, during or immediately after the receivership ends. It is common for a receivership to begin and for the company to enter liquidation during the receivership. The practicalities of this usually involve the liquidator waiting in the wings for the administrative receivership to terminate before the liquidator steps in to finish off whatever remains of the company.

Under section 44, as soon as the company enters liquidation, the administrative receiver's agency of the company is said to terminate. It does not, though, terminate the receivership. The enforcement of the debenture is dealt with outside the operation of the liquidation.[62]

The real problem with liquidation being said to terminate the receiver's agency is that it is not entirely clear what this means. On first sight, it suggests that the receiver can no longer continue to act as receiver of the company's assets. This is not the case. It does prevent the receiver from committing the company to new liabilities.[63] It prevents the receiver from carrying on the business of the company. The receiver cannot call up uncalled capital.[64] The receiver is, though, still capable of acting to get in and realise the secured assets.[65] As part of this power, the receiver can begin or continue proceedings in the company's name to get in assets subject to the debenture.[66] It should be borne in mind that the receiver

---

[61] For detailed consideration see H. Picarda, *The Law Relating to Receivers, Managers and Administrators*, 3rd edn, London: Butterworths (2000), Chapter 14.

[62] See e.g., *Strong v Carlyle Press* [1893] 1 Ch 268.

[63] See e.g., *Gosling v Gaskell* [1897] AC 575.

[64] See e.g., *Re Henry Pound, Son & Hutchins* (1889) 42 Ch D 402.

[65] See e.g., *Re Henry Pound, Son & Hutchins* (1889) 42 Ch D 402 and *Sowman v David Samuel Trust Ltd* [1978] 1 WLR 22. See also P. Millett, 'The Conveyancing Powers of Receivers after Liquidation' (1977) 41 Conv 83.

[66] See e.g., *Gough's Garages Ltd v Pugsley* [1930] 1 KB 615.

who continues to act after the termination of the agency of the company does not become the agent of the debenture holder.[67] The receiver will act as principal in continuing to realise the secured assets.

6.9.2 *Distribution of proceeds*

An administrative receiver's function is, if it is possible, to realise enough of the charged assets to pay off the appointing debenture holder. This may involve merely running a business for a period of time, in order to allow the income produced to pay off the debt. It may involve the sale of one or two large fixed assets to pay off capital and interest owing. Frequently it will require the administrative receiver to sell all the company's assets and, if feasible, to do so by selling the business as a going concern. There is often not enough money to pay off the appointing debenture holder. In practice, this may lead to the debenture holder calling in personal guarantees obtained previously from the company's directors in order to make up any shortfall.

Once the administrative receiver has completed the realisation of the secured assets (or at least as much as is necessary) payment must be made in a set order:

(1) Any secured creditor with priority over the debenture under which the administrative receiver is appointed.
(2) The administrative receiver's own costs, expenses and remuneration.
(3) Fixed changes contained within the debenture under which the administrative receiver is appointed.
(4) Debts due to preferential creditors under section 40. This is now limited to certain claims by employees and levies on coal and steel production.[68]
(5) The remaining sum is payable to the holders of floating charges (charges which as created were floating charges – section 251 of the Act).[69]
(6) If any money remains, it will be handed over to any junior incumbrancers. If none exist and the company is in liquidation, the surplus must be paid to the liquidator. If neither of these two exists, the surplus is returned to the company itself.[70]

---

[67] It is possible for the receiver to become the agent of the debenture holder if the debenture holder instructs the receiver on how to act and the receiver acts upon such instructions. This is something most lenders will be loathe to do as it will involve the lender in potential liability for the acts of the receiver; see *American Express International Corpn v Hurley* [1985] 3 All ER 564.

[68] See section 386 and Schedule 6 of the Act.

[69] For floating charges created after the coming into force of section 176A of the Act, a prescribed percentage, likely to amount to 10 per cent of the company's net assets, is first deducted for the satisfaction of unsecured creditors. This will not have any effect on the vast majority of administrative receiverships which will, by definition, usually be commenced under debentures executed prior to section 176A coming into force.

[70] See e.g., *Seabrook Estate Co Ltd v Ford* [1949] 2 All ER 94 – the receiver is not a debtor of the company so that the amount in his or her hands cannot be attached by an execution creditor.

Once the assets are realised and the receiver is able to distribute the proceeds, the receiver will need to be clear as to which assets are subject to fixed securities and which are subject to floating securities. Preferential creditors have priority over floating charges only. Administrative receivers do not generally make any distribution to unsecured creditors (except for the very limited operation in administrative receivership of the new section 176A of the Act, where a prescribed percentage of company assets, after payment of fixed charges, the administrative receiver's expenses and the preferential creditors, needs to be set aside for unsecured creditors prior to payment out under the floating charge).

6.9.3 *Termination*

Receivership will usually come to an end when the receiver has completed the task of realising enough assets to pay off the appointing debenture holder and the money has been handed over. Once the receiver's duties are over, the receiver simply lets the Registrar of Companies know that he or she is vacating office under section 45(4) and the receivership is over.

In addition to this possibility, a receiver may cease to hold office due to death, removal by the court, ceasing to be a licensed insolvency practitioner or by resignation. If the receiver vacates office for any reason other than death, he or she must again notify the Registrar of Companies under section 45(4).

6.10 Availability of administrative receivership after the Enterprise Act 2002

The relevance of administrative receivership will slowly recede as the provisions of the Enterprise Act 2002 take effect. The remedy of appointing an administrative receiver is largely abolished in relation to debentures entered into after the commencement of the Act. Section 250 of the Enterprise Act inserts a new section 72A into the Act. It provides that the holder of a 'qualifying floating charge' may not appoint an administrative receiver. The meaning of this phrase is given in para 14 of the newly inserted Schedule B1. The prohibition on appointment applies only to charges created on or after the date the provision comes into effect. It overrides any provision to the contrary contained in any agreement. Debenture holders, whose floating charges are executed after the Enterprise Act comes into force, are generally no longer able to appoint an administrative receiver, but can instead appoint an administrator out of court.

The government White Paper (*Productivity and Enterprise: Insolvency – A Second Chance* (July 2001) Cm 5234), which led to the Enterprise Act 2002, suggested a number of radical amendments to insolvency law. As we have seen, administrative receivers owe their primary duty to the debenture holder, only secondary duties to the company and others interested in the equity of redemption and no duty at all to unsecured creditors. The fact that administrative receivership is not a collective procedure has led to its slow lingering demise. The importance of administration is set to increase dramatically. It is, as we shall see in Chapter 7, a procedure where the administrator controls the company's business for the benefit of all creditors, not just the main secured creditor. It is also a procedure where the administrator has a power and may owe a duty to put together a rescue package for the company. An administrative receiver has no such power or duty.

It will be decades before the above general prohibition on administrative receivership takes full effect. As existing debenture holders will still be able to, it is likely that they will continue to appoint administrative receivers, at least in the medium term, rather than opting wholesale to appoint administrators. It will be crucial for proposed administrative receivers to check the date of the debenture before accepting an appointment. If 'appointed' under a new debenture the receiver will be invalidly appointed and may be liable to the company as a trespasser.

The generality of the above prohibition is cut down slightly by a list of exceptions contained in sections 72B–72F. In the following circumstances an administrative receiver may still be appointed even under debentures executed after the commencement of the Enterprise Act:

(1) *Capital Market* – if the charge is contained in a capital market arrangement where a company incurs, or is expected to incur, a debt of at least £50 million.
(2) *Public Private Partnership* – if a project company is financed partly by public and partly by private money and the purpose of the company is to assist a public body in the discharge of its functions.
(3) *Utilities* – project companies carrying on regulated utility businesses such as the provision of electricity, gas, water, telecommunications, postal services or railways.
(4) *Project Finance* – other project companies where the company incurs, or is expected to incur, a debt of at least £50 million.
(5) *Financial Market* – companies whose property is subject to a market charge (meaning given under section 173 Companies Act 1989), a system charge (see SI 1996/1469) or a collateral security charge (see SI 1999/2979).
(6) *Registered Social Landlord* – if the company is a registered social landlord (meaning given in Part 1 of the Housing Act 1996).

Except for these situations, new debentures no longer carry the power to appoint an administrative receiver. It is only in these six situations that administrative receivers will be appointed under floating charges created after the commencement of the Enterprise Act. It is only in such circumstances that administrative receivers are required to set aside the prescribed percentage of company assets for unsecured creditors under section 176A. This fund is not set aside in administrative receiverships commenced under floating charges created before the Enterprise Act.

The Enterprise Act does not affect the ability to appoint non-administrative receivers, such as LPA receivers, under any debentures whenever created but, as such receivers are in practical terms unlikely to be appointed under a floating charge, there is very little likelihood of the prescribed fund being set aside in non-administrative receiverships.

Chapter 7

Administration

7.1 Introduction

This chapter deals with administration which, along with receivership, voluntary arrangement and schemes of arrangement under section 425 of the Companies Act 1985, is one of the non-terminal insolvency procedures a company may enter. When a company finds itself in financial trouble it generally has four options:

(1) immediate winding up;
(2) return to profitable trading through some agreement with creditors, if necessary, such as a voluntary arrangement or the less common scheme of arrangement under section 425 Companies Act 1985;
(3) if security covers all or virtually all the company's property and includes a floating charge (executed prior to the commencement of the Enterprise Act 2002) the company may invite the debenture holder to appoint an administrative receiver or have one forced upon it; or
(4) bring in an administrator as an external manager to consider possibly rescuing the company. If company rescue is not possible, the administrator may be able to turn the business around and dispose of the business as a going concern and, in so doing, save the economic unit of the business and the jobs which go with it. The administrator may find that the best that can be achieved is a disposal of the company's assets which at least obtains a better price than would be achieved upon an immediate winding up. After the sale, the company, by that point an empty shell, will be wound up.

This chapter will look at how an administrator is appointed, the function of the administrator, the administrator's powers and duties and how the administration is conducted. The great benefit of administration and its defining characteristic is that it creates what is commonly referred to as a moratorium on actions against the company. While the administrator is in office, creditors are generally prevented from enforcing their rights against the company. This temporary freedom from creditor harassment is designed to allow the administrator time and space to put together a package to ameliorate the company's financial position.

When administration was introduced, its original purpose was to fill a gap. The Cork Committee recognised that often a company's business could be saved by its entering administrative receivership. This potentially positive result could only be achieved where a floating charge holder with security over the whole or substantially the whole of the company's undertaking existed. Administration was designed to be a similar process to administrative receivership, but one which could be initiated where no administrative receivership was possible. Somewhat ironically, it is now set to take over from administrative receivership.

As we have seen in Chapter 6, the Enterprise Act 2002 has had a dramatic effect on administrative receivership. It has also had a considerable effect upon administration.

7.1.1 *Changes under the Enterprise Act 2002*

Section 248 and Schedule 16 of the Enterprise Act 2002 replace the former administration regime under Part II of the Insolvency Act 1986 with a new Schedule B1 to the 1986 Act. As was explained in Chapter 6, the most far reaching change made by the 2002 Act is that, in most circumstances where a floating charge is created after the Act, the power of the floating charge holder to appoint an administrative receiver is replaced with the power to appoint an administrator instead. One of the perceived benefits of appointing an administrative receiver has always been the speed and relative lack of expense involved in the appointment. In order to allow debenture holders the ability to appoint an administrator with similar ease and speed, the new provisions have changed the way in which administrators are appointed. The purposes of an administration have been redrafted in different terms. The powers given to an administrator in order to achieve the purpose of the appointment have remained broadly the same as before.

The move to the new law has not been a totally clean break. The old administration regime under Part II of the Insolvency Act 1986 still applies with various appropriate modifications to a number of specific types of organisation. The old regime's special arrangements remain applicable (under section 249 of the 2002 Act) to the following types of company:

(1) water companies (under the Water Industry Act 1991);
(2) railway companies to which railway administration orders apply (under the Railways Act 1993 and according to section 19 of the Channel Tunnel Rail Link Act 1996);[1]

---

[1] See e.g., *Re Railtrack plc* [2002] 2 BCLC 308.

(3) air traffic controlling companies (under the Transport Act 2000);
(4) London Underground private public partnership companies (under the Greater London Authority Act 1999);
(5) building societies (under the Building Societies Act 1986).

Partly due to the fact that the old regime remains in effect (albeit in a small minority of modified cases) and partly because it is usually easier to understand current law if one has some knowledge of how the law has developed, it is intended to refer where appropriate to the old regime as well as dealing in detail with the new regime. Some outline knowledge of the old law may also assist when reading some of the cases decided under the former regime. As will be seen, most of the substantial changes have occurred in how the administration is commenced. The purpose of administration has been amended but the effect of administration upon third parties and the powers and duties of administrators remains largely as before and so previous case law remains relevant in interpreting the new provisions.

In the rest of this chapter the phrase 'the old regime' will be used to describe the administration system under Part II of the 1986 Act. The phrase 'the new regime' will be used when dealing with Schedule B1 of the 1986 Act (as inserted by the Enterprise Act 2002). References to paragraphs will be to provisions in Schedule B1.

7.1.2 *Nature of administration*

The nature of administration has changed somewhat. Under both the old and the new regimes, administration is in essence a temporary measure which either lays the foundations for the rescue of the company, for example, by the approval of a voluntary arrangement, or for the winding up on a more favourable basis than would be achieved by an immediate winding up. Under the old regime the administrator did not generally distribute company assets to its creditors. An important aspect of the new regime is the administrator's power to pay out preferential and secured creditors.

Under the old regime the administrator was appointed by the court with the aim of achieving a certain statutory aim or aims. The procedure was intended as an alternative to administrative receivership where no one creditor had security including a floating charge over the whole or substantially the whole of the company's undertaking and so no creditor could appoint an administrative receiver. Under the new regime, administration has taken over from administrative receivership as the only option open to a debenture holder (if the floating charge is created after the new regime comes into force). The administrator may still be appointed by the court but will usually be appointed out of court (although still deemed to be an officer of the court). Rather than having a list of statutory grounds upon which the court would make the order under the old regime, the new regime talks about the purpose of the administration. The primary purpose of the administration now is to rescue the company.

Under both the old and the new regimes, administration gives the company breathing space. This moratorium on creditor actions allows the company or its business to be rescued or for some other beneficial result to be achieved.

7.2 Appointment of administrator

7.2.1 *Procedure for appointment under the old regime*

The only way to put the company into administration under the old regime was by court order. The petition to the court could be made by the company, its directors, a creditor or creditors, or by the clerk of a magistrates' court. The petition had to be served on certain persons, most importantly any person with the power to appoint an administrative receiver. If, prior to the hearing of the petition, the debenture holder appointed an administrative receiver, the petition was dismissed. The debenture holder therefore had an effective power of veto over the possible administration order. In practice, this restriction led to only a relatively small number of administration orders being made. Administrative receivership tended to be the preferred option of debenture holders not least because the receiver owes his or her primary duty to the appointing debenture holder.

Along with the petition, an independent report (under the Insolvency Rules 'IR' rule 2.2) would be filed. This report, produced by an independent insolvency practitioner, would usually sway the court. If the report was positive (as invariably it was), claiming that the grounds for the order were likely to be achieved, the court would make the order. The statutory grounds for the order, under section 8, were that the company was, or was likely to become, unable to pay its debts and that one or more of the following purposes could be achieved:

(1) the survival of the company, and the whole or any part of its undertaking, as a going concern;
(2) the approval of a voluntary arrangement under Part I of the Act;
(3) the sanctioning of a scheme of arrangement under section 425 Companies Act 1985;
(4) a more advantageous realisation of the company's assets than would be effected on a winding up.

On presentation of the petition a statutory moratorium on actions against the company came into effect (section 10) which was continued after the order was made (section 11).

7.2.2 *Procedure for appointment under the new regime*

A company enters administration when an administrator is appointed (para 1). An administrator must be a licensed insolvency practitioner (para 6). An administrator may be appointed in three ways:

(1) by the court making an administration order under para 10;
(2) by the holder of a qualifying floating charge under para 14;
(3) by the company or its directors under para 22.

A company cannot usually enter administration if the company is in administration already, is in liquidation[2] or is subject to an effective administrative receivership.[3]

7.2.3 *Appointment by the court*

A court may still make an administration order in a similar way to how it could under Part II of the Act. There are a number of important differences to the procedure. The court must be satisfied that the company is, or is likely to become, unable to pay its debts and also that the order is reasonably likely to achieve the purpose of the administration (para 11). Under a similar provision under the old regime the word 'likely' was interpreted as meaning there was 'a real prospect' the purpose could be achieved (*Re Harris Simons Construction Ltd* [1989] 1 WLR 368 per Hoffman J as he then was).[4] A race horse whose odds were 5-1 to win the Derby was 'likely' to win the race in the opinion of Hoffman J. A 5-1 chance that a statutory ground for an administration order could be achieved was 'likely' and therefore an order would, where such probability existed, be made.

Under para 12, an application for an order may be made by one or more of the following:

(1) the company;
(2) its directors (which term includes a majority of the directors under para 105);
(3) one or more of its creditors. If the application is made by the holder of a floating charge with the power to appoint an administrator out

---

[2] But see the exception contained in para 37.
[3] See para 39.
[4] Although Peter Gibson J in *Re Consumer & Industrial Press Ltd* (1988) 4 BCC 68 had expressed a view that 'likely' meant 'likely, on a balance of probabilities' or 'more probably than not' (and this view had been followed in *Re Manlon Trading Ltd* (1988) 4 BCC 455 by Harman J) both Peter Gibson and Harman JJ later approved the 'real prospect' test of Hoffman J (in *Re SCL Building Services Ltd* (1989) 5 BCC 746 and *Re Rowbotham Baxter Ltd* [1990] BCC 113 respectively). See also Vinelott J in *Re Primlaks (UK) Ltd* (1989) 5 BCC 710.

of court under para 14, there is no requirement to show that the company is or is likely to become unable to pay its debts (para 35). Although it seems unlikely that the floating charge holder, who could appoint an administrator out of court, would wish to apply to the court for an appointment, there is one situation where the power may be useful. The power to appoint out of court cannot be exercised where the company is already subject to a winding-up order. In such circumstances the floating charge holder can apply to the court for an administration order which will result in the winding-up order being discharged (para 37)); or

(4) the chief executive of a magistrates' court (under section 87A of the Magistrates' Courts Act 1980 where the court has imposed a fine on the company).

As soon as is reasonably practicable after the application is made, the applicant must notify any person who has or may be entitled to appoint an administrative receiver or who may be entitled to appoint an administrator out of court. This provision ensures that any debenture holder with a security including a floating charge over the whole, or substantially the whole, of the company's undertaking is aware of the application and can effectively pre-empt the court application by appointing either an administrative receiver or asking the court to appoint the debenture holder's choice as administrator, as the case may be. If an administrative receiver is effectively in post[5] by the time the application for an administration order is heard, the application must be dismissed (unless the debenture holder who appointed the receiver consents to the order – para 39). The debenture holder's power of veto under the old regime survives into the new. As long as the administrative receiver is appointed before the court hearing, the receiver will generally take precedence over the administration application. Under para 36, a debenture holder with the power to appoint an administrator out of court can apply to the court to have a specified person appointed as administrator in place of the person proposed by the administration applicant.

At the hearing of the application the court may:

(1) make the administration order;
(2) dismiss it;
(3) adjourn unconditionally or conditionally;
(4) make an interim order (which may restrict the exercise of the company directors' powers and/or may invest various discretions in the court

---

[5] The court may make the order notwithstanding the administrative receivership if it thinks the security under which the appointment was made is liable to be avoided under section 238 (transaction at an undervalue), section 239 (preference) or section 245 (avoidance of certain floating charges) of the Act.

itself or an insolvency practitioner to act in relation to the company pending further development);

(5) wind the company up; or

(6) make such other order as it thinks appropriate (para 13).

If an administration order is made, it takes effect on the date specified in the order, or if none, at the time the order is made.

Under the new regime, there is as yet no express requirement as to what needs to be included within an application for an administration order. Only when amendments are made to the Insolvency Rules will it become apparent what will be needed to persuade the court to make the order. As things stand there appears no need to prepare an IR rule 2.2 independent report under the new regime. It remains to be seen if, in practice, such a report is not, in some form, still seen as a necessary requirement. Without such a report or witness statement by the intending administrator it is difficult to see where the evidence can come from for the court to exercise its power to make the order.

7.2.4 *Appointment by a floating charge holder*

A floating charge holder's ability to appoint an administrative receiver under a charge created after the commencement of the new regime has been almost totally abolished. Instead the holder of a 'qualifying floating charge' may appoint an administrator out of court under para 14. A floating charge will be 'qualifying' for these purposes if either on its own or together with other securities it relates to the whole or substantially the whole of the company's undertaking. In addition, the debenture must either:

(1) state that para 14 applies to the floating charge or otherwise purport to give the debenture holder the power to appoint an administrator; or

(2) purport to give the debenture holder the power to appoint an administrative receiver.

The new regime applies to floating charges created after its commencement but also permits the holder of a pre-existing floating charge (with power to appoint an administrative receiver) to appoint an administrator. It may be that, if the big institutional lenders perceive that administration works as well for them or better than administrative receivership, administrative receivership may become outmoded extremely swiftly.

A debenture holder considering appointing an administrator out of court is free to appoint once the charge has become enforceable under its own terms with certain important caveats:

(1) There may be another holder of a 'qualifying floating charge' over the company's undertaking who has priority over the debenture holder. Priority is decided by which floating charge is created first (subject to a different priority being agreed between the parties). Two business days' notice must be given to any holder of a prior floating charge (para 15) before the debenture holder can appoint. No notice need be given if the prior floating charge holder agrees to the appointment in writing.

(2) No appointment may be made if an administrative receiver is in office (para 17).

(3) No appointment may be made if the company is already in administration (para 7).

(4) No appointment may be made if the company is in liquidation (para 8).

(5) No appointment may be made if a provisional liquidator has been appointed under section 135 (para 17).

A person who appoints an administrator under para 14 must file with the court a notice of appointment (and other documents to be prescribed). The notice of appointment must contain a statutory declaration to the effect that the appointor holds a qualifying floating charge which has become enforceable and that the statutory requirements for appointment have been complied with (it is an offence to make false statements or statements not reasonably believed to be true in the statutory declaration). The notice of appointment must also contain the consent of the administrator to act and a statement to the effect that, in the proposed administrator's view, the purpose of the administration is reasonably likely to be achieved (reliance may be made for this purpose on information supplied by the directors).

The appointment takes effect from the filing of the notice of appointment. The appointor must notify the administrator (and such others as are prescribed) as soon as is reasonably practicable that the notice of appointment has been filed.

If the appointment under para 14 proves to be invalid, for example, because the floating charge was not qualifying or had not become enforceable, the court may order that the appointor indemnify the 'administrator' for loss arising from the invalid appointment (para 21).

7.2.5 *Appointment by the company or its directors*

Under para 22 either the company itself (by a members' resolution in general meeting) or the directors may appoint an administrator. An appointment by the directors includes an appointment made by a majority of the directors (para 105).

No appointment under para 22 is possible if the company is already in administration or liquidation (paras 7 and 8). In addition, no appointment under para 22 can be made if in the previous 12 months the company has been in administration following either an application by the company or directors to the court under para 12 or by the appointment of an earlier administrator by the company or directors under para 22 (para 23). To similar effect, no appointment may be made under para 22 if in the previous 12 months the company had the benefit of a moratorium under Schedule A1 of the Act or a voluntary arrangement flowing from such a moratorium failed prematurely within the 12-month period (para 24).

Further restrictions on the ability of the company or directors to appoint an administrator are found in para 25. No appointment may be made if a petition for the winding up of the company or an application for an administration order is pending. Following the idea that debenture holders retain some priority say on the insolvency of the company, no appointment may be made under para 22 if an administrative receiver is in office.

Under para 26 a person proposing an appointment under para 22 must give at least five business days' written notice, including details of the proposed administrator, to any debenture holder who may be entitled to appoint either an administrative receiver or an administrator under para 14 (and such other parties who are prescribed, if any).

A copy of the notice must be filed at court as soon as is reasonably practicable (para 27). This copy must be accompanied by a statutory declaration, in the prescribed form, by the proposed appointor to the effect that:

(1) the company is or is likely to become unable to pay its debts;
(2) the company is not in liquidation;
(3) as far as the declarant is aware there is no restriction under the Schedule preventing the appointment; and
(4) such other information as may be prescribed.

It is an offence to make false statements or statements the declarant does not reasonably believe to be true in the statutory declaration.

Once the five business days' notice to the debenture holder have expired (or the debenture holder has given written consent to the appointment) the appointment can be made.[6]

The appointor must file a notice of appointment in the prescribed form (and any other documents prescribed) with the court. The appointor must make a statutory declaration to the effect that the appointor has the power to make the appointment, that the Schedule has been complied with, and that the information given in the statutory declaration filed with the notice of intention remains accurate. Again, it is an offence to make false statements or statements the declarant does not reasonably believe to be true in the statutory declaration.

---

[6] It must be made within 10 business days of the date of filing the notice of intention to appoint at court (para 28).

The notice of appointment must be accompanied by a statement by the administrator that he or she is willing to act; that the purpose of the administration is reasonably likely to be achieved; and such other information as may be prescribed. The administrator is entitled to rely on any information given by the directors for this purpose (para 29).

The appointment takes effect when the notice of appointment is filed (para 31). The appointor must inform the administrator (and such other persons as may be prescribed) as soon as is reasonably possible after filing.

At any time prior to the filing of the notice of appointment under para 29, the appointment can be effectively vetoed where an administrator is appointed by the court or by a debenture holder out of court (paras 7 and 33). As with most other methods of appointing an administrator, no appointment may be made if the company is in liquidation (para 8).

If the appointment under para 22 proves to be invalid, for example, because the directors had no authority to appoint, the court may order that the appointor indemnify the 'administrator' for loss arising from the invalid appointment (para 34).

7.3 Process of administration

7.3.1 *Purpose of administration under the new regime*

Once an administrator is appointed he or she must act with the purpose under para 3(1) of:

(a) rescuing the company as a going concern, or
(b) achieving a better result for the company's creditors as a whole than would be likely if the company were wound up (without first being in administration), or
(c) realising property in order to make a distribution to one or more secured or preferential creditors.

In keeping with the case law under the old regime (see *Re Charnley Davies Ltd* [1990] BCC 605, where an administrator was judged by the standards of an ordinary, skilled insolvency practitioner) there is a general duty on the administrator to 'perform his functions in the interests of the company's creditors as a whole' (para 3(2)) and to perform his functions as quickly and efficiently as is reasonably practicable (para 4).

The primary purpose of any administration is to rescue the company as a going concern (para 3(1)(a) above). A rescue for these purposes will involve the company itself remaining intact with all or a substantial part of its business as a going concern. It will most likely involve some agreement with the company's creditors such as a company voluntary arrangement under Part I of the Act or a scheme of arrangement under section 425 of the Companies Act 1985. A proposal whereby the business is sold off leaving the company as an empty shell will not constitute a rescue for these purposes. One could question the wisdom of giving primacy to the survival of the company rather than to the survival of the business as a going concern. Time will tell whether the primary purpose of administration is frequently achieved or whether most administrations end up pursuing the secondary objective.

Only if the administrator thinks that rescuing the company is not reasonably practicable, or that the objective contained within para 3(1)(b) above would achieve a better result for the creditors as a whole, can the administrator not attempt a rescue of the company. Experience from the past as to how insolvency practitioners have operated, in both administrations and administrative receiverships, suggests that in practice this is likely to be the most common of the three possible purposes. Company rescue is usually a very difficult goal to achieve. The time and expense involved in turning a company around may be prohibitive, especially where a simple sale of the business to a buyer could be effected quickly and relatively cheaply. There is likely to be more money left for the creditors if a quick sale can be achieved, rather than if the company undertakes a long and expensive rescue package.

If the administrator believes that neither the objectives in para 3(1)(a) or (b) is reasonably practicable, he or she may carry out his or her functions with the purpose listed in para 3(1)(c) instead. This would be so if there was clearly only enough money in the company to pay some of the secured or preferential creditors. In such a scenario, owing a duty to act in the interests of the company's creditors as a whole would be a nonsense, as unsecured creditors would have no interest in the result of the administration. If this is the case, the administrator must act in such a way that does 'not unnecessarily harm' the interests of the creditors (para 3(4)(b)).

Examples of three scenarios highlighting how each of the three possible purposes for an administration are intended to operate in practice are given in the Explanatory Notes to the Enterprise Act 2002. The example given where rescue of the company should be possible under para 3(1)(a) is as follows:

Company A is operating at a profit and has excellent products, a loyal customer base and a healthy order book. However, major investment in a new IT system, which is late and over budget, has knocked the company off its business plan, its cash flow has suffered and it is unable to pay its debts. The company has been placed in administration and the administrator has had an offer for its business that would provide sufficient funds to pay the secured creditors and give 35p in the pound for unsecured creditors. However, the administrator has determined that the problems are short-term and they can be resolved and will not have any ongoing effect. The company's

bankers have given their support to the administrator's plans to continue
trading, the company's business is profitable and the administrator
is confident that the company can be rescued by trading its way out of its
current financial difficulties, and provide 65p in the pound for unsecured
creditors within 12 months. The administrator puts his proposals to
the creditors.

The rescue here is reasonably practicable in that the company's bankers
are supporting a business which is essentially sound. If the bank's support
was not forthcoming and there was no other source of finance available,
rescue may not be reasonably practicable. The decision of the administrator will be respected and, as long as the commercial decision to attempt
a rescue or to refuse to attempt a rescue is a decision which a reasonable
administrator could make, the administrator will incur no liability for
breach of duty.

If the administrator decides that company rescue is not reasonably
practicable, he or she must then consider how he or she can instead at
least achieve a better result for the company's creditors than would be
accomplished by an immediate winding up. This secondary purpose may
also be pursued if the administrator thinks it will achieve a better result for
the company's creditors as a whole than a company rescue (even if rescue
may be reasonably practicable). This may involve the breaking up of the
company's various businesses into saleable undertakings, usually on a
going concern basis. A going concern sale invariably nets a better sale
price than a sale of a company's individual assets. The example of where
para 3(1)(b) might apply given in the Explanatory Notes is as follows:

> **Company B** has good products and a sound customer base. The company is
> making losses, its plant and machinery are outdated and its overheads and
> debts have been rising for some time. The company has been placed in
> administration and the administrator has determined that there are no funds
> available to maintain its trading operation or invest in new machinery and it is
> therefore not reasonably practicable to rescue the company. The administrator
> has reviewed the company and determined that a sale of its businesses on a
> going concern basis would provide a better return than a break-up sale of its
> assets. The administrator markets the businesses and the best offer he or
> she receives would provide sufficient funds to pay the secured creditors and
> give 40p in the pound for unsecured creditors. The administrator reports to
> the creditors at a meeting and explains why it was not reasonably practicable
> to rescue the company.

If company rescue is not feasible and a going concern sale is not viable
either, the administrator falls back on para 3(1)(c) which allows the
company's property to be realised in order to make a payment to one or
more secured or preferential creditors. In this situation there will, by
definition, be no money to distribute to the company's unsecured
creditors (apart from a possible distribution of a percentage of floating
charge assets under section 176A). Despite the fact that the unsecured

creditors will not receive a distribution and therefore appear to have no interest in the administration, the administrator must 'not unnecessarily harm' the interests of the creditors of the company as a whole (para 3(4)). This phrase appears to be redolent with difficulty. It is an unusual provision not least because it has no statutory precedent. It remains to be seen how the courts will interpret it. Importantly, it does seem to impose upon the administrator a duty to consider the interests of unsecured creditors even where they appear to have no financial interest.

One of the difficulties with the wording of para 3 is that this third purpose can only be adopted if neither of the first two is reasonably practicable. As the second purpose is to achieve a better result for the creditors generally than an immediate winding up would achieve, it begs the question that if this cannot be reasonably achieved, why not put the company into winding up immediately. The task of the administrator in this context will look very much like that of a liquidator in that any distributions which can be made will be made. The company will thereafter be no more than an empty shell. In such circumstances an administration can, upon its ending, go straight into dissolution without the need for an intervening winding up. The example given in the Explanatory Notes of where para 3(1)(c) may apply is as follows:

> **Company C** is a service company whose business and reputation were built around its excellent standards of customer service. But a number of key personnel have recently left, the quality of the company's service and its reputation have suffered badly, customers have become dissatisfied and the company is no longer able to attract and retain business. It has been making losses for a number of months and is unable to pay its debts. The company is then placed in administration. The administrator reviews the company and concludes that its business is not viable and a sale is not possible. The administrator markets the company's assets and realises funds that are sufficient to make a part-payment to the secured creditors and there are no funds available to pay unsecured creditors, except for those resulting from the operation of the ring-fence (under s176A). The administrator reports to the creditors and explains why it was not possible to achieve a company rescue or a better return for unsecured creditors.

7.3.2 *Effect of administration*

Under para 40, if the court makes an administration order, it shall also dismiss any pending winding-up petition. If the administrator is appointed by a floating charge holder under para 14, any winding-up petition is suspended. Under para 41 where an administration order is made any administrative receiver must vacate office (this will only have occurred if either the appointing debenture holder consents, or the court believes the appointing debenture holder's security is vulnerable to attack by an administrator). In any type of administration, the administrator may request any other type of receiver, e.g., an LPA receiver, to vacate office.[7]

7.3.2.1 *Moratorium on actions*

Arguably the most important characteristic of administration is the fact that it frees the company temporarily from creditor harassment. It achieves this by the imposition of what is usually referred to as a moratorium on actions against the company. The rights that any third parties have against the company are in no way destroyed or reduced. The third parties are merely prevented from enforcing those rights while the company is in administration (without first obtaining the requisite consent). The moratorium is couched in very wide terms and is designed to protect the company for a period whereby it can sort out its financial problems without having its creditors nipping at its heels by repossessing goods, executing judgments, distraining for unpaid rent and so on. It can keep its premises, stock etc. intact while proposals can be put to the creditors as a whole. No creditor in theory is permitted to ignore the moratorium without the consent of the court or agreement of the administrator. The new regime has adopted very similar wording to the old regime in terms of the detail of the moratorium and so it seems certain that the courts will regard the previous case law as authoritative under the new system.

The whole purpose of administration might be frustrated if the moratorium only began as soon as the administrator was appointed. For example, in the absence of a moratorium, judgment creditors who became aware of an intention to put the company into administration may decide to act quickly to execute their judgments against company property. Suppliers to a company may decide to repossess goods supplied on retention of title or hire purchase terms. A landlord may act swiftly to distrain for any unpaid rent. To prevent this type of frustration of the administration before it has even started, there is provision for an interim moratorium (discussed shortly). Although the moratorium is extremely restrictive of creditors enforcing their rights against the company, it is possible to ask the court for leave to enforce and, in addition, once the administrator is appointed, he or she may consent to the creditor's proposed action. A breach of the moratorium in the absence of appropriate permission will, it seems, lead to a liability in damages (*Euro Commercial Leasing Ltd v Cartwright & Lewis* [1995] BCC 830).

---

[7] Where an administrative or other receiver vacates office, the receiver's remuneration is charged on such of the company's assets previously held by the receiver. The receiver's claim takes priority over the security held by his appointor. Payment may have to wait, though, as the receiver's rights are subject to the moratorium on actions against a company in administration (para 41).

7.3.2.2 *Interim moratorium*

The interim moratorium under para 44 comes into effect in the case of an application to the court for an administration order as soon as the application is made and continues until the order is made or until the application is dismissed. If the administration is commenced by an appointment by a floating charge holder under para 14, the moratorium is effective from the date a copy of the notice of intention to appoint is filed at the court. It continues until either the appointment is made or the period of five business days since the filing expires without an appointment being made. This appears to be a superfluous provision as the appointment by a floating charge holder under para 14 is effective when a notice of appointment is filed at court. The substantive moratorium comes into effect at this point. Also, there is no need under para 14 to file a notice of intention to appoint with the court.

If the company or directors are attempting to appoint an administrator, the interim moratorium is effective from the time when a copy of the notice of intention to appoint is filed with the court under para 27. The interim moratorium continues until the appointment is made or ten business days have passed without an appointment being made.

The interim moratorium is in the same terms as the substantive moratorium which takes effect upon the appointment of an administrator (ignoring any reference to the consent of the administrator as obviously at this stage there is no administrator). Exceptionally, the interim order does not prevent the following actions being taken:

(1) a winding-up petition may be presented but only if on public interest grounds or by the Financial Service Authority under section 367 of the Financial Services and Markets Act 2000;
(2) an administrator may be appointed under para 14 by the holder of a qualifying floating charge;
(3) an administrative receiver may be appointed and such a receiver may carry out his or her functions.

7.3.2.3 *Moratorium following administrator's appointment*

As soon as the administrator is appointed, the interim moratorium is replaced with the substantive one (paras 42 and 43). Once in administration:

(1) No resolution to wind up the company may be passed and no winding-up order may be made (unless the winding-up order is on the grounds of public interest or the petition was presented by the Financial Services Authority under section 367 of the Financial Services and Markets Act 2000).

In addition, none of the following actions may be taken without either permission of the court or the consent of the administrator:

(2) No step may be taken to enforce security over the company's property.

The term 'security' is defined in section 248 of the Act as meaning 'any mortgage, charge, lien or other security.'[8] The meaning of what is the company's 'property' is defined in section 436 as including 'money, goods, things in action, land and every description of property wherever situated and also obligations and every description of interest, whether present or future or vested or contingent, arising out of, or incidental to, property.' In *Bristol Airport plc v Powdrill* ([1990] Ch 744) Sir Nicholas Browne-Wilkinson V-C said (at 759): 'it is hard to think of a wider definition of property'. The case itself is illustrative of the meaning of both security and property in this context:

> An airline owed an airport money for use of its facilities. Under section 88 of the Civil Aviation Act 1982 the airport claimed a statutory right to retain aircraft held by the company under a seven year lease. The Court of Appeal in interpreting the meaning of section 248 *eiusdem generis* held that the statutory right claimed did fall within the idea of 'a lien or other security'. Although the company was not the full beneficial owner of the aircraft, its position as leaseholder was sufficient interest to make the aircraft 'property' of the company.

Under the terms of the old moratorium under section 11 of the Act as originally drafted, there were a number of cases discussing whether or not a landlord's right to forfeit a lease by peaceable re-entry could amount to the enforcement of a 'security'.[9] A most instructive discussion as to what amounts to a 'security' interest is given by Lightman J in *Razzaq v Pala* ([1998] BCC 66). His lordship states that a security interest involves the debtor conferring an interest in his or her property on the creditor which allows the creditor, following default, to enforce the debt against the property. This right is defeasible upon payment of money. This is consistent with the concepts of mortgages, charges and various types of liens. It does not fit the idea of a landlord's right to peaceable re-entry.

(3) No step may be taken to repossess goods in the company's possession under a hire purchase agreement.

---

[8] Contractual liens are within the moratorium – see the unreported decision of Hart J in *London Flight Centre (Stansted) Ltd v Osprey Aviation Ltd* (3 July 2002).

[9] See e.g., *Exchange Travel Agency Ltd v Triton Property Trust plc* [1991] BCLC 396, *Re Olympia & York Canary Wharf Ltd* [1993] BCLC 453, *Razzaq v Pala* [1998] BCC 66 and *Re Lomax Leisure Ltd* [1999] 2 BCLC 126. The courts finally concluded that the remedy of forfeiture by peaceable re-entry did not amount to a security interest. This meant that the remedy was not prevented by the administration moratorium. Express provision to include it was made by section 9 of the Insolvency Act 2000. The remedy is now expressly mentioned as being included within the para 43 moratorium.

For these purposes 'hire purchase agreement' includes a conditional sale agreement, a chattel leasing agreement and a retention of title agreement (para 111). The facts of *Re Atlantic Computer Systems plc* ([1992] Ch 505) show how important this aspect of the moratorium can be:

> The company held a large number of computers under both hire purchase and long lease agreements. The company sublet these computers to a number of end users. During the administration, the sub-lessees continued to make their rental payments to the company but the administrator did not pass any of these funds onto the owners of the computers who were owed money by the company under the various agreements. The Court of Appeal made a number of important points, some of which we will look at shortly. For present purposes it suffices to say that the moratorium was effective to prevent the owners repossessing the computers as they were considered to be still in the 'company's possession' notwithstanding the fact that they had been sublet. Repossession was therefore only possible either with the consent of the administrator or leave of the court.

Property is still in a company's 'possession' under a hire purchase agreement even if the agreement states that the company entering administration has the effect of terminating the agreement. For the purposes of the moratorium the agreement is still regarded as effective (*Re David Meek Plant Ltd* [1994] 1 BCLC 680).

(4) A landlord (which term includes a person to whom rent is payable) may not exercise a right of forfeiture by peaceable re-entry in relation to premises let to the company.

At common law a landlord has the right peaceably to re-enter tenanted premises following default by the tenant. In practice the re-entering may be anything but a lay person's idea of peaceable. The effect of exercising this self-help remedy will usually be to terminate the lease. If this remedy was available against a company in administration which traded from leasehold premises it would have a severe impact upon any rescue plan and would frustrate the main aim of the legislation. As mentioned above, this remedy was not originally included within the Act's moratorium, but was introduced by the Insolvency Act 2000.

(5) No legal process may be instituted or continued against the company or the company's property. Legal process expressly includes legal proceedings, execution (by judgment creditors) and distress (a self-help remedy frequently used by landlords whereby goods on the tenanted premises are seized and may be sold to cover unpaid rent).

The term 'legal process' under the old regime has been interpreted as meaning any process which requires the assistance of the court. It does not therefore include such matters as the service of a contractual notice making time of the essence or terminating a contract for repudiatory breach (*Re Olympia & York Canary Wharf Ltd* [1993] BCLC 453). It would seem also not to cover such matters as set-off and a bank's right to combine accounts. The term 'legal proceedings' did not appear in the wording of the old regime's moratorium; instead it merely referred to 'other proceedings'. Under the wider terminology of the old regime, 'other proceedings' was held to include both legal and quasi-legal proceedings such as arbitration (*Bristol Airport plc v Powdrill* [1990] Ch 744). It did not include an application by a competitor to have the company's statutory aviation licence revoked (*Air Ecosse Ltd v Civil Aviation Authority* (1987) 3 BCC 492). Neither did it include an application to register a charge against the company out of time (*Re Barrow Borough Transport Ltd* [1990] Ch 227). An application by an employee to an industrial tribunal under what is now the Employment Rights Act 1996 was included (*Carr v British International Helicopters Ltd* [1993] BCC 855). It remains to be seen whether the courts interpret the new narrower wording any differently to the old wording.

It is generally thought that existing floating charge holders who have decided to enforce their security will generally stick with the tried and trusted option of appointing an administrative receiver. In circumstances where the terms of the moratorium may have a beneficial effect on the realisation of the company's assets, the floating charge holder may prefer to take up the newly available option of appointing an administrator. Such a situation may arise where the company trades from leasehold premises and the landlord is threatening to distrain for unpaid rent. If this occurs the floating charge holder's security is likely to be extremely vulnerable and any chance of an administrative receiver being able to sell the business as a going concern would be limited. The appointment of an administrator would, on the other hand, bring into force the moratorium and could conceivably be crucial in saving the company or the business and at the same time ensuring the security of the floating charge holder remains intact.

7.3.2.4 *Permission of the court*

Although during the period that the moratorium is in force virtually all action against the company is prevented, there are two exceptions to this rule. First, if the administrator agrees to the action being taken, the moratorium is lifted. This may be the case where, for example, some of the company's machinery is held under a hire purchase contract, the administrator has no use for the machinery and the owner wants to repossess.

Second, if the administrator does not agree to the lifting of the moratorium, the creditor or other third party must apply to the court for permission to take action. The leading case on how the court is to approach the exercise of its discretionary power to grant permission is *Re Atlantic Computer Systems plc* ([1992] Ch 505), the brief facts of which were given above. Not surprisingly in the circumstances, the owners of the computers, who were receiving no rental payments from the company, wanted to repossess the computers. The Court of Appeal granted permission and laid down at some considerable length the matters the court would take into account in an application for permission to lift the moratorium (per Nicholls LJ at 542–544).[10] Here is a summary of the points made:[11]

(1) The party seeking permission must always make out a case.
(2) Where the party seeking permission to exercise his proprietary rights over his own property, such as by repossessing his own goods, then if this repossession is unlikely to impede the purpose of the administration, the court would normally grant permission.
(3) In other cases, the court must undertake a balancing exercise. The interests of the party claiming to repossess must be balanced with the interests of the other creditors.
(4) As part of this balancing exercise due weight needs to be given to the owner's proprietary rights. The owners of such property as the computers should not have to finance indirectly the administration for the benefit of unsecured creditors. This was effectively what was going on in the case.
(5) It will usually be the case that permission will be granted if significant loss would be caused to the owner by refusal. However, as part of the balancing exercise, if substantially greater loss would be caused to others by the grant of leave, that may outweigh the projected loss caused to the owner. In making this judgment the court looks at a number of factors. The company's financial position, its ability to make payments under the agreements (arrears and current liabilities), the administrator's proposals, the effect on those proposals of granting permission, the effect on the owner of refusal, the duration of the administration and the conduct of the parties will all be relevant considerations.
(6) If permission is refused, the administrator may be ordered to act in a certain way to ensure fairness.

7.3.3 Formalities upon appointment

As soon as an administrator is appointed, he or she must carry out a number of matters as soon as is reasonably practicable (para 46). He or she must

(1) send a notice of appointment to the company;
(2) obtain a list of the company's creditors;

---

[10] See also *Re Meesan Investments Ltd* (1988) 4 BCC 788 and *Re Polly Peck International plc (No4)* [1997] 2 BCLC 630.
[11] See also *Re City Logistics Ltd* [2002] 2 BCLC 103 where repossession of retention of title goods was permitted but delayed until a specific date.

(3) send a notice of appointment to all creditors of whom he or she is aware;

(4) publish a notice of appointment in the prescribed manner so that others are aware that the company is in administration;

(5) send a notice of appointment to the Registrar of Companies within seven days of the appointment (for these purposes the date of appointment is the date of the order if the administrator is appointed by the court, or if appointed out of court, the relevant date is the date upon which the appointor gives the administrator notice of the appointment).

Breach of para 46 without reasonable excuse is an offence.

Under para 47 the administrator, as soon as reasonably practicable after appointment, must request a statement of affairs from any of the partici-pants in the company (usually officers or employees of the company). The statement of affairs must be verified by the person giving it by a statement of truth. The statement of affairs will be in a prescribed form and will contain details of the company's property, debts and liabilities (including details of any security over the company's property). A person required to give a statement of affairs must do so within 11 days of receiving the request (subject to the administrator or court extending the period). A failure to comply with a requirement under this paragraph without reasonable excuse is an offence.

7.3.4 *Administrator's proposals*

The administrator's job is to put together some proposals in an attempt to satisfy one of the three statutory purposes under para 3(1) detailed above. Under para 49, a statement of the proposals is sent, as soon as is reasonably practicable after the appointment, to the Registrar of Companies and to the company's creditors and members. The maximum time the adminis-trator has for issuing the statement of proposals is eight weeks after the company has entered administration (this period may be extended by the court under para 107).

The statement must explain why, if this is the conclusion the adminis-trator has reached, the administrator thinks that neither of the purposes mentioned in para 3(1)(a) and (b) (company rescue or a better deal for the creditors generally than an immediate winding up would achieve) can be achieved. If rescue seems reasonably practicable the statement may include a proposal for a company voluntary arrangement (under Part I of the Act) or a scheme of arrangement (under section 425 of the Companies Act 1985).

The creditors, who are sent a statement of the administrator's proposals, must at the same time be invited to an initial creditors' meeting. This meeting should be held as soon as is reasonably practicable but must be held within 10 weeks of the company entering administration (again the court may extend this time period under para 107). The proposals will be put to the creditors for their approval.

Under para 52, there is no requirement to call an initial creditors' meeting if:

(1) the company has sufficient property to pay all the creditors in full; or
(2) the company has insufficient property to make any payment to unsecured creditors (other than under section 176A – the prescribed percentage deduction in favour of unsecured creditors of monies available to a floating charge holder); or
(3) the administration cannot achieve either rescue of the company or a better result for creditors generally than under an immediate winding up (the purposes listed in para 3(1)(a) and (b) respectively).[12]

The creditors' meeting is to be conducted in accordance with rules, which at the time of writing have yet to be produced. Under the previous regime under Part II of the Act, the administrator's proposals needed to be approved by a simple majority in value of the unsecured creditors.[13] It is likely that the new rules will mirror the old when detailing how the creditors' meeting operates.

Under the new regime (as with the old), the interests of secured and preferential creditors are protected in that, although they have no vote at the creditors' meeting in regard to their secured or preferential debt (they can vote any unsecured balance), the administrator's proposals may not include any action which would affect the priority of such debts, or, in the case of secured creditors, their right to enforce their security, without the respective creditors' consent (para 73). This in effect means, that if such creditors are not treated, under the terms of the proposal, in a way which recognises their priority, any approval of the proposals may be challenged.

The initial creditors' meeting may approve the administrator's proposals without modification, or with modification (if the administrator consents to the changes), or fail to approve the proposal (paras 53 and 55). The administrator must report the decision of the meeting to both the court and the Registrar of Companies. Any substantial changes to an approved proposal must be agreed to by a further creditors' meeting. Failure by the creditors' meeting to agree to the initial proposal or any further amendments will usually lead to the court discharging the administrator (para 55).

The creditors' meeting may also form a creditors' committee. This committee may require the administrator to attend on the committee on seven days' notice and to provide it with information about the exercise of the administrator's functions (para 57).

---

[12] This is subject to the right under para 52(2) of creditors holding at least 10 per cent of the company's total debts to requisition a meeting.

[13] See IR 2.18–2.30 generally for details.

Anything which is required or permitted to be done by a creditors' meeting may also be accomplished by correspondence between the administrator and the creditors (para 58). This is potentially a very useful way to obtain the creditors' consent to a particular course of action without the need to call formally a creditors' meeting. Time and expense may be saved by using this mechanism.

7.4 Duties of an administrator

The administrator must as soon as he or she takes office take control of the company's property (para 67). The administrator shall use his or her statutory powers (as detailed below) to manage the company in accordance with any proposals which have been approved by a creditors' meeting or according to any directions given by the court (para 68).

If a creditor or member can show that the administrator is acting or proposes to act in a way which unfairly harms the interests of the creditor or member (alone or in common with other creditors or members), he or she may apply to the court. An application may also be made by a creditor or member if the administrator is not performing his or her functions as quickly or efficiently as is reasonably practicable (para 74). The court has a wide discretion in terms of the type of order it may make if the ground for the application is made out. In particular the court may regulate the administrator's exercise of his or her functions, may require the administrator to do or not to do a specified thing, order a creditors' meeting to be called, or provide for the administrator's appointment to cease.

The rights given to members and creditors under para 74 are similar to the old regime's provisions contained in section 27 of the Act. The only real difference is that under the previous provision the applicant had to show that the conduct complained of was 'unfairly prejudicial' to, rather than conduct which 'unfairly harms', the interests of the applicant. It is difficult to discern any real difference between these two phrases and it seems likely that case law under the old regime will remain highly influential in interpreting the new regime.

The case of *Re Charnley Davies Ltd* ([1990] BCC 605) considered an application under section 27 by an aggrieved creditor who claimed the administrator had sold the company's business at an undervalue. No real guidance on the meaning of what would constitute conduct 'unfairly prejudicial to the interests' of creditors or members in this context was given by the court. Drawing an analogy with section 459 of the Companies Act 1985, clearly 'interests' means something wider than legal rights. An allegation that the creditors' legal rights had been interfered with was held not to be necessary under section 27 nor would it necessarily be sufficient. Under section 27 it had to be shown that the management of the company was being conducted in a manner unfairly prejudicial to the creditors' interests. Unlawful conduct may point to this but is not a necessary requirement.

Millett J (as he then was) held that the allegation of negligence was not made out on the facts. Even if it had been, a sale at a negligent undervalue would not necessarily fall within the section. Under section 27 much depended on the nature of the administrator's actions which were being complained about. If the applicant was complaining about conduct which showed insufficient regard to the interests of creditors or members then an application under section 27 would be appropriate. If the allegation involved a breach of duty, the correct procedure would be to have the administration order discharged, have the company placed into compulsory liquidation and have the newly appointed liquidator bring a claim against the administrator for misfeasance under section 212 of the Act.[14] The result of this is that, although the court recognised that administrators were subject to the same duties owed by all professionals to exhibit the standard of care one would expect from an ordinary skilled practitioner, the enforcement of this duty by an individual creditor was somewhat indirect as it involved putting the company into liquidation.

The awkwardness of the result of *Charnley Davies* has been reversed under the new regime. Under para 75 the court may examine the conduct of an administrator. The persons who can bring an application for such an examination are:

(1) the official receiver;
(2) the administrator of the company;
(3) the liquidator of the company;
(4) a creditor of the company;
(5) a contributory of the company.

An application under this provision must allege that the administrator:

(1) has misapplied or retained money or other property of the company;
(2) has become accountable for money or other property of the company;
(3) has breached a fiduciary or other duty in relation to the company; or
(4) has been guilty of misfeasance.

If found liable by the court it may order the administrator:

(1) to repay, restore or account for money or property;
(2) to pay interest;
(3) to contribute a sum to the company's property by way of compensation for breach of duty or misfeasance.

---

[14] See also *MTI Trading Systems Ltd v Winter* [1998] BCC 591 where the court discouraged use of section 27 to revisit commercial decisions by the administrator.

What para 75 does, in effect, is to incorporate into administration a right to bring an action which in liquidation is contained within section 212 of the Act.[15] The importance of this provision is that it permits a creditor or guarantor of the company to bring an action directly against the administrator even after the administrator has been discharged if, for example, the administrator had conducted a sale of the company's business at an undervalue, or carried on the day-to-day management of the company negligently.

There has been a conspicuous absence of case law where administrators have been sued for breach of duty.[16] As administration slowly begins to take over from administrative receivership as the most common non-terminal corporate insolvency procedure, it is likely that under para 75 the actions of administrators will be called into question and liability for breach of equitable or common law duties may become more frequent. In addition to equitable or common law duties, the administrator is now under a statutory duty under para 3(2), subject to an exception, to perform his or her functions in the interests of the company's creditors as a whole. Although the courts have not recently considered in any detail the nature of administrators' duties, it seems likely, following the receivership case of *Medforth v Blake* ([1999] BCC 771), that the courts may be keen to ensure that administrators, who owe duties to all the company's creditors, are made liable for any lapse in professional competence. It must be remembered that the administrator is also an officer of the court (para 5) and is therefore subject to the court's control and the ethical requirements imposed by the rule in *Ex Parte James* ((1874) LR 9 Ch App 609).

7.5 Powers of an administrator

The administrator acts as the company's agent (para 69). The administrator may 'do anything necessary or expedient for the management of the affairs, business and property of the company' (para 59(1)). In addition to this very widely phrased catch-all power, administrators are also given a wide range of specific powers. It is difficult to imagine an administrator acting outside the parameters of these powers, but as an extra safeguard, third parties who deal with an administrator in good faith and for value need not inquire whether the administrator is acting within his or her powers.

In common with administrative receivers, administrators have all the powers listed in Schedule 1 of the Act. In addition to these powers an

---

[15] See generally Chapter 43.
[16] G. Moss, 'Administrators' Duties and Liabilities' (1999) 12 *Insolvency Intelligence* 25.

administrator may also remove or appoint a director (para 61); call a meeting of creditors or members (para 62); and may apply to the court for directions in connection with his or her functions (para 63).

An administrator has the same powers as a liquidator to apply to the court to upset transactions at an undervalue (under section 238); preferences (under section 239); extortionate credit bargains (under section 244); and floating charges (under section 245).[17]

Administrators will usually look to continue the company's business, at least for a limited period of time. As part of carrying on the company's business, it may be necessary or commercially sensible to dispose of assets subject to floating or fixed charge security or to hire purchase, retention of title or leasing agreements.

Under para 70 an administrator may dispose of assets subject to a floating charge as if such assets were not subject to the charge. The floating charge holder's rights are protected in that its security interest is transferred to the proceeds of sale or to any further assets purchased with the proceeds of sale.

If the administrator wants to dispose of property subject to a security which is not a floating charge or which is subject to a hire purchase agreement, he or she must obtain the consent of the court (paras 71 and 72 respectively). A hire purchase agreement for these purposes is defined under para 111 as including a conditional sale agreement, a chattel leasing agreement and a retention of title agreement. The power may prove useful where the administrator is attempting to sell the business as a going concern and some crucial assets of the business, such as its premises or machinery, are subject to a fixed charge or hire purchase contract. Much of the company's stock in trade may be subject to retention of title clauses. The court will only make an order if it thinks that the disposal is likely to promote the purpose of the administration. As a condition of making such an order the net proceeds of the sale of the secured asset and any extra amount required, so as to produce a total amount equal to the asset's market value as determined by the court, must be paid to the secured creditor.[18]

7.5.1 *Disposal of assets without a creditors' meeting*

We have seen above that the administrator has the power to dispose of any assets of the company. If rescuing the company is not reasonably practicable the adminstrator can look to exercise his or her power of sale to sell the business as a going concern. We have also seen that the

---

[17] For a detailed discussion of these provisions see Chapters 36, 37, 39 and 40.

[18] The powers under paras 70 and 71 are similar to the powers that an administrative receiver has under section 43 of the Act. The power under para 72 to sell goods subject to hire purchase agreements is unique to administrators.

administrator is under a duty to prepare proposals and to call a creditors' meeting to consider those proposals within 10 weeks of the commencement of the administration. A real problem, in practice, is what the administrator should do if he or she realises immediately that the only realistic option is to sell the business off quickly. There may be only one potential buyer and that buyer may be in a hurry. The deal either happens in the first week or so of the administration, or it will not happen at all.

The administrator is in a difficult position here. The administrator has a statutory duty to call a creditors' meeting and to act in accordance with any proposals there approved. He or she also owes a duty to realise the assets in the most efficient way as regards the creditors of the company in general. A quick sale without calling a creditors' meeting would make a subsequent meeting pointless as there would be nothing left to gain approval for. To wait to call a meeting and to lose the buyer would have the creditors alleging negligence.

This particular quandary existed equally under the old regime. The solution to it can be gleaned by considering some of the cases decided under the old regime. Initially the courts seem to have been in two minds what to order. In an unreported decision on 21 January 1987 (noted without any apparent disapproval by Millett J in *Re Charnley Davies Ltd* [1990] BCC 605 at 610) Vinelott J decided that the administrator did have power to sell the company's entire undertaking without recourse to a creditors' meeting. In *Re Consumer and Industrial Press (No 2)* ((1988) 4 BCC 72) Peter Gibson J stated that only in quite exceptional circumstances would the court approve a disposal of all the company's assets prior to a creditors' meeting. In *Re NS Distribution Ltd* ([1990] BCLC 169) Harman J stated that the decision to dispose of a single asset was a decision administrators could and should make for themselves under their Schedule 1 powers, without the need for the court's direction. In considering Peter Gibson J's decision in *Consumer and Industrial*, Harman J was able to distinguish the cases as in *NS* there was no question of a disposal of all the company's assets, but merely a single asset. This would not have the effect of frustrating the purpose of the creditors' meeting.[19] There is perhaps a lack of logic which says that the disposal of some assets can be done without a meeting whereas the sale of all assets requires a meeting. The power itself listed in Schedule 1 makes no such distinction.

The matter was settled in *Re T & D Industries plc* ([2000] BCC 956).

> The joint administrators of two connected companies decided, two weeks into the administration, that they wished or may wish to dispose of some or even all of the companies' assets as a matter of some urgency without calling a creditors' meeting. They sought the court's opinion as to whether the court's approval was necessary before the assets could be sold.

---

[19] Useful reference could also be made to *Re Smallman Construction Ltd* (1988) 4 BCC 784, *Re PD Fuels Ltd* [1999] BCC 450, *Re Montin Ltd* [1999] 1 BCLC 663 and *Re Osmosis Group Ltd* [2000] BCC 428.

Neuberger J decided that the court's permission was unnecessary and should not usually be sought in such circumstances. His lordship laid down seven principles to guide administrators:[20]

(1) In normal circumstances, a creditors' meeting should be held. Administrators will need time to put together their proposals and in some cases, this may lead to delay. The sooner the adminstrator makes the proposal the better. The administration should be conducted in a speedy and efficient manner.[21]

(2) An administrator may have to make urgent and important commercial or administrative decisions. This is the job of the administrator. Administrators cannot ask the court to make the decisions for them and use the court as a 'sort of bomb shelter'.[22]

(3) Administrators should not take unfair advantage of the creditors. There will be situations where an administrator must make urgent decisions without being able first to call a creditors' meeting. However, depending upon the importance of the decision and the time available, some consultation with the creditors should be made. If time is short, it should still be possible to speak with some at least of the major creditors. The decision as to the form of the consultation and the decision following the result of such consultation is a decision for the administrator.

(4) It may be that the administrator, or some other party such as one of the creditors, will occasionally have to consider applying to the court for directions. If, for example, the creditors have not agreed with a proposed course of action and the administrator has good reason for seeking guidance rather than making up his or her own mind.

(5) If an application is made to the court it would be very unusual for the court to be able to give any real assistance without an *inter partes* hearing and where the decision is essentially either an administrative or commercial one. Some degree of comfort may be taken from the results of the limited consultations.

(6) If the matter is of sufficient importance and there is time, the administrator may ask the court to order a creditors' meeting on short notice.

(7) Where the administrator is proposing a disposal of all the company's assets without a creditors' meeting, he or she should bear in mind that an eventual creditors' meeting will be substantially ineffective. The weight given to this factor must depend on all the facts of the individual case.

The conclusion to be drawn from this is that the decision is one for the administrator, who must act as the reasonable insolvency practitioner and make the decision personally. The time available; the pressure to do the deal; the availability of another deal; the possibility of some creditor consultation, must all be borne in mind before the decision is made. If the decision is not reasonable, the administrator may be liable for breach of duty.

---

[20] See also S. Elboz, '*T&D Industries plc* – the seven principles – new guidance for administrators in disposing of assets' (1999) 15 IL&P 183 and H. Roberts, '*T&D Industries plc* revisited: further guidance for administrators in disposing of assets' (2000) 16 IL&P 61.

[21] This final point is reiterated in para 4 which states the administrator 'must perform his functions as quickly and efficiently as is reasonably practicable'.

[22] See also *Re Ciro Citterio Menswear plc* [2002] EWHC 897.

7.5.2 *Remuneration and expenses of the administrator*

Upon the administrator ceasing to hold office (whether due to resignation, death, removal from office, or because his or her appointment ceases to have effect) para 99(3) states:

(1) that his remuneration[23] and expenses are charged on and payable out of property of which he had custody or control immediately prior to the cessation of office; and
(2) are to be paid out in priority to any floating charge holder.

7.6 Contractual liability in administration

7.6.1 *Existing contracts*

The administrator acts as agent of the company (para 69). This agency is similar to that of an administrative receiver in that the company has no power to terminate it. The appointment of an administrator does not in itself terminate existing contracts with the company although many contracts will expressly state the appointment brings the contract to an end.[24]

As agent of the company the administrator incurs no personal liability on contracts of the company. He or she is entitled to continue contracts on behalf of the company. This may involve the continued occupation of land held under a lease or the use of chattels under hire purchase, leasing or retention of title contracts. If the administrator decides not to pay out under these existing contracts, the moratorium prevents the creditors from enforcing their rights against the company by forfeiture or repossession without obtaining the permission of the court. Having said this, it is usual for an administrator to pay such creditors, at least for the use of the assets during the administration. Although not enforceable strictly by the creditors as expenses of the administration, if such payments are made they will be treated as legitimate expenses. If the administrator does not pay, the creditors are likely to succeed in an application to the court for permission to enforce their rights. Alternatively, they may bring an action under para 74 claiming the administrator is acting in a manner which unfairly harms their interests. If they sit back and do nothing, they are highly unlikely to be paid.[25]

---

[23] Under the old regime the Insolvency Rules dealt with the quantum of the administrator's remuneration (see IR rules 2.47–2.50). The new rules are likely to replicate this system. The remuneration was set by the creditors' committee or, if one did not exist, by the creditors' meeting.

[24] See e.g., *Re David Meek Plant Ltd* [1994] 1 BCLC 680.

[25] For an example of a landlord who lost out in such a way, see *Spring Valley Properties Ltd v Harris* [2001] BPIR 709.

7.6.2 *New contracts*

An administrator does not incur personal liability, as does an administrative receiver, on any new contracts entered into by the administrator on behalf of the company. It is only the company which is liable on such contracts. However, when the administrator's appointment is ended, a sum payable in respect of a debt or liability arising out of a contract entered into by the administrator shall be charged on, and payable out of, property over which the administrator had custody or control and is payable in priority to the administrator's own remuneration and expenses (para 99(4)). This right to be paid out ahead of even the administrator is commonly referred to as 'super priority'.

7.6.3 *Employment contracts*

In Chapter 6 we considered the personal liability incurred by an administrative receiver who is deemed to have adopted a contract of employment. The development of receivership law on this point goes hand in hand with the law applicable in administration. Similar rules apply to employees' rights in both procedures. It is important to note that the big difference is that an administrator incurs no personal liability under an adopted employment contract. The employee is still well protected despite the lack of personal liability of the administrator. If a contract of employment is adopted by the administrator, under para 99(5) the employee's entitlements are paid out ahead even of the administrator's own remuneration and expenses (the other example of 'super priority').

The House of Lords decided in *Powdrill v Watson sub nom Re Paramount Airways Ltd (No 3)* ([1995] 2 AC 394) that if an administrator keeps an employee on for longer than 14 days after the commencement of the administration, the administrator is deemed to have adopted the employee's contract. The employee is then entitled to be paid 'wages or salary' for the period of time worked after the contract has been adopted.

For these purposes 'wages or salary' include:

(1) a sum payable in respect of a period of holiday (for which purpose the sum shall be treated as relating to the period by reference to which the entitlement to holiday accrued);
(2) a sum payable in respect of a period of absence through illness or other good cause;
(3) a sum payable in lieu of holiday;
(4) in respect of a period, a sum which would be treated as earnings for that period for the purposes of an enactment about social security; and
(5) a contribution to an occupational pension scheme (para 99(6)).

Employees may also be entitled to payment for work carried out prior to the administration, in part anyway, due to their claim as preferential creditors[26] and may have a statutory right to other payments out of the National Insurance Fund.

7.7 Ending administration[27]

7.7.1 *Distributions to creditors*

One of the practical problems encountered under the old regime was caused by the absence of a power for the administrator to make distributions to creditors. In simple terms the problem was as follows. Section 387 states the relevant date for assessing which debts are preferential. Prior to the abolition of the Crown preference, the Crown in the form of the Inland Revenue and Customs and Excise was the largest preferential creditor in virtually all insolvencies. Under the pre-Enterprise Act 2002 regime, if a company went from administration into liquidation, a most common occurrence even if the administration had been a success, the date for ascertaining preferential status was different depending upon whether the liquidation was voluntary or compulsory. This was a crucial difference from the preferential creditors' point of view.

If the liquidation was voluntary, the relevant date for deciding which debts were preferential was the date of the commencement of the liquidation (the date of the members' resolution to wind up). If it was a compulsory liquidation, the relevant date was the date of the commencement of the administration. Under the old regime where the Inland Revenue could claim up to 12 months' unpaid PAYE deductions and Customs and Excise could claim up to six months' unpaid VAT, the relevant date was crucial to the Crown making a decent recovery. If the administration had gone on for a year or so, during that period any tax returns due to the Crown would almost certainly have been met by the administrator. Any claims by the Crown to any outstanding unpaid tax would normally relate to the period prior to the commencement of the administration. In order for such claims to be preferential debts, it would be necessary for the relevant date to be the date of the administration, not the liquidation. From the Crown's point of view, following the administration, it would therefore want the company to go into compulsory

---

[26] For details of the position of employees in the preferential debts regime, see Chapter 32.

[27] In addition to the termination of the administration in the ways hereafter discussed, under paras 87–98 an administrator may be replaced due to resignation, removal, ceasing to be qualified, or death.

liquidation rather than voluntary liquidation. Only in this way would the Crown retain its preferential status for debts owed prior to the administration. If the company went into voluntary liquidation, the Crown would probably lose most, if not all, of its preferential status.

The problem facing the administrator was that a compulsory liquidation is far more expensive to fund than a voluntary liquidation. In order to act in the best interests of the company's general unsecured creditors, the administrator would wish to seek a voluntary liquidation. In order to ensure the preferential creditors maintained their preferential status, a compulsory liquidation would be necessary.

There were various attempts to solve this conundrum with administrators making various different applications to the court.[28] A rather fudged compromise solution to this problem was eventually reached in *Re UCT (UK) Ltd* ([2001] 1 BCLC 443). The court sanctioned an arrangement whereby, just prior to being discharged by the court, the administrators made a payment to themselves upon trust for the preferential creditors (calculated as if the company were entering a compulsory winding up). Upon discharge, the company would be placed into voluntary liquidation. The preferential creditors were paid out and the other unsecured creditors of the company had the benefit of the cheaper voluntary winding up.[29]

In contrast to the old regime, under para 65 an administrator has the power to make a distribution to the company's creditors. Such distributions are generally limited to secured and preferential creditors and are subject to the rules contained in section 175 as to priority of payments. A distribution under para 65 to any other type of creditor is possible but may only be made with the permission of the court. The administrator has a power to make a payment otherwise than in accordance with para 65 if he or she thinks it likely to assist achievement of the purpose of the administration. The administrator may now simply pay out the preferential creditors, calculated by reference to the date that the company entered administration. The administrator may then move to either put the company into voluntary liquidation under para 83 or to institute a procedure to dissolve the company under para 84 (see below). The relevant date for deciding who are preferential creditors in a liquidation following an administration is now the date the company entered administration regardless of whether the liquidation is compulsory or voluntary.[30]

---

[28] See e.g., *Re Mark One (Oxford Street) plc* [2000] 1 BCLC 462, *Re Norditrack (UK) Ltd* [2000] 1 BCLC 467 and *Re Powerstore (Trading) Ltd* [1998] 1 BCLC 90. See also I. West, 'Exiting administrations (Part 1) – who bears the cost?' (1999) 15 IL&P 42 and J. Brier, 'Exiting administrations (Part 2) – when the purposes of an administration order may be achieved by avoiding compulsory liquidation' (1999) 15 IL&P 44.

[29] See S. Frieze, 'Exit from Administration' (2001) 14 *Insolvency Intelligence* 41.

[30] See the amended section 387 of the Act.

7.7.2 *Automatic end (paras 76–78)*

The administrator will automatically vacate office one year from the date the administration commenced. This term may be extended by the court for such period as the court deems necessary.

The period may also be extended by up to six months with the consent of the creditors. Consent of the creditors for this purpose involves all the secured creditors agreeing and more than 50 per cent in value of the unsecured creditors who respond to the request. If the administrator has stated under para 52(1)(b) that no distribution is possible to unsecured creditors, the consent of all the secured creditors must be obtained and the consent of more than 50 per cent in value of the preferential creditors who respond.

An administration can only be extended once by consent. It cannot be extended by consent after the court has already granted an extension. There is no limit on the number of times the court can grant an extension. Once the administrator's term of office has expired it cannot be extended by either consent or court order.

If the administration is extended by the court, the administrator must as soon as is reasonably practicable notify the Registrar of Companies. If the extension is by consent, in addition to notifying the Registrar, the administrator must also file a notice of extension at the court.

7.7.3 *Court ending on application of administrator (paras 79, 81 and 82)*

If the administrator was appointed by the court and the administrator thinks that the purpose of the administration has been sufficiently achieved, he or she may apply for the appointment to cease.

In whatever way the administrator was appointed, the administrator shall apply to the court to end the administration if he or she thinks the purpose of the administration cannot be achieved; or that the company should not have entered administration; or if a creditors' meeting requires the administrator to apply.

A creditor of the company may apply to court to end the administration on the grounds of an improper motive on the part of the person who appointed the administrator (if appointed out of court), or by the applicant to the court (if the administrator is appointed by the court).

During the administration it is possible for the court to order a winding up of the company in the public interest under section 124A of the Act, or section 367 of the Financial Services and Markets Act 2000. Such a winding-up order will usually entail the administration coming to an end.

7.7.4 *Termination of administration where objective achieved (para 80)*

If the administrator is appointed out of court and believes that the purpose of the administration has been sufficiently achieved, he or she may file a notice to that effect with the court and the Registrar of Companies. Upon filing, the administration comes to an end. Notice must subsequently be sent to all creditors.

7.7.5 *Converting administration into creditors' voluntary liquidation*

It was noted above how under the old regime, it became desirable, but by no means straightforward, to end an administration and immediately put the company into creditors' voluntary liquidation. Under para 83 this transition is made considerably more straightforward.

If the administrator has exercised his or her powers to make a distribution to the secured and preferential creditors and there is money available for the company's unsecured creditors, the administrator may register a notice with the Registrar of Companies, converting the administration into a creditors' voluntary liquidation. The administrator must thereafter file a copy of the notice with the court and send a copy to all the company's creditors.

The effect of filing the notice is that the administration comes to an end and the company is wound up as if a resolution for voluntary winding up was passed on the day of filing. The creditors under the winding up have the usual powers to appoint the liquidator but if no person is appointed in that way, the administrator continues as liquidator.

7.7.6 *Administration to dissolution*

If the administrator has made a distribution to secured and preferential creditors and there is no money left for a distribution to the unsecured creditors, he or she may file a notice to this effect with the Registrar of Companies and send a copy to the court and to all the creditors. The effect of filing the notice is that the administration comes to an end and the company is deemed to be dissolved three months later. This is a sensible provision in that in these circumstances there is clearly no point in the company undergoing the further procedure of a formal winding up with the extra time and expense involved.

Chapter 8

Company Voluntary Arrangements

8.1 Introduction

When a company finds itself in financial difficulty it may attempt to come to some arrangement with its creditors. It may be that the company has short-term cash flow problems and may need its creditors to accept some delay in receiving payment. It may be that the company runs into difficulty where one of its major customers drops the company or itself becomes insolvent. In these circumstances, the company's underlying business may be sound, but it cannot afford to pay all its creditors all that it owes them. Although the company's controllers may consider putting the company immediately into liquidation, it may prove to be more beneficial to the company's creditors to come to some arrangement whereby the creditors are paid less than they are owed, but the amount paid is more than the creditors could expect on a winding up. If the creditors can be persuaded to agree to some such agreement the company may be saved.

The problem with a company negotiating an informal agreement with its creditors is that it will not be binding upon the creditors. The other problem likely to arise is that all the creditors may not agree to an arrangement. It will only take one creditor to break ranks and bring an action to enforce his or her debt and any proposed arrangement will immediately fall apart. The Cork Committee recognised that there was a need for a simple procedure to be introduced, where the will of the majority of creditors in agreeing to a debt arrangement could be made binding on a minority. Entering into a company voluntary arrangement (hereafter 'CVA') with its creditors is usually the most effective way to achieve this. Sections 1–7B of the Act contain the primary legislation governing CVAs.

There are other ways of rescuing a company in distress which will be discussed in outline later. As we have seen, the approval of a CVA is one of the ways in which a company in administration can achieve the primary object of company rescue. These two procedures are often seen together in practice, as the moratorium given by administration allows time and protection from creditor interference for the administrator to draft a proposal for a CVA. Note that when this happens the procedure to put the company into administration must first be followed and then, if the requisite majority of creditors support the proposing of a CVA, the administrator will draft the proposal and call meetings of both members and creditors to consider its approval. Both procedures will need to be followed.

It is, of course, possible for the directors of a company to propose a CVA without first putting the company into administration. This option suffers from the weakness that there is no moratorium on actions against the company while the CVA proposal is being prepared. Creditors may therefore frustrate a possible CVA by enforcing their rights prior to the meetings called to approve the proposal. This weakness of the CVA system has, in theory, been remedied, at least for small companies. The Insolvency Act 2000 has introduced a procedure for a company to obtain a moratorium in order to put together a CVA without the need first to put the company into administration. How often the 2000 Act's CVA provisions will be used in practice seems uncertain. Under the new administration regime introduced by the Enterprise Act 2002, it is now far easier to put a company into administration. It may be that administration proves to be the favoured route for companies wishing to obtain a moratorium while it puts together a CVA proposal.

As we shall see later, an individual debtor may propose an individual voluntary arrangement (hereafter 'IVA'). The law regarding IVAs is broadly the same as for CVAs. For this reason, in this chapter we shall be considering some IVA cases as well as those dealing with CVAs. The difference between IVAs and CVAs historically has been that an individual proposing an IVA has always been able to ask the court for an Interim Order while the IVA proposal is being prepared. The Interim Order acts as a temporary moratorium against certain creditors enforcing their rights while the proposal for the IVA is put together and put to a meeting of the individual's creditors.

8.1.1 *What is a company voluntary arrangement?*

When one first reads Part I of the Act and Part I of the Rules, one is immediately struck with how little detailed guidance is given as to what a CVA should look like or do. There were originally only seven sections and 30 rules. Even though these have been added to, there is still a distinct lack of detail in places. The provisions look particularly sparse when compared with, for example, the amount of legislation dealing with liquidation. In order to obtain a clear understanding of CVAs, much depends on judicial decisions and *dicta*. The whole idea of pushing through a CVA is to prevent the creditors putting the company into winding up. The way this goal is achieved is by offering the creditors a better deal than they would realise in a liquidation. The statutory effect of a CVA is that, once it has been agreed by the requisite majorities of members and unsecured creditors, it becomes binding on all unsecured creditors who had notice of and were entitled to vote at the meeting, even if they voted against the proposal.

The CVA regime has not proven as successful as it had been hoped when the Cork Committee recommended its creation back in 1982. There are two main reasons for this. The first is that the arrangement cannot be made binding upon secured or preferential creditors without their consent. The second perceived problem is that there was no provision within the CVA regime, as originally drafted, for a moratorium on creditor action while the proposal was drawn up and considered. It has always been possible to put the company into administration, and at the same time obtain the benefit of the moratorium, before putting together a proposal for a CVA. The problem of this route, in practice, was the time and expense of obtaining an administration order was often prohibitive. Due to this second weakness, the CVA provisions of the Insolvency Act 2000 were passed in order to allow small companies to obtain a moratorium, pending a draft CVA proposal, without the need to put the company into administration.

Under section 1 of the Act, the CVA itself may take one of two forms (or be a combination of the two). It may be:

(1)   a 'composition of debts' whereby the company agrees to pay only a certain proportion of the debt it owes, for example, 50p in the pound.

Or,

(2)   a 'scheme of arrangement' whereby the company agrees to pay its creditors in full but cannot pay them immediately. The scheme may be merely a moratorium. Usually a scheme is drawn up with a schedule as to when the creditors will be paid and the amounts of each payment. Schemes may include the granting to creditors of an interest in the company. This may be in the form of a debt-equity swap, whereby the creditor exchanges its debt for an equity shareholding in the company (such as with Marconi). If a company is large the scheme may take the form of a complex reconstruction of the company (possibly involving a takeover of the company by a purchaser who is able to inject expertise or capital).[1]

A CVA may be either what is termed a 'trading' or an 'assets' based CVA. A 'trading' voluntary arrangement will usually state that the company agrees to pay a certain amount each month to the supervisor of the CVA who

---

[1] See the discussion in *March Estates plc v Gunmark Ltd* [1996] 2 BCLC 1 and *Commissioners of Inland Revenue v Adam & Partners Ltd* [2001] 1 BCLC 222.

will, for the duration of the arrangement, distribute the funds according to the terms of the CVA. The CVA may go on for a number of years. The 'assets' based CVA will usually be to the effect that certain assets will be sold and the proceeds used to pay off the creditors the agreed amount. The supervisor will usually hold cash or other assets on behalf of the company's creditors. The supervisor is usually understood to be holding such assets on trust for the creditors subject to the terms of the CVA.

Prior to looking at the procedure to approve and make binding a CVA, it may be useful to become familiar with what information must be included in a CVA. The Rules contain a list of matters which must be included in a proposal for a CVA (rule 1.3(1) and (2):

(1) The directors' proposal shall provide a short explanation why, in their opinion, a voluntary arrangement under Part I of the Act is desirable, and give reasons why the company's creditors may be expected to concur with such an arrangement.

(2) The following matters shall be stated, or otherwise dealt with, in the directors' proposal—

    (a) the following matters, so far as within the directors' immediate knowledge—

        (i) the company's assets, with an estimate of their respective values,

        (ii) the extent (if any) to which the assets are charged in favour of creditors,

        (iii) the extent (if any) to which particular assets are to be excluded from the voluntary arrangement;

    (b) particulars of any property, other than assets of the company itself, which is proposed to be included in the arrangement, the source of such property and the terms on which it is to be made available for inclusion;

    (c) the nature and amount of the company's liabilities (so far as within the directors' immediate knowledge), the manner in which they are proposed to be met, modified, postponed or otherwise dealt with by means of the arrangement, and (in particular)—

        (i) how it is proposed to deal with preferential creditors (defined in section 4(7)) and creditors who are, or claim to be, secured,

        (ii) how persons connected with the company (being creditors) are proposed to be treated under the arrangement, and

        (iii) whether there are, to the directors' knowledge, any circumstances giving rise to the possibility, in the event that the company should go into liquidation, of claims under—

            section 238 (transactions at an undervalue),

            section 239 (preferences),

            section 244 (extortionate credit transactions),

            or

            section 245 (floating charges invalid);

    and, where any such circumstances are present, whether, and if so how, it is proposed under the voluntary arrangement to make provision for wholly or partly indemnifying the company in respect of such claims;

(d) whether any, and if so what, guarantees have been given of the company's debts by other persons, specifying which (if any) of the guarantors are persons connected with the company;

(e) the proposed duration of the voluntary arrangement;

(f) the proposed dates of distributions to creditors, with estimates of their amounts;

(g) the amount proposed to be paid to the nominee (as such) by way of remuneration and expenses;

(h) the manner in which it is proposed that the supervisor of the arrangement should be remunerated, and his expenses defrayed;

(i) whether, for the purposes of the arrangement, any guarantees are to be offered by directors, or other persons, and whether (if so) any security is to be given or sought;

(j) the manner in which funds held for the purposes of the arrangement are to be banked, invested or otherwise dealt with pending distribution to creditors;

(k) the manner in which funds held for the purpose of payment to creditors, and not so paid on the termination of the arrangement, are to be dealt with;

(l) the manner in which the business of the company is proposed to be conducted during the course of the arrangement;

(m) details of any further credit facilities which it is intended to arrange for the company, and how the debts so arising are to be paid;

(n) the functions which are to be undertaken by the supervisor of the arrangement;

(o) the name, address and qualification of the person proposed as supervisor of the voluntary arrangement, and confirmation that he is (so far as the directors are aware) qualified to act as such; and

(p) whether the EC Regulation[2] will apply and, if so, whether the proceedings will be main proceedings, secondary proceedings or territorial proceedings.

8.2 Procedure

8.2.1 *Procedure to approve a company voluntary arrangement*

The main procedure under the Act will be considered first. We shall then look at the new procedure under Schedule A1 of the Act introduced by the Insolvency Act 2000.

Under section 1 of the Act, the persons who may commence the procedure leading to a CVA will be the directors of the company, unless the company is in liquidation or administration, in which cases the procedure will be initiated by the liquidator or administrator as the case may be.

---

[2] See SI 2002/1307.

If the directors begin the process, under section 2, they must approach a person authorised to act as 'nominee'. The Act states that the directors will submit to the nominee a proposal for a CVA along with a statement of the company's affairs (essentially details of the company's liabilities and assets). In practice, what usually happens is that the directors will initially approach an insolvency practitioner and with his or her professional assistance will draft the proposal in advance.

The nominee has 28 days (or longer with leave of the court) to prepare a report to the court. If the nominee's report is positive, in that the nominee's professional opinion is that the proposal has a reasonable prospect of being approved and implemented, the nominee then proceeds to call meetings of the company's members and unsecured creditors. The nominee must send notices of the meetings including copies of the proposal and statement of affairs (sections 2 and 3). The time, date and venue of these meetings will have been included in the report to the court.[3] As it is usual for the nominee to have had a hand in the drafting of the proposal, it is extremely unlikely that the report to the court will be negative. It should be noted that although a report is made to the court, this is largely a matter of record only. The court does not become judicially involved in the CVA unless a problem arises.

If the company is in liquidation or administration, the nominee will be the liquidator or administrator. No report to the court is necessary and the office holder proceeds without any formality to call the meetings (section 3(2)). Copies of the proposal must still be sent out to the members and creditors together with a copy of the statement of affairs (or summary of its contents) which the liquidator or administrator will have received in his or her respective capacity.

A CVA becomes effective after the proposal has been approved. Modifications to the proposal may be made at these meetings (although generally both meetings must agree to any changes). Under section 4(3) and (4) the proposal cannot affect the rights of secured or preferential creditors without their consent.

The nominee will normally act as chairman at both meetings.[4] The members' meeting is conducted according to the voting rights in the company's articles. An ordinary resolution is required to approve the CVA (rule 1.18). Votes at the creditors' meeting are calculated according to the amount of the creditor's unsecured debt as at the date of the meeting (or the date of the company going into liquidation or administration as the

---

[3] Under rules 1.9 and 1.13, the meetings must be held not less than 14 days, nor more than 28 days, after the report is filed at the court. The meetings must be called on at least 14 days' notice. The meetings need not occur on the same day (there may be a gap of up to seven days) but the creditors' meeting must usually be held first in time (see rule 1.21).

[4] Detailed provisions dealing with how the meetings are summoned and the respective voting rights of the members and creditors at those meetings are found in rules 1.13–1.21.

case may be).[5] If a creditor's debt is partly secured, he or she may vote at the meeting in respect of the unsecured part (*Calor Gas v Piercy* [1994] BCC 69).

A creditor who is owed a debt for an unliquidated amount may vote at the meeting. For the purposes of voting, the unliquidated debt shall be valued at £1 unless the chairman agrees[6] to put a higher value on the debt. The default position here, that an unliquidated claim should be valued at £1, is a welcome amendment to the Rules[7] in that disputes as to how the chairman should or should not have valued such claims are very difficult to resolve. Unless there is a good reason to value the claim differently, it seems that a chairman should normally apply the £1 valuation.

The chairman of the creditors' meeting shall decide upon the entitlement of persons wishing to vote. The chairman may admit or reject a claim and, if in doubt, must allow the vote, but mark it as objected to. If the objected vote is subsequently found to be invalid, the court may order a new meeting to be held. An application against a decision of the chairman must be made to the court within 28 days (rule 1.17A).

The creditors' meeting must approve the proposal by a majority in excess of three-quarters in value of the creditors present in person or by proxy and voting on the resolution. Other resolutions proposed at the creditors' meeting must be passed by a simple majority in value (rule 1.19). Any resolution is invalid if those voting against it include more than half in value of the creditors who are not persons connected with the company.[8]

Section 4A of the Act, introduced by the Insolvency Act 2000, states that the proposal is approved if either:

(1) both the creditors' and members' meetings vote in favour of it; or
(2) if the proposal is approved only by the creditors' meeting (any member may, within 28 days, apply to the court to object).

This provision effectively gives the whip hand to the creditors by allowing their vote to take primacy over any differing view at the members' meetings. Once approved, the chairman of the meetings shall report the result to the court and thereafter the CVA will be implemented (section 4(6)). The nominee will usually be the chairman of the meeting and will usually continue as supervisor of the CVA.

The main perceived weakness of the CVA procedure is that as soon as the creditors' meeting is called the creditors are on notice that the company

---

[5] See IR rule 1.17.

[6] For the meaning of 'agrees' in this context see *Re Cancol Ltd* [1995] BCC 1133 and *Doorbar v Alltime Securities Ltd* [1995] BCC 1149. 'Agrees' does not mean that the chairman has to agree with the creditor an amount, it means that the chairman agrees that he will put a value on it.

[7] See the Insolvency (Amendment) (No 2) Rules 2002 SI 2002/2712 at para 8.

[8] For the meaning of 'connected' see section 249.

is in financial trouble. Although the creditors may wait for the meeting to see the terms of the proposal, it is more likely that many of them will wish to act to protect their position. As there is no moratorium in force preventing creditor actions, creditors who are quick off the mark may achieve a better result for themselves than waiting to be bound by the CVA. For example:

- a floating charge holder may appoint an administrative receiver or administrator;
- a fixed charge holder may enter into possession and sell the charged assets;
- a supplier of goods on retention of title terms or the owner under a hire purchase or leasing agreement may repossess goods;
- an unsecured creditor may seek to obtain judgment and enforce that judgment; and
- a landlord may distrain for unpaid rent or take action to forfeit the lease.

If the company had first been put into administration, the moratorium under that procedure would safeguard the company's assets pending the creditors' meeting. The expense of acquiring an administration order (under the pre-Enterprise Act 2002 regime) and having an administrator running the company was frequently prohibitive for small companies at least. The prospects of a successful CVA being implemented without the benefit of the moratorium are limited. The number of companies entering into CVAs under the old regime was relatively small compared to other insolvency procedures and particularly relative to the number of individuals entering IVAs. Arguably this is because the original 1986 regime assumed that administration (and its moratorium) would be available to all companies, when in fact in practice it was not. The problem encountered, namely, the way in which the courts dealt with administration petitions, meant that, in practice, obtaining the order was in itself too expensive a process for many companies. The irony of the present system is that it is far easier to put the company into administration nowadays, after the Enterprise Act, and therefore the requirement for a separate moratorium procedure under the Insolvency Act 2000 looks like it might be surplus to requirements, especially when one considers some of the detail as to how the 2000 Act's provisions operate.

8.2.2 *Procedure under Schedule A1*

The Insolvency Act 2000 amends the 1986 Act by the insertion of a new section 1A and a new Schedule A1. Broadly speaking, the effect of this amendment is to allow directors of 'small companies' to obtain a short moratorium for their company during which a CVA proposal can be put to the creditors. The meaning of 'small companies'[9] for this purpose is taken from the definition contained within section 247(3) of the Companies Act 1985, which states that to be eligible, the company must satisfy at least two of the following requirements:

(1) its annual turnover does not exceed £2.8 million;
(2) its balance sheet total does not exceed £1.4 million; and
(3) it has no more than 50 employees.

A company cannot take advantage of this procedure if:

(1) the company is in administration, liquidation (including where a provisional liquidator is in post), administrative receivership or is already subject to a CVA; or
(2) in the previous 12 months a moratorium has been in force in relation to the company which did not result in a CVA being approved or did result in a CVA which has ended prematurely (para 4 of Schedule A1).

If the company is eligible, the directors shall submit to the nominee the proposed CVA and a statement of the company's affairs. The nominee must reply to the directors stating whether or not, in his or her opinion:

(1) the proposal has a reasonable prospect of being approved and implemented;
(2) the company is likely to have sufficient funds available during the moratorium period to enable it to carry on its business; and
(3) meetings of the company's members and creditors should be called to consider the proposal (para 6(2) of Schedule A1).

The nominee is entitled to rely on the information furnished by the directors unless he or she has reason to doubt its accuracy (para 6(3) of Schedule A1).

In order to obtain the moratorium the directors file with the court a copy of the proposal, a statement of affairs of the company, a statement that the company is eligible and that the nominee has the favourable opinions listed above (para 7 of Schedule A1). The moratorium comes into effect upon these documents being filed. The moratorium ends after 28 days, or earlier upon both the creditors' and company meetings being held (para 8 of Schedule A1). The moratorium may be extended for a further two-month period by the agreement of both meetings (para 32 of Schedule A1). Once in effect, the moratorium must be advertised and notice of it given to:

---

[9] Banks and insurance companies are ineligible under para 2 Schedule A1 of the Act.

- the company;
- any creditor who has petitioned for a winding-up order against the company; and
- the Registrar of Companies.

Its existence must be stated on all business documents (para 16 of Schedule A1) and the company cannot obtain credit of £250 or more without disclosing the moratorium (para 17 of Schedule A1).

The moratorium itself, not surprisingly, is in very similar terms to that imposed in administration (para 12 of Schedule A1). It contains one very important addition which affects a floating charge holder's rights. Such a debenture holder is prevented from appointing an administrative receiver and cannot appoint an administrator either (leave of the court will not enable either of these things to happen). The powers that a debenture holder has in the administration regime are absent here. Futhermore a floating charge is prevented from crystallising during the moratorium (paras 13 and 43 of Schedule A1).

During the moratorium the company continues under the managerial control of the directors and may dispose of assets in the ordinary course of business. Any other disposal is only possible if there are reasonable grounds for believing that it will benefit the company and the creditors' committee (if there is one) or the nominee (if there is not a committee) approve the disposal.

The company has similar powers, under para 20 of Schedule A1, to dispose of assets subject to fixed charges or hire purchase agreements (defined to include conditional sale, chattel leasing and retention of title agreements) as an administrator has under paras 71 and 72 of Schedule B1. A court order or creditor consent is again needed to exercise this power and the proceeds from the sale must go to pay off the creditor. If a reasonable price is not realised the company must make up the shortfall. The power under para 20 to sell floating charge assets is also similar to the power an administrator has under para 70 of Schedule B1. Once floating charge assets are sold the charge in effect moves to the proceeds of sale or substituted property. The power to deal with floating charge assets is drafted in an ambiguous way and, on a purely literal interpretation, it seems that the company can only deal with assets subject to a floating charge with the consent of the debenture holder, or leave of the court. If this were the case, as the floating charge will be over all the company's property both present and future, the company will be effectively paralysed. Although capable of a more purposive interpretation, such inherent uncertainty is not likely to encourage the use of the new regime.

During the moratorium the nominee is under a duty to monitor the company's affairs in order to form an opinion as to whether the CVA remains one with a reasonable prospect of being approved and implemented, and that the company is likely to have enough money to continue to run the business (para 24 of Schedule A1). Again the nominee has the right to rely on information received by the directors unless he or she is put on enquiry. If the nominee believes that the CVA is no longer viable, he or she must withdraw his or her consent to act and the moratorium is thereby terminated (para 25 of Schedule A1).

While the moratorium is in force the nominee may be replaced by the court on an application by the directors who allege a breach of duty by the nominee or that there are other circumstances whereby it is inappropriate for the nominee to continue (para 28 of Schedule A1). A director, member, creditor or third party affected by the moratorium can bring an action against the nominee challenging any decision made. Of more concern to the nominee is the power of any creditor (where the company does not intend to bring an action itself) to apply to the court on the basis that an action or decision of the nominee has caused loss to the company (para 27 of Schedule A1).

The meetings are called and held in much the same way as under the substantive provisions of the Act as detailed above. The way in which the CVA is dealt with after the summoning of the two meetings is essentially the same.

8.3 Transparency

The Cork Committee which recommended the introduction of voluntary arrangements recognised that there had been a similar type of arrangement available under the Bankruptcy Act 1869. This fell into disuse early on, mostly due to scams, assets being concealed, creditors being manufactured and arrangements generally not producing the returns which had been promised. Under the modern voluntary arrangement procedure it is crucial that in any proposal there is transparency, otherwise the creditors will not agree to it. The proposal will need to give a transparently accurate picture of the company's existing state of affairs. For example:

- Are the assets valued independently?
- Are suppliers and customers still in place?
- Are any third party funds being put into the CVA and, if so, are they reliable?

The proposal will need to have a realistic prospect of achieving a certain outcome. During its term, the assets and income subject to it will need to be held securely. The financial result for creditors must be better than they would receive under alternative insolvency procedures. Certain creditors, for example, the preferential creditors, will have standard demands regarding full payment and how long they will wait. From the company's point of view, it will want a full discharge from its liabilities.

Criminal offences may be committed by a director of the company who does not deal with the nominee and creditors honestly and openly. If an officer of the company makes any false representation or fraudulently does or omits to do anything, for the purpose of obtaining the members' or creditors' approval, he or she commits an offence (section 6A).

8.4 Effect of approval

The effect of the CVA being approved (under the terms of section 4A) is explained by section 5. The approved CVA takes effect as if made by the company at the creditors' meeting and binds every person who:

(1) was entitled to vote at either meeting (whether or not he or she was present or represented at the meeting in question); or
(2) would have been so entitled if he or she had had notice of the meeting;

as if he or she were a party to the CVA.

The CVA therefore binds the company's unsecured creditors even if they had no notice of the creditors' meeting, or did have notice and either did not attend and vote, or did attend and voted against the proposal.

A person entitled to vote at either meeting (whether or not that person had notice of the meeting) may apply to the court (section 6(2) also allows a liquidator or administrator of the company to apply) on the grounds that:

(1) the CVA unfairly prejudices the interests of a creditor, member or contributory of the company; or
(2) that there has been some irregularity at the meeting.

On a finding of unfair prejudice or material irregularity, the court may revoke or suspend the approval of the CVA and/or order that further meetings be called to consider a revised proposal (section 6(4)).

8.4.1 *Creditors with no notice of the meeting*

The terms of section 5 have recently been amended by the Insolvency Act 2000. The voluntary arrangement provisions of the 2000 Act only came into force on 1 January 2003. It is as yet unclear exactly how the new section 5 will be dealt with by the courts. It is reasonably clear why it was changed. Under the previous wording of section 5, only creditors who had notice of the meeting were bound by the arrangement. If notice was, for example, sent to the creditor, but at the wrong address, even though the proceedings at the meeting would be valid, the creditor who had not received notice was not bound by the arrangement. As the creditor was not bound by the terms of the arrangement there was nothing to prevent him or her from serving a statutory demand and proceeding to petition for the winding up of the company.[10]

8.4.2 *The unknown creditor*

Under the previous wording of section 5, there was also the problem of the unknown creditor who is not discovered until after the CVA is being implemented. Such a creditor would not be bound by the CVA and would have an election as to remedy. Again there would be nothing to stop the creditor petitioning for the company's winding up. Some CVAs seek to provide for this issue by allowing a supervisor to permit the unknown creditor to participate in the CVA. One of the problems with this is that these late entries may have a significant impact upon the prospective rate of return agreed to at the creditors' meeting. Being included within the CVA in this way usually produces the best result possible for the unknown creditor. Where effectively the whole of the assets have been put into the CVA, liquidation will generally not provide anything for the unknown creditor. The new wording of section 5 includes such unknown creditors who are consequently bound by the CVA.

8.4.3 *Future or contingent creditors*

Another problem, which existed under the previous wording of section 5, was how to deal with future or contingent creditors. There is no guidance under the Act as to the meaning of a 'creditor'. Case law has developed in this context to include within the meaning of 'creditor' a person owed either present or future debts.[11]

If a company holds premises under a long lease, it would commonly be the case that the landlord would be owed some pre-CVA rent and would also be prospectively owed rent in relation to the future. This type of future liability would be recognised by the chairman of the creditors' meeting and a figure to represent future rent would be given to the landlord for voting purposes in respect of the CVA. The landlord would therefore be

---

[10] See e.g., *Re A Debtor (No 64 of 1992)* [1994] BCC 55 – an IVA case but the reasoning of which would equally apply to a CVA.

[11] See e.g., the Court of Appeal decision in *Doorbar v Alltime Securities Ltd* [1995] BCC 1149 affirming Knox J ([1994] BCC 994), *Re Cancol Ltd* [1995] BCC 1133, *Re Sweatfield Ltd* [1997] BCC 744 and *Beverley Group plc v McClue* [1995] BCC 751.

bound in relation to both existing and future rent.[12] The amendments made by the 2000 Act now recognise that a creditor who is owed a debt for an unliquidated amount can vote at the meeting. For the purposes of voting, the debt shall be valued at £1 unless the chairman agrees[13] to put a higher value on it.[14]

Certain types of contingent creditors create unique problems. Consider the case of *RA Securities Ltd v Mercantile Co Ltd* ([1994] BCC 598):

> A CVA was entered into by a company which had previously had a lease assigned to it by the original tenant. The main issue was the effect the arrangement had on a landlord's claim against the original lessee who was not a party to the CVA (but who remained liable for rent under privity of estate principles[15]). Under the terms of the CVA the landlord agreed to accept surrender of the lease from the company (the subsequent lessee). The original lessee claimed that this released it from any liability for future rent under the lease. Jacob J decided that the CVA was only binding as between the parties to it. Although the landlord was bound by it with regard to its claim against the subsequent lessee, the original lessee, not being a party to the CVA, could not claim benefit from it and therefore remained liable for future rent if the landlord did not accept surrender of the lease. The problem with this from the point of view of the CVA is that the original lessee would be liable to pay the landlord but could then claim on its indemnity from the subsequent lessee. As the subsequent lessee is in CVA, it will not be able to pay and the original lessee could then act to put the subsequent lessee into liquidation and, in so doing, destroy any chances of the CVA being a success. Although the landlord was bound by the CVA, there was no voluntary acceptance by the landlord to accept some other performance under the lease. Jacob J utilised privity of contract principles to decide who may claim benefit from a CVA and who may not. As Lord Coleridge CJ said in 1874 '[n]ow it has always been a cardinal point of bankruptcy law that a discharge under it of an insolvent debtor unable to pay his debts in full does not release his solvent co-debtor' (*Megrath v Gray* (1874) LR 9 CP 216 at 229–230). Jacob J explained how the original lessee could avoid liability to the landlord. The original lessee could have claimed the benefit of the CVA if it had been a party to it. Assuming the original lessee as a contingent creditor had notice of and was entitled to vote at the creditors' meeting convened to consider the CVA proposal, it could have claimed the benefit of the surrender called for by the arrangement.

The new wording of section 5 now states that the CVA binds every person entitled to vote at the meeting even if he or she has not received notice of it.

---

[12] See e.g., *Doorbar v Alltime Securities Ltd* [1995] BCC 1149 and *Burford Midland Properties Ltd v Marley Extrusions Ltd* [1994] BCC 604. In the latter case future and contingent creditors were held to be excluded from the terms of the arrangement.

[13] For the meaning of 'agrees' in this context see *Re Cancol Ltd* [1995] BCC 1133 and *Doorbar v Alltime Securities Ltd* [1995] BCC 1149. 'Agrees' does not mean that the chairman has to agree with the creditor an amount, it means that the chairman agrees that he will put a value on it.

[14] See the new wording of rule 1.17.

[15] Note the amendment to such liability made by the Landlord and Tenant (Covenants) Act 1995.

This would include co-debtors as in *RA Securities*, others subject to types of secondary liability such as guarantors, as well as other types of future or contingent creditors.[16] The terms of the CVA should therefore deal with such potential liabilities. If co-debtors are to be released under the terms of the arrangement, this must be made expressly clear. The courts are unlikely to imply such a term.[17]

The CVA should also be clear as to what rights a creditor with a claim for an unliquidated amount has under the arrangement. If agreement cannot be reached as to the creditor's entitlement, the creditor may wish to bring an action in court to quantify the amount. The CVA should be drafted in a way to avoid this.[18] A creditor who feels that the CVA is unfairly prejudicial to his or her interests, or that there has been some material irregularity at or in relation to the creditors' meeting, can apply to the court under section 6.

8.4.4 *Other effects*

Once the CVA is approved, if the company is in liquidation, the winding-up proceedings will usually be stayed by the court on the CVA taking effect. To similar effect, if the company is in administration the court will usually discharge the administrator.

The nominee will usually be the person to become the supervisor of the CVA. This occurs as soon as the proposal is approved. Any creditor or other person dissatisfied by the conduct of the supervisor may apply to the court. The court has a wide discretion to make any order it thinks fit. It can specifically confirm, reverse or modify any act or decision of the supervisor. It may also replace the supervisor (section 7).

8.5 Unfair prejudice or material irregularity

A creditor, member, nominee or (if the company is in liquidation or administration) the liquidator or administrator may apply to the court under section 6 on one or both of the following grounds:

---

[16] See also *Johnson v Davies* [1998] 2 BCLC 252.

[17] See *Greene King plc v Stanley* [2002] BPIR 491 for an example of an IVA where the court held that it was possible for the arrangement to release the principal debtor but to have rights against sureties retained.

[18] For an example of this type of claim arising where an employee sued his or her previous employer, now in CVA, for wrongful dismissal see *Alman v Approach Housing Ltd* [2001] BPIR 203.

(1) that the CVA unfairly prejudices the interests of a creditor, member or contributory of the company; or

(2) that there has been some material irregularity at or in relation to the members' or creditors' meetings.

A similar provision exists for IVAs under section 262.

If the court is satisfied that the ground for the application is made out, it may revoke or suspend the approvals given by the meetings and/or order further meetings be called to consider the original or a revised proposal.

There is no guidance in the Act as to the meaning of 'unfair prejudice'. Some general guidance may be obtained from the case law under section 459 of the Companies Act 1985 which uses the same term. It is apparent from Harman J's judgment in *Re Primlaks (UK) Ltd (No2)* ([1990] BCLC 234), that the unfair prejudice complained of may be towards a particular creditor or a specific class of creditors or to all the creditors generally. The unfair prejudice must be brought about by the terms of the arrangement itself, not from some external agreement. It must relate to some discriminatory treatment of a creditor or creditors.[19]

Conduct which might be viewed as unfairly prejudicial would include a CVA under which unsecured creditors were treated differently from one another. As well as including situations where an obvious preference was granted to a particular creditor or class of creditors it can also include more subtle variations on this theme. For example, in the IVA case of *Re A Debtor (No 101 of 1999)* ([2000] BPIR 998):

> An individual debtor who carried on business as a race horse trainer was in great financial difficulty and the Inland Revenue had petitioned for his bankruptcy. He proposed an IVA. The Inland Revenue and Customs and Excise were each owed a sum of money as unsecured non-preferential creditors. The majority of the debtor's debts were owed to friends of the debtor. These friends agreed not to participate in the IVA on the understanding that the debtor would eventually turn his business around and pay them off some time in the future. A sum of £20,000 was made available by an unnamed third party which was to be used to pay the Crown creditors approximately 19 per cent of their overall debt (£77,000). Due to the overwhelming majority of debt being held by the debtor's friends, with the friends voting in favour of it, the IVA was approved at the creditors' meeting. The Crown voted against the IVA and after the meeting applied to the court claiming its terms were unfairly prejudicial. The court agreed with the Crown. The terms of the IVA meant that the friends suffered no significant detriment as they retained all their rights and remedies against the debtor and were not subject to the moratorium under the IVA. Paying off the Crown with about a fifth of what it was owed, effectively eliminated a large amount of competing debt from the friends' point of view. This benefit cost the friends nothing. The friends were

---

[19] See in particular the following IVA cases: *Re A Debtor (No 259 of 1990)* [1992] 1 All ER 641 at 643 per Hoffman J, *Re A Debtor (No 222 of 1990) ex parte Ireland* [1992] BCLC 137 at 145 per Harman J and *Re A Debtor (No 87 of 1993)* [1996] BCLC 63 at 86 per Rimer J.

not paying the £20,000 to the Crown, and at the same time, none of the debtor's assets were being used up in paying the Crown. There would therefore be more available for the friends from the debtor's assets. The advantages given to the friends under the terms of the IVA were approved due to the voting power of the friends. The Crown creditors were not given the chance of remaining in the same position as the friends. The court ordered the IVA to be revoked if it were not varied by the debtor and the creditors.

A 'material irregularity' would seem to mean any breach of the Act or Rules with regard to the running of the meetings. Minor breaches would not be viewed as material nor would breaches which would make no difference to the result of the vote. For example, if a creditor was not given notice of the meeting even though the creditor's existence was known about, this would be an irregularity in relation to the meeting. If the creditor in question was only owed a relatively small amount and therefore his or her vote would have made no difference to the result, the irregularity would not be material.[20] If a creditor is not given notice of a meeting but should have been, it will usually be a material irregularity not to permit the creditor to vote if he or she turns up at the meeting.[21] Refusal to accept a proxy sent by facsimile message may be a material irregularity.[22] If false or misleading information is provided in a statement of affairs which leads to the arrangement being approved, this will amount to a material irregularity.[23] The irregularity need not relate purely to the convening or conduct of the meeting itself but may relate to the statement of affairs, one of the documents considered at the meeting.

8.6 Theoretical basis of voluntary arrangements

The courts have on several occasions attempted to explain the nature of a voluntary arrangement. It has been variously called a contract, a trust and a statutory binding. Previous types of formal agreements by a debtor with his or her creditors, such as under the Deeds of Arrangement Act 1914, have been accepted as contractual in nature even though the party who holds the assets subject to the deed and who carries out the terms of the deed is labelled the trustee.[24]

The decision of Morritt J in *Re McKeen* ([1995] BCC 412) was delivered in 1992 although not reported until later. The case determined the effect

---

20 See e.g., *Re A Debtor (No 259 of 1990)* [1992] 1 All ER 641.
21 See e.g., *Re Debtors (Nos 400 IO and 401 IO of 1996)* [1997] BPIR 431.
22 See e.g., *Commissioners of Inland Revenue v Combeer and White* [1996] BPIR 398.
23 See e.g., *Re A Debtor (No 87 of 1993) (No2)* [1996] BPIR 64.
24 See e.g., the Cork Report at 144.

of a bankruptcy order on a pre-existing IVA where the petition for the order was made by a creditor not bound by the IVA. His Lordship decided that the bankruptcy order did not terminate the IVA. The creditors who were parties to the IVA were 'bound by a contract imposed under statute' (at 416). The IVA could have included provision for its termination in the event of bankruptcy but as it had not done so the matter fell to be decided upon construction of the Act. The Act was silent as to the fate of an IVA in this situation. A bankrupt's estate is subject to the rights which any other person may have in the property comprising the estate. The trustee thus took the bankrupt's estate subject to the rights of the creditors under the IVA.

Morritt J clearly regards the IVA as taking effect as a form of statutory contract where there is 'no restriction on the proposals which a debtor may put forward to his creditors' (at 415). There is freedom of contract to include any provision, for example, the creditors may agree to a provision which excludes them from sharing in any property acquired after the date of the IVA. There was no mention in the arrangement itself that the supervisor was to hold property on trust for the creditors, nor had such an argument been put forward by counsel. The terms of the IVA provided for the assets comprised in the arrangement to be applied for the benefit of the arrangement creditors. Their rights under the arrangement were purely contractual and were such as to bind a subsequent trustee in bankruptcy who took the property comprised in the arrangement.

In *RA Securities Ltd v Mercantile Credit Co Ltd* ([1994] BCC 598), discussed above, Jacob J refers to the CVA as a 'statutory binding' rather than a statutory contract. It is difficult to see that there is any practical difference between the two phrases. His Lordship utilises privity of contract principles to decide who may claim benefit from a CVA and who may not.

Factually similar to *RA Securities* was *Burford Midland Properties Ltd v Marley Extrusions Ltd* ([1994] BCC 604) which turned upon the construction of a CVA. His Honour Judge Roger Cooke construed the arrangement as not including liability for future rent which was enough to decide the issue. In making various *obiter* statements the judge agreed to construe the CVA 'like any other commercial agreement' (at 611). Although in no way conclusive, this suggests a contractual approach to construction.

A different approach to the nature of a voluntary arrangement was taken in *Re Leisure Study Group Ltd* ([1994] 2 BCLC 65).

> The action was brought by an administrative receiver of a company which had previously entered into a CVA with its creditors. The terms of the arrangement provided for the company to make monthly payments to the supervisor, a distribution to be made to the creditors every three months. The administrative receiver, as agent of the company, claimed to be entitled to funds held by the CVA supervisor. Harman J rejected the claim. His lordship discussed section 1(2) which defines a proposal for a voluntary arrangement to be one which provides for an insolvency practitioner 'to act in relation to a voluntary arrangement either as trustee or otherwise for the purpose of

supervising its implementation'. According to Harman J the term 'trustee' was 'the most obvious' and 'most appropriate word' to use to describe what the supervisor was doing. He was holding the legal title to property on behalf of the creditors bound by the arrangement who were beneficially entitled to the property. The company had no claim on such money.

The decision in *Re Leisure Study* is also interesting from the point of view of a debenture holder. If the debenture holder agrees to the CVA (it cannot be binding upon it without its consent) and the CVA fails prematurely, the debenture holder may find that most, if not all, of the floating charge assets have been swallowed up under the CVA in favour of the unsecured creditors. This potentially disastrous result needs to be considered before a debenture holder gives its consent to a CVA.

The decision in *Re Bradley-Hole* ([1995] BCC 418) also adopted the terminology of the trust.

> A debtor had entered into an IVA with his creditors under which he agreed to the whole of his assets being available for the benefit of his creditors along with the net profits from his trading as the landlord of a public house. Subsequently the debtor was made bankrupt on the petition of a creditor whose debt had been incurred after the IVA had been approved. The issue before the court was whether or not the IVA was terminated by the bankruptcy order. Rimer J accepted counsel's submissions that the arrangement took effect 'as if it were in the nature of a statutory contract between the debtor and the participating creditors'. Under the terms of the arrangement the supervisor held the assets on trust for the IVA creditors. The creditors as beneficiaries could compel performance of the terms of the arrangement. The bankrupt retained no beneficial interest in the assets which was capable of vesting in the trustee in bankruptcy.

In *Davis v Martin-Sklan* ([1995] BCC 1122), Blackburne J explained that the approval of the arrangement gave rise to 'a species of statutory contract' binding the debtor and the creditors. Later in his judgment his lordship refers to the 'trusts' upon which the supervisor held money subject to the arrangement, notwithstanding the fact that there was no provision in the arrangement expressly declaring that the money was to be held on trust.

> In *Re Halson Packaging Ltd* ([1997] BCC 993) the court had to consider the effect on funds held by the supervisors of a CVA of the company entering creditors' voluntary liquidation. The terms of the arrangement provided for the company to make monthly payments to the supervisors who would distribute the money to the creditors. The company was unable to trade through its problems and the creditors and the supervisors decided that the company should be wound up. A voluntary liquidation was deemed to be less expensive than a compulsory winding up. At the time of the commencement of the winding up the supervisors held approximately £80,000 under the CVA. The cessation of business and liquidation of the company necessarily brought the arrangement to an end in the sense that there could be no further payments made to the supervisors. As to the £80,000 still held by the supervisors Judge

Maddocks construed the wording of the CVA. He decided that the arrangement expressly created a trust of these funds in favour of the creditors. There was no provision terminating this trust in the event of liquidation and so the CVA continued with regard to the assets still held by the supervisors. The trust was expressly created by the terms of the CVA. Judge Maddocks stated the effect of the arrangement was 'of a contract as between the creditors, and as between the creditors as a class, and the company'. Unless there are overriding reasons not to do so, the terms of the contract will be given effect. The money held by the supervisors remained subject to the trust in favour of the CVA creditors and could not be claimed by the liquidator.

The company in *Re Arthur Rathbone Kitchens Ltd* ([1998] BCC 450) entered into a CVA but was unable to keep up the monthly payments required by its terms. Subsequently, the company entered creditors' voluntary liquidation, which in turn was followed by a compulsory liquidation. Judge Roger Kaye QC found that although there was no express provision creating a trust of the assets in the supervisor's hands, 'it is clear that the scheme as a whole imposes a trust on the supervisor to receive and apply the funds he receives in accordance with the terms of the CVA'. The finding of Harman J in *Leisure Study* on the same point is cited in support of this conclusion.

The nature of a voluntary arrangement appears to have been largely settled by the Court of Appeal in *Johnson v Davies* ([1998] 2 BCLC 252):

> J and J were sureties of a lease taken in the name of the company they owned. J and J subsequently sold the company to C, C and H (the purchasers). J and J had the benefit of an indemnity from the purchasers in relation to any liability they might incur under the surety. The company entered receivership and did not pay its rent under the lease. J and J were called on to pay and did pay the rent. H subsequently entered into an IVA with his creditors including J and J. J and J thereafter tried to enforce the indemnity against C and C. C and C claimed that the release of H under the terms of the IVA also released them from liability under the indemnity. Their argument was that the release of one co-debtor released all. The Court of Appeal, in a detailed account of the law relating to debtor arrangement from the previous century, decided upon a contractual approach. Under previous statutory forms of debt arrangements, there were clear provisions expressly stating that co-debtors were not released. Under the new voluntary arrangement regime, things had changed. The answer in any particular case depended only upon a construction of the terms of the voluntary arrangement. It must be construed as if it were a 'consensual agreement' between the debtor and all the creditors bound by it. The terms of the IVA in question did not release C and C from their liability as co-debtors.

Proposals for voluntary arrangements may therefore contain provisions which release co-debtors or sureties as well as the principal debtor. Under the terms of the new section 5, persons who benefit from an express release of their coterminous liability under the arrangement, because they are contingent creditors of the debtor, are bound by the terms of the arrangement and can therefore enforce the terms of the arrangement against other creditors who are also parties. If the effect of releasing a party from coterminous liability unfairly prejudices a creditor, that creditor may complain to the court. Subject to that, the arrangement takes effect as if it were a consensual agreement.

The case law appears at first sight to contain some inconsistencies of approach. Sometimes the arrangement seems to be called a contract and at other times a trust or statutory binding. The answer to this potential conundrum is to be found in the courts' consistency of approach in each case of construing the wording of the Act and the arrangement itself.

Subsections 5(2) (CVAs) and 260(2) (IVAs) both state that the effect of approval of the arrangement is that it binds every person entitled to vote (whether or not he or she had notice of the creditors' meeting) as if he or she were a party to the arrangement. This has been recognised as the language of contract and results in the courts construing the terms of the arrangements as contracts. A voluntary arrangement is not a voluntary contract in that parties can be bound by an arrangement even if they do not approve its terms. This point led Jacob J in *RA Securities* to regard an arrangement as a statutory binding rather than a contract as it does not have all the consequences of a voluntary contract. Other judges seem content to call it a 'statutory contract' which by definition distinguishes it from voluntary contracts.

Often the terms of the voluntary arrangement provide either expressly or by implication[25] for the supervisor to hold assets under the arrangement on trust for the creditors. In the absence of any such express or implied provision Harman J in *Leisure Study* construed section 1(2) as leading *prima facie* to a conclusion that the supervisor is acting in relation to the voluntary arrangement as trustee. The subsection refers to the supervisor acting in relation to the arrangement 'as trustee or otherwise for the purpose of supervising its implementation'.

Although the supervisor may act as trustee, the Act expressly recognises the possibility that he or she may also act in some other capacity for the purpose of supervising the voluntary arrangement. Under rules 1.23 and 5.21, after the approval of an arrangement, the company and the debtor respectively must 'do all that is required for putting the supervisor into possession of the assets included in the arrangement'. Putting the supervisor into possession is not the same as transferring title to hold on trust for the creditors. It is therefore clearly possible, depending on the terms of the arrangement, for the supervisor to be controlling the debtor's assets without necessarily constituting himself as legal owner and trustee. This would seem to be the situation in *McKeen* where Morritt J recognised the IVA creditors' contractual rights as surviving the bankruptcy order even though there was no trust of the IVA assets in their favour. Although it is usually the case that the supervisor will hold on trust for the creditors, it is

---

[25] See e.g., *Re Arthur Rathbone Kitchens Ltd* [1998] BCC 450.

not necessarily so and the issue will be dependent upon construction of the arrangement and the statutory provisions.

A possible analogy might be drawn between the usual case of a voluntary arrangement creating a trust and the usual case of an unincorporated association. Due to its lack of legal personality, an unincorporated association cannot hold property in its own name and therefore legal persons must hold the property for it. The interests of the members of the association are purely contractual and there is no suggestion that, although property is being held on a bare trust for the members, the trustees owe them fiduciary duties. Walton J explained it thus in *Re Bucks Constabulary Fund Friendly Society (No 2)* ([1979] 1 WLR 936):

> [T]here will accordingly be one or more trustees in whom the property which is acquired by the association will be vested . . . [T]he trust deed . . . may add that the trustee holds the assets on trust for the members in accordance with the rules of the association.

If this analogy is accepted, the responsibilities of a supervisor under a voluntary arrangement can be seen as purely contractual in a similar way to the duties owed by trustees of an unincorporated association. The supervisor's functions are to carry out the terms of the arrangement. If he or she breaches the terms of the statutory contract, remedies are available under the Act. The supervisor's responsibilities range no wider than the terms of the arrangement and the Act.

Even if this reasoning is correct a cautious supervisor should still ensure the inclusion of an express provision in the arrangement itself similar to the CVA at issue in *Rathbone* which stated: 'The supervisor shall have no duties or responsibilities except as may be expressly set out here or imposed by the Act or Rules'.

8.7 Duties of the nominee and supervisor

As we have seen, there are various statutory duties owed by the nominee, the chairman and subsequently the supervisor. These deal with the initial appraisal of the proposal, the calling and holding of meetings and supervising the voluntary arrangement in accordance with the Act and the terms of the arrangement. Any breach of the statutory duties owed by a person acting in these capacities gives creditors the right to apply to court. The court has wide powers, for example, to remove and replace a nominee or supervisor, to overturn a decision of the meetings and to regulate the supervision of the arrangement generally.[26] In addition, the nominee or

---

[26] See generally sections 6 and 7.

supervisor is under a duty to report to the Secretary of State if it appears that any past or present officer of the company has been guilty of any offence in relation to the voluntary arrangement (section 7A).

One obvious difference between the 1986 and 2000 (small company) versions of the CVA is that, in the latter, the nominee is subject to a greater number of express statutory duties. As well as forming an initial opinion of the viability of the CVA (applicable under both schemes) a supervisor under the 2000 CVA regime must continue to monitor the position and must withdraw if his or her opinion changes (paras 6(2) and paras 24–5 of Schedule A1).

A cautious nominee will require a good deal of information, both at the outset and during the moratorium. The time and expense involved in this process may mean that, in practical terms, the whole purpose of the 2000 Act's CVA provisions is somewhat lost. The post 2002 administration regime looks at least as attractive a proposition.[27]

It has been clearly stated by Harman J in *Re A Debtor (No 222 of 1990)* ([1993] BCLC 233) that a nominee, in preparing a report on a proposal and in acting as chairman of the meetings, must exercise a professional independent judgment. This duty arises from the terms of the Act. The duty to act professionally is owed to the court, the creditors and possibly even to the debtor. The court is to receive a report from a qualified person skilled and experienced in such matters who exercises professional judgment in deciding whether or not the proposal should go ahead. If the conduct of the nominee is not that of a competent insolvency practitioner, the duty is breached. If this is the case, the nominee/chairman may, exceptionally, be held personally liable for (at least some of) the costs of the creditors.

In addition to the requirement that a nominee must carry out statutory duties professionally, the court has added to these duties when the nominee is put on notice that he or she may have been misled in some way by the debtor. In *Greystoke v Hamilton-Smith* ([1997] BPIR 24), Lindsay J laid down three examples of how a nominee should act, once the fullness and candour of the debtor's information has been called into question. In such circumstances, the nominee must take such steps as would be reasonable to be satisfied that:

(1) the debtor's true financial position does not appear to differ substantially from that which is to be put to the creditors;

(2) the proposal, in broad terms, has a reasonable prospect of being implemented in the manner proposed (this idea has now become part of the nominee's express statutory duties under section 2(2)(a) as amended by the Insolvency Act 2000); and

(3) in broad terms, there is 'no already-manifest yet unavoidable prospective unfairness' under the terms of the proposal.

---

[27] See also A. Smith and M. Neil, 'The Insolvency Act 2000' (2001) 17 IL&P 84.

The Court of Appeal in *King v Anthony* ([1998] 2 BCLC 517) appears to approve of Harman J's characterisation of a nominee/chairman's duty in *Re A Debtor*. In *King* the primary issue was whether or not a creditor could sue the supervisor of the voluntary arrangement for breach of his statutory duties in a private law tort action. The Court held that such a claim was not sustainable. The duties owed by a nominee/chairman/supervisor were created by statute and only if the statute did not contain a remedy for creditors could they maintain a private law action. Under the Act, there are provisions which permit a creditor (and others) to complain of the acts of the nominee/chairman/supervisor who is an officer of the court. As an officer of the court, the court itself has wide powers to control the proper performance of the statutory powers. There can be no private law action for breach of statutory duties.

Some attempts have been made to bring private law actions against a nominee or supervisor.[28] The only real prospect of such actions being successful is for the person bringing the action to show that the acts complained of were carried out by the nominee or supervisor, but in some other capacity, such as professional advisor. The problem often facing a nominee/chairman/supervisor is that he or she may have a long-standing professional relationship with the debtor company. In acting as nominee or supervisor of the CVA various statutory duties are owed to the company. In carrying out his or her functions and advising the various parties as to what is happening, he or she must be careful to make it clear in what capacity he or she is acting. The decision in *Prosser v Castle Sanderson Solicitors* ([2002] EWCA Civ 1140) (unreported 31.7.02) highlights this problem:

> P, who owned shares in a property development company, had proposed an IVA with his creditors which was approved but ultimately was unsuccessful. P sued the solicitor A and insolvency practitioner S who had been advising him for negligence. S had acted as nominee. The alleged negligence was a failure to advise P to seek an adjournment of the creditors' meeting. The creditors' meeting was hostile to the proposed IVA as a crucial proportion of the creditors demanded the immediate winding up of the property development company instead of, as the proposal suggested, allowing it to continue to trade. A short five-minute adjournment was called. During this short adjournment, P retired to discuss the matter with A and S. P asked whether he had any alternative to an immediate winding up. He was told he did not. Neither A nor S raised the possibility of P asking for an adjournment of 14 days in order to allow further time to consider the matter. A accepted that he owed P a duty of care during the discussion. S denied he owed a duty. Despite recognising the decision in *King*, the court held that S did owe a duty during the discussion. It decided that S was not acting in the

---

28 See e.g., *Heritage Joinery v Krasner* [1999] BPIR 683 where the court appears to entertain a claim in negligent misrepresentation against a nominee. The court does not consider the judgment in *King* and therefore may be regarded as *per incuriam*.

capacity of nominee during this conversation, but was acting as he had done previously as a professional advisor. The court emphasised the need for a nominee to make clear in what capacity he is acting at any time. On the facts S lost, as he could show no recoverable loss.

The consequence of *King* is that a nominee or supervisor, acting in that capacity, does not appear to owe any duties in contract or tort to the debtor or creditors. Although the case of *Pitt v Mond* ([2001] BPIR 624) suggests that a nominee may be made liable in tort for negligent advice given to the debtor, this may be better viewed as an example of negligent professional advice *per se*, rather than negligence in acting as nominee. It would seem also to be true from *King* that a supervisor does not owe any enforceable fiduciary duties to the creditors or company. Although assets are commonly held on trust by the supervisor, if he or she acts inappropriately in relation to such assets, the creditors or company can only apply to court, as the expert supervisory body, to enforce the terms of the Act or the terms of the arrangement. This appears to give supervisors unnecessary protection and is not consistent with the courts' approach to administrative receivers or administrators.

8.8 Variation of a voluntary arrangement

It is commonly the case that, during the lifetime of a CVA, circumstances may change, necessitating some amendment to the terms of the arrangement. The projected income of the business or proceeds of sale of certain assets may not be as high as originally forecast. In such circumstances, the terms of the CVA may need to be varied. Obviously, this requires the consent of the creditors and members, as they are the parties under the statutory hypothesis to the arrangement. There is no provision in the Act dealing with variation. The requisite majority needed to vary the CVA will depend upon the facts.

In *Raja v Rubin* ([1999] BCC 579) the Court of Appeal had to consider how an IVA could be varied where there was no express variation clause in the IVA itself. The supervisor believed that as long as more than 75 per cent of the unsecured creditors consented to the variation, that being the requisite majority needed initially to approve the IVA, that would suffice. The court disagreed. As the IVA was contractual in nature, all the parties bound under the terms of the Act were in effect bound by a contract. All parties to the contract who were entitled to share in the debtor's assets needed to consent in order for the variation to be valid.

In *Horrocks v Broome* ([1999] BPIR 66) the court considered the validity of an express variation clause written into the IVA. The court held the clause to be valid but pointed out that it only permitted variations or modifications, which could have been validly included in the original proposal by the debtor. The required majority of creditors under the clause was the same as under the Act, that is, greater than 75 per cent in value of the creditors needed to agree. Other prohibitions needed to be read into the clause, such as the continued protection of the position of secured and preferential creditors.

8.9 Termination of a voluntary arrangement

A CVA may be a success or a failure. It may run its course and the company may pay all the CVA creditors out under the terms of the arrangement, enabling the company to return to beneficial trading. It may be that, in fact, the company's business does not generate enough income to satisfy the CVA creditors and the terms of the CVA are breached. It may be that although the CVA creditors have received, for example, their monthly payments under the terms of the arrangement, it has largely been at the expense of post-CVA unsecured creditors. The supervisor may adjudge the company to have defaulted under the CVA and may take action to put the company into liquidation. Creditors bound by the CVA may take action upon the arrangement being breached to put the company into liquidation. It may be that post-CVA creditors petition for a winding up. In situations where the CVA itself cannot continue to operate, questions have been asked as to what exactly has happened to the CVA. Frequently, a company in CVA may be wound up. If the supervisor is still holding assets under the terms of the CVA to distribute to the CVA creditors, can this be done, or must the supervisor hand the money over to the liquidator? Does the liquidation terminate the CVA or does the CVA survive?

The courts have considered this problem a number of times. Until recently, the courts' development of the law on termination of voluntary arrangements was somewhat complex and illogical. The Court of Appeal, in *Re NT Gallagher & Son Ltd* ([2002] BCLC 133), has recently given wise guidance on the appropriate way to deal with such matters. Before dealing with the decision in *Gallagher*, it may be appropriate to consider how the courts previously dealt with the ending of a voluntary arrangement. This will put the *Gallagher* decision into some perspective.

(1) **Breach**

(a) The voluntary arrangement itself frequently will provide for matters which constitute breach and authorise the supervisor to issue a certificate or notice that the voluntary arrangement is deemed to have failed. Some voluntary arrangements direct the supervisor to petition (under section 7(4)(b)) for the winding up of the company, others give a discretion to do so. It has been assumed that such action by the supervisor will terminate the CVA.

(b) If it is costing more to chase the company than is being recovered, the supervisor ought to petition for the company's winding up. This will cause the CVA to terminate.[29]

(2) **Liquidation**

(a) A creditors' voluntary liquidation has been held not to terminate the CVA.[30]

(b) A winding-up order based upon the directors' petition has been held not to terminate the CVA.[31]

(c) A winding up based upon a non-voluntary arrangement creditor petition has been held not to terminate the CVA.[32]

(d) A winding-up order based upon a voluntary arrangement creditor petition on the grounds of breach of the CVA has been held to terminate.[33]

(e) A winding-up order based upon the supervisor's petition has been held to terminate.[34]

The logic of these decisions can be briefly explained as follows. If the liquidation or other act is based upon the CVA failing in some way, for example, where the supervisor or creditors are bound under the CVA petition, it has been assumed by the courts that the creditors would wish the arrangement to come to an end. If the liquidation is brought about by matters outside the CVA, for example, a voluntary winding up or winding up on petition of directors or non-CVA creditors, the CVA does not terminate.

This strange logic has now been overruled by *Gallagher*. The facts in the case are fairly typical:

A civil engineering company found itself in financial difficulty largely as a result of a substantial contractual dispute with one of its clients. The CVA was intended to keep the company going until the litigation surrounding the dispute could be settled. Under the terms of the CVA new debts were to be paid out of trading income and in addition to this, monthly payments were to be made to the supervisor for distribution to the CVA creditors. The

---

[29] See e.g., the *obiter* statement by Chadwick J in *Vadher v Weisgard* [1997] BCC 219 at 221.

[30] See e.g., *Re Halson Packaging Ltd* [1997] BCC 993, *Re Arthur Rathbone Kitchens* [1997] 2 BCLC 280 and *Welsby v Brelec* [2000] 2 BCLC 576.

[31] See e.g., *Re Excalibur Airways* [1998] 1 BCLC 436.

[32] See e.g., *Re Bradley-Hole* [1995] 2 BCLC 163, *Re McKeen* [1995] BCC 412 and *Re Kudos Glass Ltd* [2001] 1 BCLC 390.

[33] See e.g., *Kings v Cleghorn* [1998] BPIR 463.

[34] See e.g., *Re Arthur Rathbone Kitchens Ltd* [1998] BCC 450 and *Davis v Martin-Sklan* [1995] 2 BCLC 483.

supervisor was required to petition for the company's winding up if the company defaulted. Despite a number of defaults the supervisor did not petition. Eventually the company entered creditors' voluntary liquidation. The contractual claim remained unresolved. The supervisor held over £500,000 under the CVA which had not been distributed to the CVA creditors. The company's post-CVA debts were £2,525,649 and its total liabilities were £5,066,890. Apart from its contractual claims the company's assets amounted to £98,000. The main issue was what should happen to the money held by the supervisor. The Court of Appeal held that the trusts of the CVA had not been terminated and therefore the money was distributable under its terms.

The court emphasised that the type of liquidation or the identity of the petitioner (if it were a compulsory liquidation) was irrelevant. It laid down new guidelines which are both logical and easy to follow:

(1) Where a CVA or IVA provides for moneys or other assets to be paid to, or transferred, or held for the benefit of CVA or IVA creditors, this will create a trust of those moneys or assets for those creditors.
(2) The effect of the liquidation of the company or the bankruptcy of the debtor on a trust created by the CVA or IVA will depend on the provisions of the CVA or IVA relating thereto.
(3) If the CVA or IVA provides what is to happen on liquidation or bankruptcy (or failure of the CVA or IVA), effect must be given thereto.
(4) If the CVA or IVA does not so provide, the trust will continue notwithstanding the liquidation, bankruptcy or failure and must take effect according to its terms.
(5) The CVA or IVA creditors can prove in the liquidation or bankruptcy for so much of their debt as remains after payment of what has been or will be recovered under the trust.[35]

The position is therefore greatly simplified. The provisions of the arrangement are to be given effect. It would be usual for the creditors to require a provision to be inserted stating that the assets held by the supervisor are to be held for the creditors' benefit when the company is wound up. This is the default position if the arrangement is silent on the issue. This is a very positive development from the point of view of the creditors bound by the voluntary arrangement. It may, though, have some knock-on consequences. In any post-voluntary arrangement creditors will almost certainly not be paid if the arrangement fails prematurely. Such creditors may not even be aware that the company is in CVA as there are generally no publicity requirements for a company in CVA.[36] The decision in *Gallagher* may lead to difficulties in companies obtaining continued financing during the CVA.

---

[35] [2002] BCLC 133 at 150 per Peter Gibson LJ.
[36] The only exception to this is if the company has the benefit of a moratorium under the provisions for small companies introduced by the 2000 Act (see para 16 Schedule A1).

Once the final distributions are made by the supervisor it comes to an end. All that remains to be done is for the supervisor to send notice to the Registrar of Companies, the court and the creditors and members bound by the CVA notifying them that the arrangement has been fully implemented or (as the case may be) has terminated. The notice must be sent within 28 days of the final distributions. Accompanying the notice must be a copy of a report by the supervisor summarising all receipts and payments made by him or her, any departure from the proposal as originally approved and the reasons why (if that is the case) the arrangement has terminated (rule 1.29).

Chapter 9

Individual Voluntary Arrangements

9.1 Introduction

In the same way that companies may enter into company voluntary arrangements (hereafter 'CVAs') with their creditors, so too individuals may enter individual voluntary arrangements (hereafter 'IVAs') with their creditors. The basic idea as to what a voluntary arrangement is and how it operates is the same for both types. Most of what has been discussed in Chapter 8 on CVAs will apply to IVAs. The fundamental principles remain the same, and the provisions in Part VIII of the Insolvency Act (hereafter 'the Act') which deal with IVAs are similar to those under Part I of the Act which deal with CVAs. There are, of course, some obvious differences, for example, there will be no members' meeting called in an IVA. There are some less apparent differences which will be highlighted as we come across them.

The IVA is a way to avoid bankruptcy (an IVA can even be approved after the debtor has been made bankrupt). It is more effective than a purely informal arrangement as, once it is approved, it will bind all the debtor's creditors. No one creditor of the debtor can break ranks and petition for the debtor's bankruptcy.

Prior to the introduction of the IVA in 1985, the only way a debtor could enter into a binding arrangement with his or her creditors was under the Deeds of Arrangement Act 1914. One of the main weaknesses of that Act (which incidentally remains in force today) is that any dissenting creditor could still petition for the debtor's bankruptcy. As the execution of a Deed of Arrangement was itself, under the Bankruptcy Act 1914, a ground upon which a bankruptcy order could be made (referred to as an 'act of bankruptcy'), such deeds were frequently ineffective to save the debtor from bankruptcy. Although still possible in theory, Deeds of Arrangement have, in practical terms, been completely overtaken by the IVA. Another relatively formal way in which a debtor can deal with his or her debts is by way of a county court administration order under section 112 of the County Courts Act 1984 (not to be confused with company administration orders under the Act). The county court administration order will be considered briefly in Chapter 10.

IVAs have proven far more popular than CVAs. There are various possible reasons for this. The most important thing to a creditor is getting paid. Under an IVA, a creditor is likely to see far more of his or her money being paid than under a bankruptcy.[1] The administrative costs of running an IVA are considerably less than those of a formal bankruptcy. The IVA has had, from its inception, a moratorium on creditor actions written into its framework. The debtor can ask the court for an 'interim order' which protects the debtor from creditor harassment in a similar way that a company entering administration is protected. The interim order procedure is far less expensive than the old company administration order procedure and has proven popular. When the IVA was first introduced it was assumed that an interim order would be required in all cases. Recent amendments made by the Insolvency Act 2000 now allow for an IVA to be approved without the need to obtain first an interim order. One other possible benefit that an IVA has over a CVA is that the consequences of its failure will usually result in the debtor's bankruptcy. The immediacy of such a threat hanging over the head of the debtor may serve to concentrate the mind more than with a CVA failing and the company entering liquidation. The effect of the failure of an IVA is more personal.

9.2 Procedure

The procedure may begin in one of two ways (soon to be three when the provisions of the Enterprise Act 2002 come fully into force). An interim order may or may not be sought. If an interim order is sought, this must be acquired before the nominee reports as to whether or not a creditors' meeting should be called to consider the proposal. If no interim order is sought, the procedure begins with the nominee's consideration of the proposal. In either case, the nominee will report on the proposal to the court. If the court's view of the proposal is positive it will order a creditors' meeting to be summoned. The two procedures effectively join each other at this point and the procedure is thereafter the same.

---

[1] See K. Pond, 'New rules and new roles for the individual voluntary arrangement' (2002) 18 *Insolvency Law and Practice* 9 at 9.

9.2.1 *Procedure where an interim order is made*

An application may be made for an interim order under section 253 of the Act where a debtor intends to make a proposal for an IVA. An IVA is defined in the same way as a CVA as being a composition of debts or a scheme of arrangement. The proposal must provide for a qualified person to act as nominee where he or she has consented to act. The application may be made, if the debtor is an undischarged bankrupt, by the debtor, the trustee in bankruptcy or the official receiver. In such circumstances, if the debtor wishes to make an application, he or she must first give notice to the official receiver and, if there is one, the trustee in bankruptcy. If the debtor is not currently subject to a bankruptcy order, the debtor may make the application but only under section 255 if in a position whereby he or she could petition for his or her own bankruptcy.[2]

Prior to an application by the debtor, he or she must give a copy of his or her proposed IVA[3] to the intended nominee. On the basis of the draft proposal, the nominee will consider whether or not to consent to act. It is likely that in practice the nominee will have lent professional assistance in the drafting of the proposal and so, in such circumstances, the nominee's consent is a formality. The application for the interim order is then made, accompanied by an affidavit detailing (rule 5.7):

(1) the reasons for the application;
(2) particulars of any execution, distress or other legal process which the debtor is aware has been commenced against the debtor;
(3) that the debtor is either an undischarged bankrupt or is able to petition for his or her own bankruptcy;
(4) that no previous application for an interim order has been made by or in respect of the debtor in the previous 12 months;[4]
(5) the name of the nominee and the nominee's consent to act.

Under section 254, the application for an interim order prevents a landlord from forfeiting by peaceable re-entry any premises let to the debtor without leave of the court. The application also allows the court to forbid any such landlord from levying distress for unpaid rent and to stay

---

[2] The debtor cannot apply for an interim order if the debtor has obtained his or her discharge from bankruptcy, as the debtor is no longer able to petition for his or her own bankruptcy – see *Wright v Official Receiver* [2001] BPIR 196. The debtor cannot make an application if the debtor has petitioned for his or her own bankruptcy where the petition is pending and the court has under section 273 of the Act appointed an insolvency practitioner to inquire into the debtor's affairs with a view to a possible IVA being proposed (section 253).

[3] The proposal must contain under IR rule 5.3 the same details as are required in a CVA under IR rule 1.3. See Chapter 8 for the full contents.

[4] Under section 255(1)(c) the court will not make an interim order if there has been a previous application in the previous 12 months. See *Hurst v Bennett (No2)* [2002] BPIR 102.

any action, execution, or other legal process against the property or person of the debtor. This form of moratorium is similar to that which takes effect when action is taken to put a company into administration. The main differences are that the moratorium is not as extensive under an interim order and the stay on creditor actions is not automatic, except for the prohibition on peaceable re-entry, and is therefore at the discretion of the court. The court for these purposes includes any court where proceedings are currently pending against the debtor.

Upon receipt of the application, the court will set a return date for the hearing. At least two days' notice of the hearing must be given:

(1) where the debtor is a bankrupt, to the bankrupt, the official receiver and, if there is one, the trustee in bankruptcy (all these persons except obviously whichever one is the applicant will be given notice); and

(2) where the debtor is not a bankrupt, to any creditor who, to the debtor's knowledge, has presented a bankruptcy petition against the debtor; and

(3) in either case the nominee who has agreed to act (rule 5.7).

The court may make the interim order if it thinks it would be appropriate to do so for the purpose of facilitating the consideration and implementation of the debtor's proposal (section 255(2)). The persons given notice of the hearing may make representations at it. The court will not make the order if the proposal is not viable. If it appears to the court that the application is being used as a means to postpone an inevitable bankruptcy order, the court will not make the order.[5] In *Re O'Sullivan* ([2001] BPIR 534) the court refused to make an interim order because the size of the nominee's fee was considered to be too high (on the facts £1,000 would have been acceptable but not the £2,500 proposed). The court laid down a number of guidelines for the court to follow in considering an application for an interim order:

(1) The court has an unlimited discretion in reaching its decision. This discretion must be exercised in a judicial manner with due regard to the statutory scheme.

(2) The proposal should be one which has a real prospect of being implemented in the manner proposed and this is one of the matters on which the nominee should be satisfied in order to make a favourable report to the court.

(3) Although not a necessary requirement, the court should look to see that the IVA offers a reasonable prospect of a better recovery for the creditors in financial terms than would be achieved in a bankruptcy.

(4) The general test is that the proposal should be serious and viable.

---

[5] See e.g., *Re Cove* [1990] 1 All ER 949, *Hook v Jewson Ltd* [1997] 1 BCLC 664, *Cooper v Fearnley* [1997] BPIR 20, *Greystoke v Hamilton-Smith* [1997] BPIR 24, *Knowles v Coutts & Co* [1998] BPIR 96 and *Hurst v Bennett (No2)* [2002] BPIR 102.

(5) The court should not permit the application to become the means of postponing the making of a bankruptcy order in circumstances where there is no apparent likelihood of benefit to creditors from such a postponement.

(6) The court should be satisfied that the creditors' meeting should be called. It should not merely 'rubber stamp' views expressed by the nominee in his or her report.

(7   The decision as to the merits or otherwise of the proposal is not a decision for the court. The creditors must be left to decide upon the proposal even where the benefits are small.

(8) Where it has become evident that there is no prospect that the requisite majority of creditors can be achieved, no creditors' meeting should be called.

9.2.1.1 *Effect of the interim order*

Under section 252, the effect of the order is to impose a moratorium on actions against the debtor. The interim order lasts for 14 days beginning with the day after the order is made (section 255 (6)). It prevents any bankruptcy petition being presented against the debtor or being proceeded with. A landlord is prevented without leave of the court from forfeiting a lease by peaceable re-entry and from distraining for unpaid rent.[6] No other proceedings, execution[7] or other legal process may be commenced or continued against the debtor or his or her property without leave of the court. The terms of the moratorium are similar to those which apply in a company administration except, importantly, there is no restriction on a secured creditor enforcing security, nor on an owner under a hire purchase or retention of title contract repossessing goods. Cases decided under the administration regime would apply equally under the interim order.

9.2.1.2 *Nominee's report on debtor's proposal*

The nominee must, before the interim order expires, submit a report to the court under section 256. The report is the exact equivalent of the nominee's report in a CVA context under section 2. The nominee must approach the task in an objective and professional manner.[8] The report

---

[6] These restrictions were not present in the original Act but were added by the Insolvency Act 2000. Previously, this gap in the moratorium could destroy any chance of the IVA being a success. See e.g., *Re A Debtor* (No 13A-IO of 1995) [1996] BCC 57 and *McMullen & Sons v Cerrone* [1994] BCC 25.

[7] See e.g., *Re Peake* [1987] CLY 215 where an interim order was used to prevent the sheriff completing an execution over the debtor's goods.

[8] See Chapter 8 and in particular *Greystoke v Hamilton-Smith* [1997] BPIR 24.

must state whether, in the nominee's opinion, the proposal has a reasonable prospect of being approved and implemented and, if so, that a meeting of the debtor's creditors should be called to consider it. Details of where and when the meeting should be held must also be reported. In order to enable the nominee to make the report, the debtor must submit the draft proposal and a statement of affairs to the nominee (this may already have been done). If the nominee fails to submit the report within the 14-day period of the interim order, the court may replace the nominee and extend or renew the interim order period to allow the new nominee time to report. A nominee may apply for an extension of the interim order period if more time is needed to prepare the report. If, after receiving the report, the court is satisfied that a meeting of creditors should be called, it may extend the interim order to cover the time up to the meeting. This prevents any creditor obtaining a march on the other creditors by enforcing rights prior to the consideration of the proposal by the creditors' meeting.

9.2.2 *Procedure where no interim order is made*

Under section 256A[9] it is now possible for a debtor to propose an IVA without the need first to acquire an interim order. This procedure is available to a debtor or an undischarged bankrupt. If the individual is already bankrupt, he or she must first give notice of the proposal to the official receiver and, if one exists, the trustee in bankruptcy of the estate.[10]

In order to enable the nominee to prepare a report to the court, the debtor must submit to the nominee a copy of the draft proposal and a statement of affairs. The nominee will then report to the court (within 14 days). The report is in the same form as above. The nominee must state his or her opinion as to whether or not the proposal has a reasonable prospect of being approved and implemented and whether a creditors' meeting ought to be summoned to consider it. Details of where and when the meeting should be held must also be included. Again, the court has the power to replace a nominee who does not report in time. On an application by the nominee the 14-day period may be extended.

9.2.3 *Creditors' meeting*

Unless the court directs otherwise, following a positive report to the court, the nominee will proceed to call a creditors' meeting at the time, date and

---

[9] Inserted by the Insolvency Act 2000.

[10] The debtor cannot make a proposal under section 256A if he or she has petitioned for his or her own bankruptcy where the petition is pending and the court has under section 273 of the Act appointed an insolvency practitioner to inquire into the debtor's affairs with a view to a possible IVA being proposed.

place stipulated in the report. All creditors of whom the nominee has notice are summoned to the meeting. If the debtor is an undischarged bankrupt the creditors include:

(1) every person who is a creditor in respect of a bankruptcy debt; and
(2) every person who would be such a creditor if the bankruptcy had commenced on the day on which notice of the meeting is given (section 257).

At the meeting any modifications to the proposal must be consented to by the debtor. The proposal cannot affect the right of a secured creditor to enforce security unless the creditor consents. Similarly, the priority of a preferential creditor cannot be affected without consent (section 258).

Where the debtor is an undischarged bankrupt, votes are calculated according to the amount of a creditor's debt as at the date of the bankruptcy order. Where the debtor is not a bankrupt and an interim order is in force, votes are calculated according to the amount of a creditor's debt as at the date of the interim order. Where the debtor is not a bankrupt and an interim order is not in force, votes are calculated according to the amount of a creditor's debt as at the date of the meeting (rule 5.21(2)).

As with CVAs, a creditor whose debt is for an unliquidated amount, or whose value is not ascertained, may vote in respect of that debt and for voting purposes the debt shall be valued at £1 unless the chairman of the meeting agrees to put a higher value on it (rule 5.21(3)). The chairman will again usually be the nominee. The chairman must decide as to an individual creditor's entitlement to vote. A creditor's claim may be rejected in whole or in part. The chairman's decision as to voting entitlement is subject to a right of appeal to the court by the debtor or any creditor. If the chairman is in doubt whether a claim should be admitted or not, he or she should mark it as objected to and allow votes cast in respect of it. Such votes may subsequently be declared invalid if the court sustains an appeal (rule 5.22).

In order to approve the IVA at the creditors' meeting, a majority of more than three-quarters in value of creditors present in person or by proxy and voting is needed (rule 5.24). Any other resolutions passed at the meeting require a simple majority in value. Only unsecured creditors can vote. A secured creditor may vote in respect of any debt which is unsecured.[11] Any resolution is invalid if those voting against it include more than half in value of the creditors, with notice of the meeting and who are entitled to vote, who are not associates[12] of the debtor.

---

[11] See *Calor Gas v Piercy* [1994] BCC 69.
[12] Section 435 of the Act defines the meaning of 'associate'. It includes *inter alia*, spouse, brother, sister, uncle, aunt, nephew, niece, lineal ancestor, lineal descendent, partner, employee and employer.

9.2.4 *Effect of approval*

Where the creditors' meeting approves the IVA it takes effect as if made by the debtor at the meeting, and binds every person who:

(1) was entitled to vote at the meeting (whether or not he or she was present or represented at it); or
(2) would have been so entitled if he or she had had notice of it,

as if he or she were a party to the arrangement (section 260). This is the same as for CVAs.

Any interim order ceases to have effect after the IVA is approved. If the interim order stayed a bankruptcy petition, once the IVA is approved the petition is deemed to have been dismissed unless the court orders otherwise (section 260(5)). If the debtor is an undischarged bankrupt the court may do one of two things once the IVA is approved. The court may annul the bankruptcy order and/or give directions with regard to the bankrupt's estate to facilitate the implementation of the voluntary arrangement. A bankruptcy order will not be annulled during the period when an application against the decision of the creditors' meeting is pending or could be brought (section 261(2)).[13] A new section 261 of the Act, introduced under section 264 and Schedule 22 of the Enterprise Act 2002, will, when in force, oblige the court to annul the bankruptcy order once the IVA is approved and the period for objecting to the court has elapsed.

9.2.5 *Unfair prejudice or material irregularity*

In much the same way as with CVAs a number of people have the right, under section 262 of the Act, to apply to the court on the basis that the terms of an IVA are unfairly prejudicial to interests of a creditor, or that there has been some material irregularity at or in relation to the creditors' meeting. The meanings of unfair prejudice and material irregularity have been considered in Chapter 8 on CVAs and the reader is directed to that discussion. The persons who can apply to the court are the debtor, any person entitled to vote at the creditors' meeting whether or not that person had received notice of the meeting, the nominee and, if the debtor is an undischarged bankrupt, the trustee in bankruptcy or the official receiver.

It the court is satisfied that the IVA is unfairly prejudicial to a creditor's interests, or that there was some material irregularity in relation to the meeting, it may revoke or suspend any approval given at the meeting

---

[13] An application may be brought within 28 days of the report to the court.

and/or direct that a further creditors' meeting be called to reconsider the original proposal or to consider a revised proposal. Any interim order which is in effect prior to the original meeting will normally be extended to cover the period up to any new meeting which has been directed.

A creditor who is aggrieved at the approval of an IVA has an additional option, which is not available in a CVA context. A creditor bound by an IVA has the right to petition for the bankruptcy of the debtor under section 264(1)(c) of the Act.[14] The grounds for such a petition are found in section 276:

(1) that the debtor has failed to comply with his or her obligations under the IVA; or
(2) that information which was false or misleading in any material particular or contained material omissions, was contained in documentation provided by the debtor leading to the approval of the IVA, or was otherwise made available by the debtor to his or her creditors at or in connection with the creditors' meeting; or
(3) that the debtor has failed to do anything which may reasonably have been required by the IVA supervisor.

This provision permits a creditor or supervisor to petition for the debtor's bankruptcy if the debtor fails to comply with the requirements of the IVA. In addition, it permits a petition if misleading or false information was provided to the creditors in the process of the creditors' consideration of the proposal, or where there was a material omission in such information. An example of where this provision was successfully used by a creditor, who would it seems have failed in a complaint of unfair prejudice or material irregularity at or in relation to the meeting, is *Cadbury Schweppes plc v Somji* ([2001] 1 WLR 615):

> S owed approximately 7.6 million US dollars and proposed an IVA, the terms of which provided that 380,000 US dollars would be distributed among S's creditors over a period of 18 months. The money was to be provided by S's father. No other third party funds were mentioned in the proposal. The first creditors' meeting was adjourned after the creditors refused to approve the proposal. Three of S's main creditors representing 45 per cent of the overall debt opposed the proposal. The three creditors were Cadbury Schweppes (23 per cent) and two banks (22 per cent). After the adjourned creditors' meeting, J, an acquaintance of S, approached Cadbury and the banks. He offered to buy the debts which S owed to them if they voted in favour of the IVA. The offers were for considerably more than was on offer under the terms of the IVA (Cadbury was offered 250,000 US dollars, and the banks 240,000 US dollars). The banks agreed to the deal but Cadbury refused, stating that any funds which were available should be made available to all of S's creditors

---

[14] For an example of such action see *Davis v Martin-Sklan* [1995] BCC 1122. The supervisor of the IVA has the same power.

pro rata. The deal was to be kept confidential. There was no mention of it in the terms of the IVA itself. S was aware of the negotiations but did not know any deal had been agreed to until at the reconvened creditors' meeting the banks voted in favour and the IVA was approved. Cadbury applied to the court for revocation of the IVA under section 262 on the ground of unfair prejudice and alternatively under section 264 on the ground that the information provided by the debtor was false or misleading or contained material omissions. The Court of Appeal upheld the first instance decision which made a bankruptcy order under section 264. The bankruptcy order did not automatically mean the IVA was terminated. The terms of the IVA were literally true, in that the only third party funds to be made available under the proposal were to come from S's father, the failure to mention J's intervention meant that the proposal was misleading and this was a material omission. It was material because had the creditors known of it, it would have been likely to make a difference to the way in which the creditors would have considered and assessed the proposal. The court at first instance had held the claim of unfair prejudice must fail. Any unfairness complained of must be due to the terms of the IVA, not by matters outside it. As the complaint here related to the negotiated agreement made outside the IVA itself, it could not be included under section 262. The Court of Appeal did not expressly uphold this reasoning but did refer to the 'fairly strong' line of authority supporting it.[15]

The effect of providing false or misleading information may therefore have an adverse effect on the IVA and may lead to the possible bankruptcy of the debtor. In addition, there may also be criminal consequences. A debtor who, for the purpose of obtaining the approval of the IVA, makes any false representation or fraudulently does or omits to do something, commits an offence (section 262A). If it appears to a nominee or supervisor that the debtor has committed an offence in connection with the IVA, he or she must report this to the Secretary of State. Subsequently, the Secretary of State or Director of Public Prosecutions may bring a prosecution.

9.2.6 *'Fast track' IVA*

Sections 263A–263G of the Act introduce a new 'fast track' IVA procedure for undischarged bankrupts where the official receiver is to act as nominee.[16] This new procedure is added by section 264 and Schedule 22 of the Enterprise Act 2002 and is likely to come into force in 2004.

The 'fast track' procedure will be available wherever the debtor is an undischarged bankrupt, no interim order is applied for and the official receiver is specified as being the nominee in relation to the proposed IVA

---

[15] See also N. Griffiths, 'Voluntary Arrangements after Somji' (2001) 17 IL&P 104.

[16] Section 389B of the Act, when in force, will allow the official receiver to act as nominee or supervisor where the debtor proposing the IVA is an undischarged bankrupt. This is not restricted to the fast track procedure.

(section 263A). The procedure begins with the debtor submitting a proposal for an IVA, along with a statement of affairs, to the official receiver. If the official receiver thinks that the proposal has a reasonable prospect of being approved and implemented, he or she may make arrangements for creditors (who are creditors in respect of bankruptcy debts) to consider the proposal (section 263B).[17] The new section 263B leaves it open for the Secretary of State to provide for the creditors to approve the proposal in some way other than by calling a creditors' meeting. Importantly, the creditors will be asked to approve the proposal but cannot make any modifications to it (section 263B(4)(c)). It is either approved or rejected as it stands.

As soon as is reasonably practicable after the creditors have made their decision, the official receiver must communicate their decision to the court. If the proposal is approved it takes effect and binds the debtor and all those creditors entitled to vote on the proposal (section 263D(2)). The debtor, a creditor, the official receiver or the trustee in bankruptcy (if there is one) may apply to the court for the IVA to be revoked on the grounds of unfair prejudice or material irregularity. Such an application must be made within 28 days of the official receiver's report to the court (section 263F).

Once the IVA has been approved, the official receiver may apply to the court, which must annul the bankruptcy order. Such an application may only be made after the period for objecting to the IVA has lapsed (or such longer period where an application objecting to the IVA is pending or an appeal in relation to the application is pending) (section 263D(3) and (4)).

Once approved the IVA is implemented in the same way as any other IVA.

9.3 Implementation and supervision of the IVA

Once the IVA is approved, the nominee will usually continue as supervisor and implement the terms of the IVA (section 263 and rule 5.25). Immediately the IVA is approved, the debtor, or, where the debtor is an undischarged bankrupt, the official receiver or trustee in bankruptcy, must do all that is required to put the supervisor into possession of the assets included in the arrangement (rule 5.26). A report of what happened at the creditors' meeting must be prepared by the chairman (usually the

---

[17] Only once the official receiver has made arrangements for the creditors to consider the proposal, or informed the debtor that he or she does not intend to make such arrangements, can an application for an interim order be made under section 253.

same person who acted as the nominee and will act as supervisor). It must be filed at the court within four days of the meeting (rule 5.27) and immediately thereafter sent to all the debtor's creditors of whom the chairman is aware (section 259 and rule 5.27(4)) and to the Secretary of State (rule 5.29).[18]

If the debtor or any creditor is dissatisfied by any act, omission or decision of the supervisor, he or she may apply to the court. The court may make such order as it thinks fit, including confirming, reversing or modifying any decision by the supervisor, replacing the supervisor or otherwise giving the supervisor directions (section 263).

As part of his or her role the supervisor must keep accounts and records of his or her dealings in connection with the IVA and must provide an abstract of such matters every 12 months to the court, the debtor and the creditors bound by the IVA (rule 5.31).

9.4 Ending of the IVA

The rules as to when an IVA terminates are the same as with CVAs. The Court of Appeal's decision in *Re NT Gallagher & Son Ltd* ([2002] BCLC 133) lays down general guidelines which were discussed in Chapter 8 but are repeated here for convenience:

(1) Where a CVA or IVA provides for moneys or other assets to be paid to, or transferred, or held for the benefit of CVA or IVA creditors, this will create a trust of those moneys or assets for those creditors.
(2) The effect of the liquidation of the company or the bankruptcy of the debtor on a trust created by the CVA or IVA will depend on the provisions of the CVA or IVA relating thereto.
(3) If the CVA or IVA provides what is to happen on liquidation or bankruptcy (or failure of the CVA or IVA), effect must be given thereto.
(4) If the CVA or IVA does not so provide, the trust will continue notwithstanding the liquidation, bankruptcy, or failure and must take effect according to its terms.
(5) The CVA or IVA creditors can prove in the liquidation or bankruptcy for so much of their debt as remains after payment of what has been or will be recovered under the trust.[19]

---

[18] The Secretary of State has a duty to maintain a Register of Voluntary Arrangements open to public inspection, containing brief details of all IVAs. If an IVA is subsequently revoked by the court, the entry on the Register is completely deleted. If an IVA is fully implemented or otherwise terminates, the entry is deleted after two years have elapsed.

[19] [2002] BCLC 133 at 150 per Peter Gibson LJ.

The provisions of the arrangement are to be given effect. It would be usual for the creditors to require a provision to be inserted stating that the assets held by the supervisor are to be held for the creditors' benefit in the event of the debtor being made bankrupt. This is the default position if the arrangement is silent on the issue.

Once the final distributions are made by the supervisor to the creditors, the IVA comes to an end. All that remains to be done is for the supervisor, not later than 28 days after the final completion or termination of the IVA, to send a notice to that effect to the court, Secretary of State, debtor and all creditors bound by the IVA. The notice is accompanied by a copy of a report summarising all receipts and payments made by the supervisor and explains any difference in how the IVA was actually implemented as compared to the proposal as approved. Once these reports have been sent, the supervisor may vacate office (rule 5.34).

Chapter 10

Other Types of Arrangement

10.1 Introduction

If a company or an individual is insolvent, creditors may be entitled to wind up the company or to bankrupt the individual. It will frequently be more beneficial for creditors if an arrangement of some sort can be made with the debtor. Liquidation and bankruptcy often produce poor returns to the creditors. An arrangement such as a voluntary arrangement, as discussed in Chapters 8 and 9, may be a way of maximising the debtor's assets. An arrangement may have the knock-on beneficial effect of allowing the business of the company or individual to continue and, hopefully, be restored to financial health.

A list of the advantages of some form of arrangement for the creditors might include the following:

- An independent person may act as manager of the arrangement and advise the creditors and safeguard the creditors' interests.
- The prospect, often through continued trading of the business, of a better return than if a winding up or bankruptcy occurs.
- The opportunity to continue to supply goods and services to the debtor (preferably on a cash on delivery basis).
- Avoidance of contracts in progress being cancelled (which would be likely in a winding up or bankruptcy).
- The flexibility of schemes, which can allow for a wide range of possible arrangements.
- The possible sale, at least where the debtor is a company, of the business as a going concern in the future. This is likely to produce more funds than if the business assets were sold off piecemeal under a liquidation or bankruptcy.

Advantages for the debtor individual or company would include:

- The avoidance of the stigma of bankruptcy or liquidation.
- The continuation of the business.
- The avoidance of investigations by a liquidator or trustee in bankruptcy.
- The end of immediate creditor pressure.

The aim of any scheme is to obtain agreement whereby the creditors' rights against the debtor are in some way modified or adjusted, in such a way that the creditors obtain some benefit which would not be available if the arrangement did not exist. The manner in which the rights are modified will depend upon the circumstances.

A frequent problem in practice is that the debtor may not wish to face the looming financial crisis. The debtor may believe, optimistically, that the business can trade through its current difficulties without having to come to some agreement with its creditors. Even if a problem is recognised, the debtor may be reluctant to cede control of the business to an outsider.

From the creditors' position, different considerations need to be addressed. Some creditors may be owed only a relatively small amount and will therefore not be unduly concerned by the problems facing the debtor. Others may be depending upon being paid a large part of the debt owed in order to stay in business themselves. If the debtor is a particular creditor's main customer, the loss of the debtor's continued custom may have a serious effect on the viability of the creditor's business. Creditors may be in a weak position in that they may have to accept an arrangement or face being paid nothing in a winding up or bankruptcy.

A crucial early question is to consider what form any proposed arrangement should take. It may either be formal, such as a CVA or IVA, or informal. Which type of arrangement is appropriate will depend upon the particular circumstances. Relevant factors to consider will include the size of the company, the number of creditors, the nature of the debts, the nature of the business and the opinions of any major creditors.

The remainder of this chapter will first consider informal arrangements and, second, formal arrangements other than CVAs and IVAs.

10.2 Informal arrangements

For the most part, informal arrangements involve privately negotiated agreements which are subject to the general law of contract. They may be negotiated with one large creditor or a few creditors. The danger of negotiating with only one creditor is that the debtor remains open to attack from his or her other creditors. Usually informal arrangements involve a moratorium on the existing debt. From the debtor's point of view, the absence of publicity of the debtor's financial problems is a major advantage of an informal arrangement and may assist in the business maintaining its goodwill. The costs of an informal arrangement will usually be less than a formal agreement. It will usually also be less time consuming to set up and to operate.

The main problem with informal arrangements is they are marked by a degree of uncertainty, especially if all the creditors do not agree to the proposal. If the debtor does subsequently enter some formal insolvency procedure, the creditors will have wasted time, effort and money in considering and agreeing to the arrangement. Any payments received by creditors under an informal arrangement may potentially be attacked by a subsequent liquidator, administrator or trustee in bankruptcy as voidable preferences.

Frequently, an informal arrangement will result from the debtor approaching individual creditors. There may be a meeting of creditors called to discuss and debate any proposal. Any vote on the proposal will not serve to bind dissentient creditors. If most of the creditors agree to an informal proposal, but some do not, it may be the case that the dissenters have to be paid out, otherwise they could act to frustrate the whole plan by forcing a liquidation or bankruptcy of the debtor. Depending on the circumstances, it may even be possible for some creditors to provide extra funding to pay out the dissenters.

Informal arrangements, by their very nature, have their limitations. They are more likely to succeed where there are only a small number of creditors, in that the negotiations will be easier and the chance of having dissenting creditors is reduced.

Prior to agreeing to an arrangement, the creditors will wish to have full disclosure of the debtor's affairs and some idea of the debtor's ability to fulfil commitments under the proposal. Creditors will need to be convinced that they are helping to finance a continuing business likely to bear fruit, not just paying out to finance other creditors.

It is crucial that major creditors are involved. There will need to be a degree of trust and a reasonable working relationship between the creditors and the debtor. Specifically, any arrangement will need to state the extent of the credit to be allowed to the debtor during the lifetime of the arrangement. It will normally be necessary for any secured creditors to agree not to enforce their security. Some mechanism enabling the creditors to monitor effectively the company's progress may also be required.

A real problem in practice may be that the creditors have developed a distrust of the business's managers. Creditors may have been misled by the managers. For obvious reasons, the creditors may have no confidence in the managers being able to continue to manage the business in a prosperous way. The diplomacy skills of a financial adviser may be crucial in reaching an agreement.

The arrangement, once agreed to, should be reduced to writing. This will help to ensure that there is no confusion as to what exactly has been agreed. If the agreement is under seal it will be enforceable by all parties to it, regardless of whether or not consideration has been provided. A deed containing the terms of the arrangement and signed by all parties and is therefore useful from the debtor's point of view, as the debtor will probably not be providing any consideration for the creditors agreeing to vary their claims against the debtor.

The deed will indicate what the creditors are to surrender and what benefits they are to receive in place of such rights surrendered. If the arrangement is substantial, it would be prudent for the creditors to establish a small committee to monitor the effectiveness of the arrangement and to report back to the other creditors. The arrangement may also provide for the appointment of a financial adviser who can have unrestricted access to the debtor's books and be able to attend management meetings. Such a person would report findings to the creditors.

10.2.1 *The 'London Approach'*[1]

It is a basic truism that the larger the debt owed by a company, the less likely its bankers are to take precipitate action against it. A very large company will frequently be financed by several banks. If such a company falls into financial difficulty, several things can happen. It may enter some formal insolvency procedure such as CVA, administration or liquidation. One particular creditor may take action against the company. If the creditor is secured it may appoint a receiver. In a scenario where the company has been financed by several banks, if one bank decides to call in its loan and enforce its rights against the company, this will generally have a very negative effect on the company, its business, its employees and on its other creditors. The so-called 'London Approach' has been developed to deal with this type of situation.

The origins of the 'London Approach' can be traced back to the financial crisis in the early 1970s when the Bank of England became involved in a number of large-scale failures. Over the years, the Bank became involved as an honest broker and adviser in a number of situations where large companies had failed, owing a number of lenders significant amounts. In order to lessen the Bank's overt intervention in such insolvencies, in 1990 the Bank discussed with a number of large London-based banks the adoption of principles of best practice. The resulting 'London Rules' have now developed into what is referred to as the 'London Approach'.

---

[1] For an in-depth consideration of this subject see J. Armour and S. Deakin, 'Norms in Private Insolvency: The "London Approach" to the Resolution of Financial Distress' (2001) 1 *Journal of Corporate Law Studies* 21.

In very outline terms the 'London Approach' involves two phases. The first phase is where a company notifies its banks that it is in trouble and would like to initiate what is called a 'workout', whereby the company attempts to trade out of its difficulties, hopefully with the support of its bankers. The banks involved then collectively agree a form of moratorium in favour of the company. The banks will not take any enforcement actions against the company and existing lines of credit are kept open. Further working capital may need to be provided to keep the company going. Any such new money is given priority status over pre-existing debt. During this period, a team of accountants investigate the company's position and the team's findings are used by the banks collectively to decide what to do next. If the business can be saved, some restructuring will usually be called for. If the business cannot be saved, the costs incurred up to this point are shared *pro rata* between all the participating banks.

If a rescue is feasible, one bank will lead the restructuring negotiations. The lead bank will also act as a go-between for the company, the accountants and the other banks. The ultimate result of the negotiations may be a typical compromise of debt or some form of debt equity swap (as occurred with Marconi), or frequently something considerably more complicated. The banks will share the financial benefit of allowing the company to avoid formal insolvency. The 'London Approach' is a collective procedure which benefits all its participants, in that although a particular bank may benefit from sitting on its legal rights in certain situations, over a period of time the adoption of the cooperative 'London Approach' prevents any huge losses to any particular bank at any particular time and leads to many businesses being turned around. All the investigations and negotiations are kept secret so as not to destroy confidence in the company involved.

The 'London Approach' would appear to be extremely successful. Although no official figures are available for this secret process, an idea of its success may be gauged by the relatively small number of large companies which enter formal insolvency procedures.

10.3 Formal arrangements for companies

10.3.1 *Schemes of arrangement under the Companies Act 1985*

Under section 425 of the Companies Act 1985 a company can enter into a scheme of arrangement which is binding on all its creditors. Although potentially an alternative to a CVA, such a scheme is more complex and cumbersome and will usually take a good deal longer to set up than a CVA. A section 425 scheme tends to be used only in respect of reasonably large companies and can involve full-scale company reconstructions, for example, a reduction of the company's capital. There is no provision for a moratorium[2] on creditor actions during the planning period for a scheme and so it may be necessary to combine a scheme with first putting the company into administration.[3] This would prevent any particular creditor from acting to frustrate the purposes of the scheme. In practice, a scheme is often entered into by first putting the company into liquidation or provisional liquidation and asking the court to stay all proceedings against the company while the liquidator acts to obtain the approval of the company, its creditors and the court.[4]

The procedure to enter into a section 425 scheme is court led. It is commenced with an application to the court. The company, a creditor, a member or a liquidator (if there is one) may apply to the court. The scheme may affect the respective rights of the company and its creditors (or a class of creditors) or the company and its members (or a class of them). The court may order that meetings of creditors and/or members affected by the proposed scheme are summoned. The meetings must approve the scheme by a majority of three-quarters in value of the creditors or members present and voting. After the meetings have approved the scheme there is a second hearing. If the court sanctions the scheme at this hearing, it becomes binding on all the company's creditors or members (as the case may be).

In most corporate insolvency situations, there appear to be few advantages of using a section 425 scheme rather than a CVA. Prior to recent changes to CVAs, it was suggested[5] that a section 425 scheme could, in certain circumstances, be of more use than a CVA, as the scheme binds all the company's creditors, whereas a CVA could fail to bind creditors who were not given notice of the creditors' meeting. The recent changes to CVAs make this potential advantage far less likely. A CVA now binds all creditors entitled to vote at the creditors' meeting (whether or not present or represented at the meeting in question), or who would have been so entitled if they had had notice of the meeting. It seems unlikely that a scheme would now bind a wider number of creditors than a CVA. Despite the disadvantages of being more expensive and time consuming than a CVA, section 425 schemes are still used and sometimes deemed more appropriate where the company is being reconstructed.[6]

---

[2] See e.g., *Booth v Walkden Spinning and Manufacturing Co Ltd* [1909] 2 KB 368.

[3] See e.g., *Re Polly Peck International plc* [1996] BCC 486.

[4] If a petition for winding up has been presented to the court and a scheme is proposed, the court will usually order the winding-up proceedings to stand over and stay proceedings against the company pending the approval or otherwise of the scheme (*Bowkett v Fuller's United Electric Works Ltd* [1923] 1 KB 160.

[5] R. Goode, *Principles of Corporate Insolvency Law*, 2nd edn, London: Sweet & Maxwell (1997) at 22–23.

[6] See e.g., *Re Equitable Life Assurance Society* [2002] 2 BCLC 510 and B. Isaacs, 'The Equitable Life Scheme of Arrangement Sanction Hearing: Classes, Human Rights and Fairness' (2002) 15 *Insolvency Intelligence* 49.

10.4 Formal arrangements for individuals

10.4.1 *County court administration orders*

At the other end of the scale to the 'London Approach' and section 425 schemes is the county court administration order,[7] which may only be made in relation to very small-scale individual debtors. The administration order was first introduced by the Bankruptcy Act 1883 and, to a large extent, it appears that it has never really fulfilled its potential for benefiting small debtors.

The current regime is to be found in the County Courts Act 1984. Under section 112 of this Act, an administration order may be made over the estate of an individual whose total indebtedness does not exceed £5,000. This total amount of debt would usually include within it, for example, any mortgage or car loan.[8] In consequence, the administration order is only of use where the debtor owes small debts and has no, or only negligible, assets. In order for the court to make an order, the debtor must be subject to a court judgment which the debtor is unable to pay. The order is in effect an instalment payment plan. The application for the order can only be made by the debtor. The application must state whether or not the debtor is proposing to pay creditors in full, or if full payment is not intended, how much will be paid. The debtor will be required to make regular payments into court of an agreed amount and to specify this amount in the application. A list of creditors must be provided to the court and this list will be included in a schedule to the order.

The order provides for such payments over such period as to what the court seems practicable in the circumstances. The court may make provision for future earnings or income to be brought within the order. The order may be reviewed periodically if the debtor's circumstances change. The order prevents creditors, whose names are included in the schedule to the order or whose names were notified to the court prior to the order being made, from enforcing their debts against the debtor without leave of the court (section 114 of the County Courts Act 1984). The order also prevents creditors whose names are included in the

---

[7] This is not to be confused with the administration order available for companies under the Insolvency Act 1986.

[8] Assuming that the debtor has defaulted under such loans, this will normally result in the whole of the debt becoming payable on demand and this will usually take the total debt outside the £5,000 limit.

[9] Section 112(4) County Courts Act 1984. The exception to this rule is that a creditor owed more than £1,500 may petition within 28 days of being notified of the order. Under section 115(1) execution may be levied if the debtor's assets exceed £50 in value. A landlord's power to distrain for unpaid rent for up to six months prior to the date of the order also remains (section 116).

schedule to the order from petitioning for the debtor's bankruptcy[9] without leave of the court.

The court acts as an intermediary between the debtor and the creditors. Money paid into court is distributed by the court to the creditors according to the terms of the order. The court makes a deduction to cover administration costs of up to 10p in the pound of the money received. Creditors are generally treated equally under the order. There is no preferential debts regime applicable to administration orders. If all the creditors are paid out the order is superseded and the debtor is discharged from all the debts owed to the scheduled creditors (section 117 of the County Courts Act 1984).

There are a number of weaknesses associated with county court administration orders. Perhaps the most obvious is that the limit on the debtor's overall debt is set at £5,000. If this limit was lifted, it is likely that such orders would become far more popular. A number of other difficulties have been identified and largely remedied by the provisions contained in section 13 of the Courts and Legal Services Act 1990. The problem is these new provisions have still not been brought into force. Once in force, they will allow a debtor to apply for an order even if no judgment has been obtained. A creditor with a judgment against the debtor would be able to apply for an order. The court itself, on its own motion, could make an order. The upper limit on indebtedness would go, allowing far greater access to the order. An order would be limited to a duration of three years, ostensibly tying its lifetime to that of a normal bankruptcy under the pre-2002 system. The basic idea of this provision is to persuade creditors that they are getting no worse a deal than they would under a bankruptcy.

The court would also have the option, under the proposed new system, of imposing an order restricting enforcement of a judgment against the debtor, rather than making an administration order. Continued supply to the debtor of mains gas, electricity and water would be protected during the period the administration order is in force. An administration order could contain a composition of the debts owed. This provision will allow the court to order that the debtor's creditors are paid a lesser amount than that owed.

These amendments may never see the light of day. The county court administration order is one of many matters being considered by the Lord Chancellor as part of his long-running review of the civil enforcement system. It may remain in place with some amendments or it may end up being replaced by some new mechanism.

References

Allen & Overy, 'Secured creditors and CVAs' (2002) 13 *Practical Law for Companies* 80.

Allen & Overy, 'Rent and receivers' (2002) 13 *Practical Law for Companies* 84.

Armour, J. and Deakin, S., 'Norms in Private Insolvency: The "London Approach" to the Resolution of Financial Distress' (2001) 1 *Journal of Corporate Law Studies* 21.

Bailey, E., Groves, H. and Smith, C., *Corporate Insolvency Law and Practice*, 2nd edn, London: Butterworths (2001).

Baister, S., 'Voluntary arrangements – the failures' (2002) 99 LSG 37.

Berry, C., Bailey, E. and Schaw-Miller, S., *Personal Insolvency Law – Law and Practice*, 3rd edn, London: Butterworths (2001).

Berg, A., 'Duties of a Mortgagee and a Receiver' [1993] JBL 213.

Bloxam, P. and Tilbrook, L., 'Productivity and Enterprise: Insolvency – A Second Chance' (2002) 5 *Receivers, Administrators and Liquidators Quarterly* 59.

Brier, J., 'Exiting administrations (Part 2) – when the purposes of an administration order may be achieved by avoiding compulsory liquidation' (1999) 15 *Insolvency Law and Practice* 44.

Elboz, S., '*T&D Industries plc* – the seven principles – new guidance for administrators in disposing of assets' (1999) 15 *Insolvency Law and Practice* 183.

Farrar, J., 'Recent Developments in the Law of Receivers' (1975) JBL 23.

Farrar, J., 'The Crystallisation of a Floating Charge' (1976) 40 Conv 397.

Fealy, M., 'Receivers' Duties: a return to orthodoxy' [1994] NILQ 61.

Fletcher, I., *The Law of Insolvency*, 3rd edn, London: Sweet & Maxwell (2002).

Frieze, S., 'Exit from Administration' (2001) 14 *Insolvency Intelligence* 41.

Goode, R., *Principles of Corporate Insolvency Law*, 2nd edn, London: Sweet & Maxwell (1997).

Green, T., 'Receivership – a comparative summary' (1994) 10 *Insolvency Law and Practice* 143.

Gregory, R. and Walton, P., 'Fixed and Floating Charges – A Revelation' [2001] LMCLQ 123.

Gregory, R. and Walton, P., 'Brumark and the Privy Council – was the Curia In?' (2002) 5 *Receivers, Administrators and Liquidators Quarterly* 25.

Griffiths, N., 'Voluntary Arrangements after Somji' (2001) 17 *Insolvency Law and Practice* 104.

Harper, A., 'Mortgagees and County Court Administration Orders' (1997) 13 *Insolvency Law and Practice* 43.

Hunter, M., 'The Nature and Functions of a Rescue Culture' (1999) JBL 491.

Isaacs, B., 'The Equitable Life Scheme of Arrangement Sanction Hearing: Classes, Human Rights and Fairness' (2002) 15 *Insolvency Intelligence* 49.

Keay, A. and Walton, P., 'Preferential Debts: An Empirical Study' (1999) 3 *Insolvency Lawyer* 112.

Lightman, G. and Moss, G., *The Law of Receivers and Administrators of Companies*, 3rd edn, London: Sweet & Maxwell (2000).

Manson, E., 'The Growth of the Debenture' (1897) 13 LQR 418.

McCormack, G., *Proprietary Claims and Insolvency* London: Sweet & Maxwell (1999).

McCormack, G., 'Receiverships and the rescue culture' (2000) 2 CofiLR 229.

McDonald, I. and Moujalli, D., 'A Very English Concept: the Receiver Appointed Out Of Court' (2001) 14 *Insolvency Intelligence* 76.

McKnight, A., 'The Reform of Corporate Insolvency Law in Great Britain – the Enterprise Bill 2002' (2002) 17 JIBL 324.

Milman, D., 'Receivers as Agents' (1981) 44 MLR 658.

Milman, D. and Durrant, C., *Corporate Insolvency: Law and Practice*, 3rd edn, London: Sweet & Maxwell (1999).

Moss, G., 'Administrators' Duties and Liabilities' (1999) 12 *Insolvency Intelligence* 25.

Pennington, R., *Pennington's Corporate Insolvency Law*, 2nd edn, London: Butterworths (1997).

Picarda, H., *The Law Relating to Receivers Managers and Administrators*, 3rd edn, London: Butterworths (2000).

Picarda, H., 'Receivers and the duty of care: a short walk in the foothills of *Medforth v Blake*' (2002) 5 *Receivers, Administrators and Liquidators Quarterly* 1.

Pond, K., 'New rules and new roles for the individual voluntary arrangement' (2002) 18 *Insolvency Law and Practice* 9.

Roberts, H., '*T&D Industries plc* revisited: further guidance for administrators in disposing of assets' (2000) 16 *Insolvency Law and Practice* 61.

Sealy, L., 'Mortgagees and receivers – a duty of care resurrected and extended' (2000) 59 CLJ 31.

Smith, A. and Neill, M., 'The Insolvency Act 2000' (2001) 17 *Insolvency Law and Practice* 84.

Stevenson, M., 'The Enterprise Bill 2002 – a move towards a rescue Culture' (2002) 15 *Insolvency Intelligence* 51.

Thomson, H., 'A practical view of the receiver's relationship with other office holders – the liquidator' (2000) 16 *Insolvency Law and Practice* 74.

Tribe, J., 'The role of directors in receivership: who should bring actions for loss suffered by the company and defend any counterclaim?' (2001) 4 *Receivers, Administrators and Liquidators Quarterly* 335.

Walton, P., '*Buchan v Secretary of State for Employment*' (1997) 3 *Receivers, Administrators and Liquidators Quarterly* 155.

Walton, P., 'Voluntary Arrangements – the Nature of the Beast' (1998) 3 *Receivers, Administrators and Liquidators Quarterly* 277.

West, I., 'Exiting administrations (Part 1) – who bears the cost?' (1999) 15 *Insolvency Law and Practice* 42.

Part III

Provisional Liquidation

Before we move on to terminal insolvency administrations, we should address an administration which can be most important and which can be regarded as an interim administration. Provisional liquidation is a form of administration that can be used to ensure a company is controlled by an office-holder while winding up proceedings or some rescue option is being considered by the debtor and the creditors. There is an analogous procedure in bankruptcy, although not used anywhere near as frequently. This involves the appointment of an interim receiver after the presentation of a bankruptcy petition and before a bankruptcy order is made (section 286). The task of the interim receiver is very similar to that of a provisional liquidator.

Throughout this Part, except where indicated to the contrary, any reference to 'the Act' or to section numbers will be references to the Insolvency Act 1986. Except where indicated to the contrary, any reference to 'the Rules' or to rule numbers will be references to the Insolvency Rules 1986 (SI 1986/1925).

Chapter 11

Provisional Liquidation[1]

11.1 Introduction

Before dealing with the administration of liquidation, it is appropriate and timely to consider an administration that might occur shortly before the advent of liquidation, namely provisional liquidation. After the presentation of proceedings to obtain a court order for the liquidation of a company, an application may be made for the appointment of a provisional liquidator; the court has the power, pursuant to section 135(1) of the Insolvency Act ('the Act'),[2] to make such an appointment (section 135(2)). The effect of the appointment is to grant interim control of the company to a liquidator – control until the final determination of the liquidation proceedings.[3]

The most prevalent reason for applying for the appointment of a provisional liquidator is that there is a perception that the assets and affairs of the company are in jeopardy, primarily because the directors and/or shareholders may dissipate the assets while the liquidation proceedings are pending and that, if the assets are left in the hands of the company, the creditors might be disadvantaged if the company is eventually liquidated.

The power to appoint a provisional liquidator is a draconian power (*Re Forrester & Lamego Ltd* [1997] 2 BCLC 155 at 158), as it involves a serious intrusion on the company; the management of the company is effectively under the control of the person appointed. Practically speaking, the appointment is likely to paralyse the company commercially (*Re London, Hamburg & Continental Exchange Bank, Emmerson's Case* [1866] LR 2 Eq 231

---

[1] For a more detailed discussion, see A. Keay, *McPherson's Law of Company Liquidation*, London: Sweet & Maxwell (2001), Chapter 6. The following material draws on that chapter.

[2] All references to sections in this chapter are to sections in the Insolvency Act unless the contrary is indicated.

[3] See *Re Forrester & Lamego Ltd* [1997] 2 BCLC 155 at 158.

at 237). Therefore, courts have said that if other measures would be adequate to preserve the status quo, they should be implemented instead (*Constantinidis v JGL Trading Pty Ltd* (1995) 17 ACSR 625 at 635, 647).

Courts must consider, when hearing applications, the degree of urgency, the need established by the applicant and the balance of convenience (*Re WF Fearman Ltd* (1987) 4 BCC 139). The courts must balance the interests of the creditors against that of the company, as well as considering the public interest (*Re Pinstripe Farming Co Ltd* [1996] 2 BCLC 295 at 300; [1996] BCC 913 at 917). The court has a wide and unfettered discretion whether or not to make an appointment (*Re Union Accident Insurance Co Ltd* [1972] 1 All ER 1105 at 1109).

Effective liquidation proceedings must be in existence and they must disclose a good ground for a winding up. While not a rule of law, a provisional liquidator is not usually appointed unless it is likely, given the material before the court, that a liquidation order will be made (*ASC v Solomon* (1995) 19 ACSR 73 at 80). Appointment of a provisional liquidator is sometimes so critical that an application for it is lodged contemporaneously with the liquidation proceedings.

Although often the precursor to liquidation, the appointment of a provisional liquidator is not regarded as the beginning of a liquidation (*Object Design Inc v Object Design Australia Pty Ltd* (1997) 24 ASCR 678). Provisional liquidation is a separate administration to liquidation.

11.2 The applicant

Rule 4.25 of the Insolvency Rules provides that the following are able to apply for the appointment:

- The petitioner.
- A creditor of the company.
- A contributory of the company.
- The company.
- The Secretary of State for Trade and Industry.
- Any person who is entitled to petition for the winding up of the company.

11.2.1 *Creditors*

The majority of cases have involved a creditor as the applicant for an order. While it does not have to be the same creditor who has sought the winding up of the company, generally it will be (*Brimaud v Honeysett Instant Print*

Pty Ltd (1988) 6 ACLC 942). An example of a case where a creditor might make an application is where the directors continue to misuse funds for their own benefit or are conducting reckless ventures thereby putting company assets at risk.

In creditor applications, where the company neither consents nor opposes the application, creditors must establish a *prima facie* case for the appointment. Where there is opposition to the order, stronger evidence will be required (*Re Club Mediterranean Pty Ltd* (1975) 1 ACLR 36).

11.2.2 *Contributories*

Applications by contributories may come where there is concern over the actions of the directors, such as acting improperly or recklessly and consequently wasting assets.[4]

It is not unlikely to find contributories seeking such an order when they have petitioned for a winding up under section 122(1)(g), a provision that allows a petition for a winding-up order on the basis that it is just and equitable that the company be wound up.[5] These kinds of petitions are sometimes presented when there could be concern over a deadlock between directors.

11.2.3 *The company*

Such an application is unusual. It may occur where the company has petitioned for its own winding up. A petition might be presented as a voluntary liquidation, is not possible due to deadlock, or cannot be initiated as swiftly as necessary and the directors believe it is critical that there be an independent administrator appointed,[6] such as where directors might be liable for wrongful trading, pursuant to section 214.

11.2.4 *The Secretary of State for Trade and Industry*

The Secretary of State for Trade and Industry is able to initiate winding up proceedings, and has presented a significant number of petitions for winding up, particularly in recent years.[7] Because of the type of cases that are frequently involved the Secretary of State will often apply, in order to protect the public, for the appointment of a provisional liquidator in relation to the company's affairs.

---

[4] For an example, see the Australian case of *Re JN Taylor Holdings Ltd* (1991) 9 ACLC 1.
[5] For a consideration of the provision, see A. Keay, *McPherson's Law of Company Liquidation* at 190–207.
[6] A. Keay, *McPherson's Law of Company Liquidation* at 254.
[7] See A. Keay, 'Public Interest Petitions' (1999) 20 Co Law 296.

11.3 The application

Given the potentially far-reaching implications that an appointment can have, they have to be made to a companies court judge. If there is some doubt concerning whether the ground for winding up alleged in the petition will be successful, a court might choose to hear the application in camera (*Re London and Norwich Investments Ltd* [1988] BCLC 226), that is, in private.

The application must reveal a good ground before an appointment will be made (*Re McLennon Holdings Pty Ltd* (1983) 1 ACLC 786). A court has a discretion whether to appoint and, if there are sufficient grounds, make the appointment on what terms it deems fit (rule 4.25(4)). Where an appointment is made, the court must give notice forthwith to the official receiver (rule 4.25A(1)). If the provisional liquidator is not the official receiver, then the court will give notice to the provisional liquidator at the same time as it gives notice to the official receiver (rule 4.25A(2)).

Applications have been made *ex parte*,[8] but they are exceptional and the general rule is that an order will not be made on such an application, as the company should be served with notice of the application, unless this is not practical (*Re London and Manchester Industrial Association* (1875) 1 Ch D 466).[9]

11.4 The basis for an appointment

Section 135 fails to set out any grounds as to when an appointment may be made (*Re Forrester & Lamego Ltd* [1997] 2 BCLC 155 at 158), so we are thrown back to the case law. A court is likely to begin its deliberations from the position that the appointment would be an exceptional step. In *Re Tamaris plc*,[10] Neuberger J stated that he was wary about making orders as he was concerned that it might open the floodgates, with petitioners thinking that an appointment would be made as a matter of course.

It is impossible to compose an exhaustive set of circumstances in which an appointment will be made (*Re Club Mediterranean Pty Ltd* (1975) 1 ACLR 36 at 39), but it can be said that the most common situation that will lead to an appointment is where the assets of the company are clearly in jeopardy (*Re Marseilles Extension Railway and Land Co* [1867] WN 68; *Re A Company (No. 003102 of 1991)* [1991] BCLC 539). The need for urgency

---

[8] For example, see *Re A Company (No 007070 of 1996)* [1997] 2 BCLC 139 at 142.

[9] For a case where the court accepted an *ex parte* application, see *Re A Company (No 007070 of 1996)* [1997] 2 BCLC 139.

[10] Unreported, but discussed in E. Husband, 'Application by a petitioning company for the appointment of a provisional liquidator' (2000) 16 IL&P 3 at 4–5.

will usually cause a court to act (*Re Hammersmith Town Hall Company* (1877) 6 Ch D 112). Other cases which will precipitate an order will be: paralysis of the company because of disputes between shareholders or directors; a conflict of interest that a director has between his or her own personal interest and the company's interest, and the affairs of the company are in jeopardy (*Re Club Mediterranean Pty Ltd* ((1975) 1 ACLR 360); or where there is a need for a speedy and urgent investigation of the affairs of the company (*Re A Company (No 007070 of 1996)* ([1997] 2 BCLC 139 at 142).

It will be noted that there has been, in the discussion thus far, emphasis on appointment because of a well-grounded fear concerning a dissipation of assets. However, it must be stated that there is no authority demanding that this fear be established before an application is successful. For instance, in *Re Highfield Commodities Ltd* ([1984] 1 WLR 149; [1984] BCC 99, 277) a provisional liquidator was appointed in circumstances where the company had misled investors so as to induce them to make risky speculations.[11] On a frequent number of occasions petitions presented by the Secretary of State for Trade and Industry have been followed by successful applications for an appointment, because of allegations of misconduct made against the directors.[12]

The essential thing that an application must establish is that there is a need for an interim control of the company pending the winding up of the company and only an appointment will ensure the maintenance of the status quo (*Re Dry Docks Corporation of London* (1888) 39 Ch D 306).

A court might consider some of the following in deciding whether to make an appointment (*Re Mackay Investments Pty Ltd* (1996) 14 ACLC 319 at 321):

- whether the assets will be dissipated in the interim period between the presentation (filing) of the petition to wind up and the winding-up order being made;
- whether the petitioner has established a *prima facie* case for a winding up of the company;
- whether the applicant has established a *prima facie* case that he or she has the necessary standing to bring the petition to wind up.

A provisional liquidator may be appointed even where a voluntary liquidation is being conducted.[13] An order may well not be made, as it would add to the costs, if there are no grounds for suggesting that the public interest demanded a thorough investigation of the company. If an application follows the presentation of a petition for the winding up of

---

[11] Also, see *Re Comstrad Ltd* (unreported, September 27, 1995, High Court, Carnwath J) and referred to in *Re Forrester & Lamego Ltd* [1997] 2 BCLC 155 at 159.

[12] For example, *Re a Company (No 007070 of 1996)* [1997] 2 BCLC 139.

[13] For example, see *Securities and Investments Board v Lancashire and Yorkshire Portfolio Management Ltd* [1992] BCC 381; *Re A Company (No 007070 of 1996)* [1997] 2 BCLC 139.

a company which is already in voluntary liquidation, the court may appoint a provisional liquidator where the liquidator is in a position of conflict of interest, or is also the liquidator of a related company which is in voluntary liquidation and the affairs of the two companies are intertwined (*Re P Turner (Wilsden) Ltd* [1987] BCLC 149 (CA); *Re Pinstripe Farming Co Ltd* [1996] 2 BCLC 295; [1996] BCC 913).

In ending this section of the chapter, it is appropriate to emphasise the point that courts have a discretion as to whether they make appointments and it is not possible to give a list of situations where an appointment will ensue (*ASC v Solomon* (1995) 19 ACSR 73).

11.5 The order

Courts have a discretion as to the form of order that they will make if the application is successful. According to the Rules, the order must identify the functions that the provisional liquidator is to fulfil in relation to the affairs of the company (rule 4.26(1)). In addition it should state the nature and a short description of the property of which possession is to be taken.[14]

Orders will usually circumscribe the liquidator's powers so that he or she will only take custody of company assets and, where appropriate, carry on the business of the company. Sometimes the appointee is given all of the powers of a liquidator.[15] The courts are given power to confer the functions on a provisional liquidator which they feel are appropriate (section 135(4)) and may, in the order, limit the powers he or she may carry out (section 135(5)). If the applicant believes that a provisional liquidator should have unusual powers and can make out a case, these powers should be carefully and clearly stated in the order.

11.6 The effect of an appointment

There is no change to the company upon the making of an order in the sense that the company continues to exist and its identity is not altered (*P & C Connell Pty Ltd (prov liq app) v The Electicity Trust of South Australia* (1990) 8 ACLC 975 at 979) and there is no termination of the contracts of

---

[14] P. Davies *et al*, *Palmer's Corporate Insolvency*, vol 1, London: Sweet & Maxwell (1986) at para 1.111/1.

[15] A. Keay, *McPherson's Law of Company Liquidation* at 263.

the company (*BCCI v Malik* [1996] BCC 15 at 17). The main effects are, probably, that: the directors are displaced (*Re Oriental Bank Corp; Ex parte Guillemin* (1884) 28 Ch D 634; *In re Mawcon Ltd* [1969] 1 WLR 78; *In re Union Insurance Co Ltd* [1972] 1 WLR 640); the liquidator takes control of the company (*Amfrank Nominees Pty Ltd v Connell* (1990) 8 ACLC 319); and the liquidator takes custody or control of all the property of the company (section 144(1)).

As with liquidation and administration, when a company is in provisional liquidation no proceedings can be commenced or prosecuted against the company or in relation to its property without the leave of the court (section 130(2)). As one would expect, secured creditors, however, can enforce their security and may appoint a receiver and manager.

While it would not be regularly done, a provisional liquidator may apply, under section 236, to examine officers of the company, any persons known or suspected to have in their possession any company property or supposed to be indebted to the company, or any persons the provisional liquidator thinks are capable of giving information concerning the promotion, formation, business, dealings, affairs or property of the company.[16]

11.7 The provisional liquidator

Either the official receiver or any other fit person (section 135(2)) may be appointed as provisional liquidator, although in practice it is nearly always the former. The latter is a reference to an insolvency practitioner who is qualified to act in relation to the company.[17]

As he or she is appointed by the court the provisional liquidator is an officer of the court and is under a duty not to mislead the court (*Re Western National Earthmoving Corporation Pty Ltd* (1998) 16 ACLC 885). Unlike administrative receivers, a provisional liquidator does not represent any creditor or class of creditors, rather he or she acts pursuant to the direction of the court (*Re BCCI (No 2)* [1992] BCLC 579).

The primary role of the provisional liquidator is to preserve the status quo pending the hearing of the winding-up petition so that the company's assets will be available to those entitled to them (*Re Dry Docks Corporation of London* (1888) 39 Ch D 306; *Pacific & General Insurance Ltd (in liq) v Home & Overseas Insurance Co Ltd* [1997] BCC 400 at 406). Hence, in exercising

---

[16] See below at 366 for a discussion of examinations pursuant to section 236.
[17] See section 390. For a recent example where an insolvency practitioner was appointed, see *In re Grey Marlin Ltd* [1999] 2 BCLC 658. For an explanation as to who can act, see Chapter 4.

powers conferred by the court, he or she must keep the role as preserver of the status quo in mind. It might be appropriate for the liquidator to curtail the company's business and thereby reduce costs, safeguarding the company's assets (*Re Union Accident Insurance Co Ltd* [1972] 1 All ER 1105).

The provisional liquidator may invoke court powers so as to require any person who has in his or her control or possession any property, books, papers or records to which the company appears to be entitled to give them up to the provisional liquidator (rule 4.185(1)).

While the function of the provisional liquidator is primarily to take hold of the assets of the company and maintain the status quo, it might be in the ultimate interests of the creditors and members of the company that the assets of the company be sold off quickly. This can only be done where the provisional liquidator has the power to sell. It would probably be prudent for the provisional liquidator to seek court directions where there is no legal obligation to sell but where it is believed that it is the correct course of action (*Northbourne Developments Pty Ltd v Reiby Chambers Pty Ltd* (1990) 8 ACLC 39).

It would appear that while the main task of a provisional liquidator is to preserve the status quo, if appropriate, he or she might be entitled to reduce a company's liability for wages and rent by discontinuing parts of the company's business, as this relates to protecting the assets (*Re Union Accident Insurance Co Ltd* [1972] 1 All ER 1105 at 1112).

In the same vein as a liquidator, a provisional liquidator has imposed on him or her fiduciary duties to the company. The provisional liquidator is the agent of the company and is able to employ agents, but, like liquidators and directors of companies, he or she is not permitted to delegate the duties of a provisional liquidator (*Star v Silvia* (1994) 12 ACLC 600).

If the petition which has been presented against the company does not lead to a winding-up order, the provisional liquidator may retain out of the company's assets such sums or property as may be required to meet remuneration and expenses, except where a court directs to the contrary (rule 4.30(3A)). It is not usual for the court to order that an unsuccessful petitioner pay the costs of the provisional liquidator, but there have been cases where courts have made such orders (*Re Walter L Jacob & Co Ltd* (1987) 3 BCC 532).

11.8 The termination of the appointment

The provisional liquidation usually terminates when either there is a winding-up order, or the petition to wind up is dismissed or withdrawn (*Re Kingscroft Insurance Co Ltd* [1994] 2 BCLC 80). But, of course, there are other events which will see the provisional liquidation terminated. Chief among these is if the provisional liquidator is removed by order of the court (section 172(1)). An application to remove might come from the creditors if they are unhappy at the way that the provisional liquidator is discharging his or her duties. Certainly, if a majority of creditors support removal, the court will take that into account, but the view of the creditors is not decisive (*Re Giant Resources Ltd* [1991] 1 Qd R 107 at 115). Circumstances which will see a provisional liquidator removed includes where he or she is subject to: conflicts of interest; bias; or an appearance of bias.

Termination of an appointment can be ordered by a court on its own motion or on the application of the appointee, the petitioner, a creditor or a contributory (rules 4.25(1) and 4.31(1)).

In cases where a winding-up order is made, the provisional liquidator might well become the liquidator. If not, the provisional liquidator must, where the liquidator is not the official receiver, account to the liquidator and transfer to him or her any money, property, books and papers of the company over which he or she has custody (section 234(2)).

References

Davies, P., *et al., Palmer's Corporate Insolvency*, vol 1, London: Sweet & Maxwell (1986).

Husband, E., 'Application by a petitioning company for the appointment of a provisional liquidator' (2000) 16 *Insolvency Law and Practice* 3.

Keay, A., 'Public Interest Petitions' (1999) 20 Co Law 296.

Keay, A., *McPherson's Law of Company Liquidation*, London: Sweet & Maxwell (2001).

Moss, G. and Phillips, M., 'Provisional liquidators: new uses for an old remedy' (1993) 6 *Insolvency Intelligence* 1.

Part IV

Winding Up

In Part II we considered the insolvency of companies, but in the context of them being able, by taking some action, to continue to carry on business and eventually extricate themselves from their financial problems. We call this corporate rescue. Unfortunately, not all companies can be rescued. First, there are those which enter some process in order to see if rescue is possible, but they continue to fall deeper into debt or simply cannot make any headway and meet their responsibilities under the terms of any rescue package. Second, other companies are not even able, because of the fact that their financial position is so bad, to consider some rescue process. With both types of companies the only thing that can be done is to end the life of the company. This is known as dissolution. Before being dissolved the company will enter a process known as winding up or liquidation and this process prepares the company for dissolution.

Ever since the mid-nineteenth century, companies have been able to be wound up. Over the years winding up has been the most prevalent way of resolving the insolvency of a company. At times, particularly during recessions such as occurred at the end of the late 1980s and the early 1990s, there have, in fact, been a significant number of liquidations, primarily because of insolvency. And notwithstanding the focus on rescue in recent years and the advent of new insolvency administrations, such as those considered in Part II, as well as their greater employment and the relatively good economic conditions enjoyed in the past few years, liquidation still remains the most frequently employed way of dealing with insolvency. One only needs to point to the statistics for 2001–2002. In that year there were a total of 18,627 liquidations in Great Britain, made up of 2,744 members' voluntary liquidations, 10,676 creditors' voluntary liquidations and 5,170 compulsory liquidations (DTI Company Report for 2001–2002, p 36). It is probably fair to say that in general terms all of the companies which went into creditors' voluntary winding up and most of those entering compulsory winding up were insolvent.

In this Part we examine the primary aspects of winding up, from the time when a company enters the process until the time when it is dissolved (in effect, corporate death). In our discussion we use 'winding up' and 'liquidation' interchangeably, notwithstanding the different origins of the two expressions. In law and practice no effective distinction is made between them.

Throughout this Part, except where indicated to the contrary, any reference to 'the Act' or to section numbers will be references to the Insolvency Act 1986. Except where indicated to the contrary, any reference to 'the Rules' or to the rule numbers will be references to the Insolvency Rules 1986 (SI 1986/1925).

Chapter 12

Introduction to Winding Up

12.1 The nature of winding up

Although companies have perpetual succession and cannot die as humans can, it may be appropriate that a company's existence ceases. The end of a company comes when it is dissolved. Liquidation is the process that prepares a company for dissolution. Winding up does not consist of an order that a company be wound up; rather, it means the process whereby the assets of a company are collected and realised, the resulting proceeds are applied in discharging all its debts and liabilities and any balance which remains after paying the costs and expenses of winding up is distributed among the members according to their rights and interests, or otherwise dealt with as the constitution of the company directs.[1] Although, naturally, where an insolvent company is being wound up there will be no assets that will be available for distribution to the members.

Liquidation is a legislative creation, presently regulated, primarily, by the Insolvency Act.[2] The provisions which regulate, and have regulated in the past, liquidations originate from bankruptcy laws; so many of the concepts provided for in bankruptcy have been, over the years, pressed into service with the necessary adaptations to allow for the company form. The first Statute that regulated the winding up of companies was the Companies (Winding Up) Act of 1844.[3]

While the most prevalent reason for liquidation is insolvency (and this chapter focuses on liquidations resulting from insolvency), there are other

---

[1] A. Keay, *McPherson's Law of Company Liquidation* London: Sweet & Maxwell (2001) at 1. See *Ayerst v C & K (Construction) Ltd* [1976] AC 167 for a useful discussion by the House of Lords as to the nature of liquidation.

[2] The Companies Act 1985 is of some relevance also.

[3] For a discussion of the history of the law of winding up, see A. Keay, *McPherson's Law of Company Liquidation*, Chapter 1.

reasons why companies go into liquidation. In other words, companies that are solvent may be wound up. For instance, the controllers of a company may wish to sell its business but the buyer may only want the assets and not the company form. The company's assets will be transferred and unless the controllers have a use for the corporate shell they may wish to dissolve it.[4] Often such a corporate shell is sold to someone who wishes to incorporate a company. It is usually less expensive to purchase a dormant company than to incorporate a fresh company. A second instance where a solvent company can be wound up is where a winding up is petitioned for, under section 122(1)(g), on the basis that it is just and equitable that this occurs.[5]

At the outset the point needs to be made again that the word 'liquidation' is used interchangeably, in practice, with 'winding up' and in this book no distinction will be made between the two terms.

Where a company is wound up because of insolvency, the process is initiated because the company has no realistic chance of resolving its financial malaise by continuing to carry on business. In most cases, some form of corporate rescue is not workable (or too expensive) because of the severity of the company's financial difficulties. In such cases, the general unsecured creditors will acknowledge that they will not receive the full amount of their debts but know that the company will be wound up equitably and in an orderly fashion by an independent person, the liquidator.

Liquidation is an essential aspect of corporate insolvency law as there must be some process available for administering the affairs of a company which is insolvent and where either the members wish to resolve the problem of insolvency (or, in some cases, other difficulties such as deadlock in the company), or one or more of the creditors want to see the company placed in the hands of an independent person and the company's assets sold up to satisfy (partially) the debts owed. It is undoubtedly the case that, notwithstanding the greater use made of administration under Part II of the Insolvency Act and company voluntary arrangements, liquidation continues to be the most prevalent form of insolvency administration for companies.

As stated earlier, liquidation derives from the concept of bankruptcy for individuals and many bankruptcy principles have been adopted by liquidation law. But, the ultimate aim of liquidation and bankruptcy differ. While the latter's is to provide for the discharge of a debtor's liabilities and allow him or her to have a fresh start in life, the aim of liquidation is to prepare companies for their death in the form of dissolution.

---

[4] This will follow a members' voluntary liquidation.

[5] For discussion of winding up on this ground, see A. Keay, *McPherson's Law of Company Liquidation* at 190–207.

Liquidation is, like bankruptcy, a procedure of an inherently collective nature[6] in that each creditor exchanges the right to take action to enforce the debt owed, for a right to share in the collective proceedings administered by the liquidator. That is, the primary beneficiary of the proceedings is the general group of unsecured creditors, each of whom is affected by the bankruptcy or winding up, albeit to different degrees.[7] Therefore, winding up should not be seen as a means of enforcing a judgment[8] and courts will not permit a creditor to obtain a collateral personal advantage from liquidation.[9] When a company is being wound up because of insolvency the members of the company have no interest in the assets (*Ayerst v C & K (Construction) Ltd* [1976] AC 167 (HL)) – the process involved is a collective procedure to bring about the distribution of the assets to the creditors according to their pre-liquidation entitlements. If there was no collective procedure, then creditors would enforce their debts and it would produce a 'first come, first served' situation that would be disorderly.

12.2 The purposes of winding up

The purposes of the liquidation of insolvent companies can probably be reduced to three:

- First, it provides a procedure that allows for an equitable and fair distribution of the assets of the debtor company among its creditors. This means that one creditor cannot be unfairly favoured *vis-à-vis* the others.
- Second, liquidation aims to provide for the winding up of a company that is hopelessly insolvent. In such circumstances it is necessary for the good of the community to put an end to the company's trading.
- Third, liquidation is designed to allow for an investigation of the company's affairs, with particular emphasis on the circumstances that precipitated the winding up. Such an investigation may reveal improper or dishonest conduct by officers of the company or others associated with the company that should be punished by prosecution or civil action.

---

[6] See *Re Western Welsh International System Buildings Ltd* (1985) 1 BCC 99, 296 at 99, 297 per Harman J; *Re Lines Bros Ltd* [1983] Ch 1 at 20 per Brightman LJ; Report of the Insolvency Law Review Committee, *Insolvency Law and Practice*, Cmnd. 8558 (1982) at paras 224–227, 232 ('Cork Report').

[7] Cork Report at para 232.

[8] *Re International Tin Council* (1987) 3 BCC 103 at 118; and affirmed on appeal in (1988) 4 BCC 653 at 658–9 (CA).

[9] For example, see *Re A Company* [1894] 2 Ch 349; *Re A Company* [1983] BCLC 492.

12.3 An overview of winding up

If a company is insolvent it may be wound up in one of two ways. Either a creditor will force its liquidation through a court order (known as *compulsory liquidation*) or the members of the company will resolve to wind up their company under the watchful eyes of the creditors (known as a *creditors' voluntary winding up*).

Whichever procedure is initiated, a liquidator will administer the winding up of the affairs of the company and he or she becomes the agent of the company.

While there are important distinguishing features between voluntary and compulsory winding up, many of the aspects of the administration that will occupy the time of a liquidator are common to both modes of winding up. In fact, there are few practical differences between the administration process for the voluntary winding up of an insolvent company and the administration process for the compulsory winding up of an insolvent company. There are greater distinctions between liquidations of solvent and insolvent companies. There are, of course, marked differences with the procedure that leads to compulsory winding up as opposed to voluntary winding up.

The liquidator has the task of ascertaining the property of the company and in some cases will have to recover property to which he or she is entitled as liquidator, but which is in the hands of some other person or entity.

The liquidator possesses wide powers to enable both the affairs of the company to be investigated and the discovery of the extent of the company's property. Once the liquidator has discovered and, if necessary recovered, the property of the company, he or she is required to realise the property and distribute the proceeds among the creditors, taking into account the rules established by the Insolvency Act and the Insolvency Rules.

The proceeds of the company's realised property is distributed rateably and equally among all creditors who succeed in proving that they are owed money by the company and that the debt is legally recoverable. Such debts are known as *provable debts* and the procedure involved in establishing the debt is known as *proving the debt*. Creditors who have proved their debt are paid dividends from the realised property.

Once the liquidator has completed the winding up of the affairs of the company it will be dissolved and this, in effect, represents the death of the company.

Part IV is primarily concerned with explaining the process involved in winding up, what are its effects, the role of the liquidator and the nature and procedure of dissolution. Other matters of importance to liquidation are discussed in other parts of the book that deal with the matters as they not only affect liquidation but other administrations. These Parts are VI (Administration of Estates), VII (Creditors), VIII (Swelling the Asset Pool) and IX (Misconduct).

Chapter 13

Creditors' Voluntary Winding Up[1]

13.1 Introduction

As discussed in Chapter 12, there are two types of winding up that an insolvent company can be subject to: *creditors' voluntary winding up* or *compulsory winding up*. There is another form of voluntary winding up, known as *members' voluntary winding up*, but this form of administration may only be invoked where a company is solvent. Hence, we will not consider this kind of winding up except in passing.[2] It is worth stating at this point that before a members' voluntary liquidation can proceed:

> The directors of the company are required to make a written declaration to the effect that they have made an inquiry into the affairs of the company and at a meeting of directors they have formed the opinion that the company will be able to pay its debts in full within 12 months of the commencement of the winding up (section 89(1)).

This declaration is known as the *declaration of solvency*.

This chapter focuses on voluntary liquidation and explains how this form of insolvency administration can be initiated.

Voluntary liquidation, as the title might suggest, involves the company voluntarily entering the liquidation process. This is to be contrasted with compulsory liquidation where winding up is imposed on the company by the court. Whichever of the two kinds of voluntary liquidation is to be initiated, the starting point is the resolution of the members of the company that the company wind up. Contrary to what is often thought, a creditors' voluntary liquidation is not initiated by the creditors. If creditors want to see a winding up then, unless they can persuade the members of

---

[1] For a more detailed discussion, see A. Keay, *McPherson's Law of Company Liquidation*, London: Sweet & Maxwell (2001), Chapter 2.

[2] For a discussion of members' voluntary liquidation, see A. Keay, *McPherson's Law of Company Liquidation*, at 33–8.

the company to convene a meeting and pass a resolution to wind up, they must look for a compulsory winding up, which involves commencing winding-up proceedings in the court and the seeking of a court winding-up order. This will be considered in Chapter 14. Unlike compulsory liquidation, where the court must get involved, in the voluntary mode of winding up, the court may well not become involved. In fact it will usually only be involved if:

- the liquidator, a member, or a creditor asks it to determine a question which arises in the liquidation, or to exercise any of the powers which the court has in a compulsory winding up under section 112;
- there is some disagreement between people involved in the winding up; or
- the liquidator takes action to recover property disposed of improperly before the advent of the winding up.

Voluntary winding up is an extra-judicial procedure for liquidating a company. As such it represents a practical expression of the policy of permitting the creditors and contributories in winding up to manage what in substance are their own affairs (*Re Wear Engine Works Co* (1875) 10 Ch App 188 at 191 per James LJ).

With a members' voluntary winding-up the members are in control. Where there is a creditors' voluntary winding up, the creditors have the primary interest in the winding-up process as they will not be paid in full, the company being insolvent. The creditors have ultimate control in such a process, although it must be noted that while the liquidator will, in many cases, take notice of the creditors' views or concerns, his or her primary function is to adhere to the law and to act independently, so he or she cannot be forced by the creditors to do their will. But the creditors are entitled to appoint the liquidator[3] and fix remuneration (rule 4.127(5)), to sanction the exercise of powers in winding up (section 165), and to set up a liquidation committee to assist and supervise the liquidator in the performance of duties (section 141). The members or contributories (the title given to members once the winding-up process is set in train), on the other hand, are effectively excluded from participating in such matters[4] and in this and several other respects, creditors' voluntary winding up is much closer to winding up by the court than to members' voluntary winding up. Creditors' voluntaries are more numerous than members' voluntaries.[5]

---

[3] See section 100.

[4] Although the contributories may be involved in the establishment of a liquidation committee: section 141.

[5] In the period of 1992–1999 there were 69,949 creditors' voluntary liquidations and 21,304 members' voluntaries in England and Wales: Insolvency Service Website at http://www.insolvency.gov.uk/information/statistics.htm.

The attraction of a voluntary liquidation for the members and directors of a company that is insolvent is probably twofold. First, the winding up will usually be quicker than a compulsory one. This is particularly attractive for creditors for they should receive a distribution earlier than where court proceedings are involved. Second, it is less likely that a company undergoing voluntary winding up will attract quite the same amount of investigation. Besides the earlier receipt of a distribution from the assets of the company, the creditors will often be attracted to creditors' voluntary liquidation because it should be less costly and, therefore, the creditors' distributions should be greater.

The fact that the company is insolvent may become apparent in one of two ways: either the directors may be unable to make the declaration of solvency required before a members' voluntary liquidation may proceed (section 89), or the liquidator in a members' voluntary winding up may form the opinion that the company will not be able to pay its debts in full within the period specified in the declaration. The procedure for putting the company into creditors' voluntary winding up varies accordingly.[6]

13.2 The procedure

13.2.1 *No declaration of solvency*

The directors should be aware that once they have determined that the company is unable to pay its debts and they are unable to make a declaration of solvency in line with section 89, the directors should ensure that they do not incur any further debts, because they could be held liable for those debts pursuant to section 214 (wrongful trading).[7]

13.2.1.1 *The members' meeting*

A meeting of the members must be convened and one of the following must be passed at the general meeting for a winding up to commence (section 84):

- an ordinary resolution[8] that the company is to wind up. This will suffice where the articles of the company fixed a period for the duration of the company, the period has expired and the articles provided that at the end of the duration of the company dissolution was to occur;

---

[6] Creditors' voluntary winding up apparently commences with the passing of the resolution to wind up: section 86.

[7] For a discussion of this, see below at 523.

[8] This involves a resolution passed by a simple majority of members. This is rare.

- a special resolution[9] that the company be wound up;
- an extraordinary resolution[10] to the effect that the company cannot, because of its liabilities, continue in business and that it is advisable to wind up (section 84(1)).

At the meeting the members are entitled to appoint a liquidator. The liquidator is, before the meeting of the creditors is held, limited as to what can be done. All that a liquidator is permitted to do, without court approval, is, according to section 166:

- to take into custody or under control all property to which the company is, or appears to be, entitled;
- to dispose of perishable goods and other goods the value of which is likely to diminish if not disposed of forthwith; and
- to do all things necessary to protect the company's assets (section 166(2)(3)).

Once a liquidator is appointed, the powers of the directors come to an end except to the extent that the liquidation committee, when and if appointed, or the creditors approve of the powers continuing (section 103). The office of director does not terminate because if it did directors would not be able to convene the subsequent creditors' meeting, at which one of them must preside according to the Act.

If the members do not appoint a liquidator, the directors retain their powers, prior to the creditors' meeting, but they are unable to exercise these powers without the approval of the court except for the preparing of the statement of affairs and the calling of the creditors' meeting.[11] But directors are able, where no liquidator has been appointed and before the creditors' meeting, to dispose of perishable goods and other goods of value which are likely to diminish in value if not disposed of forthwith (section 114(3)). The rationale for the restrictions is to ensure that the assets of the company are protected from dissipation during the period between the members' meeting and the appointment of a liquidator at the creditors' meeting.

---

[9] This is where there is a resolution passed with a majority of not less than three-fourths of members entitled to vote and voting at a general meeting of which not less than 21-days' notice, indicating the intention to propose the special resolution, has been given: Companies Act 1985, section 378. The 21-days' notice may be waived by the majority of members as outlined in section 378(3) if it agrees that a proposal may be put to the members with less than 21-days' notice.

[10] This is where there is a resolution passed with a majority of not less than three-fourths of members entitled to vote and voting at a general meeting where notice has been given indicating the intention to propose the extraordinary resolution: Companies Act 1985, section 378.

[11] Section 114(2). If the directors do not comply with this provision they are liable to a fine (the statutory maximum): section 114(4).

13.2.1.2 *The creditors' meeting*

The company is to cause a meeting of its creditors to be summoned for a day not later than the fourteenth day following the day on which the company meeting is to be held to consider a resolution for winding up (section 98(1)). The meeting of creditors must be preceded by at least seven clear days' notice sent by post to every creditor (section 98(1)(b))[12] and notice of the meeting must be advertised once in the *London Gazette* and once at least in two newspapers circulating in the locality of the company's principal place of business in Great Britain during the six months immediately preceding the day on which were sent the notices summoning the company meeting at which it was resolved that the company be wound up (section 98(1)(c), (5)). The notice of meeting must state one of two things.[13] Either the name and address of a person who is qualified to act as an insolvency practitioner in relation to the company (normally the person who has been nominated as the liquidator of the company) and who will provide creditors prior to the creditors' meeting with information concerning the company's affairs as may reasonably be required (section 98(2)(a)), or, the less expensive option, providing a place in the locality of the principal place of business where, on the two business days falling next before the day on which the meeting is to be held, a list of the names and addresses of creditors is available for inspection at no charge (section 98(2)(b)).

The directors must prepare, not more than 14 days before the date of the resolution to wind up, a statement of the affairs of the company (rule 4.34(4)). This statement is then laid before the creditors' meeting when it is held (section 99(1)(b)). The directors must appoint one of their number to preside at the creditors' meeting (section 99(1)(c)).[14] The statement, which must be verified by affidavit by some or all of the directors, is required to include:

- particulars of the company's assets, debts and liabilities;
- the names and addresses of creditors;
- securities held by creditors and dates on which the securities were given; and
- other details prescribed (section 99(2)).

---

[12] Failure to notify a creditor may invalidate the meeting unless the court otherwise orders. See *F.V. Saxton & Sons Ltd v R. Miles (Confectioners) Ltd* [1983] 2 All ER 1025.

[13] If the company fails, without a reasonable excuse, to comply it is guilty of an offence and liable to a fine (section 98(6)). The fine is the statutory maximum: Schedule 10. The statutory maximum is £5,000 according to section 32 of the Magistrates' Courts Act 1980 as amended by section 17 of the Criminal Justice Act 1991.

[14] If the director fails to attend or preside at the meeting then he or she is, unless having reasonable excuse, guilty of an office and liable to a fine: section 99(3). The fine is the statutory maximum (Schedule 10).

At the meeting of creditors, the directors are to cause either the director presiding at the meeting or another person who is aware of the company's affairs to present a written or oral report which will update the statement of affairs already prepared by indicating any material transactions affecting the company and occurring between the date of the making of the statement and the date of the meeting (rule 4.53B(1)).

If the members nominated a liquidator at their prior meeting then he or she must attend the meeting of creditors and report on any exercise of liquidator's powers during the period between the members' meeting and the creditors' meeting (section 166(4)). Customarily, the liquidator will attend the meeting notwithstanding the fact that there has been no cause to exercise any of the powers of a liquidator.

At the meeting of creditors, which will, in practice, be held shortly after the members' meeting and at the same place (provided that the place is convenient to the majority in value of the creditors), the creditors may nominate a person(s) to act as liquidator (section 100(1)) and, in the event of difference with the nomination of the members, the creditors' nomination prevails over the nomination made by the members at the company meeting (section 100(2)). However, it is possible for any director, member or creditor to apply to court, within seven days of the nomination of liquidator by the creditors' meeting, for a direction either that the company's nominee shall be liquidator either jointly with or instead of the person nominated by the creditors, or appointing someone else as liquidator instead of the person nominated by the creditors (section 100(3)). Understandably, the creditors may feel that the person nominated by the members is not sufficiently independent to investigate the company's affairs thoroughly and safeguard their interests and so they may well nominate a different person as liquidator.[15] The fact that ordinarily the creditors' choice for liquidator takes precedence indicates the fact that in a creditors' voluntary winding up the creditors, who are the main stakeholders, should feel that they have control of the process and that they are able to nominate a truly independent practitioner. If two or more liquidators are appointed then the resolution should indicate whether the liquidators are to exercise their powers and duties jointly or separately (section 231(2)). If at any subsequent point no liquidator is acting, for one reason or another, then the court has the power to appoint a liquidator (section 108(1)).

Besides nominating a liquidator the creditors may, at the section 98 meeting or subsequently,[16] appoint a liquidation committee of not more than five persons (section 101(1)). The members, either at the meeting at which the winding-up resolution was passed, or at a subsequent meeting, may

---

[15] See the comments of Hoffmann J (as he then was) in *Re Palmer Marine Insurance Surveys Ltd* [1986] BCLC 106 at 111.

[16] The creditors may not, at the time of the section 98 meeting, feel that it is necessary to appoint a liquidation committee, but later events or revelations from investigations might cause them to reconsider.

appoint up to five persons to act as members of a committee of liquidation (section 101(2)). However, the right of the members to appoint members of a liquidation committee is restricted in the sense that the creditors may resolve that all or any of the persons appointed to a liquidation committee ought not be members of the committee. The mechanics surrounding these committees, and their role, is discussed later.[17] Suffice to say at this stage, these committees consist of creditors and contributories who, *inter alia*, assist and supervise the liquidator.

No other resolutions besides the resolutions just discussed can be made at the meeting, except for the following:[18]

- where no liquidation committee has been established, a resolution specifying the terms of the liquidator's remuneration or a resolution to defer consideration of the question of remuneration;
- if two or more liquidators have been nominated, a resolution indicating whether acts are to be done by both or all of them, or only by one of them;
- a resolution to adjourn the meeting for no more than three weeks;
- other resolutions that the chair feels right to allow for special reasons.

All resolutions at a creditors' meeting will only pass if a majority (not in number, but according to value) of the creditors' present and voting, in person or by proxy, are in favour (rule 4.63(1)). So, in contrast with voting in core company law issues, the amount owed to each creditor is the crucial issue. For instance, if A Ltd is in liquidation and has three creditors, X, who is owed £90,000, Y, who is owed £20,000 and Z, who is owed £60,000, what X decides to do will be critical. X can win a vote on his own as the amount owed to him is greater than that which is owed to the other two creditors combined.

To be able to vote, a creditor must have lodged and had accepted, pursuant to rule 4.70, a proof of debt (rule 4.67(1)(a)), and a proxy, if a creditor is to vote by proxy (rule 4.67(1)(b)), although the chair of the meeting has the power to permit a creditor to vote even if no proof has been lodged if satisfied that the non-lodgement was due to circumstances beyond the control of the creditor (rule 4.68). Proof of debt is explained in Part VII, but in a nutshell, it is a form in which a creditor sets out what is owed and what is the nature of the debt. Usually, unsecured creditors are entitled to vote in respect of the total debt owed to them. However, a secured creditor is only entitled to vote in respect of the balance over and above the value of the security as estimated by him or her (rule 4.67(4)). So, if a secured creditor is owed £200,000 and the security over which it has a charge is estimated to be worth only £160,000, the creditor is entitled to vote and its vote is worth £40,000.

---

[17] Below at 256–8.
[18] See rules 4.53 and 4.52(1)(c), (d), (f), (g).

13.2.2 *Liquidator decides the company is insolvent*

As mentioned earlier, if a liquidator forms the opinion, during the course of a members' voluntary winding up, that the company will not be able to pay or provide for payment of its debts within the period stated in the declaration of solvency, he or she must, as soon as practicable, take one of the courses of action prescribed by section 95, which involves the directors doing what is required when they initiate the process for a creditors' voluntary winding up, i.e., where no declaration in relation to solvency can be made. *Inter alia*, the liquidator is required to (section 95(2)):

- summon a meeting of the creditors for a day not later than the twenty-eighth day after the day on which he or she formed the opinion about the company's debts; and
- send notices of the creditors' meeting to the creditors by post not less than seven days before the day on which the meeting is to be held.[19]

The liquidator is to lay before the creditors' meeting, which has been convened, a statement of the affairs of the company (in the prescribed form) and attend and preside at the meeting (section 95(3)).

The creditors are able, at their meeting, if they wish, to replace the liquidator (rules 4.53 and 4.52(1)(a)). The only other resolutions which can be passed at the meeting are (rules 4.53 and 4.52(1)(b), (c), (d), (f), (g)):

- to establish a liquidation committee;
- where no liquidation committee has been established, a resolution specifying the terms of the liquidator's remuneration or a resolution to defer consideration of the question of remuneration;
- if two or more liquidators have been nominated, a resolution indicating whether acts are to be done by both or all of them, or only by one of them;
- a resolution to adjourn the meeting for no more than three weeks;
- other resolutions that the chair feels right to allow for special reasons.

From the time of the creditors' meeting the Act applies as if the declaration of solvency had not been made and the creditors' meeting and the company meeting at which it was resolved that the company be wound up were the meetings referred to in section 98, and hence the liquidation proceeds as a creditors' voluntary winding up (section 96), with the procedure described earlier applying.[20]

---

[19] Instead of the sending of individual notices to creditors the liquidator could obtain a court order that notice be given by public advertisement: rule 4.59(1).

[20] Any appointment made or committee established by a meeting held under section 95 is deemed to have been made or established by a meeting held in accordance with section 98: section 102.

13.2.3 *After the creditors' meeting*

In the event that the winding up lasts for more than a year the liquidator has to summon both creditors' and members' meetings at the end of the first year from the commencement of the winding up and the end of each succeeding year, or the first convenient date within three months from the end of the relevant year or such longer period as the Secretary of State permits (section 105(1)). The liquidator is to lay before the meeting an account of his or her acts and dealings and of the conduct of the winding up during the prior year (section 105(2)).[21] If the liquidation is a conversion from a members' voluntary liquidation and the creditors' meeting held under section 95 is held three months or less before the end of the first year from the commencement of the winding up, the liquidator is not required to summon a meeting of creditors at the end of the year (section 105(4)). But a members' meeting would still have to be convened. The obvious reason for the fact that there is no obligation to call a creditors' meeting is that convening a second meeting so soon after the section 95 meeting, would, more than likely, be pointless.

Other meetings may be convened from time to time to address any matters that may arise during the liquidation process. For instance, the liquidator may need to obtain the approval of the creditors, where there is no liquidation committee, if he or she wishes to exercise the powers in Schedule 4, Part 1 of the Act (section 165(3)). The liquidator is able to convene meetings of creditors or contributories at any time to ascertain their wishes concerning any matters relating to the liquidation (rule 4.54(1)).

---

[21] It the liquidator fails to comply with this requirement then he or she is liable to a fine (one-fifth of the statutory maximum): section 103(3) and Schedule 10.

Chapter 14

Compulsory Winding Up[1]

14.1 Introduction

Compulsory liquidation is a statute-defined procedure that enables a person to apply to the court for an order that the affairs of a company be wound up. The name given to this mode of winding up is based on the fact that the company being wound up is not winding up voluntarily, although in certain cases the company may consent to such a winding up.

This chapter explains a number of features of compulsory liquidation, including how it can be initiated, what grounds can be relied on, who can seek a winding up and the court process leading to a winding-up order.

While the Act, in section 124(1), allows a broad range of persons to initiate compulsory liquidation proceedings, the most prevalent petitioners are creditors. Probably well over 90 per cent of compulsory liquidations are commenced by creditors. Consequently, this chapter essentially focuses on the applications of creditors for winding-up orders. Although section 122(1) provides a number of grounds on which an application for compulsory liquidation can be based, the most common, and the one of which creditors usually avail themselves, is that the company is unable to pay its debts, i.e., it is insolvent (section 122(1)(f)). This ground will be the focus of this chapter.

---

[1] For a more detailed discussion, see A. Keay, *McPherson's Law of Company Liquidation*, London: Sweet & Maxwell (2001), Chapters 3–5.

14.2 The basis for winding up

Section 122(1) enumerates the following grounds for the making of a winding up order:

- The company has passed a special resolution that it be wound up by the court (section 122(1)(a)).
- The company is a public company which was registered on or after 22 December 1980[2] and it has not for more than a year since its registration been issued with a certificate of compliance with the share capital requirements (section 122(1)(b)).[3]
- The company is an old public company which failed to re-register as either a public or a private company by 22 March 1982 (section 122(1)(c)).[4]
- The company has not commenced business within one year of its incorporation or has suspended its business for a whole year (section 122(1)(d)).
- The company is not a private company limited by shares or guarantee and its membership has reduced below two (section 122(1)(e)).[5]
- The company is unable to pay its debts (section 122(1)(f)).
- The court is of the opinion that it is just and equitable that the company should be wound up (section 122(1)(g)).

There is no doubt that the last two grounds are by far the most important and most commonly invoked ones. We will only really concern ourselves with the insolvency ground, although there is nothing to stop a winding up order being made against an insolvent company on grounds other than its inability to pay debts.[6] This is rare.

---

[2] The date on which a new definition of 'public company' came into operation: The Companies Act 1980 (Commencement No 2) Order 1980 (SI No 1980/1785).

[3] See the provisions in Companies Act 1985, section 117.

[4] The Companies Act 1980, section 8, required public companies (known as 'old public companies') to re-register as either public or private companies. See section 1 of the Companies Consolidation (Consequential Provisions) Act 1985 for the definition of 'old public company'.

[5] In such a case the members of the company may be personally liable for the company's debts contracted during this period: Companies Act 1985, section 24.

[6] For a discussion of the other grounds, see A. Keay, *McPherson's Law of Company Liquidation*, Chapter 2.

14.3 Petitioners for winding up

The application that commences winding-up proceedings is called a 'petition' (traditionally this was a prayer of the applicant). Those who can present a petition for the winding up of a company are (section 124(1)):

- The company.
- The directors.
- Any creditor(s), including a contingent or prospective creditor, of the company.
- A contributory or a personal representative of a contributory.[7]
- The clerk of a magistrates' court.
- All or any of the above, together or separately.

Also, other provisions permit a petition to be presented in certain circumstances by:

- the Secretary of State for Trade and Industry;[8]
- the official receiver (section 124(5));
- the Attorney-General (Charities Act 1993, section 63); and
- the Bank of England or Financial Services Authority (Banking Act 1987, section 92).

A company may be the subject of a petition presented by the supervisor of a CVA that the company entered into (section 7(4)(b)) as well as being the subject of a petition presented by either the administrative receiver or administrator of the company (para 60 of Schedule B1 and section 42 together with Schedule 1, para 21).

As already noted, most winding-up orders are made on petitions presented by creditors on the basis that the company is insolvent and far exceed all other kinds of petitions which come before the courts. This is understandable in view of the fact that insolvency is the reason for most of the liquidations that occur and that presentation of the winding-up petition is the only means by which a creditor can have the company wound up and so obtain payment of the debt owed.

Next in order of frequency and importance are contributories' petitions. These are usually presented with the object of procuring a return of members' capital, or of putting a stop to fraudulent, oppressive

---

[7] Subject to section 124(2).

[8] Sections 124(4) and 124A, Financial Service Act 1986, section 72. See A. Keay, 'Public Interest Petitions' (1999) 20 Co Law 296.

or unjust conduct in the company's affairs; in practice, however, such petitions are comparatively rare, since these objects can generally be attained by the simpler method of winding up voluntarily, or by an application for relief under section 459 of the Companies Act 1985 which avoids the necessity for winding up.

Probably the next most frequent petitioner is the Secretary of State for Trade and Industry who seeks an order in the public interest.[9]

Our focus will be on petitions presented by creditors on the basis that the company is unable to pay its debts. Other permitted petitioners may rely on this ground, but rarely do so. Creditors' petitions will be discussed in detail shortly.

At the hearing of the petition for winding up, the court is granted a discretion as to what order it makes. It may, of course, order winding up. However, alternatively it may adjourn the hearing of the petition, make an interim order or any other order which it thinks fit (section 125(1)).

14.4 The hearing of the petition

If, at the hearing of the petition for a winding up order, the court is satisfied both that the alleged ground exists and that the petitioner is qualified to bring a petition, it may order the company to be wound up; but since it possesses a discretion in the matter (section 125(1)), it may refuse the order if there appears to be some good reason for doing so.

Prospective petitioners must be aware of the fact that if a winding-up order is dismissed a petitioner, whoever the petitioner is, might, conceivably, be the subject of a tortious claim by the company for malicious presentation of winding-up proceedings. Such claims are not common, but have been launched from time to time.[10] An alternative claim that might be open to a company where a petition has been dismissed is for damages based on the fact that the petitioner was abusing the process of the court.[11]

---

[9] In the 1996–1997 year the Department of Trade and Industry's Companies Report indicates that 35 companies were wound up pursuant to a petition presented by the Secretary of State. For the 1997–1998 year the number increased markedly to 77 (DTI's Companies Report for 1997–1998).

[10] For instance, see *Partizan Ltd v O J Kenny & Co Ltd* [1998] 1 BCLC 157. For a detailed discussion of the issue, see A. Keay, 'Claims for Malicious Presentation: The Peril Lurking on the Sidelines for Petitioning Creditors' [2001] *Insolvency Lawyer* 136.

[11] For example, see *QIW Retailers Ltd v Felview Pty Ltd* (1989) 7 ACLC 510 where the claim succeeded.

14.5 Winding up unregistered companies[12]

The winding up of unregistered companies is covered in Part V of the Act. Section 221(1) of the Act enables courts in England and Wales to wind up companies which are not registered in this jurisdiction.[13] In winding up such companies all of the provisions of the Act and the Companies Act 1985 relating to winding up apply to an unregistered company with the exceptions and additions mentioned in section 221. 'Unregistered company' is defined in section 220(1) as any association or company except for a company registered in any part of the United Kingdom under the Joint Stock Companies Act or under the legislation (past or present) relating to companies in Great Britain. An unregistered company cannot enter voluntary winding up (section 221(4)).

In order to determine the jurisdiction for winding up, an unregistered company is deemed to be registered in England and Wales or Scotland if its principal place of business is situated in those countries or if it has a principal place of business in both countries (namely, England and Wales or Scotland) and the principal place of business situated in that part of Great Britain in which proceedings are being instituted is, for all purposes of the winding up, deemed to be the registered office of the company (section 221(3)).

There are no specific principles laid down as to when such companies will be wound up; the matter is squarely within the discretion of the courts. Companies, the winding up of which could be performed adequately in their jurisdiction of incorporation, will not ordinarily be wound up in England and Wales (*Re Standard Contract and Debenture Corporation* (1892) 8 TLR 485; *Re Jarvis Conklin Mortgage Co* (1895) 11 TLR 373). The court must be satisfied that that there is a sufficient connection between the company and the jurisdiction before the court can justify setting its winding up procedures in motion over a body which is *prima facie* beyond the limits of territoriality (*Re Real Estate Development Co Ltd* [1991] BCLC 210 at 217).

14.6 The making of a winding-up order

If the court orders winding up then the winding up is deemed to have commenced at the time of the presentation of the petition (section 129(2)), unless there was, before the presentation, a resolution passed by

---

[12] For further discussion of this subject, see A. Keay, *McPherson's Law of Company Liquidation* at 60–5.

[13] See the comments of Sir Richard Scott V-C in the Court of Appeal in *Banco Nacional de Cuba v Cosmos Trading Corp* [2000] 1 BCLC 813 at 816–17.

the company for voluntary winding up. In the latter case, the winding up is deemed to have commenced at the time of the passing of the resolution to wind up (section 129(1)). If a winding-up order is made by a court, under para 13(1)(e) of Schedule B1 when hearing an application for an administration, the commencement of winding up is the date of the order (section 129(1A)).

On the making of a winding-up order the liquidator of the company is, automatically, the official receiver, but he or she may be replaced, at a later stage, by a private qualified insolvency practitioner who is appointed by a creditors' and contributories' meeting.[14] The liquidator, whether the official receiver or a private liquidator, is responsible to the court and acts subject to its directions and is one of its officers.

14.7 An order following voluntary winding up

Where a company is being wound up voluntarily, a court may make a winding-up order on the petition of a contributory or a creditor (sections 116 and 124(5)). Any creditor of the company, whether a pre- or post-voluntary liquidation creditor, may petition (*Re Bank of South Australia (No.2)* [1985] 1 Ch 578; *Re Greenwood and Co* [1900] 2 QB 306). Also, section 124(5) provides that the official receiver or any person authorised to act as such may petition for the compulsory winding up of a company that is in voluntary liquidation.[15]

But a petitioner is not entitled to a winding-up order without showing some good reason for it (*Re Surplus Properties (Huddersfield) Ltd* [1984] BCLC 89; *Re J D Swain Ltd* [1965] 1 WLR 909; [1965] 1 All ER 761).[16] It has to be shown that it would be detrimental to the interests of creditors to allow voluntary liquidation to continue (*Re Universal Drug Supply Association* [1873] WN 125; *Re Riviera Pearls Ltd* [1962] 1 WLR 722; *Re Medisco Equipment Ltd* [1983] BCLC 305; (1983) 1 BCC 98, 944; *Re Magnus Consultants Ltd* [1995] 1 BCLC 203) and an order would not be made against the wishes of the majority (*Re JD Swain Ltd* [1965] [1965] 1 WLR 909 at 913, 915, 916; [1965] 1 All ER 761 at 764, 765, 766 (CA); *Re Zirceram Ltd* [2000] 1 BCLC 751 at 758) unless good reason was suggested for not giving effect to those wishes. In considering the wishes of the majority, the views of creditors who are also members should not be given the same

---

[14] Insolvency Act, section 136(1)–(5). In the 1996–1997 year the official receiver remained the liquidator in 78 per cent of cases: Companies Report 1997.

[15] For example, see *In re Lubin, Rosen and Associates Ltd* [1975] 1 WLR 122; *Re Surplus Properties (Huddersfield) Ltd* [1984] 1 BCLC 89.

[16] See the comments of Lawrence Collins QC (sitting as a deputy High Court judge) in *Re Zirceram Ltd* [2000] 1 BCLC 751 at 758.

weight as those of the outside creditors (*Re Medisco Equipment Ltd*). Obviously one primary reason for giving ample weight to the views of the majority is the fact that the majority has the largest stake in the company's assets (*Re Zirceram Ltd* at 758). In cases where the majority of creditors oppose a court winding up, the petitioner will have to demonstrate a clear advantage to be gained, or some prejudice to be avoided, if a court winding up occurred (*Re Medisco Equipment Ltd*; *Re Magnus Consultants Ltd* [1995] 1 BCLC 203). The court will take account of both the quantity and the quality of the claims of the petitioner on the one hand and, on the other hand, the creditors opposing winding up (*Re Gordon & Breach Science Publishers Ltd* [1995] 2 BCLC 189; [1995] BCC 261). If it is established that the voluntary winding up will be more beneficial for creditors than a compulsory winding up then a petition will be dismissed (*Re Medisco Equipment Ltd*).

Courts will tend not to make an order where the voluntary liquidation is nearly finalised and the liquidator undertakes to cover any losses incurred by the company due to his or her lack of care and to complete the winding up quickly (*Re J Russell Electronics Ltd* [1968] 1 WLR 1252; [1968] 2 All ER 559). In *Souster v Carman Construction Co Ltd* ([2000] BPIR 371 at 380) P W Smith QC (sitting as a deputy High Court judge) thought that it was a factor in the decision he took to make a winding-up order that the voluntary liquidator's actions and investigations had not progressed significantly.

A person might want to see a company ordered to be wound up by the court when it is already subject to voluntary liquidation for a number of reasons. For instance, it may be felt that the directors have been able to exert improper influence over the liquidator and that there is a need for more rigorous investigation of the affairs of the company by a liquidator who is regarded as independent,[17] or the liquidator is not acting with due diligence and the winding up is subject to delays (*Re Hewitt Brannan (Tools) Co Ltd* [1990] BCC 354).

Orders winding up companies have been made because of a range of reasons, such as:[18] the creditor lacks confidence in the liquidator and he or she is not seen as independent (*Re Palmer Marine Insurance Surveys Ltd* [1986] 1 WLR 573; [1986] BCLC 106; (1986) 1 BCC 99, 557; *Re Roselmar Properties Ltd (No2)* (1986) 2 BCC 99, 157; *Re Falcon RJ Development Ltd* [1987] BCLC 437; (1987) 3 BCC 146; *Re Zirceram Ltd* [2000] 1 BCLC 751 at 760),[19] the voluntary liquidator has admitted into proof inflated or

---

[17] For example, see *Re Lowestoft Traffic Services Ltd* (1986) 2 BCC 98, 945; *Re Gordon & Breach Science Publishers Ltd* [1995] 2 BCLC 189; [1995] BCC 261; *Re Inside Sports Ltd* [2000] BCC 40.

[18] A. Keay, *McPherson's Law of Company Liquidation* at 149–50.

[19] The liquidator should not only be independent, but seen to be independent: *Re Lowestoft Traffic Services Ltd* (1986) 2 BCC 98, 945; [1986] BCLC 81; *Re Magnus Consultants Ltd* [1995] 1 BCLC 203.

non-substantiated claims against the company (*Re Magnus Consultants Ltd*; *Re Gordon & Breach Science Publishers Ltd* [1995] 2 BCLC 189; [1995] BCC 261), the voluntary liquidator is not impartial (*Re Pinstripe Farming Co Ltd* [1996] 2 BCLC 295; [1996] BCC 913), the voluntary liquidator had transferred company assets to associated companies for inadequate consideration (*Re Palmer Marine Insurance Surveys Ltd* [1986] 1 WLR 573; [1986] BCLC 106; (1986) 1 BCC 99, 557), or there is a need for speedy investigation of the company's affairs (*Re William Thorpe & Son Ltd* (1988) 5 BCC 156). If a voluntary winding up commenced after the presentation of the winding-up petition, that is more likely to lead to a court winding up the company compulsorily (*In re Lubin, Rosen and Associates Ltd* [1975] 1 WLR 122).

If a winding-up order is made by a court then all actions taken in the earlier voluntary liquidation are deemed to be taken validly unless the court, on proof of fraud or mistake, directs to the contrary (section 129(1)).

Where the liquidator's unfitness is established, it may be preferable simply to have him or her removed[20] and another appointed by way of replacement rather than to resort to the more drastic remedy of having the company wound up by the court.

14.8 Creditors' petitions[21]

If a creditor of a company has demanded repayment of a debt from a company and not been paid, the creditor might issue normal court proceedings to recover the debt or commence the process that leads to the initiation of winding-up proceedings. If the former action is taken and a judgment obtained, the creditor might still not get paid so, at that point, he or she will probably need to commence winding-up proceedings against the company. Insolvency is the ground usually relied upon in all creditors' petitions (section 122(1)(f)) and *prima facie* an unpaid creditor has a right to a winding-up order against a company which fails to pay its debts. The court admittedly has a discretion to refuse the order, but, despite some suggestions to the contrary,[22] a creditor does not act improperly by presenting a petition without attempting to obtain payment by other means (*Re St Thomas' Dock Co* (1876) 2 Ch D 116 at 118–119; *Re Borough of Portmouth Tramways Co* [1892] 2 Ch 263). So, a creditor might choose to forego normal legal proceedings prior to seeking a winding-up order.

---

[20] As to which, see below at 275.
[21] A. Keay, *McPherson's Law of Company Liquidation*, Chapter 3.
[22] See, for example, *Re Exmouth Docks Co* (1873) 17 Eq 181; *Re Herne Bay Waterworks Co* (1878) 10 Ch D 42.

In seeking a winding-up order, the creditor is not obtaining an order for his or her benefit. Rather, an order is for the benefit of the class of creditors of which he or she is a member (*Re Western Welsh International System Buildings Ltd* (1985) 1 BCC 99, 296; *Re Richbell Strategic Holdings Ltd* [1997] 2 BCLC 429). In other words, the right to an order is not an individual right, but a representative one (*Re Crigglestone Coal Co* [1906] 2 Ch 327 at 331–332).

14.8.1 *The creditor as petitioner*

To be a qualified petitioner for a winding-up order, a creditor must be owed a valid debt. A debt that is not legally enforceable does not qualify (*Re South Wales Atlantic Steamship Co* [1875] 2 Ch D 763). The creditor must be owed a debt that has not been paid at the time of the presentation of the petition (*Re William Hockley Ltd* [1962] 1 WLR 555). In *Re North Bucks Furniture Depositories Ltd* ([1939] 2 All ER 549) it was said that 'creditor', in relation to a petition for winding up, includes every person who has a right to prove in a winding up and this includes contingent and prospective creditors (rule 13.12). A contingent creditor is someone 'towards whom, under an existing obligation, the company may or will become subject to a present liability on the happening of some future event or at some future date' (*Re William Hockley Ltd* at 558). A contingent liability exists if there is a doubt whether there will be a debt owing at all (*Re Dummelow* (1873) LR 8 Ch 997 at 1001). There must be an existing obligation and the obligation must be able to be valued or estimated. A prospective creditor is one who is indebted in a sum of money not immediately payable.[23]

A creditor who is fully or partly secured is entitled to apply for a winding up; there is no obligation on the creditor to realise the security held before commencing winding-up proceedings (*Re Alexander's Securities (No 2)* (1983) 8 ACLR 434).

There are three specific provisions of the Act which limit the rights of creditors to present petitions. First, there is para 44 of Schedule B1 (with para 43) which provides that once an application for an administration order has been presented or notice of the intention to appoint an administrator has been filed at court, no proceeding or process, and this would include a winding-up petition (except for those presented under section 124A of the Insolvency Act or section 367 of the Financial Services and Markets Act 2000 – see para 42(4) of Schedule B1), may be commenced. Second, no winding-up order may be made against a company which is subject to administration pursuant to Part II of the Act without the consent of the administrator or leave of the court (para 42(3) of Schedule B1). Third, section 5(2)(b) provides that a company voluntary arrangement binds all creditors who had

---

[23] A. Keay, *McPherson's Law of Company Liquidation*, at 76–7.

notice of the meeting at which an arrangement was approved[24] and who were entitled to vote at the meeting, so it prevents a creditor who falls within section 5(2)(b) from petitioning to wind up a company.[25]

14.8.2 *Insolvency as a ground for winding up*

While there are many grounds on which winding-up proceedings can be based, insolvency is the most common and is the one on which we focus.

If a creditor is owed money by a company, the proper remedy for the creditor against the company, if it is insolvent, is to petition under section 124(1) for a winding-up order on the ground that the company is unable to pay its debts.[26] Unable to pay debts is defined in section 123(1), (2). The subsections enumerate four instances where a company in England and Wales will be deemed to be unable to pay its debts. These are:

- the company failed to comply for three weeks with a written demand served on it left at its registered office where the demand was given by a creditor owed a debt in excess of £750 and the demand required the payment of the amount due (section 123(1)(a));
- execution or other process issued on a judgment or order of any court in favour of a creditor of the company was returned wholly or partly unsatisfied (section 123(1)(b));
- it is proved to the satisfaction of the court that the company is unable to pay its debts as they fall due (section 123(1)(e));
- it is proved to the satisfaction of the court that the value of the company's assets is less than the amount of its liabilities after taking into account the company's contingent and prospective liabilities (section 123(2)).

Where the first two are employed, the company is presumed to be unable to pay its debts without its inability to pay actually being proved,[27] and the company has the burden of rebutting that presumption. In the last two cases, evidence of insolvency has to be adduced and, if the court is satisfied concerning the proof, the company is found insolvent as a matter of fact. The third and fourth cases were discussed in Chapter 2 and are known as *cash flow insolvency* and *balance sheet insolvency*. As it is not always easy, in terms of both time and costs, either to establish that a company is unable to pay its debts as they fall due, or that the value of the company's assets are outweighed by its liabilities,[28] creditors tend either to rely on the

---

[24] See section 3.
[25] See *Beverley Group plc v McClue* [1995] 2 BCLC 407; [1995] BCC 751.
[26] See section 122(1)(f).
[27] These instances are the same as those applying in relation to bankruptcy: section 268(1).
[28] The creditors do not usually have access to the company's books and records, they cannot obtain information from company officers and the position of the company may well be disputed.

failure of the company to comply with a demand or to establish insolvency on a cash flow basis; the non-satisfaction of execution process is not commonly invoked. It has been held that a court is entitled to find the company actually insolvent (on a cash flow basis) from the fact that the company has not paid invoices (*Re DKG Contractors Ltd* [1990] BCC 903).

While a creditor is able to establish the fact that a company is unable to pay its debts through one of the routes discussed above, it does not mean that a winding-up order will be automatically made; the court has an unfettered discretion (section 125(1)). The company might be able to establish that it is solvent, thereby rebutting the presumption of insolvency relied on by the creditor. Nevertheless, a court may still make a winding-up order if the company does not dispute the fact that it owes money to the creditor who has requested payment, because non-payment gives rise to a legitimate suspicion of inability to pay (*Cornhill Insurance plc v Improvement Services Ltd* [1986] 1 WLR 114; (1986) 2 BCC 98,942). But in *Re A Company (No 006798 of 1995)* ([1996] 2 BCLC 48; [1996] BCC 395) Chadwick J (as he then was) said that courts would not be easily satisfied that a company was unable to pay its debts from the fact of non-payment of a debt where the debt had not been demanded.

Petitioners must be able to establish that the company is unable to pay its debts at the time of the hearing of the petition as well as when the petition was presented (*Re Fildes Bros Ltd* [1970] 1 WLR 592).

14.8.2.1 *Statutory demand*[29]

A company is presumed to be insolvent where it neglects to comply with a statutory demand pursuant to section 123(1)(a). The demand will require the company on which it is served to pay the sum due by it within three weeks and if the company neglects to pay the sum due, or to secure or compound for it,[30] to the reasonable satisfaction of the creditor it will be presumed to be unable to pay debts.[31] Courts have frequently emphasised that demands should not be used as a fast-track alternative to taking action in the courts for recovery of alleged debts.[32] Notwithstanding this, statutory demands have often been served on companies by creditors who have no intention of filing winding-up proceedings. They are employed as

---

[29] For a more detailed discussion, see A. Keay, *McPherson's Law of Company Liquidation*, at 92–101.

[30] A compounding of the debt occurs when the creditor and the debtor company come together by mutual agreement in an existing arrangement to the reasonable satisfaction of the creditor at that time.

[31] It will not be until the hearing of the petition that a court will consider the reasonableness of an offer to compound or secure for a debt: *Re A Debtor (No 415/SD/93)* [1994] 1 WLR 917; [1994] 2 All ER 168.

[32] A. Keay, *McPherson's Law of Company Liquidation*, at 92.

a strategy to get a company to pay a debt (often where all else has failed) by instilling fear (the creditor hopes) in the company that the creditor may wind it up. The company does not know, in most cases, whether the creditor is intent on seeing the matter through to a winding-up order, or whether it is a pure bluff.

(a) The demand

A demand must be in the prescribed form.[33] According to the Act and the Rules the demand must satisfy the following requirements:

- it must be in writing (section 123(1)(a) and rule 4.4(2));
- it must be dated (rule 4.4(3));
- it must specify the date on which the debt claimed was incurred and the consideration for it, e.g., services rendered (rule 4.5(1)). If the consideration for the debt is not stated, that constitutes a defect in the demand, but it may not invalidate the demand if there is no prejudice to the debtor and no indication that the debtor would have complied with a demand which was not defective (*Re A Debtor (No 1 of 1987)* [1988] 1 All ER 959);[34]
- the demand must state: its purpose and the fact that if the demand is not complied with then proceedings may be issued for the winding up of the company; the time in which compliance is to take place if the initiation of winding-up proceedings is to be avoided; the methods of compliance available to the company, namely the company may pay the debt or secure or compound[35] for that amount to the creditor's satisfaction within three weeks of the demand being served on the company (rule 4.6(1));
- it must provide details as to how one of the company's officers or representatives can communicate with one or more persons named with a view to the securing or compounding of the debt (rule 4.6(2));
- it must be signed by the creditor or by someone who states that he or she is authorised to make the demand on behalf of the creditor (rule 4(3)). Creditors that are companies may sign through the agency of a director, the secretary or an executive officer of the company. If the creditor is a partnership a partner may sign on behalf of the partnership;
- it must be served by leaving it at the registered office of the company (section 123(1)(a)).

The same requirements essentially apply to demands which are served under section 268 on debtors who are individuals and the law that has developed in relation to those demands will apply, where appropriate, in relation to demands served on companies.

---

[33] Rule 4.5. The form is 4.1 in Schedule 4 to the Rules.

[34] Affirmed by the Court of Appeal ([1989] 1 WLR 271; [1989] 2 All ER 46).

[35] It was said in *Re A Debtor (No 32 of 1993)* [1995] 1 All ER 628 that an offer by a debtor of £15,000 in full settlement of a debt over £33,000 was an offer to compound for a debt.

(b) The debt

Demands must only include claims for liquidated amounts; unliquidated claims are not debts within the provisions. Where a demand claims significant amounts that were not due, it is likely to be regarded as causing substantial injustice and would be set aside.[36] The debt at the time of the demand should be due and payable. The debt must be such that the creditor is entitled to claim immediate payment of it, i.e., a debt that is due and payable.[37]

While creditors are not required to obtain a judgment or order in relation to the debt claimed before serving a demand, the benefit of doing so is that if a judgment or order is obtained, in general, the company is then unable to argue that the debt is disputed on *bona fide* and substantial grounds;[38] to argue that there remains a genuine dispute over the debt, the company would have to establish that the judgment or order was obtained by fraud (*Bowes v Hope Life Insurance and Guarantee Society* (1865) 11 HLC 389; 11 ER 1383). While creditors with judgments occupy an advantageous position, a court still retains a discretion to refrain from making a winding-up order at the hearing of the petition.

It seems, although apparently not decided conclusively, that a creditor is not allowed to serve a multiple number of demands on the one company for different debts (*Sentinel Financial Management Pty Ltd v Entercorp Finance Pty Ltd* (1997) 15 ACLC 201). After some confusion over the years it is now established that a person may serve a demand if he or she is an assignee of the debt owed, on the condition that if the assignee is paid then that will discharge the debt.[39]

Creditors must be aware that if they serve a demand on a company then, whether or not they are aware that the debt on which the demand is based is disputed on substantial grounds, they risk being held liable for the costs of the company if it applies for an order restraining the presentation of a petition (*Cannon Screen Entertainment Ltd v Handmade Films (Distributors) Ltd* (1989) 5 BCC 207 at 209).

(c) Service

The demand must be served on the company by leaving it at its registered office (section 123(1)(a)). In the unlikely situation where no registered office of the company exists, service has been allowed in the past to be effected at the company's place of business (*Re Fortune Copper Mining Co* (1870) LR 10 Eq 390).

---

[36] See *Portrait Express (Sales) Pty Ltd v Kodak (Australasia) Pty Ltd* (1996) 14 ACLC 1095.

[37] Section 123(1)(a) states 'then due'. See *Re European Life Assurance Co* (1869) 9 Eq 122 at 127; *Re Bryant Investment Co Ltd* [1974] 1 WLR 826.

[38] The following indicate that in bankruptcy there will be no going behind the judgment at the demand stage, but there may be an opportunity to do that at the hearing of the petition: *Practice Note* [1987] 1 WLR 119; *Re a Debtor (No 657/SD/91)* [1993] BCLC 180; *Cartwright v Staffordshire and Moorlands District Council* [1998] BPIR 328 (CA).

[39] But an equitable assignee is not able to serve a demand – it must be served by the person who holds the legal title to the debt: *Re Steel Wing Co* [1921] 1 Ch 349.

(d) Opposing a demand

In bankruptcy there is a procedure (rules 6.1–6.5) (discussed at 314) for filing an application to set aside a demand, but there is no similar procedure in the Act or Rules for a company to do so. What a company has to do if it wishes to resist a demand is to apply to the court for an injunction that restrains the presentation of a petition while the issue of indebtedness is resolved.[40] An application is only likely to succeed if the company can demonstrate that there is a genuine dispute concerning the existence of the debt claimed in the demand (*Re Janeash Ltd* [1990] BCC 250). But the task before the courts in determining whether a genuine dispute does in fact exist is often a difficult one. A court will not embark on any extended inquiry in order to determine whether there is a genuine dispute (*Mibor Investments Pty Ltd v Commonwealth Bank of Australia* (1993) 11 ACSR 362 at 366) and a court will not decide 'contested issues of fact or law which have a significant or substantial basis' (*Spencer Constructions Pty Ltd v G & M Aldridge Pty Ltd* (1997) 15 ACLC 1001 at 1009).

Creditors must be aware that it is an abuse of process if a demand is served while including a debt which is disputed on genuine grounds or includes a claim for an excessive sum with the intention of pressurising the company to pay more than that which is due (*Re London and Paris Banking Corp* (1875) 19 Eq 444).

14.8.2.2 *Unsatisfied execution*

Another way of establishing inability to pay debts is to serve on the debtor execution or other process, issued on a judgment, decree, or order of any court in favour of a creditor, and it is returned unsatisfied in whole or in part (section 123(1)(b)).[41] Successful parties in litigation are entitled to execute on the judgment or order that has been given. What usually occurs is that 'execution is carried out by the sheriff or an officer at the sheriff's office, who will attend at the premises of the company to see if there are any property that can be seized and then sold to pay for what is owed.'[42]

The frequent form of execution which is employed and is often returned 'unsatisfied' is the writ of *fieri facias*, and the effect of section 123(1)(b) is that insolvency is presumed if the return to such a writ is without effect. It appears that courts are able to go behind the return in order to determine whether the execution was in fact unsatisfied and may even investigate the judgment on which proceedings were based

---

[40] See *Practice Direction* [1988] 1 WLR 988; [1988] 2 All ER 1024.
[41] The assets realised must not only satisfy the amount of the debt but also the costs of execution.
[42] A. Keay, *McPherson's Law of Company Liquidation*, at 83.

(*Re Railway Finance Co* [1866] 14 WR 785). Also, a court may exercise its discretion to refuse a winding-up order if is satisfied that the petitioner for winding up has been guilty of an abuse of process.

14.9 Injunction to restrain the presentation or the advertising of the petition

Winding-up proceedings are formally commenced by the presentation to a court of a petition. Courts are able, on the application of the company, to grant an injunction restraining the presentation or advertising of a petition.[43] So a company, where it knows that a petition is imminent, might consider making an application to restrain the presentation or advertising of a petition. The primary concern of a company would be that if a petition was presented, and more so if it was advertised, it could well damage the company's business.[44] Petitions have to be advertised after presentation and not less than seven days after the service of the petition on the company, nor less than seven days before the hearing (rules 4.11(2)(b)). This provision enables the company to have time in which to take legal advice and to apply for an injunction.

The jurisdiction to grant injunctions in this context is used sparingly and applicants must establish clear and persuasive grounds for an injunction (*Bryanston Finance Pty Ltd v De Vries (No2)* [1976] Ch 63 at 78 (CA); *Coulson Sanderson & Ward Ltd v Ward* (1986) 2 BCC 99, 207 at 99, 214–99, 215 (CA); *Re Normandy Marketing Ltd* [1994] Ch 198; [1993] BCC 879; *Re A Company (No 007923 of 1994)* [1995] 1 WLR 953; [1995] BCLC 440; [1995] BCC 634). The applicant is subject to a heavy burden (*Coulson Sanderson & Ward Ltd v Ward* (1986) 2 BCC 99, 207 at 99, 214–99, 216). In *Coulson Sanderson & Ward Ltd v Ward* Slade LJ said that unless the company could present evidence which showed that *prima facie* a petition would be bound to fail it would not be able to establish an abuse of process. A court will in fact only grant an injunction if the applicant is able to establish on the evidence a *prima facie* case for holding that the petition would constitute an abuse of process (*Coulson Sanderson & Ward Ltd v Ward* at 99, 215), as the power to grant an injunction emanates from the court's jurisdiction to prevent an abuse of process.[45]

---

[43] For a use of the power, see *Mann v Goldstein* [1968] 1 WLR 1091; *Coulson Sanderson & Ward Ltd v Ward* (1986) 2 BCC 99, 207.

[44] The courts have accepted this concern: *Mann v Goldstein* [1968] 1 WLR 1091; *Coulson Sanderson & Ward Ltd v Ward* (1986) 2 BCC 99, 207; *Re A Company (No 007923 of 1994)* [1995] BCC 634.

[45] For example, see *Charles Forte Investments Ltd v Amanda* [1964] Ch 240; *Mann v Goldstein* [1968] 1 WLR 1091 at 1093; *Bryanston Finance Pty Ltd v De Vries (No2)* [1976] Ch 63 at 78 (CA).

The court may restrain advertisement of the petition if the petitioner knows that the company has a defence on which it intends to rely at the hearing of the petition (*Re A Company (No 003079 of 1990)* [1991] BCLC 235; [1991] BCC 683; *Re A Company (No 0012209 of 1991)* [1992] 1 WLR 351; [1992] 2 All ER 797; [1992] BCLC 865; *Re A Company (No 004502 of 1988)* [1992] BCLC 701). However, it has been established that just because a petitioner has a bad motive for obtaining a winding-up order, that is not sufficient for a court to restrain presentation (*Bryanston Finance Pty Ltd v De Vries (No2)*; *Coulson Sanderson & Ward Ltd v Ward*). Where a company has an alleged cross-claim against the creditor which is greater than the debt owed, but it has not been subjected to litigation, the court is to refrain from granting an injunction to restrain the presentation of a petition; the issue of the cross-claim is to be considered by a court in exercising its discretion at the hearing of the petition (*Re A Company (No 006273 of 1992)* [1992] BCC 794 at 795). In *Re A Company (No 009080) of 1992)* ([1993] BCLC 269) the court declined to grant an injunction to restrain the advertising of a petition because, while the company's cross-claim exceeded that of the creditor's claim, the company was insolvent and arguably only solvent companies can demonstrate that they will suffer damage if a petition is presented or advertised should succeed.

An injunction may be granted: where the company can demonstrate that the person who will be the petitioning creditor has no standing to present a winding-up petition (*Re A Company (No 008790 of 1990)* [1991] BCLC 561; [1992] BCC 11); where the debt claimed by the prospective petitioner is disputed bona fide;[46] or where the evidence suggests that the creditor is trying to force the company into paying its alleged debt under threat of winding-up proceedings, without permitting time to enable the company to consider its position (*Pacific Communication Rentals Pty Ltd v Walker* (1993) 12 ACSR 287).

14.10 Winding-up procedure

It is not intended to set out the procedure that is followed in winding up in any detail.[47] What is discussed below are the most important features, given the purpose of this work.

---

[46] *Re A Company (No 00751 of 1992)* [1992] BCLC 869. If the company is solvent but the debt claimed in a demand is undisputed, courts have refused to restrain the petition on the basis that non-payment of the debt is evidence from which it can be inferred that the company is insolvent: *Cornhill Insurance plc v Improvement Services Ltd* [1986] 1 WLR 114; (1986) 2 BCC 98, 942.

[47] For a detailed discussion of the procedure, see A. Keay, *McPherson's Law of Company Liquidation* at 150–75.

14.10.1 *Presenting the petition*

Winding-up proceedings are initiated by a petition that must conform to the prescribed form[48] and state the nature of the relief sought and the grounds upon which it relies; in fact, the person petitioning is limited to the grounds mentioned in the petition (*Re Fildes Bros Ltd* [1970] 1 WLR 592; *Re Armvent Ltd* [1975] 1 WLR 1679). The petition is presented (filed) at the registry of the appropriate court (rule 4.7(1)) and this action is critical, because it fixes the commencement of winding up (if there is a winding-up order made subsequently) which is important when it comes to any claims by a liquidator in respect of pre-liquidation transactions that can be adjusted by a court (under sections 238–246).[49] An affidavit must also be filed verifying the matters stated in the petition (rules 4.7 and 4.12(1)). The petition that is filed must be accompanied by a receipt to the effect that the petitioner has paid a deposit (rule 4.7(2)). This money is transmitted to the official receiver and will be used by him or her to carry out his or her duties if and when the petition is successful and a winding-up order is made. An appropriate court official seals each copy of the petition presented and they are issued to the petitioner (rule 4.7(5)). The court fixes a venue for the hearing and this is indorsed on each copy of the petition issued (rule 4.7(6)).

Petitions may be defective in some way, but they will not be held to be invalid because of any formal defects or by any irregularity, unless the court, before which an objection to a petition is made, considers that substantial injustice has been caused by the defect or irregularity and the injustice is unable to be remedied by court order (rule 7.55).

14.10.2 *Service of the petition*

After the petition has been presented, it must be served on the company at its registered office,[50] unless the company itself is the petitioner (rule 4.8(1), (2)). Service can be undertaken in several ways, as set out in rule 4.8(3). If service pursuant to one of these ways is not practicable, the court is at liberty to direct or approve another way by way of a substituted service order (rule 4.8(6)).

The petition must be served seven clear days before the hearing (rule 11.2(a)), but as the petition must be advertised at least seven business days before the hearing and the petition must be advertised at least seven business days after service (rule 11.2(b)), service will usually be effected 14 business days before the hearing.[51]

---

[48] Form 4.2 of Schedule 4 to the Rules (rule 4.7) for petitions by persons other than contributories; Form 4.14 of Schedule 4 to the Rules for contributories (rule 4.22).

[49] See Part VIII.

[50] It has been held that where a company is served at the address which is the registered office according to the records at Companies House then even if that is an old address the petition should not be struck out: *Re Corbenstoke Ltd* [1989] BCLC 496.

[51] A. Keay, *McPherson's Law of Company Liquidation* at 154.

14.10.3 *Advertising the petition*

The petitioner must advertise the presentation of the petition once in the *London Gazette*, unless the court directs otherwise.[52] Where the petitioner is other than the company then, according to rule 4.11(2)(b), advertising must occur no less than seven business days after the date of service on the company and not less than seven days before the hearing date. Advertising is intended to give other creditors and contributories an opportunity of supporting or opposing winding up, as well as notifying the public of the petition (*Applied Data Base Ltd v Secretary of State* [1995] 1 BCLC 272). A second reason for advertising is to put on notice those who might trade with the company during the time from the presentation of the petition and until it is determined and who might be affected by section 127(see pp 236–41): *Re A Company (No 007923 of 1994)* [1995] 1 WLR 953; [1995] BCLC 440; [1995] BCC 634. In this latter case the Court of Appeal said that the first reason set out above was the primary one.[53]

14.10.4 *Substitution of creditors*

The Rules (rule 4.19) permit the court to substitute another creditor (if he or she had been entitled to apply for a winding up (rule 4.19(2)) as petitioner in place of one who:

● has failed to advertise the petition within the prescribed time or such extended time as the court may allow (rule 4.19(1)(a));
● is not entitled to apply (rule 4.19);
● consents to withdraw the petition, allows it to be dismissed, consents to an adjournment, fails to proceed with it at the hearing (rule 4.19(1)(b));[54] or
● who appears at the hearing but fails to apply for an order in the terms of the prayer in the petition (rule 4.19(1)(c)).

The substituted petitioner is obliged to rely on the ground alleged in the original petition and must show that he or she had a right to apply for a winding-up order on that ground at the time of the original petition (*Re Elgar Heights Pty Ltd* (1985) 3 ACLC 480). While it is usually creditors who apply to be substituted as petitioners, contributories may apply.[55]

Substitution is permitted so that proceedings can continue and to allow all creditors to take advantage of them and to ensure that where a ground for winding up has been established against a company, the company does

---

[52] Rule 4.11(1). Although not strictly necessary, petitioners often also advertise in a London or local newspaper. This was required prior to the advent of the Act and Rules.
[53] Also, see para 2.1 of Practice Direction [1999] BPIR 441; [2000] BCC 927.
[54] See *Re Wavern Engineering Co Ltd* (1987) 3 BCC 3.
[55] See *Re Bryant Investment Co Ltd* [1974] 1 WLR 826.

not escape, except where there is fair dealing with all of its creditors (*DMK Building Materials Pty Ltd v Baker Timbers Pty Ltd* (1985) 3 ACLC 729; (1985) 10 ACLR 16). The creditor seeking to be substituted must rely on the ground set out in the petition for winding up, which will usually be inability to pay debts, although it is not necessary to establish the ground in the same manner as the original petitioner sought to do (*Re Elgar Heights Pty Ltd* at 482).

A substitution is in the court's discretion. The court has to balance two competing policies when considering its decision. First, insolvent companies should not be allowed to continue to trade to the detriment of existing and future creditors, but should be wound up as expeditiously as possible. Second, a court should not allow winding up to be used as a debt-collecting mechanism or as an instrument of oppression by a creditor whose debt is subject to genuine dispute (*South East Water v Kitoria Pty Ltd* (1996) 14 ACLC 1328).[56] Once a substitution order is made, the successful creditor has standing to pursue the petition (*Kelvingrove (1993) Pty Ltd v Paratoo Pty Ltd* (1998) 16 ACLC 964 at 966).

14.10.5 *The hearing*

The hearing of a creditor's petition for winding up is usually a quite formal affair, particularly if, as so often happens, neither the company nor any other creditor appears to oppose the petition. A hearing 'seldom involves more than the reading of the requisite affidavits, applications for leave to make any necessary amendments, and the formal pronouncement of the winding-up order.'[57] No one besides the company and the petitioner have the right to be heard at the hearing (*Re Ibo Investment Trust Ltd* [1903] Ch 26), although other persons are able to appear either if they give, according to rule 4.16, notice of intention to appear or the court gives leave.

The court may make one of a number of specific orders at the hearing in relation to the petition to wind up a company in insolvency. It may (section 125(3)):

- grant a winding-up order;[58]
- dismiss the petition even if a ground has been proved on which a winding-up order may be made;
- adjourn the hearing conditionally or unconditionally;
- make an interim or other order; or
- any order which it thinks fit.

---

[56] A. Keay, *McPherson's Law of Company Liquidation* at 164.
[57] A. Keay, *McPherson's Law of Company Liquidation* at 165.
[58] The court may post-date the order: *Re Doncaster Permanent Benefit Building and Investment Society* [1863] 11 WR 459.

While it has sometimes been said that there is a rule that a petitioner, who can prove that a debt is unpaid and that the company is insolvent, is entitled to a winding-up order, it must be acknowledged that the court has a broad discretion under section 125. Consequently, courts are able to refuse to make a winding-up order even when the grounds for one have been established.[59] This power is, however, fairly strictly regulated and is exercised in accordance with relatively well defined principles. It can be said that courts are only justified in refusing to make an order on the petition of an unpaid creditor in the following cases:

(1) the petitioner's debt amounts to less than £750;
(2) the debt is *bona fide* disputed by the company;
(3) the petition constitutes an abuse of process;
(4) the company has paid or tendered payment of the petitioner's debt;
(5) winding up is opposed by other creditors;
(6) the company is in the process of being wound up voluntarily; and
(7) the English and Welsh courts are not the most appropriate jurisdiction for the issues to be resolved.[60]

Not all of these warrant any consideration. Point(6) was discussed earlier in this chapter, and the next sections examine three of the other reasons for dismissal.

14.10.5.1 *Disputed debt*

There is a broad general principle that a winding-up order will not, as a matter of discretion, be made on a debt which is *bona fide* disputed, provided that the dispute is based on some substantial ground (*Mann v Goldstein* [1968] 1 WLR 1091 at 1098–1099; *Re Selectmove Ltd* [1994] BCLC 349; *Re Richbell Strategic Holdings Ltd* [1997] 2 BCLC 429; *Re UOC Corp; Alijour v Ary* [1997] BCC 377 (CA); *TJ Ross (Joiners) Ltd v High Range Developments Ltd* 2000 SCLR 161); the petition should be struck out (*In re Gold Hill Mines* (1882) 28 Ch D 210 (CA); *Re A Company (No 0013734 of 1991)* [1993] BCLC 59; *Re Claybridge Shipping Co SA* [1997] 1 BCLC 572 (CA)). Historically, the major reason for a court exercising its discretion and refusing to make a winding-up order has been where there is a *bona fide* dispute based on some substantial ground concerning the debt which is the subject of the proceedings. The rule is set out in the case of *Mann v Goldstein* by Ungoed-Thomas J:

> I would prefer to rest the jurisdiction on the comparatively simple propositions that a creditor's petition can only be presented by a creditor, that the winding-up jurisdiction is not for the purpose of deciding a disputed debt

---

[59] See *Re P & J MacRae Ltd* [1961] 1 WLR 229 at 238.
[60] A. Keay, *McPherson's Law of Company Liquidation* at 108.

(that is, disputed on substantial and not insubstantial grounds) since, until a creditor is established as a creditor he is not entitled to present the petition and has no *locus standi* in the Companies' Court; and that, therefore, to invoke the winding-up jurisdiction when the debt is disputed (that is on substantial grounds) or after it has become clear that it is so disputed it is an abuse of the process of the court. (at 1098–1099)

A reason for this rule is that a petitioner whose debt is disputed is not qualified to present a petition for a winding-up order (*Mann v Goldstein* [1968] 1 WLR 1091; *Re Selectmove Ltd* [1994] BCLC 349); the petitioner is not a creditor if it turns out that the company was justified in refusing to pay (*Mann v Goldstein* [1968] 1 WLR 1091 at 1098; *Re Lympne Investments Ltd* [1972] 1 WLR 523 at 527; *Stonegate Securities Ltd v Gregory* [1980] 1 Ch 576). A second reason is that the companies' jurisdiction is not to be used for deciding factual disputes between litigants in relation to a debt (*Re Selectmove Ltd*). But, the primary reason is that a winding-up petition is not to be used for the improper purpose of forcing what is a solvent company to pay a disputed debt which would be discharged as soon as the company's liability was actually demonstrated to exist (*Re Imperial Silver Quarries* [1868] 14 WR 1220; *Re Imperial Hydropathic Hotel Co* (1882) 49 LT 147 at 150), and irreparable damage could be caused to the company if a winding-up order was made (*Cadiz Waterworks Company v Barnett* (1874) LR 19 Eq 182). However, while a petition will normally be dismissed, courts have, on occasions, said that a court always has a discretion whether or not to make a winding-up order, even if a dispute exists (*Re Claybridge Shipping Co SA* [1981] Com LR 107; [1997] 1 BCLC 572 (CA)). But, in the Court of Appeal decision in *Re Bayoil SA* ([1998] BCC 988; [1999] 1 BCLC 62), Nourse LJ said that where a company disputes a petition on substantial grounds then 'the dismissal of the petition in such a case is not, at any rate, initially, a matter for the discretion of the court' (at 990;66). While the comment was only *obiter*, it was the view of an appellate court judge and it is likely to be relied on in subsequent cases.

The rule that a dispute over a debt founding the petition will lead to dismissal, while no more than a rule of practice (*Re Claybridge Shipping Co SA*), is applied across the board, except in special circumstances. The position in England, according to the majority of case law, is that a court is to dismiss a petition where there is a substantial dispute over the debt founding the petition even if the company is clearly insolvent.[61] However, there is authority to suggest that courts should modify the general approach even where a *bona fide* dispute occurs, if the company is found to owe some sum to the petitioner.[62]

---

[61] See A. Keay, 'Insolvent Companies Which are Able to Dispute Debts Owed to Petitioning Creditors: Should they be Wound Up?' (1998) 19 Co Law 230.

[62] See *Re Steel Wing Company* [1921] 1 Ch 349; *Re Tweeds Garages Ltd* [1962] 1 Ch 406; *Re Bydand Ltd* [1997] BCC 915.

To ensure dismissal of a petition where it is alleged that the debt relied on in the petition is disputed, a company must demonstrate that the dispute must be genuine and *bona fide*, both in the sense that it must be honestly believed to exist by those who allege it (*Stonegate Securities Ltd v Gregory* [1980] Ch 576 at 580; [1980] 1 All ER 241 at 243–244 (CA)) and in the sense that the belief must be based on reasonable (*Stonegate Securities*) or substantial (*Re Welsh Brick Industries Ltd* [1946] 2 All ER 197 at 198; *Taylor Industrial Flooring Ltd v M & H Plant Hire (Manchester) Ltd* [1990] BCLC 216; [1990] BCC 44 (CA); *Re A Company (No 0010656 of 1990)* [1991] BCLC 464 at 466) grounds. Whether or not there is a dispute on substantial grounds is a matter to be decided in each case.[63] The dispute envisaged must involve, to a substantial extent, disputed questions of fact which demand the consideration of oral evidence together with cross-examination (*Re Lympne Investments Ltd* [1972] 2 All ER 385 at 389). Evidence must be adduced which supports the argument of the company that there is a substantial dispute.[64] The courts will be wary of the case where a company seeks to raise multiple objections to a petition in order to cast doubts on the petitioner's case and to claim that a debt is disputed if the objections are not able to be determined on affidavit evidence and without cross-examination (*Re A Company (No 006685 of 1996)* [1997] 1 BCLC 639).

Courts may, if there is an alleged dispute concerning the petitioner's debt, try to ascertain what is the true position between the company and the petitioner, namely whether the company does in fact owe the alleged debt.[65] But this is rarely done, as such a course of action is often time-consuming and the Companies' Court is 'wholly unsuited to the determining of contested issues of fact on winding-up petitions' (*Re A Company (No 0010656 of 1990)* at 467).

The usual practice has been in the past, where the debt is disputed at the winding-up hearing, to dismiss the petition outright,[66] but the court has power under section 125(1) to adjourn the hearing conditionally or unconditionally and the court has on a few occasions exercised this power in order to allow the petitioner to bring an action to establish the debt (*Re Catholic Publishing Co* (1864) 33 LJ Ch 325; *Re QBS Pty Ltd* [1967]

---

[63] In *Re FSA Business Software Ltd* [1990] BCC 465 Warner J held that there was not a substantial dispute.

[64] *Re Great Britain Mutual Life Assurance Society* (1880) 26 Ch D 246. In *Re A Company (No 0013734 of 1991)* [1993] BCLC 59 Robert Kaye QC (sitting as a Deputy Judge of the Chancery Division) said that as the evidence of the company could not be seriously challenged as far as the dispute over the petitioner's debt was concerned, he struck out the petition.

[65] For example, see *Brinds Ltd v Offshore Oil NL* (1986) 2 BCC 98, 916 (PC); *Re Janeash Ltd* [1990] BCC 250.

[66] *Palmer's Company Precedents*, Part 2 at 27; *Re Martin Wallis & Co.* (1893) 37 Sol Jo 822; *Re Meaford Manufacturing Co.* (1919) 46 OLR 252; *Strata Welding Alloys Pty Ltd v Henrich Pty Ltd* (1980) 5 ACLR 442. Compare *Re Claybridge Shipping Co SA* [1981] Com LR 107; [1997] 1 BCLC 572 (CA).

Qd R 218; *Re DJ & SR Campbell Building Contractors Pty Ltd* (1983) 7 ACLR 696; *Brinds Ltd v Offshore Oil NL* (1986) 2 BCC 98, 916 (PC)). Courts have also taken this approach where the company impugns a judgment on what the debt claimed in the petition is based, in order to enable the company to take proceedings to have the judgment set aside for fraud (*Bowes v Hope Life Insurance and Guarantee Society Ltd* (1865) 11 HLC 389; 11 ER 1383).

In like manner the courts have generally ordered the striking out of petitions where the company has a set-off or cross-claim against the company and it is equal to, or greater than, the petitioner's debt. It now appears that there are only two situations where the courts will not order dismissal of the petition. First, where there are special circumstances in existence which warrant the petition to remain standing. Second, where, taking the cross-claim of the company into account, the company still owes money to the petitioner.[67]

14.10.5.2 *Abuse of process*

(a) Generally

The court has an inherent power to prevent abuse of its process and may, in its discretion, dismiss it with costs (*Re Gold Hill Mines* (1883) 23 Ch D 210; *Re A Company* [1973] 1 WLR 1566; *Re A Company (No 00751 of 1992)* [1992] BCLC 869; *Re A Company (No 0012209 of 1991)* [1992] 1 WLR 351; [1992] 2 All ER 797; [1992] BCLC 865). In determining if the petitioner has committed an abuse of process, the court is able to consider the conduct of the petitioner both before and after the presentation of the petition (*QIW Retailers Ltd v Felview Pty Ltd* (1989) 7 ACLC 510; *Re Doreen Boards Ltd* [1996] 1 BCLC 501). Initiating winding-up proceedings where there is a disputed debt is one instance of an abuse of process.

Courts have held that the petitioner for a winding-up order could be abusing process in other circumstances. These circumstances are:[68]

- The proceedings are bound to fail.
- The proceedings are commenced for some improper purpose. For instance, the petitioner is seeking to use the process in order to force the company into paying what is allegedly owed without giving the company an opportunity to establish what the position is with the alleged debt and having it determined whether the debt is properly payable (*Baillieu Knight Frank (NSW) Pty Ltd v Ted Manny Real Estate Pty*

---

[67] See *In re Bayoil SA* [1998] BCC 988; [1999] 1 BCLC 62 (CA); *Atlantic & General Information Investment Trust Ltd v Richbell Information Services Inc* [2000] 2 BCLC 779. Also, see A. Keay, 'Disputing Debts Relied On By Petitioning Creditors Seeking Winding Up Orders' (2001) 22 Co Law 40.

[68] A. Keay, *McPherson's Law of Company Liquidation* at 131–2.

Ltd (1993) 10 ACSR 539 at 541; *Dewina Trading Sdn Bhd v Ion International Pty Ltd* (1996) 21 ACSR 535).

● Issues will arise in the proceedings of a kind that are inappropriate for resolution in winding-up proceedings, such as where substantial issues as to the existence of the alleged debt need to be considered (*Re A Company (No 006798 of 1995)* [1996] 2 BCLC 48; [1996] BCC 395).

● Premature advertising of the petition (rule 4.11(2)(b)).

(b) Costs

'If a petition is struck out on the basis of constituting an abuse of process the court has a discretion as to the order it makes as to costs. Normally the petitioner will be liable for the costs of the company.'[69] Where appropriate, a court may order that some other person, other than the petitioner, pay the costs personally (*Re A Company (No 006798 of 1995)*). For example, the solicitor for the petitioner if he or she was to swear the affidavit verifying the petition and stated in the affidavit that he or she believed that the company was unable to pay its debts as they fell due, yet this belief was not held (*Re A Company (No 006798 of 1995)*).

(c) Claims for abuse of process

If one uses a legal process to achieve a purpose other than for which it was designed and as a result to cause someone to suffer damage, one commits a tort.[70] At the heart of the action is the fact that the person who originally commenced proceedings used the process for some purpose other than the attainment of the claim in the action.[71] The original proceedings may have been commenced with an ulterior purpose in mind or to attain a collateral advantage (*Goldsmith v Sperrings Ltd* [1977] 1 WLR 478 at 498; *Speed Seal Ltd v Paddington* [1985] 1 WLR 1327 at 1335; *QIW Retailers v Felview Pty Ltd* (1989) 7 ACLC 510). In *QIW Retailers v Felview Pty* it was held that there was an abuse of process. The petitioner's real objective, in initiating winding-up proceedings, was, according to the court, to force the directors of the company to negotiate in relation to his attempt to take over the company (at 521).

14.10.5.3 *Creditor opposition to the petition*

If the petitioner is an unsecured creditor, the right to have a winding up belongs to the class of unsecured creditors, so all, those supporting and those opposing the petition, are entitled to be consulted (*Re Crigglestone*

---

[69] A. Keay, *McPherson's Law of Company Liquidation* at 133.

[70] *Halsbury's Laws of England*, 4th edn, vol. 45 at para 1381.

[71] See the bankruptcy case of *Re Majory* [1955] Ch 600 where Lord Evershed MR said that an abuse of process involved taking proceedings not for the purpose for which such proceedings are designed and exist (ibid at 623). A majority of the Court of Appeal in *Goldsmith v Sperrings Ltd* [1977] 1 WLR 478 at 490, 503 agreed with this comment.

Coal Co [1906] 2 Ch 327). This is in line with the general principle that winding up is a collective process designed to benefit the general body of creditors. The general policy of the law is to treat the creditors themselves as being in the best position to decide what is in their interests (*Re Crigglestone Coal Co*). Therefore, if a majority in value of the unsecured creditors oppose a winding-up order, the court can exercise its discretion and refrain from making an order (*Re P & J MacRae Ltd* [1961] 1 WLR 229). It appears that it is necessary for a court to balance the right of a creditor, who cannot obtain payment of an undisputed debt which is presently owing, to a winding-up order (*Re Crigglestone Coal Co; Re P & J MacRae Ltd*) on the one hand, as against the fact that the majority in value of creditors may wish the company to continue, on the other. The court may say that the petitioner is entitled to an order but the court, in exercising its discretion (which is overriding) (*In re Chapel House Colliery Co* (1883) 24 Ch D 259), might nevertheless decide to refrain from making the order because of the attitude of the majority of creditors and the fact that the creditors can demonstrate good reasons for their attitude (*Re P & J MacRae Ltd*).

Section 195 recognises the collective nature of winding up for it grants the court a discretion to have regard for the wishes of the creditors in relation to all matters affecting a winding up. Therefore, it would appear that courts have a legislatively endowed right to consider the views of the creditors. In calling meetings of creditors for the purpose of ascertaining their wishes in accordance with section 195, the court is required to have regard to the 'value of each creditor's debt'.[72] This is the basis for the principle that the courts are, in determining whether an order should be made, to allow that the wishes of the majority of creditors *prima facie* to prevail. At one time it seemed that this was an absolute rule and that the court itself had to give effect to those wishes. But in *Re P & J MacRae Ltd*, the Court of Appeal unanimously held that majority opposition to winding up did not preclude the exercise of the court's discretionary power to make an order on the petition (at 235, 238).[73]

If the case is that an overwhelming proportion of the creditors in number and value oppose the order for good reason and the petitioning creditor is virtually alone, then in the absence of special circumstances the court will make a decision according to the wishes of the majority (*Re P & J MacRae Ltd; Re ABC Coupler & Engineering Co* [1961] 1 WLR 243 (CA)). But not all creditors will be seen as equal. In the exercise of discretion the weight to be given to those creditors opposing a winding-up order will vary according to the number and value of the creditors and the nature and quality of their debts (*Re P & J MacRae Ltd*). If the petitioner seeks a compulsory winding up and the majority of the creditors oppose winding

---

[72] A. Keay, *McPherson's Law of Company Liquidation* at 139.
[73] This view was followed recently in *Re Lummus Agricultural Services Ltd* [1999] BCC 953.

up, then *prima facie* the petitioning creditor is entitled to a winding up unless there are some additional reasons for deciding to the contrary and in favour of the majority (*Re J D Swain Ltd* [1965] 1 WLR 909 (CA)). If, on the other hand, the petitioner seeks a compulsory winding up and the majority of the creditors are opposed to it on the basis of good reasons then 'for the wishes of the petitioner to overrule those of the majority of the creditors there must be some special reason why the wishes of the majority should be overridden'.[74]

> While the views of creditors with vested interests in the company, such as the directors of the company and creditors who are associated with the company, will not be disregarded [*Re Medisco Equipment Ltd* [1983] BCLC 305; (1983) 1 BCC 98, 944], they will carry far less weight when it comes down to working out majorities [*Re H J Tompkins Ltd* [1990] BCLC 76] and may well be discounted [*Re Lummus Agricultural Services Ltd* [1999] BCC 953 at 958].[75]

The question of what constitutes a 'good reason' for the wishes of the majority in opposing the order to hold sway is largely one of fact and will rely heavily on the circumstances of each case. But some guidance is afforded by the decided cases. The following are examples of matter that a court might well take into account where a petition is resisted by a majority of creditors:

- prospect of payment is reasonable;
- there is an absence of assets;
- commercial propriety dictates that an investigation of the affairs of the company should take place.

14.11 Stay of winding-up proceedings

Liquidation means that the company is subject to a change of status[76] involving certain legal consequences that are discussed in Chapter 15. While its corporate status and powers are not affected by the liquidation, the fact is that the company exists, after the commencement of winding up, only so that it can be wound up, and then dissolved. The directors' powers pass to the liquidator and there are restrictions on what can be done with company property. This all happens because of statutory enactment and so the company of its own motion cannot revert to its

---

[74] *Re JD Swain Ltd* [1965] 1 WLR 909 at 914–915 (CA). See *Re Television Parlour plc* (1988) 4 BCC 95.

[75] A. Keay, *McPherson's Law of Company Liquidation* at 141.

[76] See *Thomson v Henderson's Transvaal Estates Ltd* [1908] 1 Ch 765 per Buckley LJ at 778.

former state. It can only be achieved by obtaining an order of the court staying proceedings in the winding up (section 147(1)). Such orders are most commonly applied for where the company has paid off all its debts and wishes to re-commence business, or where it is desired to give effect to a plan of reconstruction,[77] or a scheme of arrangement (*Re Stephen Walters & Sons* [1926] WN 236),[78] or a proposal for the entering into of a company voluntary arrangement.

Section 147(1) provides that the court is empowered at any time after ordering the winding up of a company, on the application of the liquidator, official receiver, any creditor or any contributory, to order the staying of winding-up proceedings either altogether or for a limited time and on such terms and conditions as the court thinks fit. Before making an order the court is entitled to ask the official receiver to deliver a report in relation to any facts or matters that, in the opinion of the official receiver, may be relevant to the application (section 147(2)). Usually companies are not permitted to apply for a stay where they are appealing the making of winding-up orders (*Re A & BC Chewing Gum Ltd* [1975] 1 All ER 1017). In applications for a stay, the court has a discretion (*Re Telescriptor Syndicate Ltd* [1903] 2 Ch 174 at 180) whether or not to stay proceedings and while there are no firmly binding rules (*Re Calgary and Edmonton Land Co Ltd* [1975] 1 All ER 1046 at 1051), this discretion is exercised pursuant to certain principles, many of which derive from those used in bankruptcy when considering applications for annulments (*Re Telescriptor Syndicate Ltd*). Before exercising its discretion the court has to find some valid reason why it should do so (*Aetna Properties Ltd (in liq) v GA Listing & Maintenance Pty Ltd* (1994) 13 ACSR 422). So, an applicant for a stay must make out a convincing case (*Re Calgary and Edmonton Land Co Ltd* [1975] 1 All ER 1046; [1975] 1 WLR 355) and if a court has doubts, a stay should not be ordered (*Re Calgary and Edmonton Land Co Ltd*; *Re Lowston Ltd* [1991] BCLC 570).

Where there is an application for a stay, the interests of the liquidator, the creditors and the members are considered (*Re Calgary & Edmonton Land Co Ltd*). Courts will not order a stay merely because all of the creditors agree to it and it will benefit them (*Re Telescriptor Syndicate Ltd* at 180), although the agreement of the creditors will be a matter that is considered by the court in coming to its decision (*In re Hester* (1889) 22 QBD 632 at 634, 636 and in the appeal at 640, 641). A court will determine whether a stay would be detrimental to commercial morality and the

---

[77] *Re Patent Automatic Knitting Machine Co* [1882] WN 97; *Re Steamship 'Titian' Co* (1885) 58 LT 178; *Re Egnia Pty Ltd (in liq)* (1991) 9 ACLC 1561; (1991) 5 ACSR 781. In such a case the liquidator's opinion is to be taken into account: *Remiliotis v Tenth Anemot Pty Ltd* (1994) 13 ACSR 650 at 652.

[78] In *Re Bristol Victoria Pottery Co* [1872] WN 85, a stay was ordered to enable conversion to voluntary winding up.

interests of the public (*In re Hester*).[79] A court will be concerned that an insolvent company is not given a licence to return to trading (*Re Telescriptor Syndicate Ltd*). Matters which a court may take into account are:

- directors have not complied with their duty to assist the official receiver;
- an investigation is warranted into aspects of the promotion, formation or demise of the company; and
- the business affairs of the company require investigation (*Re Telescriptor Syndicate Ltd*).

If there is evidence of misfeasance or improper activities the court will deny a stay (*Re Calgary and Edmonton Land Co Ltd*).

With voluntary liquidation an application may be made under section 112 for a stay (*Re Serene Shoes Ltd* [1958] 1 WLR 1087; [1958] 3 All ER 316; *Re Calgary and Edmonton Land Co Ltd*). There can be no doubt that section 147 applies to voluntary winding up as well as compulsory winding up (*Re South Barrule Slate Quarry Co* (1869) 8 Eq 688; *Re Calgary & Edmonton Land Co Ltd*). The section can be invoked 'at any time during the winding up of a company'.

The winding-up process ends on a stay order being made; all[80] proceedings in relation to the winding up may be made by the court at any stage following a winding-up order. This means that the whole effect of winding up ceases and the company can resume its business and affairs as if no winding up existed.

An alternative that is now available is for the company to apply for the winding-up order to be rescinded pursuant to rule 7.47(1).

If a compulsory winding up follows a voluntary, and the former is stayed, the voluntary liquidation proceeds (*Re Bristol Victoria Pottery Co Ltd* (1872) 20 WR 569).

---

[79] See the bankruptcy case of *In re Flatau* [1893] 2 QB 219. According to the Report of the Insolvency Law Review Committee in *Insolvency Law and Practice*, Cmnd 8558, 1982, ('the Cork Report'), 'it is a basic objective of the law to support the maintenance of commercial morality' (at para 191).

[80] The court has no power to stay only part of the proceedings: *Re European Assurance Society* [1872] WN 85.

Chapter 15

The Aftermath of the Advent of Winding Up

15.1 Introduction

The advent of a winding up has an impact on several stakeholders in the company. This chapter explores the extent of the impact.

15.2 On the company itself

15.2.1 *The entity and powers of the company*

First, it should be emphasised that the corporate personality remains unaffected; however, there are many effects that warrant mentioning. Following the advent of winding up there is to be no carrying on of the company's business except for the limited purpose of winding up. Also, while most of the powers of the company remain, winding up does cause a general prohibition upon its power to dispose of property. This is partly the result of the Act itself, but principally it is because of the fact that on winding up the company's affairs are removed from the control of the directors and control is bestowed on the liquidator, whose powers are circumscribed by statute to dealing with the assets for the purpose of winding up the company. In the case of voluntary winding up, section 87 provides[1] that the company is to cease to carry on business as from the commencement of the winding up,[2] but that the corporate state and corporate powers of the company shall continue until dissolved (section 87(1)).

---

[1] See *Midland Counties District Bank Ltd v Attwood* [1905] 1 Ch 357.
[2] See *Willis v Association of Universities of the British Commonwealth* [1965] 1 QB 140.

There is no comparable statutory provision with respect to compulsory winding up, but it has always been assumed that a liquidation of this type does not affect the corporate personality of the company (*Reigate v Union Manufacturing Co* [1918] 1 KB 592, 606), and that the powers of the company are not restricted by the fact that it has gone into liquidation (*Re Woking Urban District Council Act* [1914] 1 Ch 300). A liquidator in a voluntary liquidation has the power to carry on its business so far as is necessary for its beneficial disposal (*Re Great Eastern Electric Co Ltd* [1941] 1 Ch 241). Part III of Schedule 4 to the Act indicates that a liquidator in a compulsory liquidation also has the power to carry on its business so far as is necessary for its beneficial disposal.

15.2.2 *Name*

By way of warning to persons who might deal with a company in liquidation, every invoice, order for goods and business letter issued by or on behalf of the company, being a document on which the name of the company appears, must contain a statement that the company is being wound up (section 188(1)) and this is done by inserting the words 'in liquidation' in brackets after the name of the company; hence, ABC Ltd (in liquidation). If this is not done, the company could be liable to a fine and so might any officer and liquidator of the company who knowingly and wilfully authorises or permits the default (section 188(2)).

Section 216 prohibits the re-use of a company's name, except in limited circumstances, where the company has entered insolvent liquidation.[3] This is done so as to prevent the so-called Phoenix Syndrome.[4] This has usually involved[5] an unscrupulous trader who operated through a limited liability company that he or she ran down, with the result that it had substantial debts owed to unsecured creditors. The trader might put the company into receivership or into voluntary liquidation and then purchase, on behalf of another company which he or she controls, the company's business as a going concern from the receiver or liquidator. Thereafter, the latter company re-commences the business conducted by the former company. The new company might operate the business of the insolvent company from the same premises and/or with the same staff as its predecessor. Hence, the business is seen as rising from the ashes (of insolvency) like the mythical Phoenix.

---

[3] This means that at the time of entering liquidation, the company's assets are insufficient for the payment of its debts and other liabilities and the expense of winding up: section 216(7).

[4] See *Re Lightning Electrical Contractors Ltd* [1996] BCC 950. For a recent and extensive discussion of the syndrome, see D. Milman, 'Curbing the Phoenix Syndrome' [1997] JBL 224; S. Griffin, *Personal Liability and Disqualification of Company Directors* Oxford: Hart Publishing (1999) at 99–116.

[5] For an example, see *Western Intelligence Ltd v KDO Label Printing Machines Ltd* [1998] BCC 472.

15.2.3 *Ownership of property*

While winding up divests the company of the beneficial interest in its property, the legal title remains in the company (*Re Oriental Inland Steam Co* (1874) 9 Ch App 557; *Ayerst v C & K (Constructions) Ltd* [1976] AC 107 (HL)).

Liquidators may apply (section 145(1)) for and obtain an order vesting in them all of any part of the property of the company, in which case it vests in liquidators in their official capacity (*Graham v Edge* (1888) 23 QBD 683) and enables them to bring and defend legal proceedings in respect of it in their own name.[6] But, as liquidators merely become the agents of companies, which retain legal ownership of the property, they cannot be sued personally if the property is vested in them. Winding up does not, as with bankruptcy,[7] cause an automatic transfer of company property to the liquidator.[8]

Neither creditors nor members acquire any proprietary interest in the property by reason, or in consequence, of winding up.

15.2.4 *Dispositions of property*

15.2.4.1 *Compulsory winding up*

While winding up does not affect the company's ownership of its property, its powers of dealing with that property are limited significantly. Section 127 avoids any disposition of property of the company[9] made after the commencement of winding up, unless the court otherwise orders. The commencement date will, most often, be the date of the presentation of the petition to wind up.[10]

The purpose of section 127 is to ensure that the assets are divided rateably among the creditors (*Re Liverpool Civil Service Association* (1874) 9 Ch App 511; *Re Civil Service & General Store Ltd* (1889) 58 LR 220 at 221; *Re J Leslie Engineers Co Ltd* [1976] 1 WLR 292 at 304). Lord Cairns said that the particular object of a precursor of section 127 was to:

> prevent during the period which must elapse before a petition is heard the improper alienation and dissipation of the property of a company *in extremis*.[11]

---

[6] Section 145(2). See *Russian & English Bank v Baring Bros & Co* [1935] 1 Ch 120 at 125, 133–135; [1936] AC 405 at 435.

[7] See section 306.

[8] *Re Oriental Inland Steam Co* (1874) 9 Ch App 557 at 560; *Bank of Scotland v MacLeod* [1914] AC 311 at 321; *Re HJ Webb & Co* [1922] 2 Ch 369 at 388, affirmed *sub nom Food Controller v Cork* [1923] AC 647 at 671; *Ayerst v C & K (Construction) Ltd* [1976] AC 167 (HL); *Tanning Research Laboratories Inc v O'Brien* (1990) 8 ACLC 248 at 255.

[9] Cf *Re Branston & Gothard Ltd* [1999] BPIR 466.

[10] Section 127 has no effect in relation to any disposition made by an administrator while a winding-up petition is suspended pursuant to para 40 of Schedule B1 (section 127(2)).

[11] *Re Wiltshire Iron Co* (1868) 3 Ch App 443 at 447. See also *Coutts & Co v Stock* [2000] BCC 247.

The disposition rendered void is void at the time it took place (*National Acceptance Corp Pty Ltd v Benson* (1988) 12 NSWLR 213 at 221; (1988) 6 ACLC 685 at 691).

Section 127 can be seen as being constituted by three elements:

- a disposition of property;
- the disposition occurred after the commencement of the winding up; and
- no court order has been made to the effect that the disposition is not void.

(a) Disposition of property[12]

The words 'disposition of property' in section 127 are to be given a wide meaning (*Re Dittmer Gold Mines Ltd (No. 3)* [1954] St R Qd 275 at 282; *Sheahan v The Workers' Rehabilitation and Compensation Corporation* (1991) 9 ACLC 735) and has been held to apply to a broad range of forms of disposition. The disposition, to be affected by section 127, might be made by the company or a third party or made directly or indirectly, but any *bona fide* purchaser for value without notice of the winding-up proceedings would not be liable.[13]

The operation of section 127 causes special problems, especially for banks of companies in liquidation.[14] When a company pays money *into* its bank account after the commencement of the winding up this constitutes a disposition of property of the company within the provision, whether the company's account is in debit or in credit (*Re Gray's Inn Construction Co Ltd* [1980] 1 WLR 711; [1980] 1 All ER 814). As soon as the bank credits an amount collected in reduction of the company's overdraft, it makes a disposition on the company's behalf in its own favour, discharging *pro tanto* the company's liability on the overdraft (*Re Gray's Inn Construction Co Ltd*). Contrast the situation where a bank collects cheques drawn on third parties and pays them into the account of a company which is in credit before the payment in, because in such a case there is not a disposition of property (*Re Barn Crown Ltd* [1994] 1 WLR 147; [1984] BCLC 186; [1984] BCC 381).

Other problems exist where there are payments *out* of the company's bank accounts. Here the law appears to be uncertain. A distinction may have to be made between the case where the company's account is overdrawn and the case where the account is in credit. It is clear that where the former occurs, there is a disposition of property of the company within section 127 (*Re Gray's Inn Construction Co Ltd*). The leading case on this issue is *Re Gray's Inn Construction Co Ltd*.

---

[12] For a detailed discussion, see A. Keay, *McPherson's Law of Company Liquidation* London: Sweet & Maxwell (2001) at 285–93.

[13] See *Re J Leslie Engineers Co Ltd* [1976] 1 WLR 292; [1976] 2 All ER 85.

[14] See A. Keay, 'Dispositions of Company Property Post-Presentation of Winding-up Petitions and the Plight of Banks' [2001] *Restitution Law Review* 86.

In that case a petition for the winding up of a company was presented on 3 August. The company was wound up by court order on 9 October. During the period between these dates the company's bank continued to accept payments in and out of the company's account. About £25,000 was paid in and about £24,000 paid out during this time and the company's account was overdrawn during this period. On 3 August the account was overdrawn to the extent of £5,322 and by 9 October the state of the account was overdrawn by £4,464. The account was, at its highest point during the period, overdrawn by £7,000 and the lowest point was less than £3,600. The company's liquidator issued proceedings for a declaration that the amounts credited and debited to the company's account from 3 August to 9 October were dispositions that were void under section 127. Templeman J found for the bank, but on appeal the Court of Appeal upheld the liquidator's appeal.

Buckley LJ, who delivered the leading judgment in the Court of Appeal explained that when a customer of a bank is overdrawn and pays a sum from a third party into that account, the customer is discharging his or her indebtedness to the bank (at 715–716; 817). His Lordship went on to say that:

'It may well be the case . . . that in clearing a third party's cheque and collecting the amount due on it, the bank acts as the customer's agent, but as soon as it credits the amount collected in reduction of the customer's overdraft, as in the ordinary course of banking business it has authority to do in the absence of any contrary instruction from the customer, it makes a disposition on the customer's behalf in its own favour discharging *pro tanto* the customer's liability on the overdraft' (at 716; 817).

The Court of Appeal in *Re Gray's Inn Construction Co Ltd* did not need to consider where the company's account in the relevant period covered by section 127 is in credit, but Buckley LJ said that he did not see this being any different from the case before him, namely where the account is in debit (at 716; 817). In a later decision of the Court of Appeal, in *Bank of Ireland v Hollicourt (Contracts) Ltd (in liq)* ([2000] 1 WLR 895; [2000] BCC 237), the Court refused to accept that *Gray's Inn* stood for the proposition that all cheques drawn after the presentation of a petition in favour of third parties on the company's bank account, whether it is in credit or debit, involve a disposition of the amount of the cheque in the bank's favour and are void, with the consequence being that the bank may be liable for the amounts of the dispositions so far as the amounts cannot be recovered from the payees.

In *Hollicourt (Contracts) Ltd (in liq) v Bank of Ireland*, a petition was presented against a company on 5 February and was advertised on 26 February. The company's bank continued to honour cheques drawn on the company's account until 16 May. This was due to human error. The bank's employees failed to see the advertisement even though there were procedures for checking petitions which had been advertised. From 5 February until 16 May £156,200 was paid out of the account and £146,285 was paid in. During this period, apart from two brief times when H was overdrawn, the company was in credit. The liquidator of H attempted under section 127, but failed, to recover amounts paid out of the account, from the recipients of the payments. So, the liquidator looked to gain satisfaction from the bank. The bank argued, on the basis of several Australian decisions,[15] that where a company's account is in credit, only the recipient of any payment by cheque, and not the bank, could be regarded as receiving a disposition for the purposes of section 127. The issue in the case was whether section 127 made the bank, in continuing to operate the account on the company's instructions, liable for the amounts paid out on the cheques, or did section 127 only make the payees of the cheques liable? Blackburne J held for the liquidator. Consequently, the bank appealed.[16] The Court of Appeal held that section 127 only invalidates the dispositions by the company to the payees of the cheques. Mummery LJ, whose judgment was approved of by the other members of the Court (Peter Gibson and Latham LJJ), accepted the two points made by counsel for the bank, namely, first, that:

'[W]here a company pays a creditor by cheque drawn on an account in credit between the date of a petition and the winding up order, there is a disposition of the company's property in favour of the creditor falling within section 127. But it is contended that the judge was not required by principle nor by authority to hold (and he was wrong in holding) that there was another relevant disposition of the company's property in favour of the Bank when the Bank debited the Company's account with the sum paid to the creditor and that that disposition was avoided by section 127, so as to render the bank liable to restore the Company's account to its pre-disposition condition' (at 295–296).

The second point, and connected to the first, was related to the extent of the consequences of the statutory avoidance under section 127. Mummery LJ accepted that Blackburne J was wrong to hold that the legal effect of applying section 127 to the dispositions was to avoid the transactions between the Bank and the company as banker and customer, as well as the dispositions of the company's property as between the company and the payees of the cheques. His Lordship, after noting the rationale for section 127 and the fact that the provision is restitutionary, said that:

'In our judgment the policy promoted by section 127 is not aimed at imposing on the bank restitutionary liability to a company in respect of the payments made by cheques in favour of the creditors, in addition to the unquestioned liability of the payees of the cheques. The Bank operated the Company's account as agent for the Company . . . The section impinges on the end result of the process of payment initiated by the Company, i.e., the point of ultimate receipt of the Company's property in consequence of a disposition by the Company. The statutory purpose . . . is accomplished without any need for the section to impinge on the legal validity of intermediate steps, such as banking transactions, which are merely part of the process by which dispositions of the Company's property are made. This is not a restitutionary situation where the Bank has been unjustly enriched as against the Company . . .' (at 296).

---

[15] *Re Mal Bower's Macquarie Electrical Centre Pty Ltd* [1974] 1 NSWLR 254; *Re Loteka Pty Ltd* (1989) 7 ACLC 998.
[16] *Hollicourt (Contracts) Ltd v Bank of Ireland* [2000] 2 WLR 290.

In *Hollicourt (Contracts) Ltd (in liq) v Bank of Ireland* Mummery LJ said that when applying the legislative policy of section 127 the conclusion one came to was that the only dispositions of the company's property were the payments to the payees of the cheques drawn after the petition was presented (at 297). Section 127 requires a disposition which amounts to an alienation of a company's property. The Bank was merely obeying the order of its principal to pay out the principal's money. At no time was the beneficial ownership of the property of the company transferred to the bank, and there was no alienation of company property following the giving of the cheques (at 297).

Importantly, Mummery LJ opined that any decision under section 127 did not depend, as far as the position of the bank was concerned, on whether the company's account was in credit or overdrawn.

It has been frequently suggested, certainly until recent decisions, that when a company goes into liquidation it is considered advisable for its bank to apply for an order under section 127 providing that the company's bank account be frozen as at the date of the presentation of the winding-up petition and that all further dealings on the existing account be stayed from that date (*Re Gray's Inn Construction Co Ltd* [1980] 1 WLR 711 at 719, 720; [1980] 1 All ER 814 at 821). Moreover, it could require all subsequent dealings to be on a new and separate account. Prudence dictates that the bank should ask for the order to state that the bank is not under any obligation to ensure that transactions are in the ordinary course of business, or that the consideration given to the company represented market value for what the company disposed of.[17] Some have felt that these orders are necessary in order to protect the bank against a subsequent challenge to payments made out of the company's account after the date of the presentation of the winding-up petition.[18] *Hollicourt (Contracts) Ltd v Bank of Ireland* ([2000] 2 WLR 290 at 293) accepted that it was normal and prudent practice for banks to freeze existing company accounts when it becomes aware of the presentation of a petition and for the bank to require all subsequent dealings to be on a new and separate account in respect of which a validation order may be obtained.[19] The Court seemed to give its imprimatur to such action (at 293).

(b) Remedies

It is not altogether clear whether section 127 operates automatically on winding up or whether it only operates at the election of the liquidator. In other words, are liquidators given an automatic remedy or do they first have to elect to avoid the disposition? It is submitted that the basis for the

[17] See *Re A Company (No 00687 of 1991)* [1991] BCLC 133; [1991] BCC 210.
[18] *Re Gray's Inn Construction Co Ltd* [1980] 1 WLR 711 at 720; [1980] 1 All ER 814 at 821. Buckley LJ said that if a bank does not apply for a validation order and continues on then it is risky and it must bear the consequences.
[19] See *Re A Company (No 007130 of 1998)* [2000] 1 BCLC 582 for a case where a bank was unsuccessful in obtaining a validation order.

former is stronger, for 'void' means void for all purposes related to or incidental to the administration of the winding up, and any disposition rendered void is void at the time it took place.

(c) Validation of dispositions
The impact of section 127 is not absolute, as the court has a discretionary[20] power to declare that dispositions shall not be void.[21] The rationale for this, according to *Re Wiltshire Iron Co* ((1868) 3 Ch App 443), was that if a company is trading, and if transactions in the ordinary course of business that are entered into *bona fide* were not permitted, then the persons interested in the assets of the company could be prejudiced (at 446). Anyone applying for what is called a 'validation order', namely an order that the disposition is not void, has the onus of establishing the fact that the order should be made (*Re Rushcutters Court Pty Ltd (No. 2)* (1978) ACLC 29, 965).

In exercising their discretion courts should seek to ensure that there is justice as between the unsecured creditors and those who claim under the transaction under scrutiny (*In re Tramways Building & Construction Co Ltd* [1988] 1 Ch 293). Each case is determined on the particular circumstances, according to what is just and fair (*Re Steane's (Bournemouth) Ltd* [1950] 1 All ER 21; *Re Clifton Place Garage Ltd* [1970] Ch 470 at 491, 492). The courts will permit dispositions where they are made honestly, in the ordinary course of business and for the benefit of the company,[22] such as the payment of wages of employees or payments on supplies to enable the company to fulfil a contract that appeared to be profitable (*Re Webb Electrical Ltd* (1988) 4 BCC 230 at 234). A situation where no validation would be ordered is where the payment at issue was made to benefit directors of the company (*Re Burton & Deakin Ltd* ([1977] 1 WLR 390). Generally courts will validate dispositions which are shown to have been necessary in order to preserve the assets of the company, or increase the value of the company's assets (*Re Wiltshire Iron Co* (1868) 3 Ch App 443; *Re Gray's Inn Construction Co Ltd* [1980] 1 WLR 711 at 719; [1980] 1 All ER 814 at 820; *Re Fairway Graphics Ltd* [1991] BCLC 468 at 469).

Arrangements that are clearly for the benefit of the company and creditors as a whole have a reasonable chance of being validated. The transaction that is most commonly validated is one that permits the company to continue trading, because that might well benefit everyone (*Re Atlas Truck Service Pty Ltd* (1974) 24 FLR 220).

---

[20] *Re Steane's (Bournemouth) Ltd* [1950] 1 All ER 21 at 24–25. There are many factors which a court can consider in making its decision. See A. Keay, *McPherson's Law of Company Liquidation* at 299–300.

[21] Given the legal and practical problems which may arise if the court attempted to remake the bargain between the parties, the court is reluctant to validate particular parts of a transaction: *Jardio Holdings Pty Ltd v Dorcon Construction Pty Ltd* (1984) 2 ACLC 574.

[22] *Re Oriental Bank Corp* (1884) 28 Ch D 634; *Re Burton & Deakin Ltd* [1977] 1 WLR 390; *Re Webb Electrical Ltd* (1988) 4 BCC 230; *Denney v John Hudson & Co Ltd* [1992] BCLC 901; *sub nom Re SA & D Wright Ltd* [1992] BCC 503 at 506 (CA).

In *Re Park Ward & Co Ltd* ([1926] Ch 828) the court validated the granting of a debenture to a company that had lent the company money so that the company could pay its workers. If the loan had not been granted then the company would have had to close down. The upshot was that the loan and the subsequent payment of the workers ensured that the company could be sold as a going concern which benefited creditors.[23]

Courts have refused to grant validation orders where the disposition was going to benefit only one creditor to the detriment of the other unsecured creditors of the company (*Re Rafidain Bank* [1992] BCC 376).

The following principles detailed by the Court of Appeal in *Denney v John Hudson & Co Ltd*[24] are helpful in deciding when a court might validate a disposition:

- The discretion of the court is subject to the general principles that apply to the exercise of any discretion and to the limitations flowing from general insolvency law principles placed on the discretion.
- The assets of a company at the time of the commencement of the winding up are to be distributed *pari passu* among the unsecured creditors.
- On occasions it may be beneficial to the company and the unsecured creditors that it be permitted to dispose of some of its assets during the period between the presentation of the petition and the making of a winding-up order.
- When deciding whether to make a validation order the courts must ensure that the unsecured creditors are not prejudiced.
- The courts have to balance the desirability of the company carrying on business (an assessment of which is often speculative) with the possible prejudice to creditors.
- Save in exceptional circumstances a court should not validate a transaction which leads to one creditor being paid in full and the others only receiving a dividend.
- If a transaction is carried out in good faith when the parties are not aware of the presentation of the petition then, unless there is an indication that the transaction was an attempt to give a preference, it will normally be validated.

15.2.4.2 *Effect of the making of a void disposition*

While a disposition made after the commencement of winding up is void, if the recipient of the disposition fails to return it following a liquidator's demand being made, a liquidator will have to commence legal proceedings.

---

[23] In like manner the court in *Re TW Construction Ltd* [1954] 1 WLR 540; [1954] 1 All ER 744 validated the giving of an overdraft to enable the company to continue to trade.

[24] [1992] BCLC 901; *sub nom Re SA & D Wright Ltd* [1992] BCC 503.

The liquidator usually will not have to establish more than a disposition of property within section 127 and the point of time it was made.[25]

While a liquidator will be the usual applicant for an order setting aside a disposition, it has been held in *Mond v Hammond Suddards* ([1996] 2 BCLC 470 at 473) that proceedings are not restricted to the liquidator. Also, according to that case, section 127 does not provide a power of recovery, as do provisions like section 214 (wrongful trading),[26] because section 127 merely states that dispositions are void. As a consequence any sum or property obtained by a liquidator could be claimed by a charge-holder.

15.2.4.3 *The impact of the Human Rights Act 1998*

It may well be argued that section 127 is not compatible with the rights set out in the European Convention on Human Rights in that the provision affects two rights of a company. First, the company's right to property under Article 1. Second, where section 127 applies there is a determination of the company's civil rights without a fair hearing, and this is a breach of Article 6.[27] In addition, it might be pointed out that the company will probably incur costs in obtaining a validation order if it wishes that a disposition is to be effective.[28] It has been contended that the riposte to these arguments is that the company's right to property is only temporary and the action of section 127 does not determine the company's rights, as it only operates until either a winding-up order is made or the petition is dismissed. In any event the company can apply for a validation order in relation to any disposition.[29]

15.3 On directors

When a company enters insolvent liquidation the management of the company passes from the directors to either the official receiver in a compulsory liquidation or a private insolvency practitioner in a voluntary liquidation.

---

[25] Unlike with the recovery of preferences there is no need to be concerned with any subjective elements.

[26] See below at 523–32.

[27] M. Simmons and T. Smith, 'The Human Rights Act 1998: the practical impact on insolvency' (2000) 16 IL&P 167 at 168.

[28] Editorial (2000) 16 IL&P 165.

[29] Ibid.

15.3.1 *Powers*

In a creditors' voluntary winding up, the powers of the directors cease except in so far as they may be continued under the sanction of the liquidation committee (or if no such committee, the creditors) or the liquidator (section 103). It is unusual for directors' powers to be continued except for the purpose of exercising some power which is not given to the liquidator, such as sale or forfeiture of shares.[30] Section 114(3) indicates that the directors are able to both dispose of perishable goods and other goods the value of which are likely to diminish if they are not disposed of immediately and to do all that is necessary to protect company assets.

There is no provision in the Act that addresses the situation in relation to powers of liquidators in compulsory liquidations. However, it seems that it has been universally accepted that in winding up by the court, the powers of the directors come to an end with the appointment of a permanent liquidator.[31] Importantly, though, it has been held that directors retain residuary powers allowing them to appeal against a winding-up order (*Re Union Accident Insurance Co Ltd* [1972] 1 WLR 640; *Re Reprographic Exports (Euromat) Ltd* (1978) 122 SJ 400).

15.3.2 *Office*

Doubt surrounds whether the appointment of the liquidator brings to an end the office of directors. There are no provisions that touch upon voluntary winding up. However, it is submitted that there are two reasons why the office of director does not come to an end. First, the Act permits directors to exercise certain powers in some circumstances after the commencement of winding up. Second, there is case law to the effect that the office of directors does not end (*Midland Counties District Bank Ltd v Attwood* [1905] 1 Ch 357). After saying that, the offices of executive directors are terminated on winding up as they hold these positions as employees (*Fowler v Broad's Patent Night Light Co* [1893] 1 Ch 724).

The position in relation to compulsory winding up is also unclear. However, because of the decision of the Court of Appeal in *Measures Brothers Ltd v Measures* ([1910] 2 Ch 248) one can assert with some authority that on a court winding up occurring, the appointment of the directors terminates automatically (at 254, 256, 259). The fact that the position of director ends in one mode of liquidation and not in another seems to be anomalous, as there appears to be no justification for the difference.

---

[30] See e.g. *Re Fairbairn Engineering Co* [1893] 3 Ch 450.

[31] *Re Oriental Inland Steam Co* (1874) 9 Ch App 557 at 560; *Re Ebsworth & Tidy's Contract* (1889) 42 Ch D 23 at 43; *Fowler v Broad's Patent Night Light Co* [1893] 1 Ch 724; *Re Farrow's Bank* [1921] 2 Ch 164 at 173; *Re Mawcon Ltd* [1969] 1 WLR 78; cf. also *Gosling v Gaskell* [1897] AC 575 at 587; *Re Union Accident Insurance Co Ltd* [1972] 1 WLR 640 at 642.

If a director acts in relation to the affairs of the company following the termination of office, that action will be binding on the company if the liquidator subsequently ratifies the action. The danger for directors is that if there is no ratification then the director may be personally liable (*Measures Brothers Ltd v Measures*).

15.3.3 *Responsibilities*

Directors, as well as former and current officers of the company, have certain responsibilities imposed upon them by the Act, including the obligation to cooperate with the liquidator. Directors are to give to the liquidator information concerning the company, its promotion, formation, business, dealings, affairs or property and to attend the liquidator at such times as is reasonably required by the liquidator (section 235(2)). Section 208 provides that if directors fail to do certain things, such as disclose to the liquidator all of the company's property and deliver up to the liquidator all parts of the property of the company of which they have control and/or custody, they are committing an offence. The duty that directors have in this regard is a continuing requirement (section 235(2)).

In a compulsory winding up, the official receiver may, on the making of a winding-up order, require the directors, among others, to make out and submit a statement of affairs of the company (section 131(1)). If a director fails, without reasonable excuse, to fulfil the requirements of section 131 he or she is liable to a fine. If a person fails to comply with section 131 then the official receiver may apply to the court for an order.[32]

15.4 On company contracts

One cannot make general statements about the consequence of winding up in relation to company contracts, as each contract depends upon its nature and terms and the events leading up to, and surrounding, the winding up (*Re Tru-Grain Co* [1921] VLR 653). No legislative provision covers the issue. Liquidation does not, in itself, terminate the contracts of a company (*BCCI v Malik* [1996] BCC 15 at 17). The result is, on the one hand, that liquidation will have no effect upon a contract; however, on the other hand, it might lead to a situation that terminates the contract.[33]

---

[32] Rule 7.20(1)(a). See *Re Wallace Smith Trust Co Ltd* [1992] BCC 707.

[33] *Re Tru-Grain Co* [1921] VLR 653. Sometimes it has the effect of accelerating the time for payment of sums due under the contract, as in *Re South Brisbane Theatre Ltd* [1940] QWN 18.

If winding up has no effect *per se* on the contract, it will continue until the liquidator either repudiates or disclaims it.[34] Where the winding up operates to discharge the contract, it could occur in one of two ways: either by frustration – in which case the obligations of both parties are at an end – or by breach, in which case the other party will be entitled to prove for damages in the winding up. Where a liquidator advises that he or she is unable to complete a contract, the other party may be able to regard this as an immediate breach and sue for damages (*Ogdens Ltd v Nelson* [1905] AC 109 at 113(HL)). The nature and terms of the contract itself will determine whether the liquidation discharges the contract by breach or by frustration.

More frequently, winding up will result in a breach of contract for which the company will be liable in damages. This is the case even though the company may have gone, or been forced to go, into liquidation because of inability to pay its debts.

> In *Re Premier Products Ltd* ([1963] NZLR 368)[35] a company had agreed to supply certain paint products at fixed prices for a period of five years. It then became unable to pay its debts and went into voluntary liquidation before the expiration of that period. Leicester J considered that the agreement to supply paint for five years was in unqualified terms and the company was guilty of a breach of contract when it went into liquidation and so prevented itself from doing what it had agreed to do.

Contracts of employment are usually going to be affected by winding up. The rule is that a winding-up order, from its publication date,[36] operates as notice of dismissal to all the company's employees (*Re General Rolling Stock Co* (1866) 1 Eq 346; *Re Oriental Bank Corp; MacDowell's Case* (1886) 36 Ch D 366). The result is that employees either entitled to a period of notice or employed for a fixed term or for life, have a claim in damages for a breach of contract.[37]

Sometimes the liquidator will determine that it is appropriate to carry on the business of the company and in such a case that it is also appropriate to continue the employment of some or all of the company's employees. The notice of dismissal, in the form of the publication of the winding-up order, may be waived and the employee's employment continues under the existing contract with the company (*Re English Joint Stock Bank; Ex parte Harding* (1867) 3 Eq 341; *Re Associated Dominions Assurance Society Ltd* (1962) 109 CLR 516). The fact that this is the state of affairs must be made quite clear. It is possible that a liquidator does not waive the dismissal, but then re-employs an employee on fresh terms.

---

[34] See section 178(3)(a); as to damages caused by disclaimer: section 178(6). See below at 384–95 for greater discussion of disclaimer and the effects thereof.

[35] See also *Reigate v Union Manufacturing Co* [1918] 1 KB 593.

[36] Notice dates from publication of the order: *Re General Rolling Stock Co; Chapman's Case* (1866) 1 Eq 346.

[37] See *Re RS Newman Ltd* [1916] 2 Ch 309.

The balance of authority seems to suggest that the position is not the same in voluntary liquidation as it is with compulsory liquidation. For instance in *Midland Counties Bank v Attwood* ([1905] 1 Ch 357) it was held that voluntary liquidation did not operate to dismiss the employees of the company. However, it is submitted that this is not the case for all liquidations. If a company goes into voluntary liquidation because of insolvency, the resolution to wind up indicates the fact that the company is not able to perform its obligations under the employment contract and as a consequence it acts as a dismissal notice.[38]

If a liquidator is going to transfer the company's business, or part of it, he or she must ensure compliance with the Transfer of Undertakings (Protection of Employment) Regulations 1981[39] in relation to the liabilities of the company for its employees. The Regulations only apply to transfers in creditors' voluntary liquidations (as well as receiverships and administrations).[40] A transfer will not operate to terminate the contract of employment of any person employed by the company (regulation 5). On the completion of the transfer the rights, powers, duties and liabilities of the company under or in connection with any transfer are transferred to the transferee and anything done before the transfer is completed by or in relation to the company in respect of a contract of employment shall be deemed to be done by or in relation to the transferee (regulation 5(2)). Prior to the actual transfer of the business the liquidator is obliged to inform the appropriate representatives of employees who are affected (that is, the appropriate trade unions) of, *inter alia*, the transfer, the reasons for it and the legal, economic and social implications of it.[41]

15.5 On members

The effect of winding up is to bind all members and converts them into a category that is known as 'contributories' (*Re Hull & County Bank* (1886) 15 Ch D 507 at 511). There are three major matters to mention.

First, with companies limited by shares, members are liable to pay any amount unpaid on their shares to the extent that debts remain owing after

---

[38] See *Fowler v Commercial Timber Co Ltd* [1930] 2 KB 1.
[39] SI 1981 No 1794. The Regulations were made on 14 December 1981 under the European Communities Act 1972, section 2. Regulations 10, 11 and 11A were amended in 1995 (SI 1995/2587). For discussions of the Regulations, see, for example, R. Hepple, 'The Transfer of Undertakings (Protection of Employment) Regulations' (1982) 11 ILJ 29; S. Frisby, 'TUPE or not TUPE: Employee Protection, Corporate Rescue and "One Unholy Mess"' [2000] Cfi LR 249.
[40] See regulation 4.
[41] Regulation 10(2). The consequences of a failure to inform are set out in regulation 11.

the realisation of the assets of the company.[42] Those who were members within the year before the commencement of winding up (section 74(2)(a)) are liable in the same manner as present members if the present members are unable to satisfy what is owed by the company (section 74(2)(c)). This only applies in respect of debts incurred before the past members ceased to be members (section 74(2)(b)).

Second, as a result of the operation of section 127, any transfer of shares made after the commencement of winding up is void unless sanctioned by the court, in the case of compulsory winding up, or by the liquidator in voluntary winding up (section 88).[43] The reason for this prohibition is to prevent a shareholder from evading liability as a contributory by transferring shares to some impecunious person after winding up has commenced.[44]

Third, sections 88 (voluntary) and 127 (compulsory) provide that no alteration in the status of a member of the company should be valid[45] when occurring after winding up has commenced. Such a prohibition is aimed at alterations in status designed to relieve a member of the obligation to contribute (*Re Blaina Colliery Co* [1926] WN 30). An alteration would seem to encompass any transaction the effect of which is to terminate membership altogether or to convert the status of a contributory from that of present member to past member after winding up has commenced. However, it does not include the change of status that necessarily follows the removal of a shareholder from the register in pursuance of either the power of the court or the liquidator to sanction transfers in winding up (*Re National Bank of Wales* [1897] 1 Ch 298 at 306, 312).

15.6 On legal proceedings

15.6.1 *Proceedings commenced against the company*

15.6.1.1 *Compulsory winding up*

(a) Generally
When a winding-up order is made all proceedings and actions are automatically stayed under section 130(2), which provides that no proceeding shall be proceeded with or commenced against the company or its property except by leave of the court and subject to such terms as are imposed by the court. The rationale for this is that it is not appropriate for

---

[42] See section 74(1) (2)(d).

[43] Section 88. If the liquidator refuses to sanction the transfer an application could be made to the court under section 112.

[44] See *Rudge v Bowman* (1865) LR 3 QB 659 at 695 per Blackburn J.

[45] In a compulsory winding up the court may, however, validate such alterations: section 127.

the liquidator to be harassed by litigants, which would diminish the estate of the company; rather the liquidator is to preserve the limited assets of the company for distribution among all the persons who have claims upon them (*In re David Lloyd & Co* (1877) 6 Ch D 339 at 344). Later cases have also indicated that the provision is intended to oblige all claimants to submit to the procedural scheme established in winding up. It is less expensive and more orderly if any claims against the company can be dealt with in the usual way that is used for the proving of claims (*Ogilvie-Grant v East* (1983) 7 ACLR 669 at 672). So, the objects of section 130(2) are: to avoid the inconvenience and expense of litigation;[46] and to oblige all claimants to submit to the procedural scheme established in winding up (*Ogilvie-Grant v East*), which provides for an orderly process of winding up.

Of importance is the fact that the time in which a creditor has to commence proceedings under the Limitation Act 1980 stops running on the making of a winding-up order (*Re General Rolling Stock Co* (1872) LR 7 Ch App 646 at 649–650; *Re Cases of Taff's Wells Ltd* [1992] BCLC 11 at 17; [1991] BCC 582 at 586–587); therefore, a creditor does not have to initiate proceedings after the advent of winding up in order to preserve his or her rights.

Section 130(1) refers to the staying of any 'proceeding' and any 'action'. These terms are not interpreted restrictively. The former has been said to be an inclusive term which may be used to include any kind of action (*Re Keystone Knitting Mills' Trade Mark* [1929] 1 Ch 92, 102) and includes criminal proceedings (*R v Dickson* [1991] BCC 719). Similarly, 'action' should be given a wide meaning (*Langley Constructions (Brixham) Ltd v Wells* [1969] 1 WLR 503. 509). It covers counterclaims (*Langley Constructions (Brixham) Ltd v Wells* [1969] 1 WLR 503; [1969] 2 All ER 46), but it has been held that lodging an appeal (*Humber & Co v John Griffiths Cycle Co* (1901) 85 LT 141 (HL) and applying for security for costs against the company (*Pasdale Pty Ltd v Concrete Constructions* (1996) 14 ACLC 554; *BPM Pty Ltd v HPM Pty Ltd* (1996) 14 ACLC 857) are not actions or proceedings for which leave of the court is required.

(b) Leave to proceed
While section 130 stays proceedings and actions, the law does allow a person to obtain leave either to initiate or continue proceedings against a company. Whether leave to proceed will be granted will depend very much on each case's facts (*In re Kentwood Constructions Ltd* [1960] 1 WLR 646). It is certainly not granted readily. It is quite clear that the courts will

---

46 *Re David Lloyd & Co* (1877) 6 Ch D 339 at 344; *Ogilvie-Grant v East* (1983) 7 ACLR 669 at 672; *Zempilas v JN Taylor Holdings Ltd* (1991) 9 ACLC 287; *Vagrand Pty Ltd (in liq) v Fielding* (1993) 10 ACSR 373. The requirement of leave enables there to be an orderly winding up and avoidance of a multiplicity of actions (*Ogilvie-Grant v East; Zempilas v JN Taylor Holdings Ltd; Vagrand Pty Ltd (in liq) v Fielding*).

not engage in a consideration of the merits of a claim against a company (*Re BCCI (No 4)* [1994] 1 BCLC 419). If a party does proceed without securing leave, any claim or other originating process initiated following the beginning of winding up and served on the company is a nullity (*Roberts Petroleum Ltd v Bernard Kenny Ltd* [1983] 1 All ER 564).

An applicant for leave must establish that there is a serious or substantial question to be tried (*Vagrand Pty Ltd (in liq) v Fielding* (1993) 11 ACLC 411; (1993) 10 ACSR 373), and it must be affirmatively established that the claim has a solid foundation. So, leave is not granted where the applicant's claim is futile.

In determining whether to grant leave the courts have an absolute discretion,[47] and an appellate court will not readily interfere with the exercise of a discretion (*Thomas Plate Glass Co v Land & Sea Telegraph Construction Co* (1871) 6 Ch App 643; *Re Pacaya Rubber & Produce Co* [1913] 1 Ch 218 (CA)). There are not a lot of guidelines for courts in the exercise of the discretion. It has been said that courts are to do what is right and fair in all of the circumstances (*Re Aro Co Ltd* [1980] Ch 196; *Re Exchange Securities & Commodities Ltd* [1983] BCLC 186 at 195; *Canon (Scotland) Business Machines Ltd, Noter* [1992] BCC 620; [1993] BCLC 1194). Other factors which have said to be important in determining whether leave should be granted are 'the amount and seriousness of the claim, the degree of complexity of the legal and factual issues involved, and the stage to which the proceedings, if already commenced, may have progressed' (*Ogilvie-Grant v East* (1983) 7 ACLR 669, 672 per McPherson J).

In considering an application courts will examine whether there is a good cause of action, whether the action will affect the orderly winding up of the company and whether any action would prejudice the other creditors (*Re Gordon Grant and Grant Pty Ltd* (1982) 1 ACLC 196; (1982) 6 ACLR 727). The court may extend leave to a creditor to prosecute or initiate legal proceedings and impose conditions, such as the usual requirement that the creditor will not attempt to enforce against the company any judgment obtained without the leave of the court (*Re Gordon Grant and Grant Pty Ltd* (1982) 1 ACLC 196; (1982) 6 ACLR 727; *Re Coastal Constructions Pty Ltd (in liq)* (1994) 13 ACSR 329).

Where a party is seeking equitable relief such as a declaration or an injunction, it is a factor in favour of the giving of leave that such relief can only be secured by a successful application to the court (*Wyley v Exhall Gold Mining Co* (1864) 33 Beav 538; 55 ER 478; *Vagrand Pty Ltd (in liq) v Fielding* (1993) 11 ACLC 411 at 414).

It appears that the cases where leave has been granted are able to be placed under two principal headings. First, where the nature of the

---

47 *Thomas Plate Glass Co v Land & Sea Telegraph Construction Co* (1871) 6 Ch App 643; *Re Pacaya Rubber & Produce Co* [1913] 1 Ch 218 (CA); *Re Aro Co Ltd* [1980] Ch 196; [1980] 1 All ER 1067.

applicant's claim demands leave. An example is where the claim is for his or her own property which is in the hands of the company (*Re David Lloyd & Co* (1877) 6 Ch D 339; *Re Lineas Navieras Boliviarnas SAM* [1995] BCC 666). Second, where the balance of convenience and the requirements of justice demand that leave be given (*Fielding v Vagrand Pty Ltd* at 174). The question would have to be fundamentally one of expedience and convenience,[48] and leave will not be granted where the proposed action raises issues which are able to be dealt with in the liquidation proceedings with equal convenience and less delay and expense (*Re Exchange Securities & Commodities Ltd* [1983] BCLC 186 at 196). An example is a claim for which the company is insured and an insurance company will stand behind the company to pay any judgment (*Re Gordon Grant and Grant Pty Ltd*). Also, any claims which are likely to be more difficult (*Thames Plate Glass Co v Land & Sea Telegraph Co* (1871) 6 Ch App 643) or more expensive (*Re Joseph Pease & Co* [1873] WN 127) to settle in winding up rather than by action at law are usually allowed to proceed. If a liability of the company is only able to be admitted to proof provided that it is liquidated by a judgment, then leave will normally be granted.

15.6.1.2 *Voluntary winding up*

While there is no equivalent in voluntary winding up to section 130(2), the practice is for the court, upon application by the liquidator under section 112(1), to exercise its power[49] of staying actions and proceedings after commencement of voluntary winding up,[50] in order to effect the same result as section 130(2).

15.6.2 *Proceedings on behalf of the company*

When assuming office the liquidator will take advice as to whether proceedings commenced prior to the beginning of winding up are likely to be successful. The ultimate decision taken is often substantially influenced by the state of the level of the company's assets and funds.

---

[48] See also *Re Queensland Mercantile Agency Co* (1888) 58 LT 878; *Ogilvie-Grant v East* (1983) 7 ACLR 669; *Re Exchange Securities & Commodities Ltd* [1983] BCLC 186; *Fielding v Vagrand Pty Ltd (in liq)* (1992) 9 ACSR 505 (affirmed on appeal ((1993) 10 ACSR 373). For this reason it is not necessary for the applicant to establish that he or she is a secured creditor before the court will grant leave: *Re Aro Co Ltd* [1980] Ch 196; [1980] 1 All ER 1067.

[49] Under section 126.

[50] See *Westbury v Twigg Co Ltd* [1892] 1 QB 77; *Freeman v General Publishing Co* [1894] 2 QB 380; *Anglo-Baltic & Mediterranean Bank v Barber* [1924] 2 KB 410.

15.7 On creditors

The principal object of the statutory scheme which regulates winding up is to ensure that the property of an insolvent company shall, on its winding up, be rateably applied in satisfaction of its liabilities equally[51] and that this is done orderly. It would be antithetical to this if creditors were able to retain the right of enforcing their claims in the ordinary way.[52] Hence, section 128(1) declares any attachment, sequestration, distress, or execution put in force against the property of the company after the commencement of winding up to be void. On liquidation creditors no longer have personal rights against the company; they are exchanged for rights against a fund consisting of the company's assets that is administered by the liquidator for the benefit of those entitled to claim on the fund under the Act (*Re Lines Bros Ltd* [1983] Ch 1 at 14).

Aspects of the effect on creditors are discussed in Part VII.

---

[51] See section 107 (voluntary winding up) and rule 4.181(1) (compulsory liquidation). Also, see *Webb v Whiffin* (1872) LR 5 HL 711 at 735.

[52] For statements of the principle of rateable division in relation to this section, see *Re Redman (Builders) Ltd* [1964] 1 WLR 541 at 546; *Re Lines Bros Ltd* [1983] Ch 1 at 20.

Chapter 16

The Players in a Liquidation

16.1 Introduction

There are a number of persons that are involved either directly or indirectly in the liquidation of an insolvent company. This chapter discusses the major ones. The primary person involved, the liquidator, is the subject of Chapter 17.

16.2 The official receiver

Official receivers may play various roles in relation to the winding up of an insolvent company. First, when a company is wound up by court order, the official receiver automatically, except in two cases, becomes the liquidator of the company, at least for a while (section 136(2)), and continues in this role until another person becomes liquidator. The situations where the official receiver does not become the liquidator on the making of a winding-up order are: where a winding-up order immediately follows the end of administration under Part II of the Insolvency Act and in such a case the court may appoint the former administrator as liquidator (section 140(1)); where a winding-up order is made when there is a supervisor of a company voluntary arrangement, the court may appoint the supervisor as liquidator at the time of the making of the winding-up order (section 140(2)).

At any time while liquidator of a company, the official liquidator may summon separate meetings of the company's creditors and contributories for the purpose of choosing a person to be liquidator of the company in place of the official receiver (section 136(4)). The person appointed must, as we will see shortly, be a licensed insolvency practitioner. The official receiver may, at any stage, apply to the Secretary of State for Trade and Industry for the appointment of another person to assume the position of liquidator of a company (section 137(1)). If the official receiver is replaced as the liquidator of a company, he or she may still play an important part as far as compulsory liquidations are concerned. For instance, the official receiver is under a duty to investigate the causes of the failure of the company and the promotion, formation, business, dealings and affairs of the company and to make such report (if any) as is thought fit (section 132(1)). Also, the official receiver is entitled, at any time before the company's dissolution, to apply for the public examination of certain persons, such as the officers of the company (section 131(1)).[1]

Official receivers are at liberty to apply to the court for directions in relation to any matter affecting a liquidation (rule 10.3). The official receivers are duty bound, like liquidators, pursuant to the Company Directors' Disqualification Act 1986 (section 7(3)), to report to the Secretary of State any director, past or present, of an insolvent company who appears to be unfit to be concerned in the management of a company.[2] If there is no liquidation committee then the functions of a committee are vested in the Secretary of State (section 141(5)). In such a situation the functions may be exercised by the official receiver (rule 4.172(1)).

16.3 The general meeting of the company[3]

With voluntary liquidations the liquidator must convene annual meetings of members (contributories) (section 105) and a final meeting of members once the affairs of the company are fully wound up (section 106).

When dealing with winding-up issues the court is entitled to have regard to the wishes of creditors and contributories (section 195(1)). This is a statutory manifestation of one of the policies on which insolvency law is based, namely, that, in all matters relating to winding up, those who have financial interests in a distribution from an insolvent company's funds should be consulted wherever and whenever it is practicably feasible to do so.

How much the creditors and contributories actively participate in the processes of winding up will often depend largely upon the attitude of the liquidator, who may be more or less willing to seek and act upon their

---

[1] See below at 361–6.

[2] Official receivers are empowered to bring disqualification proceedings: *Re Minotaur Data Systems Ltd* [1999] 2 BCLC 766 at 772 (CA).

[3] For more detailed discussion, see A. Keay, *McPherson's Law of Company Liquidation* at 410–17.

advice. In general it is true to say, however, that in voluntary winding up the influence of creditors and contributories is stronger than it is in compulsory winding up, since in the latter the liquidator is primarily responsible to the court for the manner in which he or she discharges the liquidator's duties; but in both cases there is a discernible, though sometimes ill-defined, power in creditors or contributories to control the conduct of the liquidation.

Liquidators may well convene meetings in order to seek advice on certain matters, such as the need for some third party, usually an insurer, to agree to indemnify the liquidator for the costs in litigation in exchange for a portion of any judgment sum. Even though the approval of creditors or contributories may not, in many cases, be legally obligatory, the advantage for the liquidator of obtaining approval is to give some degree of protection if charges of misfeasance or negligence are later brought against the liquidator.

In some situations liquidators are obliged to call meetings for approval of actions that they are contemplating. Besides that, liquidators are subject to an express statutory duty to have regard to directions given by resolutions of creditors or contributories in general meeting.[4] This does not mean that a liquidator must do what a meeting determines, for he or she is certainly not bound by a direction which conflicts with the proper execution of the duties of a liquidator (*Re David Hamilton Ltd* [1928] NZLR 419), but it does indicate the importance of liquidators consulting the meeting before taking action in serious matters.

Meetings are held:

- where on the liquidator's own motion he or she calls a meeting of creditors or contributories in order to ascertain their wishes on a particular matter (section 168(2));
- where the liquidator is directed by resolution of the creditors or contributories to summon a meeting or is requested to do so by not less than one-tenth in value of the creditors or contributories;[5]
- in the case of a creditors' voluntary winding up, where annual meetings are required (section 105);
- in the case of members' voluntary winding up which has continued for more than one year, annual general meetings of the company must be summoned so as to enable the liquidator to give an account of his or her acts and dealings and of the conduct of the winding up during the preceding year (section 93);

---

[4] See section 168(2) for compulsory winding up and rule 4.54(1) for voluntary winding up.

[5] Section 168(2) requires the liquidator to convene a meeting when requested in writing to do so by not less than one-tenth in value of the creditors. Rule 4.61(1) provides that the costs of a meeting so convened shall be paid by the person upon whose request the meeting is convened; and that person shall before the meeting is convened deposit with the liquidator such sum as may be required as security for the payment of expenses.

- in the case of members' voluntary winding up, the liquidator must, as soon as the affairs of the company are fully wound up, call a final general meeting of the company for the purpose of presenting the liquidator's final account showing how the winding up has been conducted;[6] and
- where, pursuant to section 195(1), the court directs that a meeting of creditors or contributories be held in order to ascertain their wishes on some matter relating to the winding up.

16.4 The liquidation committee[7]

In compulsory or creditors' voluntary liquidations a liquidation committee may be appointed and it consists of creditors and contributories who, *inter alia*, assist and supervise the liquidator

16.4.1 *Compulsory liquidation*

There are two ways that a committee can be set up in a compulsory winding up. First, where meetings of creditors and contributories have been called for the purpose of appointing a liquidator, the meetings may choose to establish a liquidation committee (section 141(1)). Second, a liquidator, who is not the official receiver, may at any time convene separate meetings of the creditors and contributories in order to see if a liquidation committee should be established (section 141(2)).

Where there is a difference between the meeting of creditors and the meeting of contributories as to whether there should be a committee, then the committee shall be established unless there is a court order which provides to the contrary (section 141(3)).

It is provided in the Rules that in a compulsory winding up, where a committee is established, other than by the contributories, the committee is to consist of at least three, and not more than five, creditors who are elected by the creditors pursuant to section 141 (rule 4.152(1)). In a creditors' voluntary winding up, the only requirement is that the committee must have three members before it is established (rule 4.152(2)). Any creditor, other than one whose debt is fully secured can act as a member of a committee provided that a proof of debt has been lodged and the proof has neither been wholly disallowed for voting purposes, nor wholly rejected for purposes of distribution of dividend (rule 4.152(3)).

---

[6] Sections 94 (members' voluntary) and 106 (creditors' voluntary).
[7] For more detailed discussion, see A. Keay, *McPherson's Law of Company Liquidation* at 417–26.

As the court has no express power to interfere with the composition of a validly appointed committee, it may, in exercising its general powers in relation to winding up, consider influencing the composition so as to ensure that no creditor or class of creditors with a substantial interest is excluded from the representation which it seeks (*Re Radford & Bright Ltd* [1901] 1 Ch D 272 at 277).

16.4.2 *Creditors' voluntary liquidation*

The section 98 meeting of creditors, or a subsequent meeting, may appoint a committee of not more than five persons (section 101(1)). The members may, at a general meeting of the company, appoint a number of persons, up to five, to serve on a committee that has been established (section 101(2)). The same rules that apply to compulsory windings up, as far as representatives of committee members go, apply equally to creditors' voluntary windings up.

16.4.3 *Position of committee members*

A fiduciary position is occupied by committee members in relation to the creditors and contributories (*Re Geiger* [1915] 1 KB 439 at 447; *Re Bulmer* [1937] Ch 499 at 502; *Re Security Directors Pty Ltd (in liq)* (1997) 24 ACSR 558) and that prevents them from obtaining a profit from their office or from allowing their own interests to conflict with their duty as committee members.

The Rules provide, *inter alia*, that a committee member, or a person who has been a committee member during the last 12 months, is not permitted to (rule 4.170):

- receive from the company's assets any payment for services given or goods supplied in connection with the winding up;
- obtain any profit from the winding up;
- acquire any assets of the company;

unless the approval of the court is obtained beforehand, or where the transaction is made as a matter of urgency, or by way of a contract already in force before the company went into liquidation, and the leave of the court is secured for the transaction where it is satisfied, after full disclosure of the circumstances, that the person will be giving full value in the transaction.

16.4.4 *Powers*

The liquidation committee has a number of powers in compulsory winding up, such as being able:

- to grant or withhold approval for the compromise of certain debts owed to the company (section 167(1)(a) and Part I of Schedule 4);
- being able to grant or withhold approval for the bringing or defending of legal proceedings in the name of the company (section 167(1)(a) and Part I of Schedule 4);
- to receive notice that the liquidator is going to dispose of property to a person connected with the company (section 167(2)(a));
- to receive notice that the liquidator is going to employ a solicitor to assist in the carrying out of his or her functions (section 167(2)(b)).

If the liquidation committee refuses to approve a course of action where the liquidator needs approval, the liquidator may apply to the court, which will have regard for the opinion of the committee, but is able to overrule the committee's decision (*Re Northern Assurance Co Ltd* (1915) 113 LT 989). But the liquidator should not seek court approval with respect to something that he or she knows the committee will not sanction, without first seeking the opinion of the creditors and contributories (*Re Consolidated Diesel Engine Manufacturers Ltd* [1915] 1 Ch 192).

16.5 The Insolvency Service

The position and role of the Insolvency Service was discussed in Chapter 4 and it is not intended to deal with it here, save to say that the Service is, as it is with all insolvency administrations, concerned about liquidations.

16.6 The Secretary of State for Trade and Industry

The Secretary of State is the political head of the Department of Trade and Industry. Her role is to regulate the formation, management and insolvency of companies. Again the role of the Secretary of State was touched on briefly in Chapter 4.

In some cases the Secretary of State has the power to present a petition for the winding up of a company.[8] Also, as part of the power to initiate and approve insolvency rules and regulations, the Secretary of State may, subject to the Act and the Rules, make Regulations with respect to any

---

[8] For example, see section 124A and see above at 208.

matter provided for in the Rules as relates, *inter alia*, to the carrying out of the functions of a liquidator and a provisional liquidator with respect to the following matters arising in a winding up:[9]

- The preparation and keeping by liquidators and provisional liquidators of books, accounts, and other records, and their production to such persons as may be authorised or required to inspect them.
- The auditing of liquidators' accounts.
- The manner in which liquidators are to act in relation to the books, papers and records of insolvent companies and the manner of their disposal.
- The supply, in an insolvent winding up, by liquidators to creditors, members of companies, contributories and liquidation committees of copies of documents relating to the insolvency and the company's affairs.
- The manner of distribution of assets by liquidators including provision with respect to unclaimed funds and dividends.
- The manner in which moneys coming into the hands of liquidators during the winding up is handled and invested and the payment of interest on sums which have been paid into the Insolvency Services Account.
- The amount to be paid to the official receiver by way of remuneration when acting as provisional liquidator or liquidator.

The Secretary of State may exercise the functions of a liquidation committee where none exists.[10] The Secretary of State has a duty to monitor the activities of insolvency practitioners, which of course includes liquidators and their records and accounts.[11] The Secretary of State has a role to play in determining the release of liquidators. First, she may give a release to a liquidator who has resigned or been removed.[12] Where the official receiver has acted as the liquidator of a company and gives notice that the winding up of the affairs of the company have been, for practical purposes, completed, he or she has a release from the time that the Secretary of State determines (section 174(3)). In relation to a private liquidator who has been removed from office by the court or the Secretary of State, or who has vacated office under section 172(5) or (7), and the creditors have passed a resolution against his or her release, the liquidator's release will be effective from the time determined by the Secretary of State (section 174(4)). The Secretary of State also determines

---

[9] Much of the following also applies to bankruptcies.
[10] Section 141(4), (5). The same applies where the liquidator is the official receiver.
[11] Insolvency Practitioners' Regulations 1990, regulation 18.1.
[12] See above at 278–82.

the time of the release of a liquidator who has held the final meeting of a winding up and the creditors have, at that meeting, resolved against the liquidator having a release (section 174(5)).

The Secretary of State has the power to apply to the court for the disqualification of a director and this might well be exercised following the liquidation of an insolvent company.[13]

---

[13] Company Directors' Disqualification Act 1986, section 7(1). See below at 558–65.

Chapter 17

The Liquidator[1]

17.1 Introduction

The most important player in a winding up is the liquidator. The liquidator is the one who administers the liquidation for the creditors. The principal object of winding up is, of course, to have the assets of the company collected and realised, its debts and liabilities discharged and any remaining balance distributed among the members. These are typically the functions of the liquidator and it is the liquidator, and only the liquidator, who is entitled to perform them. As there are large numbers of liquidations in a year and the liquidator is such an important person in the administration of liquidations, the work of this office-holder warrants significant attention.

17.2 Appointment

17.2.1 *The appointee*

The Act provides that companies in compulsory liquidation must be wound up by either the official receiver or persons qualified as insolvency practitioners in relation to companies (section 230(3)). The official receiver was discussed both in Chapter 4 and Chapter 16, so the balance of this section of the chapter deals with the appointment of licensed insolvency practitioners who are in private practice.

---

[1] For a detailed study of the liquidator, see Chapters 8 and 9 of A. Keay, *McPherson's Law of Company Liquidation*, London: Sweet & Maxwell, (2001). For more discussion of the work of a liquidator in administering a winding up, see Part VI.

Originally liquidators needed no specific professional qualifications. But the Act changed this state of affairs so as to ensure that so far as possible only competent and reliable persons will be entrusted with windings up.[2] A person acts as an insolvency practitioner when he or she acts as a liquidator (section 388(1)). It is an offence to act as an insolvency practitioner in relation to a company if one is not qualified to do so (section 389).

One or more persons are entitled to act as joint liquidators, if they are qualified (section 231(1)), and it is not uncommon to have more than one liquidator, particularly where the winding up is complex and demanding.

The critical aspect with a liquidator is that he or she must be independent and must be seen to be independent and impartial (*Re Contract Corp* (1872) 7 Ch App 207). Liquidators must ensure that they do not put themselves in situations where there is a conflict of interest between their own interests and that of the creditors (*Re Contract Corp* (1872) 7 Ch App 207; *Re Sir John Moore Gold Mining Co* (1879) 12 Ch D 325; *Silkstone Coal Co v Edey* [1900] 1 Ch 167; *Re Rubber & Producers' Investment Trust Ltd* [1915] 1 Ch 382; *Re Gertzenstein Ltd* [1937] Ch 115). As the liquidator must be impartial, any suggestion that the prospective appointee might be biased should mean that he or she is not to be appointed (*Re West Australian Gem Explorers Pty Ltd* (1994) 13 ACSR 104; (1994) 12 ACLC 256). It is necessary that any proposal to appoint a person as the liquidator of a company with which he or she has had a prior link be carefully scrutinised (*Re National Safety Council of Australia (Victoria Division)* (1989) 15 ACLR 355; (1989) 7 ACLC 602), so that there can be no allegation of bias.

If an insolvency practitioner gives, or agrees or offers to give, any valuable consideration to any member or creditor of a company with a view to securing his or her own appointment or nomination as liquidator, the practitioner is liable to a fine (section 164; Schedule 10).

17.2.2 *The method of appointment*

In a compulsory winding up the official receiver becomes the liquidator of the company at the time of the making of the order and continues in this role until another person becomes liquidator. The most usual occurrence is that the official receiver is replaced at meetings of the creditors and contributories of the company.[3] The meetings are called by the official receiver (section 136(4)) at his or her volition, or in response to the requirement of one-quarter in value of the creditors (section 136(5)(c)).

---

[2] See Chapter 12.
[3] See section 139.

Where both a creditors' and a contributories' meeting are held and both nominate, as they are entitled, the liquidator will be the person nominated by the creditors (section 139(3)). Where the creditors do not make a nomination, then the liquidator will be the nominee of the contributories. Where the two meetings nominate two different persons then any contributory or creditor may apply to the court, within seven days from the day on which the creditors made a nomination, for an order either that the person nominated by the contributories be liquidator alone or jointly with the person nominated by the creditors, or some other person be appointed instead of the person nominated by the creditors (section 139(4)).

For a creditors' voluntary winding up, the liquidator is appointed by the company in general meeting (section 91(2)), and, while not required, this is invariably done at the same meeting as that at which the resolution for voluntary winding up is passed.[4] At the subsequent meeting of creditors, the creditors may nominate a person(s) to act as liquidator (section 100(1)) and, in the event of difference, their nomination prevails over the nomination made by the members at the company meeting (section 100(2)), though it is possible for any director, member or creditor to apply to court, within seven days of the nomination of liquidator by the creditors' meeting, for a direction either that the company's nominee shall be liquidator either jointly with, or instead of, the person nominated by the creditors, or appointing someone else as liquidator instead of the person nominated by the creditors (section 100(3)).

Once the position of liquidator is determined, if there are any subsequent vacancies in the office of liquidator, they may be filled by the creditors.[5] If at any stage there is no liquidator acting then the court has the power to appoint a liquidator (section 108(1)).

If a creditors' voluntary winding up occurs as a result of being a conversion from a members' voluntary winding up, namely where the liquidator appointed under a members' voluntary believes that the company will be unable to pay its debts within the time stated by the directors in their statement of solvency made under section 89 and the liquidator convenes a creditors' meeting pursuant to section 95, then any appointment of a liquidator at that meeting of creditors is deemed to have been made under section 98 (section 102).

---

[4] Where there is proper notice of the proposed winding-up resolution, express notice of the proposal to appoint a liquidator is not necessary: *Re Trench Tubeless Tyres Co* [1900] 1 Ch 408.

[5] Section 104. Where there is a need to fill a vacancy a meeting of creditors may be convened by any creditor, or where there was more than one liquidator the meeting may be convened by the liquidator(s) who intends to continue in office: rule 101A.

17.3 Liquidator's position

The actual status of a liquidator is not clear. Although sometimes referred to as a trustee, he or she is not. But clearly a liquidator is a fiduciary and owes fiduciary obligations to the company and the body of creditors and if these are not complied with, the claim is for a breach of statutory duty and not for a breach of trust (*Pulsford v Devenish* [1903] 2 Ch 625).

What is clear is that the liquidator is the agent of the company (*Re Silver Valley Mines Ltd* (1882) 21 Ch D 381 (CA); *Knowles v Scott* [1891] 1 Ch 717; *Stewart v Engel* [2000] BCC 741; [2000] 2 BCLC 528; [2000] BPIR 383), giving him or her power to bind the company[6] without personal liability (*Stead Hazel Co v Cooper* [1933] 1 KB 840). An effect of the liquidator being an agent is that the liquidator is bound by those things which bound the company and he or she can be in no better position than the company (*A-G (Canada) v Standard Trust Co of New York* [1911] AC 498; *Multinational Gas & Petroleum Co Ltd v Multinational Gas & Petroleum Services Ltd* [1983] 1 Ch 258). The liquidator's agency is rather unusual in the sense that the liquidator is in control of the actions of the principal. Also the liquidator's duties are subject to the overriding duties set out in the Act to pay the funds collected from the sale of the company's assets to the creditors.[7] While discharging the powers of an agent of the company, the liquidator is not generally personally liable and this includes the case where contracts are made on behalf of the company (*Stead Hazel & Co v Cooper* [1933] 1 KB 840). Liquidators are only liable if they contract in such a way as to make it plain that they are undertaking personal liability (*Stewart v Engel* [2000] BCC 741; [2000] 2 BCLC 528). In *Stewart v Engel* the liquidator of a company entered into in a contract which included a clause that provided that the liquidator entered into the contract as agent of the company and the clause excluded any personal liability on the part of the liquidator. Subsequently, when it was attempted to enforce the contract against the liquidator, the court held that the clause not only excluded the liquidator from being liable in contract, it also excluded liability for negligence.

In effect, a liquidator is a hybrid composite with elements of fiduciary trustee, agent, and (in some instances) officer of the court,[8] although a liquidator in a voluntary liquidation is not an officer of the court (*Re Hill's Waterfall Estate & Gold Mining Co* [1896] 1 Ch 947 at 954; *In re Knitwear (Wholesale) Ltd* [1988] 1 Ch 275). A liquidator in a compulsory winding up, whether or not appointed by the court, is an officer of court[9] and under

---

[6] See *Re Farrow's Bank Ltd* [1921] 2 Ch 164.
[7] *Knowles v Scott* [1891] 1 Ch 717. See sections 107 and 143(1).
[8] A. Keay, *McPherson's Law of Company Liquidation* at 370.
[9] See *Re Contract Corporation: Gooch's Case* (1872) 7 LR Ch App 207 at 211; *Re Timberland Ltd: Commissioner for Corporate Affairs v Harvey* (1979) 4 ACLR 259 at 281, 286.

the control of the court (section 167(3)). The liquidator is not a servant of the court in the same sense as a court official (*Re Dominion Trust Co: Critchley's Case* (1916) 27 DLR 580), but a liquidator is a representative of the court (*Re Timberland Ltd: Corporate Affairs Commission v Harvey* (1979) 4 ACLR 259 at 286) and is accountable to the court.

17.4 Duties of liquidators

The principal duties of the liquidator are enumerated in section 143, and are: to ensure that the assets of the company are got in, realised and distributed to the creditors and, if there is a surplus, it is distributed to the persons entitled to the assets.[10] How these duties are discharged is, for the most part, left to the judgment of the liquidator.

In carrying out his or her duties, a liquidator is to act with common sense and judgment (*Re Windsor Steam Coal Co* [1929] 1 Ch 151 at 159).

It is clear that the liquidator not only owes a duty to the company, but also to its creditors (*Pulsford v Devenish* [1903] 2 Ch 625 at 632, 637; *James Smith & Sons (Norwood) Ltd v Goodman* [1936] Ch 216 at 231–232; *A & J Fabrications Ltd v Grant Thornton* [1998] 2 BCLC 227 at 231) and if a liquidator fails to fulfil this duty then the creditors may take action against the liquidator.

17.4.1 *Fiduciary duties*

These duties, emanating from the fact that liquidators are fiduciaries, are strictly enforced by the courts. A primary duty is to act honestly and to exercise powers *bona fide* for the purpose for which they are conferred[11] and not for any private or collateral purpose. In addition, two further duties of major importance follow from the fiduciary relationship. First, the liquidator must not allow private interests to come into conflict with duties (*Re Corbenstoke Ltd (No2)* [1990] BCLC 60 at 62). Second, in discharging the duties he or she must at all times act in a totally impartial way as between the various persons interested in the property and liabilities of the company.

It is only if it can be established that the liquidator deliberately engaged in the action that constituted the breach that a liquidator is liable (*Charlie Pace v Antlers Pty Ltd (in liq)* (1998) 16 ACLC 261 at 275).

---

[10] See *Ayerst v C & K (Construction) Ltd* [1976] AC 167 at 177 (HL).

[11] A liquidator who exercises powers in good faith after taking proper advice is not open to challenge: *Re Burnells Pty Ltd (in liq); Ex parte Brown and Burns* (1979) 4 ACLR 213.

17.4.1.1 *Refraining from a conflict of duty and interest*

In accordance with the principle of equity that those occupying fiduciary positions are not to permit their personal interests to conflict with the interests of those whom it is their duty to protect, liquidators are not permitted, either directly or indirectly, to profit from their office otherwise than to the extent expressly allowed by law, namely receipt of the remuneration allowed them (*Re Gertzenstein Ltd* [1937] Ch 115). Consequently, they are only entitled to their authorised remuneration and any benefit over and above this is a profit which the liquidator has no right to retain.

Another aspect of the liquidator's fiduciary duty is that he or she is unable to enter into contracts with the company and if a liquidator purchases company property without disclosing any interest in the transaction, the contract is liable to be rescinded (*Silkstone Coal Co v Edey* [1900] 1 Ch 167) and the property restored to the company.

17.4.1.2 *A duty to act with impartiality*

Liquidators must not act as the agent of, or represent, any particular interest or group of interests (*Re Lubin, Rosen & Associates Ltd* [1975] 1 WLR 122 at 126). In many respects the liquidator's functions are quasi-judicial and therefore he or she is under a duty to act impartially whenever there is a conflict between the interests of creditors and contributories,[12] or between the creditors of different companies which are being wound up by him or her (*Re City & County Investment Co* (1877) 25 WR 342).

17.4.2 *Duties of skill and care*

A high standard of care and diligence is required of a liquidator in the performance of his or her duties (*Re Windsor Steam Coal Co* [1929] Ch 151 at 165; *Re Home and Colonial Insurance Co Ltd* [1930] 1 Ch 102 at 125). The liquidator is duty bound to complete the winding up within a reasonable time (*Re House Property & Investment Co* [1954] Ch 576 at 612) without needlessly protracting it.[13] The liquidator must demonstrate a degree of skill and care that conforms to the responsibility that the nature of the office places upon the liquidator, who is a well-paid professional person (*Re Windsor Steam Coal Co* [1929] Ch 151 at 165).

In considering the actions of liquidators, courts are not to be hasty in criticising them, as they are often found in difficult positions. Certainly

---

[12] See *Re Rubber & Produce Investment Co* [1915] 1 Ch 382.

[13] See *Re House Property & Investment Co* [1954] Ch 576 at 612; *Re Timberland Ltd; Commissioner for Corporate Affairs v Harvey* (1979) 4 ACLR 259; *Charlie Pace v Antlers Pty Ltd (in liq)* (1998) 16 ACLC 261 at 273.

courts should not judge a liquidator's conduct with hindsight (*Re Windsor Steam Coal Co* [1929] Ch 151).

The liquidator owes a duty of care to the creditors, shareholders and those guaranteeing the debts of the company when realising assets (*Re Macrae & Henderson* 1989 SLT 523). If liquidators fail to exercise their duties of skill and care then they may suffer two forms of penalty. First, they may be subject to a claim for damages. Second, their right to claim remuneration may be lost (*Re Silver Valley Mines* (1882) 21 Ch D 381).

17.4.3 *Duty to exercise discretion*

The liquidator is obliged to use his or her own discretion in the management of the affairs and property of the company and the distribution of the assets;[14] liquidators are not to delegate the exercise of their discretion to others where professional judgement is required, although they may appoint an agent to do any business which they are unable to do (para 12 of Part III of Schedule 4).

17.4.4 *Specific duties*

There are a number of more specific duties that are imposed on liquidators by either statute or the common law. These may be divided into broad duties which include a number of functions and more specific duties that are procedural in character.[15]

17.4.4.1 *Publishing and filing notice of appointment*

Within 14 days of appointment, a liquidator in a creditors' voluntary liquidation must publish a notice of appointment in the *Gazette* and to file a copy of the notice with the Registrar of Companies (section 109). Notice of appointment must also be given, where the meeting of creditors or contributories or the meeting of the company has appointed the liquidator, in such newspaper as he or she thinks is most appropriate for ensuring that the appointment comes to the notice of the company's creditors and contributories (rule 4.106(1)).

In a compulsory winding up, copies of the winding-up order are to be sent by the official receiver (rule 4.21(1)) to the registered office of the company, or if there is no registered office, the company's principal or last known principal place of business (rule 4.21(2)), and a copy to the

---

[14] See *Re London and Mediterranean Bank: Ex parte Birmingham Banking Co* (1868) 3 Ch App. 651.
[15] For a more in-depth consideration, see A. Keay, *McPherson's Law of Company Liquidation* at 460–501.

Registrar of Companies (rule 4.21(3)). The official receiver is to cause the order to be inserted in the *Gazette* and such newspaper as the official receiver selects (rule 4.21(4)).

17.4.4.2 *Providing statement of affairs and report*

The official receiver must send a report to creditors and contributories with respect to the proceedings in the winding up and the state of the affairs of the company and a copy is to be filed in court (rule 4.43). Where a statement of affairs has been submitted and filed in court, the official receiver is to send out to creditors and contributories a report containing a summary of the statement and such observations as is thought fit in relation to the statement and the affairs of the company in general (rule 4.45(1)).

17.4.4.3 *Settling a list of contributories*

Liquidators must determine which of the company's members are contributories of the company, namely those who are liable to contribute to the company on a winding up (section 79). The court has the duty to settle a list of contributories (section 148(1)) and this power is delegated to liquidators in compulsory liquidations (section 195) and to liquidators in voluntary liquidations (section 165(4)(a)).

17.4.4.4 *Retaining records, books and accounts*

It is necessary for the liquidator on demand to produce to the Secretary of State, and permit her to inspect, any accounts, books and other records kept either by the liquidator or by a previous liquidator.[16]

Under the Insolvency Practitioners' Regulations 1990[17] liquidators must maintain a record of the course of the liquidation and maintain it for 10 years beyond release.[18] It must be produced to the professional body to which a practitioner belongs and by virtue of which the practitioner is a licensed insolvency practitioner and to the Secretary of State on reasonable notice.[19]

In all compulsory and creditors' voluntary liquidations[20] a liquidator is required to prepare and keep separate financial records for the company

---

[16] Insolvency Regulations 1994, regulation 15(1) (SI 1994/2507).
[17] SI 1990/439, regulations 16–20.
[18] Ibid at regulation 20. The matters of which records are to be kept are set out in Schedule 3 to the Regulations.
[19] Ibid at regulation 18.
[20] Insolvency Regulations 1994, regulation 10(1).

and such other records as are required to explain the receipts and payments entered in the financial records and relating to the carrying on of business, including an explanation of the source of any receipts and the destination of any payments.[21]

In compulsory liquidations the liquidator is to obtain and retain bank statements relating to any local bank account set up in the name of the company.[22] Administrative, financial and trading records of the company have to be retained for a period of six years following the vacation of the office of liquidator.[23]

17.4.4.5 *The collection of property*

An important task of the liquidator when appointed is to take custody, or have control, of all the property to which the company is, or appears to be, entitled (section 144(1)). It is the liquidator's duty to immediately take possession of the books, deeds and documents of the company; and investigate where any missing assets are, as well as obtaining possession of the assets of the company. With respect to assets of which physical possession cannot be obtained, e.g., book debts owing to the company, the liquidator should perfect his or her title as far as possible.

To assist liquidators, section 234, which provides that the court may require any person of the company to deliver to the liquidator any money, property or books to which the company appears to be entitled, and is applicable to liquidators in voluntary liquidations (section 234(2)).[24] In order to collect some property or money, it might be necessary for a liquidator to take legal proceedings. Some of the sorts of actions in which a liquidator might engage are discussed in Part VIII.

17.4.4.6 *The investigation of the affairs of the company*

Liquidators are obliged to investigate the affairs of companies in liquidation, including their promotion and formation and the way that a company's business has been conducted. This is in order to locate and collect the property of the company, and to prosecute any delinquent officers of the company. This matter is discussed in more detail in Chapter 25 but a few words are appropriate here.

In a compulsory winding up, the official receiver may, on the making of a winding-up order, require, by notice, some or all of the persons referred

---

[21] Ibid at regulation 10(2).
[22] Ibid at regulation 10(3).
[23] Ibid at regulation 13(1).
[24] The provision also applies to provisional liquidators, administrators and administrative receivers.

to in section 131(3) to make out and submit to him or her a statement of affairs of the company (section 131(1)). The persons referred to in section 131(3) are the former officers of the company, those who have taken part in the formation of the company at any time within one year of the date of the winding-up order, employees of the company and former employees in employment within one year of the winding-up order and those who are or have been in the year before the date of the winding-up order officers or employees of a company which is or was in the year before the winding-up order an officer of the company being wound up. The statement of affairs may lead the official receiver to further investigations. In any event the official receiver has the duty, under section 132, to investigate the cause of the failure of the company, if it has failed, and to investigate generally the promotion, formation, business, dealings and affairs of the company.

The official receiver may determine that it is necessary to seek the public examination of certain persons, namely the past or present officers of the company, liquidators, administrators or receivers of the company, or such persons who have been concerned, or taken part, in the promotion, formation, or management of the company (section 133(1)).

As part of the investigation the liquidator might seek, under section 236, the examination of the following persons:[25]

- An officer of the company.
- Anyone who is known or suspected to have in his or her possession any property of the company or who is supposed to be indebted to the company.
- Anyone whom the court thinks is capable of giving information concerning the promotion, formation, business, dealings, affairs or property of the company.

17.4.4.7 *The preserving of assets*

As the company's property is to be realised for the creditors, the liquidator must ensure that he or she protects and preserves the assets of the company (*Cleve v Financial Corp* (1873) 16 Eq 363, 381) including, perhaps, the insurance of property where appropriate. As the value of the company's business might rapidly deteriorate if trading activities were brought to a sudden end, and in order to preserve the goodwill of the business, it might be proper that the liquidator carries on the business for a period during the winding up. Paragraph 5 of Schedule 4 permits the carrying on of business in so far as this is necessary for the beneficial winding up of the business. The liquidator must have reasonable grounds for believing

---

[25] See section 236(2).

that carrying on the business is beneficial or else he or she may be held personally liable for any loss sustained.

> In *Re Centralcast Engineering Ltd* [2000] BCC 727 a liquidator allowed the continuation of trading when it was clear that she should have realised the assets quickly. The company liabilities grew considerably due to the continuation of trading. As a result the liquidator was held liable for misfeasance.

17.4.4.8 *The realisation of assets*

The central aim of insolvent winding up is, of course, to liquidate the assets so that the proceeds can be paid to creditors in order to satisfy the liabilities of the company. The liquidator is authorised by paragraph 6 of Schedule 4 to sell or otherwise dispose of all or any part of the property of the company. Where, as frequently happens, property of the company is burdened by mortgages or charges or otherwise subject to securities, the liquidator is entitled to deduct a reasonable sum to meet the cost of realisation before applying the proceeds in paying the principal debt and any outstanding interest to the secured creditor (*Re Marine Mansions Co* (1867) 4 Eq 601; *Lathom v Greenwich Ferry Co* (1892) 36 Sol Jo 789: *Re Universal Distributing Co* (1933) 48 CLR 171 at 174).

The liquidator is at liberty to sell the company's property in any manner he or she determines is appropriate, namely by tender, by private contract or by public auction. Advice may need to be sought as to what would be the best way to sell items of property. For the most part it might be proper for liquidators to take advice on what is the value of property so that they ensure that property is not sold at below value. In disposing of property it must be acknowledged that it is unlikely that a liquidator will be able to sell the assets for what they would have been worth had the company been a going concern, as buyers will often be aware that property is part of the estate of a company which is in liquidation and consequently they could drive a hard bargain. The terms of sale are a matter for the discretion of the liquidator, but the liquidator's fundamental duty is to realise the assets of the company in the most efficient way and to obtain the highest possible price for the assets.

17.4.4.9 *Determining and discharging liabilities*

There is a general obligation to pay all liabilities, whether present or future, certain or contingent, ascertained or sounding only in damages.[26] Initially, the liquidator is to determine the extent of the

---

[26] See Chapter 9 of Part 4 of the Rules and rule 12.3. As to priority of payment of debts, see section 175.

liabilities and the identity of the respective creditors. The liquidator can do this to some degree by examining the books of the company and the statement of affairs under section 99, in creditors' voluntary winding up, and in a compulsory winding up the statement of affairs submitted under section 131, if there is one (*Butler v Broadhead* [1975] Ch 97). Additionally, the liquidator should invite claims by advertisement and, if necessary, by contacting creditors personally when he or she knows of them and they have failed to prove their debts (*Pulsford v Devenish* [1903] 2 Ch 625 at 631; *Re Armstrong-Whitworth Securities Co* [1947] Ch 678; *Austin Securities Ltd v Northgate & English Stores Ltd* [1969] 1 WLR 529).

The general rule is that the liquidator is to pay or discharge only those liabilities that are legally enforceable. However, regard must be had for the principle that if an officer of the court is under an obligation of conscience then the court will direct the officer to fulfil that obligation (*Star v Silvia* (1994) 12 ACLC 600 at 603). Courts will not permit their officers to take courses of action or to take advantage of a technical position in law where it would be dishonourable (*Re John Bateson & Co Ltd* [1985] BCLC 259 at 261). This is referred to as 'the rule in *Ex parte James.*' The rule is derived from bankruptcy law, where it provides that a trustee in bankruptcy will not be permitted to take advantage of strict legal rights if this has the effect of unjustly enriching the estate at the expense of an innocent claimant. In *Re Condon; Ex parte James* ((1874) 9 Ch App 609), the trustee was ordered to restore moneys paid under a mistake of law which would otherwise have been irrecoverable. Since the early part of the last century, courts in England have treated *Ex parte James* as standing for a wider principle than dealing with the recovery of payments made pursuant to a mistake of law.[27] Apparently, the enrichment of the officer is the most significant element[28] and it does not matter how that occurred.

The reason for the application of the rule in bankruptcy is that the trustee is an officer of the court and, as such, will not be permitted to do anything which would be regarded as dishonourable or unconscionable for an ordinary person to do.[29] The rationale is that the courts must separate themselves from any actions which do not measure up to proper standards of probity and fair dealing.[30]

---

[27] For example, see *In re Clarke* [1975] 1 WLR 559. I. Dawson in 'The Administrator, Morality and the Court' ([1996] JBL 437 at 454) submits that the rule may be subsumed under the law of restitution (at 461).

[28] For example, see *Green v Satangi* [1998] BIPR 55.

[29] See *Scranton's Trustee v Pearce* [1922] 2 Ch 87; *Downs Distributing Co v Associated Blue Star Stores Ltd* (1948) 76 CLR 465 at 482–3.

[30] I. Dawson, 'The Administrator, Morality and the Court' [1996] JBL 437 at 443. See *Re Tyler* [1907] 1 KB 865 at 871.

Courts have applied the rule to a liquidator in compulsory winding up (*Re Regent Finance & Guarantee Corp* (1930) 69 LJ Ch 283; [1930] WN 84; *Re Clifton Place Garage Ltd* [1970] Ch 477 at 491; *Re Associated Dominions Assurance Co* (1962) 109 CLR 516; *Re Wyvern Developments Ltd* [1974] 1 WLR 1097) on the basis that the liquidator is an officer of the court. The rule applies also to official receivers (*Re Wyvern Developments Ltd* [1974] 1 WLR 1097 at 1105). There are divergent cases on whether liquidators in voluntary liquidation are subject to the rule. They are not officers of the court, but it might be argued that it brings the law into disrepute if the rule's application depends on what kind of liquidation has been initiated. Notwithstanding this, it might be appropriate for voluntary liquidators to disregard the rule and let a court decide on the application of the person who is allegedly aggrieved.

17.5 Powers of the liquidator

17.5.1 *Statutory powers*

While the powers of a liquidator in compulsory and in creditors' voluntary winding up are essentially the same, different provisions apply to each form of winding up and therefore it is more convenient to deal with them separately.

17.5.1.1 *Compulsory winding up*

The primary powers of the liquidator are provided by section 167 and Schedule 4 of the Act. Most of these powers are directed to specific duties which are bound to be carried out.

In exercising powers, the liquidator is constantly subject to the control of the court[31] and the court may make a determination on what a liquidator has done, when hearing the application of a creditor or a contributory concerning the actions of the liquidator. However, courts are not keen to interfere with a liquidator unless he or she is acting absurdly (*Leon v York-O-Matic Ltd* [1966] 1 WLR 1450) or unreasonably (*Pitman v Top Business Systems Ltd* [1984] BCLC 593; *Re Greenhaven Motors Ltd* [1997] BCC 547). Section 167, in conjunction with Schedule 4, provides that some of the powers are only able to be exercised with the approval of the court, which may be given retrospectively (*Re Patrick Plains Free Press Newspaper Co* (1892) 3 BC (NSW) 49) in cases of urgency (*Re London Metallurgical Co* [1897] 2 Ch 262),

---

[31] See section 167(3).

or of the liquidation committee.[32] Notwithstanding that, others can be exercised without approval.[33] Below we mention the most important powers.

(a) Effecting compromises
Approval is required to effect compromises with the company's creditors and debtors (Para 3 of Schedule 4), carrying on the company's business (Para 5 of Schedule 4) and the bringing or defending of legal proceedings (Para 4 of Schedule 4). Nevertheless, the court occasionally authorises the liquidator to exercise all these powers without first applying for its approval or consent (*Re Rochdale Property & General Finance Co* (1879) 12 Ch D 775).

A compromise will only be approved if the court believes that it is for the benefit, and serves the interests, of the creditors (*Re Edennote Ltd (No.2)* [1997] 2 BCLC 89; *Re Greenhaven Motors Ltd* [1999] BCC 463; [1999] 1 BCLC 635 (CA)). In *Re Bank of Credit and Commerce SA (No. 4)* ([1995] BCC 453) the court permitted the liquidators to enter into a contribution agreement. Under the agreement, claims between companies in the BCCI group, which were in liquidation, and the majority of shareholders were settled in exchange for a payment into the winding up by the shareholders. The court was satisfied that this course of action represented the only chance for the Bank's depositors (and creditors) to get anything from the company.

(b) Commencing or defending proceedings
While liquidators are able to initiate proceedings in their own names (*Re Silver Valley Mines* (1882) 21 Ch D 381), any decision to commence proceedings in the name of the company must be approved (paras 3A and 4 of Schedule 4).[34]

In proceedings taken in the name of the company then, while an order for security for costs may be made against the company pursuant to section 726 of the Companies Act 1985,[35] no liability will usually be imposed on the liquidator as far as costs go (*Re Wilson Lovatt & Sons Ltd* [1977] 1 All ER 274), absent the exceptional case[36] where a court decides

---

[32] See Parts I and II of Schedule 4.
[33] See Part III.
[34] It is expressly stated in para 3A of Schedule 4, as a result of section 253 of the Enterprise Act 2002, that all liquidators must gain sanction for initiating proceedings under sections 213, 214, 238, 239, 242, 243, or 423. These sections, apart from sections 242 and 243 that only apply to Scotland, are discussed in some detail in Part VIII.
[35] For a discussion of this issue, see D. Milman, 'Security for Costs: Principles and Pragmatism in Corporate Litigation' in B.A.K. Rider (ed.), *The Realm of Company Law,* London: Kluwer Law International (1998) at 167; A. Keay, *McPherson's Law of Company Liquidation,* at 441–4.
[36] See the discussion by K. de Kerloy, 'The Personal Liability of Liquidators and Administrative Receivers for the Costs of an Unsuccessful Action' (2000) 4 RALQ 13 at 17–18 as to what might be deemed exceptional.

to exercise its power, under section 51(1) and (3) of the Supreme Court Act 1981, to order costs against a non-party.[37]

(c) Selling company assets
This is something that will occur in nearly every liquidation, and is the way that the liquidator will get funds to pay creditors. This power is contained in paragraph 6 of Schedule 4 and can be exercised without any sanction.

(d) Acting for the company
The power is to be found in paragraph 7 of Schedule 4, and includes executing documents in the name, and on behalf, of the company. No court or liquidation committee sanction is needed.

(e) Appointing agents
Liquidators will need to appoint agents who are able to bring special abilities to an aspect of the liquidation, e.g., solicitors, auctioneers and real estate agents.

(f) The incidental power
This power is contained in paragraph 13 of Schedule 4 and authorises the liquidator to do all such things as are necessary for winding up the affairs of the company and distributing its property. This is an extremely wide power (*Re Cambrian Mining Co* (1882) 48 LT 114 at 116; *Mercantile Credits Ltd v Dallhold Investments Pty Ltd* (1994) 15 ACSR 230 at 233) and permits the liquidator to do anything which may be thought expedient with reference to the property of the company (*Re Cambrian Mining Co*; *Butterell v Docker Smith Pty Ltd* (1997) 23 ACSR 149; (1997) 15 ACLC 307).

17.5.1.2 *Supplementary powers*

Some supplementary powers are provided in section 168 for compulsory liquidations. They are the power:

- to summon general meetings of the creditors and contributories for the purpose of ascertaining their wishes (section 168(2));
- to apply to the court for directions in relation to any particular matter arising in the winding up (section 168(3));
- to use his or her own discretion in the management of the assets and the distribution among the creditors (section 168(4)).

---

[37] For example, see *Aiden Shipping Co Ltd v Interbulk Ltd* [1986] AC 965 (HL); *Globe Equities Ltd v Globe Legal Services Ltd* (1999) BLR 232; *The Times*, April 14, 1999 (CA); *National Justice Compania Naviera SA v Prudential Assurance Co Ltd (No.2)*, *The Times*, October 15, 1999 (CA).

17.5.1.3 *Delegated powers*

There are powers conferred by the Act upon the court, the exercise of which is delegated to the liquidator. The powers delegated are:

- the holding and conducting of meetings of creditors and contributories to ascertain their wishes (section 160(1)(a));[38]
- the settling of lists of contributories and, where required, the rectifying of the register of members (section 169(1)(b));
- the collection and application of the assets (section 169(1)(b));[39]
- the requiring of the payment, delivery, conveyance, surrender or transfer of money, property, books and papers (section 160(1)(c));[40]
- the making of calls (section 160(1)(d));[41] and
- the fixing of a time within which the debts and claims must be proved (section 160(1)(e)).[42]

Given that the powers come from the court, the liquidator acts as an officer of the court in exercising these powers.

17.5.2 *Voluntary winding up*

Section 165 regulates the powers of liquidators in voluntary liquidations.

Court or liquidation committee (or, if there is no committee, a meeting of the creditors) approval must be obtained where liquidators exercise the powers contained in Part I of Schedule 4 (section 165(2)(b)).

Liquidators are permitted to exercise all of the powers contained in Parts II and III of Schedule 4 without any need to secure approval (section 165(3)), but if they wish to take legal proceedings pursuant to any of sections 213, 214, 238, 239, 242, 243 or 423 then they must secure sanction (para 3A of Schedule 4). These sections involve actions taken to recover money or property disposed of by the company prior to winding up, and they are, save for sections 242 and 243 which apply only to Scotland, discussed in detail in Part VIII. Liquidators are allowed to exercise two court powers: the settling of a list of contributories (section 165(4)(a)) and the making of calls (section 165(4)(b)).

---

[38] See rule 4.54.
[39] See rule 4.179(1).
[40] See rule 4.195.
[41] See rule 4.202.
[42] See section 153.

17.6 Remuneration

A liquidator is able to claim remuneration for services rendered in relation to the winding up of the company (rule 4.127(1)). Where the official receiver is the liquidator, remuneration is calculated in accordance with the scale of fees enumerated in Part 5 of the Insolvency Regulations 1994 (SI 1994/2507). A licensed insolvency practitioner acting as a liquidator may calculate remuneration in one of two ways. Either, in the same manner as the official receiver, as a percentage of the value of the assets realised or distributed, or a combination of the two figures, or on the basis of the time properly spent in attending to the winding up (rule 4.127(2)).

In circumstances where a voluntary liquidation precedes a compulsory winding up, the remuneration of the voluntary liquidator will have priority over the expenses of the winding up (rule 4.129).

The remuneration of the liquidator is payable from the company's assets as part of the expenses of winding up. In cases of insufficient assets to pay the expenses of winding up, the expenses are paid out in accordance with the order of priority provided for in rule 4.218(1) of the Rules.[43] The remuneration of the liquidator does not attract a high priority. The court has, in compulsory liquidations, a discretion as to the order in which the expenses of winding up are to be paid,[44] but this discretion will not be exercised so as to enable the liquidator to have remuneration in priority to other expenses which would normally rank ahead of remuneration, except where exceptional circumstances exist (*Re Linda Marie Ltd (in liq)* (1988) 4 BCC 463 at 472).

With both compulsory winding up and creditors' voluntary winding up the amount of remuneration is, in the first instance, to be determined by the liquidation committee, if there is one (rule 4.127(3)). Where there is none, or it makes no determination, remuneration is fixed by resolution passed at a creditors' meeting (rule 4.127(5)). In making a determination, both the committee and the meeting are to have regard to several factors. These are: (rule 4.127(4)):

- The complexity of the winding up.
- Any responsibility of an exceptional kind which fell on the liquidator.
- The effectiveness with which the liquidator appears to be carrying out (for an interim assessment), or appears to have carried out, his or her duties.
- The value and nature of the assets with which the liquidator has had to deal.

---

[43] See below at 400–13.
[44] Section 156; also see rule 4.220. The same right would exist in voluntary liquidations due to section 112.

Rule 4.127(6) provides that remuneration is to be in accordance with the scale provided for the official receiver, where not fixed as above.

If remuneration is determined by a liquidation committee the liquidator may request a meeting of creditors to increase it (rule 4.129). Where a liquidator is not satisfied with the decision of the liquidation committee or the resolution of the creditors' meeting, or what the official receiver's scale under rule 4.127(6) would provide, he or she may apply to the court for an order increasing the amount or rate (rule 4.130(1)). If a creditor believes the remuneration fixed for a liquidator is excessive then, with the agreement of 25 per cent in value of the creditors, an application may be made to the court for an order reducing the liquidator's remuneration (rule 4.131(1)).

Liquidators are not able to claim remuneration in relation to work which was not within the scope of his or her duties, or that was not necessary (*Reiter Bros Exploratory Drilling Pty Ltd* (1994) 12 ACLC 430 at 436). Remuneration will be denied where a reasonable amount of skill has not been exercised.

17.7 The end of the appointment

If a practitioner ceases to be qualified to act as an insolvency practitioner (such as becoming a bankrupt) then his or her position as liquidator in relation to existing windings up is automatically terminated.[45] But the more frequent occurrences which see the termination of office are resignation, removal and release.

17.7.1 *Resignation*

A liquidator in compulsory winding up is only permitted to resign in those circumstances set out in rule 4.108(4) and after giving notice to the court (section 172(6)). These circumstances are:

- ill-health;
- an intention to cease to practise as an insolvency practitioner;
- a conflict of interest or change of personal circumstances which precludes or makes impracticable the further discharge of the duties of a liquidator.

Before resigning, a liquidator must convene a meeting of creditors for the purpose of receiving the resignation. The notice of the meeting must

[45] Section 172(5). See *Re Bridgend Goldsmiths Ltd* [1995] 2 BCLC 208 at 209.

be accompanied by an account of the liquidator's administration of the liquidation and include a summary of receipts and payments and a statement by the liquidator that he or she has reconciled his or her account with that which is held by the Secretary of State (rule 4.108(3)).

Except where the creditors' meeting decides against the liquidator being released, the liquidator is automatically released once his or her resignation is effective under rule 4.109.

If a creditors' meeting does not accept the resignation, the liquidator may apply, in a compulsory or creditors' voluntary liquidation, to the court and it may give leave to the liquidator to resign (rule 4.111(1)).

17.7.2 *Removal*

A liquidator may be removed by either the court or a meeting of creditors in relation to compulsory (section 172(2)) and creditors' voluntary (sections 171(2)(b), 172(3)) windings up. If a creditors' meeting is convened to consider the removal of a liquidator then the meeting must be specially convened for that purpose.

A meeting of the creditors is to be summoned for the purpose of replacing the liquidator if it is requested by not less than one-half in value of the company's creditors (section 171(3)).

Where liquidators are appointed by the Secretary of State then the Secretary of State may, by direction, remove them (section 172(4)).

If a creditors' meeting cannot be convened or a resolution to have the liquidator removed is lost, then an application to the court for removal may be considered. Section 108(2) provides, in relation to voluntary winding up, that a liquidator may, on cause shown, be removed by the court. There is no such provision in relation to compulsory winding up, but rule 4.119(2), together with past case law, indicates that the same criteria applies, i.e., that a cause must be shown for removal to be ordered.

An applicant for removal must demonstrate that he or she is qualified to make the application and that he or she is a proper person to make the application (*Deloitte Touche AG v Johnson* [1999] BCC 992 at 997(PC)). This means that the applicant has a legitimate interest in the relief sought (*Deloitte Touche*). A creditor would certainly qualify, as would the liquidator (*Re Stella Metals Ltd (in liq)* [1997] BCC 626), even if he or she is no longer qualified to act as a liquidator (*Re AJ Adams (Builders) Ltd* [1991] BCC 62).[46] It was held in *Re Corbenstoke Ltd (No 2)* ([1990] BCLC 60) that an application for the removal of a liquidator can only be properly made by someone with an interest in the outcome of a liquidation and if a company is insolvent then a contributory has no such interest, and cannot apply (at 61–62).

---

[46] Section 172(5) provides that a liquidator is to vacate office if he or she ceases to be a qualified insolvency practitioner.

To show cause for removal it is not necessary to establish a personal grievance against the liquidator – it is sufficient if it can be proved that the liquidation is not being handled so as to benefit the interests of the persons mainly interested in the winding up (*Re Rubber and Produce Investment Trusts* [1915] 1 Ch 382). In *Re Adam Eyton Ltd* ((1887) 36 Ch D 299) the court said if to leave the liquidator in post would be against the interests of the liquidation, this meaning the interests of all those who are interested in the company being liquidated, then the court could remove him or her (at 303–304). So, a court is acting properly if it removes a liquidator because the creditors have lost faith in him or her and this loss of faith is reasonable in the circumstances (*Re Edennote Ltd* [1996] BCC 718 (CA).

In a similar way, Millett J (as he then was) said, in *Re Keypack Homecare Ltd* ((1987) 3 BCC 558), that courts should not limit or define the kind of cause which is required as circumstances vary widely and it may be appropriate to remove a liquidator even where there was nothing against the liquidator, either personally or in his or her conduct. In this case the liquidator was removed even though there was no evidence of misconduct or wrongdoing on the part of the liquidator, but according to Millett J the liquidator had not pursued proceedings against the directors as vigorously a he could have. Liquidators are expected to be efficient, vigorous and unbiased in their conduct and if a liquidator has not met these requirements courts will have no hesitation in removing him or her (*AMP Enterprises Ltd v Hoffman, The Times*, August 13, 2002). But courts will not remove a liquidator simply because his or her conduct has fallen short of the ideal in a couple of respects, for if this was not the case the courts would be, in effect, encouraging creditors who had not had their preferred liquidator appointed to apply for removal (*AMP Enterprises Ltd v Hoffman*).

In considering the position of a liquidator the courts will examine whether there is any real risk of the liquidator not being able to act impartially or objectively in relation to the company's affairs (*Tracker Software International Inc v Smith* (1997) 24 ACSR 644 at 646). Liquidators have been removed where their independence or fiduciary position has been compromised. Conflict of interest is a classic case for removal (*Re Charterlands Goldfields Ltd* (1909) 26 TLR 182; *Re Corbenstoke Ltd (No 2)* (1989) 5 BCC 767). Also, impropriety, misconduct, or unfitness may be sufficient and may be satisfied by proof of some breach of duty (*Re Scotch Granite Co* (1868) 17 LT 538; *Re Baron Cigarette Machine Co* (1912) 28 TLR 294) or want of efficiency (*Re Federal Bank of Australia* (1893) 20 VLR 199) or appearance of partiality (*Re London Flats Ltd* [1969] 1 WLR 711). In general the views of the creditors and contributories will be considered by a court as these persons are usually the best judges of what is in the interests of the liquidation (*Re Association of Land Financiers* (1878) 10 Ch D 269; *Re Oxford Building & Investment Co* (1883) 49 LT 495). But, while their wishes are relevant, they are certainly not decisive (*Re Mercantile Finance & Agency Co* (1894) 13 NZLR 472; *Re George Bond & Co* (1932) 32 SR (NSW)

301). In the case of *Re Edennote Ltd* ([1996] 2 BCLC 389 at 398) Nourse LJ (with whom Millett LJ agreed) said that the creditors' loss of confidence in a liquidator must be reasonable.

Courts will not remove their own officer without careful consideration and without compelling reasons. They will pay regard to the impact of removal on the liquidator's professional standing and reputation (*Re Edennote Ltd* [1996] 2 BCLC 389 at 398). But even if removal may lead to the discredit of a liquidator, courts should not fail to remove in appropriate cases (*AMP Enterprises Ltd v Hoffman, The Times*, August 13, 2002). Notwithstanding this, removal of a professional is not to be undertaken lightly, and those who submit that a liquidator should be removed are under a duty to establish at least a *prima facie* case that this is for the general advantage of the persons interested in the winding up (*Re Mercantile Finance & Agency Co* (1894) 13 NZLR 472).

What has become quite an issue in recent years is where a liquidator decides to leave a firm to which he or she belongs and is willing to have another member of the firm (qualified as a insolvency practitioner and therefore able to act as a liquidator) take over his or her role as liquidator; the liquidator is unable to resign as this does not qualify under the circumstances provided for in rule 4.108(4). However, the courts have, on occasions, been ready to permit the circumvention of the relevant procedures and to make orders removing a practitioner from multiple offices and to appoint an appropriate replacement. The courts have asked whether the convening of meetings of creditors which are required by the Rules would serve a useful purpose (*Re Parkdown Ltd* (unreported, High Ct, Harman J, 15 June 1993); *Re Sankey Furniture Ltd* [1995] 2 BCLC 594 at 600 and 601). If a practitioner has resigned from his or her firm for other employment which does not allow him or her to discharge the duties of a liquidator adequately, the court may well make an order removing the liquidator and directing that another member of the firm to which the liquidator previously belonged is to assume the position of liquidator (*Re Equity Nominees Ltd* [1999] 2 BCLC 19).

> In *Re Alt Landscapes Ltd* ([1999] BPIR 459) two practitioners, A and B, applied for their removal as office-holders for a number of insolvent estates, including liquidations. The practitioners were partners in the Manchester office of a large accounting firm. The day-to-day affairs of the insolvencies were conducted by C, a senior manager in the firm's Liverpool office. The firm decided to close its Liverpool office and C was successful in obtaining employment in another Liverpool firm. One of the partners of the new employer, D, was a licensed insolvency practitioner. A and B applied to be removed and replaced by D, with C continuing to retain day-to day control of the insolvencies. Lloyd J decided that it was appropriate to make the orders sought.

Courts have had more of a problem when the liquidator is moving firms and is required by his or her agreement with the former firm to pass over the office to a member of that former firm. In *Re Sankey Furniture Ltd*

([1995] 2 BCLC 594) the court denied a removal order as the liquidator
was able to continue to act as a liquidator, but with another firm (at 603).
In such a case the court said that the creditors should be consulted (at 603).
Yet in *Re A & C Supplies Ltd* ([1998] BCC 708) Blackburne J was willing to
remove a liquidator and replace him in relation to a substantial number
of liquidations with one of his former partners in the same firm. The
liquidator had sought to resign from the partnership, in order to move to
another firm, and his partners had served him with an expulsion notice
excluding him from the partnership premises. His Lordship distinguished
Re Sankey Ltd, on the basis that the liquidator's resignation from his firm
meant that he would not have access to the relevant files or necessary
resources to enable him to carry out his duties as liquidator, whereas the
liquidator in *Re Sankey Furniture Ltd* could have continued to function by
continuing to employ the services of his former firm or move the work to
his new firm (*Re A & C Supplies Ltd* at 715). Blackburne J was particularly
concerned about the cost involved in calling creditors' meetings in many
administrations.

In *Re Equity Nominees Ltd* ([1999] 2 BCLC 19) the court sought to
reconcile the approaches taken in *Re Sankey Furniture Ltd* and *Re A & C
Supplies Ltd*. The court said that the 'short-cut approach' used in cases like
Re A & C Supplies Ltd was a practical and sensible approach in certain
circumstances and, subject to the imposition of conditions and safeguards,
could be employed. The removal and replacement of the liquidator was
ordered along with the sending of a letter to all creditors within a short
time explaining the effect of replacing the liquidator and their right to
have him discharged (*Equity Nominees* at 23–26). A similar result was
achieved in *Cork v Rolph* (*The Times*, December 13, 2000). In this latter case
the court accepted that replacing the liquidator with a former colleague
and advising creditors by way of a block advertisement in the *London
Gazette* in relation to each administration was the least expensive course of
action to take.

17.8 The supervision of liquidators[47]

First, we can note that both a liquidation committee, if appointed, and
the creditors are able to, in a sense, supervise the work of liquidators.
The liquidation committee, and its role, was discussed in Chapter 16. The
creditors can, of course, informally monitor the work of a liquidator and if
a creditor is able to muster the support of a tenth in value of all creditors,

---

[47] See A. Keay, *McPherson's Law of Company Liquidation*, at 501–8; A. Keay, 'The Supervision
and Control of Liquidators' [2000] *The Conveyancer* 295.

he or she is able to force the liquidator to convene a meeting of the creditors (section 168(2)). A court is able to override the duty of a liquidator to convene such a meeting and may direct a liquidator not to convene a meeting (*Re Barings plc: Hamilton v Law Debenture Trustees Ltd* [2001] All ER (D) 171).

More importantly, some statutory provisions allow for the courts to supervise the activities of liquidators. There are a number of ways that the law safeguards parties from the action of liquidators. One was mentioned earlier in the chapter, in the context of removal of liquidators. Sections 171 and 172 enable courts to take into account the conduct of liquidators and inquire into complaints made and ultimately remove a liquidator.[48]

17.8.1 *Court examination of the conduct of liquidators*

Courts are permitted by section 212(3) to consider the conduct of liquidators when hearing applications from creditors, contributories or the official receiver in relation to complaints of misfeasance. The courts may order a liquidator to repay, restore, account for money or property or contribute such sum to the assets of the company by way of compensation in relation to any misfeasance or breach of fiduciary or other duty as the court thinks fit.[49]

17.8.2 *Review of the acts or decisions of liquidators*

Section 168(5), as far as compulsory liquidations, enables courts, on an application by a person who is 'aggrieved' by an act, omission or decision of a liquidator, to review what a liquidator has done. The same action can be taken in voluntary liquidations through the operation of section 112 (*Re Hans Place Ltd* [1992] BCC 737 at 741). It must be said that courts are reluctant to interfere with a decision of a liquidator and will not do so unless the decision of the liquidator is such that no reasonable liquidator could, properly instructed and advised (*Associated Provincial Picture Houses Ltd v Wednesbury Corp* [1948] 1 KB 223; [1947] 2 All ER 680; *Re Edennote Ltd* [1996] BCC 718 at 722 ; [1996] 2 BCLC 389 at 394 (CA)), in the circumstances arrive at it (*Re Hans Place Ltd: Re Greenhaven Motors Ltd* [1997] BCC 547; *Re Edennote Ltd: Hamilton v Official Receiver* [1998] BPIR 602).

> In *Hamilton v Official Receiver* ([1998] BPIR 602) the official receiver in his capacity as liquidator of a company refused to assign to a person who previously controlled the company in liquidation, a speculative claim which the company had against a firm of solicitors. The court took the view that the

---

[48] See above at 279.
[49] This is discussed in more detail in Chapter 44.

refusal was unreasonable because this was the only offer made in relation to the assignment of the cause of action and the official receiver had no interest in taking action himself. An order was made directing the official receiver to assign the action to the former controller.

The rationale for granting the courts power to review actions or omissions of liquidations is to ensure that the duties and powers of liquidators are properly exercised (*Craig v Humberclyde Industrial Finance Ltd* [1999] 1 WLR 129; [1998] 2 BCLC 526 (CA)).

When conducting a review of a decision courts will give great weight to commercial decisions made by liquidators (*Re Edennote Ltd* [1996] BCC 718 at 720; [1996] 2 BCLC 389 at 394; *Mitchell v Buckingham International plc* [1998] 2 BCLC 369 at 390 (CA)).

17.8.3 *Control of the court*

Finally, under section 167(3) the powers of a liquidator in a compulsory liquidation, conferred by that section, and incorporating the ones in Schedule 4, are subject to the control of the court. In fact a creditor or contributory may apply to the court in relation to any exercise or proposed exercise of any of the powers. This court role also applies to voluntary liquidations through the agency of section 112.

Clearly there is some overlap between section 167(3) and section 168(5) (*Re Edennote Ltd* [1996] BCC 718 at 721; [1996] 2 BCLC 389 at 393). Having said that, section 168(5) appears to be broader than section 167(3) as it permits applications by 'an aggrieved person' while section 167(5) is limited to creditors and contributories. Furthermore, section 168(5) is wider as it is not, as is section 167(5), only applied to addressing applications in relation to powers granted to the liquidator under section 167 and Schedule 4.

Chapter 18

Dissolution[1]

18.1 Introduction

A company continues in liquidation until it is dissolved (*Re Working Project Ltd* [1995] BCC 197) and this is the case notwithstanding the fact that the period of liquidation is lengthy. Dissolution is the final act in the life of the company and will constitute the final act to complete the liquidation, unless assets or funds of the company remain unclaimed or undistributed in the hands of the liquidator (rule 4.223(2)). Despite the apparent finality of dissolution, in certain circumstances a company might in fact come back to life following dissolution.

This chapter deals with process of dissolution and devotes some space to consideration of the resurrection of dissolved companies. The dissolution procedure is essentially the same whether the company has been wound up compulsorily or voluntarily, but because of some differences, particularly in section and rule references, the two kinds of liquidation are dealt with separately.

18.2 The process

18.2.1 *Compulsory winding up*

Dissolution occurs automatically at the end of a three-month period following the Registrar of Companies' registration of the receipt of either the return from a private liquidator that the final meeting

---

[1] For more detailed discussion, see A. Keay, *McPherson's Law of Company Liquidation*, London: Sweet & Maxwell (2001) at 868–98.

required under section 146 has been summoned and held, or in the case of the official receiver, notice that the winding up is complete (section 205(1)(2)).[2] Dissolution may be deferred by the direction of the Secretary of State where an application is received from the official receiver, or a person whom the Secretary of State deems to be interested in the winding up (section 205(3)). The period of the deferral is in the discretion of the Secretary of State (section 205(3)), but the decision of the Secretary of State may be the subject of an appeal to the courts (section 201(4)).

18.2.2 *Voluntary winding up*

Similarly, where a company has been subject to a creditors' voluntary winding up, dissolution occurs automatically on completion of the liquidation. Completion takes place three months after the Registrar of Companies registers the fact that he or she has received the liquidator's final account and return stating that the final meeting under section 106 has been held (section 201(1), (2)).[3]

The court may, on the application of the liquidator or a person whom the court deems to be interested in the winding up, defer dissolution to a date it sees fit (section 201(3)).

18.2.3 *Early dissolutions*

The Act also provides a procedure for dissolution in compulsory liquidations where it would be a waste of time and money for a company, given its lack of realisable assets, to be taken through the formal processes discussed earlier. This may occur if it appears to the official receiver, as the liquidator of a company, that the realisable assets of the company are insufficient to cover the expenses of the winding up and, if the affairs of the company do not require any further investigation, the official receiver may apply to the Registrar of Companies for the company's early dissolution (section 202). Prior to initiating an application, the official receiver is required to give 28 days' notice to creditors and contributories, as well as to an administrative receiver if one has been appointed, that he or she has decided to apply for early dissolution (section 202(3)). The time when notice is given signifies the end of the duty of the official receiver to perform the functions of office in relation to the company, absent applying for an early dissolution (section 202(4)). When the

---

[2] The Registrar is obliged to register the return of the liquidator forthwith when it is received: section 205(2).

[3] This action is administrative: *Re Wilmott Trading Ltd (in liq) (Nos 1 and 2)* [1999] 2 BCLC 541.

Registrar receives an application from the official receiver, it must be registered immediately and after three months the company is dissolved automatically. The Secretary of State is entitled at some time before the elapse of the three months to give directions under section 203 in relation to the dissolution of the company (section 202(5)).

The Act permits interested parties to contest the decision to apply for early dissolution. Where the official receiver gives notice of an intention to make an application pursuant to section 202, any creditor, contributory or administrative receiver may apply to the Secretary of State for directions (section 203(1)) if:

- the realisable assets of the company are sufficient to cover the winding-up expenses;
- the affairs of the company require further investigation; or
- there is any other reason why the early dissolution of the company is inappropriate (section 203(2)).

18.2.4 *Administration to dissolution*

Where administration has occurred it is possible that dissolution might follow administration, rather than requiring liquidation to occur before dissolution can take place. If the administrator has made a distribution to secured and preferential creditors and there is no money left for a distribution to the unsecured creditors, he or she may file a notice with the Registrar of Companies and send a copy to the court and to all the creditors (para 84 of Schedule B1). The effect of filing the notice is that the administration comes to an end and the company is deemed to be dissolved three months later (para 84(6)).

18.3 The consequences of dissolution

These are extensive. The primary consequence is that the corporate existence of the company ends (*Re Pinto Silver Mining Co* [1878] 8 Ch 273; *Video Excellence Pty Ltd v Cincotta* (1998) 28 ACSR 389; *Top Creative Ltd v St Albans District Council* [1999] BCC 999; [2000] 2 BCLC 379 (CA)).

After dissolution no one can act on behalf of the company (*Salton v New Beeston Cycle Co* [1900] 1 Ch 43). The debts and obligations of the company are totally extinguished (*Re Pinto Silver Mining Co* [1878] 8 Ch 273; *Re Austral Family Homes Pty Ltd (in liq)* (1992) 8 ACSR 322) and it is unable to commence legal proceedings (*Video Excellence Pty Ltd v Cincotta* (1998) 28 ACSR 389).

18.3.1 *Proceedings*

As mentioned above, when a company's registration has been cancelled it is not able to commence legal proceedings.[4] Also, it is not able to defend proceedings, but that is of marginal import given the fact that dissolution prevents actions from being brought against the company (*Deutsche Bank v Banque des Marchands de Moscou* (1932) 158 LT 364). Also, proceedings against former officers of the company in order to obtain contribution to the assets are not permitted (*Coxon v Gorst* [1891] 2 Ch 73; *Bentinck v Cape Breton Co* (1892) 36 Sol Jo 328).

18.3.2 *Property*

Upon dissolution any estate or interest in real property that belonged to the corporation goes to the Crown by escheat (*Re Strathblaine Estates Ltd* [1948] Ch 162) and the company's personal property is taken by the Crown as *bona vacantia* (*Re Wells* [1933] Ch 29). Property vesting in the Crown may be disposed of and this is the case notwithstanding the fact that the company could be reinstated at a later date.[5] Where property does vest in the Crown, it may disclaim property which vests as *bona vacantia* by a notice signed by the Crown representative (section 656(1) of the Companies Act 1985). If the Crown does disclaim then the property is deemed not to have vested in the Crown under section 654 of the Companies Act 1985 (section 657(1)) and a person who is interested in the property may seek a vesting order.[6]

18.3.3 *Third party rights against insured companies*

As proceedings cannot be commenced against a dissolved company, if a person has a claim, then an application must be made to the court for the company's reinstatement. It is sometimes the case that persons who were injured by the dissolved company during its life and prior to its dissolution, do not wish to claim against the company's assets, but against the company's insurer.[7] However, it will still be incumbent on the person who was injured to apply for the reinstatement of the company and the injured person can then seek to establish the liability of the insured company (*Post Office v Norwich Union Fire Insurance Society Ltd* [1967] 2 QB 363).

---

[4] See *MH Smith (Plant Hire) Ltd v Mainwaring* [1986] BCLC 342; (1986) 2 BCC 262; *Bradley v Eagle Star Insurance Co Ltd* [1989] AC 957; [1989] 1 All ER 961.
[5] The issue of resurrection is discussed below at 289–95.
[6] See 293.
[7] For further discussion of this area, see A. Keay, 'The Pursuit of Legal Proceedings Against Dissolved Companies' [2000] JBL 405.

18.3.4 *Dealings of others with the company*

When dealing with a company that is dissolved, the legal position is the same as when there is a dealing with a company that has not yet been formed. In such cases there can be no claim against the company, as it does not exist for legal purposes. At common law a person purporting to contract on behalf of a non-existent company (one not yet formed) may not be liable in a personal capacity. That person would be liable if aware that the company was not in existence and it was indicated to be his or her intention to be personally bound (*Kelner v Baxter* (1866) LR 2 CP 174). Consequently, if directors of the dissolved company purported to make contracts with third parties on behalf of the company, it is probable that they would be liable personally (*In re Lindsay Bowman Ltd* [1969] 1 WLR 1443 at 1445). Persons purporting to deal with the dissolved company may have an action against the erstwhile agent for breach of warranty of authority, just as that person might if dealing with someone purporting to act on behalf of a company not yet formed (*Collen v Wright* (1857) 8 E & B 647; 120 ER 242; *Black v Smallwood* (1966) 117 CLR 52).

18.4 Reinstatement[8]

18.4.1 *General*

While not occurring frequently, it is not unusual for a company to be reinstated under either section 651 or section 653 of the Companies Act 1985. The former provision deals primarily with companies that have been dissolved following their winding up, while the latter relates essentially to the case where a company has been struck off the register of companies by the Registrar (*Re Test Holdings (Clifton) Ltd* [1970] Ch 285 at 289). To strike off, the Registrar must have reasonable cause to believe that a company is not carrying on business or in operation.[9] The case law generally seems to say that someone who wishes to apply for reinstatement has a choice under which provision to apply, provided that the applicant is included within the category of persons who are entitled to apply (*Re Test Holdings (Clifton) Ltd* [1970] Ch 285 at 288; *Re Thompson & Riches Ltd* ([1981] 1WLR 682 at 688; *In re Townreach Ltd* [1995] Ch 28).

---

[8] This section of the chapter draws on A. Keay, 'The Pursuit of Legal Proceedings Against Dissolved Companies' [2000] JBL 405.

[9] A. Keay, *McPherson's Law of Company Liquidation* at 871–3.

The provisions have very different wording and this has caused some problems in the past and, it appears, continues to do so. Section 651(1) states that:

> Where a company has been dissolved, the court may on an application made for the purpose by the liquidator of the company or by any other person appearing to the court to be interested, make an order, on such terms as the court thinks fit, declaring the dissolution to have been void.

Section 653(2) provides that:

> The court, on an application by the company or the member or creditor made before the expiration of 20 years from publication in the Gazette of notice under section 652 [striking off the register], may, if satisfied that the company was at the time of the striking off carrying on business or in operation, or otherwise that it is just that the company be restored to the register, order the company's name be restored.

In broad terms, orders under either provision has the same effect in that a company is reinstated as a legal personality. However, there are critical differences in the effects resulting from orders under the two provisions.

The main purpose behind section 651 is to permit the distribution of property which belonged to the company before the dissolution and was, for some reason, not distributed (*Re Servers of the Blind League* [1960] 1 WLR 564; 2 All ER 298; *Re Oakleague Ltd* [1995] 2 BCLC 624; [1995] BCC 921). Nevertheless, many applications are brought by persons who wish to pursue proceedings against the dissolved company, but cannot do so until reinstatement occurs (*Re Forte's (Manufacturing) Ltd* [1994] BCC 84 at 87; *sub nom Stanhope Pension Trust Ltd v Registrar of Companies* [1994] 1 BCLC 628 at 632).[10]

Section 653(3) states if an order of reinstatement is made then the company is deemed to have continued in existence as if its name had not been struck off. The provision goes on to state that a court may 'give such directions and make such provisions as seem just for placing the company and all other persons in the same position (as nearly as may be) as if the company's name had not been struck off'.

Where proceedings against a company that has been struck off are a nullity, the practice is for courts to stay such proceedings while the plaintiff applies for the company's reinstatement. If the application succeeds then the court might end the stay and order the restoration of the substantive proceedings.

Lords Sumner and Blanesburgh, two of the majority judges in *Morris v Harris* ([1927] AC 252) placed emphasis on the difference between sections 651 and 653. Lord Sumner said that an order voiding dissolution under section 651 did not mean that dissolution was deemed not to have taken place, thereby reversing the order of dissolution. While, as

---

[10] See the comments of Harman J in *In Re Workvale Ltd* [1991] 1 WLR 294 at 296.

we have seen, an order under section 653 means that the company is deemed to have continued in existence as if its name had not been struck off (at 257).

> The reason for distinguishing the provisions is their respective wording.
> The difference in wording has meant that courts have said that the result of
> a section 653 reinstatement is that the company is treated as having continued
> to exist during the period of its dissolution – regarded as never having been
> dissolved and it follows that transactions which were carried out in the interim
> between striking off and restoration to the register are also validated . . . The
> words in section 653(3) which allow a court to give such directions and make
> such provisions as seem just for placing the company and all persons in the
> same position so far as possible, as if the name of the company had not been
> struck off, are present to prevent the hardship which might otherwise result
> from the statutory fiction of treating the company as continuing to exist.[11]
> (footnote in the original omitted)

18.4.2 *Applications*

18.4.2.1 *Voiding the dissolution under section 651*

The application for a voiding order under section 651 must be made by the liquidator of the company or by any other person appearing to the court to be interested (section 651(1)). To be regarded as interested in the voiding of dissolution, an applicant must have a proprietary or pecuniary interest in having a company revived under section 651. Those regarded as persons interested in the company and able to apply are: a person who requires the company to meet a liability that would otherwise remain unpaid (*Re Forte's (Manufacturing) Ltd* [1994] BCC 84; *sub nom Stanhope Pension Trust Ltd v Registrar of Companies* [1994] 1 BCLC 628); a person who had not been appointed as liquidator of the company, but had acted as liquidator (*Re Wood and Martin (Bricklaying Contractors) Ltd* [1971] 1 WLR 293; [1971] 1 All ER 732); and the Secretary of State where he or she wishes to commence disqualification proceedings against the company's directors (*In re Townreach Ltd* [1995] Ch 28; [1994] 3 WLR 983).

Applications are often instituted by persons who wish to bring proceedings against the company or to enable the orderly distribution of assets which were only discovered after the commencement of dissolution (*Re Oakleague Ltd* [1995] 2 BCLC 624; [1995] BCC 921). Also, the case law reveals situations where it has been discovered subsequent to the completion of the winding up that the affairs of the company were managed most improperly.

---

[11] A. Keay, *McPherson's Law of Company Liquidation* at 879–80.

Any application under section 651 has to be made within two years of the dissolution of the company (section 651(4)) and if this occurs, the order can be made even though the two-year period has ended by the time of the order (*Re Scad Ltd* [1941] Ch 386 at 387). It has been held that whether or not a declaration voiding a dissolution is to be made under section 651 is within the unfettered discretion of the courts (*Re Servers of the Blind League* [1960] 1 WLR 564; [1960] 2 All ER 298).

It has been held that where a restoration order is sought so as to permit a prospective claimant in personal injuries' proceedings against the company, a direction under section 651 should not be made unless the application has been brought to the notice of all parties who might be expected to oppose restoration, including insurers of the company (*Smith v White Knight Laundry* [2001] All ER (D) 152 (CA)).

18.4.2.2 *Restoration of the company to the register*

Section 653 permits the company or any member or creditor of the company that has been struck off and who feels aggrieved by the striking off, to apply for the company to be restored to the register. It is somewhat curious that the company is entitled to apply at a time when it does not actually exist. The application must be made within 20 years from the publication of the notice under section 652 (that the company is dissolved) and the court has a discretion, if satisfied that the company was at the time of the striking off carrying on business or in operation or it is otherwise just, as to whether the company should be restored to the register (section 653(2)).[12]

Applicants for restoration, i.e., creditors and members, are required to have an interest in the company coming back to life and the interest relied on must not be minimal (*Re Lindsay Bowman Ltd* [1969] 1 WLR 1443). Another curious thing is that a liquidator who was appointed to the dissolved company is not empowered to bring an application.[13] The applicant must be aggrieved at the time of the dissolution of the company and the circumstances that cause the applicant to be aggrieved cannot have arisen subsequent to dissolution (*Re AGA Estate Agencies Ltd* (1986) 2 BCC 99, 257). However, it is our view that the approach taken in Scotland of permitting persons to apply for restoration when the circumstances leading to them being aggrieved occurred after dissolution, which can give them the right to apply under section 653 (*Conti v Ueberseebank* [2000] BCC 172), is to be preferred.

---

[12] It was held in *In re Belmont & Co Ltd* ([1952] Ch 10 at 15) by Wynn-Parry J that courts have an inherent power to restore companies to the register.

[13] See *Re Wood & Martin (Bricklaying Contractors) Ltd* [1971] 1 WLR 293; [1971] 1 All ER 732; *Re Proserpine Pty Ltd and the Companies Act* (1980) 5 ACLR 603.

When it comes to interpreting 'creditor' in section 653, a broad approach will be employed (*Re Harvest Lane Motor Bodies Ltd* [1969] 1 Ch 457 at 462; [1968] 2 All ER 1012 at 1015) and a person who had a genuine claim that had not been satisfied because dissolution intervened, or whose claim only arose after dissolution, will be included (*Ealing Corporation v Jones* [1959] 1 QB 384 at 392; *Deputy Commissioner of Taxation v Lanstel Pty Ltd* (1997) 15 ACLC 25). Notwithstanding this, applicants ought to be prudent and to rely on both section 653 and section 651 in the same application (in the alternative); it is likely that such a person would fall under the category of interested persons within section 651(1).

Once a court is satisfied that the company had been carrying on business at the time of the striking off, it has a broad discretion to reinstate where it feels that it is just to do so. An example of a case where it would be just to reinstate is where the applicant needs the company to be restored to permit the filing of proceedings against the company. A second instance is where the applicant has a claim against the company and there is an insurer standing behind the company (*Re Priceland Ltd* [1997] BCC 207).

Section 653 is usually employed where the company was struck off the companies register. If that is the case, a court will decline to make an order unless it is convinced that the reason for the striking off has been remedied.[14] In general terms courts will make the order sought and revive the company and it is only in exceptional cases that they will refuse to accede to the application (*Re Priceland Ltd*).

18.4.3 *Effect of orders that terminate dissolution*

The consequence of orders made under either sections 651 or 653 is that the name of the company is restored to the register of companies. Where property vested as *bona vacantia* in the Crown on dissolution, it will re-vest in the company no matter what provision was relied on in the application to restore, and this is done automatically (*Re CW Dixon Ltd* [1947] Ch 251 at 255). If the Crown had property vested in it and it accordingly disposed of it during the period of the company's dissolution, nothing can be done about the disposition (Companies Act 1985, section 655(1), (2)). Notwithstanding that, the company may claim a sum that is equal to the amount of any consideration that the Crown received for the property, or the value of any such consideration at the time of the disposition (Companies Act 1985, section 655(2)).

---

[14] For example, see *Shire Court Residents Ltd v Registrar of Companies* [1995] BCC 821.

18.4.3.1 *The effect of voiding dissolution*

In *Morris v Harris* Lord Blanesburgh, one of the judges in the majority, said that when an order avoiding dissolution was made:

> The company is restored to life as from the moment of dissolution, but, continuing a convenient metaphor, it remains buried, unconscious, asleep, and powerless until the order declaring the dissolution to have been void is made. Then, and only then, is the company restored to activity ([1927] AC 252 at 269).

Section 651(1) allows courts to make an order voiding a dissolution. Then section 651(2) states:

> Thereupon such proceedings may be taken as might have been taken if the company had not been dissolved.

In *Morris v Harris* Lord Sumner, in his speech, took the view that the aim of the provision was to give a fresh start to proceedings which could not be commenced while the company was in a state of dissolution, as the company did not exist, but which could, once a voiding order had been made, be instigated (at 259). The result is that the provision removes a bar to proceedings in the future, but does not retrospectively validate proceedings that have been commenced (at 258).[15]

There has been a general willingness to follow[16] the views of the majority judgments, and the views of dissenting judges have been forgotten; apparently no court or judge has sought to approve of dissenters' opinions. Notwithstanding this, the Court of Appeal in *Smith v White Knight Laundry* ([2001] All ER (D) 152) has said that section 651(1) does enable a court to declare the dissolution of a company void on such terms as it thinks fit and, in doing so, a court can adjust the limitation consequences of the voiding order so as to produce a just result in the circumstances.

18.4.3.2 *The effect of restoration*

Where an order of restoration under section 653 is made, the company is deemed to have continued in existence as if its name had not been struck off.[17] Additionally, the court is able to make provision in its order

---

[15] For elaboration on this issue, see A. Keay, *McPherson's Law of Company Liquidation* at 891–6.

[16] For example, see *Re Lewis & Smart* [1954] 1 WLR 755; *Foster Yates & Thom Ltd v HW Edgehill Equipment Ltd, The Times,* November 30, 1978; (1978) 122 Sol Jo 860; *Re Mixhurst Ltd* [1994] 2 BCLC 19; *Bianchi v Crewe & Sons Pty Ltd* (1996) 14 ACLC 1658; *Re Philip Powis Ltd* [1997] 2 BCLC 481.

[17] Section 653(3) of the Companies Act 1985. See *Top Creative Ltd v St Albans District Council* [1999] BCC 999; [2000] 2 BCLC 379 (CA).

for the placing of the company and all other persons in the same position as nearly as may be as if the company's name had not been struck off (*Re Priceland Ltd* [1997] BCC 207; *Re Blenheim Leisure (Restaurants) Ltd (No.2)* [2000] BCC 821 at 831; *Top Creative Ltd v St Albans District Council* [1999] BCC 999; [2000] 2 BCLC 379 (CA)).

So, the effect of reinstatement is that the company is treated as having continued to exist during the period of its dissolution. It is seen as never having been dissolved. Consequently, transactions entered into in the period between the company's striking off and its restoration to the register are validated.

References

Bailey, E., Groves, H. and Smith, C., *Corporate Insolvency Law and Practice*, 2nd edn, London: Butterworths (2001).

Dawson, I., 'The Administrator, Morality and the Court' [1996] JBL 437.

de Kerloy, K., 'The Personal Liability of Liquidators and Administrative Receivers for the Costs of an Unsuccessful Action' (2000) 4 *Receivers, Administrators and Liquidators Quarterly* 13.

Finch, V., *Corporate Insolvency Law: Perspectives, and Principles*, Cambridge: Cambridge University Press (2002).

Finch, V., 'Public Interest Liquidation: PIL or Placebo' [2002] *Insolvency Lawyer* 157.

Fletcher, I.F., *The Law of Insolvency*, 3rd edn, London: Sweet & Maxwell (2002).

Goode, R.M., *The Principles of Corporate Insolvency Law*, 2nd edn, London: Sweet & Maxwell (1997).

Frisby, S., 'TUPE or not TUPE: Employee Protection Corporate Rescue and "One Unholy Mess"' [2000] 4 *Company Financial and Insolvency Law Review* 249.

Galatopoulos, A., 'Cross-Claims, Winding up and Judicial Discretion: An Overview' [1999] *Insolvency Lawyer* 240.

Hepple, R., 'The Transfer of Undertakings (Protection of Employment) Regulations' (1982) 11 ILJ 29.

Keay, A., 'Insolvent Companies Which are Able to Dispute Debts Owed to Petitioning Creditors: Should they be Wound Up?' (1998) 19 Co Law 230.

Keay, A., 'Public Interest Petitions' (1999) 20 Co Law 296.

Keay, A., 'The Supervision and Control of Liquidators' [2000] *The Conveyancer* 295.

Keay, A., 'The Pursuit of Legal Proceedings Against Dissolved Companies' [2000] JBL 405.

Keay Andrew, R., *McPherson's Law of Company Liquidation*, London: Sweet & Maxwell (2001).

Keay, A., 'Disputing Debts Relied On By Petitioning Creditors Seeking Winding Up Orders' (2001) 22 Co Law 40.

Keay, A., 'Claims for Malicious Presentation: The Peril Lurking on the Sidelines for Petitioning Creditors' [2001] *Insolvency Lawyer* 136.

Keay, A., 'Dispositions of Company Property Post-Presentation of Winding-up Petitions and the Plights of Banks' [2001] *Restitution Law Review* 86.

Milman, D., 'Curbing the Phoenix Syndrome' [1997] JBL 224.

Milman, D., 'Security for Costs: Principles and Pragmatism in Corporate Litigation', in B.A.K. Rider (ed.), *The Realm of Company Law*, London: Kluwer Law International (1998).

Milman, D. and Durrant, C., *Corporate insolvency: law and practice*, 3rd edn London: Sweet & Maxwell (1999).

Moss, G. and Segal, N., 'Insolvency Proceedings: Contract and Financing' (1997) 1 *Company Financial and Insolvency Law Review* 1.

Part V

Bankruptcy

Bankruptcy legislation in England dates back to 1542. Although significant changes were made to bankruptcy law in 1825 and 1883, many of the principal concepts remained unchanged up to the mid-1980s. Modern bankruptcy law is, procedurally, considerably simpler than its predecessor. A student of modern bankruptcy law who reads cases decided under the former Bankruptcy Acts will come across such concepts as 'acts of bankruptcy' (formerly the grounds upon which a person could be made bankrupt), 'receiving orders' (an intermediate stage in the bankruptcy procedure) and 'the doctrine of reputed ownership' (whereby the bankrupt's estate could, in certain circumstances, claim assets which appeared to be in the ownership of the bankrupt even if, in fact, they belonged to another). Students of the current law have been saved a good deal of trouble.

The modern regime is largely based upon the rules and procedures present in the compulsory liquidation of companies. There are a number of necessary differences between bankruptcy and liquidation, as the law is dealing with a real person and not a merely legal person. Although greatly simplified, when compared with the previous system, modern bankruptcy regime is far from stultified. The law continues to evolve and new innovations relating to discharge and preferential debts have been introduced by the Enterprise Act 2002.

Througout this Part, except where indicated to the contrary, any reference to 'the Act' or to section numbers will be references to the Insolvency Act 1986. Except where indicated to the contrary, any reference to 'the Rules' or to rule numbers will be references to the Insolvency Rules 1986 (SI 1986/1925).

Chapter 19

Introduction to Bankruptcy

19.1 Introduction

We have just considered the liquidation of companies. The equivalent procedure for individuals is bankruptcy. Bankruptcy, like liquidation, is a collective process whereby a trustee in bankruptcy (bankruptcy's counterpart of the liquidator) is appointed to administer the estate of an insolvent debtor. The debtor can only be made bankrupt by a bankruptcy order of the court. The debtor's estate, subject to certain exceptions, will automatically vest in the trustee. The trustee will attempt to maximise the assets available to pay as much as possible to the creditors.

The law and procedure in bankruptcy is broadly similar to that in compulsory liquidation with necessary differences. There will obviously be no members' meetings as an individual does not have members. The ultimate result of a liquidation is that the company is dissolved and ceases to exist. In the bankruptcy of an individual, the debtor will not cease to exist and instead has the benefit of a discharge from all the bankruptcy debts at the end of the bankruptcy. The effect of discharge is generally that the slate is wiped clean and the vast majority of discharged bankrupts may start again with all the debts wiped away by the bankruptcy process.

The concept of discharge is a great privilege in that without it the debtor would remain liable forever on debts which will frequently have reached an unmanageable size. Historically bankruptcy and the consequent discharge from debts was only available to debtors who could show that they were traders. Only in 1861 did bankruptcy become available to non-traders as well. The discharge permits the debtor to be given a fresh start and is in such a context seen as a form of rehabilitation.

In addition to the benefit to the debtor of becoming discharged from the accumulated burden of his or her debts, bankruptcy is a collective procedure. Under the bankruptcy process, creditors are generally treated equally. This equality rule, known as the *pari passu* rule, is subject to a number of exceptions but to some extent prevents all the debtor's creditors engaging in a free-for-all rush to enforce their claims against the debtor. The administration of the bankrupt's estate is dealt with in an orderly manner by the trustee.

Although bankruptcy is a privilege, it attracts a very negative connotation in that there remains a social stigma attached to bankruptcy. During the period that a bankrupt remains undischarged, a number of disabilities are imposed on the bankrupt. Even after discharge, a debtor's credit history will be severely damaged. Any prospective lender who undertakes a credit search and finds a prospective borrower has previously been adjudicated bankrupt will be reluctant, to say to the least, to lend the discharged bankrupt money.

The law on bankruptcy underwent a considerable overhaul following the implementation of the Cork Committee's recommendations. The law is now found principally in Part IX of the Insolvency Act 1986. In this Part of the book, references to section numbers or to 'the Act' refer to the Insolvency Act 1986. References to rules or to 'the Rules' are references to the Insolvency Rules 1986 (SI 1986/1925). The previous law contained within the Bankruptcy Act 1914 has been largely replaced and so the case law on previous provisions is not authoritative under the new regime. Although certain concepts remain essentially the same and so older cases may be persuasive in certain situations, the courts have made it clear that the 1986 regime is a new scheme and is to be interpreted afresh without the fetters of previous authority.[1]

It should be borne in mind that many insolvent debtors can deal with their financial problems without recourse to bankruptcy. Some form of informal arrangement may be the solution. Many consumer debtors may find that an arrangement brokered by a Citizens Advice Bureau or some other debt counsellors will greatly ameliorate their situation. A county court administration order may assist if the debts are relatively minor. As we have seen, individual voluntary arrangements are popular ways of reaching an arrangement with creditors even where some creditors are against such a proposal. One of the great problems for debtors is their ignorance of the legal mechanisms available to them. Many will be unaware of the possibilities short of bankruptcy. Many will continue to suffer oppressive conduct on the part of their creditors and will not know that it is possible for a debtor to petition for his or her own bankruptcy.

---

[1] See e.g., *Re A Debtor (No1 of 1987)* [1989] 1 WLR 271 at 276 and *Smith v Braintree District Council* [1990] 2 AC 215 at 237–8.

19.2 Outline of bankruptcy procedure

Prior to looking at bankruptcy law and procedure in some detail there follows a brief summary of the bankruptcy procedure.

It must first be established whether or not the debtor is capable of being made bankrupt. The types of debt owed and the types of creditor owed those debts may need to be considered. It will need to be established that the debtor is subject to the bankruptcy jurisdiction of the English courts.

A petition will need to be presented to the court. The petitioner will usually be a creditor or the debtor. Voluntary bankruptcy is the term used to describe the situation where the debtor petitions against himself or herself. If the petitioner is a creditor, it will need to be shown that the debtor owes a debt of at least £750. Both types of petition are heard by the court. The court may make the bankruptcy order, dismiss the petition or, in certain circumstances, instruct an insolvency practitioner to consider whether a voluntary arrangement is possible and would be a better solution than a bankruptcy order.

Once the bankruptcy order is made, the bankruptcy is deemed to have commenced. The official receiver is initially appointed as receiver and manager of the estate to protect and preserve it for the benefit of the creditors. The official receiver may continue in office as the trustee in bankruptcy or a trustee from the private sector may be appointed by the bankrupt's creditors.

The official receiver is under a duty to obtain a statement of affairs from the bankrupt and to investigate the reasons for the insolvency. The official receiver must also establish the value of the estate. The official receiver may apply for a public examination of the bankrupt. At such an examination the bankrupt is questioned on oath (or affirmation), for example, on the events that led to the bankruptcy or the whereabouts of certain assets.

If the value of the estate is sufficient, the official receiver will call a meeting of creditors to appoint a private sector trustee in bankruptcy. The creditors may also set up a creditors' committee to represent the creditors throughout the bankruptcy.

Once appointed the estate vests in the trustee, in that he or she controls it, is responsible for it and can sell it. There are certain types of asset which do not vest. The trustee must realise the estate and distribute the proceeds to the creditors according to statutory priority rules. Distribution is only made to creditors with provable debts. The trustee has wide powers to get the estate property in and, for example, to avoid antecedent transactions entered into by the bankrupt.

Once the estate has been fully administered the bankrupt will be discharged. Depending on the circumstances the discharge will occur automatically after two or three years of the order or, where the debtor has been bankrupt in the previous 15 years, the discharge must be applied for and the court will only grant discharge if it is satisfied that it is proper to do so.

The rules relating to discharge are about to be changed. The relevant provisions of the Enterprise Act 2002 are due to come into force in 2004. Once in force, bankrupts will be automatically discharged within one year of the order, but may be subject to a bankruptcy restrictions order or undertaking, which will restrict the debtor in a similar way to the current company directors' disqualification regime, for between 2 and 15 years.

19.3 Who can be made bankrupt?

Before considering in detail the rules relating to debtors' or creditors' petitions it is necessary first to consider who can be made bankrupt. Under section 265 of the Act there needs to be some geographical connection between the debtor and the court's jurisdiction in England. A petition may only be presented against a debtor if the debtor is either:

(1) domiciled in England and Wales;
(2) personally present in England and Wales on the day on which the petition is presented; or
(3) at any time in the period of three years ending with that day:
  (a) has been ordinarily resident, or has had a place of residence, in England and Wales, or
  (b) has carried on business in England and Wales.

It can be seen from this that the court's jurisdiction is wide and could conceivably catch a debtor who has never actually been to England and Wales as long as the debtor has a business within the jurisdiction. It should be noted that the EU Regulation on Insolvency Proceedings (1346/2000) may apply to an individual debtor. If the Regulation applies, insolvency proceedings may only be commenced in a Member State where the debtor has a centre of main interests or in a state where the debtor has an establishment.

It is outside the scope of this book to consider how insolvent partnerships are dealt with but the following general points should be noted. Unless incorporated under the Limited Liability Partnerships Act 2000, a partnership is not a legal entity and will not have a legal personality distinct from the individual partners. If a partnership owes money to its creditors, the creditors may decide to sue the individual partners separately or sue them in the name of the partnership. If the partnership is insolvent, it may be wound up under Part V of the Act as if it were an unregistered company (Insolvent Partnerships Order 1994 (SI 1994/2421)). Such a liquidation of the partnership and its assets may have the knock-on effect of separate bankruptcy proceedings against the partners individually. If the partnership itself is not being wound up, it is still possible and indeed common for bankruptcy proceedings to be brought against the individual partners.

19.4 Who can petition?

Under section 264 of the Act the following persons may petition for a debtor's bankruptcy:

(1) the debtor himself or herself;
(2) one of the debtor's creditors, or more than one of them petitioning jointly;
(3) the supervisor of, or any person (other than the debtor) who is for the time being bound by, a voluntary arrangement proposed by the debtor and approved under Part VIII of the Act.

Chapters 20 and 21 will concentrate on the debtor's and creditor's petitions. For consideration of the third type of petition please refer to the discussion in Chapter 9.

Chapter 20

Debtor's Petition

20.1 Introduction

It has for many years been the case that an individual debtor can seek the protection of the bankruptcy procedure by way of the presentation of the debtor's own petition. The effect of presenting the petition immediately removes the debtor's estate from separate enforcement proceedings by unsecured creditors.

Under section 272 of the Act, a debtor can only be made bankrupt if he or she is unable to pay debts that are owed. The sole ground for a debtor's petition is in fact the inability to pay debts. If the debtor can pay debts which are currently enforceable and due, the debtor cannot petition for his or her own bankruptcy. There is no minimum debt level which must have been reached. The test is based upon the debtor's ability to pay currently due debts.[1] In *Re A Debtor, ex parte the Debtor v Allen (No17 of 1966)* ([1967] Ch 590):

> A debtor owed £2,400. Judgment was obtained by a creditor and the court ordered the debt to be paid by instalments of a little over a pound a week. The debtor petitioned against himself on the grounds that he was unable to pay his debts. The debtor was hoping to be made bankrupt and get discharged from the full debt of £2,400. The court made the order but it was annulled on appeal on the basis that he could pay all the debts due i.e., the weekly instalments.

The petition must contain details of:[2]

(1) the debtor's place of residence;
(2) the debtor's occupation or business;
(3) any names other than the debtor's true name used either in business or otherwise;

---

[1] See e.g., *Re Coney* [1998] BPIR 333.
[2] See IR rule 6.38–6.39.

(4) a statement that the debtor is unable to pay his or her debts and requests a bankruptcy order;

(5) whether or not the debtor has, in the previous five years, been made bankrupt, been subject to a voluntary arrangement or county court administration order;

(6) if there is in force an individual voluntary arrangement, details of the supervisor must be given.

Under section 285, at any time when proceedings on a bankruptcy petition are pending the court may stay any action, execution or other legal process against the property or person of the debtor. The court, or any court where proceedings are pending, may stay proceedings or allow them to continue on such terms as it thinks fit. Once a bankruptcy order is made, creditors are generally prevented from commencing any action against the bankrupt or claiming any remedy against the property or person of the bankrupt. The creditors' rights to enforce their claims are stayed.

Any attempt by the debtor to petition for bankruptcy to protect himself or herself from creditor harassment in the short term and then later withdraw the petition after the protection is obtained is prevented by section 266. This section states that a petition can only be withdrawn with the consent of the court. A debtor cannot therefore use the expedient of a bankruptcy petition to create a temporary lull in creditor enforcements and then later unilaterally withdraw the petition.

The court has the power to refuse to consider a petition if its presentation amounts to an abuse of process. Under section 375 the court has a wide power to 'review, rescind or vary' any order. The court may also annul a bankruptcy order under section 282 where it is of the opinion that the order should not have been made. An example from the old pre-1986 law is *Re Betts* ([1901] 2 KB 39):

> The debtor had evaded committal proceedings against him twice before by presenting bankruptcy petitions against himself. Such petitions protected him from enforcement proceedings. The third attempt to remove himself from his creditors' actions failed when the court rescinded the order made. The court pointed out that it was by no means illegal to obtain protection from one's creditors by petitioning for bankruptcy. It was just that on the facts, the debtor was clearly abusing his legal privilege.[3]

The petition must be accompanied by a statement of the debtor's affairs which contains particulars of the debtor's creditors and debts and other liabilities. The fee for such a petition is £120 (SI 1999/687). Upon filing the court sends notice to the Chief Land Registrar for registration in the register of pending actions. If the court can be persuaded that it is necessary for the protection of the debtor's property, it may (under section 286) at any time after the presentation of the petition appoint the official receiver

---

[3] See also *Re Bond* (1888) 21 QBD 17.

to be interim receiver of the debtor's property. The interim receiver has wide powers under section 287 to act as receiver and manager to protect the property pending the hearing of the petition.

The petition, together with three copies and the statement of affairs accompanied by two copies, must be filed at court. A deposit of £250 must also be paid.[4] This deposit goes towards covering the costs of the official receiver. One copy of the petition is returned to the debtor. One copy of the petition together with a copy of the statement of affairs is sent to the official receiver. The remaining copy petition and statement are retained by the court to be sent to an insolvency practitioner if one is appointed under section 273 to consider a possible voluntary arrangement.[5]

A bankruptcy commences on the day on which the order is made and continues until the bankrupt is discharged (section 278).

20.2 Consideration of possible voluntary arrangement

Under section 273 the court will not make a bankruptcy order in the following circumstances:

(1) if a bankruptcy order were made the amount of the unsecured bankruptcy debts would be less than the small bankruptcies level (currently £20,000 under the Insolvency Proceedings (Monetary Limits) Order 1986 (SI 1986/1996));

(2) if a bankruptcy order were made the estate would be equal to or more than the minimum amount (currently £2,000 (SI 1986/1996);

(3) the debtor has not in the previous five years either been made bankrupt or entered into a composition or scheme with his or her creditors; and

(4) it would be appropriate to appoint a person to prepare a report which may lead to an individual voluntary arrangement being approved.

The policy behind section 273 is to discourage bankruptcy wherever possible. The Act assumes that it may be more appropriate to consider a voluntary arrangement where the debts are not enormous and there is at least some value in the estate. The insolvency practitioner appointed, under section 273, must submit a report to the court stating whether or not the debtor is willing to make a proposal for a voluntary arrangement. The report will also state whether or not meetings of the debtor's creditors

---

[4] See IR rule 6.42 and Insolvency Fees Order 1986 (SI 1986/2030). The payment of the deposit is mandatory and this requirement is not a breach of a debtor's human rights – see *R v Lord Chancellor, ex parte Lightfoot* [1999] 4 All ER 583.

[5] See IR rule 6.42.

should be called to consider such a proposal. Depending upon the contents of the report the court may decide to make a bankruptcy order. If the voluntary arrangement proposal seems feasible the court may make an interim order to ensure that creditor harassment does not interfere with the putting of the proposal to the creditors as a whole. The voluntary arrangement regime contained within Part VIII of the Act applies to the situation thereafter, as if the whole thing had been commenced as a voluntary arrangement.

The procedure under section 273 does not apply where the petition is brought by a creditor.

20.3 Certificate of summary administration

Under section 275, if the court makes a bankruptcy order in circumstances that:

(1) the total debts owed by the debtor are less than the small bankruptcies level (£20,000); and
(2) the debtor has not within the previous five years been made bankrupt or entered into a composition or scheme with his or her creditors,

the court will usually issue a certificate of summary administration. The main consequence of this is that the debtor will be automatically discharged after two years rather than the normal three years.[6]

---

[6] See section 279.

Chapter 21

Creditor's Petition

21.1 Introduction

The most common way for a bankruptcy order to be made is on the petition of a creditor. The law and procedure in this area is based upon and has much in common with a creditor's petition for the compulsory liquidation of a company.[1]

Under section 383 of the Act, a creditor is defined for the purposes of bankruptcy as a person to whom any 'bankruptcy debt' is owed. In relation to a creditor's petition a creditor is defined as any person who would be a creditor in the bankruptcy if a bankruptcy order were made on that petition. 'Bankruptcy debt' is defined in section 382 and includes the following:

(1) any debt or liability to which the debtor is subject at the commencement of the bankruptcy;
(2) any debt or liability to which the debtor may become subject after the commencement of the bankruptcy (including after discharge) by reason of any obligation incurred before the commencement of the bankruptcy.

Liability in tort is included as long as the cause of action arose prior to the commencement of the bankruptcy. The debt may be present or future, certain or contingent, for a fixed sum or unliquidated or capable of being ascertained by fixed rules or as a matter of opinion.

The definition of debt for these purposes would include debts which have been assigned to third parties although the assignee may have difficulty in petitioning unless the assignment satisfies section 136 of the Law of

---

[1] See Chapter 14.

Property Act 1925.[2] Most debt factoring agreements will satisfy section 136 and so this should not be a problem for debt factors wishing to put the debtor into bankruptcy.

21.2 The petition

Where a single debt is owed to two or more joint creditors, a bankruptcy petition can only be brought if all the joint creditors are a party to it.[3] It is possible, if no single creditor is owed the minimum statutory level of debt, for two or more creditors to join in presenting a petition on the basis that the aggregate amount is at least as much as the bankruptcy minimum.[4]

Although the definitions mentioned in the introduction above suggest that a creditor may petition for the debtor's bankruptcy on the basis of a future or contingent debt, the matter is clarified by section 267 which lays down a number of qualifications for the presentation of a petition:

(1) The petition must be in respect of one or more debts owed by the debtor and the petitioning creditor must be a person to whom the debt is owed. The section permits a joint petition by more than one creditor in which case each of the petitioning creditors must be owed at least one of the debts; and

At the time of the petition:

(2) the amount of the debt is at least the amount of the bankruptcy level, currently £750;
(3) the debt must be for a liquidated sum payable either immediately or at some certain, future time;
(4) the debt is unsecured;
(5) the debt is one which the debtor appears either to be unable to pay or to have no reasonable prospect of being able to pay; and
(6) there must be no pending application to set aside a statutory demand served in relation to the debt.

Some important points may be made in light of this. The debt, required to be for at least £750, must be owed at the time the petition is presented.

---

[2] If the assignment is only an equitable assignment, the assignee will in theory need to join the assignor to the petition. *Re Baillie* (1875) LR 20 Eq 762 suggests that an equitable assignee can petition without such joinder but the position remains somewhat uncertain.
[3] See *Brickland v Newsome* (1808) 1 Camp 474.
[4] See *Re Allen, Re A Debtor (No 367 of 1992)* [1998] BPIR 319.

Under IR rule 6.30, if the petitioning creditor fails to appear at the hearing or withdraws, the court may substitute another creditor to take the original petitioning creditor's place. This can be done as long as the substitute would have been entitled to petition himself or herself on the date of the presentation of the petition.

Contractual entitlements to interest may be added to the principal sum in calculating the overall debt. Costs of failed enforcement proceedings cannot be added to take the debt over the bankruptcy level.[5] Any right of set-off under section 323 must be taken into account before any final figure is reached. If the debt has been reduced below the bankruptcy level by the time of hearing of the petition,[6] the petition cannot continue without substitution of the petitioning creditor under rule 6.30.

The debt must be liquidated at the date of the petition or at some certain future time. Outstanding tort claims cannot, by definition, be liquidated until the court makes an award. Contractual claims will usually be for a certain amount and will therefore be liquidated.[7] The liability must be an existing liability even if it is not payable until some future specific moment. The liability cannot be one that is contingent on the occurrence of some event.

As the bankruptcy process does not prevent a secured creditor from enforcing his or her security, such a creditor is prevented from petitioning for a bankruptcy.[8] Under section 269 a petitioning debt need not be unsecured if the creditor agrees to give up the security upon bankruptcy, or the petition is made in respect of an unsecured part of the debt owed.

Section 267 states that the debtor must appear to be unable to pay or have no reasonable prospect of paying the debt. The debtor's inability to pay debts is defined in section 268. There are only two ways in which it can be shown that the debtor is unable to pay currently due debts:

(1) the creditor has served a statutory demand on the debtor and the demand has not been satisfied or set aside within three weeks of service; or
(2) execution or other process issued in respect of a judgment debt in favour of the petitioning creditor has been returned unsatisfied in whole or in part.

In order to show that a debtor has no reasonable prospect of being able to pay a debt which is payable at some future time, the creditor may serve on the debtor a statutory demand requiring the debtor to establish that there is a reasonable prospect that the debtor will be able to pay the debt when it falls due. If the demand is not satisfied within three weeks,

---

[5] See e.g., *Re Long* (1888) 20 QBD 316.
[6] See e.g., *Re A Debtor (No 459 of 1928)* [1929] 1 Ch 170.
[7] See e.g., *Re King, ex parte Furber* (1881) 17 Ch D 191.
[8] See section 285(4). For the meaning of security, see Chapter 29.

the creditor will have established the statutory ground. Reliance on a statutory demand is the more prevalent way of demonstrating inability to pay debts.

21.2.1 *Statutory demand*

The use of the statutory demand procedure was introduced into bankruptcy law under the 1985/1986 legislation. It is borrowed from the similar procedure which has existed for many years in relation to compulsory liquidations (and discussed at 216–219). The procedure is fairly straightforward and as long as the demand is completed and served competently the creditor is fairly certain of success. If the demand is not satisfied by the debtor, inability to pay debts will, in most instances, have been proved.

It will not usually be fatal to a statutory demand that it contains errors as to the amount claimed.[9] If the amount claimed is greater than the amount in fact owed, the court will not generally invalidate the demand as long as the amount owed is at least equal to £750.[10] Similarly, if part of a debt is disputed, as long as the undisputed part is at least £750, the courts will not set aside the demand.[11] The rationale for this flexible approach seems to be that there is no real point in requiring absolute accuracy where it is apparent that the debtor cannot pay.

21.2.2 *Expedited petition*

It is extremely common for a petitioning creditor to have served a statutory demand upon the debtor. It is a straightforward and certain process. The only potential problem with it is in circumstances where the creditor is reluctant to wait the three-week period before serving the petition. If there is evidence that there is a serious possibility that the debtor's property or the value of it will be significantly diminished during that period, the creditor may present the petition before the three weeks have elapsed.[12] Although no bankruptcy order can be made before the three-week period is up, it does allow for an interim receiver to be appointed under section 286, or for the court to order a stay on actions against the debtor under section 285. An interim receiver fulfils a similar role to the provisional liquidator discussed in Part III. The law applying to provisional liquidators has been applied to interim receivers and vice versa.

---

[9] See generally *Re A Debtor* [1989] 1 WLR 271 and D. Milman, 'Statutory Demands in the Courts: A Retreat from Formalism in Bankruptcy Law' [1994] Conv 289.

[10] See e.g., *Re A Debtor* [1992] 1 WLR 507.

[11] See e.g., *Re A Debtor* [1993] BCLC 180.

[12] See e.g., *Re A Debtor (No22 of 1993)* [1994] 1 WLR 46.

21.2.3 *Application to set aside a statutory demand*

As mentioned above, a petition cannot be presented on the basis of a statutory demand where there is an application pending to set aside the statutory demand. Under IR rule 6.4, the debtor has 18 days from the date of service of the statutory demand to challenge it. The effect of an application challenging the statutory demand is that the three-week period for compliance ceases to run and is in effect frozen. If an application is made it prevents the presentation of a bankruptcy petition by the creditor until after the application is heard and determined by the court. The application may be dismissed without notice to the creditor if the court thinks that no sufficient cause is shown. If it is apparent to the court that the debtor is just trying to delay the inevitable, it will immediately dismiss the application and time will begin to run again on the three-week compliance period. Otherwise, the court will hear the application and make a decision on the evidence currently available to it. At least seven days' notice must be given of the hearing.

The statutory demand may be set aside if:

(1) the debtor appears to have a counterclaim or set-off which equals or exceeds the amount of the debt specified in the statutory demand;[13]
(2) there appear to be substantial grounds for disputing the debt;[14]
(3) a secured creditor has served the statutory demand and the court is satisfied that the security equals or exceeds the debt claimed;
(4) the court is satisfied on other grounds that the demand should be set aside.

Under category (4) the courts have emphasised that procedural inaccuracies will not lead to a statutory demand being set aside unless it can be shown that it would be unjust not to do so. If the demand overstates the amount owed but it is clear that the debtor cannot pay his or her own debts, there will be no injustice to the debtor.[15] If the application fails, the court will make an order authorising the creditor to present a bankruptcy petition forthwith or after a date specified in the order.[16]

21.2.4 *Unsatisfied execution*

The second way in which a creditor can show that the debtor is unable to pay his or her debts is to prove that execution or other process issued in respect of a judgment debt has been returned unsatisfied in whole or in

---

[13] See e.g., *Re Bayoil SA* [1999] 1 WLR 147 – a company case whose reasoning is relevant to individuals.
[14] See e.g., *Re A Debtor* [1989] 1 WLR 271 and *Re A Debtor* [1992] 2 All ER 664.
[15] See *Re A Debtor* [1989] 1 WLR 271.
[16] See generally IR rules 6.4 and 6.5.

part. This provision, as with the statutory demand procedure, is modelled on its long-standing equivalent in corporate insolvency. One difference is that the judgment debt in bankruptcy must be a debt owed to the petitioning creditor.[17] A debt owed to another creditor will not be able to be used by the petitioning creditor. Where the debtor is appealing against the judgment debt, the bankruptcy court, on hearing the petition, should consider whether the appeal has a reasonable prospect of success. If not, the court may proceed to make the order.[18]

In order to show that the execution is returned unsatisfied, a genuine attempt to execute the judgment must have been made. If the judgment is executed by a writ of *fi fa*, it must be shown that the sheriff has levied execution and that the goods available were insufficient to satisfy the judgment. It is not enough for the sheriff to have returned the writ unsatisfied because he or she could not gain access to the debtor's premises.[19]

21.3 Procedure[20]

It is not intended to deal exhaustively with the procedure, but a few words are warranted in this regard. Many aspects of the procedure mirror the compulsory liquidation procedure for companies. The creditor's petition must be on the correct form[21] and must clearly and in some detail identify the debtor and the debt being claimed. The following details must be given in relation to the debtor:

(1) name, place of residence and occupation;
(2) business names used if different from true name;
(3) nature of business and address of business;
(4) other names used by the debtor.

The debt must be identified as to the amount owed, the consideration furnished for it (if any), when the debt was incurred or became due, any interest claimed, and that the debt is for a liquidated amount due either immediately or payable at a certain date in the future. There must also be a statement that the debtor is unable to pay a presently due debt or

---

[17] The court will only look behind a judgment debt if it is shown that the judgment was obtained by fraud, collusion or represents a miscarriage of justice – *Dawodu v American Express Bank* [2001] BPIR 983.

[18] See e.g., *Westminster City Council v Parkin* [2001] BPIR 1156.

[19] See e.g., *Re A Debtor (No 340 of 1992)* [1992] 2 All ER 211.

[20] See IR Chapter 2.

[21] Forms 6.8–6.10.

appears to be unable to pay a debt due in the future. If a statutory demand has been served on the debtor, details of when and how it was served must be included. If relevant, details of an unsatisfied execution must be given.

The petition must be filed at the court, technically referred to as the presentation of the petition. The fee for presentation of a creditor's petition is £150 (SI 1999/687). The statements made in the petition must be verified by affidavit. Two copies must also be filed. One is for service on the debtor and the other to be exhibited to an affidavit verifying service. The affidavit of service must be filed at the court. At the time of filing the petition the creditor must pay a deposit of £300 (SI 1986/2030). If a statutory demand has been employed an affidavit verifying service of the demand must be served. Upon filing, the court must notify the Chief Land Registrar who will register the petition in the register of pending actions.

When these formalities have been satisfied, the court will set a date for the hearing. Usually at least 14 days' notice must be given of the hearing from the date of the service of the petition. The court may agree to a shorter notice period, for instance, if the debtor has absconded. If the debtor wishes to defend the petition, a notice specifying the grounds for objecting must be filed with the court not less than seven days prior to the return date. Other creditors as well as the petitioning creditor may attend the hearing and either support (the usual case) or oppose the petition.

The debtor may choose not to appear, but this may not prevent the court from proceeding with the hearing.

Under section 271 the court will not make an order unless it is satisfied that the debt, in the case of a debt payable at the time of the petition, has not since the date of the petition been paid, secured or compounded. In the case of a future debt the court will not make an order unless it is satisfied that the debtor has no reasonable prospect of being able to pay it when it falls due.

The petition may be dismissed if the court is satisfied that the debtor is able to pay all his or her debts or that the debtor has made an offer to secure or compound the debt and the offer has been unreasonably refused by the creditor.[22] In *Re A Debtor (No 32 of 1993)* ([1994] 1 WLR 899), the court decided that whether a creditor's refusal was reasonable or not is to be judged from the position of the hypothetical creditor. The court must be satisfied that no reasonable hypothetical creditor would have refused the offer. An offer to take part in an individual voluntary arrangement is not an offer for these purposes as the decision whether to accept or not is not one solely for the creditor.[23]

Generally speaking, the court will make a bankruptcy order if it is satisfied that the statements in the petition are true and that the debt has not been paid, secured or compounded.[24]

---

[22] See generally *Re Gilmartin* [1989] 1 WLR 513.

[23] See *Re a Debtor (No 2389 of 1989)* [1991] Ch 326.

[24] See IR rule 6.25.

Chapter 22

Effects of Bankruptcy

22.1 Introduction

After considering how a person becomes bankrupt, we examine in this chapter the effects that bankruptcy brings. Once a bankruptcy order is made by the court, the subsequent procedure and legal effects are the same regardless of whether the petition had been presented by a creditor or the bankrupt. The order will state the date of the presentation of the petition and the time and date of the order itself. The date of the order is the date of the commencement of the bankruptcy. The bankruptcy is deemed to have commenced at the earliest moment of that day. The order will also contain a notice requiring the bankrupt to attend the office of the official receiver immediately following service of the order. Copies of the order are sent to the official receiver who then serves one copy on the bankrupt. The official receiver will also notify the Chief Land Registrar who will register the bankruptcy order in the register of writs and orders affecting land. This has the effect of giving notice to any third parties who propose any dealing with the land of the bankruptcy order. The official receiver will also publish a notice of the order in the *London Gazette* and such newspapers as the official receiver sees fit.[1]

In general terms, the bankrupt's estate automatically vests in the trustee in bankruptcy as soon as the trustee is appointed. This is the most important effect as far as the property of the bankrupt is concerned. For the purposes of this chapter it is sufficient to be aware that even if the bankrupt's estate has not yet vested in the trustee, as soon as the order is made, the official receiver, under section 287 of the Act, acts as receiver

---

[1] See generally IR rules 6.33, 6.34, 6.45 and 6.46. These publicity requirements may be stayed pending an appeal by the bankrupt against the order. In such circumstances, third parties dealing with the bankrupt in ignorance of the bankruptcy would be generally outside the collective bankruptcy process as the debts incurred by the bankrupt would be incurred after the commencement of the bankruptcy and consequently void under section 284 of the Act.

and manager of the bankrupt's estate. The official receiver is under a duty to protect the estate pending appointment of a trustee (who may be a private sector insolvency practitioner or the official receiver himself or herself). The appointment of the official receiver prevents the bankrupt dealing with any assets in the estate after the order is made.

The official receiver is under a duty to investigate the conduct and affairs of every bankrupt.[2] The bankrupt must cooperate by providing information and the official receiver may require the bankrupt to attend personally at any reasonable time.[3]

22.2 Dispositions of property by the bankrupt after the petition

Under section 284, any disposition of property or payment of money by the bankrupt after the date of the petition is void, unless approved by the court at the time or subsequently. A third party who receives property or payment prior to the date of the bankruptcy order is protected as long as that person has acted in good faith, for value and without notice of the petition (section 284(4)(a)). Where the bankrupt incurs a debt after the bankruptcy order to, for example, the bankrupt's bank, the debt is deemed to have been incurred prior to the date of the order unless the bank had notice of the order at the time the debt was incurred (section 284(5)).

Where the bankrupt is a trader, under section 344, any general assignment of the trader's existing or future book debts is void against the trustee in bankruptcy as regards book debts not paid before the date of the presentation of the petition (unless in the unlikely event that such an assignment is registered under the Bills of Sale Act 1878). Such assignments will usually be made by way of security to cover the bankrupt trader's borrowing.

Although after the bankruptcy order is made, the bankrupt is still technically the owner of his or her property pending appointment of the trustee, the bankrupt loses his or her powers of disposition over the property comprised in the estate. Any attempt at disposing of assets will generally be void under section 284. The bankrupt must deliver up possession of his or her estate to the official receiver, including all books and records relevant to the estate.[4] Further, similar duties are imposed upon the bankrupt, once a trustee is appointed, so far as cooperating with the trustee.[5]

---

[2] Note the new section 289 of the Act to be introduced when the Enterprise Act 2002 comes into force. The new provision gives the official receiver a discretion as to whether or not to carry out an investigation.

[3] See Chapter 25.

[4] See section 291 of the Act.

[5] See section 333 of the Act.

22.3 Loss of property

The basic philosophy of bankruptcy is that in exchange for handing over virtually all that the bankrupt owns to be sold off for the benefit of the creditors, the bankrupt will, at a later point in time, be released from all the debts owing. The bankruptcy estate vests automatically in the trustee at such time as the trustee is appointed. This is not as straightforward as it sounds, due to the various legal characteristics that different types of assets may possess. Although the bankrupt's assets must be made available to the creditors, some assets and some income must be left with the bankrupt in order to permit him or her and his or her family to survive physically. Assets such as the matrimonial home cause their own particular problems with issues of joint ownership and families being in residence. The estate's claim on the bankrupt's pension entitlement is again not easily assessed.

As soon as the trustee in bankruptcy is appointed, under section 306 the bankrupt's estate immediately vests in the trustee. Such vesting occurs automatically without the need for any formal conveyance, assignment or transfer.

The meaning of property for these purposes is defined in section 436 to include 'money, goods, things in action, land and every description of property wherever situated and also obligations and every description of interest whether present or future or vested or contingent, arising out of, or incidental to, property.' The definition is extremely wide and appears to include almost any type of proprietary interest imaginable.

In addition, the 'bankrupt's estate' is defined in section 283. It comprises all 'property' belonging to or vested in the bankrupt at the commencement of the bankruptcy. It expressly does not apply to:

(1) such tools of the trade, books, vehicles and other items of equipment as are necessary to the bankrupt for use personally by him in his employment, business or vocation; and

(2) such clothing, bedding, furniture, household equipment and provisions as are necessary for satisfying the basic domestic needs of the bankrupt and his or her family;

(3) property held by the bankrupt on trust for any other person;

(4) certain types of dwelling house tenancies such as assured tenancies under Part I of the Housing Act 1988, protected tenancies under the Rent Act 1977, secured tenancies under the Housing Act 1985.[6]

The property that vests in the trustee is the property owned by the bankrupt at the date of the bankruptcy order even though the trustee will not be appointed for many weeks after the order. The trustee takes the property 'subject to equities' and cannot therefore ignore the rights of

---

[6] The provisions of section 308A should be noted which allow a trustee in spite of section 283 to claim such tenancies.

secured creditors[7] or the rights of set-off which an unsecured creditor may have.[8] In addition to the property in existence at the date of the order, the trustee may be able to claim other assets which were disposed of by the bankrupt between the date of the petition and the date of the order. As we have seen, any such dispositions will generally be void under section 284. There may be circumstances which permit the trustee to swell further the assets available to the estate by attacking transactions entered into prior to bankruptcy, such as transactions at an undervalue, preferences, extortionate credit bargains and transactions defrauding creditors.[9]

Property over which the bankrupt has only personal rights, such as a non-assignable periodic tenancy, cannot be regarded as property falling into the bankrupt's estate.[10] If the bankrupt has any rights of action against a third party they will vest in the trustee.[11] Compensation for personal injury is seen as a personal right rather than proprietary and will not vest.[12] Income-related social security benefits do not vest.[13] As can be seen from these examples it is by no means easy to predict which type of assets the courts will view as purely personal and therefore will not vest or which type of assets are truly property interests which will vest.

22.3.1 *Reasonable replacement*

Tools of the trade covered by Section 283 may involve literally a workman's tool bag and its contents, but is wider than that. A businessman may need to have a car in order to do business and get to meetings. A car would, in such circumstances, be a tool of the businessman's trade. Even though a bankrupt's tools of the trade are excepted from the estate, it may be the case that if, taking the example of the businessman's car, the car is worth a great deal of money and a replacement could be acquired for less than the sale price of the car, the trustee may take action to claim the car.

Under section 308, where property is excluded from the estate by virtue of it comprising tools of trade or household effects, if the trustee believes that the realisable value of that property exceeds the cost of a reasonable replacement, the trustee may claim that property for the estate. Upon serving the notice on the bankrupt the property identified immediately vests in the trustee. The trustee's title relates back to the date of the bankruptcy order except as against a purchaser in good faith, for value and

---

[7] See e.g., *Re Wallis* [1902] 1 KB 719.

[8] See e.g., *Bradley-Hole v Cusen* [1953] 1 QB 300.

[9] See Chapters 36, 37, 38 and 40.

[10] See *London City Corp v Brown* (1990) 60 P&CR 42. See also *Re Rae* [1995] BCC 102.

[11] See e.g., *Nelson v Nelson* [1997] BPIR 702 and *Khan-Ghauri v Dunbar Bank plc* [2001] BPIR 618.

[12] See e.g., *Lang v McKenna* [1997] BPIR 340. For an example of a cause of action which involved partly personal claims and partly claims for loss of property see *Mulkerrins v PriceWaterhouse Coopers* [2001] BPIR 106.

[13] See e.g., *Mulvey v Secretary of State for Social Security* [1997] BPIR 696.

without notice of the bankruptcy. The trustee must apply funds in the estate to the purchase of a reasonable replacement item for use by the bankrupt. A replacement is reasonable if it is 'reasonably adequate' for meeting the needs met by the other property.

22.3.2 *After-acquired property*

Although the cut-off date for assessing what falls within the estate is the date of the bankruptcy order, under section 307 of the Act the trustee may claim property acquired by the bankrupt after the date of the bankruptcy order. The bankrupt is under a duty to inform the trustee if he or she becomes entitled to any after acquired property.[14] If the bankrupt, for example, inherits some money or has the benefit of some other form of windfall, the trustee may serve a written notice on the bankrupt.[15] Once served upon the bankrupt this has the effect of vesting the after acquired property in the trustee as from the date the property was acquired. The trustee cannot claim the property from a third party who has acquired it in good faith, for value and without notice of the bankruptcy.

22.3.3 *Income of the bankrupt*

Section 307 deals with after acquired property of a capital nature. It does not apply to any income the bankrupt may earn from his or her trade or profession.[16] This does not mean that the trustee cannot make a claim for such income. Under section 310 the trustee may apply to the court for an income payments order. The effect of such an order is that a part of the bankrupt's income, while the bankrupt remains undischarged, must be paid over to the trustee. The court will not order an amount to be paid over which reduces the bankrupt's income to below the level which the court believes is necessary for meeting the reasonable domestic needs of the bankrupt and his or her family. In most cases the income payments order will continue as long as the bankruptcy order is in force. In most cases, where discharge occurs automatically after three years, the income payments order will cease to be effective.

Under the new regime for discharge to be introduced when the Enterprise Act 2002 is fully effective, all bankrupts will be automatically discharged after one year. Section 310 is amended for the purposes of the new regime to allow an income payments order to continue in force for up

---

[14] See IR rule 6.200.

[15] For an example of section 307 operating see *Pike v Cork Gully* [1997] BPIR 723 where the bankrupt unsuccessfully claimed that money in an account was income from his business.

[16] See e.g., *Supperstone v Lloyd's Names Association Working Party* [1999] BPIR 832. For a discussion of the distinction and a consideration of how income payments orders work see G. Miller, 'Income Payments Orders' (2002) 18 IL&P 43.

to three years. Also under the new regime, if the amount to be paid over to the official receiver or trustee in bankruptcy can be agreed between the bankrupt and the trustee, there will in future be no need to obtain a court order. Instead, an income payments agreement will be entered into under section 310A. This legally binding agreement will be enforceable as if it were an income payments order. This will undoubtedly save money in that no court order will have to be obtained.

22.3.4 *Pension rights*

Pension rights of the bankrupt have created a number of difficult questions. The courts have generally held that such rights will vest in the trustee unless under the terms of the pension policy the rights have been effectively forfeited.[17] The courts have held that the inclusion of a non-assignment clause in the pension policy will not prevent the benefits under the policy from vesting in the trustee.[18] Parliament has recognised that the impact of this case law can be very harsh on bankrupts who may lose all their pensions, even though they have been paying into them for several decades. To remedy this perceived injustice, the provisions of the Welfare Reforms and Pensions Act 1999 have introduced new sections 342A, B and C of the Act. It is generally now the case that personal pension schemes as well as occupational pension schemes are excluded from the estate of a bankrupt. Only if 'excessive' contributions have been made will the trustee be able to claim back some of the money tied up in the pension fund. If the bankrupt is receiving income from the pension, the trustee retains the option of applying for an income payments order with regard to any income over and above that needed for the reasonable domestic needs of the bankrupt and his or her family.

22.3.5 *Bankrupt's home*

The most valuable item of property which the bankrupt owns will frequently be his or her home. Even where the home is mortgaged, in times of high property values, the value to the bankrupt, known as the equity, may be substantial. Although this is good news for the bankrupt's creditors, the bankrupt and possibly his or her family may be rendered homeless by a sale. The law attempts to balance this impossible conflict by recognising the rights of both the creditors and the family. In effect, sections 335A–338 of the Act allow for the sale of the family home to be delayed for up to one year from the date of the vesting of the estate in the

---

[17] See e.g., *Re Landau* [1998] Ch 223, *Caboche v Ramsay* [1997] BPIR 377, *Re the Trusts of the Scientific Investment Pension Plan* [1998] BPIR 410 and *Patel v Jones* [2001] EWCA Civ 779.

[18] See *Krasner v Dennison* [2001] Ch 76 approving *Re Landau.*

trustee. After the year expires the interests of the creditors are deemed to be paramount and further postponement of the sale will only be possible if there are exceptional circumstances.

The bankrupt spouse may be joint owner of the matrimonial home under a trust of land with his or her spouse or former spouse or may be sole beneficial owner. Where there is joint ownership, the trustee will usually wish to obtain an order of sale under section 14 of the Trusts of Land and Appointment of Trustees Act 1996 for the home to be sold. The trustee will thereby be able to obtain the value of the bankrupt spouse's share in the home. Under section 335A of the Act, the court will make such order as it thinks just and reasonable having regard to:

(1) the interests of the creditors;
(2) where the application is made in respect of the family home:
    (a) the conduct of the spouse or former spouse so far as it contributed to the bankruptcy;
    (b) the needs and financial resources of the spouse or former spouse; and
    (c) the needs of any children; and
(3) all the circumstances of the case other than the needs of the bankrupt.

After one year of the vesting of the interest in the home in the trustee, the court shall assume, unless the circumstances are exceptional, that the interests of the creditors outweigh all other considerations.

In order to convince the court that exceptional circumstances exist, it is usually necessary to show that, for example, the spouse is seriously ill and a forced sale of the home would have a serious effect on the spouse's health.[19] An example of this is *Claughton v Charalamabous* ([1998] BPIR 558):

> After a year had elapsed since the bankruptcy order, the trustee in bankruptcy applied under section 14 of the Trusts of Land and Appointment of Trustees Act 1996 for an order of sale of the home jointly owned by the bankrupt and his wife. Under the terms of section 335A the court found exceptional circumstances existed. The wife of the bankrupt was aged 60 years. She suffered from chronic renal failure and chronic osteoarthritis with the consequence that she could only walk with the aid of a Zimmer frame and then only with great difficulty. She needed a wheelchair. The home was fitted with a chair lift which was necessary for her needs. A move of house would have necessitated her having to move to a ground floor property or a nursing home. Her life expectancy and the way in which she lived were exceptional circumstances. The court ordered that the home be sold but the sale to be postponed until such time that the wife permanently vacated the home or died, whichever event occurred sooner.

Where there is evidence that the bankrupt has transferred either all or a part share in the home to the non-bankrupt spouse prior to bankruptcy,

---

[19] For examples of 'exceptional circumstances' in this context see e.g. *Re Citro* [1991] Ch 142, *Judd v Brown* [1997] BPIR 470, *Re DR Raval* [1998] BPIR 389 and *Re Bremner* [1999] 1 FLR 558.

the trustee may attack the transaction as one entered into at an undervalue under section 339.[20] This is what happened in the *Claughton* case, which we have just discussed. Prior to the trustee's application for an order for sale he had to bring an action under section 339 to upset the deed of gift made by the bankrupt to his wife of his half share in the matrimonial home just prior to his petition against himself. Transaction avoidance provisions may be used to upset property adjustment orders made on divorce under section 24 of the Matrimonial Causes Act 1973.[21]

Similar provisions apply where the bankrupt is the sole beneficial owner of the family home. Under section 336, the bankrupt's spouse is unable to acquire any statutory right of occupation under the Family Law Act 1996, following the date of the bankruptcy petition. If a right of occupation has been effectively acquired prior to this date, the spouse's right gives rise to a charge on the home which is binding on the trustee. Any application for an order of sale will be considered by the court taking into account the same factors as for a proposed sale where the spouse is a joint owner (listed above).

A third possibility is where the bankrupt owns the home and lives there without a spouse but children who are minors do live there. This may be the case where the bankrupt owns the home but cohabits with a partner with whom the bankrupt has children. In addition to the above provisions, under section 337, if the bankrupt has a beneficial interest in the home and any persons under the age of 18 lived there at the time of both the bankruptcy petition and the order, the bankrupt has the following rights against the trustee:

(1) if in occupation the right not to be evicted without the trustee obtaining leave; and
(2) if not in occupation, a right with leave of the court to enter and occupy the home.

The court may make such order as it thinks is just and reasonable having regard to the interests of the creditors, the bankrupt's financial resources, the needs of the children and all the circumstances of the case. Again, in the absence of exceptional circumstances, the creditors' interests will be paramount after one year. The serious illness of a child may constitute exceptional circumstances.

Under section 313, if the trustee is for any reason unable to realise the bankrupt's interest in a dwelling house, the trustee may apply to the court for a charging order to be made over the interest in favour of the estate. This provision allows the trustee to complete the administration of the bankruptcy with the charging order still outstanding. When eventually the interest in the dwelling house is realised the benefit still goes to the creditors.

[20] See generally Chapter 36.
[21] See e.g., *Re Kumar* [1993] 2 All ER 700 and *Re Flint* [1993] 1 WLR 537.

When in effect, the Enterprise Act 2002 will introduce a new section 283A into the Act. This new section provides that where the bankrupt has an interest in his or her home, unless the trustee has acted to realise or charge the interest or otherwise come to some agreement in relation to it, within three years of the bankruptcy order, the interest reverts back to the bankrupt.

The 2002 Act also includes a new section 313A. This provides for the dismissal of any application for orders for sale, possession or a charging order in respect of the bankrupt's residence where the value of the bankrupt's interest is below a level to be prescribed in secondary legislation.

22.4 Release from creditor harassment

Under section 285(1) of the Act, at any time after a petition has been presented, the court may stay any action, execution or other legal process against the debtor.[22] Upon the bankruptcy order being made, the bankrupt can, generally speaking, no longer be sued by his or her creditors. Under section 285(3), no creditor with a debt provable in the bankruptcy may have any remedy against the person or property of the bankrupt.[23] This is subject to a number of exceptions, notably a secured creditor may still enforce security[24] and special rules apply to execution creditors and landlords.[25]

Under section 281(6) of the Act and IR rule 12.3(2), any obligation arising under an order made in family proceedings is not provable in the bankruptcy. This therefore does not release the bankrupt from the liability to pay, for example, periodical payments or a lump sum payment to a former spouse. If the bankrupt defaults on either type of obligation there is not much the spouse can do about it. The spouse of the bankrupt is unable to enforce an order for periodical payments by proving in the bankruptcy. As the bankrupt loses control of his or her capital assets upon being declared bankrupt, any transfer of a lump sum will not be possible. The spouse can only wait until the bankrupt is discharged before trying to enforce the payment.

In theory, debts not provable in the bankruptcy may still be enforced but the court has a discretion to stay such proceedings. As a general rule, if the proceedings are punitive in nature, for example, contempt of court

---

[22] See e.g., *Re Eileen Davies* [1997] BPIR 619.

[23] For an explanation of which debts are provable see Chapter 34.

[24] See e.g., *Re X* [1996] BPIR 494 – a spouse's claim to a lump sum payment in family proceedings is not a provable debt under IR rule 12.3(2) and therefore is not subject to the limits imposed by section 285(3). A landlord's power of peaceable re-entry is similarly outside the provision, see *Razzaq v Pala* [1998] BCC 66. Also see the limitation in section 285(5).

[25] See Chapter 31.

proceedings, the court will not order a stay. Where the proceedings are intended to force payment of money a stay will be ordered. In *Smith v Braintree District Council* ([1990] 2 AC 215):[26]

> The House of Lords had to consider whether the meaning of 'other legal process' under section 285(1) included orders of committal for non-payment of rates. Their Lordships decided that it was included and reinstated the Registrar's order staying the committal. The underlying purpose of section 285 was to protect the bankrupt's estate for the benefit of all the creditors and therefore committal proceedings intended to force the payment of rates fell within the section. To order otherwise might allow the local authority to obtain an advantage over the other unsecured creditors. Criminal proceedings would be outside the scope of the section but quasi-criminal proceedings such as these which are designed to coerce payment of a debt are within the section.

The effect of section 285(3) is to force virtually all the bankrupt's unsecured creditors to take part in the collective process that is bankruptcy.

22.5 Personal consequences

In order that the bankrupt's estate is got in and distributed efficiently and fairly to the creditors, the law imposes a number of duties upon the bankrupt. Generally speaking breach of such duties leads to criminal sanctions against the bankrupt. In addition to such liability, an undischarged bankrupt is subject to a number of restrictions imposed in the public interest.

22.5.1 Criminal liability

Failure on the part of the bankrupt to cooperate with the official receiver or trustee in bankruptcy (if there is one) by handing over property belonging to the estate and to provide information required by the relevant office holder will, in the absence of reasonable excuse, constitute a contempt of court.[27]

A number of criminal offences may be committed by an undischarged bankrupt. It will be a defence for the bankrupt to show that he or she had no intent to defraud or to conceal the true state of affairs. It is interesting to note that some of these offences are committed by the bankrupt after adjudication whereas some others are committed only in retrospect by conduct carried out prior to the bankruptcy which but for the bankruptcy would probably not be an offence. The possible offences are:[28]

---

[26] A case decided under section 285(1) but the principles apply to section 285(3) as well.
[27] See sections 291 and 333 of the Act.

(1) non-disclosure of property comprised within the estate;
(2) non–delivery of property comprised within the estate or concealment of any debt or property of £500 or more;
(3) non-delivery of all books, papers and other records which relate to the estate;
(4) making any material omission in any statement, e.g., makes up fictitious losses or expenses to account for a gap in any records;
(5) fraudulent disposal of assets prior to commencement of bankruptcy;
(6) absconding the jurisdiction with property, which should be delivered up to the official receiver or trustee, which has a value in excess of £500;
(7) fraudulent disposal of property acquired on credit but not paid for, in the year prior to the bankruptcy;
(8) obtaining credit of more than £250 without disclosing bankruptcy;
(9) engaging in business under a name different from that in which he or she was declared bankrupt;
(10) failure to keep proper accounts in the two years prior to the petition (section 361);
(11) increased the extent of insolvency by gambling or hazardous speculations in the two years prior to the petition (section 362).

Most of these offences are discussed in Chapter 46 of the book.

The court has wide powers to order the arrest of either a debtor subject to a bankruptcy petition or an undischarged bankrupt and to seize any books, papers, records, money or goods in that person's possession. The grounds upon which the court may act are contained in section 364 and are:

(1) there are reasonable grounds for believing that the person has or will abscond with a view to avoiding or delaying payment of debts or to disrupt the bankruptcy proceedings;
(2) that person is about to remove goods with a view to preventing or delaying the official receiver or trustee in bankruptcy from taking possession of them;
(3) there are reasonable grounds for believing that person has concealed or destroyed, or is about to, any goods or records which might be of use in the administration of the bankruptcy;
(4) that the person has removed goods exceeding £500[29] without the consent of the official receiver or trustee;
(5) that the person has failed to attend an examination ordered by the court.

---

[28] See Chapter VI of Part IX of the Act (sections 350–363) and the discussion in I. Fletcher, *The Law of Insolvency*, 3rd edn, London: Sweet & Maxwell (2002), Chapter 13. Also, see Chapter 46 below.
[29] Insolvency Proceedings (Monetary Limits) Order 1986 (SI 1986/1996).

Under section 371 the court may order that for a period of up to three months at a time, the Post Office must redirect the bankrupt's post to the official receiver or trustee.[30]

22.5.2 *Personal restrictions*

While a bankrupt remains undischarged, he or she is subject to a number of restrictions or legal disabilities:

(1) A bankrupt suffers the same disability as a director of a company who is subject to a company directors' disqualification order or undertaking. A bankrupt cannot without leave of the court, act as a director of or, directly or indirectly, take part in the promotion, formation or management of a company. Breach of this restriction constitutes a criminal offence.[31]

(2) A bankrupt cannot sit or vote in the House of Lords, be elected to, sit or vote in the House of Commons, nor sit or vote in a committee in either House. An MP who becomes disqualified has effectively six months to have the bankruptcy order annulled, otherwise at the end of this period the MP's seat shall be vacated.[32]

(3) A bankrupt cannot be elected to, or be a member of, a local authority.[33]

(4) A bankrupt cannot be appointed, or act as, a Justice of the Peace.[34]

(5) A bankrupt cannot act as an insolvency practitioner.[35]

(6) A bankrupt cannot hold a solicitors' practising certificate.[36]

The provisions of the Enterprise Act 2002 make a number of amendments to the restrictions placed upon an undischarged bankrupt. Disqualification from sitting as an MP, a Justice of the Peace or a member of a local authority is largely removed. The offences under sections 361 and 362 of the Act are repealed. In addition, under the 2002 Act, a new regime of bankruptcy restrictions orders will operate to extend the restrictions imposed upon bankrupts for a set period of time after discharge.[37]

---

[30] For a discussion of this power from a human rights viewpoint see e.g., C. Gearty, 'Insolvency and Human Rights' [2000] *Insolvency Lawyer* 68 and N. Pike, 'The Human Rights Act 1998 and its impact on Insolvency Practitioners' [2001] *Insolvency Lawyer* 25.

[31] See sections 11 and 13 of the Company Directors Disqualification Act 1986 and *R v Brockley* [1994] BCC 131.

[32] See section 427 of the Act. The provisions of subsections 6A to 6C extend this provision to members of the Scottish Parliament, the Welsh Assembly and the Northern Ireland Assembly.

[33] See section 80 of the Local Government Act 1972.

[34] See section 65 of the Justices of the Peace Act 1997.

[35] See section 390 of the Act.

[36] See section 12 of the Solicitors Act 1974.

[37] See Chapter 24.

Chapter 23

The Trustee in Bankruptcy

23.1 Introduction

As we have seen in the previous chapters, as soon as the bankruptcy order is made the official receiver is appointed as receiver and manager of the bankrupt's estate pending appointment of a trustee in bankruptcy. The official receiver has a number of duties to carry out prior to a trustee taking office. The official receiver must carry out an investigation into the reasons for the bankruptcy.[1] As part of the information gathering exercise the bankrupt (or others involved with the bankrupt) may be summoned to a private or public examination by the court.[2]

If the bankruptcy was commenced by a debtor's petition, the official receiver will have received a copy of the bankrupt's statement of affairs. If the petition was commenced other than by a debtor's petition, the bankrupt must submit a statement of affairs to the official receiver not more than 21 days after the date of the bankruptcy order (section 288). The statement of affairs will usually be required to cover the two-year period prior to the bankruptcy order. Creditors of the bankrupt will be sent a summary of the statement and the official receiver's comments on it.

Any accounts that the bankrupt has relating to his or her affairs in the three years prior to the petition may be requested by the official receiver. Further information relating to the bankrupt's affairs generally may need to be provided by the bankrupt (section 291). Once the official receiver's investigation is completed, a report must be made to the court (section 289).

---

[1] Note the new section 289 of the Act to be introduced when the Enterprise Act 2002 comes into force. The new provision gives the official receiver a discretion as to whether or not to carry out an investigation.

[2] See Chapter 25.

23.2 Appointment of the trustee

As soon as is practicable within 12 weeks of the bankruptcy order the official receiver must decide whether to summon a meeting of the bankrupt's creditors for the purpose of appointing a trustee of the bankrupt's estate (section 293). If a certificate of summary administration has been issued, no creditors' meeting will be called. Instead, the official receiver will automatically become the trustee in bankruptcy (section 297). The decision as to whether or not to call a meeting will depend upon how much the estate is worth. If the estate is so depleted and the deficiency so large that there is no likelihood of a dividend being paid to the unsecured creditors, the official receiver will usually not call a meeting. The reason for this is that in such a situation it is highly unlikely that a private sector insolvency practitioner would agree to act, as there would not be sufficient funds to pay for his or her remuneration. The trustee's fees and costs would be paid out ahead even of the preferential creditors. Once the trustee's fees are paid, assuming there is enough in the estate to cover them, there may be no money left for any of the creditors. In such circumstances, the only sensible solution will be for the official receiver to continue to act as trustee instead. The costs of the official receiver are frequently not met by the value in the estate and, in such circumstances, there is no alternative but for the costs of the estate's administration to fall upon the State.

If the official receiver decides not to call a creditors' meeting (the expense of such a meeting having to be met out of assets within the estate), any creditor may still request the official receiver to summon such a meeting. The only exception to this is where a certificate of summary administration has been issued in which case the creditors cannot requisition a meeting. If at least one-quarter in value of the bankrupt's creditors appear to support the request the official receiver must call the meeting (section 294).[3]

If the official receiver decides not to call a creditors' meeting, he or she must give notice of the decision to the court and all the creditors of whom he or she is aware. Upon giving notice to the court, the official receiver becomes the trustee in bankruptcy (section 293(3)).

23.2.1 *Creditors' meeting*

Where a meeting of creditors is called, notice of it must be given to the court and to every known creditor of the bankrupt. Creditors must be given at least 21 days' notice of the meeting. The meeting must also be advertised publicly (rule 6.79). The official receiver will usually act as chairman of the meeting (rule 6.82). The official receiver may require the bankrupt to attend (rule 6.84).

---

[3] The costs of calling the meeting may lie with the requisitionists, see IR rules 6.80, 6.87 and 6.88.

The business conducted at the meeting is largely limited to the appointment of a trustee in bankruptcy, fixing of the trustee's remuneration and the establishment or not of a creditors' committee (rule 6.80). Resolutions are passed by a majority in value of those present and voting, in person or by proxy (rule 6.88).

A creditor will only be entitled to vote if proof of debt has been lodged by the time and date specified in the notice of the meeting. This must not be more than four days prior to the meeting. The chairman of the meeting has the power to admit or reject a creditor's proof. A creditor has a right of appeal against the chairman's decision. In cases of uncertainty, the chairman should allow the proof and mark the claim as objected to. The vote may subsequently be invalidated by the court, which may order a further meeting to be called if the vote was crucial to the decisions made at the meeting (rules 6.93 and 6.94).

Secured creditors cannot vote at the creditors' meeting. The creditor may decide to surrender the security and vote the whole debt or value the security and vote only in respect of the unsecured balance (rules 6.93 and 6.98). A creditor owed an unliquidated or unascertained amount can only vote where the chairman agrees to put an estimated minimum value on the debt.[4]

If a creditors' meeting is held but it fails to appoint a trustee, the official receiver must decide whether or not to refer the matter to the Secretary of State. If the referral is made, the Secretary of State may either make an appointment or decline to do so. If no referral is made by the official receiver or if the Secretary of State makes no appointment, the official receiver will report this fact to the court and upon service of this notice the official receiver is appointed as trustee (section 295). In certain special cases listed in section 397, the court may be asked to appoint a trustee.

23.2.2 Commencement of appointment of trustee

Under section 292 of the Act, only a person qualified to act as an insolvency practitioner may be appointed as a trustee in bankruptcy. The appointment takes effect only if that person accepts the appointment in accordance with the Insolvency Rules.[5] Where the creditors' meeting has appointed the trustee, the chairman certifies the appointment but only after the appointee has confirmed he or she is qualified to act and agrees to the appointment. The appointment takes effect at the time specified in the certificate of appointment, which will normally be the date of the certificate. The trustee must forthwith give notice of the appointment in such newspaper as he or she thinks appropriate for ensuring that the appointment comes to the notice of the bankrupt's creditors.

---

[4] See IR rule 6.93, *Re Rickett* [1949] 1 All ER 737, and the discussion of the meaning of 'agrees to put a value' contained in Chapter 8 of Part II in relation to voluntary arrangements.
[5] See rules 6.120–6.125.

Under section 306, the bankrupt's estate vests automatically in the trustee immediately on the appointment taking effect without any need for any formal conveyance, assignment or transfer. Upon appointment, the official receiver must act to put the trustee into possession of the estate.

23.2.3 *Creditors' committee*

As we have seen, the creditors' meeting may set up a creditors' committee (section 301). There can be no committee if the official receiver is the trustee. The primary function of the committee is to act as representatives of the general body of creditors. Its job is to ensure that the trustee acts in accordance with the Act and Rules in relation to the keeping of accounts and records. The committee may require the trustee to send to the committee members a report on the progress of the bankruptcy administration. Certain powers of the trustee can only be exercised with the consent of the committee. The committee must consist of between three and five creditors. Meetings of the committee are called by the trustee at times and venues chosen by the trustee. The first meeting must take place within three months of the trustee's appointment or the committee's establishment (whichever is the later date). The trustee must call a meeting if one is requested by a member of the committee. The tendency is only to have committees where an estate is sizeable or there is likely to be significant litigation.

23.3 Administering the estate

23.3.1 *Trustee's duties*

In many ways the duties of trustees mirror those imposed on liquidators and discussed earlier in Chapter 17. Under section 305, the trustee is under a duty to get in, realise and distribute the bankrupt's estate. Subject to the provisions of the Act, the trustee has a wide discretion as to how this duty is satisfied.[6] If the trustee is not the official receiver, the trustee must furnish the official receiver with such information, permit inspection of such books, papers and other records and give such assistance as the official receiver may reasonably require.

---

[6] As an officer of the court the trustee must act honourably in carrying out his or her functions under the Rule in *Ex parte James* (1874) 9 Ch App 609. For two examples of conduct which did not fall foul of the Rule see *Boorer v Trustee in Bankruptcy of Boorer* [2002] BPIR 21 and *Mountney v Treharne* [2002] BPIR 556.

The trustee, on appointment, must immediately take possession of the estate and realise it in such a way as to maximise the return to creditors. If the value of the estate permits, the trustee must pay a dividend to the creditors after having first deducted a sum to cover the expenses of the bankruptcy (section 324).

The trustee is required to maintain financial records and to handle all monies and fees in accordance with the Insolvency Regulations (SI 1994/2507) which essentially oblige the trustee to bank with the Insolvency Services Account held by the Secretary of State at the Bank of England. Receipts and payments made by the trustee must be recorded on a daily basis. Administrative records of all meetings of creditors or the creditors' committee which have been held must be kept.

Under section 303 of the Act, if the bankrupt or any creditor or other person is dissatisfied by an act, omission or decision of the trustee, an application may be made to the court. The court may either confirm, reverse or modify any act or decision of the trustee. This power to apply to the court is rarely used in practice and it appears difficult to persuade the court that a creditor is justifiably dissatisfied.[7]

Under section 304 of the Act, the trustee may be found liable for breach of duty.[8] This provision is equivalent to section 212,[9] which applies to liquidators. The bankrupt, a creditor, the official receiver or the Secretary of State may bring an action. The grounds for an action are:

(1) that the trustee has misapplied or retained, or become accountable for, any money or other property comprised in the estate; or
(2) that the estate has suffered loss due to any misfeasance or breach of fiduciary or other duty by the trustee.

The court may order the restoration of money or property or a payment compensating the estate for loss caused by the trustee's actions.

23.3.2 *Trustee's powers*

In order to carry out the administration of the bankruptcy estate, the trustee is given wide powers. In order to ensure the trustee is able to get in the property in the estate, he or she has power to take possession of all books, papers and other records relating to the estate. In order to get in the bankrupt's property the trustee has all the powers of a receiver of the High Court and can consequently ask the court to enforce such acquisition and retention of property.

---

[7] For a very limiting approach to the section see *Port v Auger* [1994] 1 WLR 862.
[8] See e.g., *Green v Satsangi* [1998] BPIR 55.
[9] Discussed below at 553–8.

In addition to the powers to avoid prior transactions discussed in Part VIII of the book, a trustee has a number of powers given by section 314 and under Schedule 5 of the Act to assist in the job of getting in and realising the estate. The first group of powers listed in section 314(2) and Part I of the Schedule require the trustee to obtain the consent of the creditors' committee, or if there is none the court, before he or she can exercise them. These powers include the following:

(1) to carry on any business of the bankrupt so far as may be necessary for its beneficial winding up;
(2) to bring or defend any action or legal proceedings relating to the property comprised in the estate;
(3) sell assets on credit terms;
(4) mortgage or pledge estate assets for the purpose of paying off debts;
(5) exercise an option for the benefit of the creditors;
(6) compromise any liabilities of the estate or refer disputes to arbitration.

A second group of powers listed in Part II of Schedule 5 and various other sections of the Act may be exercised without any need to obtain permission:

(1) to sell any assets within the estate;
(2) to give good receipt to debtors of the estate;
(3) to exercise any powers under the Act such as attacking prior transactions as transactions at an undervalue or preferences;[10]
(4) to transfer shares in a company in the same way as the bankrupt would have been able to if he or she had not become bankrupt;
(5) to inspect and, if desired, redeem goods subject to a pledge, pawn or other security (section 311);
(6) to summon a meeting of the creditors or the creditors' committee (if there is one) (section 314 and rule 6.153).

A third group of powers listed under Part III of Schedule 5 are termed ancillary powers and are intended to ensure that the trustee has capacity to do certain fairly essential things. Part III gives to the trustee in his or her official name powers to:

(1) hold property of any description;
(2) make contracts;
(3) sue and be sued;
(4) enter into engagements binding upon the trustee and any successors in office;
(5) employ an agent;
(6) execute any power of attorney, deed or other instrument.

---

[10] Note that once the provisions of the Enterprise Act 2002 come into effect, the trustee will need consent of the court or creditors to exercise these powers (see section 262 of the 2002 Act).

23.3.3 *Trustee's remuneration*

The trustee's remuneration is set by the creditors' committee if there is one or by the creditors' meeting in default. The remuneration may either be a fixed percentage of the value of the assets in the estate which are realised or distributed, or by reference to the time taken by the trustee and his or her staff in dealing with the administration of the estate (rule 6.138).

23.3.4 *Resignation, removal or vacation of office by the trustee*

Under sections 298, 299 and 300 of the Act, the trustee may cease to hold office in a number of ways. The trustee may resign by giving notice to the court. Prior to giving such notice the trustee must inform the creditors and the official receiver. Resignation is only possible on the grounds of ill health, that the trustee is retiring from insolvency practice, or some circumstance has occurred, for example, a conflict of interest has arisen, which prevents the trustee from continuing in office. The earlier discussion on this topic in dealing with liquidators is most pertinent.[11]

The trustee must vacate office if he or she ceases to be a qualified insolvency practitioner.

The trustee may be removed by the court or by a creditors' meeting convened for that purpose. The court or the creditors (as the case may be) may replace the trustee with another insolvency practitioner at the time of the removal. If the official receiver is the trustee he or she can only be removed by the creditors' meeting if the official receiver thinks fit, the court so directs or the meeting is requested by at least one quarter in value of the creditors.

If the administration of the estate is complete, the trustee must call a final meeting of creditors under section 331 and thereafter give notice to the court that the meeting has occurred and that the trustee is vacating office.

23.4 Distribution to creditors

As we have seen, the trustee is under a duty to get in and realise the bankrupt's estate. The final matter the trustee has to deal with is the distribution of the proceeds of the disposal of the estate among the bankrupt's creditors. The way in which the trustee goes about this task is to get the creditors to prove their debts.[12] Once the trustee has received what are known as 'proofs of debt' from all the creditors with provable debts (or at

---

[11] See above at 278–82.
[12] For an explanation of proof of debts, see Chapter 34.

least all the trustee is aware of), the trustee must then rank the debts owed according to the statutory order and pay out the creditors accordingly. If, as will be the case with an insolvent estate, there is not enough money to pay all the creditors, those with a higher priority in the statutory ranking will get paid first. If there is enough to pay some only of a particular class each member of that class is paid a rateable proportion of what he or she is owed.[13]

Creditors who get paid by the trustee are said to receive a dividend from the estate. The trustee may pay a dividend fairly early on in the administration of the estate (known as an 'interim dividend') and, indeed, is under a statutory obligation to pay a dividend whenever he or she holds sufficient funds for the purpose. The trustee must always retain enough money to pay the expenses of the bankruptcy. In making any distribution the trustee must make provision for:

(1) any bankruptcy debt which appears to be due to persons who, by reason of the distance of their place of residence, may not have had sufficient time to tender and establish their proofs;
(2) any bankruptcy debts which are the subject of claims which have not yet been determined; and
(3) any disputed proofs and claims (section 324).[14]

Once a dividend is declared it cannot be disturbed by a creditor who has not participated in the dividend who later proved that he or she should have been paid. Such a creditor is entitled to be paid out of any money for the time being available for the payment of any further dividend, in priority to any further dividend (section 325).[15]

The order in which the bankrupt's liabilities must be paid is as follows.[16]

23.4.1 *Expenses of the bankruptcy*

The trustee must retain such sums as are necessary to pay for the expenses of the bankruptcy. The expenses include various costs, fees and charges which are listed extensively in rule 6.224. Things listed include, for example, the expenses properly incurred by the official receiver and trustee in getting

---

[13] This is not the case with the expenses of the bankruptcy where a hierarchy of payment is contained within rule 6.224. See 413–15.
[14] For the detailed provisions dealing with declaration of dividends see IR Part 11 and Regulation 23 of Insolvency Regulations 1994 (SI 1994/2507). See 417–20.
[15] Although it is usual for a dividend to be paid in cash, it is possible, with the permission of the creditors' committee, for the trustee to pay a dividend *in specie* (see section 326). This may be particularly useful when a specific asset is difficult to sell for one reason or another.
[16] See generally section 328 of the Act. Please note that secured creditors will usually have looked to their security and enforced their debts outside the administration of the bankruptcy.

in and realising the estate and the remuneration of the trustee and anyone employed by the trustee in the running of the bankrupt's business. The expenses of the bankruptcy are listed in a strict order.[17] This ranking is the order in which each head of expense is paid. As the remuneration of the trustee is ranked very low down the list, it is no coincidence that in a very poor estate, a private sector trustee cannot be persuaded to take the bankruptcy. In such an estate there will frequently be no money to pay the remuneration of the trustee. As we have noted above, in such situations no private sector trustee will be appointed. The official receiver will act as trustee.

23.4.2 Pre-preferential debts

Under section 328(6) certain types of debts, under specific statutory pro-visions, are given priority in the distribution, even over preferential debts. Such debts may be referred to as pre-preferential debts. The following are the two most common examples of such debts (for other instances see p 414).

(1) Where the bankrupt is deceased, funeral and testamentary expenses are pre-preferential debts.[18]
(2) Where the bankrupt had engaged an apprentice or articled clerk, the fact of the bankruptcy may lead to the termination of the apprentice-ship or clerkship (as the case may be). Where money has been paid to the bankrupt by or on behalf of the apprentice or clerk, the trustee in bankruptcy may, under section 348 of the Act, repay the fee to such extent as the trustee deems reasonable.[19]

23.4.3 Preferential debts

After the commencement of the Enterprise Act 2002, the number of pref-erential creditors has been greatly reduced. The effect of this change is that the Crown has virtually lost its status as a preferential creditor. Section 386 and Schedule 6 of the Act (as amended) detail the categories of pref-erential debts. Schedule 6 of the Act contains the following preferential debts:

(1) any sums payable in relation to occupational pension schemes (para 8);
(2) remuneration of employees for up to four months prior to the relevant date subject currently to a maximum payment of £800 (para 9);

---

[17] See 414–15.
[18] See Art 4(2) Administration of Insolvent Estates of Deceased Persons Order 1986 (SI 1986/1999).
[19] In addition to this right the apprentice or clerk may apply to the Secretary of State for payment out of the National Insurance Fund under the provisions of the Employment Rights Act 1996. See Chapter 32.

(3) any amount of employees' holiday pay accrued in respect of any employment prior to the relevant date (para 10);

(4) any sum loaned and used for the specific purpose of paying employees' remuneration (para 11);

(5) levies on coal and steel production (para 15A).

It will be seen that in most insolvencies the only preferential debts remaining are those relating to employees' rights. There is no financial limit on the preferential status of contributions which should have been made by an insolvent employer to occupation pension schemes of employees. Similarly, there is no limit on the payment of accrued holiday pay. There is, crucially, a limit on the preferential status of unpaid wages or salary. Although in theory up to four months' back pay may be claimed, this is limited by an overall maximum amount payable of £800.

In a bankruptcy, if the assets prove insufficient to meet all the claims of preferential creditors, each preferential creditor's claim ranks equally and so must suffer equal abatement.

23.4.4 *Ordinary debts*

If there is any money left in the estate once the preferential creditors have been paid, the next class to be paid is the ordinary unsecured creditors. If, as is likely, there is not enough to pay all the ordinary debts, each creditor's claim ranks *pari passu* with the others and will abate proportionately (section 328(3)). If a dividend is capable of being paid to the ordinary creditors it will usually be expressed as a payment of so many pence in the pound.

23.4.5 *Interest (accrued since the commencement of the bankruptcy)*

Creditors are allowed to prove in the bankruptcy for interest on their debts accrued up to the date of the bankruptcy (section 322). They are only allowed a payment in regard to interest accrued after the bankruptcy order, if all the preferential and ordinary creditors have been paid in full. For the purposes of the payment of interest payable after the commencement of bankruptcy, preferential and ordinary creditors are treated together. Preferential creditors have no priority to such payments of interest. If there is enough money in the estate to pay interest, preferential and ordinary creditors have equal claims to such funds. Again, if there is not enough money to satisfy all the claims for interest, they abate equally. There is a maximum rate of interest which can be claimed.[20]

---

[20] See section 17 of the Judgments Act 1838. The current rate is 8 per cent (SI 1993/564).

23.4.6 *Postponed debts*

Section 328(6), as well as identifying certain pre-preferential debts, also recognises that specific statutory provisions may also have the effect of postponing the priority of certain types of debts. These types of debts are referred to as postponed debts. For example, under section 329 any debt owed to the spouse of the bankrupt is a postponed debt and payable only after the five classes of debt listed above. The justification for this rule is mainly the prevention of fraud. It would be easy for the spouse of a bankrupt to set up an alleged loan agreement between the spouse and the bankrupt and to claim some priority in the bankruptcy. This provision largely prevents any such claim being successful.[21]

23.4.7 *Surplus (if any payable to the bankrupt)*

In the unlikely event that there is any money left in the estate after the payment of the above six classes of creditors, under section 330(5) of the Act, the surplus must be returned to the bankrupt. In such circumstances, the bankrupt may attempt to have the bankruptcy order annulled under section 282 of the Act.

23.5 Ending the administration of the bankrutpcy

Once the administration of the estate is finished, in that the trustee has realised as much of the estate as possible without needless protraction of the trusteeship, the trustee may declare a final dividend and must call a final meeting of creditors.[22] At the final meeting the trustee reports to the creditors on how the administration of the estate went. The creditors decide whether or not the trustee should be released from the trusteeship.[23] If the creditors decide the trustee should be released, the trustee notifies the court and the date of such notification is the date of the trustee's release. If the creditors refuse to release the trustee, the trustee must apply to the Secretary of State who decides when the release is to occur.

---

[21] See also section 3 of the Partnership Act 1890 for an example of a business loan, the repayment of which is relegated to the status of postponed debt.

[22] Under section 332, a final meeting may be called even if the trustee has not been able to realise the bankrupt's share in any dwelling house. In order to call the final meeting it will usually be necessary to show that the trustee has applied for and either been granted a charging order over the home under section 313, or had the application rejected.

[23] See sections 331, 298 and 299 of the Act. No final meeting of the creditors is called where the official receiver is the trustee. The official receiver is released upon giving notice to the Secretary of State that the administration of the estate is for practical purposes complete.

Chapter 24

Discharge

24.1 Introduction

We have seen in Chapter 23 how the estate of the bankrupt is administered and how the creditors' interests are looked after by the trustee. The realisation and distribution of the estate is one major aspect of bankruptcy. The major benefit from the bankrupt's viewpoint is that eventually, either before or after the estate has finally been distributed, the bankrupt is discharged from all the bankruptcy debts he or she owed at the date of the bankruptcy order. Discharge from bankruptcy brings to an end the disabilities suffered by a bankrupt, discharges the bankrupt from his or her debts and permits the bankrupt, in effect, to start afresh with a clean slate. Bankruptcy commences with the day of the bankruptcy order and continues until the individual is discharged (section 278 of the Act).

Depending upon the circumstances, the discharge may be automatic after a certain period of time has elapsed, or the bankrupt may be forced to apply to the court for discharge. The provisions of the Enterprise Act 2002 will have a major impact upon the rules governing discharge when the relevant provisions come into effect, estimated to be during the 2004 financial year. After these provisions become operative, automatic discharge will apply to all bankrupts. The important proviso to this rule is that the court may make a bankruptcy restrictions order against the discharged bankrupt, which has the effect of continuing the disabilities felt by a bankrupt for a further period of time. As we shall see, the bankruptcy restrictions order regime bears some similarity to the company directors' disqualification regime. Both are intended to be proceedings brought in the public interest to protect the public from unscrupulous individuals.

In addition to discharge bringing the end to a bankruptcy, it is also possible for the bankruptcy order to be annulled. This matter will be briefly considered at the end of this chapter.

24.2 Current system of discharge

24.2.1 *Automatic discharge*

As long as the bankrupt has not been an undischarged bankrupt in the 15 years prior to the bankruptcy order, the bankruptcy will be discharged automatically once a period of time has elapsed. The exact period will vary depending upon whether or not the bankruptcy was a small bankruptcy where a certificate of summary administration was issued by the court. If the bankruptcy was one with a summary administration, the bankrupt will be automatically discharged two years after the bankruptcy order was made (section 279(2)(a) of the Act). Where the bankruptcy is not one with a certificate of summary administration, the period is three years from the date of the bankruptcy order (section 279(2)(b)). It can therefore be seen that for most bankrupts, certainly those who have been made bankrupt for the first time, discharge occurs automatically with the passing of time.

A bankrupt who would normally expect to be discharged after the three-year period has elapsed may have this period extended. Under section 279(3), the official receiver[1] may apply to the court for an order to the effect that time will cease to run. The grounds for such an application will be that the bankrupt has not been complying with his or her obligations as a bankrupt. If the official receiver has suspicions that the bankrupt is hiding property or is otherwise being less than candid in giving information relating to the estate, the official receiver may apply for the suspension of time leading to the bankrupt's automatic discharge. The court may suspend the running of time for a set period or until certain conditions have been fulfilled. For instance, in *Holmes v Official Receiver (Re A Debtor No 26 of 1991)* ([1996] BCC 246) time was suspended to allow a public examination of the bankrupt to be conducted.[2]

24.2.2 *Discharge by the court*

Where the bankrupt has been an undischarged bankrupt at any time in the 15 years prior to the current adjudication, the only way the bankrupt may achieve his or her discharge is by order of the court (section 280 of the Act). It should be noted that the 15-year period does not run from the date of the previous bankruptcy order, but covers any time when the individual was an undischarged bankrupt. If the prior bankruptcy was a 'normal'

---

[1] Only the official receiver may apply for such an order. It is not open to the petitioning creditor to apply (*Hardy v Focus Insurance Co Ltd* [1997] BPIR 77).
[2] See also *Jacobs v Official Receiver* [1999] 1 WLR 619.

bankruptcy, in that there was no certificate of summary administration issued, automatic discharge from the second bankruptcy will only be available if the first bankruptcy order was made in excess of 18 years before the current bankruptcy order was made.

An application under section 280 may only be made after the end of five years from the date of the current bankruptcy order. The court has a wide discretion either to refuse to discharge, to order the discharge absolutely or to order the discharge subject to conditions. The conditions may apply to any future income or property acquired by the bankrupt being made available to the bankruptcy creditors.

Once the bankrupt has applied to the court for his or her discharge, notice must be given to the official receiver, the trustee in bankruptcy (if there is one) and to every creditor with an unsatisfied claim against the estate (rule 6.217). In advance of the hearing the official receiver prepares a report on the bankrupt's conduct both before and during the current bankruptcy and any dividends which have been paid or are likely to be paid to the creditors. The official receiver is an officer of the court and the court will in normal circumstances place great reliance upon the report in deciding whether or not to order the discharge. The bankrupt has the opportunity to dispute any statements made in the report (rule 6.218).

There are no modern reported decisions on how the court exercises its discretion in these cases. Generally, the court will look to ensure that the bankrupt has acted reasonably, that the creditors have been paid or will be paid all that can be expected in the circumstances and that the bankrupt will not constitute a risk to the public if the bankruptcy order is discharged.

24.2.3 *Effect of discharge*

Whether discharge comes about automatically or by court order, its effect on the bankrupt will be the same. Generally, from the date of the discharge, the bankrupt is released from all bankruptcy debts[3] and is freed from all the personal restrictions which apply to all undischarged bankrupts.[4] Essentially, the slate is wiped clean and the bankrupt is given a fresh start. The creditors of the bankrupt have had their rights to enforce their claim against the bankrupt personally, replaced with the right to prove in the bankruptcy. The creditors cannot chase the bankrupt for payment after the bankruptcy order is made nor after the bankrupt is discharged from all of his or her bankruptcy debts. In practice this is not quite so

---

[3] Defined in section 382 of the Act. See Chapter 34.
[4] See Chapter 22.

simple as it appears as the bankrupt's credit rating will have plummeted and a discharged bankrupt will usually find it difficult to obtain business finance or a lender willing to provide money, for example, to buy a car or a house.

There are a number of exceptions to the general release of the bankrupt listed in section 281 of the Act.

It is possible that the bankrupt is discharged before the trustee has completed the administration of the estate. Section 281(1) therefore provides that discharge does not affect the carrying out by the trustee of the administration of the estate. This also includes the right of creditors to continue to prove their bankruptcy debts existing at the date of the bankruptcy order. The point of this provision is that although the discharge operates to release the bankrupt from the debts owed at the date of the bankruptcy order, his or her estate remains liable for those debts after the bankrupt is discharged from them. As an additional point, the discharge does not prevent secured creditors from realising their security after discharge to pay off debts from which the bankrupt has now been discharged (section 281(2)).

Discharge does not operate to release a bankrupt from liabilities arising out of any fraud[5] or fraudulent breach of trust perpetrated by the bankrupt (section 281(3)) nor generally from any liability in respect of a fine imposed for a criminal offence (section 281(4)).

The discharged bankrupt is only released from certain types of bankruptcy debt to such extent and on such conditions as the court may direct (section 281(5)). Such debts include those arising from a liability to pay damages for personal injury arising from an action in negligence, nuisance, breach of statutory, contractual or other duty, or under the Consumer Protection Act 1987. Debts arising from family proceedings are also within section 281(5).[6]

Under section 281(6) the bankrupt is not discharged from certain prescribed debts which are not provable in the bankruptcy. One example of this is contained within rule 6.223 of the Rules, whereby the bankrupt is not released from any obligation arising under a confiscation order under section 1 of the Drug Trafficking Offences Act 1986 or under section 71 of the Criminal Justice Act 1988.

Although the bankrupt is released from bankruptcy debts, any person with coterminous liability on such debts, such as a business partner or guarantor, is not released from his or her liability (section 281(7)).

---

[5] The meaning of 'fraud' in this context requires a fraud in the sense of deceit. Equitable fraud or unconscionable conduct will not suffice – see *Mander v Evans* [2001] BPIR 902.

[6] The definition of 'family proceedings' is provided by section 281(8) and adopts the definition contained in the Magistrates' Courts Act 1980 and the Matrimonial and Family Proceedings Act 1984.

24.3 Effect of Enterprise Act 2002 on discharge

The most far-reaching change to individual insolvency law brought about by the Enterprise Act 2002 is in relation to the discharge of bankrupts and how bankrupts are dealt with after discharge. The provisions of the 2002 Act which relate to individual insolvency (save for the abolition of the Crown's status as preferential creditor) are due to be brought into force in the financial year 2004. Section 256 of the 2002 Act replaces section 279 of the Act with a new provision. The new section 279 provides for discharge of all bankrupts one year after the bankruptcy order (discharge will still operate to discharge the bankrupt from his or her bankruptcy debts subject to the exceptions discussed above). The one-year period may be reduced if the official receiver files a notice stating that further investigation into the bankrupt's conduct and affairs is unnecessary, or has been concluded. Due to the reduction of the discharge period to one year the whole regime of summary administration is repealed (para 2 of Schedule 23 of the Act). The aim of reducing the discharge period to one year is to allow individuals who have been made bankrupt, frequently through no fault of their own, to get back on their feet more quickly.

It will still be possible for discharge to be suspended if there is evidence that the bankrupt is failing to comply with his or her statutory obligations (section 279(3) and (4)).

Transitional provision is made by Schedule 19 to deal with bankrupts who are subject to a bankruptcy order made prior to the commencement of the relevant provisions of the 2002 Act. In this situation, neither the old nor the new law applies. Instead, the date of discharge will be one year from the date of commencement of the new section 279 or earlier if the two- or three-year (as the case may be) discharge period is due to end before that date.

Where the bankrupt has been an undischarged bankrupt in the 15 years prior to the current bankruptcy order being made, the bankrupt is discharged automatically five years from the date of commencement or earlier if an order under section 280 of the Act is made.

24.3.1 *Restrictions on the bankrupt after discharge*

In order that the public is still protected from 'dishonest' or blameworthy bankrupts, a new section 281A of the Act is introduced which deals with bankruptcy restrictions order ('BROs') and bankruptcy restrictions undertakings ('BRUs'). Section 281A gives effect to a new Schedule 4A of the Act. The purpose of this new provision is to ensure that bankrupts who are culpable in some way for their insolvency remain subject to a number of restrictions even after they are discharged from their bankruptcy. As we shall see, there are a number of similarities between the new BRO or BRU procedures and the procedure whereby a director of a company may become subject to a disqualification order or undertaking, for example, a BRO may only be made for between 2 and 15 years' duration. This is the same for most director disqualification orders.

A BRO may be made by the court only on the application of the Secretary of State or the official receiver on a direction from the Secretary of State. This mirrors the procedure for a director's disqualification order. In deciding whether or not to grant a BRO the court will take account of the bankrupt's conduct either before or after the making of the bankruptcy order. In particular, para 2 of Schedule 4A states that the court shall take account of the following matters (the list is not exhaustive and bears some comparison with Schedule 1 of the Company Directors' Disqualification Act 1986):

(1) failing to keep records which account for a loss of property by the bankrupt in the period beginning two years prior to the petition and ending with the date of the application for the BRO (the criminal offence of failing to keep proper records under section 361 of the Act is repealed by section 263 of the 2002 Act. The effect of failure to keep proper records will therefore in future be one of the matters the court will take account of in deciding whether to make a BRO);

(2) failing to produce records of that kind on demand by the official receiver or trustee;

(3) entering into a transaction at an undervalue (under section 339 of the Act);

(4) giving a preference (under section 340 of the Act);

(5) making an excessive pension contribution;

(6) failing to supply goods or services which were wholly or partly paid for which gave right to a claim provable in bankruptcy;

(7) trading at a time prior to the bankruptcy order, when the bankrupt knew or ought to have known that he or she was unable to pay his or her own debts (this is similar to the common allegation in directors disqualification proceedings not contained in the statutory list but added to by case law of 'trading while insolvent');

(8) incurring a debt prior to the bankruptcy order, which the bankrupt had no reasonable expectation of being able to pay;

(9) failure to account for loss of property or an insufficiency of property to meet bankruptcy debts;

(10) carrying on any gambling, rash and hazardous speculation or unreasonable extravagance which may have materially contributed to or increased the extent of the bankruptcy (the criminal offence of gambling and speculation under section 362 of the Act is repealed by section 263 of the 2002 Act. The effect of gambling and speculation will therefore in future be one of the matters the court will take account of in deciding whether to make a BRO);

(11) neglect of business affairs of a kind which may have materially contributed to or increased the extent of the bankruptcy;
(12) fraud or fraudulent breach of trust;
(13) failure to cooperate with the official receiver or trustee in bankruptcy;
(14) whether the bankrupt was an undischarged bankrupt at some time during the period of six years prior to the bankruptcy order.

It remains to be seen how much guidance the courts will take, if any, from the case law on directors disqualification, but as there is so much discussion of public policy considerations and 'unfit' conduct of directors within that case law, some general guidance at least seems likely to be taken.

In the absence of the court's permission for a longer period to apply, an application for a BRO must be made within one year of the bankruptcy order (para 3 of Schedule 4A). Without anything further, this tight deadline in which to bring the application would cause considerable difficulty in practice. Experience from directors' disqualification cases, where the deadline is two years from the onset of insolvency, shows that it is not at all easy to put together a watertight case in such a short period of time. Even if the court was happy to allow late applications for BROs, the problem from a public policy point of view is that the bankrupt would be discharged after a year and it may be several months, if not years, before any BRO may be ordered. In order to avoid this absurd result para 5 of Schedule 4A allows for an interim BRO to be made. As long as the application for the substantive BRO has been made, the court may make an interim BRO if it thinks that there are *prima facie* grounds to suggest that the application for the BRO will be successful and it is in the public interest to make the order. The interim order has the same effect as a substantive BRO and will run until the application has been heard or a BRU has been entered. This provision is likely to cause a good deal of difficulty in practice. The Secretary of State has to ensure that a *prima facie* case is established so that an application, at least, for a substantive BRO may be made. The problems of deciding whether a *prima facie* case has been made out without the need for some form of mini trial of the issues have been experienced elsewhere in the area of minority shareholder protection. Applications for interim BROs may become commonplace in practice and, if this happens, it seems likely that they will generate a good deal of case law.

Instead of having to go to court for a BRO, a bankrupt may offer a BRU to the Secretary of State under para 7 of Schedule 4A. The effect of a BRU, if accepted by the Secretary of State is the same as if the court had made a BRO. This mirrors the position with directors' disqualification orders and undertakings.

The Secretary of State has a statutory duty to maintain a register of BROs and BRUs.

24.3.2 *Effect of BRO or BRU*

The purpose of the new discharge regime is to release automatically those bankrupts perceived to be not to blame for their financial difficulties. Bankrupts who are proven culpable due to their conduct before or during the bankruptcy will still benefit from automatic discharge after one year, but where a BRO is made or a BRU agreed, they will remain subject to many of the restrictions imposed upon them prior to the discharge. The BRO or BRU continues to enforce bankruptcy restrictions.

Schedule 21 of the Act amends some of the restrictions imposed upon a bankrupt under the old regime and extends these restrictions to an individual who is subject to an interim BRO, a BRO or a BRU. The restrictions imposed are as follows:

(1) the individual cannot act as a receiver or manager of a company's property on behalf of a debenture holder (the new section 31 of the Act);

(2) the individual cannot obtain credit above the prescribed limit without disclosing that he or she is subject to the interim BRO, BRO or BRU (as the case may be) (section 360 of the Act as amended);

(3) the individual cannot trade in a name other than that under which the individual was made bankrupt (section 360 of the Act as amended);

(4) the individual is disqualified from acting as an insolvency practitioner (section 390 of the Act as amended);

(5) the individual is disqualified from acting as a company director (the new section 11(1) of the Company Directors' Disqualification Act 1986); and

(6) the individual is automatically disqualified from sitting as an MP. His or her seat must be vacated immediately (similar provision is made for the Scottish Parliament, the Welsh Assembly and the Northern Ireland Assembly – section 426A of the Act. Note that this system of automatic disqualification only applies where the individual is made bankrupt and subsequently made subject to a BRO or a BRU in England or Wales. No longer will a non-culpable MP have to vacate his or her seat within six months of bankruptcy. There is no equivalent BRO or BRU regime in Scotland or Northern Ireland, and so the old rules will continue to apply if an individual is made bankrupt in Northern Ireland or sequestrated in Scotland). A peer made subject to a BRO or BRU is disqualified from sitting and voting in the House of Lords.[7]

---

[7] Bankrupts will no longer be prevented from sitting as Justices of the Peace or automatically disqualified from serving as a member of a local authority. If an individual becomes subject to a BRO or BRU, he or she will be prevented from serving as a member of a local authority. The removal of bankrupt Justices of the Peace is left to the wide discretionary powers of the Lord Chancellor.

As with bankrupts prior to receiving their discharge, breach of an interim BRO, a BRO or a BRU after discharge will result in an offence being committed.

24.4 Annulment

If a bankruptcy order is annulled by the court, the effect of the annulment is as if the bankruptcy order was never made (section 282 of the Act). The annulment may occur whether or not a bankrupt has been discharged. Obviously, it is likely that the official receiver or trustee in bankruptcy will have taken a number of steps in the administration of the bankruptcy prior to any annulment and any action taken by them remains valid notwithstanding the annulment.[8] Upon annulment any property vested in the trustee shall instead be vested in such person as the court shall appoint, usually reverting to the bankrupt.

The grounds upon which the court may annul a bankruptcy order are:

(1) that on any grounds existing at the time the order was made, the order ought not to have been made (section 282(1)(a));
(2) that the bankruptcy debts and the expenses of the bankruptcy have all either been paid or secured to the satisfaction of the court (section 282(1)(b); or
(3) the bankrupt's creditors approve an individual voluntary arrangement (section 261 (and section 263D once the provisions of the Enterprise Act 2002 are brought into force)).

Under the first ground, the court may annul a bankruptcy order if it should never have been made. Essentially what the court needs to see is evidence that the prescribed formalities leading to an order have not been properly carried out to the serious detriment of the bankrupt. If there has been some form of 'abuse of process' in acquiring the order, the court may intervene to order annulment. The court can only act on the basis of facts which existed at the date the order was made.[9] It may often be the case, that facts existed at the date the court made the order but such facts were not made available to the court at the time of its deliberations. An example of this type of situation is *Henwood v Customs & Excise* ([1998] BPIR 339):

> The hearing was of an application for leave to appeal. A bankruptcy order had been made against the applicant on the petition of Customs & Excise and related to sums of money owed by the applicant in the nature of unpaid

---

[8] For an interesting consequence of this rule see *More v More* [1962] Ch 424.
[9] See section 282(1)(a) of the Act and *Re A Debtor (No 68 of 1992)* [1993] TLR 69.

VAT. There was evidence that the applicant, to his own admission, had underpaid a sum of £300 VAT for the period December 1990 to June 1992. At this time Customs & Excise prepared a statutory demand in the sum of £6,549 for that same period. The following month Customs & Excise sent a schedule to the applicant showing he in fact owed £3,487 for the period December 1989 to June 1992. A month later Customs & Excise presented a petition in the sum of £6,549. The applicant filed a notice of opposition disputing the amount owed. There followed a number of adjourned hearings. Subsequently, an affidavit sworn by a trainee legal executive at Customs & Excise's solicitors exhibited the schedule in the sum of £3,487 for the period December 1989 to June 1992. At a further adjourned hearing, in his absence, the applicant had instructed solicitors to attend but they did not show up. The court made a bankruptcy order against the applicant. The applicant applied for an annulment on the grounds that the petition was erroneous. At the annulment hearing, the applicant attended but his solicitors were delayed in traffic. The application was dismissed. The applicant appealed but his appeal was dismissed. In the meantime, the applicant had paid the sum of £3,487 which it had subsequently been agreed was the true sum owed for the period prior to December 1990. The consequence of all this was that a bankruptcy order had been made on the basis of a debt owed relating to a period not claimed in the petition. The debt owed for the period claimed in the petition was £300 only, not enough by itself for an order to be made (less than £750). In addition to this the court was not aware at the time of the order being made of the reasons for the non-appearance of the applicant's solicitors. The Court of Appeal gave leave to appeal. The Court likened its powers to annul a bankruptcy order to its powers to set aside a statutory demand where there was a dispute on substantial grounds.

Under the second ground for annulment, the bankrupt must show that all his or her bankruptcy debts and the expenses of the administration of the bankruptcy have been paid or secured for, to the satisfaction of the court. It seems in order to show the debts have been dealt with, the creditors must have first proved their debts.[10] Under rule 6.211 of the Rules, all debts proved must have been paid in full. If a debt is disputed, the bankrupt must give such security (in the form of money paid into court or a bond entered into with approved sureties), as the court considers adequate to satisfy any sum that may subsequently be proved due to a creditor.

Where an undischarged bankrupt enters into an individual voluntary arrangement with his or her creditors, the court has a discretion to annul the bankruptcy order under section 261.[11] A new section 261, introduced under section 264 and Schedule 22 of the Enterprise Act 2002, will, when in force, oblige the court to annul the bankruptcy order once the IVA is approved and the period for objecting to the court has elapsed.

When the provisions of Schedule 4A of the 2002 Act come into effect, annulment will operate differently on any BRO or BRU currently in force,

[10] See e.g., *Re Robertson* [1989] 1 WLR 1139.
[11] See Chapter 9.

depending upon the type of annulment. Where a bankruptcy order is annulled under section 282(1)(a), any BRO or BRU in respect of the bankrupt shall also be annulled. If a bankruptcy order is annulled for some other reason, it shall not affect any BRO or BRU. The BRO or BRU will continue in force.

References

Berry, C., Bailey, E. and Schaw-Miller, S., *Personal Insolvency Law – Law and Practice*, 3rd edn, London: Butterworths (2001).

Briggs, N. and Sims, H., 'Escaping Bankrutpcy – Applications to Annul' [2001] *Insolvency Lawyer* 2.

Dawson, I., 'The Administrator, Morality and the Court' [1996] JBL 437.

Elwes, S., 'Bankruptcy and Disability Payments' (2002) 23 Bus LR 9.

Fletcher, I., *The Law of Insolvency*, 3rd edn, London: Sweet & Maxwell (2002).

Gearty, C., 'Insolvency and Human Rights' [2000] *Insolvency Lawyer* 68.

Hunter, M., *Muir Hunter on Personal Insolvency* (looseleaf) London: Sweet & Maxwell.

Jackson, T., *The Logic and Limits of Bankruptcy* (Harvard Press, 1986).

Jones, J., 'The Trusts of Land and Appointment of Trustees Act 1996 – the case law in relation to bankruptcy so far' (2001) 23 *Journal of Social Welfare and Family Law* 353.

Keay, A., 'Insolvent Companies Which are Able to Dispute Debts Owed to Petitioning Creditors: Should they be Wound Up?' (1998) 19 Co Law 230.

Keay, A., 'Balancing Interests in Bankrutpcy Law' (2001) 30 *Common Law World Review* 206.

Keay, A., 'Disputing Debts Relied On By Petitioning Creditors Seeking Winding Up Orders' (2001) 22 Co Law 40.

Miller, G., 'Applications by a trustee in bankruptcy for sale of the family home' (1999) 15 *Insolvency Law & Practice* 176.

Miller, G., 'Income Payments Orders' (2002) 18 *Insolvency Law & Practice* 43.

Milman, D., 'Statutory Demands in the Courts: A Retreat from Formalism in Bankruptcy Law' [1994] Conv 289.

Pike, N., 'The Human Rights Act 1998 and its impact on Insolvency Practitioners' [2001] *Insolvency Lawyer* 25.

Rose, D., *Lewis' Bankruptcy Law*, 11th edn, Sydney: Law Book Co (2000).

Toube, F., 'Challenging the Trustee's Remuneration' (2002) 15 *Insolvency Intelligence* 63.

Warren, E., 'Bankruptcy Policy' (1987) 54 *University of Chicago Law Review* 775.

Part VI

Administration of Insolvent Estates

In this Part we consider some of the major aspects concerning the administration of formal insolvencies, of both individuals and companies. When office-holders are appointed to insolvent estates they will be required to complete certain formalities and it will be prudent for them to carry out other functions to ensure that both the estate is administered as well as it can be and the creditors receive all the benefits to which they are entitled. As the discussion purports to deal with all of the kinds of insolvency administrations encompassed by this book, it is necessary to handle matters in general terms. However, in places it is thought appropriate to deal with specific issues encountered by particular office-holders. In a book of this nature it is not possible to consider all aspects of the administration process, but we endeavour to examine the primary ones and refer readers to other sources for more detailed examinations.

Througout this Part, except where indicated to the contrary, any reference to 'the Act' or to section numbers will be references to the Insolvency Act 1986. Except where indicated to the contrary, any reference to 'the Rules' or to rule numbers will be references to the Insolvency Rules 1986 (SI 1986/1925).

Chapter 25

Investigations and Examinations

25.1 Introduction

One of the primary roles of the majority of office-holders whom we discuss in this book is to carry out investigations of the affairs of the insolvent. Mainly in this chapter we are focusing on the work of administrators and liquidators of companies, the official receiver in relation to both companies and individuals and trustees of bankrupt estates. This is not meant to imply that other kinds of office-holders do not engage in investigations. In fact, when referring to investigations in general terms, all office-holders must undertake some basic investigations. But a good portion of the work of liquidators and trustees is investigative. Much of what follows considers investigations which all administrators, liquidators, trustees and official receivers will perform, but in places it will be necessary to focus on one particular kind of office-holder who has a legislative duty to carry out some specific investigative task(s). For example, there rests upon a liquidator a public responsibility to investigate past activities connected with the company and, in appropriate cases, to report certain findings to the Director of Public Prosecutions.

Examinations can be seen in many ways as part of the investigation process and as examinations have been so important over the years and a large body of law has grown up in relation to them, a significant part of the chapter is devoted to considering them.

The primary purpose of investigations is to enable the office-holder who comes, generally, to an estate with little knowledge of its affairs to ascertain what has occurred in relation to the affairs of the person or company.

25.2 Investigations

25.2.1 *General*

The extent of an office-holder's investigations will depend on the size of the company or the estate of an insolvent person. With both insolvent companies and persons, the nature of the affairs and assets of the insolvent and the circumstances surrounding the advent of the insolvency administration will also be of interest. Additionally, with companies the attitude of the officers may be of importance. Often the office-holder will have to be judicious in engaging in investigations as there may not be sufficient funds to support detailed investigations unless the creditors support such endeavours, and they may well be reluctant to do so given the fact that they are almost certainly not going to recover what they are owed.

The investigative process has a number of aims, but principally they are: to discover the assets to which the estate can lay claim; to ascertain whether the claims of creditors are valid; and to discover what was the reason for the failure of the insolvent.[1] The investigative role of administrators, liquidators, official receivers and trustees in bankruptcy is recognised by the Act and the case law. These office-holders are to ascertain if there have been any improper activities in the management of companies. For instance, under section 132, the official receiver is required, in a compulsory winding up, to investigate the following:

- if the company had failed, the cause of the failure; and
- the promotion, formation, business, dealings and affairs of the company.

Likewise where a person enters bankruptcy the official receiver has a similar duty of investigating the conduct and affairs of the bankrupt (section 289).

Directors of an insolvent company have a duty to cooperate pro-actively with the official receiver while the latter is discharging his or her duties (*R v McCredie* [2000] BCC 817; [2000] BCLC 438 (CCA)).

25.2.2 *The official receiver*

It is appropriate to consider initially the role of the official receiver in investigating insolvent estates, as it will be the official receiver who often is involved first in the investigation task. Our concern here will be with compulsory liquidations and all forms of bankruptcies.

---

[1] Cork Report at para 238.

25.2.2.1 *Compulsory winding up*

In the course of investigating a compulsory winding up, the official receiver may, on the making of a winding-up order, require, by notice, some or all of the persons referred to in section 131(3) to make out and submit a statement of affairs of the company (section 131(1)).[2] The persons referred to in section 131(3) are the former officers of the company, those who have taken part in the formation of the company at any time within one year of the date of the winding-up order, employees of the company and former employees in employment within one year of the windingup order and those who are or have been in the year before the date of the winding-up order officers or employees of a company which is or was in the year before the winding-up order an officer of the company being wound up.

If the persons required by the official receiver to provide a statement of affairs fail to do so, then the official receiver may apply to the court to obtain an order to enforce compliance (Insolvency Rules ('the Rules'), rule 7.20(1)(c);[3] *Re Wallace Smith Trust Co Ltd* [1992] BCC 707).[4] The statement is often of such critical importance to the official receiver as it enables the official receiver to begin to understand the company's affairs and activities to use it as the starting point in the search for assets of the company and ascertain the role of the officers of the company in the affairs of the company. The statement, when investigated, may lead the official receiver to seek a public examination of the officers of the company under section 133.

The statement of affairs will be of assistance usually to the official receiver in discovering the assets of the company and deciding whether to apply for an examination of officers and others in relation to the company's affairs. The statement will be filed in court and is open to inspection (rule 7.28). While section 433 probably permits the statement under section 131 to be used in subsequent civil proceedings, it cannot be used in most criminal proceedings since the amendment of section 433 in 1999 (as a result of the enactment of the Youth Justice and Criminal Evidence Act).[5] Now, as a result of the decision of the European Court of Human Rights in *Saunders v United Kingdom* ([1997] EHRR 313; [1998] 1 BCLC 362; [1997] BCC 872), section 433(2) provides that no evidence relating to the statement may be adduced and no question relating to it may be asked by or on behalf of the prosecution unless evidence relating to the statement is adduced

---

[2] For further discussion concerning the statement of affairs, see A. Keay, *McPherson's Law of Company Liquidation*, London: Sweet & Maxwell (2001) at 306–8.

[3] All references to rules in this chapter are to rules in the Insolvency Rules 1986 unless the contrary is indicated.

[4] According to this case a public examination under section 133 could be a legitimate way of obtaining the information that should be provided in a statement of affairs.

[5] See section 59 and Schedule 3, cl.7(1).

in the proceedings by the maker of the statement. While most criminal proceedings are covered by the prohibition in section 433(2), proceedings relating to offences under the Act, *inter alia*, are not covered. This also applies in relation to statements submitted in bankruptcies and discussed below.

Besides possibly seeking a public examination under section 133 to enhance the official receiver's investigations, the official receiver may also seek a private examination under section 236. These examinations are discussed in more detail later in this chapter.

The official receiver is required, where it is thought fit, to make a report concerning the investigation of the affairs of a company in compulsory liquidation (section 132(1)). In making out this report the official receiver is acting as the official receiver and not in the capacity of a liquidator. If the official receiver has not discovered anything of note, it is appropriate that no report be prepared, thereby avoiding the incurring of unnecessary costs. Any report made is, in relation to any proceedings, *prima facie* evidence of the matters stated in it (section 132(2)). It is likely that where a decision is made to proceed against officers of the company for wrongful trading under section 214 or misfeasance under section 212, or for disqualification of a director of the company pursuant to the Company Directors' Disqualification Act 1986, any report will of substantial use.

25.2.2.2 *Bankruptcy*

The official receiver is required, save where there is a certificate for summary administration in effect, to investigate the conduct and affairs of the bankrupt and to make a report to the court, as is thought fit, concerning the investigation (section 289(1))(this will change after the Enterprise Act provisions become operative). With summary administrations the official receiver has a discretion whether or not to investigate (section 289(5)).

While a statement of affairs of the insolvent company is a matter of the discretion of the official receiver in liquidation, bankrupts must submit a statement of affairs. In the situation where the debtor presents his or her own petition, then a statement must accompany the petition (section 272(2)) and contain details of both the debtor's creditors and debts and the assets of the debtor (section 272(2); rule 6.68). The official receiver may require further disclosure at a later date (rule 6.66). Where a debtor becomes bankrupt as a result of a creditor's petition being presented, then the bankrupt must, within 21 days from the commencement of bankruptcy, submit a statement to the official receiver (section 288(1)). The official receiver may give the bankrupt a longer period in which to submit or even release the bankrupt from the obligation to submit a statement (section 288(3); rule 6.62(1)). The contents of the statement are as for a statement accompanying a debtor's petition (section 288(2); rule 6.59).

Where a statement is filed, whether pursuant to a debtor's petition, or following a bankruptcy order on a creditor's petition, it must have been verified by affidavit (rules 6.60(2), 6.70(1)).

The official receiver is able to require that the bankrupt provides accounts covering the three years prior to bankruptcy and a court order can be secured for accounts that relate to earlier years (rules 6.64–65, 69–71). The official receiver is at liberty to require the bankrupt to attend at his or her offices as is reasonable in order to assist the administration of the estate (section 291(4)).

As with liquidation, the official receiver is entitled to apply for a public examination, but only of the bankrupt (section 290(1)). An application for an examination must be made, unless the court orders to the contrary, if one of the creditors so requests and not less than a half of the creditors in value agree (section 290(2)).

25.2.3 *Company liquidators*

The liquidator, whether it be the official receiver or a qualified insolvency practitioner, must locate and recover assets, ascertain the circumstances that precipitated the liquidation, investigate the conduct of present and former officers of the company and to explore whether they or others may have committed criminal offences and, where necessary, provide information to prosecuting authorities.[6] To this end the liquidator will usually conduct informal interviews of company employees and those officers who are cooperative, speak to creditors of the company and examine the company's books, records, cash receipts, bank accounts, dealings with others and disposal of assets. Other officers and people connected with the company may be interviewed but they may not be co-operative and hence, as we will see shortly, other measures may need to be embraced.

If, in the course of his or her investigations, the liquidator of an insolvent company (in compulsory or voluntary liquidations) arrives at the view that a director is not fit to be involved in the management of a company,[7] he or she is to report the director to the Secretary of State for Trade and Industry.[8]

---

[6] See section 218. The provision is discussed below at 565–6.

[7] Section 9 of Company Directors' Disqualification Act 1986 together with Schedule 1 to that Statute provides some guidance for practitioners as to what unfitness for office involves. Also, see Department of Trade and Industry Guidance Notes on Disqualification of Directors (July 1996).

[8] Company Directors' Disqualification Act 1986, section 7(3) with section 6(1). This also applies to people acting as shadow directors: section 22(4)(5). The report is not privileged: *Re Barings plc (in administration); Secretary of State for Trade and Industry v Baker* [1998] Ch 356; [1998] 1 BCLC 16. A report by voluntary liquidators is to be in accordance with Form D1 of the Schedule to the Insolvent Companies (Reports on Conduct of Directors) Rules 1996 (SI 1996/1909). See rule 3(1) of these Rules.

In compulsory liquidations, the official receiver might continue on as the liquidator of a company, but more often than not the creditors will resolve that a private insolvency practitioner be appointed to act as the liquidator. But the following really is applicable to either the official receiver or a private practitioner. In compulsory liquidations, the official receiver will already have done some investigative work when a liquidator is appointed and there will usually be a statement of affairs from which the liquidator can work. Where we have a creditors' voluntary liquidation, the liquidator will have a statement of affairs which has been prepared pursuant to section 99 and which contains those matters which must be found in a statement of affairs required by the official receiver in a compulsory winding up, as the basis for investigations into the company.

Section 235 provides an informal procedure to allow liquidators to obtain information (*Re Arrows Ltd (No4)* [1994] BCC 641 at 643 per Lord Brown-Wilkinson (HL)). It requires the persons who are mentioned in that section to assist the official receiver or liquidator by providing information and attending him or her when reasonably required. The persons mentioned in the provision are (section 235(3)):

- the officers and former officers of the company;
- those who have taken part in the formation of the company at any time within one year of the date of the winding-up order;
- employees of the company and former employees in employment within one year of the winding-up order and are in the official receiver's opinion capable of giving information which he or she requires;
- those who are or have been in the year before the date of the winding-up order officers or employees of a company which is or was in the year before the winding-up order an officer of the company being wound up; and
- anyone who has acted as the administrator, administrative receiver or liquidator of the company.

If a person fails, without reasonable excuse, to comply with this obligation, then that person is liable to a fine and, for continued contravention, to a daily default fine (section 235(5)).

A liquidator or official receiver should, ordinarily, seek to use applications for formal examinations pursuant to either section 133 or section 236 sparingly, primarily on grounds of cost, but also to save time and possibly to prevent alienating relevant persons.[9]

---

[9] A. Keay, *McPherson's Law of Company Liquidation* at 772.

25.2.4 *Trustees in bankruptcy*

Trustees have a similar role and function to liquidators. As with compulsory liquidations, the official receiver may remain as trustee, or he or she may be replaced by a private practitioner who is appointed at a creditors' meeting following the making of a bankruptcy order. To assist his or her investigations, the trustee is entitled to require, provided that it is reasonable, information from the bankrupt relating to the bankrupt's affairs and to have the bankrupt attend at his or her offices (section 333(1)).

25.3 Public examinations[10]

25.3.1 *General*

To facilitate the need of official receivers to ascertain what has happened to a company which has entered liquidation or a person who has become bankrupt, there may be a need to examine certain persons and the examination of such persons may be ordered by the courts (sections 133, 290). So, we are only dealing with official receivers in this part of the chapter. Examinations ordered only on the application of official receivers are held in public. Examinations for a hearing in private may be instigated by an official receiver, but also at the instigation of administrators, liquidators and trustees. Private examinations (section 236, 336) are considered later in the chapter.

The point should be made at the outset that public examinations are not sought as a matter of fact by an official receiver, nor are private examinations for that matter. All examinations are expensive and may be inappropriate. They are frequently needed when companies have come to a calamitous end and the persons who managed the companies, and therefore responsible for the companies' state of affairs, should be subjected to public examination (*Re Seagull Manufacturing Co Ltd (in liq)* [1993] BCLC 1139 (CA)).

It is inappropriate to use public examinations merely to enforce compliance with a person's failure to cooperate with the official receiver. If there is non-compliance then it is more appropriate for the official receiver to apply to the court pursuant to rule 7.20 (which also applies to all office-holders) asking it to make such orders as are necessary to require persons to fulfil their obligations (*Re Wallace Smith Trust Co Ltd* [1992] BCC 707). But a public examination could be a legitimate way of obtaining the information that should be provided in a statement of affairs under

---

[10] For a detailed discussion, see ibid at 779–88.

either section 131(companies) or section 272(2) or section 288(2) (individuals) (*Re Wallace Smith Trust Co Ltd*).

Examinations in both bankruptcy and liquidation law have a long lineage. The first bankruptcy statute in 1542 provided a mechanism for bankrupts to be examined and this procedure was adopted in a general fashion in the Joint Stock Companies Winding Up Act 1844 in relation to those involved with companies that were in liquidation (section 15). The examination provision empowered the court to summon and examine persons who were thought to be capable of giving information about the property and past transactions of the insolvent. But the primary purpose of examinations of this kind was to assist the office-holder in discovering and locating assets of the company. Examinations have always suffered from a number of shortcomings. They were essentially administrative in nature and were held in private and creditors, contributories and members of the public were not present. Also, their value as a means of scrutinising the company's affairs was considerably diminished by the fact that the person summoned was privileged from answering incriminating questions.

However, in the later years of the nineteenth century Parliament made provision for the examination in public of insolvents and those connected with their affairs. In relation to companies this included promoters and officers of the company.[11] Examinations may be sought where the official receiver is concerned to investigate suspected misconduct and/or concealment of actions etc. and where it is appropriate for some degree of publicity. The function of the examination is sometimes to gain information, where persons have failed to comply with some other statutory requirement, such as the filing of a statement of affairs.

The law that has developed applies in general to both bankruptcies and liquidations, the examination for the latter having been based on the bankruptcy provision. Consequently, unless necessary, the following discussion does not distinguish between examinations in bankruptcy from examinations in liquidations. Before discussing elements that are common to examinations in the two forms of administration we will briefly consider those matters that ought to be raised separately in relation to bankruptcy and liquidation.

25.3.2 *Pre-examination issues*

In *Re Seagull Manufacturing Co Ltd (in liq)* ([1993] BCLC 1139 at 1145 (CA)) it was said that section 133 was intended by Parliament to fulfil the purposes contained in the Cork Report, namely:

---

[11] See Companies (Winding Up) Act 1890, section 8. For points of similarity and distinction between public and private examinations: see *Re Great Kruger Gold Mining Co* [1892] 3 Ch 307 at 313.

(a) to form the basis of reports, which the Official Receiver may have to submit to the Department concerning the affairs of the company; for example concerning possible offences by officers of the company and others; (b) to obtain material information for the administration of the estate which cannot as well be obtained privately; and (c) to give publicity, for the information of creditors and the community at large, to the salient facts and unusual features connected with the company's failure.

Before the introduction of section 133, public examinations in liquidations, but not in bankruptcies, were rarely used. The Cork Report called for a greater use of such examinations.[12] Section 133 is most likely to be invoked where there is a concern over public interest factor, where fraud or other improper conduct may have taken place.

In relation to winding up, public examinations can be employed in any compulsory liquidation, but they are generally only utilised in insolvent liquidations. Applications may be made for examinations in voluntary liquidations under section 112 (*Re Campbell Coverings Ltd (No2)* [1954] Ch 225; *Re Serene Shoes Ltd* [1958] 1 WLR 1087; *Bishopsgate Investment Management Ltd (in prov liq) v Maxwell* [1992] Ch 1 at 24 and 46; [1992] BCC 222 at 232 and 249 (CA)).

An important purpose of a public examination is to inform the public of what has happened in relation to failed companies (*Re Civil Naval & Military Outfitters Ltd* [1899] 1 Ch 215 at 239; *Friedrich v Herald & Weekly Times Ltd* (1990) 1 ACSR 277; 8 ACLC 109). The publicity may cause people to supply liquidators with helpful information relating to the liquidation (*Friedrich v Herald & Weekly Times Ltd*). Also, the procedures existence is designed to act as a deterrent, so that the adverse publicity and other effects of the examination process, which often follow upon testimony that indicates fraudulent activity, will operate as a warning to other persons (*Friedrich v Herald & Weekly Times Ltd*). In fact public examinations in winding up or bankruptcy sometimes lead, ultimately, to criminal prosecution.

The only person that may be examined in bankruptcy is the bankrupt (section 290(1)). However, in winding up there is a range of people who may be examined, and the range is broad. The following may be examined under section 133:

- present or past officers of the company;
- persons who have acted as a liquidator, administrator or receiver or manager of the company;
- anyone who has been concerned, or has taken part, in the promotion, formation or management of the company (section 133(1)).

---

[12] See paras 653–7.

The official receiver may, in his or her discretion, decide to apply for an examination at any time, in a liquidation, prior to dissolution (section 133(1)) and, in bankruptcies, at any time before discharge (section 290(1)). Official receivers must apply for examinations in relation to liquidations where requested by one-half in value of the creditors of the company or three-quarters in value of the company's contributories (section 133(2)). The creditors' or contributories' request is subject to the court being able to override the request. This also applies to bankruptcy (section 290(2)).

An application for examination must be served on the prospective examinee.

Where the applicant is the official receiver, the court has no discretion and must direct that an examination of the person mentioned in the application be held at a particular time on an appointed date (section 133(3), 290(3); *Re Casterbridge Properties Ltd* [2002] BCC 453; [2002] BPIR 428). In liquidations, the court's order is to be served on the examinee forthwith (rule 4.211(1)),[13] whereas in bankruptcy the order is required simply to be sent to the bankrupt (rule 6.172(1)). A court is able to order, under rule 12.12, that it be served on a person who is outside the jurisdiction and resident abroad, even if the person is not a British subject (*Re Seagull Manufacturing Co Ltd (in liq)* [1993] Ch 345; [1993] BCC 241 (CA)). The normal policy of not applying statutes outside of the jurisdiction except where the statute expressly provides does not operate because the intention of Parliament is that these examinations must be permitted so as to enable effective investigations of corporate collapses (*Re Seagull Manufacturing Co Ltd (in liq)* (CA)).

In circumstances where a liquidation examination is based on section 133(1)(c), namely that the prospective examinee has been concerned, or has taken part, in the promotion, formation or management of the company, the application must be accompanied by a report from the official receiver indicating the grounds which suggest that the examinee was concerned, or did take part, in the promotion, formation or management of the company. The prospective examinee may apply for rescission of the order. The court may rescind if it is satisfied that the named examinee does not fall within section 133(1)(c).

On an application to set aside an order for an examination, the court has to place adequate weight on the following factors: the mandatory nature of the original order of examination; the special role of the official receiver; and the special duties of the official receiver under section 132 (*Re Casterbridge Properties Ltd* [2002] BCC 453; [2002] BPIR 428). The examinee has the burden of establishing the fact that the original order ought to be discharged (*Re Casterbridge Properties Ltd*).

---

[13] The case of *Re Seagull Manufacturing Co Ltd (in liq)* [1993] Ch 345 at 359; [1993] BCC 241 at 248 indicates that this means that service is to be effected as soon as is reasonably practicable.

25.3.3 *The examination*

Examinations are held in open court and the registrar or judge before whom it is held has an unfettered discretion in determining how the examination ought to be conducted and what questions may be asked (*In re North Australian Territory Company* (1890) 45 Ch D 87 at 93; *Re Maville Hose Ltd* [1938] 1 Ch D 32 at 40), with only relevant questions being allowed (*In re Pennington; ex parte Pennington* (1888) 5 Mor 268 at 269).

At an examination the liquidator or trustee, any person appointed as special manager of the insolvent's property or business and any creditor who has tendered proof and any contributory may take part and question the examinee (sections 133(4), 290(4)). All those involved in an examination may, with the court's approval (notice being given either at the hearing or in advance of it), appear by solicitor or counsel. A significant part of what is said below also applies to private examinations.

Examinees are examined on oath and must answer all such questions asked (rules 4.215(1), 6.175(1)). It is a requirement that examinees give the best answers that they are able and, where necessary, supplemented by documents (*In re Richbell Strategic Holdings Ltd (in liq) (No2)* [2000] 2 BCLC 794). An examinee is not able to claim the privilege against self-incrimination in relation to any question[14] and a refusal to answer, on the basis of self-incrimination, means that the examinee is in contempt of court (*Bishopsgate Investment Management Ltd (in prov liq) v Maxwell* [1992] Ch 1; [1992] 2 All ER 856; [1992] BCLC 475; [1992] BCC 222 (CA)). Self-incriminating answers of an examinee are able to be used in evidence in criminal proceedings where those proceedings are brought pursuant to the Act.

The examinee is entitled to be legally represented by a solicitor, with or without counsel, at his or her own expense and the examinee's legal representative may put such questions as the court may allow for the purpose of enabling the examinee to explain or qualify any answers which have been given and may make representations on behalf of the examinee (rules 4.215(3), 6.176(2)).

The role of the court is to ensure that there is fair play (*Re Mondelphous Engineering Associates (No2) Ltd (in liq)* (1989) 7 ACLC 220) and to this end the court is given a discretion to allow or disallow questions (rules 4.215(1), 6.175(1)). A court may disallow questions which: have already been asked; are asked merely for the purpose of satisfying personal spite or vindictiveness; and, not asked in good faith in order to the benefit of the creditors, contributories or the public (*Re London & Globe Finance Co* [1902] WN 16). Notwithstanding these restrictions, an office-holder is

---

[14] *Re Atherton* [1912] 2 KB 251; *Re Paget* [1927] 2 Ch 85; *Re Jeffery S. Levitt Ltd* [1992] BCC 137 (affirmed by the Court of Appeal ([1992] BCC 202)); *Bishopsgate Investment Management Ltd (in prov liq) v Maxwell* [1992] Ch 1; [1992] 2 All ER 856; [1992] BCLC 475; [1992] BCC 222 (CA).

permitted to delve into the circumstances relating to the foundation for the examination and this might, of course, open up another line of inquiry which should be pursued to ascertain the truth (*Re Spedley Securities Ltd (in liq); Ex parte Potts* (1990) 2 ACSR 152).

Unusually for proceedings in a common law system, the power to examine is inquisitorial in nature (*In re Metropolitan Bank* (1880) 15 Ch D 139 at 142; *Ex parte Willey; In re Wright* (1886) 23 Ch D 118 at 129; *Rees v Kratzmann* (1965) 114 CLR 63), with the examinee not being called by a party to the proceedings; the examinee is the witness of the court.

Important features of examinations are: the court's task is to gather evidence from the examinee (*Barton v Official Receiver* (1977) 29 FLR 195 at 203); questions are not put to strengthen a party's case; there is no such thing as examination-in-chief or cross-examination (*In re Greys Brewery Company* (1883) 25 Ch D 400 at 404); and questions are not limited to a matter pertinent to some disputed issue, as is the case with normal litigation – questions can be wide-ranging provided that they are relevant to the affairs of the insolvent.[15]

An examinee must, except where there is reasonable excuse, attend the examination. Failure to attend examinations as ordered constitutes a contempt of court (sections 134(1), 290(5)). The Act provides in relation to a section 133 examination, but not to a section 290 examination, that if either an examinee fails to attend an examination and has no reasonable excuse, or there are reasonable grounds for believing that the examinee has absconded, or is about to abscond, with a view to avoiding or delaying the examination, the judge or registrar may cause an arrest warrant to be issued (section 134(2)). If the examinee appeals against the making of an arrest warrant and fails, then he or she is close to contempt and may be ordered to pay, on an indemnity basis, the costs of the official receiver (*Re Avatar Communications Ltd* (1988) 4 BCC 473). If an examinee is arrested pursuant to an order of the court, the court may authorise the examinee to be retained in custody until such time as the court may order (section 134(3)).

25.4 Private examinations[16]

The official receiver and other office-holders have the right to apply to have certain persons examined in private under section 236 for companies and section 366 for individuals. These kinds of examination are more frequent than public examinations. They might, in exceptional cases, be held in open court (*Bishopsgate Investment Management Ltd v Maxwell* [1992] 2 All

---

[15] A. Keay, *McPherson's Law of Company Liquidation* at 786–7.
[16] For a detailed discussion, see A. Keay, *McPherson's Law of Company Liquidation* at 788–819.

ER 856 at 874 (CA)). The material in this section of the chapter applies equally to both companies and individual insolvencies, unless the contrary is indicated.

The office-holder will be seeking to obtain, by interrogation, information about matters which the books of the company or the bankrupt on the one hand, or private interviews on the other, have failed to disclose. As with public examinations, the examinee is cross-examined on oath and bound to answer incriminating questions.

An application for an examination must be made in writing and must be accompanied by a brief statement[17] of the grounds on which the application is made (rule 9.2(1)). The statement is confidential (*Re Aveling Barford Ltd* [1989] 1 WLR 360; (1988) 4 BCC 548), but the court has the discretion to order that it be available for inspection (rule 9.5(2)).

The application is made to a registrar of the Companies Court, who may refer it to a judge, or a district judge where the application is made in the county court. An application will be governed by Article 6 of the European Convention on Human Rights, namely the right to a fair hearing.

While the Rules permit an application to be made *ex parte*,[18] the general rule, as a result of some recent case law, is that applications must be made *inter partes*,[19] unless there are compelling reasons for an *ex parte* application, such as a need for urgency or concern over the likelihood of documents disappearing (*Re Maxwell Communications Corporation plc* [1994] BCC 741 at 747; *Re PFTZM Ltd (in liq)* [1995] 2 BCLC 354; [1995] BCC 280). This is in accordance with the general principle that a person is entitled to be heard before the making of an order of far-reaching impact.[20] It is likely anyway that *ex parte* hearings will not be permissible because of the Human Rights Act; it may be argued that an *ex parte* hearing is not consistent with Article 6 of the European Convention on Human Rights which gives persons the right to be heard.

25.4.1 *Rationale for examinations*

Private examinations tend to be the last resort for office-holders, except where it is critical that they obtain evidence on oath, because of the cost of the process. Every effort will be made to obtain information needed through interviews, especially of company officers or the bankrupt. But, if

---

[17] In the Court of Appeal in *Re British and Commonwealth Holdings Ltd* [1992] Ch 342 at 385, 388 Woolf LJ indicated unequivocally that the statement should be brief.

[18] Rule 9.2(4). This was the practice in past years: *Cornhill Insurance plc v Cornhill Financial Services Ltd* [1993] BCLC 914 at 961(CA).

[19] *Re PFTZM Ltd (in liq)* [1995] 2 BCLC 354; [1995] BCC 280; *Re Murjani* [1996] 1 BCLC 272; [1996] BCC 278; [1996] BPIR 325. In the latter case Lightman J was dealing with an application in bankruptcy (under section 366), but his Lordship indicated that the rule applied to an application in corporate insolvency as well as in bankruptcy (at 335).

[20] Ibid.

the officers of the company or the bankrupt prevaricate or are recalcitrant, examination might be the only alternative. Also, examinations might be sought where there is a refusal to attend an informal interview, or to answer questions adequately.

The reasons why an office-holder may seek to examine someone are, *inter alia*:

- the office-holder might want the answers to questions on oath, feeling that the answers will have greater veracity;
- the office-holder might want the answers on oath and recorded in court transcript to be used as evidence in further proceedings against the examinee, or to be of assistance in prosecuting proceedings against some other person, such as a creditor to whom an alleged preference was given;
- where there may be grounds for taking proceedings either against promoters, managers or others involved with an insolvent company during its life in liquidations or associates of a bankrupt in bankruptcies.[21]

Courts have a discretion whether to order an examination (rule 9.3(1)). This discretion is informed by some established principles. First, justice and fairness must demand that an order be made (*Re BCCI (No7)* [1994] 1 BCLC 458). Second, the discretion must involve a careful balancing of the interests and factors involved, including taking into account the purpose of the examination power and whether the making of an order would be unreasonable, unnecessary or oppressive (*Re British & Commonwealth Holdings plc (No.2)* [1993] AC 426; [1992] BCC 977 (HL)). Other factors that a court could well take into account are: the purpose of an examination; the reasonable requirements of the office-holder to wind up the company or the bankrupt estate; the oppression of the prospective examinee; and the width of the order sought (*Re British & Commonwealth Holdings plc (No.2)*).

Where orders for examination are made, examinees might apply to set aside the orders. The grounds often relied on are that the examination would be unreasonable or oppressive (*Cornhill Insurance plc v Cornhill Financial Services Ltd* [1993] BCLC 914 at 961 (CA)). Courts, when hearing such applications, will balance the same factors as when initially deciding whether to order an examination.

25.4.2 *The function of examinations*

The function of examinations, for individual and corporate insolvents, was considered by Buckley J in *Re Rolls Razor Ltd* ([1968] 3 All ER 698). His Lordship said that the power to examine is granted so that courts are able to assist a liquidator 'to discover the truth of the circumstances' surrounding the insolvent's affairs and to enable the office-holder, as effectively and

---

[21] A. Keay, *McPherson's Law of Company Liquidation* at 789.

inexpensively as possible, to fulfil his or her role in putting the insolvent's affairs in order. The examination process is aimed at permitting the office-holder to carry out all aspects of the insolvency administration, including discovering and getting in any assets (*Re Rolls Razor Ltd* at 700).[22] The Court of Appeal in *Re Esal (Commodities) Ltd* ([1989] 1 BCLC 59 at 70) and Lord Slynn in giving the leading speech in *Re British and Commonwealth Holdings plc (No2)* ([1992] BCC 977 at 983) approved of what Buckley J had to say.

It has been held that examinations are to enable the office-holder to ascertain whether any substantive proceedings can be initiated or whether defences against proceedings that have already been, or are likely to be, issued against the insolvent can be set up,[23] as well as allowing for the investigation of misconduct (*Re Arrows Ltd (No4)* [1994] BCC 641).

It is also of note that section 236 is to be read in conjunction with the provisions that precede it, namely sections 234 and 235 (*Re Pantmaenog Timbers Co Ltd* [2002] BCC 11 at 27 (CA)). Applied to bankruptcy it means that sections 291 and 365 need to be taken into account when considering section 366.

25.4.3 *The nature of examinations*

What has been said already in relation to public examinations is generally applicable here. Like public examinations, this power is a very broad and unusual[24] power that is inquisitorial in nature (*Ex parte Willey; In re Wright* (1886) 23 Ch D 118 at 129; *Re Rolls Razor Ltd (No.2)* [1970] Ch 576 at 591; [1969] 3 All ER 1386 at 1396; *Re Esal (Commodities) Ltd* [1989] 1 BCLC 59 at 64, 70 (CA)).

Sections 236 and 366 are far-reaching provisions and courts have, out of concern for possible abuse, indicated that the power must be exercised carefully in order that the examinee is not unfairly disadvantaged (*Re North Australian Territory Company* (1890) 45 Ch D 87 at 93; *Ex parte Willey* (1883) 23 Ch D 118 at 128; *Re Rolls Razor Ltd (No.2)* [1970] Ch 576 at 591; [1969] 3 All ER 1386 at 1396). The courts are careful not to permit unnecessary or unfair impinging on the rights of a person to privacy and confidentiality (*Hamilton v Oades* (1989) 166 CLR 486; *Grosvenor Hill (Queensland) Pty Ltd v Barber* (1994) 120 ALR 262 at 267). The power is an

---

[22] See *Re Pantmaenog Timbers Co Ltd* [2002] BCC 11 (CA).

[23] For example, see *In re Gold Company* (1897) 12 Ch D 77; *Re Hugh J. Roberts Pty Ltd (in liq)* (1970) 91 WN (NSW) 537 at 540–541; *Re Castle New Homes Ltd* [1979] 2 All ER 775 at 788.

[24] *In re Imperial Continental Water Corporation* (1886) 33 Ch D 314 at 316; *In re Scharrer; ex parte Till* (1888) 20 QBD 518 at 522; *Re Rolls Razor Ltd (No.2)* [1970] Ch 576 at 591; [1969] 3 All ER 1386 at 1396; *Re Spiraflite Ltd* [1979] 2 All ER 766 at 768; *Re British & Commonwealth Holdings plc (No.2)* [1992] Ch 342 (CA) and affirmed on appeal by the House of Lords at [1993] AC 476; *First Tokoyo Index Trust v Gould* [1996] BPIR 406; *Re Atlantic Computers plc* [1998] BCC 200.

invasion of the privacy and confidentiality of a citizen,[25] but the courts seek to limit this intrusion as much as possible. Notwithstanding this concern over privacy, the courts will also take into account the need of the office-holder to obtain assistance in undertaking the administration of the insolvent's affairs. The consequence is that the courts have to engage in a balancing exercise between the needs of the office-holder and any possible oppression that might be suffered by the examinee.[26]

The enactment of the Human Rights Act 1998 is likely to lead to challenges to sections 236 and 366 and/or their application in the future in British courts, given the kind of provisions that these sections are and their far-reaching nature.

25.4.4 *The examinee*

The following are able to be examined in relation to insolvent companies (section 236):

● officers of the company;
● any persons known or suspected to have in their possession any property of the company or supposed to be indebted to the company; or
● any persons whom the court thinks capable of giving information concerning the promotion, formation, business, dealings, affairs or property of the company (section 236(2)).

The people who are frequently examined are the directors, company secretary, company's solicitor, company's accountant, company's auditors and the bank manager of the branch where the company's accounts are kept.

In a bankruptcy the persons who may be examined under section 366 are:

● the bankrupt or the bankrupt's spouse or former spouse;
● any person who is known or believed to have any property comprised in the bankrupt's estate in his or her possession or to be indebted to the bankrupt;
● any person appearing to the court to be able to give information concerning the bankrupt or the bankrupt's dealings, affairs or property.

An applicant for an examination must provide reasonable grounds for the belief that the prospective examinee is able to give information which

---

[25] See *Re Paulson; ex parte Granada Television Ltd v Maudling* [1976] 2 All ER 1020.
[26] The balancing exercise that the courts must perform is discussed in *Re Esal (Commodities) Ltd* [1989] 1 BCLC 59 at 71 (CA); *Cloverbay Ltd (Joint Administrators) v Bank of Credit and Commerce International SA* [1991] BCLC 135 at 138 (CA); *Re British and Commonwealth Holdings plc* [1992] BCC 977 at 984 per Lord Slynn; *Re Atlantic Computers plc* [1998] BCC 200 at 209–210; *Joint Liquidators of Sasea Finance Ltd v KPMG* [1998] BCC 216 at 220.

may assist the office-holder, but it is unlikely that a court will dismiss an application unless it constitutes either oppression or an abuse of process (*Re Metropolitan Bank* (1880) 15 Ch D 139 (CA); *Re Embassy Art Products* (1987) 3 BCC 292; *Re Adlards Motor Group Holdings Ltd* [1990] BCLC 68).

25.4.5 *The extent of examinations*

As already mentioned, the courts will ensure that the jurisdiction granted by sections 236 and 366 are exercised cautiously (*Re Atlantic Computers plc* [1998] BCC 200), and they will be careful to make sure that the permissible extent to which the power can be put is not abused. The cases indicate that courts have granted more freedom to office-holders in recent years, in both their applications and questions asked during the course of examinations, because of the significant concern demonstrated in relation to fraudulent conduct, particularly by company officers.[27]

The difficulty that court have had at times is to successfully strike the balance between allowing the public interest of permitting examinations to ensure the efficient administration of insolvent administrations and protecting the private interests of individual examinees; courts have to weigh up the need to uncover wrongdoing with the possible oppression of the innocent party (*Morris v European Islamic Ltd*, unreported, June 8, 1999, Neuberger J). To ensure that there is a fair balance, the courts have the power to prevent questions and lines of questioning if they believe that they are too wide and fall outside what is permitted in examinations (*Re Aveling Barford Ltd* [1989] 1 WLR 360; (1988) 4 BCC 548). While courts have an unfettered discretion in adjudicating on what questions may be asked of the examinee, there are some well-established principles that have been formulated.[28] The fundamental principle is that questions must be necessary in the interests of the insolvent administration (*Re Embassy Art Products* (1987) 3 BCC 292) (that the office-holder has a reasonable need for the information sought (*Re Galileo Group Ltd* [1998] 2 WLR 364; [1998] 1 BCLC 318)) and it should not be unfairly oppressive on the examinee (*Re Norton Warburg Holdings Ltd* (1983) 1 BCC 98,907; *British & Commonwealth Holdings plc (Joint Administrators) v Spicer* [1993] AC 426; [1992] BCC 977).

In accordance with the fact that more latitude is given to office-holders today, courts accept that the views of office-holders are entitled to be given a good deal of weight (*Re Norton Warburg Holdings Ltd*; *Re Embassy Art Products*; *Cloverbay Ltd (Joint Administrators) v Bank of Credit and Commerce International SA* [1991] BCLC 135 at 146 (CA); *Joint Liquidators of Sasea Finance Ltd v KPMG* [1998] BCC 216 at 220)), and the office-holder does

---

[27] See the comments of Lord Browne-Wilkinson in *Re Arrows Ltd (No4)* [1994] BCC 641 at 650.
[28] See the comments of Browne-Wilkinson V-C and Nourse LJ in *Cloverbay Ltd (Joint Administrators) v Bank of Credit and Commerce International SA* [1991] BCLC 135 at 138, 144.

not have to demonstrate an absolute need for the information sought (*Cloverbay Ltd (Joint Administrators) v Bank of Credit and Commerce International SA* (CA)). In *Cloverbay Ltd (Joint Administrators) v Bank of Credit and Commerce International SA* Browne-Wilkinson V-C (with whom Nourse LJ agreed)[29] said that courts, in engaging in balancing the requirements of the office-holder as against the possible oppression of the examinee, should consider the importance to the office-holder of obtaining the information and the degree of oppression to the examinee (at 141). According to The Vice-Chancellor, the things that courts should take into account are: office-holders have no knowledge of the insolvent's affairs when they are appointed and often relevant documents and papers are not able to be located; the test for determining whether an examination should be held is not whether the office-holder has an absolute need for the information, but whether obtaining the information is a reasonable requirement (at 142); usually office-holders have a stronger case for examining officers or former officers of the company in corporate insolvency and the bankrupt in bankruptcy compared with the examination of third parties (at 142); as court orders for oral examination of persons is more likely to be oppressive, application for orders for the production of documents are more likely to be granted.[30]

Later, in *Re British & Commonwealth Holdings plc (No.2)* ([1992] Ch 342 (CA)) Ralph Gibson LJ said, and this was approved of by the House of Lords,[31] that the following principles should be considered by a court: the court has an unfettered discretion whether or not to permit an examination; the exercise of the discretion involves balancing the office-holder's requirements as against possible oppression to the prospective examinee; the power is to enable the court to help the office-holder discharge his or her function as effectively and as speedily as possible.[32]

The courts will be especially concerned to prevent examinations being used to conduct fishing expeditions,[33] namely initiating the process without any clear suspicions or information (*Re Maundy Gregory* [1935] 1 Ch 65).

The courts have been particularly concerned about protecting examinees where an office-holder seeks to examine someone who is likely to be a party to (or a witness at the hearing of) legal proceedings which the office-holder is either contemplating or has already commenced.[34] The reason for the concern is that the office-holder may endeavour to secure significant

---

[29] McGowan LJ dissented in relation to the overall outcome.

[30] *Cloverbay Ltd (Joint Administrators) v Bank of Credit and Commerce International SA* [1991] BCLC 135 at 142. This was also accepted by a differently constituted Court of Appeal in *Re British & Commonwealth Holdings plc (No.2)* [1992] Ch 342 at 372.

[31] [1993] AC 426.

[32] *Re British & Commonwealth Holdings plc (No.2)* [1992] Ch 342 at 370–2.

[33] *Re Maundy Gregory* [1935] 1 Ch 65 at 74; *Re Castle New Homes Ltd* [1979] 2 All ER 775 at 790; *Re James McHale Automobiles Ltd* [1997] 1 BCLC 273; [1997] BCC 202.

[34] For a detailed discussion of this issue, see A. Keay, *McPherson's Law of Company Liquidation* at 799–805.

forensic advantages in the conduct of contemplated or pending litigation. In carrying out their balancing exercise the courts have, at times, found it difficult to make decisions. In exercising their discretion, courts might well make a distinction between examinees who are insiders (directors, secretaries etc.) in, or associates of, the insolvent and those who are not.[35]

It is clear that office-holders will be permitted to initiate and conduct examinations so at to enable them to decide whether to commence, or defend existing, proceedings, as a possible cost-saving device (*In re Gold Company* (1897) 12 Ch D 77). It is when an office-holder tries to gain some advantage in proposed or existing litigation that the courts will prevent examinations (*Re Spiraflite Ltd* [1979] 2 All ER 766 at 769). But an office-holder will not be prevented from examining a person either merely because he or she has completed litigation against the respondent (*Re JT Rhodes Ltd* (1986) 2 BCC 99,284), or because an office-holder has decided to proceed, or has initiated proceedings, against the examinee (*Re JT Rhodes Ltd*; *Re Castle New Homes Ltd* [1979] 2 All ER 775 at 782). The main problem is where litigation has already been commenced, because the examination would normally be used to improve the position of an office-holder in the litigation and this will not be allowed by a court (*Re Spiraflite Ltd* [1979] 2 All ER 766 at 769; *Re Castle New Homes Ltd* [1979] 2 All ER 775 at 789). In *Joint Liquidators of Sasea Finance Ltd v KPMG* ([1998] BCC 216 at 221) Robert Walker J said, in relation to the issue, that:

> [I]t remains a sound principle that, 'if the liquidator is seeking merely to dot the i's and cross the t's of a fairly clear claim by examining the proposed defendant to discover his defence, the balance would come down against making the order' . . . The jurisdiction under section 236 is not to be used to vary the ordinary rules of procedure in litigation so as to enable office-holders to obtain, for instance, the advantage of premature discovery . . . (at 221).

An example of a case where an office-holder was not able to examine is *Re Sasea Finance Ltd* ([1999] 1 BCLC 559; [1999] BCC 103). There a liquidator was seeking an examination as a precursor to the bringing of a negligence claim against the prospective examinee or his or her firm. The liquidator had administered interrogatories, but had not received answers. The court found that the purpose of an examination was not to secure information, rather it was designed to obtain damaging admissions prior to the commencement of the negligence action.

But, even if an office-holder has already commenced proceedings, the court might still order an examination if the office-holder is able to convince the court that he or she wishes to obtain information that, while it might pertain to the action, is to be given in order to enable the office-

---

[35] *Cloverbay Ltd (Joint Administrators) v Bank of Credit and Commerce International SA* [1991] BCLC 135 at 142. See G. Moss, 'Getting at the Truth – section 236 Examinations' (1998) 11 *Insolvency Intelligence* 41 at 43. Compare *Re Spiraflite Ltd* [1979] 2 All ER 766 at 773 per Megarry J.

holder to carry out his or her duties (*Re Brook Martin & Co (Nominees) Ltd* [1993] BCLC 328).

In the course of an examination an examinee might feel that an answer could incriminate him or her. But it has been held that an officer of an insolvent company or a bankrupt is unable to claim the privilege against self-incrimination and, therefore, refuse to answer questions.[36] The reason given for this approach is that the aim of sections 236 and 366 necessitates the abrogation of the privilege, or else an examinee could effectively stultify the investigation of the office-holder by claiming the privilege (*Re Jeffery S Levitt Ltd* [1992] BCC 137; [1992] BCLC 250; *Bishopsgate Investment Management Ltd Ltd (in prov liq) v Maxwell* [1992] Ch 1; [1992] 2 All ER 856; [1992] BCLC 475; [1992] BCC 222 (CA)).

The right to claim legal privilege is also subject to some incursions. It cannot be claimed by the solicitors of either an insolvent company or a bankrupt, in relation to documents which belonged to the company or the bankrupt,[37] as the office-holder effectively stands in the shoes of either the directors of the company or the bankrupt.[38]

If solicitors (of a company officer, any other type of person examined under section 236, a bankrupt, or other person who can be examined under section 366) are examined, they are not able to rely on the privilege in circumstances where it would be incumbent on their client to reveal the information which is the subject of the question.[39]

Notwithstanding this, sections 236 and 366 do not appear to remove the privilege in relation to those documents and information protected under the basic principles that apply generally to the privilege.

25.4.6 *The examination*

The procedure for an examination is comparable to that applying to public examinations. Any person, permitted by either sections 236 or 366 to apply for an examination, may, with the leave of the court and if the one who is the applicant does not object, attend the examination and ask questions. But, the latter can only be done through the applicant.[40] In circumstances

---

[36] *Re Jeffery S. Levitt Ltd* [1992] BCC 137; [1992] BCLC 250 (affirmed by the Court of Appeal ([1992] BCC 202)); *Bishopsgate Investment Management Ltd (in prov liq) v Maxwell* [1992] Ch 1; [1992] 2 All ER 856; [1992] BCLC 475; [1992] BCC 222 (CA); *Re A E Farr Ltd* [1992] BCC 150. Lord Browne-Wilkinson in *Re Arrows Ltd (No4)* [1994] BCC 641 mentioned the interpretation employed by these cases and did not suggest that they were wrong in implying the abrogation of the privilege (at 647). This brings liquidations in line with the position in bankruptcy. see *R v Scott* (1856) Dears & Bell 47; 169 ER 909; *Re Atherton* [1912] 2 KB 251; *Re Paget* [1927] 2 Ch 85; *Re Jawett* [1929] 1 Ch 108.

[37] *Re Brook Martin & Co (Nominees) Ltd* [1993] BCLC 328 at 336.

[38] A. Keay, *McPherson's Law of Company Liquidation* at 806.

[39] *Re Murjani* [1996] 1 BCLC 272; [1996] BCC 278; [1996] BPIR 325.

[40] Rule 9.4(2).

where an application was made as a consequence of information provided by one of the insolvent's creditors, then that creditor may, with the leave of the court and if the applicant does not object, attend the examination and ask questions, again only through the applicant.[41]

If it appears to a court, in considering any evidence which is obtained pursuant to either sections 236 or 237 on the one hand, or sections 366 or 367 on the other, that persons have in their possession any property belonging to the insolvent, the court may, on the application of the office-holder, order those persons to deliver the property to the office-holder at such time, in such manner and on such terms as the court thinks fit (sections 237(1), 367(1)). Similarly, if it appears to a court, in considering any evidence, that persons are indebted to the insolvent, the court may, on the application of the office-holder, order those persons to pay to the office-holder, at such time and in such manner as it may direct, the whole or part of the sum due, whether in full discharge of the debt or otherwise, as it thinks fit (sections 237(2), 367(2)).

25.5 Conclusion

As this chapter demonstrates, investigations are critical and very much at the heart of the functions of office-holders. They are intended to permit the office-holder to come to grips with the affairs of the insolvent and, more particularly: to discover the assets to which the estate can lay claim; to ascertain whether the claims of creditors are valid; and to discover what was the reason for the failure of the insolvent.

Examinations are sometimes an important element. They, or even the threat of them, can permit the office-holder to ascertain crucial facts and issues relating to the affairs of the insolvent.

The problem that office-holders often encounter in carrying out their investigative role is the lack of funding. This brings us to Chapter 26, as it is a matter that is taken up there.

---

[41] Rule 9.4(4).

Chapter 26

Funding[1]

26.1 Introduction

Office-holders need funds to do various things to administer the insolvent estate over which they have control. Primarily they will need funds to undertake investigations concerning the activities of certain people, such as the bankrupt and his or her associates in bankruptcy and company directors and other officers in a winding up or administration and the ascertaining and recovery of property to which the insolvent is entitled, but in the possession of someone else. As part of his or her function, the office-holder is bound to do all that can be done to augment the disposable assets of the insolvent (*Re Tavistock Ironworks Co* (1871) 24 LT 605) and is equipped, as we will see, with various statutory powers for recovering property or debts owing to the company.[2] A general power given to office-holders, and which permits them to set about recovering some property or money, is the power to bring proceedings.[3]

Office-holders might find that before the advent of insolvent administration the insolvent commenced proceedings or filed a defence to proceedings initiated by some other party. In such cases the office-holder must take legal advice to ascertain whether it is advisable and prudent to continue to prosecute or defend proceedings or to seek some form of

---

[1] For further discussion of this issue, see, for example, A. Walters, 'Forshortening the shadow: maintenance, champerty and the funding of litigation in corporate insolvency' (1996) 17 Co. Law. 165; A. Walters, 'Creditor-Funded Litigation in Corporate Insolvency' (1997) 1 CfiLR 126; R. Parry, 'Funding Litigation in Insolvency' (1998) 2 CfiLR 121; A. Keay, *McPherson's Law of Company Liquidation*, London: Sweet & Maxwell (2001) at 434–44, 470–6; A. Keay, 'Pursuing the Resolution of the Funding Problem in Insolvency Litigation' [2002] *Insolvency Lawyer* 90. This chapter draws substantially on this last article.

[2] For further discussion, see Part VIII.

[3] Section 14 together with Schedule 1, para 5 (administration), sections 165(3) and 167(1)(a) together with Schedule 4, para 4 (winding up) and section 314 together with Schedule 5, para 2 (bankruptcy).

compromise. Undertaking any of these, along with engaging in substantive investigations, will require funds. This chapter examines the problems that confront office-holders in terms of funding activities and actions that are necessary or prudent.

26.2 Legal proceedings

Legal proceedings should only be commenced or continued after careful thought, not least because of the significant costs that might be incurred. In *Re Exchange Travel (Holdings) Ltd (in liq) (No3)* ([1997] 2 BCLC 579; *sub nom Katz v McNally* [1997] BCC 784), Phillips LJ observed that the costs incurred by the liquidators in a preference action exceeded what was at stake. If proceedings are commenced, for instance, in the name of a company that is in liquidation, the defendant might well seek security for costs, on the basis that the proceedings are brought by an insolvent company. This application would be brought under section 726 of the Companies Act 1985.

If an office-holder does initiate proceedings and they fail, the office-holder will not be thanked by the creditors for the fact that the insolvent estate's funds will be used to pay a likely costs award against the insolvent. It is possible that a liquidator might even, where proceedings were brought in the name of the company, have an award of costs made against him of her under section 51(1) and (3) of the Supreme Court Act 1981. These provisions enable courts to make costs orders against non-parties in appropriate cases.[4] Such an order will only be made against non-parties who have substantial connections with the relevant proceedings (*Symphony Group v Hodgson* [1994] QB 179 at 191 (CA); *National Justice Compania Naviera SA v Prudential Assurance Co Ltd (No.2)* [2000] 1 WLR 603 (CA)), but clearly liquidators will usually fill the bill. The making of an order does not depend on whether the non-party has acted 'in bad faith, abuse of process, impropriety or procedural manipulation' (*Re Aurum Marketing Ltd* [2000] 2 BCLC 645 at 654 per Mummery LJ), but rather on whether or not in all the circumstances it is just to exercise the power (*Globe Equities Ltd v Globe Legal Services Ltd* (1999) BLR 232 at 239–240; *The Times*, April 14, 1999 (CA); *Locabail (UK) Ltd v Bayfield Properties Ltd, The Times*, February 29, 2000; *Re Aurum Marketing Ltd* [2000] 2 BCLC 645 (CA)).

---

[4] For example, see *Aiden Shipping Co Ltd v Interbulk Ltd* [1986] AC 965 (HL); *Globe Equities Ltd v Globe Legal Services Ltd* (1999) BLR 232; *The Times*, April 14, 1999 (CA); *National Justice Compania Naviera SA v Prudential Assurance Co Ltd (No.2)* [2000] 1 WLR 603 (CA). See A. Keay, *McPherson's Law of Company Liquidation*, London: Sweet & Maxwell (2001) at 436–8.

It will be incumbent on office-holders to commence many of the actions that they wish to initiate in their own names. Perhaps two of the most obvious are actions by a liquidator for the recovery of preferences under section 239 of the Act and claims for wrongful trading under section 214 of the Act. These provisions grant to the liquidator personally the right to bring proceedings in the role of liquidator and, therefore, it is necessary that the proceedings be in the name of the liquidator.[5] The right to bring proceedings was never available to the company before winding up. It has been held that an award of costs in relation to failed proceedings cannot be recouped from the funds of the company under rule 4.218(1)(a) of the Insolvency Rules (*Re MC Bacon Ltd (No2)* [1991] Ch 127; [1990] BCLC 607; [1990] BCC 430; *Re RS & M Engineering Co Ltd; sub nom Mond v Hammond Suddards* [2000] Ch 40; [1999] 2 BCLC 485 (CA); *Re Floor Fourteen Ltd (Lewis v IRC)* [2001] 2 BCLC 392 (CA)). Also, of concern for an office-holder was the holding in the Court of Appeal in *Re Floor Fourteen Ltd (Lewis v IRC)* ([2001] 2 BCLC 392), that a liquidator who succeeds in the litigation is not entitled to seek indemnity from company funds after paying the legal representatives of the liquidator and associated costs. The above decisions have now been overcome by rule 23 of the Insolvency (Amendment) (No. 2) Rules 2002, as from 1 January 2003. This rule broadens rule 4.218 with the result that expenses and costs of proceedings are recoverable as liquidation expenses. The problem that still exists is that an insolvent might not have any or few funds.

26.3 The options

There are several options technically available to an office-holder to gain funding, but they might not be either viable or fruitful in the long run.

26.3.1 *Creditor indemnity*

An office-holder may call for indemnities from creditors in relation to costs expended in prosecuting a claim and prudent office-holders have, on occasions in the past, obtained such indemnities. The Court of Appeal in *Re Exchange Travel (Holdings) Ltd (in liq) (No3)* ([1997] 2 BCLC 579) sanctioned the giving of indemnities by creditors and said that it was permissible for the liquidator in that case to agree that any fruits of the litigation would be used first to defray litigation costs paid for by creditors giving indemnities (at 588).

---

[5] See *Re Ayala Ltd (No2)* [1996] 1 BCLC 467; *Re Oasis Merchandising Services Ltd* [1997] 1 All ER 1009; [1997] BCC 282; [1997] 1 BCLC 689 (CA).

In this case Morritt LJ adverted to the fact that the obtaining of indemnities from creditors is a common practice (at 595). If effective indemnities are obtained then it will not matter if there are insufficient assets in the insolvent estate to cover an award of costs against the office-holder, or if there is an award of costs against the office-holder personally. Indemnities can also be used to cover the office-holder's own costs. Of course, office-holders must ensure that those granting indemnities are persons or entities of substance.

The problem is that so often creditors are not keen to grant indemnities as they see it as a case of 'throwing good money after bad'. The fact that office-holders have not enjoyed a great deal of success in bringing actions based on the adjustment provisions in the Act, namely sections 238, 239, 244, 245, 339, 340 and 343,[6] in particular, or the wrongful trading provision (section 214),[7] will not encourage creditors to consider indemnifying the pursuit of proceedings.

26.3.2 *Fighting funds*

In the past some office-holders in some cases have sought the establishment of 'fighting funds' by creditors.[8] These involve creditors contributing a certain number of pence in the pound proportionately in accordance with the admitted level of their proofs of debt. The advantage with such a fund is that it will not be incumbent on the office-holder 'to chase' money if he or she is ordered to pay costs. However, the office-holder must constantly monitor the level of the fund as it may be exhausted more quickly than first thought.

If the fund is exhausted and the action has not been finalised, then the office-holder may be vulnerable to personal liability.

26.3.3 *Conditional fee agreements*

More recently it has been possible for an office-holder's burden to be relieved somewhat by the use of conditional fee agreements with legal advisers.[9] However, that only means that if the office-holder is not successful his or her own lawyers do not get paid. If, as usually occurs, costs go to the victor, the office-holder will be faced with having to pay the costs of the other party.

---

[6] See, for example, D. Milman and R. Parry, 'Challenging Transactional Integrity on Insolvency: An Evaluation of the New Law' (1997) 48 NILQ 24; A. Keay, 'Preferences in Liquidation Law: A Time for a Change' (1998) 2 CfiLR 198.

[7] For example, see C. Cook, 'Wrongful Trading – Is it a Real Threat to Directors or a Paper Tiger ?' [1999] *Insolvency Lawyer* 99.

[8] G. Hamilton, 'Aspects of Official Liquidators' Personal Liability for Costs of Litigation' (1989) 7 C & SLJ 301.

[9] See Courts and Legal Services Act 1990, section 58; Conditional Fee Arrangements Order 1995 (SI 1995/1647); Conditional Fee Arrangements Regulations 1995 (SI 1995/1675).

26.4 Insurance arrangements

Another avenue for raising funds for litigation and which had become increasingly popular, is where a person or company agrees to cover the costs connected with the office-holder's litigation in exchange for a premium. There are various packages that are arranged but the two most common ones involve the premium payable being either a specified portion of any moneys recovered by the office-holder pursuant to the litigation together with any funds advanced to the office-holder, or, where the office-holder can afford it, a sum paid upfront out of the funds of the insolvent. The former appears to have been used more frequently, because more often than not office-holders either do not have the funds to commit to the venture or they wish to retain funds for some other purpose.

The problem which confronts an office-holder with this type of funding is, *inter alia*, that what he or she is doing is able to be categorised as indulging in maintenance and/or champerty. The former is the assistance or encouragement of proceedings by someone who has no interest in the proceedings nor any motive recognised by the law as justifying interference in the proceedings. The latter is a form of maintenance in that assistance or encouragement of proceedings is provided in exchange for a promise to provide a share of the proceeds of the action. The policy behind the outlawing of champerty is to stop a person from intermeddling in others' disputes where he or she has no interest, is not justified in intermeddling and does so with a view to obtaining a part of the spoils (*British Cash and Parcel Conveyors Ltd v Lamson Store Service Co Ltd* [1908] 1 KB 1006). Notwithstanding the fact that these doctrines are archaic,[10] they still will be applied in some cases. However, over time some exceptions to the doctrines have developed. One of these exceptions is the rule that a trustee in bankruptcy (and a liquidator and administrator) is able to lawfully assign any of the bare causes of action of the bankrupt that have vested in the trustee on the basis that the trustee is to receive a share of any proceeds of ensuing litigation (*Seear v Lawson* (1880) 15 Ch D 426; *Re Park Gate Waggon Works Co* (1881) 17 Ch D 234 (CA); *Ramsey v Hartley* [1977] 1 WLR 686 (CA); *Stein v Blake* [1996] 2 AC 243 (HL); *Norglen Ltd v Reeds Rains Prudential* [1998] 1 All ER 218 at 232 (HL)). This exception (referred to here as 'the insolvency exception' as it applies to liquidation and administration as well as bankruptcy) is based on the idea that the legislature has granted to the office-holder the power to realise the assets of the insolvent and the transfer of an action to an underwriter in return for the financing of it and the payment of a part of the proceeds. The assignment has been treated as a sale of property[11] and office-holders have

---

[10] See the comments of Oliver LJ in *Trendtex Trading v Credit Suisse* [1980] QB 629 at 674 (CA).

[11] See, *Grovewood Holdings Plc v James Capel & Co Ltd* [1995] BCC 760 at 764.

a power to sell the insolvent's property,[12] which includes causes of action, but, as we will see shortly, the power to sell in this respect has been interpreted restrictively.

The House of Lords in *Norglen Ltd (in liq) v Reeds Rains Prudential Ltd* ([1998] BCC 44) clearly accepted that the assignment of a chose in action was an exception to the law against champerty. However, the insolvency exception is only aimed at the outright sale of causes of action and not the sale of a right to share in the fruits of an action (*Grovewood Holdings Plc v James Capel & Co Ltd* [1995] 2 WLR 70; [1995] BCC 760).

As most of the case law has involved liquidators, it is appropriate to focus on liquidators in this part of the chapter, but recognising the fact that much of what is said applies to bankruptcy trustees and administrators.

Presently the case law restricts liquidators in two different ways. First, as we will see, it seems clear that liquidators are able to assign bare causes of action, but not able to agree to assign actions which are given to them by legislation in their role as liquidator. The view that is extant in the courts is that the liquidator is only able to assign company property, and actions given to the liquidator personally do not constitute company property. Second, there is case law that indicates that a liquidator, while able to assign a cause of action to a third party, in certain circumstances, is unable to assign a portion of the fruits of a cause of action.

A number of actions are granted to liquidators in their capacity as liquidators. Can they be assigned? In *Re Ayala Ltd (No 2)* ([1996] 1 BCLC 467) the liquidator sought to assign an action under section 127 and the court said that this was not permissible. Knox J said that such an action cannot be assigned as it is not property of the company, but involved a right given to the liquidator by legislation. Following *Re Ayala Ltd (No 2)*, Robert Walker J (as he then was), in *Re Oasis Merchandising Services Ltd* ([1995] BCC 911), refused to permit the purported assignment of a share of the recoveries in a cause of action on the basis of what was said in *Re Ayala Ltd (No 2)*. Like the latter case this involved an action brought by the liquidator (but in this case for wrongful trading under section 214) and was an action that was not the company's, but was the liquidator's. His Lordship said that an application under section 214 'cannot in my judgement be regarded simply as ordinary civil litigation. It is litigation which has, at least potentially, a public or penal element' (at 918). So, the upshot is that an action under section 214 is incapable of outright assignment (at 919). Clearly his Lordship was not willing to distinguish between assignments of bare causes of action or assignments of shares in the fruits of the action. His Lordship's decision has been upheld by the Court of Appeal (*Re Oasis Merchandising Services Ltd* [1998] Ch 170; [1997] 1 All ER 1009; [1997] BCC 282; [1997] 1 BCLC 689).

---

[12] See sections 165 and 167 and para 6 of Schedule 4 (winding up) and section 314 and para 9 of Schedule 5 (bankruptcy).

The Court of Appeal in *Re Exchange Travel (Holdings) Ltd (in liq) (No3)* ([1997] 2 BCLC 579; *sub nom Katz v McNally* [1997] BCC 784), seemed to accept the reasoning in *Re Oasis Merchandising Services Ltd* and applied it to actions involving applications for the adjustment of preferences under section 239.[13]

So, an assignment of a bare cause of action is unquestionably possible[14] and falls within the insolvency exception, but not where the action is not able to be regarded as part of the property of the company, but was given to the liquidator by legislation.

The second situation which we now will address is where a liquidator wishes to assign a portion of the fruits of an action to an insurer/underwriter.

In *Grovewood Holdings Plc v James Capel & Co Ltd* ([1995] BCC 760) the liquidator of Grovewood wished to continue legal proceedings that had been commenced at a time before the advent of the liquidation. The proceedings, against Capel, sought damages for negligence and misrepresentation. The liquidator unsuccessfully secured the financial support of the creditors and members of Grovewood. Consequently, he entered into a funding arrangement. The fundamental term of the funding arrangement was that those who funded the proceedings would, in return for agreeing to fund the action, receive half of any moneys recovered. Capel subsequently sought a stay of proceedings on the basis that the funding arrangement was champertous. All parties recognised that the arrangement was champertous. But the liquidator argued that the arrangement fell within the insolvency exception. Lightman J accepted the existence of the insolvency exception (at 764), but, importantly and crucially, his Lordship distinguished between an assignment of a bare cause of action and the assignment of a share in the proceeds of an action (at 765). His Lordship held that the former could, under the insolvency exception, be assigned, but a share of the proceeds of an action could not be as it was not a sale of company property for the purposes of paragraph 6 of Schedule 4 to the Act (at 765). His Lordship was also of the view that the term of the arrangement which provided that the company funding the proceedings would control the litigation, could not be allowed, as the liquidator had a fiduciary duty to control such proceedings (at 767).

The position taken by Lightman J has ruled out many funding arrangements. However, it must be noted that Robert Walker J in *Re Oasis Merchandising Services Ltd* (at 920) in *obiter* comments, did doubt the distinction made by Lightman J because in *Glegg v Blomley* ([1912] 3 KB 474), on admittedly different facts, it was said that the sale of the fruits of litigation was acceptable. Later, on appeal in *Re Oasis Merchandising Services Ltd* ([1997] BCC 283), again in *obiter*, the Court opined that there was much to be said for allowing a liquidator to sell the fruits of an action (at 288). More recently, Neuberger J in *Farmer v Moseley (Holdings) Ltd* ([2001]

---

[13] See R. Parry, 'Funding Litigation in Insolvency' (1998) 2 Cfi L.R. 121 at 131–2.

[14] For a recent case holding so, see *Empire Resolution Ltd v MPW Insurance Brokers Ltd* [1999] BPIR 486.

2 BCLC 572 at 578) said that it was unnecessary for him to choose between the views of Lightman and Robert Walker JJ, but if he had to he would favour the view of the latter. Notwithstanding these views, no judge in any case has expressly dissented from the opinion of Lightman J. But it might be noted that in the case of *ANC Ltd v Clark Goldring & Page Ltd* (*The Times*, May 31, 2000), the Court of Appeal seemed to accept the accuracy of a submission of counsel that the assignment of the fruits of an action does not involve champerty, because the assignment does not grant any right to prosecute the action.

Unlike *Re Oasis Merchandising Services Ltd*, if the action in *Grovewood Holdings* had been assigned outright, then that would have been acceptable as the action was one which belonged to the company. The action was an asset of the company prior to winding up.

It seems that the time has come where champerty should be laid to rest in relation to the insolvency context except only where there is clear detriment to the defendant, to creditors or to the administration of justice.[15]

26.5 Conclusion

In Part VIII we outline a number of the problems that office-holders face in bringing proceedings to recover property or money that were handed by the insolvent to third parties before the commencement of a formal insolvency administration, like liquidation. We note in Part VIII that these problems might cause an office-holder to refrain from commencing proceedings. The problems with obtaining the necessary funding to institute legal proceedings are likely to cause office-holders to question why they should be bothered with bringing proceedings, for everything seems to be against them. These problems might lead to a shortfall in litigation and this could 'undermine the effectiveness of the legislation, leading to the regulatory impact of these laws being reduced.'[16] If funding arrangements cannot be used, then in the words of Lindsay J in *Eastglen Ltd v Grafton* ([1996] 2 BCLC 279 at 292–293):

> Justice in liquidation would be even more elusive and defaulting directors and others susceptible to proceedings would have even greater incentives to ensure that the incoming liquidator would find the company completely devoid of the funds necessary to fund litigation against them.

---

[15] A. Walters, 'Forshortening the shadow: maintenance, champerty and the funding of litigation in corporate insolvency' (1996) 17 Co Law 165 at 174.

[16] R. Parry, 'Funding Litigation in Insolvency' (1998) 2 CfiLR 121.

Chapter 27

Disclaimer

27.1 Introduction

Ordinarily, office-holders are concerned about exercising control over as much property as they can. Naturally, the more property that they can control and then realise, the greater the dividend which will be paid ultimately to the creditors. However, in some insolvencies office-holders would prefer not to retain property because it is too onerous, worth little or unsaleable. Liquidators and trustees in bankruptcy are permitted, in certain cases, to disclaim property which the insolvent owned.

Liquidators and trustees would prefer to divest themselves of the property in order to avoid responsibilities and costs in relation to it. Disclaimer is allowed under statute. In disclaiming, liquidators and trustees give notice to others that they wish to make a divesture of any interest in the property; this requires those persons to whom notice has been given to mitigate their loss. The idea behind disclaimer is that if the onerous property were retained there would be a diminution of the benefits available for distribution to the creditors.[1]

The Bankruptcy Act 1869 (section 23) provided the first instance of the power to disclaim. A similar provision, in the form of section 267 of the Companies Act 1929 was applied to the corporate sphere. Now sections 178 and 315 of the Act provide the general power of disclaimer in liquidations and bankruptcies respectively.

[1] M. Mourell and J. Willoughby, 'Disclaimers of Onerous Property under section 568 of the Corporations Law' (1994) 4 *Australian Journal of Corporation Law* 63 at 67.

27.2 Scope of the power

27.2.1 *Introduction*

The power to disclaim, available to liquidators in both compulsory and voluntary liquidations and bankruptcy trustees, exists to permit an office-holder to reduce the liabilities of the insolvent. It must be made clear that if a liquidator does not disclaim, he or she is not held personally liable for the failure to perform any of the insolvent's obligations pertaining to the interest in onerous property. But, a liquidator might be held liable, in appropriate cases, for having failed to disclaim. Where a trustee in bankruptcy is concerned, he or she might be held liable personally for not disclaiming, since a bankrupt estate vests in the trustee and the trustee, unlike a liquidator (*Stead Hazel & Co v Cooper* [1933] 1 KB 480), becomes personally liable in respect of onerous property if he or she fails to disclaim it (section 315(3)(b).[2]

Office-holders may disclaim unprofitable contracts (sections 178(3)(a), 315(2)(a)). It would appear that a contract is unprofitable if the cost involved for the company in performing its obligations is greater than the benefit which the company will enjoy under the terms of the contract.[3] The court in *Re Bastable* ([1901] 2 KB 518) said that a contract was not unprofitable if the amount of profit is little. The court said that demonstrating that a better commercial bargain could be made by the liquidator compared with the bargain that was arranged originally (prior to bankruptcy or liquidation) falls well short of establishing that the contract is unprofitable. If the other party to the contract is unable or unwilling to perform his or her side of the contract, which would give the insolvent a claim for damages provided that the insolvent performed what the insolvent had agreed to do, that would not present the liquidator with sufficient justification to disclaim the contract.[4]

Besides unprofitable contracts, office-holders are able to disclaim all property which is unsaleable or not readily saleable by reason of its binding the possessor thereof to the performance of any onerous act (examples of these have been covenants to build and maintain property, as well as covenants contained in mortgages over real estate[5] and rates (*Re Middle Harbour Investments Ltd (in liq)* (1975–76) CLC 40–629)), or to the payment of a sum of money (sections 178(3)(b), 315(2)(b)).

Liquidators and trustees are not stopped from disclaiming by the fact that they have taken possession of the property, endeavoured to sell it or exercised rights of ownership over it (sections 178(1), 315(1)). But a part

---

[2] See *Titterton v Cooper* (1882) 9 QBD 473.
[3] A. Keay, *McPherson's Law of Company Liquidation*, London: Sweet & Maxwell (2001) at 488.
[4] R. Pennington, *Pennington's Corporate Insolvency Law*, 2nd edn, London: Butterworths (1997) at 151–2.
[5] For example, see *Re Mercer and Moore* (1880) 14 Ch D 287.

of an item of property cannot be disclaimed and a part retained (*Re Fussell* (1882) 20 Ch D 341 (CA)) – it is an all or nothing thing. If a person who is interested in some property of the insolvent and that person has applied in writing to the office-holder requiring the office-holder to decide whether to disclaim or not and the office-holder has not given a notice of disclaimer within 28 days, then no disclaimer can occur (sections 178(5), 316(1)).

Approval of the court for a disclaimer was once necessary, but it is not needed now.[6] Notwithstanding that, a person who is affected by the proposed disclaimer could apply to the court under either section 168(5) or 303 for a review of the official-holder's decision to disclaim.[7] If a court did decide to set aside the purported disclaimer the position pre-disclaimer would be restored.

27.2.2 *Environmental problems: a case study*[8]

It is more than likely that nowadays office-holders will more frequently encounter environmental problems. Office-holders might find that the land owned by the insolvent is so badly polluted that it cannot be sold. With polluted land the office-holder might find that the insolvent held a waste management licence, permitting the insolvent to deal with certain waste products. This was the case in *Re Mineral Resources Ltd* ([1999] 1 All ER 746; [1999] 2 BCLC 516; [1999] BCC 422).

> A liquidator of a company in voluntary liquidation purported to disclaim what was treated as a waste management licence. The licence related to a landfill site. The Environment Agency ('the Agency') sought a declaration that the liquidator of the company was unable to disclaim a licence as onerous property and that the disclaimer in this case was of no effect. The Agency argued that a licence was not 'property' within section 436 of the Act and as a consequence the liquidator could not disclaim it. The Agency's second line of argument was that even if the licence was property the provisions of the Environmental Protection Act 1990 ('EPA') prevented a use of the power to disclaim. Neuberger J held that the licence was property within section 436. As to the second argument put by the Agency his Lordship noted that there was a conflict between the environmental legislation (and in particular section 35(11) of the EPA which preserves the existence of waste management licences until they are either revoked by the Agency or the agency accepts their surrender) requiring action that promoted a healthy environment and the insolvency legislation and principles that promoted a fair and orderly winding up. Neuberger J accepted the argument of the Agency that the EPA constitutes a self-contained code relating to the grant, terms, revocation,

---

[6] Cases decided under the former law, when approval of the court was needed, are no longer relevant: *Re Hans Place Ltd* [1992] BCC 737; [1992] BCLC 768.

[7] For example, see *Re Hans Place Ltd* [1992] BCC 737; [1992] BCLC 768.

[8] For more discussion of this issue, see A. Keay and P. de Prez, 'Insolvency and Environmental Principles: A Case Study in a Conflict of Public Interests' (2001) 3 *Environmental Law Review* 90.

surrender and transfer of waste management licences and that a licence holder is able to only divest himself or herself of a licence within the provisions of the code. The learned judge acknowledged that this left no room for determination of a licence by disclaimer. Consequently, as Neuberger J found, there was a conflict between a licence being disclaimable under section 178 of the Act and the provisions of the EPA. The learned judge decided the conflict by holding that the provisions of the EPA prevailed over those of the Act. Neuberger J said that the provisions of the environmental legislation would prevail over the Act as it was in the public interest that a healthy environment was maintained. It seems that it was significant, for the decision of Neuberger J, that the effect of a licence being disclaimed was that the obligations of the licensee would end and the Agency would not be able to prove in the winding up of the company for any loss or damage experienced as a consequence of disclaimer, because the Agency would not be under any statutory or contractual duty to carry out remedial work needed and so could not claim to have sustained loss. The judge noted that if there was a need to carry out work the loser, as a result of the disclaimer, would be the public.

Later in *Re Celtic Extraction Ltd; Re Blue Stone Chemicals Ltd* ([1999] 2 BCLC 555) the Court of Appeal considered the issues raised above. The Court disagreed with the view that Neuberger J espoused that the environmental legislation should take precedence over the insolvency legislation. The Court could not agree that the provisions of the Act and the provisions of the EPA were mutually inconsistent and irreconcilable. According to the Court the EPA only provided for unilateral termination of the licence by its holder, but did not preclude termination by other statutes (at 567–568). The Court took the view that the polluter pays principle, the principle relied on by the Agency, was not applicable to cases, such as the case before the court, namely where the polluter could not pay and as a result unsecured creditors of the corporate polluter were required to end up paying (at 568). Morritt LJ emphasised that a critical element of the public policy requirement that creditors should share *pari passu* in the assets of companies in liquidation was to permit the liquidator to disclaim onerous property. His Lordship went on to say that it would require pointed and clear wording to exclude the operation of section 178 from specific items of property or specific insolvents (at 569). The Court concluded that the EPA provisions concerning termination of licences were limited to termination by the act of the parties and not where the termination was caused through the force of a statute, as occurred with disclaimer – the termination of the licence is permitted under section 178 of the Act.

Subsequently, in *In re Rhondda Waste Disposal Co Ltd* ([2000] BCC 653) a differently constituted Court of Appeal took a different approach. It must be said that the facts are distinguishable from *Re Celtic Extraction Ltd; Re Blue Stone Chemicals Ltd*, as the case revolved around whether leave was necessary before the Agency could initiate criminal proceedings. The judge at first instance had, following the approach in *Re Celtic Extraction Ltd; Re Blue Stone Chemicals Ltd*, denied leave to the Agency. Importantly for our purposes, the

Court of Appeal indicated that when the public interest dictated, as it did in this case, leave to pursue criminal proceedings ought to be given readily and the Court went on to say that the judge at first instance was wrong in not granting leave because he wrongly regarded the interests of the company's creditors as trumping all other considerations. *Prima facie* the comments in this case, while not dealing directly with the issue of disclaimer, may cast doubts on whether the view espoused in *Re Celtic Extraction* will, necessarily, be followed in the future.[9]

27.2.3 *The process*

The first step to be taken by an office-holder, when disclaiming, is to prepare and give the prescribed notice.[10] The notice is to contain particulars of the property disclaimed so as to enable the property to be identified (rules 4.187(1) or 6.178(1)). The notice must be signed by the office-holder and (with a copy) filed in the court (rules 4.187(2) or 6.178(2)). Once endorsed with the date of filing and sealed, the copy of the notice is returned to the office-holder (rules 4.187(3) or 6.178(3)). Within seven days of the notice being returned to the office-holder, copies of the notice of the disclaimer are to be sent to the persons prescribed by: rules 4.188(2) or 6.179(2) (persons with interests in leasehold property); rules 4.188(4) or 6.179(5) (those who are parties to, or have interests in, an unprofitable contract); rules 4.188(3) or 6.179(4) (every person who, to the knowledge of the office-holder, claims an interest in the property, or is under a liability in relation to the property (not including liabilities discharged by the disclaimer, no matter what the nature of the disclaimed property)); or rule 6.179(3) (in a bankruptcy where the disclaimer relates to a house and there are persons either occupying, or having a right to occupy, it). If after doing this, the office-holder discovers that persons have an interest that entitles them to receive a notice of disclaimer, the office-holder must send or give a copy of the notice to such persons. But, this obligation on the office-holder does not apply if he or she is satisfied that the persons have been made aware of the disclaimer and its date. Alternatively, the office-holder is relieved from his or her obligation if the court orders, on the application of the office-holder, that compliance is not necessary (rules 4.188(5) or 6.179(6)). To ensure that fairness is done and, perhaps, to ensure that he or she has not failed in discharging his or her duties, an office-holder may give a notice of the disclaimer to anyone who should, in the public interest, be advised of the disclaimer (rules 4.189 or 6.180).

---

[9] See A. Keay and P. de Prez, 'Insolvency and Environmental Principles: A Case Study in a Conflict of Public Interests' (2001) 3 *Environmental Law Review* 90.

[10] Sections 178(2) and 315(1). The notice is to be in accordance with Form 4.53 (rule 4.187(1)) or Form 6.61 (rule 6.178).

In the situation where there is a right to disclaim and it appears to the office-holder that there is a person who claims or may claim that he or she is entitled to an interest in the property, the office-holder is able to give notice to that person requiring the person to declare within 14 days whether he or she has a claim to any interest and, if so, the nature and extent of it.[11] If the notice does not precipitate any response, the office-holder is permitted to assume that the person has no interest in the property that will stop or hinder disclaimer (rules 4.192(2) or 6.184(2)).

A disclaimer is presumed to be effective and valid unless it is proved that there has been a breach of duty in relation to the giving of the notice of disclaimer, or either a breach of sections 178–180 (liquidations) or sections 315–319 (bankruptcies) or of the Rules (rules 4.193, 6.185).

It is in respect of leasehold interests that the power to disclaim is most commonly exercised.[12] There are specific sections, namely sections 179 and 317, which deal with the disclaimer of leaseholds. To be effective a copy of the disclaimer of a leasehold interest must be served on every person claiming under the insolvent as an underlessee or mortgagee and either no application is made under section 181 (liquidations) or 320 (bankruptcy) to the court claiming an interest before the end of the period of 14 days, commencing from the date on which the last notice was served or where a sections 181 or 320 application has been made, the court directs that the disclaimer shall take effect (sections 179(1) or 317(1)). If the court directs that the disclaimer is effective, it may also, instead of or in addition to any order it makes under either sections 181 or 320, make such orders relating to fixtures, tenant's improvements and other matters arising out of the lease as it thinks fit (sections 179(2) or 317(2)). But it was stated in *Re ITM Corp Ltd (in liq)* ([1997] BCC 554; [1997] 2 BCLC 389) that a court does not have jurisdiction to make a vesting order for the benefit of a landlord on such terms that it shall be subject to and with the benefit of existing sub-eases. More will be said about the disclaimer of leasehold interests shortly.

Where disclaimer has occurred, a person who claims a proprietary interest in the disclaimed property (*Lloyds Bank S.F. Nominees v Aladdin Ltd (in liq)* ([1996] 1 BCLC 720), or a person who is under any liability in respect of the disclaimed property (not including a liability discharged by the disclaimer), may apply to the court (sections 181(1)(2) or 320(1)(2)). The court may make an order, at the hearing of the application, for the vesting of the property in, or for the delivery to, a person entitled to make an application or a trustee for such a person (sections 181(3)(a) or 320(3)(a)).

---

[11] For liquidations, see rule 4.192(1) – the notice is to be in Form 4.55. For bankruptcy, see rule 6.184(1) – the form to be used is Form 6.63.

[12] A. Keay, *McPherson's Law of Company Liquidation* at 494. As to the difference between a contractual agreement to surrender a lease and a disclaimer, see *Torminster Properties Ltd v Green* [1983] 1 WLR 676.

27.2.4 *The effect of a disclaimer*

Essentially, the principle underlying disclaimer is that although a disclaimer is likely to affect third parties, the rights and obligations of such persons should be affected as little as possible, and only 'to the extent necessary to achieve the primary object: the release of the company from all liability' (*Hindcastle Ltd v Barbara Attenborough Associates Ltd* [1996] BCC 636 at 644 (HL) per Lord Nicholls). Following on from this, in *Capital Prime Properties plc v Worthgate Ltd* ([2000] BCC 525), Neuberger J said that when assessing the impact of disclaimer, courts are to apply a test based on commercial sense and minimising the disruption on others. Nothing in sections 178 and 315 indicates that a disclaimer undoes contractual rights and benefits that have already vested (*Capital Prime Properties plc v Worthgate Ltd*). The general effect of a disclaimer is to determine, as from the date of the disclaimer, the rights, interests and liabilities of the insolvent in respect of the property disclaimed but does not affect the rights and liabilities of any other persons, except as necessary in order to release the insolvent and his, her or its property from liability (sections 178(4) or 315(3)). Also, it must be noted that in bankruptcy a disclaimer has the effect of discharging the trustee from all personal liability in relation to the property disclaimed (section 315(3)(b)). As the act of a disclaimer usually releases the insolvent from liability,[13] those persons who are affected by the disclaimer may prove as creditors of the insolvent for the amount of the loss sustained (sections 178(6) or 315(5)),[14] together with a right to apply for a vesting order or order for delivery of the property disclaimed (sections 181(2) or 320(2)). The effect of a vesting order under either sections 181 or 320 will be taken into account for the purpose of determining the extent of the loss sustained as a result of a disclaimer (sections 181(5) or 320(5)).

There is an obligation on persons who suffer loss as a result of a disclaimer to mitigate the damage sustained (*Re Hide* [1871] 7 Ch App 28). Where a lease is disclaimed, it becomes a lease without an owner, but it does not cease to exist subject to the usual means of terminating a lease (*WH Smith Ltd v Wyndham Investments Ltd* [1994] 2 BCLC 571; [1994] BCC 699).

Unless a court makes a vesting order in relation to the interest of the insolvent that is disclaimed, that interest vests in the Crown automatically as *bona vacantia* (*Re Mercer & Moore* (1880) 14 Ch D 287). The insolvent's rights under a contract do not vest in the Crown, but will terminate. What about where land is involved?

---

[13] See *Re Katherine et Cie Ltd* [1932] 1 Ch 70.

[14] For a discussion of the principles to be applied under this provision in relation to a disclaimed lease, see *Re Park Air Services Ltd* [1996] 1 BCLC 547.

27.2.4.1 *Freehold land*

Freehold interests in land are able to be classified as onerous property (*Scmella Properties Ltd v Gesso Properties (BVI) Ltd* [1995] BCC 793 at 797). In fact the disclaimer of such property interests has increased in recent years (*Scmella Properties Ltd*). When a liquidator disclaims freehold land, the title to it revests in the Crown on the basis of escheat (*Re Mercer & Moore* (1880) 14 Ch D 287; *Scmella Properties Ltd*) unless a vesting order is made in favour of some other person, for instance, a consenting mortgagee or other incumbrancer so as to provide some form of compensation in light of the company's failure to discharge its liability.

Legal charges and leases of tenants will survive a disclaimer (*Scmella Properties Ltd*). In *Scmella Properties Ltd* a company disclaimed its freehold interest in land and over which a bank held a mortgage. The court said that as the disclaimer ended the freehold interest, the Crown became the owner, but as a mortgagee's interest survived disclaimer, the bank was able to sell its interest in the property to tenants of the property.

27.2.4.2 *Leasehold land*

The legal position resulting from a disclaimer of leasehold land is quite clear where only the lessor and the insolvent are involved.[15] The disclaimer terminates all the insolvent's liabilities (and in bankruptcy, the trustee's) and rights, and the rights of the lessor[16] and there is no need for an order vesting the property in the lessor since the effect is simply to accelerate the lessor's interest (*Hindcastle Ltd v Barbara Attenborough Associates Ltd* [1997] AC 70 at 87; [1996] BCC 636 at 644; *Re Park Air Services plc* [1999] BCC 135 at 137). Where the insolvent is the sub-lessee the original lessor is not affected (*Hill v East & West India Dock Co* (1884) 9 App Cas 448; *Re Finley* (1888) 21 Ch D 475 at 485; *Wanford Investments Ltd v Duckworth* [1978] 2 WLR 741) and is liable until the lease expires or is determined. However, things are more complicated where the insolvent is the sub-lessor.[17] In such a case the effect is to extinguish the rights and liabilities of the sub-lessee (*Re Finley* (1888) 21 Ch D 475).

In *Hindcastle Ltd v Barbara Attenborough Associates Ltd* ([1997] AC 70; [1996] BCC 636), Lord Nicholls identified three categories of leaseholds involving land where a disclaimer had an effect. They are (at 89; 644–646):

---

[15] For a general account, see *Re Finley* (1888) 21 Ch D 475; *Hindcastle Ltd v Barbara Attenborough Associates Ltd* [1997] AC 70; [1996] BCC 636 (HL).

[16] The result is that the lessor is entitled to possession but not to future rent: *Re Park Air Services plc* [1999] BCC 135 at 140 (HL).

[17] See *Re AE Realisations (1985) Ltd* [1988] 1 WLR 200; (1987) 3 BCC 136.

- a landlord and tenant are involved;
- a situation where others have a liability in relation to the lease;
- a situation where others have an interest in the property.

The most common is the first of the above situations, with the insolvent being the tenant. Here the landlord's rights are determined (*Hindcastle Ltd* at 90; 645), but he or she has, under sections 178(6) or 315(5), a right to prove in the winding up or bankruptcy for the loss sustained from the act of disclaimer, often the non-receipt of future rent.[18] There is no scope for any rights or liabilities to be preserved by sections 178(4) or 315(3) (*Hindcastle Ltd* at 90; 645).

While the liabilities of an insolvent pursuant to a lease are terminated when an office-holder disclaims an interest in the lease, this does not determine the covenants in the lease for all purposes (*Hill v East and West India Co* (1884) 9 App Cas 448; *Hindcastle Ltd v Barbara Attenborough Associates Ltd* [1994] 4 All ER 129; [1994] BCC 705 (CA); *Hindcastle Ltd* (HL)).

> In *Hindcastle Ltd v Barbara Attenborough Associates Ltd* ([1997] AC 70; [1996] BCC 636)[19] a landlord granted a lease of commercial premises to X Ltd. Later, X Ltd assigned it to Y Ltd who agreed to pay the rent and perform the lessee's covenants during the remaining part of the term of the lease. Z, one of Y Ltd's directors, agreed to guarantee the obligations of Y Ltd under the lease for a period of 10 years. Following this, Y Ltd assigned the lease to A Ltd. A Ltd subsequently entered into creditors' voluntary liquidation. Its liquidator disclaimed the lease. The landlord brought proceedings against X Ltd, Y Ltd and Z for unpaid rent and other money due both before and after the disclaimer. The landlord obtained summary judgment, and X Ltd went into compulsory liquidation and was not involved any further in the proceedings. Y Ltd went into liquidation and its liquidator argued that Y Ltd was not liable pursuant to the lease. The landlord sued Y Ltd and Z for outstanding rent and Z argued specifically that the disclaimer had the effect of ending any liability he had under the guarantee in his role as guarantor. At first instance judgment was granted in favour of the landlord. Y Ltd and Z appealed. The Court of Appeal dismissed the appeals ([1994] 4 All ER 129; [1994] BCC 705). Y Ltd and Z then appealed to the House of Lords.
>
> In the leading speech in the House of Lords, Lord Nicholls stated that just because the company's liabilities were at an end, as a result of the disclaimer, it did not mean, necessarily, that the guarantor's obligations to the landlord also terminated ([1997] AC 70 at 88; [1996] BCC 636 at 645). His Lordship went on to say that the legal rights of recourse of the guarantor could be determined without releasing the guarantor from his liability to the landlord; this liability survived the extinguishment of the guarantor's right of recourse. The problem facing their Lordships was: if the lease ended on disclaimer then the guarantor could not be held liable, but if the lease did not come to

---

[18] See section 178(6). How compensation is assessed in a leasehold situation was discussed by the House of Lords in *Re Park Air Services plc* [1999] BCC 135.

[19] This discussion of the case is based on that found in A. Keay, *McPherson's Law of Company Liquidation* at 498–9.

an end, so that rent could continue to accrue, what happens to the lease taking into account the fact that A Ltd's interest in the property had been disclaimed? Lord Nicholls pointed out that the Insolvency Act envisages the fact that a person may be liable to perform the covenants of the tenant even following a disclaimer. For instance, a vesting order can be made under section 182. His Lordship said that one must see the statute taking effect as a deeming provision so far as the preserved rights and obligations of persons other than the insolvent. In other words, while the insolvent's liability ends, the rights and liabilities of persons such as guarantors are to remain as though the lease had continued and not been determined. If no vesting order is made and the landlord takes possession then the obligations of persons such as a guarantor come to an end as far as the future is concerned. Lord Nicholls went on to explain that the fundamental purpose of having a guarantee was to ensure that if insolvency of the principal debtor eventuated the creditor would be protected, so if the liability of the guarantor was terminated by the disclaimer of the principal debtor then this would completely undo the whole idea of having a guarantee. His Lordship did note that the guarantor is able to prove in the estate of the principal debtor under section 178(6).

The upshot of *Hindcastle Ltd* is that a guarantor of the obligations under a lease and the original lessee of the lease which has been assigned are able to be classified under sections 181(2)(b) or 320(2)(b) as persons who are under a liability in respect of disclaimed property and they could apply for a vesting order. Such action might improve the position in which they find themselves, as they could rent out or use the premises. But, the better course of action would probably be 'if the landlord entered into possession, thereby determining their obligations for future rent and leaving them only liable for past amounts outstanding.'[20]

It has been recognised for a long time that if a lease, which has been assigned, is disclaimed, the continuing liability of the original lessee and anyone who guaranteed the liability of the original lessee (and assignor) is not determined (*Hill v East & West India Dock Co* (1884) 9 App Cas 448; *Hindcastle Ltd*). However, if a lease was entered into after 1 January 1996 and was assigned and the assignee disclaims then the effects on the original lessee will not be as far-reaching, for the original assignor will not be liable for future rent and fulfilling any covenants of the assignee, as he or she is automatically discharged from such liability on assignment of the lease.[21]

27.2.4.3 *Contracts*

Contracts may be disclaimed by the office-holder in the course of the winding up or bankruptcy only where they are unprofitable. Disclaimer

---

[20] A. Keay, *McPherson's Law of Company Liquidation* at 499.
[21] See Landlord and Tenant (Covenants) Act 1995, sections 1(1), (3), 5(1), (2) and 31(1).

occurs sometimes where the contract is of a kind which imposes continuing obligations, the effect being to bring the insolvent's liabilities to an end. The other party to the contract has a right to prove for damages in the winding up or bankruptcy.[22]

---

[22] See section 178(6) or section 315(5).

Chapter 28

Distribution of Property in Insolvent Estates

28.1 Introduction

This chapter focuses on the distribution of the property gathered in by a trustee in bankruptcy or a liquidator (although parts of the chapter might be relevant to other administrations) in the course of the administration of an insolvent estate, through simple collection, or recovery from third parties.

28.2 The *pari passu* principle

Once the office-holder has collected enough assets, and realised them, he or she is likely to begin discharging the liabilities of the insolvent. In liquidation the assets may be taken to include all property which belonged to the company on its winding up (section 144) and in bankruptcy it is all the property belonging to or vested in the bankrupt at the commencement of the bankruptcy and any property that is treated by the Act as falling within the category of property of the bankrupt (section 283). The general rule, embodied in section 107 for voluntary winding up, rule 4.181 of the Insolvency Rules ('the Rules') for compulsory winding up and section 328(3) for bankruptcy, is that the property of the company is to be applied in satisfaction of its liabilities equally; this is known as 'the *pari passu* principle'. For instance, section 107 states:

> Subject to the provisions of this Act as to preferential payments, the company's property . . . shall on winding up be applied in satisfaction of the company's liabilities *pari passu* . . .

As noted in Chapter 3, the *pari passu* principle providing for equality of division among creditors is one of the (if not the most) fundamental principles of the law of insolvency[1] and is at the very heart of the whole statutory schemes of bankruptcy and winding up. The principle, which has a long history and can be traced back to at least the bankruptcy statute of 1570 (13 Eliz c.7), is explained by Professor Seligson, in an often cited passage:

> Equality is equity. That maxim is a theme of bankruptcy administration – one of the cornerstones of the bankruptcy structure. All persons similarly situated are entitled to equality in treatment in the distribution of the assets of the bankrupt estate.[2]

The generally accepted aim behind the use of *pari passu* is to ensure fairness.[3] The principle's enforcement means that the inevitable social and economic costs associated with bankruptcy and liquidation are, to a degree, minimised.[4] A liquidation, particularly of large companies, for example, can lead to significant financial problems for many of those persons trading with the failed company and can lead to a chain of failed enterprises.[5]

Notwithstanding the fact that the *pari passu* principle is said to be at the heart of insolvency law, it has been eroded significantly and remains only as a theoretical doctrine.[6] Equal treatment rarely occurs because the principle does not affect the rights of certain people. First, creditors who have rights in rem, such as secured creditors; liquidation and bankruptcy do not interfere with the security rights of a secured creditor (*Re Portbase (Clothing) Ltd* [1993] BCC 96 at 108). Second, those whose claims are able to be classed as the expenses of winding up. Third, certain unsecured creditors entitled to preferential treatment.

We will now concern ourselves with the distribution of the estate to the unsecured creditors.

---

[1] R. Goode, *Principles of Corporate Insolvency Law*, 2nd edn, London: Sweet & Maxwell (1997) at 141; Report of the Insolvency Law Review Committee in *Insolvency Law and Practice*, Cmnd 8558, 1982, ('the Cork Report') at para 233; V. Finch, 'Directors' Duties': 'Insolvency and the Unsecured Creditor', in *Current Issues in Insolvency Law* (edited by A Clarke, Stevens, London, 1991), at 87.

[2] C. Seligson, 'Preferences Under the Bankruptcy Act' (1961) 15 *Vanderbilt Law Review* 115; T. Jackson, *The Logic and Limits of Bankruptcy Law*, Cambridge: Harvard University Press (1986) at 123.

[3] J. McCoid, 'Bankruptcy, Preferences and Efficiency: An Expression of Doubt' (1981) 67 *Virginia Law Review* 247 at 271.

[4] T.H. Jackson and A. Kronman, 'Voidable Preferences and Protection of the Expectation Interest' (1976) 60 *Minnesota Law Review* 971 at 989.

[5] T.H. Jackson and A. Kronman, 'Voidable Preferences and Protection of the Expectation Interest' (1976) 60 *Minnesota Law Review* 971 at 989.

[6] Cork Report at para 233.

28.3 Exceptions to *pari passu*[7]

There are a number of exceptions to the *pari passu* principle, such that one can say that the *pari passu* principle, rather than being the all-prevailing rule that it is supposed to be, is in fact more like a convenient default principle. The next part of the chapter sets out the exceptions to the principle, but it is preferable to defer more extensive discussion of some of them until later, when they are considered in the context of the order of distribution of the assets of the company.

Before going any further it is appropriate to note that secured creditors and claimants under Romalpa clauses in contracts (giving the right to retain title) are not true exceptions, as the property subject to security or retention of title does not belong to the company and so the creditors of the company are not able to claim distribution of the assets.[8] The same reasoning can be applied to property that is held in trust by the company. That property is not available to the creditors.

28.3.1 *Set-off*

The right to set-off is discussed in Chapter 33 and is provided for by rule 4.90 for liquidations and section 323 for bankruptcies. Set-off is allowed as an exception to the *pari passu* rule for reasons of policy and justice. Parke B said in *Forster v Wilson* ((1843) 12 M & W 191; 152 ER 1165) that the purpose behind permitting set-off in liquidations and bankruptcy was 'to do substantial justice between the parties, where a debt is really due from the debtor to his estate' (at 204, 1171). Injustice would be produced if the party who had dealt with the company was required to discharge the debt he or she owed to the insolvent company and only received a right to claim a dividend in the winding up (*Morris v Agrichemicals Ltd* [1996] BCC 204 at 209 (CA)).

28.3.2 *Debt subordination*[9]

On the basis that the *pari passu* principle is so fundamental to winding up, the courts have been reluctant to accede to creditors' attempts to circumvent it by having specific assets reserved for the payment of

---

[7] The discussion does not purport to be exhaustive. For more detail, see A. Keay, *McPherson's Law of Company Liquidation*, London: Sweet & Maxwell (2001) at 714–22.

[8] R.M. Goode, *Principles of Corporate Insolvency Law*, 2nd edn, at 152.

[9] For further discussion of this topic, see P Wood, *Wood on International Finance: The Law of Subordinated Debt*, London: Sweet & Maxwell (1990); B. Johnston, 'Contractual Debt Subordination and Legislative Reform' [1991] JBL 225; G. McCormack, *Proprietary Claims and Insolvency*, London: Sweet & Maxwell (1997), at 28–35; E. Ferran, *Company Law and Corporate Finance*, Oxford: Oxford University Press (1999), Chapter 16.

particular classes of debts, i.e., contracting out. This is where creditors agree to defer claims to the claims of others. It is known as debt subordination. It may take a number of forms.[10] For example, money may be advanced to a company simply on the basis that the debts of those associated with the company are postponed or it is agreed by several creditors that the party who provides the funds is given priority over them. Alternatively, a creditor might agree to rank behind some and not all of the creditors of the company.[11] The issue of subordination usually occurs when a company is in financial distress and the only way that it may continue to operate is if further funds are injected, but the provider of such funds wishes to ensure that should the company collapse, its debt will be paid in priority to others. There may be support for this kind of arrangement because without the injection of funds the company is likely to collapse. Normally, the interests of the creditors are strengthened if the company continues to operate and is able, perhaps, to haul itself out of the financial malaise in which it finds itself.

Traditionally, there have been two reasons why contracting out of *pari passu* has not been permitted. First, the House of Lords in *National Westminster Bank Ltd v Halesowen* ([1972] AC 785) held that there was a public interest factor in rules laid down for the administration of a company's assets in winding up, such as the *pari passu* principle and so creditors could not do private deals and organise priority in the way they saw fit. Second, contracting out would be unfair on the general body of creditors (*British Eagle International Air Lines Ltd v Compagnie Nationale Air France* [1975] 1 WLR 758 at 780–781 (HL)).

The starting point for examination of this area is the decision of the House of Lords in *British Eagle International Air Lines Ltd v Compagnie Nationale Air France*, where a majority refused to give effect in winding up to a contractual 'clearing house' arrangement between international airlines. Following this decision courts had to consider the balance between strict legal principle and the commercial realities that confronted companies. A wide view of the House of Lords' decision prevailed in some courts[12] with the result that all contracting out was proscribed as breaching the mandatory rule of *pari passu*, while in other courts a more liberal view was taken and the decision was given more limited application.[13] In due course greater certainty was provided to parties. The courts distinguished between two types of situations. First, where an unsecured creditor seeks to gain

---

[10] The advantages of the use of subordination of debt are summarised by Dr Ferran in *Company Law and Corporate Finance*, Oxford: Oxford University Press (1999) at 546.

[11] For example, see *United States Trust Co of New York v ANZ Banking Group Ltd* (1995) 13 ACLC 1225 (NSW CA).

[12] For example, *Re Orion Sound Ltd* (1979) 2 NZLR 574; *Carreras Rothmans v Freemans Mathews Treasure Ltd* [1985] Ch 207; [1985] 3 WLR 1016.

[13] For example, *Re Marlborough Concrete Constructions Pty Ltd* [1977] Qd 37; *Re NBT Builders Pty Ltd (in liq)* (1984) 2 ACLC 269; *Horne v Chester & Fein Property Developments Pty Ltd* (1987) 5 ACLC 245.

an advantage over other unsecured creditors without their agreement, the courts would not enforce such an agreement. Second, where an unsecured creditor enters into an agreement with the company and/or other unsecured creditors whereby his debt ranks behind that of other unsecured creditors.

The courts would permit a liquidator to distribute according to an agreement made along the lines of the second situation provided that to do so would not adversely affect any creditor not a party to the agreement, i.e., creditors not involved in the subordination agreement would receive less under that agreement than would have been received if distributions had been made on a *pari passu* basis. This approach was adopted by Vinelott J in *Re Maxwell Communications Corporation plc (No.3)* ([1993] BCC 369) where his Lordship recognised several policy matters which supported him not preventing the contracting out of the *pari passu* principle by way of subordination agreement. These policies were that: a creditor should be able to agree pre-insolvency that if insolvency ensued his debt would be subordinated when he would be at liberty after the commencement of winding up to agree to the postponement of the debt owed to him (at 376); subordination is recognised in many contexts and it is treated for accountancy purposes as if it were part of the company's capital and a creditor is entitled to assign the benefit of his or her debt to other creditors (at 380), so if subordination in these senses was recognised, yet not where there was a direct contract between the company and a creditor, it would allow form to be paramount over substance (at 381); subordination was permitted in other jurisdictions[14] and insolvencies were increasingly having international consequences (at 381–384).

While it will be helpful for an appellate court to affirm the approach taken by Vinelott J, it is preferable that Parliament takes some action by amending legislation to permit subordination in certain circumstances.

28.3.3 *Liquidation and bankruptcy expenses*

Unfortunately liquidations and bankruptcies cannot be attended to without the incurring of certain costs and expenses. For example, property must be sold and that will usually involve things like advertising costs, agency commission etc. Probably on the basis of pragmatism the legislature has provided that these expenses are paid out before unsecured creditors receive anything.[15] Details of expenses are discussed in Section 28.4 of this chapter.

---

[14] The judge considered section 501(a) of the United States' Bankruptcy Code which permits debt subordination (at 383–4).

[15] A. Keay, *McPherson's Law of Company Liquidation* at 722.

28.3.4 *Preferential creditors*

Certain unsecured creditors, while having no priority under the general law, are given express priority by legislation to payment in the administration of an insolvent estate. Such creditors are often referred to as preferential creditors. Bestowing favoured status on particular kinds of debts has been a matter of controversy for some time. Elsewhere we have even criticised the existence of priority for any kind of unsecured debt.[16] This topic is discussed further later in the chapter.

28.3.5 *Summary*

While courts have, on many occasions, said that the *pari passu* principle provides a mandatory code to be followed in insolvency administrations, exceptions to the principle abound to the point where the principle's authoritative position has been severely undermined. Exceptions to the principle have emerged in an *ad hoc* fashion and, in some cases, founded on questionable policy considerations. The result is a muddled and confusing situation.[17]

28.4 Distribution of the estate – a matter of priorities

The assets of the insolvent together with any property or funds recovered by the office-holder from others and, in relation to companies, sums collected from shareholders who had not fully paid up their shares, form a single fund which is available for the payment of the claims set out below. The issues discussed here primarily affect the distribution process in liquidation and bankruptcy and so we major on these two administrations. It is preferable for the purposes of clear exposition to deal with the administrations separately, while acknowledging that there are many similarities between the two.

28.4.1 *Liquidation*

Much of what follows applies as much to bankruptcy as it does to liquidation. However, we will focus on liquidation and deal with some issues peculiar to bankruptcy after discussing the general structure of priority in liquidations.

---

[16] A. Keay and P. Walton, 'The Preferential Debts' Regime in Liquidation Law: In the Public Interest?' (1999) 3 Cfi LR 84.

[17] A. Keay, *McPherson's Law of Company Liquidation* at 723.

The order of distribution provided for in the Act, after secured creditors other than those with floating charges have realised their security, is, through a combination of sections 107,115,175, 386, Schedule 6, and rule 4.181:

- costs and expenses of winding up (section 115);
- preferential debts (section 175(1));
- secured debts pursuant to floating charges (section 175(2)(b));[18]
- any preferential charge on goods distrained that arises pursuant to section 176(3);[19]
- general body of ordinary unsecured creditors (rule 4.181);
- post-liquidation interest on debts (section 189);
- deferred creditors – mentioned in section 74(2)(f);
- any balance is divided among the contributories pursuant to the memorandum and articles.

The last category is really only of theoretical interest in insolvency as it usually only comes into play where there is a members' voluntary liquidation. Also, the penultimate category will rarely feature in insolvent liquidations.

The following discussion is based on the above order. Primarily we will concentrate on the costs of winding up, with special treatment being given to liquidation expenses and preferential debts.

28.4.1.1 *The expenses of winding up*[20]

It is provided in rule 12.2 that all fees, costs, charges and expenses incurred in the course of winding up are to be regarded as expenses of the winding up. Expenses being granted priority is based on the notion that 'the creditors have a community of interest in having a common agent maximise a fund for distribution among them'.[21] Providing priority to expenses like this has been likened to salvage in that a liquidator must pay something for the use of property or services rendered by third parties because it can be assumed that creditors are benefiting from the use of the property or services which are necessary for the liquidator to perform his or her functions.[22]

---

[18] This is certainly the case as far as charges which crystallised by reason of, and immediately after, the commencement of winding up, and there is case law to the effect that the same situation exists in relation to charges crystallising pre-commencement of winding up.

[19] For a modern discussion of distress in the context of insolvency administrations, see P. Walton, 'The landlord, his distress, the insolvent tenant and the stranger' (2000) 16 *Insolvency Law and Practice* 47.

[20] For a helpful discussion, see G. Moss and N. Segal, 'Insolvency Proceedings: Contract and Financing' (1997) 1 Cfi LR 1.

[21] Australian Law Reform Commission, *General Insolvency Inquiry*, Report No. 45 ('the Harmer Report'), 1988 at para 717. See the comments of Vaughan Williams J in *Re London Metallurgical Co* (1895) 1 Ch 758 at 763.

[22] Ibid.

Where a liquidator has sufficient funds to pay all liquidation expenses, it is unnecessary to consider which expenses are to be paid first. But it is not unusual for there to be insufficient funds in the company so as to satisfy all costs. Consequently, rule 4.218 lists the order in which the various kinds of costs will be paid.

Rule 4.220 permits a re-ordering of the priorities in rule 4.218 and 4.219 by a court. In this respect the court's discretion is unfettered, but it is ordinarily exercised in accordance with certain well-settled principles.[23] The court has a complete discretion to apportion the assets in payment of expenses (*Re Dominion of Canada Plumbago Co* (1884) 27 Ch D 33) and where all things are equal, it would do this.

The order of payment is such that the assets of the company that are subject to a floating charge[24] are available to pay for the liquidation expenses. At one time this only applied where floating charges did not crystallise before the commencement of winding up (*Re Barleycorn Enterprises Ltd* [1970] Ch 465 at 474 (CA)). But it was held in *Re Portbase (Clothing) Ltd* ([1993] Ch 388; [1993] BCC 96) that, as a result of changes to the definition of 'floating charge', introduced by the Insolvency Act in 1986, that if a floating charge did crystallise before winding up the assets which are subject to it would also be available to pay for liquidation expenses. What was not clear was what happens where a charge crystallises before winding up and a receivership occurs. It appears that the position propounded in *Re Portbase (Clothing) Ltd* ([1993] Ch 388; [1993] BCC 96) has been adopted in relation to this issue. The Court of Appeal in *Re Leyland DAF Ltd* ([2002] 1 BCLC 571) endorsed the approach in *Re Portbase*.

Where there are hybrid charges, namely some assets are subject to a floating charge and others are subject to a fixed charge, then the liquidation expenses and preferential creditors only have priority with respect to the assets covered by the floating charge (*Re Lewis Merthyr Consolidated Collieries Ltd* [1929] 1 Ch 498 at 512 (CA)). If assets are subject to an expenses claim then section 40(2) will operate to give preferential creditors priority in the receivership.

Any post-liquidation claim that is covered under expenses of the winding up should be paid by the liquidator. The liquidator is able to agree any of the costs of any person payable from company assets, but the liquidator is entitled, where appropriate, to require the person to have his or her costs taxed by the court.

The term 'expenses' is wide and encompasses claims that have been adopted by the liquidator.[25] An example of this is where a liquidator enters a fresh contract with a third party following the commencement of liquidation. Some items are, in rule 4.218(1), specifically stated to be liquidation expenses. Rule 4.218(1) provides a priority scheme for the

---

[23] See *Re Massey* (1870) 9 Eq. 367; *Re Pacific Coast Syndicate Ltd* [1913] 2 Ch 26.

[24] This is opposed to assets under a fixed charge which are safe: *Re Lewis Merthyr Consolidated Collieries Ltd* [1929] 1 Ch 498 at 512 (CA).

[25] G. Moss and N. Segal, 'Insolvency Proceedings: Contract and Financing' (1997) 1 Cfi LR 1 at 12.

payment of post-liquidation expenses. It applies to both compulsory and voluntary liquidations (*Re Toshoku Finance UK plc* [2000] 1 BCLC 683 at 699 (CA)). Some of the expenses and costs provided for in rule 4.218(1) warrant little or no discussion. The priority set out in rule 4.218 (for all liquidations) is as follows:

(a) Expenses properly incurred in preserving, realising or getting in company assets (rule 4.218(1)(a))

The term 'expenses' has been said to cover any expenses which the liquidator might be compelled to pay in respect of preserving, realising or getting in of property of the company (*Re Beni-Felkai Mining Co* [1934] Ch 406). Consequently, it includes the costs of recovery, preservation and realisation of the assets, such as solicitors' and real estate agents' costs. Furthermore, it embraces all kinds of debts and liabilities incurred in the winding up while carrying on the business of the company (*Re Davis & Co* [1945] Ch 402; *Re Mawcon Ltd* [1969] 1 WLR 78), such as salaries and wages of employees.

Sometimes it may be necessary to apportion liabilities between liquidation and pre-liquidation periods for the purpose of determining which expenses of winding up were properly incurred and entitled to priority (*Re ABC Coupler & Engineering Co. Ltd (No. 3)* [1970] 1 WLR 702 at 709).

If a winding up commenced as voluntary but has become a compulsory one, the remuneration of the voluntary liquidator and as many of the costs and expenses of the voluntary winding up as the court allows are to be included in the expenses covered by rule 4.218 (rule 4.219). Courts tend to allow costs and expenses to rank with a priority as provided under rule 4.219, unless there is a good reason relating to the conduct of the liquidator in office not to do so (*Re Tony Rowse N M C Ltd* [1996] 2 BCLC 225 at 233; [1996] BCC 196 at 203).

After paying out this head of expenses, there may not be sufficient assets to cover other expenses, so a liquidator will seek to bring as many expenses as possible under rule 4.218(1)(a), particularly the costs of litigation. Where an action is commenced, or defended, in the name of the company before or after the commencement of winding up, if costs are awarded against the company, these may be claimed under rule 4.218(1)(a),[26] whether the company is in compulsory or voluntary winding up (*Re Wenborn & Co* [1905] 1 Ch 413; *Re Pacific Coast Syndicate Ltd* [1913] 2 Ch 26). The general rule is that the liquidator's own costs will be satisfied from the assets of the company (*Re Wilson Lovatt & Sons Ltd* [1977] 1 All ER 274), because the liquidator is carrying out a public function on the part

---

[26] *Re Trent and Humber Ship Building Co* (1869) LR 8 Eq 94; *Re Home Investment Society* (1880) 14 Ch D 167; *Re Dronfield Silkstone Coal Company (No.2)* (1883) 23 Ch D 511; *Re Pacific Coast Syndicate Ltd* [1913] 2 Ch 26; *Re London Drapery Stores* [1898] 2 Ch 684; *Re Movitex Ltd* [1990] BCC 491; [1990] BCLC 785; *Norglen Ltd v Reeds Raines Prudential Ltd* [1999] 2 AC 1 (HL). This applies to all costs, according to Lord Hoffmann in the last case cited, in the situation where a liquidator adopts an action.

of all creditors and contributories and in relation to the getting in of company assets (*Re Trent & Humber Ship Building Co; Bailey's Case* (1869) 8 Eq 94; *Madrid Bank v Pelley* (1869) 7 Eq 442; *Re Dominion of Canada Plumbago Co* (1884) 27 Ch D 33). A liquidator will be concerned where there are insufficient assets to pay parties who succeeded in litigation against the liquidator and were awarded costs. In such cases the successful litigants are entitled to require the liquidator to return any money paid to the liquidator in relation to his or her fees and expenses. The position as far as costs awarded against a liquidator where proceedings are brought in his or her name was discussed earlier in Chapter 26.[27]

The expenses of a provisional liquidator, incurred while performing his or her functions, including the carrying on the business of the company, should, where there is a subsequent liquidation, be paid out before other expenses covered by rule 4.218(1)(a) and there are insufficient assets to cover all liquidation expenses. The reason for this is that the rules give a provisional liquidator a higher priority over a liquidator for payment of remuneration, so a provisional liquidator should enjoy a higher priority for the repayment of expenses (*In re Grey Marlin Ltd* [1999] 2 BCLC 658 at 665).

(b) Expenses incurred or disbursements made by the official receiver (rule 4.218(1)(b))
An example of this is corporation tax incurred by the official receiver in carrying on the business of a company (*Re Beni-Felkai Mining Co* [1934] Ch 406).

(c) Fees payable under section 414 and remuneration payable to the official receiver (rule 4.218(1)(c))

(d) Official receiver's fees payable under section 414 for performance of general duties

(e) Security provided by a provisional liquidator, liquidator or special manager (rule 4.218(1)(e))

(f) Remuneration of any provisional liquidator (rule 4.218(1)(f))[28]

(g) Any deposit lodged on an application for the appointment of a provisional liquidator (rule 4.218(1)(g))

(h) Costs in respect of the petition for the winding-up order
Rule 4.218(1)(h) provides that the petitioner will be entitled to the costs allowed by the court in relation to the winding-up petition. Also if anyone

---

[27] Above at 377–83.
[28] See Part III.

who appears on the petition and is allowed his or her costs by the court, that person's costs come under this head.

(i) Remuneration of any special manager (rule 4.218(1)(j))

(j) Necessary disbursements made by the liquidator in the course of winding up (rule 4.218(1)(m))
This heading can cover the expenses incurred by members of the liquidation committee and their representatives if allowed by the liquidator under rule 4.169.

(k) Remuneration of anyone employed by the liquidator to perform services required or authorised under the Act (rule 4.218(1)(n))

(l) Liquidator remuneration up to that payable to the official receiver (rule 4.218(1)(n))
Liquidators are permitted to pay themselves remuneration up to the amount that is payable to the official receiver under the general regulations (*Tony Rowse N M C Ltd* [1996] 2 BCLC 225; [1996] BCC 196).

(m) The balance of the liquidator's remuneration (rule 4.218(1)(q))
If a liquidator pays the expenses of the winding up and does not have sufficient funds to pay himself or herself remuneration, the liquidator may request the creditors and members to establish a fund for the payment of the remuneration (*Tony Rowse NMC Ltd*).

Where a liquidator realises property which is subject to security, that liquidator is entitled to deduct, from the proceeds of the sale of the property and to be delivered to the secured creditor, that portion of his or her remuneration relating to the sale of the security (*Re Universal Distributing Co Ltd (in liq)* (1933) 48 CLR 171 (HC of Aust)).

28.4.1.2 *Preferential debts*[29]

What is discussed here applies equally to bankruptcy. There are some matters that are likely to apply in bankruptcies and not in liquidations and they will be obvious from the content.

---

[29] For further discussion, especially concerning the policy behind the provision of priority and some of the issues surrounding the granting of priority, see, for example, M. Shanker, 'The Worthier Creditors (and a cheer for the King)' (1975–76) 1 *Canadian Business Law Journal* 341; R.M. Goode, 'The Death of Insolvency Law' (1980) 1 Co Law 123; S. Cantlie, 'Preferred Priority in Bankruptcy' in J. Ziegel, *Current Developments in International and Comparative Corporate Insolvency Law*, Oxford: Clarendon Press 1994 at 438; J. Garrido, 'The Distributional Question in Insolvency: Comparative Aspects' (1995) 4 IIR 25; A. Keay and P. Walton, 'The Preferential Debts' Regime in Liquidation Law: In the Public Interest?' (1999) 3 Cfi LR 84.

(a) The priority scheme

Those debts that are able to be categorised as preferential debts are set out in section 386 and Schedule 6 of the Insolvency Act.[30] They apply to individual and corporate insolvencies, but the critical ones are bankruptcy and liquidation and we will limit our discussion to those administrations.

These debts are paid in priority to all other debts (section 175(1)), including, where we have an insolvent company, those owed to secured creditors who hold floating charges (section 175(2)(b)). Also, where goods or effects of the company have been distrained within three months of the date of the winding-up order, the goods and effects or the proceeds from their sale are the subject of a charge to the preferential debts (section 176(2)). If a person surrenders goods or effects or a payment relating to the sale of goods and effects of the company, that person ranks in respect of the amount received by the liquidator by way of the proceeds of sale of the goods or effects or the amount of any payment made to the company, as a preferential creditor, although his or her entitlement is limited to the remainder of the company's property (section 176(3)).[31]

Importantly, the date on which preferential debts are determined is known as the 'relevant date' and is defined in section 387. The date will differ depending upon the circumstances. It will generally be the date of the winding-up order for compulsory liquidation (section 387(3)(b)), the date of the passing of the winding-up resolution for voluntary liquidation (section 387(3)(c)) and the date of the bankruptcy order for bankruptcy (section 387(6)(b)).

In very broad terms, the Act contains the following preferential debts (which are divided into several categories):[32]

Category 1 – Inland Revenue Debts

(1) PAYE income tax deductions made from emoluments paid during the period of 12 months prior to the relevant date.[33]

Category 2 – Customs and Excise Debts

(2) Unpaid VAT for the six months prior to the relevant date.[34]
(3) Unpaid car tax, general betting duty, bingo duty, certain pool betting duty, gaming licence duty that became due in the 12 months prior to the relevant date.[35]

---

[30] For a discussion of the history behind preferential debts and the development of the law, see A. Keay and P. Walton, 'The Preferential Debts' Regime in Liquidation Law: In the Public Interest?' (1999) 3 Cfi LR 84 at 86–91.

[31] A. Keay, *McPherson's Law of Company Liquidation* at 735.

[32] Note that the Enterprise Act provides for changes to the regime when it begins to operate.

[33] Schedule 6, paras 1 and 2. The deductions referred to are those which the company would have been liable to make pursuant to section 203 of the Income and Corporations Taxes Act 1988.

[34] Schedule 6, para 3.

[35] Schedule 6, paras 4 and 5.

(4) Insurance premium tax referable to the six months prior to the relevant date.[36]

(5) Landfill tax referable to the six months prior to the relevant date.[37]

(6) Beer duty that became due in the six months prior to the relevant date.[38]

(7) Lottery duty that which became due in the 12 months prior to the relevant date.[39]

(8) Air passenger duty that became due in the six months prior to the relevant date.[40]

Category 3 – Social Security Contributions

(9) Unpaid social security contributions for the period of 12 months prior to the relevant date.[41]

Category 4 – Contributions to Occupational Pension Schemes

(10) Any sums in relation to occupational pension schemes.[42]

Category 5 – Employee Benefits

(11) Remuneration[43] of employees for up to four months prior to the relevant date subject currently to a maximum payment of £800.[44]

(12) Any amount of employees' holiday pay accrued in respect of any employment prior to the relevant date.[45]

(13) Any sum loaned and used for the specific purpose of paying employees' remuneration.[46]

Category 6 – Levies on Coal And Steel Production

(14) Levies on coal and steel production.[47]

As far as employees are concerned, there is a separate statutory scheme which provides for their protection when their employers are unable or unwilling to meet certain of their liabilities. The scheme operates in such a way that payments are made under this scheme to employees, by the

---

[36] Schedule 6, para.3A; introduced by Schedule 7, para 2 Finance Act 1994.

[37] Schedule 6, para 3B introduced by section 60 and Schedule 5, para 12(1) Finance Act 1996.

[38] Schedule 6, para 5A; introduced by Schedule 2, para 22 Finance Act 1991.

[39] Schedule 6, para 5B; introduced by section 36(2) Finance Act 1993.

[40] Schedule 6, para 5C; introduced by Schedule 7, para 13(1) Finance Act 1994.

[41] Schedule 6, paras 6 and 7. If there is more than one year's amount owing the Commissioners are able to choose any of the year's assessment for priority: *In re Pratt* [1951] Ch. 225.

[42] Schedule 6 para 8.

[43] A term defined widely in Schedule 6, para. 13.

[44] Schedule 6 para 9; the £800 figure is fixed by the Insolvency Proceedings (Monetary Limits) Order 1986 (SI 1986/1996) Article 4.

[45] Schedule 6 para 10.

[46] Schedule 6 para 11.

[47] Schedule 6 para 15A; introduced by the Insolvency (ECSC Levy Debts) Regulations 1987 (SI 1987 2093).

Secretary of State out of the National Insurance Fund under the Employment Rights Act 1996. The Secretary of State is then able to step into the shoes of the employees and take over their preferential rights to the extent that the payments made are in respect of the insolvent employers' liabilities which have preferential status under the Insolvency Act.

If a guarantor of a company debt which would have been preferential if the guarantor refrained from paying it, discharges the debt, that guarantor is able, like the Secretary of State, when making payments out of the National Insurance Fund under the Employment Rights Act 1996, to be subrogated to the rights which would be given to the original creditor. The upshot is that the guarantor is indemnified in the liquidation as a preferential creditor for the amount paid (*Re Lamplugh Iron Ore Co Ltd* [1927] 1 Ch 308). An example of this is where money is advanced to the company so that employees of the company may be paid remuneration or holiday pay.[48] The lender would be able to be subrogated to the rights of the relevant employees.

If the company's property is not sufficient to pay out the creditors who can claim as preferred creditors in full, all preferential debts rank equally between themselves and each must suffer equal abatement (section 175(2)(a)). The consequence is that all preferential debts are equal. So, if there was £30,000 available after payment of the winding-up expenses and the total amount owed to preferential creditors is £60,000, each preferential creditor will be paid 50 pence for every pound that is owed to that creditor. In that scenario, the ordinary unsecured creditors will, of course, receive nothing. Unfortunately, this is only too common an occurrence.

(b) The abolition of Crown priority
Returning to the actual categories of preferential creditors, the most important preferential debts, certainly in terms of frequently occurring and value, are those owed to employees, namely Category 5. We will consider the employees in a moment. First, it is appropriate to mention that, until the enactment of the Enterprise Act 2002, there was one other major category of preferential creditor, namely the Crown. The main claims made by the Crown were in relation to unpaid tax or unpaid VAT. The argument in favour of the priority for unremitted tax deductions and VAT payments are concerned, is that it would be unfair not to allow a preference because the debtor is acting as a tax collector and it would be inequitable if the deductions and payments increased the amount available to the unsecured creditors.[49] Across the world revenue authorities have tended to be granted some significant priority in the insolvency of companies and persons. However, in recent years a number of jurisdictions, such as Germany, Austria and Australia, have either abolished or severely

---

[48] Schedule 6, para 11.
[49] Cork Report at para 1418.

reduced the advantages that such authorities have enjoyed. The UK has now followed suit,[50] with the consequence that the Crown is now only able to claim in any insolvency administration as an ordinary unsecured creditor.

Section 251(1) of the Enterprise Act provides that the following debts will cease to have preferential status: debts to the Inland Revenue; debts due to Customs and Excise (this will include unpaid VAT); and social security contributions.

(c) Employee priority

The justification for granting priority status in winding up to the wage claims of employees has been generally stronger on moral and socio-political grounds and has been stated to be that:

> [S]alaries and wages are generally needed for, and generally expended in, the support and maintenance of the persons earning them, their wives and families and others dependent on them, and so may well be given priority, for a short period, over debts due to other creditors in the ordinary course of business and generally more nearly related to the profit and loss account of the creditor than his sustenance or that of those dependant upon him.
> (*Re Parkin Elevator Co* (1916) 41 DLR 123 at 125 per Meredith CJCP).

Not unreasonably, the employee has been regarded as being in a weak bargaining position compared to other creditors and investors. The employee priority is to 'ease the financial hardship caused to a relatively poor and defenceless section of the community by the insolvency of their employer.'[51] Due to understandable ignorance, most employees, do not, when negotiating an employment contract, think about their employer becoming insolvent and do not consequently consider requiring some form of protection should the employer fall into insolvency. The pervasive view has been that the effect of insolvency on employees will be far more devastating for employees compared with ordinary creditors, on the basis that wages are likely to be the only source of income for an employee while other creditors are able to diversify their risk and are likely to have other sources of income. However, this view fails to appreciate the fact that there are in today's world many trade creditors, such as sub-contractors providing labour, who are not in a very different position from employees. Significant numbers of people who have historically been employees have had to become sub-contractors to be able to obtain work, because employers have wished to reduce their employed labour force. These sub-contractors often work for one company and have little control over whether they work on particular projects.[52]

---

[50] For an argument against Crown priority, see A. Keay and P. Walton, 'The Preferential Debts' Regime in Liquidation Law: In the Public Interest?' (1999) 3 Cfi LR 84.

[51] Cork Report at para 1428.

[52] For further discussion along these lines, see A. Keay and P. Walton, 'The Preferential Debts' Regime in Liquidation Law: In the Public Interest?' (1999) 3 Cfi LR 84 at 99–101.

Under the preferential scheme in the Act, employees are able to claim the following:

- remuneration in respect of the whole or any part of the four months before the relevant date, not exceeding the prescribed amount (at present this is £800);[53]
- accrued holiday pay for the period of employment before the relevant date. This is payable to former employees and those whose employment was terminated at or after the relevant date;[54]
- any amount which is ordered to be paid by the company under the Reserve Forces (Safeguard of Employment) Act 1985 and it is ordered in respect of a default by the company in respect of the employee's obligations under the said Act, not exceeding the prescribed sum (at present it is £800).[55]

For a person to be able to claim priority as an employee, he or she must be employed under a contract of service with the company (*Re General Radio Co Ltd* [1929] WN 172), therefore excluding those who may be categorised as independent contractors (*Re CW &AL Hughes Ltd* [1966] 1 WLR 1369). Often, establishing whether a person is an employee or not is a difficult question. A substantial amount will depend upon the contract under which the claimant works. Also of relevance is the nature of the company's business and to the actual services performed in the past by the claimant.[56]

In recent years there has been a significant amount of case law that has considered the issue and it has been decided that in assessing whether a person is or is not an employee all relevant factors must be taken into account and one must balance those factors suggesting employment against those suggesting that the claimant is not an employee (*Ivey v Secretary of State for Employment* ([1997] BCC 145 at 146). According to *Ivey* the following questions must be considered:

- Is the person under the control of another?
- Is the person an integral part of another's organisation?
- Is the person in business on his or her own account?
- What is the economic reality between the person and the alleged employer?
- Is there mutuality of obligation between the person and the alleged employer?
- What are the respective bargaining powers of the person and the alleged employer?

---

[53] Schedule 6, para 9(b); Insolvency Proceedings (Monetary Limits) Order 1986 (SI 1986/1996).

[54] Schedule 6, para 10.

[55] Schedule 6, para 12; Insolvency Proceedings (Monetary Limits) Order 1986 (SI 1986/1996).

[56] See *Re London Casino Ltd* (1942) 167 LT 66; *Re Benalpha Products Ltd* (1946) 115 LJ Ch 193.

In *Montgomery v Johnson Underwood Ltd* (*The Times*, 9 March 2001), the Court of Appeal indicated that for one to be an employee of another the former must be under some control by the latter and that, in relation to the relevant parties, there was mutual obligation.

What has caused particular problems is whether a director of the company can also be regarded as an employee.[57] The general view is that non-executive directors cannot be regarded as employees on the basis that they are performing services for the company on their own account. In dealing with executive directors the above factors, mentioned in *Ivey*, must be taken into account. It was indicated by the Court of Appeal in *Secretary of State for Employment v Bottrill* ([1999] BCC 177) that the fact that a director holds a controlling interest in the company was only one factor in the equation, albeit probably a significant factor in deciding that the director was not an employee for the purposes of the Act (at 195).[58]

What an employee can claim by way of a priority includes wages or salary (payable for what is known as time or piece work, or earned wholly or partly by way of commission, in relation to services rendered to the company in the relevant period), holiday pay and sick pay. Also, remuneration includes any of following where it occurs in the relevant period:

- a guarantee payment under Part III of the Employment Rights Act 1996;
- any payment for time off under section 53 (to look for work or arrange training) or section 56 (ante-natal care) of the Employment Rights Act or under section 169 of the Trade Union and Labour Relations (Consolidation) Act 1992 (time off for doing union duties);
- remuneration on suspension on medical grounds or on maternity grounds under Part VII of the Employment Rights Act; or
- remuneration under a protective award under section 189 of the Trade Union and Labour Relations (Consolidation) Act 1992 (redundancy and dismissal compensation).[59]

Excluded from remuneration is any amount paid in lieu of proper notice on termination of an employee's employment under the terms of an industrial award (*Re Grabowski v Allert* (1988) 6 ACLC 545 at 551).

---

[57] For a more detailed examination, see A. Keay, *McPherson's Law of Company Liquidation* at 740–2.

[58] See *Brooks v Secretary of State for Employment* [1999] BCC 232 where the directors were controlling owners of the company and deemed not to be employees. Also, see *Connolly v Sellers Arenascence Ltd*, *The Times*, February 21, 2001.

[59] Schedule 6, para 13(2).

28.4.1.3 *Unsecured debts*

This is the category into which most creditors fall. It is a sad fact of life that these creditors receive little or nothing in many bankruptcies and liquidations.

The category refers to all debts not granted some preference or covered by security, and it does not matter at what time, before winding up, the debt was incurred. Typically, in bankruptcy and liquidation, there are insufficient funds to pay all of the unsecured creditors, so the debts abate rateably (rule 4.181 (liquidations, section 328(3) (bankruptcy)). The office-holder will calculate what amount each creditor will receive, after deciding what rate is to be applied to the debts and it will be expressed as so many pence in the pound. For example, the office-holder may find that he or she can pay 5 p in the £, that is everyone receives 5 per cent of what they are owed.

Unsecured creditors in insolvent companies have been given some help by the Enterprise Act 2002. That legislation states (section 252) that a new section 176A will be introduced into the Insolvency Act. That section provides that if there is a floating charge over company property and the company has entered liquidation, administration, provisional liquidation or receivership (section 176A(1)), then the office-holder is to make a prescribed part of the company's net property (the amount of a company's property which would, but for section 176A, be available for the satisfaction of claims of holders of debentures secured by floating charges (section 176A(6)) available for the satisfaction of unsecured debts (section 176A(2)). This requirement, known as 'top-slicing', was raised first by the Cork Report in 1982. That Report advocated the setting up of 'The Ten Per Cent Fund', namely 10 per cent of the property covered by the charge would be set aside for unsecured creditors.[60] Section 176A is an attempt to provide benefits to unsecured creditors as a consequence of the abolition of the Crown preference. If such a provision was not introduced then it is likely that in many cases floating chargeholders would be the only ones to be advantaged by the abolition.

The setting aside of funds for the unsecured creditors is not to take place where the company's net property is less than the prescribed minimum and the office-holder thinks that the cost of making a distribution would be disproportionate to the benefits (section 176A(3)). The prescribed amount will be set by Regulation.

28.4.1.4 *Post-liquidation interest on debts*

Next, if any funds remain, after paying out the unsecured creditors, interest on all debts will be paid in relation to the periods that they have been outstanding since the company entered winding up (section

---

[60] See para 1540ff.

189(2), bankruptcy – section 328(4)). The rate to be paid is the 'official rate' set out in section 189(4) (bankruptcy – section 328(5)). All interest ranks equally and no regard is to be paid to the ranking given to the debt on which the interest is based (section 189(3), bankruptcy – section 328(4)).

28.4.1.5 *Deferred debts*

There are also types of debts that are categorised as deferred debts, which are payable out of the assets remaining only after the ordinary unpreferred, unsecured debts have been satisfied in full. These comprise, *inter alia*:

- certain debts owing to a partner of the company;
- certain debts which are owing to a member of the company in his or her character as such;
- any amount for which the company is liable where it fails to redeem its own shares or carries through with an agreement to purchase its own shares before the commencement of winding up;[61]
- debts owed to persons liable for fraudulent or wrongful trading;[62]
- interest accrued on debts since liquidation (section 189(2));
- miscellaneous claims under statute (see rule 12.3(2A)).

28.4.2 *Bankruptcy*[63]

The order of distribution in bankruptcy, as one might expect, is not so complicated as it is often in liquidation. The order of distribution provided for in the Act, following permitting secured creditors to realise their security for their benefit is, through a combination of sections 328(1), (2), (3), (4), 386, Schedule 6, and rule 6.224:

- costs and expenses of bankruptcy (section 328(2), rule 6.224);
- pre-preferential debts;
- preferential debts (section 328(1));
- general body of ordinary unsecured creditors (section 328(3));
- post-bankruptcy interest on debts (section 328(4));
- deferred creditors (section 329);
- any surplus, after the payment in full of the debts of creditors together with interest, goes to the bankrupt (section 330(5)).

---

[61] See section 178(3)–(6) of the Companies Act 1985.
[62] See section 125 of the Act.
[63] Also, see 336–9.

It should be noted that in a few unusual cases some creditors will rank before the preferential debts. These are:

● Articled clerks and apprentices who worked with the bankrupt are entitled to recover part of any amount paid to the bankrupt in relation to the articles or apprenticeship if either the bankrupt, on the one hand, or the articled clerk or apprentice, on the other hand, gives notice to the trustee that the articles or apprenticeship is to terminate (section 348).
● A claim for trustee's expenses under a deed of arrangement and avoided as a consequence of the bankruptcy of the debtor (Deeds of Arrangement Act 1914, section 21).
● Where a bankrupt was an officer of a Friendly Society the trustees of the Society are ranked before the preferential debts (Friendly Societies Act 1974, section 59).
● A claim by a trustee savings bank where the bankrupt was an officer of the bank and he or she held, by virtue of his or her office, some of the bank's money (Trustee Savings Bank Act 1969, section 72).
● Reasonable funeral and administration expenses where the bankrupt is deceased (Administration of Insolvent Estates of Deceased Persons Order 1986, Article 4(2)).

That which has been discussed in the context of liquidation in relation to preferential debts, the unsecured creditors and interest payable on debts in relation to the period following a company entering winding up is equally applicable to bankruptcy. What needs to be considered now is the costs of bankruptcy and deferred debts.

28.4.2.1 *Costs and expenses of bankruptcy*

There has been far more judicial opinion on liquidation expenses compared with bankruptcy expenses and much of what has been said in relation to the former apply equally to the latter. A few comments are worthwhile. The following are the primary expenses (not exhaustive):

(a) Expenses properly chargeable or incurred by the official receiver or the trustee in preserving, realising or getting in the bankrupt's assets (rule 6.224(1)(a)).
(b) Other expenses incurred or disbursements made by the official receiver (rule 6.224(1)(b)).
(c) Remuneration payable to the official receiver under the General Regulations (rule 6.224(1)(c)).
(d) The remuneration of any interim receiver (rule 6.224(1)(f)).
(e) The costs of the petitioner and any person appearing on the petition and allowed costs by the court (rule 6.224(1)(h)).
(f) Any necessary disbursements incurred by the trustee in the course of the administration (rule 6.224(1)(m)).

(g) Remuneration payable to any person employed by the trustee to perform services for the estate (rule 6.224(1)(n)).

(h) Remuneration of the trustee (rule 6.224(1)(o)).

The remuneration that can be claimed is up to the limit of what is payable to the official receiver under general regulations.

(i) The balance of any amount to the trustee (rule 6.224(1)(q)).

This covers what is left owing over and above what would be payable on the official receiver scale and referred to in the previous point.

28.4.2.2 *Deferred debts*

This category has traditionally been directed at those who have been associated with the insolvent. Section 329 requires debts owed in relation to credit provided by a person (and interest thereon) who was the spouse of a bankrupt at the commencement of bankruptcy to be ranked after the unsecured creditors. In addition, anyone who lends money to a person who is engaging in or about to engage in a business and the lender is to receive a rate of interest dependent on profits or a share of the profits, then if the borrower goes bankrupt the lender's debt is a deferred debt.[64] In a similar position are those who either sell the goodwill in a business to a person who goes bankrupt in consideration for a percentage of the business's profits, or lend money to a person who enters bankruptcy as part of a joint venture arrangement (*Re Meade* [1951] Ch 774 at 784).

28.5 Statutory subrogation

Subrogation involves the substituting of one party's rights for the rights of another. Mention has already been made of a form of subrogation in relation to employee benefits. We have discussed the fact that employees are given, in respect of their employment benefits, a priority in winding up or bankruptcy by section 386 and Schedule 6. Then paragraph 11 of Schedule 6 provides a statutory right of subrogation to that priority to a company or person (usually banking institutions) who, prior to winding up or bankruptcy, advances money to the company for the purpose of paying debts of this kind. If the money advanced is used to pay employees

---

[64] Partnership Act 1890, section 2(3)(d)); *Re Beale* (1876) 4 Ch D 246 (CA); *Re Grason* (1879) 12 Ch D 366 (CA).

on account of priority debts, such as their wages, the company or person making the advance is entitled to claim to be a preferential creditor in place of the employees (*Re Primrose (Builders) Ltd* [1950] Ch 561; *Re Rampgill Mill Ltd* [1967] 1 Ch 1138).[65]

The company or person making the advance must establish that the money was both advanced and actually used for the purpose of paying a debt which would by virtue of paragraphs 9 and/or 10 in Schedule 6 have enjoyed priority in winding up. Where not all of the advance was used to pay employees priority type payments, the company or person who advanced the funds is only entitled to claim as a preferential creditor to the extent that the money was paid to employees who would have been entitled to be considered preferential creditors if they had not be paid.

Earlier in the chapter,[66] mention was made of a separate statutory scheme that was introduced in order to protect employees whose employer has become insolvent and unable to meet its liabilities to its workers. Employees are paid their rightful benefits by the Secretary of State from the National Insurance Fund under the Employment Rights Act 1996. Where this occurs, the Secretary of State may, under section 189 of that Act, be subrogated to the employees' preferential rights to the extent that the payments made are in respect of the insolvent employers' liabilities which have preferential status under the Insolvency Act. The benefits that are payable under section 184(1)(a) of the Employment Rights Act are: up to eight weeks arrears of pay, wages during the statutory minimum notice period;[67] up to six weeks holiday pay; and a basic award for unfair dismissal.[68] Where payments are to be calculated by reference to weekly pay the maximum amount that can be used in the calculation is £250.[69]

This scheme is beneficial to employees in three respects. First, they will be paid more quickly than by a trustee, administrator or liquidator. Second, the payments are likely to be more than would be received under the Act, as the financial limits are potentially higher e.g., 8 × £250 is more than £800 (the amount that is payable as a priority under the Act). Third, certain payments such as a basic award for unfair dismissal do not attract preferential status under the Act.

There are others who may have a statutory approved subrogated claim against insolvent companies, but this does not occur regularly. Some of the claims are:

---

[65] The lender should be entitled to this gross amount advanced for the purposes of paying wages etc. even if the amounts are deducted from the gross amount in order to pay the employees' income tax.

[66] Above at 407–8.

[67] As laid down in section 86 of the Employment Rights Act 1996.

[68] Under section 167 of the Employment Rights Act redundancy payments may in certain circumstances also be made by the Secretary of State out of the National Insurance Fund.

[69] Employment Rights (Increase of Limits) Order (SI 2002/10).

- where the company is an insurance company the Policyholders' Protection Board may be so entitled under the Policyholders' Protection Act 1975;
- where the company is an authorised institution or former authorised institution under the Banking Act 1987, the Deposit Protection Board may have a claim;
- where the company is an insurance company a third party claimant may have a claim under the terms of the Third Party (Rights Against Insurers) Act 1930.

28.6 Payment of dividends

28.6.1 *General*

When an office-holder has an accumulation of funds that do not need to be employed in running the insolvency administration, the office-holder will consider the distribution of some or all of the funds. The share in the funds that is paid to creditors is known as a dividend.

Section 324 provides that a trustee in bankruptcy is duty-bound to declare and distribute dividends to creditors when he or she has sufficient funds and after retaining adequate funds to cover bankruptcy expenses. There is no equivalent provision applying to liquidations, but the practice is certainly the same or else liquidations would be unnecessarily protracted. Naturally it is important that creditors should receive their money as soon as possible. Once a point is reached where the office-holder feels that some return to the creditors may be safely made it is usual for an interim dividend to be declared and paid to all of those who have proved their debts.[70] It must not be forgotten that all preferred creditors must, to the extent that the law requires and the assets permit, be paid in priority to any other debts or liabilities. The office-holder must ensure that sufficient funds are retained to cover further expenses of liquidation or bankruptcy and any disputed claims against the estate of the insolvent.

When paying dividends the ordinary unsecured creditors, they must be paid *pari passu*, which means that a dividend must be struck and each creditor paid an equal proportion of the amount owing to him or her.

---

[70] See rule 4.180(1). For the actual process of payment, see Insolvency Regulations 1994 (SI 1994/2507).

28.6.2 *Entitlement to payment*

As a general rule, all creditors are entitled to be paid a dividend if there are sufficient assets. But two rules might affect this general rule. First, there is the rule that in compulsory winding up a creditor may be excluded from the benefit of any distribution made before his or her debt was proved (having a claim accepted by the liquidator). Second, we have the general equitable principle, known as the rule in *Cherry v Boultbee*. Essentially this rule[71] provides that anyone who is entitled to share in a fund and is also bound to contribute to it, must contribute before he or she is qualified to take the share to which he or she is entitled. This principle is similar to, but wider than, set-off. It operates in cases where debts are not capable of being set off. For instance,[72] X Ltd and Y Ltd are both insolvent companies that are in liquidation. X is both the creditor and the debtor of Y and vice versa. X's debt to Y is incapable of being set-off because it represents a liability for unpaid calls (*Re Auriferous Properties Ltd (No. 2)* [1898] 2 Ch 428) or damages for misfeasance (*Re Rhodesia Goldfields Ltd* [1910] 1 Ch 239; *Re Leeds & Hanley Theatre of Varieties Ltd* [1904] 2 Ch 45) or some other such liability, such as a preference under section 239. In this type of case neither X nor Y's liquidator are able, because of the rule in *Cherry v Boultbee*, to claim a dividend until it has paid the full amount that it owed to the other company's liquidator first.

28.6.3 *Procedure for payment*

The Insolvency Rules contain detailed provisions describing the procedure to be followed in making distributions from the funds collected by office-holders. Chapter 11 of the Rules applies to distributions made in both winding up and bankruptcy. The major steps of the payment process are as follows: giving notice of an intention to declare and distribute a dividend (rule 4.180(1) (liquidation), section 324(1) (bankruptcy)); notice of the intended dividend is given to all creditors whose address is known to the office-holder and who have not proved their debt (rule 11.2(1)) and the notice must state an intention to declare a dividend within four months of the notice (rule 11.2(3)). If the office-holder is announcing a first dividend, notice must be given of the intended dividend by public advertisement (rule 11.2(1A)). Any notice must specify a date up to which proofs (the document in which the creditor makes the claim in the winding up) may be lodged (rule 11.2(2)). The date is the same for all creditors and must not be less than 21 days from the date of the notice.

---

[71] See *Cherry v Boultbee* (1839) 4 My & Cr 442; 41 ER 171.
[72] This example is based on A. Keay, *McPherson's Law of Company Liquidation* at 753.

During the four-month period mentioned in rule 11.2(3), an appeal may be initiated concerning the office-holder's decision on a proof. If an appeal is initiated, the office-holder may postpone or cancel a dividend (rule 11.4). If there is no appeal, the office-holder shall within the four months proceed to declare the dividend of which notice has been given (rule 11.5(1)). But if there is an appeal pending in relation to the office-holder's decision concerning any proof, no declaration of dividend is to take place except with the leave of the court (rule 11.5(2)).

The office-holder must give notice of the declaration of dividend to all of the creditors whose debts and claims have been proved (section 324(3), rule 11.6(1)).[73] The notice is to include the following particulars:

- amounts realised from the sale of assets;
- payments made in the winding up;
- any provision for unsettled claims and what funds (if any) are retained for particular purposes;
- the total amount to be distributed and the rate of the dividend;
- whether and if so when, any further dividend is expected to be declared (rule 4.186(2), section 330(2) and rule 11.6(2)).

If the liquidator finds that he or she is not able to declare a dividend or any further dividend, the notice shall contain information as to the fact:

- that no funds have been realised;
- funds realised have already been distributed or used or allocated for defraying the expenses of the liquidation or bankruptcy (rule 11.7).

Those creditors whose proofs are increased by court decisions are not entitled to disturb the distribution of a dividend declared before the date on which their proof was increased (rule 11.8(1)). Nevertheless, they are entitled to be paid, out of any available money for the time being in the office-holder's hands, dividends that were not paid to the creditors and they are entitled to be paid these amounts before funds are applied to pay any further dividends (rule 11.8(1), (2)). Where, after a creditor's proof has been admitted, the proof is either withdrawn by the creditor or expunged by decision of the office-holder or a court, or the amount of it is reduced, that creditor must repay the amount overpaid by way of dividend (rule 11.8(3)).

Office-holders must ensure that they take note of all claims of which they are cognisant, for if they ignore them they may be held personally liable to the relevant creditors (*Re Armstrong-Whitworth Securities Co* [1947] Ch 678).

---

[73] See Chapter 34 for a discussion of proving debts.

28.6.4 *Final dividend*

The final payment or distribution should occur when the office-holder has realised all of the insolvent's assets or so much of them as can, in his or her opinion, be realised without needlessly protracting the liquidation (rule 4.186(1)) or bankruptcy (section 330(1)). The office-holder must give notice in accordance with Part 11 of the Rules, in the manner outlined earlier. In the notice the office-holder will state either that it is intended to declare a final dividend or that no dividend or further dividend will be declared (*Re Armstrong-Whitworth Securities Co*). In cases where a dividend is to be declared, the notice will include the matters set out above.

Where no dividend is to be declared, or no further dividend is to be declared, the notice is to contain a statement to the effect that:

- no funds have been realised;
- the funds realised have already been distributed or used or allocated for defraying the expenses of the liquidation or bankruptcy (rule 11(7)).

In the notice, the office-holder will require all claims against the insolvent estate to be established by a specified date (rule 4.186(2) (liquidation), section 330(2) (bankruptcy)). After the specified date, the office-holder must defray any outstanding expenses of the liquidation or bankruptcy out of the insolvent's assets and if intending to declare a final dividend, declare and distribute the dividend without regard for the claim of anyone who has not proved the claim (rule 4.186(3) (liquidation), section 330(4) (bankruptcy)). A court is able to postpone the date specified in the notice on the application of any person (rule 4.186(4) (liquidation), section 330(3) (bankruptcy)).

References

Bailey, E., Groves, H. and Smith, C., *Corporate Insolvency Law and Practice*, 2nd edn, London: Butterworths (2001).

Berry, C., Bailey, E. and Schaw-Miller, S., *Personal Insolvency Law – Law and Practice*, 3rd edn, London: Butterworths (2001).

Bompas, G., *Butterworths Practical Insolvency*, Ch VI, London: Butterworths (1999).

Cantlie, S., 'Preferred Priority in Bankruptcy' in J. Ziegel, *Current Developments in International and Comparative Corporate Insolvency Law*, Oxford: Clarendon Press(1994) at 438.

Cook, C., 'Wrongful Trading – Is it a Real Threat to Directors or a Paper Tiger?' [1999] *Insolvency Lawyer* 99.

Ferran, E., *Company Law and Corporate Finance*, Oxford: Oxford University Press (1999).

Finch, V., 'Directors' Duties: Insolvency and the Unsecured Creditor' in A. Clarke (ed.), *Current Issues in Insolvency Law*, London: Stevens, (1991).

Finch, V., *Corporate Insolvency Law: Perspectives and Principles*, Cambridge: Cambridge University Press (2002).

Fletcher, I.F., *The Law of Insolvency*, 3rd edn, London: Sweet & Maxwell (2002).

Garrido, J., 'The Distributional Question in Insolvency: Comparative Aspects' (1995) 4 *International Insolvency Review* 25.

Goode, R.M., 'The Death of Insolvency Law' (1980) 1 Co Law 123.

Goode, R.M., *The Principles of Corporate Insolvency Law*, 2nd edn, London: Sweet & Maxwell (1997).

Hamilton, G., 'Aspects of Official Liquidators' Personal Liability for Costs of Litigation' (1989) 7 *Company & Securities Law Journal* 301.

Jackson, T.H., *The Logic and Limits of Bankruptcy Law*, Cambridge: Harvard University Press (1986).

Jackson, T.H. and Kronman, A., 'Voidable Preferences and Protection of the Expectation Interest (1976) 60 *Minnesota Law Review* 971.

Johnston, B., 'Contractual Debt Subordination and Legislative Reform' [1991] JBL 225.

Keay, A., 'Gone Fishing! Is it Legitimate in an Examination under section 597 of the Corporations Law?' (1991) 9 *Company & Securities Law Journal* 70.

Keay, A., 'The Parameters of Bankruptcy Examinations' (1994) 22 *Australian Business Law Review* 75.

Keay Andrew, R., *McPherson's Law of Company Liquidation*, London: Sweet & Maxwell (2001).

Keay, A., 'Pursuing the Resolution of the Funding Problem in Insolvency Litigation' [2002] *Insolvency Lawyer* 90.

Keay, A. and de Prez, P., 'Insolvency and Environmental Principles: A Case Study in a Conflict of Public Interests' (2001) 3 *Environmental Law Review* 90.

Keay, A. and Walton, P., 'The Preferential Debts' Regime in Liquidation Law: In the Public Interest?' (1999) 3 *Company Financial and Insolvency Law Review* 84.

Lightman, G. and Moss, G., *The Law of Receivers and Administrators of Companies*, 3rd edn, London: Sweet & Maxwell (2000).

McCoid, J., 'Bankruptcy Preferences and Efficiency: An Expression of Doubt' (1981) 67 *Virginia Law Review* 247.

McCormack, G., *Proprietary Claims and Insolvency*, London: Sweet & Maxwell (1997).

Milman, D., 'Priority Rights on Corporate Insolvency' in A. Clarke (ed.), *Current Issues in Insolvency Law*, London: Stevens (1991).

Milman, D. and Parry, R., 'Challenging Transactional Integrity on Insolvency: An Evaluation of the New Law' (1997) 48 NILQ 24.

Moss, G., 'Getting at the Truth – s 236 Examinations' (1998) 11 *Insolvency Intelligence* 41.

Moss, G. and Segal, N., 'Insolvency Proceedings: Contract and Financing' (1997) 1 *Company Financial and Insolvency Law Review* 1.

Mourell, M. and Willoughby, J., 'Disclaimers of Onerous Property under section 568 of the Corporations Law' (1994) 4 *Australian Journal of Corporation Law* 63.

Parry, R., 'Funding Litigation in Insolvency' (1998) 2 *Company Financial and Insolvency Law Review* 121.

Pennington, R., *Pennington's Corporate Insolvency Law*, 2nd edn, London: Butterworths (1997).

Seligson, C., 'Preferences Under the Bankruptcy Act' (1961) 15 *Vanderbilt Law Review* 115.

Shanker, M., 'The Worthier Creditors (and a cheer for the King)' (1975–76) 1 *Canadian Business Law Journal* 341.

Simmons, M. and Smith, T., 'The Human Rights Act 1998: the practical impact on insolvency' (2000) *Insolvency Law and Practice* 167.

Stallworthy, M., 'The Regulation and Investigation of Commercial Activities in the United Kingdom and the Privilege Against Self-Incrimination' [2000] ICCLR 166.

Trower, W., 'Bringing Human Rights Home to the Insolvency Practitioner' (Part 1) (2000) 13 *Insolvency Intelligence* 41.

Walters, A., 'Forshortening the shadow: maintenance, champerty and the funding of litigation in corporate insolvency' (1996) 17 Co Law 165.

Walters, A., 'Creditor-Funded Litigation in Corporate Insolvency' (1997) 1 *Company Financial and Insolvency Law Review* 126.

Wood, P., *Wood on International Finance: The Law of Subordinated Debt*, London: Sweet & Maxwell (1990).

Ziegel, J., 'Preferences and Priorities in Insolvency Law: Is There a Solution?' (1995) 39 *Saint Louis Law Journal* 793.

Part VII

Creditors

The principle of equality of division among creditors of an insolvent debtor is one of the, if not the most, fundamental principles of insolvency law.[1] It is at the heart of all the collective insolvency procedures, liquidation, bankruptcy, administration and voluntary arrangements. It is necessary to have a collective process before any equal division of assets may be accomplished. The collective nature of these procedures requires that all creditors come inside the system to ensure that individual creditors do not act on their own to reward themselves at the cost of the collective good. Creditors who are quick off the mark in enforcing their rights against a debtor can steal an advantage over other creditors as long as they act before any collective process becomes enforceable against all creditors. The equality principle is an old equitable principle, known as the *pari passu* principle. It is an example of the equitable maxim 'equity is equality'.

The underlying idea of the equality principle is to produce fairness. When a business fails it can affect many people, not just those within the business itself. Many other businesses may rely on trade with the failed business. If those other businesses lose both the steady trade they had before and all the money owed to them by the failed business, those other businesses may fail too. Their failure may have a knock-on effect to others. This phenomenon is commonly referred to as the 'ripple effect'. If all the creditors of the failed business were not treated equally, so that they each had the chance of recouping some of their money, there would be a greater risk that more creditors would fail to survive the collapse of the main debtor's business. The impact of the failed business will be spread among the business's trading partners. The pain will be shared which in theory should allow for more creditors being able to continue to trade.

[1] See e.g., R.M. Goode, *Principles of Corporate Insolvency Law*, 2nd edn, London: Sweet & Maxwell (1997) at 141 and Report of the Insolvency Law Review Committee in *Insolvency Law and Practice* Cmnd 8558 (1982) ('the Cork Report') at para 233.

This is possibly most relevant where creditors are relatively small concerns who do not wield the financial muscle to use influence or threats to extract payments prior to formal insolvency from tardy payers.

Although it sounds like a panacea for all the insolvency woes of the world, the *pari passu* principle is limited in its application. There are many types of creditors who are able to avoid falling in with the general body of unsecured creditors all being treated equally. In this Part of the book we shall look at ways in which certain types of creditor are given rights greater than the average unsecured creditors. We shall be looking at situations which may be viewed as sidestepping or leaping over the *pari passu* principle.

Creditors who have security are treated well by formal insolvency procedures. As long as the security is adequate, secured creditors will nearly always be guaranteed payment even if there is little if anything left for the unsecured creditors. Suppliers to an insolvent business who have contracted upon retention of title terms will generally be able to retrieve the goods supplied if the customer fails to pay. Other creditors will be left to see what their entitlement may be in one of the collective insolvency procedures. As we shall see, landlords have rights peculiar to themselves which may allow them to come out of the insolvency of their tenants in a better condition than other creditors. Judgment creditors who have managed to execute their judgment may have their diligence rewarded by some priority treatment in the judgment debtor's subsequent insolvency. Preferential creditors, whose name accurately depicts their nature, have priority rights over other unsecured creditors.[2] A right to set off debts from a course of dealing with an insolvent can act to soften the blow of the insolvency by leaving the person with the right of set-off in a far better financial position than other unsecured creditors.

The *pari passu* principle is fundamental but it is in practice frequently undermined by different types of creditors' priority rights.

In this Part of the book, references to section numbers or to 'the Act' refer to the Insolvency Act 1986. References to rules or to 'the Rules' are references to the Insolvency Rules 1986 (SI 1986/1925).

---

[2] See A. Keay and P. Walton, 'The Preferential Debts Regime in Liquidation Law: In the Public Interest?' (1999) 3 CfiLR 84.

Chapter 29

Secured Creditors

29.1 Introduction

A secured creditor generally has two rights: a right of action against the property over which he or she has security and a right of action against the debtor. As long as the security is adequate to pay off the creditor, the creditor will normally look to the secured assets for payment. The policy of the insolvency legislation is to give primacy to secured creditors. Where a debtor is insolvent the first to get paid out of the debtor's assets will generally be the secured creditors.

Under the Insolvency Act 1986 ('the Act'), security is defined by section 248 as 'any mortgage, charge, lien or other security'. This definition is taken to mean that the rights the creditor have are proprietary in character. The proprietary interest in the debtor's assets allows the creditor to realise the secured assets to discharge the debtor's obligation to the creditor.

Lightman J in *Razzaq v Pala* ([1998] BCC 66) states that a security interest involves the debtor conferring an interest in his property on the creditor which allows the creditor, following default, to enforce the debt against the property. This right is defeasible upon payment of money. This is consistent with the concepts of mortgages, charges and various types of liens. On the facts of *Razzaq* it did not include a landlord's right to peaceable re-entry as the landlord's right was not in property of the debtor as such and the landlord retained the right to peaceable re-entry despite payment of money.[1]

As mentioned above, if the creditor's security is adequate to cover the amount of money owed, upon default by the debtor, the creditor will usually look for payment out of the secured assets. This may be accomplished by

[1] For a further discussion of the meaning of security see *Bristol Airport plc v Powdrill* [1990] Ch 744.

entering into possession of the secured assets if the creditor is a mortgagee or by the appointment of a receiver to realise the assets in order to pay off the creditor.

Only if the security is inadequate or vulnerable to attack will the creditor consider surrendering the security and try to enforce personal rights against the debtor by, for example, obtaining judgment against the debtor and enforcing that judgment. A security may be vulnerable in a subsequent administration, liquidation or bankruptcy of the debtor as a preference, a transaction at an undervalue or in the case of corporate debtors under section 245 of the Act.

We will now look at the position of secured creditors in the various insolvency procedures under the Act. It is assumed in the following commentary that the creditor's security is valid.

29.2 Liquidation

Liquidation does not generally interfere with the rights of a secured creditor. If it did then it would, in many cases, make the taking of security valueless. One of the main purposes of taking security is to protect the creditor in the event of the debtor's insolvency. It is usually the case that a secured creditor will enforce the security outside of the liquidation. This will commonly be done, where the debtor is a company, by the appointment of a receiver to realise the company's assets and pay off the creditor. In such a situation, the liquidator, who will commonly have been appointed after the company has already entered receivership, will wait in the wings for the receiver to finish the realisation of the secured assets and only thereafter take control of the remaining assets of the company (if any). The enforcement of the creditor's security will usually take place outside of the liquidation and so the liquidator will not usually be involved in the realisation of the secured assets.

A secured creditor cannot retain security and prove for the full amount of the debt owed.[2] A secured creditor is only entitled to prove in a winding up for the whole amount of his or her debt if the creditor surrenders the security which is held. If the creditor realises the security, but it proves inadequate to pay off the whole debt, the creditor may prove for the balance owed, after deducting what was received from the realisation of the security.

---

[2] See e.g., *Moor v Anglo-Italian Bank* (1879) 10 ChD 681.

29.3 Bankruptcy

The position of a secured creditor in bankruptcy is essentially the same as in liquidation. The Act does not interfere with the secured creditor's right to enforce the security and again such enforcement will usually take place outside the trustee in bankruptcy's administration of the estate. The creditor again will be able to prove in the bankruptcy for any shortfall from the realisation of the security.

29.4 Administrative receivership

As we have seen, in the common instance of a secured creditor taking a combined fixed and floating charge over a company's undertaking, when the company defaults, the creditor will often wish to appoint an administrative receiver to realise the creditor's security (this possibility will disappear for new debentures entered into after the commencement of the Enterprise Act 2002).[3] The administrative receiver's primary function is to sell off enough of the secured assets to enable the security holder to be paid out.

Any sale of the secured assets by the administrative receiver takes effect subject to the debenture under which the receiver is appointed and any other incumbrances. The receiver cannot transfer any greater right in the assets than the company has. In order that the purchaser takes free from the debenture under which the receiver was appointed and other incumbrances, either a deed of release will be necessary or the debenture holder and the other incumbrancers will need to be made a party to the sale. As an alternative to this, the debenture holder can sell as mortgagee and appoint the receiver as its agent for that purpose. This overrides junior incumbrances whose rights attach to any surplus proceeds.[4]

It is possible, under section 43 of the Act, for an administrative receiver to sell assets subject to prior or equal ranking securities, but the approval of the court is necessary. This power may be useful to a receiver who is trying to sell the company's business as a going concern where certain important assets of the company, such as a piece of land or machinery, are subject to a prior security. In order for the court to allow the sale it must be satisfied that it would promote a more advantageous realisation of the company assets than would otherwise be possible. A condition of the court order will be that the proceeds of sale are used to pay off the security

---

[3] See Chapter 6.

[4] If the company enters liquidation only the second sale mechanism is possible as the administrative receiver will no longer be agent of the company under section 44.

holder first. If the disposal does not achieve a sum which in the court's view should have been possible by a sale in the open market, any shortfall must be made good from the other assets of the company.

29.5 Administration

The rights of a secured creditor in administration remain in place but the right to enforce the security is suspended during the period of the administration under the terms of the moratorium on creditor actions.

Prior to the appointment of the administrator an interim moratorium will come into force which is not as extensive as the substantive moratorium which applies after the administrator takes office. The interim moratorium under para 44 of Schedule B1 comes into effect in the case of an application to the court for an administration order as soon as the application is made and continues until the order is made or until the application is dismissed. If the administration is commenced by a floating charge holder under para 14 of Schedule B1, the moratorium is effective from the date a copy of the notice of intention to appoint is filed at the court. It continues until either the appointment is made or the period of five business days since the filing expires without an appointment being made. If the company or directors are attempting to appoint an administrator, the moratorium is effective from the time when a copy of the notice of intention to appoint is filed with the court under para 27 of Schedule B1. The moratorium continues until the appointment is made or 10 business days have passed without an appointment being made.

The interim moratorium is essentially in the same terms as the substantive moratorium which takes effect upon the appointment of an administrator (ignoring any reference to the consent of the administrator as obviously at this stage there is no administrator), but it does not prevent, *inter alia*, the appointment of an administrative receiver by a qualifying floating charge holder.

If a floating charge holder has the power to appoint an administrative receiver, he or she may therefore enforce the charge in this way during the interim moratorium. Such an appointment will generally prevent the appointment of an administrator.

Once an administrator is appointed the power to appoint an administrative receiver is lost. Any attempt to enforce the security thereafter will only be possible if either the administrator consents or leave of the court is obtained (para 43 of Schedule B1).

Under para 70 of Schedule B1 of the Act, an administrator may dispose of assets subject to a floating charge as if such assets were not subject to the charge. The floating charge holder's rights are protected in that its security interest is transferred to the proceeds of sale or to any further assets purchased with the proceeds of sale.

If the administrator wants to dispose of property subject to a security which is not a floating charge, such as a fixed charge or mortgage, consent of the court must first be obtained (para 71 of Schedule B1). This power may be exercised by the administrator where he or she is attempting to sell the company's business as a going concern and some crucial assets, such as the company's premises or machinery, are subject to a fixed charge. The power is similar to the power of an administrative receiver has under section 43 of the Act. The court will only make an order if it thinks that the disposal is likely to promote the purpose of the administration. As a condition of making such an order, the net proceeds of the sale of the secured asset, and any extra amount required so as to produce a total amount equal to the asset's market value as determined by the court, must be paid to the secured creditor.

29.6 Voluntary arrangements

Under section 4(3) and Schedule A1 para 31(4) in relation to company voluntary arrangements ('CVAs') and section 258(4) in relation to individual voluntary arrangements ('IVAs'), the proposal cannot affect the rights of secured creditors to enforce their security without their consent. Where a moratorium is obtained for a small company under Schedule A1, secured creditors cannot enforce their security, by the appointment of an administrative receiver or otherwise, during the period that the moratorium is in force (para 12 of Schedule A1). If an individual has obtained an interim order under section 252, this does not prevent secured creditors from enforcing their security.

If a moratorium has been obtained for a small company under Schedule A1, the company can dispose of property subject to a security only with the consent of the secured creditor or the court. If the court gives its consent to the disposal of fixed charge assets, the consent will be conditional upon the net proceeds of sale (or their market value if the proceeds are a lesser amount) being paid to the fixed charge holder. In the case of consent being given to the disposal of floating charge assets, the debenture holder will in effect have the floating charge extended over any substituted assets (para 20 of Schedule A1).

Votes at the creditors' meeting are calculated according to the amount of the creditor's unsecured debt. If a creditor's debt is partly secured, he or she can vote at the meeting in respect of the unsecured part (*Calor Gas v Piercy* [1994] BCC 69).

In relation to CVAs, the case of *Re Leisure Study Group Ltd* ([1994] 2 BCLC 65) highlights a potential pitfall for floating charge holders who agree to the CVA. If the CVA fails prematurely, it will usually be the case that some, if not all, of the floating charge assets will have been transferred to the supervisor on trust for the unsecured creditors. The floating charge holder may not have any claim to such assets. Careful consideration needs to be taken by a floating charge holder of the terms of the CVA prior to giving consent to it in order to avoid this result.

Chapter 30

Retention of Title

30.1 Introduction

It is frequently the case that on the insolvency of a debtor, there is no money left in the estate to pay unsecured creditors once the secured and preferential creditors have been paid out. One very effective protection for creditors who supply goods to a customer is to contract on terms which provide that the supplier remains the owner of the goods supplied until they have been paid for. As long as such a clause is valid it will prevent the goods supplied being swallowed up by a floating charge and will normally protect them from any other secured or preferential creditor's claim. If the goods never pass to the debtor, the debtor's creditors have no claim on them. It is usual to contract for the supplier to have the power to enter the customer's premises and repossess the goods if they are not paid for. It is also usual to state that although title to the goods is retained pending payment, risk passes on delivery to the customer. If the goods are accidentally destroyed after delivery, although they belong to the seller, the loss will fall on the customer. Despite the fact that title has not passed to the customer, the customer, as a buyer in possession, may give good title to a purchaser and so may use the goods supplied in the ordinary course of business.

Contractual terms, which allow the supplier to remain the owner of goods pending payment, are usually referred to as retention of title clauses, or sometimes reservation of title clauses or Romalpa clauses (after the case of *Aluminium Industrie Vaassen BV v Romalpa Aluminium Ltd* [1976] 1 WLR 676 which was the first modern consideration of such clauses).

There exists a large amount of case law on retention of title clauses and possibly even more academic commentary.[1] What follows is a very simple

---

[1] See e.g., I. Davies, 'Reservation of Title Clauses: A Legal Quagmire' [1984] LMCLQ 49 and S. Wheeler, 'The Insolvency Act 1986 and Retention of Title' [1987] JBL 180 and G. McCormack, 'Reservation of Title – the controversy continues' [1989] LMCLQ 198.

explanation of the main principles established by the case law. It should be borne in mind that there are many different types of clause in circulation and many cases turn upon their individual facts or the wording of the clause at issue.

Generally speaking, if the clause merely states that the supplier remains the owner of the goods until payment, the clause will be effective and enforceable. This type of clause is usually referred to as a 'simple clause'. It is important that the clause expressly states that the owner remains legal owner of the goods. If the goods are to remain only in the equitable ownership of the supplier the clause is likely to be interpreted as a charge and unless it is registered as such, where the debtor is a company, under section 395 of the Companies Act 1985, it will be void against a liquidator, administrator or other creditor of the company. The case of *Re Bond Worth Ltd* ([1980] Ch 228) deals with such a situation:

> The supplier sold synthetic fibre to the company. The company used this fibre in a manufacturing process to make carpets. The fibre had therefore undergone a manufacturing process and was no longer identifiable as the fibre supplied. The terms of the supply claimed that the supplier remained the equitable owner of the fibre and had an equitable interest in any mixed goods such as the end product, the carpet. The court refused to recognise that any trust of the carpets had been created. The clause was held to have created a floating charge only in favour of the supplier which was void for non-registration. The court viewed the clause as an attempt to give the supplier some security interest over the assets of the company. As this interest in the company's assets was defeasible upon payment of money, in that as soon as the fibre was paid for the interest lapsed, the interest could only be by way of charge.

This type of approach can be seen in subsequent cases, but the clause may not fail in totality. If part of a contract claims to retain legal ownership of the goods supplied until payment, it will generally be valid notwithstanding that other parts of the contract are deemed to be void as unregistered charges.[2] Similarly, if there is a course of dealings between the supplier and the customer, a retention of title clause may be drafted so that title to the goods supplied remains with the supplier until all monies under all the contracts have been paid (usually referred to as an 'all monies' clause).[3]

As long as the original goods supplied are still identifiable, a simple retention of title clause will be effective. In *Hendy Lennox (Industrial Engines) Ltd v Grahame Puttick Ltd* ([1984] 1 WLR 485) an engine had been supplied under a retention of title contract. The engine had been incorporated into a larger generator, but as it could be unbolted and removed intact, the reservation of title to it was valid.

Where goods undergo a manufacturing process and are therefore altered from the goods supplied, the simple retention of title clause cannot operate.

---

[2] See e.g., *Clough Mill Ltd v Martin* [1985] 1 WLR 111.
[3] See e.g., *Armour v Thyssen Edelstahlwerke AG* [1991] 2 AC 339.

Title cannot be retained in a new product, title to which the supplier has never held. A claim in *Borden (UK) Ltd v Scottish Timber Products Ltd* ([1981] Ch 25) by a supplier of resin which had been manufactured with other goods into chipboard, the end product, failed. The supplier could only claim an equitable interest in the chipboard and such an interest, being defeasible upon payment of money, could only be an interest by way of charge. Such a charge was void for non-registration.[4] Claims to mixed goods invariably fail in practice.

Another type of claim a supplier may attempt to make is to the proceeds of sale of either the original goods supplied or to mixed goods. It seems that no matter how the contract is drafted, no enforceable liability to account can be imposed in this situation. In order for such a claim to succeed, it would be necessary to show a fiduciary relationship exists between the supplier and the customer in regard to the proceeds of sale. This is highly unlikely in a commercial setting. If the interest in the proceeds only exists as long as the supplier is owed money and ceases upon payment of that money, the interest is again characterised as a charge. Such claims will almost certainly fail in a corporate context as unregistered charges.[5]

30.2 Liquidation

If a company enters liquidation and is holding assets supplied to it under a simple or all monies retention of title clause, the clause will be effective. As the assets held will not belong to the company, the liquidator will have to surrender the assets to the owner. If the clause attempts to give rights to the supplier in mixed goods or proceeds of sale, such a clause will usually be interpreted as creating a charge over the company's property and unless the clause has been registered under the Companies Act 1985, the charge will be void against the liquidator.

30.3 Administrative receivership

The position is essentially the same in administrative receivership. A simple or all monies clause will be enforceable against the receiver. A claim to mixed goods or proceeds of sale, almost certainly to be viewed as a charge, will, if it is unregistered, be void against the receiver.

---

[4] See also e.g., *Re Peachdart Ltd* [1984] Ch 131.
[5] See e.g., *Re Andrabell Ltd* [1984] 3 All ER 407.

30.4 Bankruptcy

In bankruptcy, again a simple or all monies clause will be enforceable against the trustee in bankruptcy. The more complex clauses have not been considered by the courts in this context, but if *Bond Worth* is correct in the conclusion that the complex clauses will create a floating charge, such a charge will be void in bankruptcy. The reason for this is that any attempt by an individual to create a floating charge will be void under the Bills of Sale Act (1878) Amendment 1882.

30.5 Administration

The legal position of the supplier under a retention of title clause in administration is similar to that in liquidation. If the clause is a simple or all monies retention of title clause, it will be effective so that the supplier remains the owner. If the clause attempts to give rights to the supplier in mixed goods or proceeds of sale, such a clause will usually be interpreted as creating a charge over the company's property and unless the clause has been registered under the Companies Act 1985, the charge will be void against the administrator.

Even if a simple or all monies clause is effective, the moratorium imposed by the company entering administration prevents the supplier from repossessing the goods without the consent of the administrator or leave of the court (paras 43 and 111 of Schedule B1).

In addition, the administrator has the power to apply to the court in order to sell assets subject to a retention of title clause (paras 72 and 111 of Schedule B1). This may be essential if the goods supplied are needed in order to keep the company's business going. The proceeds from the sale must go to pay off the supplier. If the market price is not realised the company must make up the shortfall.

30.6 Voluntary arrangements

Where an individual or company is proposing a voluntary arrangement, there is nothing stopping a supplier under a simple or all monies clause from repossessing the goods prior to the creditors' meeting. In the case of an individual, if an interim order has been obtained, it does not prevent a retention of title owner from repossessing the goods.

In the case of a company which has obtained a moratorium under Schedule A1 of the Act, a retention of title creditor is prevented from repossessing during the moratorium without leave of the court (paras 1 and 12 of Schedule A1). The company has similar powers to dispose of assets subject to retention of title contracts as an administrator (para 20 of Schedule A1). A court order or creditor consent is again needed to exercise this power and the proceeds from the sale must go to pay off the creditor. If the market price is not realised the company must make up the shortfall.

If the voluntary arrangement is being proposed by a company, again any complex clauses claiming rights in mixed goods or proceeds of sale will, unless registered, be void against the company's other creditors.

Again, if one accepts that such complex clauses create floating charges, in the case of an individual proposing a voluntary arrangement, such a charge will be void for breaching the terms of the Bills of Sale Act (1878) Amendment 1882.

Chapter 31

Landlords and Execution Creditors

31.1 Introduction

The basic principle of a *pari passu* distribution to all unsecured creditors of an insolvent is further encroached upon by the rights of a landlord or an execution creditor. A landlord has two distinct remedies against an insolvent tenant, namely the ancient self-help common law right to distrain the goods on the tenanted premises and the right to forfeit the lease either by obtaining a court order or again by the self-help process of peaceable re-entry. An unsecured creditor who has obtained judgment against a debtor will usually want to execute that judgment. Depending upon which type of execution is chosen and which type of formal insolvency the tenant subsequently enters, the execution creditor may remain in the ranks of the unsecured creditors or may be able to show that the judgment debt has become a secured debt.

31.2 Rights of a landlord

31.2.1 *Landlord's distress*

A landlord's power to distrain for unpaid rent 'is a remedy which enables landlords to recover arrears of rent, without going to court, by taking goods from the demised property and selling them' (*Rhodes v Allied Dunbar Pension Services* [1989] 1 All ER 1,161 at 1,163 *per* Nicholls LJ). The landlord can levy distress personally or authorise court licensed bailiffs to carry out the distraint. It may be levied as soon as rent is in arrears without prior notice to the tenant. Somewhat surprisingly perhaps, the goods distrained need not belong to the defaulting tenant.[1]

Distress has been subject to common law and statutory modifications, introduced in an entirely *ad hoc* manner over a period of a thousand years. Some restrictions have been placed upon its operation, importantly, for example, landlords of residential tenancies will usually be required to obtain the permission of the court before distraining.[2] Certain goods, those with absolute privilege, cannot be distrained at all.[3]

Distress is of particular use where the tenant is insolvent as it may enable the landlord to jump the queue of unsecured creditors. The extent to which the landlord is entitled to gain such a priority position varies considerably depending upon which insolvency procedure the tenant has entered.

31.2.2 *Forfeiture of the lease*

If the remedy of distress proves to be of little value to the landlord because, for example, there are few if any assets on the premises to distrain against, the landlord may consider forfeiting the lease. If the lease is a long lease with a substantial capital value, the landlord could be financially in a very good position if the lease is forfeited. The forfeiture brings the lease to an end and the landlord is able to obtain vacant possession of the premises. The grant of a new lease by the landlord may be at a premium or at an increased rent. Once a lease is forfeited the landlord's power to distrain is lost as there is no longer a lease under which such a right may be claimed.

It will usually be expressly stated in any lease that the insolvency of the tenant will give rise to a power in the landlord to forfeit. Failure to pay rent or the tenant entering a formal insolvency procedure will almost always be listed as events triggering the right to forfeit. Things are not quite so weighted in favour of the landlord. If the effect of forfeiture would deprive the tenant's other creditors of a valuable asset, such as a long lease with a capital value on a sale, the court may not permit forfeiture. The landlord's ability to forfeit may, in such circumstances, be viewed as an act which unjustly enriches the landlord.[4]

---

[1] See e.g., *Salford Van Hire (Contracts) Ltd v Bocholt Developments Ltd* [1995] CLC 611.

[2] If the tenancy is a protected tenancy under section 147 of the Rent Act 1977 or an assured tenancy under section 19 of the Housing Act 1988, the landlord must obtain a court order before levying distress. Landlords of other residential tenancies such as secure tenancies under the Housing Act 1985, which would include most local authorities, may continue to distrain without judicial permission.

[3] For example, wearing apparel, bedding, tools of the trade and money – section 4 of the Law of Distress Amendment Act 1888 as amended by section 89 of the County Courts Act 1984 which itself is amended by section 15 of the Courts and Legal Services Act 1990.

[4] See e.g., the House of Lords decision in *Billson v Residential Apartments Ltd* [1992] 1 AC 494.

The standard provision for forfeiture in a lease provides for the landlord to be able to re-enter the premises upon the occurrence of a number of events of default. The lease is not forfeited automatically but deemed to be voidable at the option of the landlord.[5] Once the right to forfeit has arisen, the landlord may exercise it by either making a peaceable re-entry or by bringing an action for possession. Peaceable re-entry may be in practice anything but peaceable in fact. It has the benefit of being an out of court action by the landlord and until recently could be used effectively despite a company being in administration.[6] A landlord is criminally liable if force is used and so, in normal circumstances, a writ of possession will be issued. If the writ is issued the forfeiture only becomes final once judgment for possession is obtained, which has the effect of establishing that the forfeiture is justified and that no relief against it will be granted.

31.3 Landlords and insolvent tenants

31.3.1 *Bankruptcy*

Prior to 1825 there was nothing to prevent a landlord distraining against the estate of a bankrupt tenant. Section 74 of the Bankruptcy Act 1825 introduced one mild form of limitation. Once the bankruptcy had commenced, the landlord was limited in distraining for no more than one year's rent accrued due prior to the bankruptcy order. The landlord was reduced to proving for any amount over that figure as an unsecured creditor.

This limited protection of the bankrupt's estate has survived in substance through subsequent Bankruptcy Acts. The period of one year prior to the commencement of bankruptcy was reduced to six months by section 28 of the Bankruptcy Act 1890. The relevant provision today is section 347 of the Insolvency Act 1986. Bankruptcy nowadays commences on the date of the bankruptcy order (section 278). However, in the context of distress, this is effectively backdated in that, if a landlord distrains after the petition but before the order is made, any sum realised in excess of six months' rent is to be held for the bankrupt as part of his estate. The impact on landlords of section 347 is not always too serious. For example, if rent is paid quarterly and the tenant becomes bankrupt, the landlord can still distrain at the end of the quarter for the full quarter's rent.[7]

---

[5] See e.g., *Davenport v R* (1877) 3 App Cas 115 and section 146(7) of the Law of Property Act 1925.

[6] See e.g., *Re Lomax Leisure Ltd* [2000] Ch 502, the effect of which was reversed by section 9 of the Insolvency Act 2000.

[7] See e.g., *Re Howell* [1895] 1 QB 844.

The restriction on claiming six months' rent only applies to rent due before the bankruptcy order. If subsequent to the order, the trustee in bankruptcy remains in possession of the demised premises without disclaiming the lease, the landlord can distrain for all rent accruing after the bankruptcy order.[8] Essentially this means that a trustee who remains in possession of the demised premises must pay rent for occupying the premises.

If a landlord distrains and the tenant becomes bankrupt within three months the landlord may lose some or all of the benefit of the distress under section 347(3). This subsection applies if the bankrupt's estate is insufficient to meet the debts owed to preferential creditors. If section 347(3) applies, the goods which have been distrained or the proceeds of their sale are charged for the benefit of the bankrupt's estate with the preferential debts. Therefore, although distress allows the landlord to jump the queue of unsecured creditors, it does not, in the circumstances of section 347(3), give the landlord priority at the expense of preferential creditors.

There is no restriction on a landlord forfeiting a lease upon the tenant's bankruptcy (subject to the court allowing relief against forfeiture). Section 285 of the Act provides that no person shall have a remedy in respect of a debt provable in the bankruptcy but this does not apply to forfeiture of a lease. The forfeiture is not a proceeding which enforces a provable debt, it merely brings the lease to an end.[9]

31.3.2 *Voluntary arrangements*

If the arrangement covers rent owing to the landlord, it will prevent the landlord from distraining on the basis of it, even if the landlord voted against the arrangement proposal. Unless a moratorium has been imposed, there is nothing to prevent the landlord from distraining prior to the creditors' meeting if rent is unpaid. By doing so, the landlord will avoid being bound by the arrangement. A distress at this time will almost certainly have the knock-on effect of destroying any possibility of the arrangement being workable.

Under section 252 of the Act, if an individual debtor has obtained an interim order, the effect of the order is to prevent a landlord without leave of the court from distraining for unpaid rent.[10]

If a small company has the benefit of a moratorium under the provisions of Schedule A1, para 12 of that Schedule prevents any distress being levied without leave of the court.

---

[8] See e.g., *Re Binns* (1875) 1 Ch D 285.
[9] See e.g., *Ezekiel v Orakpo* [1977] QB 260.
[10] This restriction was not present in the original Act but was added by the Insolvency Act 2000. Previously, this gap in the moratorium could destroy any chance of the IVA being a success. See e.g., *McMullen & Sons v Cerrone* [1994] BCC 25.

A landlord cannot forfeit a lease either by action or by peaceable re-entry without leave of the court, if the tenant is an individual and has the benefit of an interim order.[11] If the tenant is a small company and has the benefit of a moratorium, again the landlord cannot forfeit without leave of the court.

31.3.3 *Compulsory liquidation*

The rules for governing how distress is treated in compulsory liquidation have a different origin from the rules in bankruptcy. The first restrictions on landlords' distress in compulsory winding up came with the 1862 Companies Act. The provisions of this Act are largely replicated today. Section 126 of the Act states that at any time after the presentation of the petition, but before the making of a winding-up order, the court can, on the application of the company or any creditor or contributory, restrain any action, suit or proceeding pending against the company. Section 130 provides that after a winding-up order is made, no action, suit or other proceeding can be proceeded with or commenced against the company without leave of the court. Under section 128 any attachment, sequestration, distress or execution put in force against the company following the commencement of winding up[12] is void to all extents. Under section 128 'put in force' as it applies to distress refers to when the distress is levied initially. The distress need not have been completed by sale.

A landlord's distress has always been held to be a type of 'proceeding' for the purposes of sections 126 and 130, even though the principle upon which the courts have acted would seem, at best, questionable. The meaning of 'proceeding' usually implies a court process. In *Re Lancashire Cotton Spinning Co* ((1887) 35 ChD 656 at 661) Cotton LJ thought it:

> doubtful whether, having regard to the express words of section [128], which says, 'That any distress shall be void', it was right to say that section [130] included distress among the 'proceedings which the court might allow'.

Despite this opinion, his Lordship felt bound by previous decisions to hold that 'proceeding' included distress. The ultimate result is that a landlord can apply for leave under section 130 to distrain even after the commencement of the winding up.

A distress put in force after the commencement of winding up is void under section 128 unless the court gives leave under section 130. The courts will not usually permit a landlord to levy distress after the winding

---

[11] Peaceable re-entry was possible until the amendments made by the Insolvency Act 2000. For an example of the previous law in operation see *Re A Debtor (No 13AIO of 1994)* [1995] NPC 50.

[12] Under section 129 a compulsory winding up commences on the date of the petition.

up has commenced for rent accrued due before the winding up which is provable in the winding up. This would offend the policy of *pari passu* distribution among all the unsecured creditors.

Rent accrued due after the commencement of the winding up is, in general, required to be paid, otherwise leave will be given to distrain for it. If the landlord applies to the court for leave to distrain under section 130, he or she must usually show that it is inequitable for the liquidator to insist upon the protection of section 128. If the liquidator wishes to use the demised premises for the purposes of the winding up the rent must be met.

If the distress has been levied before the commencement of winding up, but has not been completed by sale, the court will almost certainly not restrain the sale. After the petition, but before the winding-up order, the company, any creditor or contributory may apply to restrain the distress under section 126. Once the winding-up order is made, in order to continue with the distress the landlord must apply for leave under section 130. The courts will only stay the distress if there are special reasons which show that to allow it would be inequitable. This will require evidence of fraud or unfair dealing. In this context it is not unfair dealing for the landlord to prevent the *pari passu* rule applying by sweeping off all the assets in the distress.

The rules under section 347(3) which apply in bankruptcy are largely replicated in section 176 in relation to compulsory winding up.

Prior to a winding-up order being made, a landlord can bring an action for forfeiture although once a petition for winding up has been presented, the company, a creditor or a contributory may apply for a stay of proceedings. Once a winding-up order is made, leave of the court is required to commence or proceed with the application (under section 130 of the Act).[13] It is unclear whether peaceable re-entry falls within the restrictions of sections 126 and 130 as an action or proceeding. As distress has been held to fall within these sections, it seems likely that peaceable re-entry will too.

31.3.4 *Voluntary liquidation*

In relation to voluntary liquidation there is no provision in the Insolvency Act 1986 preventing the landlord distraining. However, under section 112 of the Act, a liquidator, creditor or contributory of a company in voluntary liquidation may ask the court to exercise any power it has in relation to companies in compulsory liquidation. This includes the power to stay any distress[14] and any forfeiture. The court's discretion will be exercised on the same grounds as for a compulsory liquidation. A landlord who acts

---

[13] For guidance as to whether or not leave will be ordered see e.g., *Re David Lloyd & Co Ltd* (1877) 6 Ch D 339. Also, see 249–51.

[14] See the discussion in *Herbert Berry Associates Ltd v IRC* [1977] 1 WLR 1437.

swiftly by completing the distress before the liquidator applies to the court is safe, as the distress cannot later be invalidated.

31.3.5 *Administrative receivership*

There appears to be no restriction on a landlord distraining against the goods of a corporate tenant in administrative receivership. This is logical in that the receiver acts as the agent of the company and therefore the property charged still belongs to the company and is under the control of its agent. There is no statutory provision preventing the distress and so it should be allowed.[15]

The right to forfeit a lease is not prevented by the appointment of an administrative receiver. The receiver may be successful in applying for relief from forfeiture as the forfeiture may destroy any chance of the receivership being successful.[16]

31.3.6 *Administration*

Under the terms of the administration moratorium under para 43 of Schedule B1, no distress may be levied and no forfeiture by either action or peaceable re-entry is possible, without the consent of the administrator or leave of the court.

31.4 Execution creditors

Execution can be taken to mean 'the process for enforcing or giving effect to the judgment of the court' (*Re Overseas Aviation Engineering (GB) Ltd* [1963] Ch 24 at 39 *per* Lord Denning MR). A judgment for the payment of money may be enforced in the High Court by a writ of *fieri facias*, a third party debt order, a charging order or the appointment of a receiver. The creditor may also have the right to have the judgment enforced in the county court. A judgment for the giving of possession of land may be enforced by a writ of possession. A judgment for the delivery of goods may be enforced by a writ of specific delivery.

For the purposes of this chapter it is intended to concentrate upon the modes of execution most commonly sought by a commercial creditor,

---

[15] But see the discussion in P. Walton, 'The Landlord, his Distress, the Insolvent Tenant and the Stranger' (2000) 16 *Insolvency Law and Practice* 47 which suggests the law on this issue is by no means clear.

[16] See e.g., *Transag Haulage Ltd v Leyland DAF Finance plc* [1994] 2 BCLC 88.

namely the writ of *fieri facias*, third party debt orders and charging orders. It should be noted that the Lord Chancellor has undertaken a wide-ranging and long-running review of civil enforcement mechanisms. Changes have been made to third party debt orders and charging orders but at the time of writing no changes have yet been made to the writ of *fieri facias*.

The real issue for an execution creditor on the insolvency of the execution debtor is whether or not the execution has transformed the creditor from an unsecured into a secured creditor. The next question will be whether or not the execution creditor can enforce any newly acquired security in the formal insolvency of the debtor.

31.4.1 *Third party debt orders (previously garnishee proceedings)*[17]

In third party debt proceedings an interim order is served on a third party who is a debtor of the judgment debtor. The third party is frequently a bank with whom the judgment debtor holds an account in credit and the intention is to require the bank to pay the execution creditor rather than the judgment debtor the money held in the acccount. The procedure to obtain a third party debt order is a two-stage process. An application for an interim third party debt order is made without notice. No hearing is held. The interim order directs the third party not to make any payment to the judgment debtor which reduces the amount owed to the judgment debtor to less than the amount specified in the order. The interim order is binding upon the third party when it is served.

A return date is set for a hearing to consider whether or not to make the order final. This hearing is the second stage of the process. Unless there are grounds for objecting to the order it will be made final. The grounds upon which such objection may be made include the third party claiming a right of set-off, or some other party claiming some prior right to the money. If the order is made final it becomes enforceable against the third party as an order to pay money and can thereafter be enforced against the third party.

Under the previous enforcement regime of garnishee proceedings, the equivalent of the interim order, the garnishee order *nisi*, was expressly stated to bind the debt as from the service of the order on the garnishee:

> Such an order shall bind in the hands of the garnishee as from the service of the order on him or her any debt specified in the order or so much thereof as may be so specified.[18]

---

[17] On 25 March 2002 garnishee proceedings were abolished and replaced by third party debt orders by the Civil Procedure (Amendment No 4) Rules 2001 (SI 2001/2792) by the introduction of CPR Part 72.

[18] RSC Ord 49 rule 3(2).

If the garnishee order were made absolute, execution could thereafter issue against the garnishee's own property. It was the order *nisi*, though, which created an equitable charge over the debt.[19] The courts, despite some careless phrasing at times,[20] were consistent in deciding that a garnishee order *nisi* gave rise to an equitable charge over the debt in favour of the judgment creditor upon service of the order *nisi* on the garnishee. The debt became subject to the charge but was not transferred to the judgment creditor.

Under the new regime of third party debt orders there is no specific mention of the debt being bound by service of the interim order. There is a statement that the interim order 'becomes binding on a third party when it is served on him' but not that it is binding upon the actual debt. It is clearly binding upon the third party who is required to retain enough of the debt to satisfy the judgment and costs of the enforcement but this does not amount to the creation of any interest by way of charge or otherwise over the debt itself in favour of the judgment creditor. The upshot of this is that a third party debt order does not constitute the execution creditor a secured creditor.

31.4.2 *Charging orders*

A charging order is defined by section 1(1) of the Charging Orders Act 1979 as an order 'imposing on any such property of the debtor as may be specified in the order a charge for securing payment of any money due or to become due under [a] judgment or order'. It may be used by a judgment creditor to obtain a charge over the judgment debtor's land, stocks and shares, beneficial interest under a trust or over money held in court for the debtor. The order secures the debt but in itself does not produce any money. The procedure is similar to that involved in third party debt proceedings in that there is a two-stage process. The first stage is to obtain an interim charging order (formerly a charging order *nisi*) without a hearing. The order will subsequently be made final unless the debtor (or other interested party) can show cause as to why it should not. The creditor can enforce the charge by applying to the court for an order of sale.

There is no doubt that the interim charging order takes effect as an immediate equitable charge on the assets.[21]

---

[19] See e.g., *Cairney v Back* [1906] 2 KB 746.

[20] See the criticism by D. Hare and D. Milman, 'Debenture holders and judgment creditors – problems of priority' [1982] LMCLQ 57 at 62 of Farwell LJ's *dictum* in *Galbraith v Grimshaw and Baxter* [1910] 1 KB 339 at 343.

[21] See Charging Orders Act 1979, section 3(4), CPR rule 73.4 (2) and *Coutts and Co v Clarke* [2002] EWCA Civ 943.

31.4.3 *Writ of fieri facias*

The writ of *fieri facias* (commonly abbreviated to *fi. fa.*) may be used to execute a judgment or order for the payment of money or costs. The writ of *fi. fa.* may issue immediately upon payment becoming due which, with a judgment in the ordinary form, will mean immediately the judgment is entered. There will ordinarily be no need to serve notice of the judgment or the judgment itself on the debtor prior to the writ being issued.

The writ of *fi. fa.* is in the form of a royal direction addressed to the sheriff of the county (or bailiwick) in which the debtor's goods are situate, to seize and sell such goods of the debtor within the county as may be sufficient to satisfy the judgment, interest upon the judgment (which begins to run when judgment is entered) and the costs of the execution itself. The writ also instructs the sheriff to pay the amount levied to the judgment creditor less his or her own costs and fees. It is the duty of the sheriff in executing the *fi. fa.* to take possession of all the goods of the judgment debtor within his or her bailiwick or at least sufficient to satisfy the execution. The sheriff owes a duty to the execution creditor to seize the debtor's goods at once. Upon the sale of the goods, and the proceeds being paid over to the sheriff, the execution creditor has a right of action against the sheriff for money had and received. In practice the sheriff may decide not to remove the goods seized from the premises but may enter into what is known as a 'walking possession' agreement with the debtor. This agreement allows the goods to remain at the debtor's premises, but as the goods will be *in custodia legis*, the debtor cannot deal with them until the debt is paid.

Delivery of the writ to the sheriff is said to bind the goods of the execution debtor from the date of delivery. It is clear that title to the goods, is not altered. Any transfer by the debtor remains valid but the purchaser takes the goods subject to the rights of the execution creditor. Title to the goods is not transferred to the judgment creditor by either delivery of the writ to the sheriff nor by seizure of goods under it by the sheriff.

Title to the goods remains in the debtor until sale. Upon sale, the purchaser obtains a good title from the sheriff. At this point the debtor's title is extinguished. The sheriff is under a duty to sell and pay over the proceeds to the creditor. This is a legal duty imposed by the writ and does not constitute the sheriff as trustee for the creditor.

In *Re Clarke* [1898] 1 Ch 336 a debtor who had his goods seized under a writ of *fi. fa.*, subsequently had a receiver appointed over his affairs under the Lunacy Act 1890 on the ground that he was of unsound mind. The receiver claimed that under the Lunacy Act the lunatic debtor's assets were entitled to be protected from the execution. The Court of Appeal found that there was no power available to the court to protect the assets of the lunatic in the absence of the receiver having actually taken possession of the lunatic's assets prior to the execution. Importantly, Lindley MR stated:

It is very true that the property in goods seized under a *fi. fa.* remains in the execution debtor until sale . . . But it is no less true that after seizure and

> before sale the execution creditor is as regards those goods in the position of a secured creditor . . . He had a legal right as against the execution debtor – i.e, owner of the goods – to have the goods sold and to be paid out of the proceeds of sale.

Although no property in the goods passes to the execution creditor on seizure, the creditor at that point becomes a secured creditor. The security is in the nature of a fixed equitable charge.

31.5 Execution creditors and insolvent debtors

The foregoing discussion deals with whether or not an execution creditor becomes a secured creditor at any stage of the execution. If the judgment debtor is solvent it is likely that execution creditors will get paid out and so will not be overly concerned as to their secured status or otherwise. Where the issue becomes of greater importance is when the debtor enters a formal insolvency procedure. If the execution creditor can claim a secured interest, one would expect the creditor to be paid out in priority in any subsequent insolvency of the debtor. As will be seen, this is not quite the case. In some non-terminal procedures (voluntary arrangements and administration orders) the secured status is potentially crucial. In another non-terminal procedure (receivership) the courts have partly ignored the execution creditors' claim to be secured creditors. In terminal procedures (liquidation and bankruptcy) the Act, in the main, overrides any security interest obtained by the execution creditor unless completed prior to the liquidation or bankruptcy.

31.5.1 *Administrative receivership*

A common priority dispute exists between an execution creditor, on the one hand, and the holder of a floating charge, on the other. The dispute will frequently arise when the execution creditor has instituted enforcement procedures and the company is put into receivership before the creditor is paid out. Logic would dictate that if the execution creditor has the benefit of a security interest before the floating charge crystallises then the execution creditor should win. Unfortunately, in this area, logic has been conspicuous by its absence.

The case law is most remarkable by an almost complete absence of consideration of the rights given to execution creditors upon enforcement. The analysis, such as it is, concentrates on what rights are given to the holder of a floating charge. The most unfortunate thing about this is that the cases fall broadly into two diametrically opposed groups as to what a floating charge actually is. It is small wonder then that the case law fails to be entirely logical or consistent either on its own terms or with the wider case law determining the rights of execution creditors.

The two categories of case law differ fundamentally as to what rights in the charged property a floating charge gives to the chargee prior to crystallisation. In the early days of the floating charge, the courts wrestled primarily with two possibilities.

The first group of cases proceeded on the basis that a floating charge created an immediate interest in the charged property. This is what Professor Pennington later labelled the 'licence' theory.[22] Essentially the floating charge gave the chargee an immediate security interest in the assets but gave the chargor company a licence to continue to use the assets in the ordinary course of business. This line of cases[23] decides that the floating charge takes priority over an execution creditor even if the charge has yet to crystallise as long as the debenture is issued prior to the date of the execution.

The second line of cases views the floating charge as attaching to nothing until something happens to crystallise the charge.[24] This is what Professor Pennington calls the 'mortgage of future assets' theory.[25] In *Robson v Smith* ([1895] 2 Ch 118) a garnishee order had been made absolute prior to crystallisation and so took priority over the floating charge. The result of applying the mortgage of future assets theory to the priority dispute between an execution creditor and a floating charge holder is therefore that the execution creditor wins if the execution is complete prior to crystallisation of the floating charge.

Evans v Rival Granite Quarries Ltd ([1910] 2 KB 979) is widely regarded as settling the law as to disputes between floating charges and execution creditors. It does this by a not very convincing reconciliation of only some of the previous cases.

> In *Evans* a judgment creditor had obtained a garnishee order *nisi* and the court had subsequently made the order absolute. By this time, a floating charge holder had still not intervened sufficiently to crystallise the charge. The Court of Appeal decided that the decisive factor was whether or not the execution creditor had actually received the money owed prior to crystallisation. In arriving at this result, it found that even obtaining a garnishee order absolute prior to crystallisation did not give the execution priority. The execution must

---

[22] R. Pennington, *Company Law*, 8th edn, London: Butterworths (2001) at 539–41.
[23] *Re Standard Manufacturing Co* [1891] 1 Ch 627, *Re Opera* [1891] 3 Ch 260, *Davey v Williamson* [1898] 2 QB 194, *Simultaneous Colour Printing Syndicate v Foweraker* [1901] 1 QB 771, *Duck v Tower Galvanising Co* [1901] 2 KB 314, *Norton v Yates* [1906] 1 KB 112, *Cairney v Back* [1906] 2 KB 746. *Norton* and *Cairney* even go as far as to suggest that even after a garnishee order is made absolute, a subsequently created floating charge will still take priority.
[24] See e.g., *Taunton v Sheriff of Warwickshire* [1895] 1 Ch 734 and *Evans v Rival Granite* [1910] 2 KB 979.
[25] R. Pennington, *Company Law*, 8th edn, London: Butterworths (2001) at 539–41.

> be absolutely complete prior to crystallisation in order to win out against
> a floating charge. There was no consideration as to whether or not seizure
> by the sheriff under a *fi. fa.* or a garnishee order *nisi* being granted gave the
> execution creditor a charge in priority to the floating charge.

In order to gain priority in a receivership, the execution must be complete
prior to crystallisation. It will only be complete when the execution creditor
has the money in his or her hands or possibly when the sheriff has the
proceeds of a sale under a *fi. fa.* in his or her hands.

31.5.2 *Compulsory liquidation*

As with the law relating to distress and forfeiture, there are a number of
overlapping provisions restricting the rights of execution creditors which
apply where the debtor company is being wound up. There is no great
logic to the provisions, some apply specifically to compulsory winding up
only but may be applied in voluntary liquidation at the discretion of the
court. Some apply after the commencement of the winding up while others
only apply once the winding up has occurred. Some provisions have been
interpreted by the courts in an unlikely manner.

The policy behind the rules applying to execution creditors' rights in
winding up was summarised by James LJ in *Re Oriental Inland Steam Co*
((1874) 9 Ch App 557 at 559):

> Parliament has enacted that in the case of a winding up the assets of the
> company so wound up are to be collected and applied in discharge of its
> liabilities. That makes the property clearly trust property. It is property
> affected by the Act of Parliament with an obligation to be dealt with by
> the proper officer in a particular way. Then it has ceased to be beneficially
> the property of the company; and, being so, it has ceased to be liable to be
> seized by the execution creditors of the company.

Under section 126 of the Act, upon the presentation of a petition for a
compulsory winding up, the company, a creditor, or a contributory may
ask the court to stay execution (or other civil proceeding) against the
company. If no stay is obtained, the execution (or other proceeding) may
be continued with until such time as a winding-up order is made. In
the absence of special circumstances, the court will restrain execution in
order to ensure an equal distribution of assets among the company's
creditors.[26]

Under section 130, once a winding-up order is made, no action or
proceeding shall be proceeded with or commenced against a company
without leave of the court. Action or proceeding in this context includes
execution. It is highly unlikely that the court will grant leave to a creditor

---

[26] See e.g., *Bowkett v Fullers United Electric Motors Ltd* [1923] 1 KB 161.

to enforce a judgment against a company in compulsory liquidation as it would secure an advantage to which the creditor would not be properly entitled if the assets were to be administered in accordance with the winding-up provisions.

Under section 128 any execution put in force after the commencement of a compulsory winding up is void. The meaning of 'put in force' in the case of a *fi. fa.* is when the goods are seized and so at the same time that a charge has been created over the assets. If this does not occur until after commencement of the winding up the execution is void. Despite the very definite language of section 128, it has long been held that the court may give leave to a creditor to continue with the execution, where the process had begun, for example, the writ of *fi. fa.* had been issued, even though not 'put in force'. In the absence of special circumstances rendering it inequitable not to allow the creditor to continue with the execution, leave will be refused. If the creditor has been prevented from enforcing due to some fraud or trickery, the court may grant leave to complete the execution. It is necessary to show something greater than the 'usual delaying' tactics or excuses being employed by the non-paying company.

Under section 183 if the execution has begun prior to the winding up, the creditor can only retain the 'benefit of the execution'[27] or attachment if the process has been completed prior to the commencement of winding up. An execution against goods is 'completed' in this context by seizure and sale under a *fi. fa.* or by the making of a charging order. Attachment of a debt is completed by receipt of the debt.[28] The court has a wide discretion to set aside the liquidator's right to deny the execution creditor. In practice, in the absence of fraud or trickery, weighty reasons must exist before the court will exercise its discretion to depart from the *pari passu* principle by permitting a creditor to retain the benefit of an incomplete execution.

Under section 184, if goods have been seized by the sheriff but not yet sold and if the sheriff is given notice of a winding-up order or resolution to wind up voluntarily, the sheriff must, on request, deliver the assets seized to the liquidator. If the execution is for a sum greater than £500, after sale, the sheriff shall retain the sum of money for 14 days. If the sheriff receives notice during this period of a petition for compulsory winding up or that a meeting of members has been called to consider a voluntary winding up resolution, if a winding up results, the sheriff must pay the money over to the liquidator who has priority over the execution creditor.

---

[27] The meaning of 'benefit of the execution' under the reasoning in *Re Andrew* [1937] Ch 122 refers to the charge obtained by the execution creditor, not any money actually received by the creditor under the execution.

[28] It remains to be seen whether the new Third Party Debt Orders will be viewed as proceedings which attach a debt.

31.5.3 *Voluntary liquidation*

Although there are no similar specific provisions governing voluntary liquidations, the liquidator may apply to the court under either sections 126 or 130 to have the execution stayed or set aside, by virtue of the court's powers under section 112. The onus to show why the execution should be stayed is on the liquidator. The court's power to stay proceedings includes any situation where the proposed action threatens an equal distribution of the company's assets and so is likely to be granted to prevent an execution creditor enforcing judgment.

31.5.4 *Bankruptcy*

The ideal of equal division of the insolvent's assets free from execution creditor harassment also underpins the rules in bankruptcy. Somewhat frustratingly, the provisions, found in sections 285 and 346 of the Act, although largely mirroring those in compulsory liquidation, are drafted slightly differently. It is important to note that the commencement of the bankruptcy is the date of the bankruptcy order, not the date of the presentation of the petition.

The court may stay any executions at any time when proceedings on a bankruptcy petition are pending or when the debtor has been adjudged bankrupt. After the making of the bankruptcy order no creditor with a provable debt can obtain any remedy against the property of the bankrupt. In the event of the bankruptcy of the judgment debtor the execution creditor can retain the 'benefit of the execution'[29] or attachment or sums paid to avoid it only if it is completed prior to the commencement of the bankruptcy. Execution is complete for these purposes against goods by seizure and sale, under section 1 of the Charging Orders Act 1979 when the charging order is made or under an attachment of a debt by receipt of the debt.[30]

If the execution has been commenced by *fi. fa.* and seizure has occurred but no sale has yet been made, if notice is given to the sheriff of the judgment debtor's bankruptcy, the sheriff must, on request, hand over the goods to the estate.

Where the value of the judgment being enforced exceeds £500, even where the goods have been sold and therefore the execution deemed complete under section 346, the sheriff must not hand over the proceeds to the execution creditor within 14 days from the date of sale or while a bankruptcy petition is pending. If the sheriff is given notice of a petition

---

[29] The meaning of 'benefit of the execution' under the reasoning in *Re Andrew* [1937] Ch 122 refers to the charge obtained by the execution creditor, not any money actually received by the creditor under the execution.

[30] It remains to be seen whether the new Third Party Debt Orders will be viewed as proceedings which attach a debt.

for bankruptcy against the debtor during this 14-day period he or she must await the fate of the petition. If a bankruptcy order is made the money held by the sheriff falls into the bankrupt's estate and the sheriff must pay the proceeds, after deducting the costs of the execution, to the official receiver or trustee in bankruptcy (if there is one).

The court does have a discretion to set aside the rights of the estate in favour of the execution creditor although such applications are unlikely to be met with success.

If the amount of the judgment does not exceed £500 and the goods have been sold prior to the bankruptcy order, the sheriff must pay the proceeds to the execution creditor.

31.5.5 *Voluntary arrangements*

Voluntary arrangements cannot affect the rights of secured creditors to enforce their security unless they agree to be bound.[31]

An individual with the benefit of an interim order under section 252 of the Act has the benefit of a moratorium. No execution may be commenced or continued with during the period of the interim order without leave of the court(section 252(2)).[32] No such protection is available for companies although for small companies para 12 of Schedule A1 of the Act allows for a similar, although more extensive moratorium. If a moratorium under Schedule A1 is obtained, no creditor may commence or continue with an execution without leave of the court.

Once the voluntary arrangement is approved, it is given effect to under its own terms and will expressly prevent creditors bound under it from enforcing their rights against the debtor while the voluntary arrangement remains in force.[33]

> In the context of an individual voluntary arrangement, *Peck v Craighead* ([1995] 1 BCLC 337) considered the status of an execution creditor under a *fi. fa.* after seizure of the debtor's assets but prior to sale. In this case, the debtor proposed a individual voluntary arrangement but prior to the creditors' meeting held to consider his proposal, a judgment creditor proceeded to issue a writ of *fi. fa.* under which the sheriff seized goods. The issue was whether or not the creditor became a secured creditor for the purposes of voting on the voluntary arrangement. Section 383(2) Insolvency Act 1986 defines a security as 'a mortgage, charge, lien or other security'. Martin Mann QC held (at 341) that the judgment creditor became a secured creditor upon seizure:

---

[31] Section 4(3) of the Act for company voluntary arrangements and section 258(4) for individual voluntary arrangements. See *Calor Gas Ltd v Piercy* [1994] BCC 69.

[32] Prior to the order being made, but any time after the application to the court is made the court may stay any execution pending the hearing (section 254).

[33] See e.g., the precedent individual voluntary arrangement provided by the Association of Business Recovery Professionals (R3) at paras 4(3), 5(1) and 6(1).

> I infer that the security right which an execution creditor has under a
> *fi. fa.*, which has been acted upon by seizure, is not unlike a lien, which is a
> security right expressly contemplated by section 383(2). The fact that such
> a security right has not been enforced is nothing to the point. It is enough
> that the debtor's property in the goods is bound. It is clearly irrelevant that
> the property has not yet passed out of the debtor's hands as on completion
> of the execution by sale.

The importance of this decision is that an execution creditor who has
become secured before the voluntary arrangement is approved, is not
bound by its terms unless it has agreed to be bound. The creditor can
continue with the execution. The practical impact of this is that the
arrangement proposal will in effect have to promise the execution creditor
full payment in order to obtain its approval.

The potential problem for the execution creditor who agrees to such a
voluntary arrangement occurs in the event that the arrangement fails.
What happens to assets held by the supervisor on the premature ending of
an arrangement has been the subject of some controversy, but has recently
been settled by the Court of Appeal.[34] It is generally assumed by the courts
that if a voluntary arrangement does fail, creditors who are owed money
are returned to the position they were in prior to the arrangement being
entered into, with credit given for any sums of money received under the
arrangement while it was on foot. The problem which arises here for the
execution creditor is that if the debtor goes into bankruptcy or liquidation
following the demise of the voluntary arrangement (which would normally
be the case) then the creditor is no longer in the position of a secured
creditor. Under the provisions dealing with bankruptcy and liquidation
the creditor would be unable to continue with the execution (without leave
of the court) and would be reduced to the ranks of unsecured creditors.
The obvious consequence of this is that the execution creditor is unlikely
to see much if any of the debt owed and is reduced from a very powerful
position under the arrangement to one of great weakness.

The best advice to an execution creditor who has achieved secured
creditor status for the purposes of a voluntary arrangement is not to agree
to the proposal at all (for fear of it subsequently failing) but to forge ahead
with the execution to ensure payment. Such advice flies in the face of the
ideal of debtor rescue and rehabilitation inherent in the Act but is the
logical result of the terms of the Act.

31.5.6 *Administration*

The purpose of a company entering administration is to allow the company
to have the benefit of a moratorium from creditor action in order that the
company's business can be rescued (in whole or in part) or at least that the

---

[34] See *Re NT Gallagher and Son Ltd* [2002] 2 BCLC 133.

company's assets may be realised in a more beneficial manner than would occur in an immediate winding up. The widely drafted moratorium expressly prevents an execution being continued or commenced without leave of the court (para 43 of Schedule B1). Whether or not the execution creditor is a secured creditor is irrelevant. The execution cannot be continued.

The status of the execution creditor is relevant under para 71 of Schedule B1 of the Act. This provision permits the administrator to deal with assets subject to a security (which is not a floating charge) with leave of the court or the consent of the debenture holder. If leave to deal with secured property is obtained, the administrator must apply the proceeds of sale (or open market value if the sale achieved a lesser amount) in discharging the sums payable to the secured creditor.

If the execution creditor is deemed to be a secured creditor in the administration, the administrator can only deal with the assets subject to the execution by in effect paying off the execution creditor. Either the administrator pays off the execution creditor immediately or obtains leave of the court to deal with the charged assets and then subsequently pays off the execution creditor. If, for example, the creditor has the benefit of the sheriff's walking possession agreement over all the company's chattels, the administrator will not be able to deal with any of the chattels without first paying out the execution creditor. The execution creditor who has become a secured creditor due to the execution is therefore potentially in a very strong position in the administration.

The meaning of the term 'security' for the purposes of adminstration orders is defined by section 248 as meaning 'any mortgage, charge, lien or other security'.

In the context of an administration order Lord Browne-Wilkinson in *Bristol Airport plc v Powdrill* ([1990] Ch 744 at 760) stated:

> Security is created where a person ('the creditor') to whom an obligation is owed by another ('the debtor') by statute or contract, in addition to the personal promise of the debtor to discharge the obligation, obtains rights exercisable against some property in which the debtor has an interest in order to enforce the discharge of the debtor's obligation to the creditor. While not holding that that is a comprehensive definition of 'security', in my judgment it is certainly no wider than the ordinary meaning of the word.

The definition of security contained in section 248 is in the same terms as the definition in section 383, where in the context of voluntary arrangements the court has held that seizure under a *fi. fa.* is enough to constitute the execution creditor a secured creditor (in *Peck v Craighead* [1995] 1 BCLC 337). The definition would also seem to include an interim charging order. As submitted above, an execution creditor under an interim (or final) third party debt order will not be constituted a secured creditor for these purposes.

An execution creditor who has become a secured creditor prior to the administration is in a very strong position. Although the creditor cannot continue with the execution without leave of the court, the likelihood is that the administrator will need to use the assets subject to the security in the administration and so the execution creditor will almost be guaranteed to be paid. This position is in sharp contrast to that if the administration order is discharged and the company goes into liquidation. If the execution creditor remains unpaid at the end of the administration, the creditor will be reduced to the ranks of the unsecured creditors in the winding up.

Chapter 32

Preferential Creditors

32.1 Introduction

As we have seen, upon the insolvency of a debtor, some creditors have greater rights than others. Creditors may have protected themselves by taking security over the debtor's assets. They may have the benefit of a retention of title clause in a contract of supply. They may have specific powers available to them in their capacity as landlords who may distrain for unpaid rent or forfeit a lease. A judgment creditor may have successfully executed the judgment in order to ensure payment. Other unsecured creditors may find there is no money left in the pot to pay them off. In addition to the above creditors' individual priority rights there have always been, in one form or another, a class of unsecured creditors who are given preferential rights in any insolvency. Historically, the most important preferential creditor has been the Crown. Employees have also been given limited rights as preferential creditors. The Crown's preferential status has been abolished by the Enterprise Act 2002 and this will be discussed shortly.

At common law, the Crown's prerogative rights always gave the Crown a priority in any insolvency. The Crown would always be paid out ahead of any other unsecured creditor. This right applied in both individual and corporate insolvencies. It was only in the latter part of the nineteenth century that the Crown's prerogative rights were cut down. The preferential debts regime since then has experienced a slow erosion of the Crown's rights.

Employees' limited rights to be paid ahead of other unsecured creditors were first introduced in 1825 and remain in place today. As well as employees' preferential creditor status, employees have additional protection under the Employment Rights Act 1996.

The current preferential creditor regime is found in section 386 and Schedule 6 of the Insolvency Act 1986 (hereafter 'the Act'). As mentioned above, the Enterprise Act 2002 has greatly reduced the number of debts which are preferential. The new regime only applies to insolvencies commenced after the coming into force of the 2002 Act. The previous regime will therefore remain of importance for a number of years and we shall therefore look at both the pre- and post-2002 position.

32.2 The pre-Enterprise Act 2002 regime

Section 386 and Schedule 6 Insolvency Act 1986 detail the categories of preferential debts for both individual and corporate insolvencies. Following the Cork Committee's recommendations the Crown lost its general preference in respect of unpaid taxes. Its rights were reduced to include generally only those taxes where the debtor was in effect the tax collector on behalf of the Crown such as PAYE income tax deductions and VAT. Schedule 6 of the Act contains the following preferential debts. (It should be noted that the 'relevant date' is defined in section 387 and differs depending upon the circumstances. The relevant date will be discussed in relation to each insolvency procedure later):

(1) PAYE income tax deductions made from emoluments paid during the period of 12 months prior to the relevant date (paras 1 and 2);
(2) unpaid VAT for the six months prior to the relevant date (para 3);
(3) unpaid car tax, general betting duty, bingo duty, certain pool betting duty, gaming licence duty which became due in the 12 months prior to the relevant date (paras 4 and 5);
(4) unpaid social security contributions for the period of 12 months prior to the relevant date (paras 6 and 7);
(5) any sums payable in relation to occupational pension schemes (para 8);
(6) remuneration[1] of employees for up to four months prior to the relevant date subject currently to a maximum payment of £800 (para 9);[2]
(7) any amount of employees' holiday pay accrued in respect of any employment prior to the relevant date (para 10);
(8) any sum loaned and used for the specific purpose of paying employees' remuneration (para 11).

---

[1] A term defined widely in para 13 of Schedule 6.
[2] The £800 figure is fixed by the Insolvency Proceedings (Monetary Limits) Order 1986 (SI 1986/1996).

Since the Act first came into effect in 1986 the following Crown debts were added to the list:

(9) levies on coal and steel production (para 15A);[3]
(10) beer duty which became due in the six months prior to the relevant date (para 5A);[4]
(11) lottery duty which became due in the 12 months prior to the relevant date (para 5B);[5]
(12) insurance premium tax referable to the six months prior to the relevant date (para 3A);[6]
(13) air passenger duty which became due in the six months prior to the relevant date (para 5C).[7]

In a winding up or bankruptcy, if the assets prove insufficient to meet all the claims of preferential creditors, each preferential creditor's claim ranks equally and so must suffer equal abatement.

32.3 The post-Enterprise Act 2002 regime

Under section 251 of the Enterprise Act 2002 the provisions listed above at points 1–4 and 10–13 have been abolished. The effect of this change is that the Crown has virtually lost its status as a preferential creditor.

The only remaining preferential debts are now:

(1) any sums payable in relation to occupational pension schemes (para 8);
(2) remuneration of employees for up to four months prior to the relevant date subject currently to a maximum payment of £800 (para 9);
(3) any amount of employees' holiday pay accrued in respect of any employment prior to the relevant date (para 10);
(4) any sum loaned and used for the specific purpose of paying employees' remuneration (para 11);
(5) levies on coal and steel production (para 15A).

It will be seen that in most insolvencies the only preferential debts remaining are those relating to employees' rights. There is no financial limit on the preferential status of contributions which should have been made by an insolvent employer to occupation pension schemes of employees.

---

[3] Introduced by the Insolvency (ECSC Levy Debts) Regulations 1987 (SI 1987/2093).
[4] Introduced by Schedule 2 para. 22 Finance Act 1991.
[5] Introduced by section 36(2) Finance Act 1993.
[6] Introduced by Schedule 7 para. 2 Finance Act 1994.
[7] Introduced by para 13(1) of Schedule 7 Finance Act 1994.

Similarly, there is no limit on the payment of accrued holiday pay. There is, crucially, a limit on the preferential status of unpaid wages or salary. Although in theory up to four months' back pay may be claimed, this is limited by an overall maximum amount payable of £800. In modern times, with the advent of the national minimum wage, the four-month limitation period is unlikely to be a relevant matter in that most employees, who are owed unpaid salary for a period of over four months prior to the insolvency of the employer, will be owed a sum far greater than the £800 maximum.

In addition to the above, a separate statutory scheme exists (for insolvencies commenced both before and after the Enterprise Act) for the protection of employees whose employers are unable or unwilling to meet certain of their liabilities to their workers. Payments are made under this scheme to employees by the Secretary of State out of the National Insurance Fund under the Employment Rights Act 1996 ('the ERA'). The Secretary of State is subrogated to the employees' preferential rights to the extent that the payments made are in respect of the insolvent employers' liabilities which have preferential status under the Act.

As we have seen, the Act provides essentially for unpaid wages up to a maximum of £800 and any accrued holiday pay. Section 182 ERA provides *inter alia* for up to eight weeks' arrears of wages during the statutory minimum notice period (as laid down by section 86 of the ERA), up to six weeks' holiday pay and a basic award for unfair dismissal to be paid to an employee. 'Pay' is defined widely. Where payments are to be calculated by reference to weekly pay, the maximum amount which can be used in the calculation is £250 (SI 2002/10).

The ERA scheme is beneficial to employees as payment from the Secretary of State is likely to be quicker than from a liquidator or trustee in bankruptcy. It is also likely to be a larger payment than the employee will receive under the Act. This is because the financial limits are potentially higher, for example, 8 × £250 is more than £800. It is also more beneficial because it includes certain payments such as a basic award for unfair dismissal which does not have preferential status under the Act.

The Secretary of State makes the payments out of the National Insurance Fund and stands in the shoes of the employee in attempting to recoup such money from the liquidator. A large proportion of these payments do not have preferential status and so the Secretary of State has only limited rights of subrogation.

32.4 Liquidation

The preferential debts regime operates in liquidation to ensure preferential creditors are paid out ahead of floating charge holders and unsecured creditors (section 175). The costs of the winding up take priority over the preferential creditors (as do any fixed charge realisations which will occur outside of the liquidation). The relevant date for assessing which debts are preferential, under section 387 of the Act, will be:

(1) the date of the resolution to wind up in the case of a voluntary winding up (or where a company is being wound up by the court after it had initially been placed in voluntary liquidation); or
(2) the date of the winding up order if the company is wound up by the court; or
(3) the date of the appointment of a provisional liquidator if one was in office; or
(4) if the company is being wound up following the company being in administration, the relevant date is the date the company entered administration.

32.5 Bankruptcy

The preferential debts regime operates in bankruptcy in a similar manner to the way it acts in liquidation. Secured creditors will usually enforce their security outside the bankruptcy. The preferential creditors will be paid out after the trustee's expenses and pre-preferential debts. Preferential debts will be paid ahead of the other unsecured creditors. The relevant date for ascertaining preferential debts in bankruptcy will be:

(1) the date of the making of the bankruptcy order; or
(2) where at the time the bankruptcy order was made there was an interim receiver appointed under section 286 of the Act, the date is the date on which the interim receiver was appointed after presentation of the bankruptcy petition.

32.6 Administrative receivership

The preferential debts regime prevents the receiver from making any payment to the holder of a floating charge until the preferential creditors have been paid. The relevant date for deciding which debts are preferential is the date of the appointment of the receiver by the debenture holder.

32.7 Administration

For the purposes of assessing which creditors are preferential in the administration, the relevant date is generally the date that the company enters administration.

Under the pre-Enterprise Act 2002 regime, if a company went from administration into liquidation the date for ascertaining preferential status was different depending upon whether the liquidation was voluntary or compulsory. If the liquidation was voluntary, the relevant date for deciding which debts were preferential was the date of the commencement of the liquidation (the date of the members' resolution to wind up). If it was a compulsory liquidation, the relevant date was the date of the commencement of the administration. Under the old regime where the Inland Revenue could claim up to 12 months' unpaid PAYE deductions and Customs and Excise could claim up to six months' unpaid VAT, the relevant date was crucial to the Crown making a decent recovery.[8]

Under the new regime, an administrator has the power to make a distribution to the company's creditors. Such distributions are generally limited to secured and preferential creditors and are subject to the rules contained in section 175 as to priority of payments. The administrator may now pay out the preferential creditors, whose rights are calculated as from the date the company entered administration. The administrator may then act either to put the company into voluntary liquidation under para 83 of Schedule B1 or to institute a procedure to dissolve the company under para 84. Under the new regime, if a company goes from administration into voluntary or compulsory winding up, the relevant date is the date the company entered administration.

32.8 Voluntary arrangements

Under sections 4 and 258 of the Act, the priority of a preferential creditor, under the terms of a company or individual voluntary arrangement respectively, cannot be effected without the creditor's consent.

The relevant date for ascertaining preferential creditors under section 387 is slightly different depending upon whether the arrangement is entered into by a company or an individual.

For a company voluntary arrangement, where the company is not being wound up, the relevant date is:

---

[8] See the discussion in Chapter 7.

(1) where the company is in administration the date on which the company entered administration;
(2) if the company is not in administration the relevant date is the date on which the voluntary arrangement takes effect;
(3) if the company is a small company which obtained the benefit of a moratorium under Schedule A1 of the Act, the date is the date of filing of the requisite documents at court leading to the moratorium.

For an individual voluntary arrangement, where the individual is not an undischarged bankrupt the relevant date is:

(1) where an interim order has been made under section 252, the date of that order;
(2) in any other case, the date on which the voluntary arrangement takes effect.

Chapter 33

Set-Off

33.1 Introduction

In simple terms, set-off is the right of one party who is owed money by a second party to ensure payment from the second party by setting off the amount owed, by a reduction of the first party's liability to the second party under a separate dealing. Where a creditor and debtor have had mutual dealings, the creditor is entitled to set off against the debt which he or she is owed, any sum which the creditor owes to the debtor. A simple example would be as follows:

> A supplies grapes to B for £10,000. B uses the grapes to make wine. B sells some wine to A for £30,000. In any action by B to sue A for the £30,000, A does not need to pay B the full £30,000 and then bring a separate action to claim the £10,000 owed by B to A. A may set off the £10,000 owed by B and only need pay to B the balance, that is, £20,000.

In order for there to be a set-off, there must, by definition, be two separate claims. Set-off cannot apply where there is, for example, a current account with a continuous flow of debits and credits, as with such an account there is a running total at all times and there is always a balance payable.[1]

The law relating to set-off is extremely complex and it is not intended in this book to do more than give some general guidance as to how it operates in an insolvency context.[2] The types of set-off which are most relevant in this context are equitable set-off and insolvency set-off. If the debtor is in bankruptcy or liquidation, the provisions of the Act and the Rules respectively apply specific rules for how insolvency set-off applies. In other situations the more general rules applicable to equitable and contractual set-off will normally apply.

---

[1] See e.g., *Halesowen Presswork and Assemblies Ltd v Westminster Bank Ltd* [1971] 1 QB 1.

[2] For detailed explanation see e.g., R. Derham, *Set-Off*, 2nd edn, Clarendon Press (1996) and P. Wood, *English and International Set-Off*, 2nd edn, London: Sweet & Maxwell (1989).

33.2 Insolvency set-off in liquidation and bankruptcy

The right of set-off in bankruptcy can be found in section 323 of the Act. The wording is virtually identical to that which applies in liquidation. The right of set-off in liquidation can be found in rule 4.90 of the Rules which states:

> 4.90(1) [Application of Rule] This Rule applies where, before the company goes into liquidation there have been mutual credits, mutual debts or other mutual dealings between the company and any creditor of the company proving or claiming to prove for a debt in liquidation.
>
> 4.90(2) [Account of mutual dealings and set-off] An account shall be taken of what is due from each party to the other in respect of the mutual dealings and the sums due from one party shall be set off against the sums due from the other.
>
> 4.90(3) [Sums not to be included in account] Sums due from the company to another party shall not be included in the account taken under paragraph (2) if that other party had notice at the time they became due that a meeting of creditors had been summoned under section 98 or (as the case may be) a petition for the winding up of the company was pending.
>
> 4.90(4) [Only balance (if any) provable etc.] Only the balance (if any) of the account is provable in the liquidation. Alternatively (as the case may be) the amount shall be paid to the liquidator as part of the assets.

Some points may be made about this rule:

- Its operation is a distinct exception to the *pari passu* principle. A creditor who has the ability to set off mutual debts and credits will be in a far better position than creditors who merely prove in a bankruptcy or liquidation as unsecured creditors. The set-off creditor will have the benefit of the set-off and may therefore be paid out fully or to a significant extent. Unsecured creditors frequently receive little or nothing from the insolvency of their debtors.
- There must have been mutual credits, mutual debts or other mutual dealings between the parties before the liquidation or bankruptcy. Mutuality requires that the dealings between the parties be in the same capacity, right or interest.[3] For example, a claim by A against company B in liquidation cannot be set off against a claim by company B against A in the capacity of trustee for a third party.
- The respective claims of the parties must be based upon monetary claims. A proprietary claim such as a bailment cannot be set off against a money claim.
- Set-off is only possible in relation to claims made in the liquidation or bankruptcy which are subject to proof. If a debt could not be proved

---

[3] For a comparison on similar facts where mutuality was held to exist and not to exist respectively see *MS Fashions Ltd v BCCI* [1993] Ch 425 and *Re BCCI (No 8)* [1997] 4 All ER 568.

for in the liquidation or bankruptcy, such as a claim which has become statute barred, it cannot be set off.

- No set-off is possible in relation to mutual dealings where sums become due from the company after the other party has notice of a meeting of creditors convened for the purposes of a voluntary winding up or a petition for a compulsory winding up (or bankruptcy). As long as the contract has been entered into and the debt has become due, it seems it will not matter that it is not presently payable.

From the leading case of *Stein v Blake* ([1996] 1 AC 243) the following further points may be made. First, the rule is mandatory. If there have been mutual dealings between the parties prior to the winding up or bankruptcy, the insolvency set-off cannot be excluded by any agreement between the parties. It takes precedence over any other form of set-off not exercised before the winding up or bankruptcy.[4] Second, the set-off takes effect on the parties' respective rights as they exist at the time of the commencement of the winding up[5] or bankruptcy.[6] Separate debts cease to exist at this point. This date will be brought forward under section 323 or rule 4.90 if the other party has notice of the bankruptcy or winding-up petition or a meeting to consider a resolution to wind up the company voluntarily. Third, the courts consider what happens after the commencement of the liquidation or bankruptcy in order to give a value to the mutual claims at the date of the liquidation or bankruptcy. This is of relevance where claims are contingent in nature and can only be quantified at a later date.

33.3 Equitable or contractual set-off applicable in receivershiip

There is no specific legislative provision dealing with set-off in receivership. One must therefore consider the general position at law and in equity to ascertain if and when set-off will be possible in receivership. Where a claim and counter-claim, even if not arising from the same contract, are closely connected, equity will usually allow a set-off. The effect of this is that the mutual debts and credits are set off to prevent an inequitable result. Contractual set-off may take precedence over equitable set-off and applies wherever the parties have expressly provided in the

---

[4] See e.g., *Halesowen Presswork and Assemblies Ltd v Westminster Bank Ltd* [1971] 1 QB 1.

[5] Date of the petition in a compulsory winding up and the date of the members' resolution in a creditors' voluntary winding up.

[6] Date of the bankruptcy order.

contract for mutual credits and debits to be set off. Contractual set-off can expressly include a set-off of all sums owed or owing between the parties. It need not be limited to one particular contract but can encompass all the dealings between the parties. Express contractual set-off provisions will usually be drafted in such a way as to apply to the parties' dealings prior to the coming into force of an insolvency set-off.

An equitable set-off is available between two parties where the claims are so closely related that there is a clear connection between them. This will usually be the case where the competing claims arise from the same contract or the same subject matter.[7] The claims may be for liquidated or unliquidated amounts.

In the context of a receivership, equitable set-off will be available if the rights being set off arise before the floating charge crystallises. An example of this is the case of *Rother Iron Works Ltd v Canterbury Precision Engineers Ltd* ([1974] QB 1):

> Two companies had entered a series of contracts for the supply of goods to one another. Company A owed Company B £124 for goods supplied but not yet paid for. Company B ordered goods to the value of £159 from Company A. Before delivery or payment were possible, Company A was put into receivership by its bank which held a floating charge over the company's undertaking. The bank's floating charge crystallised at this moment. The receiver sued Company B in Company A's name for the outstanding £159. Company B claimed it was able to set off the £124 it was owed from the £159 it owed. The court agreed with Company B. The court pointed out that although when the floating charge crystallised it fixed upon the company's *chose in* action to sue Company B for £159, the debenture holder could not be in a better position than Company A itself and so took subject to the right of set-off. Company B was only liable to pay the balance of £35.

If a company in receivership continues to perform a contract which was in existence prior to the receivership, the right of set-off is retained. This is the case even if some of the debts were incurred before and some after the receivership.[8] A creditor who enters a new contract with a company which has entered receivership cannot set off against the receiver a debt owed by the company prior to the receivership. There is said to be a lack of mutuality in this situation. The parties are not dealing with one another in the same right.[9] Set-off is equally not available if the claim arises after the company has entered receivership but in relation to a pre-receivership contract. Again there is no mutuality and set-off will only be possible if the claims arise out of the same subject matter.[10]

---

[7] See e.g., *Newfoundland Government v Newfoundland Railway Co* (1888) 13 App Cas 199.

[8] See e.g., *Parsons v Sovereign Bank of Canada* [1913] AC 160.

[9] See e.g., *NW Robbie & Co Ltd v Witney Warehouse Co Ltd* [1963] 1 WLR 1324.

[10] See e.g., *Business Computers Ltd v Anglo African Leasing Ltd* [1972] 1 WLR 578.

33.4 Set-off in administration

There are again no specific legislative provisions dealing with set-off in administration. Although a company in administration has the benefit of a moratorium on creditor actions, (under paras 42 and 43 of Schedule B1 of the Act), it does not appear to prevent a claim of set-off. The moratorium expressly prevents any legal proceedings being commenced or continued against the company but this has been interpreted as only covering proceedings which require the assistance of the court (*Re Olympia & York Canary Wharf Ltd* [1993] BCLC 453). Contractual or equitable set-off, in theory, do not need the court's assistance to be claimed and therefore seem to be available to claim against a company in administration as long as the claims are sufficiently mutual or are based on the same subject matter. The problem faced by a creditor of a company in administration is that if the company in administration brings an action against the creditor, the creditor will only be able to claim set-off if the creditor's claim has already been quantified. If the creditor's claim is for an unliquidated amount requiring court action prior to being ascertained, leave of the court will need to be granted before this can occur and before any set-off can be claimed. The difficult position a creditor may be placed in can be seen from *Isovel Contracts Ltd (in administration) v ABB Building Technologies Ltd* ([2002] BPIR 525):

> Company C in administration sought summary judgment under Part 24 of the Civil Procedure Rules 1998 against Company D, in respect of a cheque which Company D had countermanded. Company D asked for a stay of the Part 24 proceedings pending the outcome of its own Part 20 claim against Company C. Company D argued that non-payment of the cheque was justified due to the failure in consideration of Company C under a building contract. The court granted summary judgment and refused any stay. A stay of judgment in bills of exchange cases should only be granted in exceptional circumstances. Company C being in administration did not constitute exceptional circumstances even though it would cause Company D problems in bringing its Part 20 claim. To grant the stay would be tantamount to permitting a set-off between Company D's liability on the cheque and any rights Company C might end up with under its Part 20 claim. The court would not extend the principles of insolvency set-off under rule 4.90 to companies in administration.

33.5 Set-off in voluntary arrangements

Again there are no specific legislative provisions dealing with set-off in voluntary arrangements. There is no prohibition on claiming the right of set-off during the period of an interim order leading to an IVA or the moratorium under the new CVA procedure for small companies introduced by the 2000 Insolvency Act. It is clear that the chairman at the creditors' meeting will set off any debts owed to the debtor from any owed by the debtor to the creditor, before putting a value on the creditor's claim for voting purposes. The voluntary arrangement itself will usually contain a provision dealing with set-off. Such a provision will be not dissimilar to the wording of section 323 of the Act. For example, the standard conditions for individual voluntary arrangements produced by R3 (the Association of Business Recovery Professionals) in March 2002 contain the following provision:

7 Mutual credit and set-off

7(1) [Application] This paragraph applies where before the commencement of the Arrangement there have been mutual credits, mutual Debts or other mutual dealings between the Debtor and any Creditor.

7(2) [Account to be taken] An account shall be taken of what is due from each party to the other in respect of the mutual dealings and the sums due from one party shall be set-off against the sums due from the other.

7(3) [No account where Creditor has notice] Sums due from the Debtor to another party shall not be included in the account taken under sub-paragraph (2) if that other party had notice at the time they became due that a bankruptcy petition relating to the Debtor was pending or that an interim order was made in relation to the Debtor.

7(4) [Restriction on post-commencement set-off] Other than as provided for in this Paragraph, set-off shall not be available in respect of any Debt or item of Property.

7(5) [Balance provable or to be paid] Only the balance (if any) of the account taken under sub-paragraph (2) is provable in the Arrangement or, as the case may be, to be paid to the Debtor or, if the Proposal so provides, to the Supervisor.

The practical effect of this provision is to incorporate the rules for insolvency set-off into voluntary arrangements. It would seem an eminently sensible provision which should ensure certainty as regards how set-off operates in voluntary arrangements. It does, of course, also bring into the arrangement a palpable breach of the *pari passu* principle which in theory could lead some creditors to apply to the court claiming the terms of the arrangement unfairly prejudice their interests.

Chapter 34

Proving Debts

34.1 Introduction

The status of creditor confers a number of rights and powers over an insolvent debtor. A creditor may petition for the winding up or bankruptcy of a debtor. A creditor may attend and vote at creditors' meetings. The most important right for an unsecured creditor is the right to prove in a winding up or bankruptcy and to receive a dividend on the final distribution of the estate. Any rights to commence or continue proceedings or to execute a judgment are usually suspended where the debtor is being wound up or is bankrupt and the creditor is instead left with the right to prove or claim the debt. As most liquidations and bankruptcies are insolvent an unsecured creditor will usually only be paid a percentage of the debt owed. This percentage payment is referred to as a dividend. Creditors will prove for their debts by completing proof forms sent out to them by the liquidator or trustee in bankruptcy (as the case may be). If a proof is rejected by the liquidator or trustee, the creditor may apply to the court to have the decision reversed.

Proving debts is only really of relevance in the terminal insolvency procedures, that is, liquidation and bankruptcy. A receiver or administrator will not usually make dividend payments to unsecured creditors. That is not their function. A receiver is in post to realise the secured assets and pay off the debenture holder. An administrator is in post to attempt a rescue of the company. If this is not possible, the administrator must attempt to realise the company's assets in as advantageous a manner as possible. Once this is accomplished, the company will usually be wound up and it will be the liquidator who will deal with the proofs of the unsecured creditors. The supervisor of a voluntary arrangement will usually have a duty to pay off unsecured creditors but this duty will arise under the terms of the arrangement itself, not under the provisions of the Act.

34.2 Liquidation

Most but not all debts owed by a company in liquidation are provable in the liquidation. Rule 13.12 of the Rules defines debts and liabilities for the purposes of liquidation as:

(1) any debt or liability to which the company is subject at the date on which it goes into liquidation;
(2) any debt or liability to which the company may become subject after that date by reason of any obligation incurred before that date; and
(3) interest accrued prior to the winding up on such debts or liabilities (see rule 4.93(1)).

Debts dealt with in a winding up will therefore be those incurred either before the commencement of liquidation (the date of the resolution or petition) or incurred after liquidation but, for example, under a contract entered into before the liquidation. The debt must be one which is legally due in the sense of being enforceable by legal process. Any contract debt which, for example, has become statute barred, cannot be the subject of proof in a liquidation.

Under rule 12.3 a debt or liability is provable whether it is present or future, certain or contingent, whether its amount is liquidated, or sounds only in damages. Any liability arising in tort is provable if the cause of action arose before the company entered liquidation. A liability includes a liability to pay money or money's worth and includes liability arising from any enactment, breach of trust, any liability in contract, tort or bailment or any liability arising out of an obligation to make restitution. The value of any debt which is not ascertained will be estimated by the liquidator and it will be the estimated amount which will be provable (rule 4.86).

The vast majority of debts owed by a company are provable in a liquidation. An example of a non-provable debt, under rule 12.3, is an obligation arising under a confiscation order under section 1 of the Drug Trafficking Offences Act 1986 or under section 1 of the Criminal Justice Act 1988.

A rare example of a case where a non-provable debt arose is *Re Kentish Homes Ltd* ([1993] BCC 212):

> Prior to the liquidation, a Law of Property Act receiver had been appointed over the company's premises. The receiver completed a contract to build some houses. By doing so the company incurred community charge liabilities to the local authority in relation to the unoccupied houses. The liquidator had not taken possession of the houses. The court decided that the local authority could not prove in the liquidation. The reason for this was that the liability to pay the community charge did not exist at the date of the commencement of the liquidation nor did it arise under a pre-existing obligation.

The rule against double proof prohibits more than one proof in respect of what is in substance the same debt. This has the consequence that a surety cannot prove in a winding up so long as the principal creditor retains a right of proof. Although the claim owed to the principal creditor and the claim of the surety under an indemnity from the company (effective when the company fails to pay in full the principal creditor) are distinct liabilities, they are in substance the same debt whether one or two claims arise out of the same liability. The rule against double proof looks at the substance rather than the form. Oliver LJ in *Barclays Bank Ltd v TOSG Trust Fund Ltd* ([1984] 2 WLR 49 at 58) explained that for the rule to apply the relationship between the two claims:

> is simply whether the two competing claims are, in *substance*, claims for payment of the same debt twice over . . . the rule against the double proofs in respect of two liabilities of an insolvent debtor is going to apply wherever the existence of one liability is dependent upon and referable only to the liability to the other and where to allow both liabilities to rank independently for dividend would produce injustice to the unsecured creditors.

Liabilities incurred after the commencement of the liquidation will rank as expenses of the liquidation rather than as provable debts.

A secured creditor may do one of four things in relation to proof of debts:

(1) realise the security and prove for any balance owing;
(2) assess the value of the security, declare the value to the liquidator and receive a dividend in relation to the balance;
(3) rely on the security for full satisfaction of the debt owed and therefore lodge no proof;
(4) surrender the security to the liquidator and prove for the whole debt owed.

34.3 Bankruptcy

The rules as to what debts are 'bankruptcy debts' are essentially the same as for liquidation. The rules, found in section 382 of the Act, largely repeat the provisions of rule 13.12 and include debts and liabilities to which the bankrupt is subject at the commencement of the bankruptcy (the date of the bankruptcy order).

Rule 12.3 applies to bankruptcy as it does to liquidation but in bankruptcy there are more debts which are not provable than in liquidation. The reason for this appears to be that a company in liquidation will cease to exist and therefore there is no possibility of a debt surviving the liquidation. An individual will survive the bankruptcy and although the bankrupt will be discharged from most debts, some liabilities do survive the bankruptcy. Any fine imposed for an offence and any obligation arising under an order made in family proceedings or under a maintenance assessment made under the Child Support Act 1991 are not provable in a bankruptcy. A bankrupt is not released from such liabilities on discharge but remains liable after discharge (section 281).

The rules in liquidation which deal with contingent creditors, double proof and secured creditors apply equally in bankruptcy.

References

Bailey, E., Groves, H. and Smith, C., *Corporate Insolvency Law and Practice*, 2nd edn, London: Butterworths (2001).

Bebchuk, L. and Fried, J., 'The Uneasy Case for the Priority of Secured Claims in Bankruptcy' (1996) 105 Yale L J 857.

Berry, C., Bailey, E. and Schaw-Miller, S., *Personal Insolvency Law – Law and Practice*, 3rd edn, London: Butterworths (2001).

Cantlie, S., 'Preferred Priority in Bankruptcy' in J. Ziegel, *Current Developments in International and Comparative Corporate Insolvency Law*, Clarendon Press (1994).

Davies, I., 'Reservation of Title Clauses: A Legal Quagmire' [1984] LMCLQ 49.

Derham, R., *Set-Off*, 2nd edn, Clarendon Press (1996).

Finch, V., 'Security, Insolvency and Risk: Who Pays the Price?' (1999) 62 MLR 633.

Fletcher, I., *The Law of Insolvency*, 3rd edn, London: Sweet & Maxwell (2002).

Garrido, J., 'The Distributional Question in Insolvency: Comparative Aspects' (1995) 4 *International Insolvency Review* 25.

Goode, R., 'Is the Law too Favourable to Secured Creditors?' (1983–4) 8 *Canadian Business Law Journal* 53.

Goode, R., *Principles of Corporate Insolvency Law*, 2nd edn, London: Sweet & Maxwell (1997).

Gregory, R., 'Romalpa clauses as unregistered charges – a fundamental shift?' (1990) 106 LQR 550.

Hare, D. and Milman, D., 'Debenture holders and judgment creditors – problems of priority' [1982] LMCLQ 57.

Keay, A., *McPherson's Law of Company Liquidation*, London: Sweet & Maxwell (2001).

Keay, A. and Walton, P., 'The Preferential Debts Regime in Liquidation Law: In the Public Interest?' (1999) 3 *Company Financial and Insolvency Law Review* 84.

Lightman, G. and Moss, G., *The Law of Receivers and Administrators of Companies*, 3rd edn, London: Sweet & Maxwell (2000).

McCormack, G., 'Reservation of Title – the controversy continues' [1989] LMCLQ 198.

McLoughlin, P., *Commercial Leases and Insolvency*, 3rd edn, London: Butterworths (2002).

Milman, D. and Durrant, C., *Corporate Insolvency: Law and Practice*, 3rd edn, London: Sweet & Maxwell (1999).

Mokal, R., 'The Search for Someone to Save: A Defensive Case for the Priority of Secured Credit' (2002) 22 OJLS 687.

Pennington, R., *Pennington's Corporate Insolvency Law*, 2nd edn, London: Butterworths (1997).

Pennington, R., *Company Law*, 8th edn, London: Butterworths (2001).

Schwartz, A., 'Security Interests and Bankruptcy Priorities Among Creditors' (1981) 10 *Journal of Legal Studies* 1.

Schwarcz, S., 'The Easy Case for the Priority of Secured Claims in Bankruptcy' (1997) 47 Duke L J 425.

Walton, P., 'The Landlord, his Distress, the Insolvent Tenant and the Stranger' (2000) 16 *Insolvency Law and Practice* 47.

Walton, P., 'Landlord's Distress – Past Its Sell By Date?' [2000] Conv 508.

Wheeler, S., 'The Insolvency Act 1986 and Retention of Title' [1987] JBL 180.

Wood, P., *English and International Set Off*, 2nd edn, London: Sweet & Maxwell (1989).

Part VIII

Swelling the Asset Pool

One of the most time-consuming and often the most demanding part of the job of office-holders is the collection of the assets of the insolvent. The office-holder will need to know what assets are legally available for division among creditors and for distribution. This was addressed in broad terms in Chapter 26. This Part considers the assets which may be able to be recovered and what actions can be initiated by an office-holder to recover assets to which he or she is entitled but which are held by others.[1] Much of the Part is concerned with discussing the law applicable to the adjustment of transactions entered into prior to winding up or bankruptcy commencing. Where a transaction entered into prior to the advent of a formal insolvency administration is adjusted in favour of the insolvent then the pool of assets available for distribution will be increased. The recovery of assets may lead to substantial and, perhaps, protracted, litigation. One of the problems that office-holders often encounter in attempting to recover assets is that they do not have sufficient funds to pursue litigation. The issue of funding was discussed in Chapter 26. While it is a significant issue in relation to the actions discussed here, no further discussion will be included in relation to funding, but readers should be aware of its practical significance.

While sections of this Part are relevant to administrations, our main focus is on liquidation and bankruptcy as it is in relation to these insolvency administrations that most actions are initiated to augment the assets available for creditors. As far as possible we will deal with provisions that are relevant to both corporate and personal insolvencies together.

---

[1] Sections 246 and 349 (the unenforceability of liens of books), and section 344 (the avoidance of general assignments of book debts), are not addressed in this Part. For a consideration of section 246, see A. Keay, *McPherson's Law of Company Liquidation*, London: Sweet & Maxwell (2001) at 611–12, and for a discussion of all of the foregoing sections, see R. Parry in *Transaction Avoidance in Insolvencies*, Oxford: Oxford University Press (2001) at 215–24.

Throughout this Part, except where indicated to the contrary, any reference to 'the Act' or to section numbers will be a reference to the Insolvency Act 1986. Except where indicated to the contrary, any reference to 'the Rules' or to rule numbers will be a reference to the Insolvency Rules 1986 (SI 1986/1925).

Chapter 35

General Principles and Concepts

35.1 Introduction

Besides the assets that are obviously owned by an insolvent, an office-holder can claim various other forms of property. A number of statutory provisions permit office-holders to recover property or money from other persons, or to avoid certain obligations. It is with these provisions that this Part is primarily concerned. The provisions considered here relate to dispositions by the insolvent in favour of third persons, particularly during the time immediately before the commencement of the insolvency administration and with special focus on persons associated with the insolvent. During this period an individual or the controllers of a company may well be aware that liquidation, administration or bankruptcy is imminent. Realising this, they may attempt to favour associated parties, or so order the affairs of the company, or in the case of individuals, their own affairs, with the result that they themselves, or some associates, are benefited at the expense of the general body of creditors. Sometimes third parties are benefited without any intention on the part of the bankrupt or the controllers of the company to act improperly or unfairly; the benefits are bestowed randomly. However, as far as the law of insolvency is concerned the reason for providing a benefit does not matter; the law in this area is preoccupied with a concern for a fair, equal and rateable distribution among the creditors and the bestowal of benefits before an administration on others is likely, generally speaking, to affect the fair distribution principle.

The law provides for a collective process in that liquidation and bankruptcy binds all unsecured creditors in relation to the assets of the insolvent that are collected and distributed among creditors. The process is supported by one of the foremost principles of insolvency law which is that there should be a fair and equal distribution of assets among the general body of creditors and creditors of the same class should be treated equally. The principle is known as the *pari passu* principle,[1] and was discussed in Chapter 28. It would be impossible to achieve equality if the law was to disregard what happened prior to winding up.

The collective process, in effect, restricts individual creditors in order to benefit the whole body of creditors. It does so by prohibiting certain transactions before the commencement of insolvent administrations. The legislature has taken the view, and it is a long established one, that transactions by which an insolvent disposed of property within a certain time zone prior to the commencement of an insolvent administration, in circumstances which are unfair to the whole group of creditors, should be subject to scrutiny, and perhaps to adjustment or avoidance. The consequence of such a policy is that transactions which effected the disposition of assets or other property and which were entered into quite legally and, in many cases, quite properly before the commencement of the administration, may be reviewed and adjusted or avoided. The assets disposed of by the insolvent may be recovered and made available to meet the claims of the creditors. A policy allowing for adjustment prevents the unjust enrichment of the party who receives the property from the insolvent to the detriment of the other creditors, if the recipient is a creditor, or to the detriment of all unsecured creditors if the recipient is not a creditor. If such transactions could not be adjusted in some way it would be open to a debtor, before the commencement of the insolvency administration, to dissipate assets in favour of whomsoever the debtor pleased and this is unlikely to be in accord with the principle of fair and equal distribution. If dissipation transpired there would be a reduction of the property that would be available to the office-holder to distribute to those creditors who had not been favoured by the debtor.

A second reason for the legislature permitting office-holders to attack transactions entered into prior to an insolvent administration is that the existence of provisions allowing for challenges to transactions might protect the assets of the insolvent and prevent the dismemberment of the insolvent's estate thereby causing the premature advent of a formal insolvency administration.[2]

---

[1] For a more detailed discussion of the *pari passu* principle, see V. Finch and S. Worthington, 'The Pari Passu Principle and Ranking Restitutionary Rights' in F. Rose (ed), *Restitution and Insolvency*, London: LLP (2000) at 1–7; V. Finch, 'Is Pari Passu Passe?' [2000] *Insolvency Lawyer* 194; R. Mokal, 'Priority as Pathology: The Pari Passu Principle Myth' (2001) 60 CLJ 581.

[2] See A. Keay, 'In Pursuit of the Rationale Behind the Avoidance of Pre-Liquidation, Transactions' (1996) 18 *Sydney Law Review* 55.

35.2 The legislative framework

The power to challenge transactions stems from sections 238–241 and sections 244–246 (sections 242 and 243 apply to Scotland only) for insolvent companies and sections 339–344 for insolvent individuals. These provisions provide for the adjustment or avoidance of the transactions entered into before an insolvent administration. Special mention needs to be made of another provision, section 423, which must be discussed in the same context as the sections mentioned earlier, even though it is not found in the same parts of the Act as the other provisions. It is a provision which applies to individuals as well as companies; it can be invoked by creditors in addition to office-holders and it is broader than the other provisions as it is not necessary for the person against whom proceedings are brought to be an insolvent or to have entered a formal insolvency administration before it can be invoked.

The most important of the above provisions are often referred to as 'the avoidance provisions', 'provisions for transactional avoidance', or 'avoiding powers' (the last phrase is the terminology used chiefly in the United States). The reason for the use of avoidance in the description of the type of proceedings which we are discussing is that originally the only provision made in relation to such transactions by statute was for the avoidance of the impugned transaction. Here, because we will consider provisions which do not provide either at all or exclusively for avoidance, it is appropriate to refer to the provisions simply as 'the adjustment provisions'.

At the outset it should be noted that the law in this area and the issues which have emanated from the decided cases is voluminous and only so much space can be devoted to this topic. For greater detail, especially concerning some of the issues and problems that exist in this area, the reader should refer to specialist works.[3]

---

[3] For example, see I.F. Fletcher, 'Voidable Transactions in Bankruptcy: British Perspectives' in J. Ziegel (ed.), *Current Developments in International and Comparative Corporate Insolvency Law*, Oxford: Clarendon Press (1994) at 297–310; D.D. Prentice, 'The Effect of Insolvency on Pre-Liquidation Transactions' in B. Pettet (ed), *Company Law in Change: Current Legal Problems*, London: Stevens (1987); D. Milman and R. Parry, 'Challenging Transactional Integrity on Insolvency: An Evaluation of the New Law' (1997) 48 NILQ 24; A. Keay, 'Preferences in Liquidation Law: A Time for a Change' [1998] 2 Cfi LR 198; A. Keay, 'The Recovery of Voidable Preferences: Aspects of Recovery [2000] Cfi LR 1; A. Keay, *McPherson's Law of Company Liquidation*, London: Sweet & Maxwell (2001), Chapter 11; R. Parry, *Transaction Avoidance in Insolvencies*, Oxford: Oxford University Press (2001).

35.3 Applicable concepts

To appreciate the provisions that allow for adjustment or avoidance one must understand some important concepts.

35.3.1 *The relevant time*

Not all pre-insolvency administration transactions can be challenged by an office-holder. Transactions must fall into certain categories. Also, for an office-holder to be able to seek an order adjusting a transaction on the basis that it is a transaction at an undervalue (sections 238, 339) or a preference (sections 239, 340), or for an administrator or liquidator to challenge a transaction on the basis that it is an invalid floating charge (section 245), the transaction must have been entered into within 'the relevant time', which is a time zone specified in the legislation. The actual time zone applicable will depend on several circumstances, including what type of transaction is alleged to have been made, but what is uniform with all transactions is that the time zone is calculated in relation to a specific date: either the onset of insolvency for companies (section 240(3)) or when a petition was presented against an individual debtor who was later adjudged bankrupt on the petition (section 341(1)).

Section 240(3) explains that 'onset of insolvency' means a number or things, depending on whether there was an administration, a straight winding up or whether an administration preceded winding up. The date is, where an administration order was made, the date of the administration application (section 240(1)(a)) and where no administration order was made (there was an appointment without court order) and the appointment was initiated by the company (or its directors) or a floating chargeholder, the date is the date on which the copy of the notice of appointment was filed with the court (section 240(1)(b)). In other circumstances where administration has occurred the date is the date when the administration takes effect (section 240(3)(c)). Where a winding up either follows conversion of administration into winding up or at the time when the appointment of an administrator ceased to have effect, the relevent time is the date on which the company entered administration (or, where relevant, the date on which the application for the administration was made or a copy of the intention to appoint an administrator was filed) (section 240(3)(d)). If the company's liquidation occurred in any other circumstances then the date of the commencement of the winding up is the onset of insolvency.

As discussed in Chapter 14, the commencement of winding up is, for voluntary liquidations, at the time of the passing of the resolution for winding up (section 86), and in compulsory liquidation, it is the time of the presentation of the petition (section 129(2)). If a winding-up order is made by a court, under para 13(1)(e) of Schedule B1 when hearing an application for an administration order, the commencement of winding up is the date of the order (section 129(1A)). For bankruptcy the relevant time is the date of the presentation of the petition on which the debtor is adjudged bankrupt (section 341(1)).

Once the office-holder has determined the date of the onset of insolvency or the date of the presentation of the petition on which the debtor is adjudged bankrupt, the office-holder must then work backwards to see what transactions fall within the time periods set out in the Act. For a transaction to be able to be challenged on the basis that it is a preference then it must have been given in the six months before the onset of insolvency or the date of the presentation of the petition on which the debtor is adjudged bankrupt (sections 240(1)(b), 341(1)(c)). This period is extended to two years when the person who was the recipient of the preference is connected with the company (except merely through employment) or an associate of the bankrupt (sections 240(1)(a), 341(1)(b)). Transactions which are categorised as transactions at an undervalue may be adjusted where they were entered into by either the company within two years of the onset of insolvency or the bankrupt within five years of the date of the presentation of the petition on which the debtor is adjudged bankrupt (sections 240(1)(a), 341(1)(a)). Floating charges will only be avoided where created within either the 12 months prior to the onset of insolvency (section 245(3)(b)), or the two-year period before the onset of insolvency and the charge was created in favour of a connected person (section 245(3)(b)), a term we will consider shortly.

35.3.2 *Insolvent*

The relevant time for determining whether a transaction is in fact able to be subject to adjustment is not only dependent on the amount of time before the onset of insolvency or the date of the presentation of the petition on which the debtor is adjudged bankrupt. There is another factor to consider when it comes to some of the adjustment provisions. Office-holders, when taking action under sections 238, 339 (transaction at undervalue), 239, 340 (preference) or 245 (creation of a floating charge) in relation to a transaction, might have to establish, besides the fact that the transaction occurred within the designated time zone, that either the insolvent was insolvent at the time of the transaction or became insolvent as a result of the transaction.[4] The provisions that refer to companies do not directly refer to the need to establish insolvency. They say that the

---

[4] See section 240(2) for transactions at an undervalue and preferences, and section 245(4) for creation of floating charges in relation to companies. Section 341(2) applies to individuals who become bankrupt.

company must have been 'unable to pay its debts'. The concept of 'unable to pay debts' is to be construed according to the way that phrase is defined in section 123. Unable to pay debts, which is a more expansive way of saying 'insolvent', is defined in section 123(1), (2) of the Act. The sub-sections enumerate six instances where a company will be deemed to be unable to pay its debts. Two instances are not applicable in England and Wales and will not be considered here. The four instances discussed earlier, in Chapter 14, were:

- the company failed to comply for three weeks with a written demand served on it left at its registered office where the demand was given by a creditor owed a debt in excess of £750 and the demand required the payment of the amount due (section 123(1)(a));
- execution or other process issued on a judgment or order of any court in favour of a creditor of the company was returned wholly or partly unsatisfied (section 123(1)(b));
- it is proved to the satisfaction of the court that the company is unable to pay its debts as they fall due (section 123(1)(e));
- it is proved to the satisfaction of the court that the value of the company's assets is less than the amount of its liabilities after taking into account the company's contingent and prospective liabilities (section 123(2)).

Section 341 includes the last two tests for establishing the insolvency of a bankrupt when a trustee is seeking to attack pre-bankruptcy transactions. So, depending on whether we are dealing with a company or an individual, it must be demonstrated that the insolvent was unable to pay its debts as they fall due (cash flow insolvency) or the value of assets are less than the amount of liabilities (balance sheet insolvency). These two tests were explained and assessed in Chapter 2.

35.3.3 *Connected persons and associates*

As mentioned above, if the party to a transaction in which an insolvent company (later in liquidation or administration) is involved falls within the definition of 'connected person', then an office-holder can challenge trans-actions that are able to be classified as preferences, if they were entered into up to two years before the onset of insolvency (section 240(1)(a)). This is to be contrasted with the period of six months (section 240(1)(b)) specified for preferential transactions where the party to the transaction is not a connected person. Similarly, in relation to the avoidance of floating charges in section 245, a floating charge will only be avoided where it was created in the 12 months before the onset of insolvency (section 245(3)(b)), whereas if a floating charge was created in favour of a connected person then the time is expanded to two years (section 245(3)(a)).

Where preferences are concerned, the same principle applies if a party to a transaction in which an insolvent person (later to become a bankrupt) is involved falls within the definition of 'associate'.

'Connected person' is defined in section 249 as a director or shadow director or an associate. But then it is necessary to go to other sections to get a complete view of the term. First, 'director' is defined in section 741(1) of the Companies Act 1985 as 'any person occupying the position of director, by whatever name called'. Second, 'shadow director' is defined in section 741(2) of the Companies Act 1985 as 'a person in accordance with whose directions and instructions the directors of the company are accustomed to act',[5] but excludes persons who are giving advice to the company in a professional capacity. Third, the expression 'associate', which is also relevant for bankruptcy, is defined broadly in section 435. 'Associate' includes a broad range of persons and relationships. Besides identifying as associates spouses and relatives, and those with whom the insolvent is associated in partnership (section 435(3)), the section seeks to define when a company is deemed to be an associate of another company. Further, section 435 explains how persons can be associates because of their control of companies (section 435(6)). The relationship between trustee and beneficiaries under some types of trust may lead to those persons deemed to be associates if the company or its associates are able to benefit under the trust (section 435(5)).[6] In addition, the provision defines 'relative' (section 435(8)).

The foregoing provisions are an attempt to prevent persons and companies associated with an insolvent, or directors of an insolvent company, from benefiting from preferences and floating charges which occurred outside of the normal time zone of six or 12 months respectively. Connected persons are specifically identified on the basis that they are likely to be aware of the financial affairs of the company and may be able to exert influence to gain some advantage. The same can be said about associates in relation to bankrupts.

---

[5] For a discussion of the ingredients of the definition, see *Re Hydrodan (Corby) Ltd* [1994] BCLC 180; [1994] BCC 161 per Millett J.

[6] See the discussion of this provision in *Re Thirty-Eight Building Ltd* [1999] 1 BCLC 416; [1999] BCC 260.

Chapter 36

Transactions at an Undervalue

36.1 Introduction

This chapter deals with transactions that have left the insolvent's estate short of funds or property, because the insolvent has either made gifts to others or received consideration of a value that is significantly less than that which was given by the insolvent and the provisions, namely sections 238 and 339, enable office-holders to challenge such transactions in an attempt to conserve the insolvent estate. Transactions entered into by a company may be challenged by either a liquidator or administrator and transactions entered into by an insolvent individual might be impugned by a trustee in bankruptcy.

While other provisions included in the adjustment sections of the Act were based directly on previous provisions in either the companies or the bankruptcy legislation, sections 238 and 339 were new provisions clearly providing that undervalued transactions could be adjusted. Now, after saying that, it must be acknowledged that the sections are, in a sense, successors to section 42 of the Bankruptcy Act 1914 (avoidance of voluntary settlements benefiting the debtor's family or associates), which provided for the avoidance of voluntary settlements. Besides saying that sections 238 and 339 are successors to section 42 of the Bankruptcy Act, it is undoubtedly true to say that the provisions have their roots in the law which first provided for the avoidance of fraudulent conveyances, in 1571. This is because the provisions are designed to prevent debtor misbehaviour, namely preventing insolvents disposing of assets, particularly to associates, at an undervalued amount just before the advent of a formal insolvency administration, thereby reducing the pool of property which would be available to the office-holder to distribute to creditors. Provisions like sections 238 and 339 are designed to discourage those in control of companies and individual debtors from transferring assets or opportunities to associates so that they benefit and the creditors of insolvents lose out.

There has been a surprising paucity of reported cases dealing with sections 238 and 339, which appears to be because of the lack of use of the section, although the provisions have produced more reported cases in recent times and recently section 238 came under the scrutiny of the House of Lords in *Phillips v Brewin Dolphin Bell Lawrie* ([2001] 1 WLR 143).

It should be noted that liquidators and trustees in bankruptcy will need, when the Enterprise Act becomes operative, to secure approval from either the liquidation committee or the court in the case of the former and the creditors' committee or the court in the case of the latter, before initiating proceedings under either sections 238 or 339 (para 3A of Schedule 4 and para 2A of Schedule 5).

36.2 Conditions for adjustment

Before a court will consider making any order adjusting a transaction at an undervalue under sections 238 and 339, an office-holder must establish the following:

- the insolvent is in liquidation, administration (section 238(1)) or bankruptcy (section 339(1));
- the insolvent, if a company, entered into a transaction at an undervalue in the two years preceding the onset of insolvency (sections 238(2), 240(3)), or the insolvent, if an individual, entered into a transaction at an undervalue in the 5 years preceding the date of the presentation of the bankruptcy petition (sections 339(1), 341(1)(a));
- at the time when the transaction was entered into a company was unable to pay its debts or it was unable to pay its debts as a result of entering into the transaction (section 240(2)), or an insolvent person was insolvent or became so as a result of entering into the transaction (section 341(2)) (in bankruptcy if the transaction occurred in the two years proceeding bankruptcy there is a presumption of insolvency).

Importantly, demonstration of any intention to defraud or injure the creditors, or that the insolvent was aware of insolvency at the time of the transaction, is not necessary.

The onus of proving insolvency is removed in circumstances where the defendant is a connected person (section 240(2)) or an associate (section 341(2)). In such a situation there is a rebuttable presumption that the insolvent was in fact insolvent at the time of the transaction.

36.3 The transaction

What a transaction at an undervalue is, is set out for insolvent companies in section 238(4) and occurs where:

(a) the company makes a gift to that person [the person subject to the proceedings] or otherwise enters a transaction with that person on terms that provide for the company to receive no consideration; or

(b) the company enters into a transaction with that person for a consideration the value of which, in money or money's worth, is significantly less than the value, in money or money's worth, of the consideration provided by the company.

The equivalent provision for individuals (section 339(3)) is almost identical save for the fact that in addition a transaction can be covered by the section if the individual enters into the transaction in consideration of marriage (section 339(3)(b)). The inclusion of this category is probably to address the fact that in equity marriage is valid consideration (*Attorney-General v Jacobs Smith* [1895] 2 QB 341) and also under the previous legislation (Bankruptcy Act 1914, section 42) marriage could render an otherwise voidable transaction valid.

'Transaction' is defined in section 436 as including 'a gift, agreement or arrangement' and it is indicated that the references to 'entering into a transaction' in the Act are to be construed accordingly. 'Transaction' is defined broadly and the courts have said that they should not strain to limit the width of the definition (*Phillips v Brewin Dolphin Bell Lawrie Ltd* [1999] BCC 557 at 565 (CA)).[1] 'Transaction' would appear to cover:

- gifts;[2]
- agreements to perform tasks for no consideration;
- purchases of property which has a market value less than the price paid;
- leases of assets over their rental value;
- dispositions of property for prices less than their market value;
- the supply of an asset on lease below its rental value;
- agreeing to pay for services a sum which exceeds their value;
- agreeing to provide services for a sum less than their value;
- providing a guarantee for no benefit or a benefit less than the value of the benefit conferred by the guarantee;
- providing security for a previously unsecured loan.[3]

---

[1] On appeal the House of Lords ([2001] 1 WLR 1430) appeared to agree with this approach.

[2] For an example of this, see *Re Barton Manufacturing Co Ltd* [1998] BCC 827; [1999] 1 BCLC 740.

[3] The transactions are based on R. Goode, *Principles of Corporate Insolvency Law*, 2nd edn, 1997 at 356–7 and para 668 of the Australian Law Reform Commission's *General Insolvency Inquiry* ('the Harmer Report'), Report No 45, 1988, Canberra.

Millett J (as he then was) in *Re MC Bacon Ltd* ([1990] BCLC 324) broke section 238 down into parts as far as a transaction is concerned. His Lordship said that the transaction must be:

(i) entered into by the company; (ii) for a consideration; (iii) the value of which is measured in money or money's worth; (iv) is significantly less than the value; (v) also measured in money or money's worth; (vi) of the consideration provided by the company (at 340).[4]

36.4 Consideration

From what Millett J said in *Re MC Bacon Ltd*, and approved of by Jonathan Parker J, in *Re Brabon* ([2000] 1 BCLC 11; [2000] BPIR 537), it is plain that a liquidator must establish a significant undervalue by proving the respective values of the consideration given by the parties to the transaction and this must be done in money terms.[5] So, in the classic case where the company sells an asset for £10,000 to X and the liquidator maintains that the asset was worth £20,000, he or she must establish the latter value.

The issue of consideration is very much central to the transaction under scrutiny and it is more important to ascertain the consideration received by the insolvent than identifying the actual transaction itself. The actual consideration given to the company by the other party to the transaction will usually be examined carefully. The House of Lords in *Phillips v Brewin Dolphin Bell Lawrie Ltd* ([2001] 1 WLR 143)[6] said that if the value of the consideration for which a company enters into a transaction is speculative, then the party who relies on the consideration is required to establish the value.[7]

The use of the word 'consideration' in sections 238(4) and 339(4) might well lead to confusion. The word is used regularly in the contract law field and in that sense it has a rather specialised meaning. It is debatable whether the word is being used in its contractual sense[8] and in

---

[4] This breakdown was approved of by the House of Lords in *Phillips v Brewin Dolphin Bell Lawrie Ltd* ([2001] 1 WLR 143.

[5] Also, see *National Bank of Kuwait v Menzies* [1994] 2 BCLC 306; [1994] BCC 119.

[6] For an analytical discussion of this case, see R. Mokal and L. Ho, 'Consideration, Characterisation and Evaluation: Transactions at an Undervalue After *Phillips v Brewin Dolphin*' (2001) 1 JCLS 359. Also, see the discussion by Dr Rebecca Parry in *Transaction Avoidance in Insolvencies*, Oxford: Oxford University Press (2001) at 90–1.

[7] In this case the House of Lords held that the party had not done so.

[8] Professor Goode assumes that it is (*Principles of Corporate Insolvency Law*, 2nd, 1997, at 360) while other commentators (E. Bailey, H. Groves, C. Smith, *Corporate Insolvency Law and Practice*, London: Butterworths (1992) at 364) take the view that it is not. The latter see the word as meaning benefit in financial terms.

the Court of Appeal in *Phillips v Brewin Dolphin Bell Lawrie Ltd* ([1999] 2 All ER 844 at 853) Morritt LJ refrained from coming to a decision one way or the other. His Lordship said that the critical thing was that there was a *quid pro quo* 'for that which it is alleged that the company disposed of at an undervalue' (at 853). In any event, the interpretation of 'consideration' is likely to have no bearing on the end result. For example, X provides £1 in exchange for a car owned by Y Ltd that is in fact worth £10,000. Although X had given good consideration in a contractual sense, the transaction would be attacked by Y's liquidator. The liquidator would argue that the transaction falls within section 238(4)(b) in that the company received consideration which is significantly less than the value of the consideration provided by the company. What is important is the value of the consideration to the one who receives it, i.e., it is subjectively evaluated.[9]

Any consideration given to a third party may be taken into account in deciding whether a transaction is at an undervalue, as might any consideration given by a third party as indicated in *Phillips v Brewin Dolphin Bell Lawrie Ltd*.

36.5 Valuation

Whether a transaction is a transaction at an undervalue will depend on the question of value. In the typical case the main issue is likely to be whether the insolvent received significantly less consideration than was given. Resolving this issue will entail a valuation in money terms of the consideration provided both by the insolvent and the other party to the transaction. It has been held that the office-holder must establish the respective values in money or money terms of the consideration given and received by the insolvent and, also, demonstrate that what was received was significantly less than what was provided.[10]

In *National Westminster Bank plc v Jones* ([2001] 1 BCLC 98; [2000] BPIR 1092) it was said that when determining whether consideration received was significantly less than the consideration passed to the debtor(s) (this was a case involving a claim under section 423), the court has to form the view as to the price which the property representing the consideration given by the defendant and that given by the debtor(s) would fetch in the open market, thus providing a 'correct valuation' (at 122; 1115). The court

---

[9] R. Parry, *Transaction Avoidance in Insolvencies* at 88 and referring to *Re MC Bacon Ltd* [1990] BCLC 324 at 340.

[10] See *Re MC Bacon Ltd* [1990] BCLC 324 at 340–341 and approved of in *Phillips v Brewin Dolphin Bell Lawrie Ltd* [1999] BCC 557 at 566 (CA).

will have to compare the value of property as against what consideration was given for it, and then consider 'in percentage or proportionate terms, how much less the consideration is than the value' (at 123; 1116).

Presently it is not possible to say what will constitute 'significantly less', as the expression has not been interpreted by the courts.[11] It is not possible to say how much less than market value constitutes 'significantly less' in any given case.

The likely difficulty that will confront office-holders is the valuing of assets that are the subject of the impugned transactions. As Professor Goode says in relation to valuing:

> [It] is not an exact science but to a considerable extent a matter of judgment as the amount a willing buyer would pay in the market when dealing with a willing seller.[12]

The difficulty of valuation is likely to be accentuated where the transaction was entered into some years before the proceedings are heard by a court.

If property was purchased by the insolvent from a person at arm's length and after it had been offered for sale publicly, this will suggest the price paid by the insolvent was market value (*Re Brabon* ([2000] 1 BCLC 11; [2000] BPIR 537)).

Sections 238(4)(b) and 339(3)(c) demand there to be an inequality of benefit and to establish this one must have cognisance of all aspects of the transaction, including any special reason for the insolvent or the other party to the transaction entering into the transaction.

> In *Agricultural Mortgage Corporation v Woodward* ([1994] BCC 688), which involved a claim under section 423 (also dealing with transactions at an undervalue (see Chapter 38)), a farmer borrowed £700,000 from a lender which took security over the farm. The farmer fell into arrears and before a deadline for the satisfaction of the arrears, he granted his wife a tenancy of the property. The farm, if there was no tenancy, was worth £1 million, but with a tenancy the farm was worth less than £500,000. It was agreed that the rent to be paid under the tenancy represented a full market rent. Judge Weeks QC (sitting as a High Court judge) found that the transaction involving the farmer and his wife constituted a transaction that was entered into by the former for the purpose of prejudicing the lender's interests within section 423. This finding was not challenged on appeal. However, his Honour said that he did not find that the transaction was entered into at an undervalue. The lender appealed to the Court of Appeal on this point and the Court of Appeal reversed the decision of Judge Weeks. The Court looked at what had in fact happened – a realistic approach. The Court took into account the fact that the result of the transaction was that the husband experienced a diminution of the value of his land and the wife was advantaged in that she was granted security of tenure in the family home, the family business

---

[11] I. Snaith, in *The Law of Corporate Insolvency*, London: Waterlow Publishers (1990) at 648 argues that a *de minimus* rule must apply.

[12] *Principles of Corporate Insolvency Law*, 2nd edn, at 69.

was saved from its creditors and she was given the chance to negotiate a large surrender value for her interest. The wife was, in effect, placed in 'a ransom position' (at 696).[13]

36.6 Defences

In defence to an application pursuant to section 238, but not under section 339, it could be argued that the company entered into the transaction in good faith, for the purpose of carrying on its business and when entering the transaction there were reasonable grounds for believing that the transaction would benefit the company (section 238(5)), for example, where a company had severe cash flow problems and it would benefit from the sale of an asset, whatever the price.[14]

To make out the defence it must be proved that the company was acting in good faith in the course of carrying on the company's business (section 238(5)(a)) and there was a belief on reasonable grounds that the transaction would benefit the company (section 238(5)(b)). There is no assessment of the state of mind or circumstances of the person receiving a benefit from the company. It may be onerous, in some cases, for a defendant to prove that the company acted with propriety. The question of whether the company entered into the transaction in good faith involves considering a subjective state of mind. This can be a problem because it is sometimes difficult to know whose subjective state of mind is relevant where a company is involved. As it is an abstraction, a company has no mind of its own – it acts through human agents.[15] It is likely that the issue of whether a company acted in good faith will rarely be the point on which a case turns. In most cases liquidators will be more concerned with denying that it could have been reasonably believed that the transaction would benefit the company.

Whether there was a belief on reasonable grounds that the company would be benefited by the transaction is a matter to be assessed at the time

---

[13] For a critique of the judgment of the Court of Appeal, see R. Parry, *Transaction Avoidance in Insolvencies* at 95–6.

[14] Professor Fletcher ('Voidable Transactions in Bankruptcy: British Perspectives' in J. Ziegel (ed.), *Current Developments in International and Comparative Corporate Insolvency Law*, Oxford: Clarendon Press (1994) at 305) submits that in such circumstances, persons acquiring assets at 'bargain' prices should be assured of retaining the benefit of their bargains.

[15] For example, see *Lennard's Carrying Co Ltd v Asiatic Petroleum Co Ltd* [1915] AC 707 at 713; *HL Bolton (Engineering) Co Ltd v T J Graham & Sons Ltd* [1957] 1 QB 159 at 172–173; *Tesco Supermarkets Ltd v Nattrass* [1972] AC 153 at 170; *El Ajou v Dollar Land Holdings plc* [1994] BCC 143 at 150. For further discussion, see A. Keay, *McPherson's Law of Company Liquidation*, London: Sweet & Maxwell (2001) at 566–8.

of the transaction. The test is objective so the belief of a company is of no assistance to it if it was not reasonably held. If no consideration was given to the company, it is more difficult to make out the defence.

36.7 Court orders

If an office-holder has proved that a transaction at an undervalue within sections 238 or 339 had been entered into, then the court is probably first going to make a declaration to that effect. Then it will consider what other orders are appropriate. Sections 238(3) and 339(2) provide that the court is to make orders that restore the position to what it would have been if the company or individual had not entered the impugned transaction. This provision encapsulates the aim of the adjustment provisions, i.e., to ensure that there is restitution by restoring the status quo. But sections 238(3) and 339(2) are not the only relevant provisions. Because section 241(1) (and section 342(1) is essentially in the same terms) provides that: 'without prejudice to the generality of sections 238(3) and 239(3) [the latter dealing with preferences], an order under either of those sections with respect to a transaction or a preference entered into or given by a company may . . .' and the provision goes on to set out a number of orders which the court may make to achieve the goal articulated in section 238(3). These orders are, in effect, examples of what a court can do, but clearly a court is not limited by the kinds of orders enumerated in sections 241 or 342; the orders set out in sections 241 and 342 indicate the wide range that court orders may take.[16] However, for the most part courts are likely to make orders which follow one or more of those in sections 241(1) or 342(1). Whatever order(s) is made by a court, it must seek to restore the position as it existed prior to the making of the transaction and to effect this objective the orders set out in sections 241(1) and 342(1) are not to be seen as restrictive. So, while the examples set out may omit orders which might be thought to be appropriate in some cases, a court is not prevented from making such an order. Importantly, the paragraphs in sections 241 and 342 apply also to transactions which are classified as preferences under sections 239 and 340 respectively.

While a court would have to make a declaration that the impugned transaction was a transaction at an undervalue, it appears debatable whether a court would have to make any other order that would effect a restoration of the insolvent's position. The problem is that sections 238(3) and 339(2) provide that the court *shall* make such order as it thinks

---

[16] Orders are not limited to situations where the property was originally owned by the company.

fit for restoring the position existing before the impugned transaction. The use of the word 'shall' is strange if the courts were to have the right to decline to make an order; the wording of the provision appears to indicate that courts have no option but to make a restoration order. Nevertheless, in *Re Paramount Airways Ltd* ([1993] Ch 223), Nicholls V-C said that despite the use of 'shall' the phrase 'such order as it thinks fit' confers an overall discretion on the court and that 'discretion is wide enough to enable the court, if justice so requires, to make no order against the other party to the transaction' (at 239).

While the paragraphs of sections 241 and 342 are merely to be regarded as examples of the orders or types of orders which a court might see fit to make to remedy the entering into of a transaction which can be adjusted, some provisions in sections 241 and 342, for example sections 241(1)(b) and 342(1)(b), will be more suited than others to transactions at an undervalue.[17]

While the legislative statement that the aim of court orders is to ensure that the status quo prior to the preference is to be restored is most laudable, there are variables that may be relevant in any given case which precipitate problems for courts in achieving the legislative objective. Courts may well find that they will be faced with problems, particularly where any property which has been transferred by, or to, the insolvent under a transaction at an undervalue has increased or decreased in value. These are issues with which a court may well have to grapple.[18]

36.8 Protecting third persons

A court order following a decision that a transaction at an undervalue was entered into may affect a third party. In such a case one must have regard for sections 241(2) or 342(2) which may provide protection for a third party. This provision, which can be relied upon by a person who was not a party to the impugned transaction but who acquired, from someone other than the insolvent, a benefit from the transaction, indicates that a court order must not prejudice any interest in property which was acquired from a person other than the insolvent in good faith and for value, or prejudice any interest deriving from such an interest. Also the order shall not require a third party who received a benefit from the

---

[17] For a discussion of the orders that can be made and how they might apply where there is a transaction at an undervalue, see A. Keay, *McPherson's Law of Company Liquidation* at 570–2; R. Parry, *Transaction Avoidance in Insolvencies* at 110–14.

[18] For a discussion, see A. Keay, 'The Recovery of Voidable Preferences: Aspects of Recovery' [2000] Cfi LR 1.

impugned transaction in good faith and for value to pay a sum to the office-holder, except where the person was a party to the transaction.

Sections 241(2A) and 342(2A) must be considered in relation to the issue of the good faith of the third party. The provisions state that where a person who acquired an interest in property from someone other than the insolvent or has received a benefit from a transaction at an undervalue at the time of the acquisition of the interest, had notice of the relevant surrounding circumstances and of the relevant proceedings, or was connected with, or an associate of, the insolvent or the person with whom the insolvent had entered the impugned transaction, then there is a presumption that the third party acquired the benefit otherwise than in good faith. Sections 241(3) and 342(4) define the meaning of 'relevant surrounding circumstances', and sections 241(3B) and 241(3C) for companies and section 342(5) for individuals, explain the meaning of 'relevant proceedings'.

Chapter 37

Preferences

37.1 Introduction

To ensure that the policy of *pari passu* distribution eventuates, transactions which affect the disposition of assets or other property before the commencement of the liquidation, administration or bankruptcy and which have the effect of reducing the dividend to be paid to the unsecured creditors, might be reviewed and adjusted.

The payment by insolvents who subsequently enter liquidation, administration or bankruptcy, of some of the insolvents' creditors could mean that those payments constitute preferences. Such payments are likely to be subject to adjustment as they would interfere with the *pari passu* principle.[1] The avoidance of preferences is designed, ostensibly, to prevent a creditor jumping to the front of the queue of the general unsecured creditors, all of whom should be paid equally and to ensure that 'an undignified scramble by creditors over available assets' is avoided.[2] This undignified scramble usually occurs because creditors fear the imminent liquidation of their debtor and they wish to improve their position and beat other creditors to getting paid, realising that not everyone will receive payment.

Where there is a preference, a creditor has received more from an insolvent before the advent of a formal insolvency administration than would have otherwise been received in the insolvency administration. This idea is to be found in sections 239(4) and 340(3). The true test of a preference is – does the transaction confer a priority or advantage on a creditor in relation to past indebtedness of the insolvent and is the

---

[1] For a more detailed discussion of the background to, and history of, preferences, see A. Keay, 'The Recovery of Voidable Preferences: Aspects of Recovery' [2000] Cfi LR 1; R. Parry in *Transaction Avoidance in Insolvencies*, Oxford: Oxford University Press (2001) at 122–5.

[2] J. O'Donovan, 'Corporate Insolvency: Policies, Perspectives and Reform' (1990) 3 CBLJ 1 at 11–12.

advantage given at the expense of other creditors who are owed debts at the time of transaction, thereby preventing an equal distribution of the insolvent's property among the unsecured creditors?

The Report of the Insolvency Law Review Committee, *Insolvency Law and Practice*[3] (known as the 'Cork Report'), gave the following as examples of preferences: paying the whole or part of a debt (the most common); providing security or further security for an existing debt; and, returning goods that have been delivered but not paid for.[4]

It should be noted that liquidators and trustees in bankruptcy will need, once the Enterprise Act begins to operate, to secure approval from either the liquidation committee or the court in the case of the former and the creditors' committee or the court in the case of the latter, before initiating proceedings under either sections 239 or 340 (para 3A of Schedule 4 and para 2A of Schedule 5).

37.2 The elements to be established for adjustment

In order for a liquidator or trustee (or administrator – this section will focus on liquidation and bankruptcy rather than administration) success-fully to attack a transaction as a preference, the liquidator or trustee has to prove that:[5]

● the insolvent must be in liquidation or bankruptcy;[6]
● the transaction was entered into at the relevant time (sections 239(2), 340(1)) (within the six-months before the onset of insolvency for companies (sections 240(1)(b)[7] and within the six months before the date of the presentation of the bankruptcy petition for individuals (section 341(1)(c)), or, if the defendant is a person connected with the insolvent, within the two years prior to either the onset of insolvency for companies or to the presentation of the bankruptcy petition for individuals) (sections 239(2), 341(1));

---

[3] Cmnd 8558, 1982.

[4] At para 1208.

[5] Morritt J, in *Re Ledingham-Smith* ([1993] BCLC 635 at 639), discussed the issues which confront a court in a preference case. See R. Parry, *Transaction Avoidance in Insolvencies* at 131–6 for instances of transactions that could be preferences.

[6] As with transactions at an undervalue, the company may also be in administration under Part II of the Act. See *Re Exchange Travel (Holdings) Ltd* [1996] BCC 933 (upheld on appeal: *sub nom Katz v McNally* [1999] BCC 291) for a preference action initiated by administrators.

[7] 'Onset of insolvency' is defined in section 240(3) in relation to straight liquidations, as the date of the commencement of winding up. According to section 129, the date of commencement, in relation to compulsory liquidations, is the date of the presentation of the petition to wind up.

- the other party to the transaction (the recipient of the preference) is one of the insolvent's creditors or a surety or guarantor for any of the insolvent's debts (sections 239(4)(a), 340(3)(a));
- the insolvent does anything which has the effect of putting the recipient of the preference into a position which, in the event of a company entering insolvent liquidation or an individual becoming bankrupt, will be better than the position he or she would have been in had the thing not been done (sections 239(4)(b), 340(3)(b));
- the insolvent was influenced in deciding to enter into the impugned transaction by a desire to enable the recipient to have a preference (sections 239(5), 340(4)); and
- at the time of, or as a result of, the giving of the preference, a company was unable to pay its debts within the meaning of section 123 (section 240(2)), or an individual was insolvent at the time of the preferential transaction or became so as a consequence of the transaction (section 341(2)).

Importantly, sections 239(6) and 340(5) provide that if a preference was given to a person connected with a company or was given to an associate of the insolvent individual, then it is presumed that the insolvent was influenced by a desire to give a preference. Section 249 defines the persons who are regarded as being connected with a company, and section 435 defines associates. So sections 239(6) and 340(5) encapsulate rebuttable presumptions, introduced to assist office-holders to recover preferences from persons who were associated with the insolvent.

Preference law then still, like its forebears, maintains an emphasis on motivation. The insolvent's motive in making a payment then is of critical importance in the determination of whether a transaction can be successfully challenged. The problem with introducing the need for any inquiry into the motives of people is that such inquiries can be complicated and ascertaining motives is always a difficult exercise. This matter will be taken up a little later in the chapter.[8]

While one might think that sections 239 and 340 provide an office-holder with a better chance of attacking a transaction as a preference, in practice this does not appear to be the case. Absent the situations where the respondent is a connected person or an associate of the insolvent who is labouring under the burden of a presumption that the insolvent had a desire to give a preference to the respondent, office-holders will often have difficulty in adducing any or sufficient evidence to impugn the transaction.

Some of the elements of a preference warrant further discussion.

---

[8] See below at 498–501.

37.2.1 *Improvement in the position of the creditor or guarantor*

Sections 239(4)(b) and 340(3)(b) provide that the office-holder must prove, *inter alia*, that the creditor or guarantor was placed in a better position than he or she would have been if the preference had not be given and, if the insolvent was a company, it entered insolvent liquidation and, if the insolvent was an individual, he or she became bankrupt. If the transaction would have the effect of disturbing the statutory order of priorities as regards payment in winding up or bankruptcy, then it has led to improvement of the recipient's position (*Burns v Stapleton* (1959) 102 CLR 97 at 104). There is no reference to the creditor enjoying an advantage over other creditors, but the fact that the creditor is in a better position than would have been the case if the transaction was not entered into, effectively he or she does have an advantage over other creditors. Sections 239(4)(b) and 340(3)(b) are providing for, in effect, a transaction which results in a creditor receiving from an insolvent more than the creditor would receive from the insolvent in respect of the debt owed if the transaction were set aside and the creditor were to prove for the debt in a winding up or bankruptcy of the insolvent. In such cases, the transaction is a preference. It is necessary to draw a comparison, i.e., between what the creditor received as a result of the transaction and what would have been received if the transaction were set aside and the creditor proved in a winding up or bankruptcy. What must be determined is: is the creditor's benefit, received under the impugned transaction, to be weighed against what would be received in the actual winding up or bankruptcy, or what would have been received had there been a hypothetical winding up or bankruptcy at the time of the transaction? We submit that it is the latter.[9]

37.2.2 *Secured creditors and granting security*

Something should be said about security given by a debtor in exchange for a contemporaneous or subsequent advance of funds. For example, Y Ltd provides X with a charge over its assets and X advances £10,000 to Y Ltd at the same time or later. This does not constitute a preference because any decrease in assets as a result of the giving of the security is matched by the provision of fresh funds to the company. In any event, the secured creditor is not a creditor in respect of past indebtedness.[10] Added to this it is settled that a payment in discharge of a valid security is not a preference.[11] But the case is different where a debtor satisfies an unpaid

---

[9] For a detailed consideration of this, see R. Parry, *Transaction Avoidance in Insolvencies* at 137–40.

[10] See *Robertson v Grigg* (1932) 47 CLR 257.

[11] See *National Australia Bank Ltd v KDS Construction Services Pty Ltd* (1987) 163 CLR 668 at 679 (Aust HC).

unsecured creditor by a payment or by the provision of security for the debt. Here the statutory order of priorities are unsettled as regards payment in winding up and bankruptcy and, therefore, there is a preference (*Burns v Stapleton* (1959) 102 CLR 97 at 104). But this is to be contrasted with the case where there is a payment to a creditor who was fully secured at the time, as this does not improve the position of the secured creditor and it does not affect the position vis-a-vis the other creditors in winding up.[12]

In the situation where some security, such as a charge or a mortgage, is created and it relates to both past indebtedness and new advances, the security is able to be attacked only as a preference and the transaction adjusted, as far as the giving of the security related to the debtor's existing indebtedness.[13] So, take the case where X lends £10,000 to Y Ltd. At a later date X agrees to lend a further sum of £20,000 to Y Ltd provided that Y Ltd grants a charge over some of its assets. The charge is only valid in so far as it secures the latter advance of £20,000. Naturally, if the security given to a person in consideration of the advance of new funds was not safe from being challenged as a preference, debtors in financial difficulties could not attract funds because potential lenders would be apprehensive of debtors going into liquidation or becoming bankrupt and the taking of security rendered otiose by the subsequent challenge of an office-holder.

37.2.3 *Influenced by a desire*

We have already noted that for there to be a preference, the insolvent must have been influenced in deciding to enter into the impugned transaction by a desire to enable the recipient to have a preference (sections 239(5), 340(4)). This is often the stumbling block to office-holders succeeding in their challenge of transactions as preferences. Why is this the case?

37.2.3.1 *Re MC Bacon Ltd*

The seminal case on the topic of preferences under the Act, *Re MC Bacon Ltd* ([1990] BCLC 324), provides us with the answer to why the need to establish that the insolvent was influenced by a desire to give a preference is a problem. While the case dealt with a company in liquidation, the principles it laid down apply equally to bankruptcies.

---

[12] A. Keay, *McPherson's Law of Company Liquidation,* London: Sweet & Maxwell (2001) at 581. See *Re Moffatt* (1940) 11 ABC 146.

[13] See *Burns v Stapleton* (1959) 102 CLR 97 (Aust HC).

In this case we have a classic state of affairs for a preference claim.[14] A bank had provided an unsecured overdraft facility to a company. The company's fortunes plummeted during late 1986 and early 1987 and it was only able to operate by using its overdraft facility to the full. The Bank became aware of the company's problems and required some security. In May 1987 a report by officers of the Bank indicated that the company was insolvent, however it was stated that it was reasonable to conclude that the company could trade out of its problems. Subsequently, a debenture was executed in favour of the bank by the company. The debenture gave a fixed and floating charge over the company's assets. Later, on 4 September 1987, an administrative receiver was appointed in relation to the company's assets. Then on 7 September 1987 a liquidator was appointed by a meeting of creditors. In due course the liquidator applied to have the debenture given to the Bank set aside on the basis, *inter alia*, that it was a preference under section 239.

The judge, Millett J (as he then was), focused on 'desire' in section 239(5) and indicated that the word was subjective. He opined that 'desire' involved positively wishing something to occur (at 335). According to his Lordship, it is not necessary to adduce direct evidence of the requisite desire as it may be inferred from the circumstances of the case,[15] but importantly the desire must have influenced the decision of the company to enter into the transaction that is the subject of the liquidator's action (at 335–336). According to the learned judge, there must be a nexus between the desire and the making of the transaction. There was no necessity to prove that the requisite desire was the only or decisive factor that caused the company to give the preference. The desire might, in fact, only be one of the factors (at 336). Also, his Lordship said that it is not necessary for the liquidator to prove that if the requisite desire had not been present then the company would not have entered into the transaction impugned (at 336).

His Lordship said that there is not necessarily a preference where there is financial assistance provided to a struggling company and then the finance provider is paid by the company. Provided that the company is motivated by commercial considerations in making the payment, and has no desire to improve the creditor's position, there is no preference (at 336).

In this case Millett J took the view that the company held the genuine belief that it could survive, but in order to do so it had to give the debenture demanded by the Bank. His Lordship found that there was no reason why the directors of the company would want to improve the Bank's position in the event of an insolvent liquidation. Also found by the judge was that the company had no motive other than a desire to avoid demand being made in relation to the amount owed pursuant to the overdraft and to enable it to continue the carrying on its business (at 337).

37.2.3.2 *The problems with desire*

One problem is that, despite what was said in *Re M C Bacon Ltd*, it is not plain what 'desire' actually entails.

---

[14] For a most expansive discussion of the case, see A. Keay, 'Preferences in Liquidation Law: A Time for a Change' (1998) 2 Cfi LR 198.
[15] Affirmed in *Rooney v Das* [1999] BPIR 404 at 406.

It is clear that the office-holder does not have to prove that the debtor had a desire to enter the transaction that is alleged to be a preference. Rather, it must be established that the debtor positively wished to improve the position of the creditor (*Re MC Bacon Ltd* [1990] BCLC 324 at 335, 336). Also, the office-holder must establish that the desire did in fact influence the decision to enter into the relevant transaction (at 336). Crucially, this involves establishing the debtor's subjective motivation (*Re MC Bacon Ltd* at 335; *Re Beacon Leisure Ltd* [1991] BCC 213 at 216; *Re Fairway Magazines Ltd* [1992] BCC 924 at 929). To establish subjective motivation is exacting. It is difficult to ascertain what a person's desire is and he or she is always likely to 'play down' his or her intention (or desire) where it might affect the person's rights or position.[16] Provisions akin to section 239 require the courts to undertake the difficult task of attempting, well after the fact, to determine what must have been the motive of the insolvent at the time of the entering into of the transaction which is challenged.[17] The Cork Committee, the majority of which recommended retaining some element of motive in the preference provision, acknowledged that ascertaining motive is 'a difficult and unsatisfactory inquiry'.[18]

Determining desire in relation to a person is hard enough, but it is even more difficult when one comes to the point of having to ascertain the desire of a corporate entity. Naturally, companies are unable to have desires, so one must consider whose desire will office-holders have to establish. In *Re Transworld Trading Ltd* ([1999] BPIR 628) it was said that it is 'necessary to explore the mind of the company which gave the preference'(at 629). The question of how one determines the state of mind of a company has been a difficult issue for courts to resolve. Probably though the basic question which will be asked is: what was the objective of the board in entering into the transaction?[19] Perhaps, on occasions, courts may take into account the mind of the person who was involved in initiating the making of the preference. The courts have said that a debtor's state of mind may be inferred from the circumstances, but, with the possible exception of the court in *Re Agriplant Services Ltd* ([1997] BCC 842) (discussed shortly), they have not been all that ready to make this inference.[20] Unless there are admissions by the directors of the debtor company or direct evidence from the minute book or a person who participated in the discussions that led to the decision, the only way that the liquidator can prove the requisite desire is by demonstrating that it is unlikely that the directors reached the decision they did without taking the

---

[16] A. Keay, *McPherson's Law of Company Liquidation*, at 586.
[17] Ibid.
[18] Para 1253.
[19] J. Verrill, 'Attacking Antecedent Transactions' (1993) 7 JIBL 485 at 489.
[20] See, for example, *Re Beacon Leisure Ltd* [1991] BCC 213; *Re Fairway Magazines Ltd* [1992] BCC 924.

desire to prefer into account.[21] While Millett J in *Re MC Bacon Ltd* (at 336) said that the test for whether a preference was in fact given is not – did the desire to improve the position of the creditor tip the scales as far as the debtor deciding to enter the transaction?[22] – it may be argued that in practice this has been the test adopted.[23]

Establishing the subjective motive of the debtor is also difficult because in practice most transactions that favour creditors are made, except where the creditors are company officers or their associates in relation to insolvent companies, or debtors who later become bankrupt or their relatives and associates, uninfluenced by any desire to improve the position of the creditors. Primarily, they are made to ensure that the debtor can continue to do business or to stop creditors pressing for payment. Additionally, it is not uncommon for debtors suffering liquidity problems to pay off creditors haphazardly and that cannot be regarded as desiring to improve a creditor's position, certainly taking the Millett interpretation of section 239.

It is submitted that any need to prove motive is outdated. It was first demanded in the eighteenth century, at a time when the notion of credit was the subject of deep mistrust in England and bankrupts considered villains.[24] Notwithstanding major changes to the way that bankruptcy was viewed, English law has never accepted the fact that the motive of the debtor was not a relevant element in challenging preferences.[25] An objective approach, whereby the office-holder only had to establish objective elements, namely all of the elements contained in sections 239 and 240 (for applications in corporate insolvency) on the one hand or sections 340 and 341 (for applications in bankruptcy) on the other hand, except the need for desire, would involve a far better test. Undoubtedly, this would take much of the uncertainty out of the law as well as giving potency to preference law.[26]

As adverted to earlier and worth repeating in more detail, the issue of desire is not a problem if the person or company against whom the office-holder is proceeding is able to be labelled as a person connected with the insolvent company or an associate of the insolvent person who subsequently becomes a bankrupt. This is because sections 239(6) and 340(5) provide that if a preference was given to a person connected with a company or was given to an associate of the insolvent individual, then it is presumed that the insolvent was influenced by a desire to give a preference.

---

[21] K. Otter, 'Influential Desire – Dominant Intention?' (1990) 3(6) *Insolvency Intelligence* 42.

[22] The argument put by the defendant bank in *Re MC Bacon Ltd.*

[23] See K. Otter, 'Influential Desire – Dominant Intention?' (1990) 3(6) *Insolvency Intelligence* 42.

[24] R. Weisberg, 'Commercial Morality, the Merchant Character, and the History of the Voidable Preference' (1986) 39 Stanford L R 3, 11–16.

[25] M. Conaglen, 'Voidable Preferences Under the Companies Act 1993' [1996] *New Zealand Law Review* 197 at 203.

[26] See A. Keay, 'Preferences in Liquidation Law: A Time for a Change' (1998) 2 CfiLR 198 for a criticism of the present position and an argument for the use of an objective test.

37.2.3.3 *After Re MC Bacon Ltd*

The reasoning in *Re M C Bacon Ltd* has been consistently applied.[27] In all of the successful cases claiming preferences given by companies, the recipient of the preference, with the exceptions of *Re Living Images Ltd* ([1996] BCC 112) and *Re Agriplant Services Ltd* ([1997] BCC 842), has been a person who is able to be classified as a connected person.[28] This provides a clear indication of the difficulty that a liquidator has in establishing that the company had the requisite desire. Of course, in cases where the creditor was a connected person or an associate of the insolvent there is a presumption that the insolvent was influenced by the requisite desire.

Re Agriplant Services Ltd is a rare case in that the necessary desire was found by the court.

> Here, the liquidator claimed that the repayment of a loan to C by the company in liquidation, A Ltd, was a preference. The relevant payment had been made shortly before A Ltd had entered voluntary winding up. The loan had been guaranteed by S, one of the two directors of A Ltd. S gave evidence to the effect that the payment was made to ensure that A Ltd's equipment was not repossessed by C, something that could occur if the loan was not paid. If the equipment was repossessed then, according to S, A Ltd could not continue to trade. S also said that he made the payment because of pressure exerted by C. Jonathan Parker J rejected the evidence of S. He found that in getting the company to pay off C, S was concerned about his own liability pursuant to the guarantee. The judge said that S was 'influenced by a desire to reduce the company's indebtedness to [C] with the consequence that his own position on an insolvent liquidation of the company would be improved' (at 851).

It seems that Jonathan Parker J was willing to make important inferences as to the motives of the directors who were behind the preferences given and this was critical to the final result.

37.2.3.4 *Commercial pressure*

The cases that have been decided under sections 239 and 340 indicate that if the decision of the debtor to enter the transaction attacked by the office-holder was influenced solely by proper commercial considerations, the office-holder will fail (*Re MC Bacon Ltd* at 336; *Re DKG Contractors Ltd*

---

[27] For example, see *Re DKG Contractors Ltd* [1990] BCC 903 at 909–910; *Re Lewis's of Leicester Ltd* [1995] BCC 514 at 523; *Re Living Images Ltd* [1996] BCC 112 at 117; *Wills v Corfe Joinery Ltd (in liq)* [1997] BCC 511 at 512; *Re Agriplant Services Ltd* [1997] BCC 842 at 848–9; *Rooney v Das* [1999] BPIR 404 at 405.

[28] For example, see *Re DKG Contractors Ltd* [1990] BCC 903; *Weisgard v Pilkington* [1995] BCC 1108; *Re Exchange Travel (Holdings) Ltd* [1996] BCC 933; *Wills v Corfe Joinery Ltd (in liq)* [1997] BCC 511; *Mills v Edict Ltd* [1999] BPIR 391; *Re Transworld Trading Ltd* [1999] BPIR 628.

[1990] BCC 903 at 910; *Re Fairway Magazines Ltd* [1992] BCC 924 at 930; *Wills v Corfe Joinery Ltd (in liq)* [1997] BCC 511 at 512). While we have never been given an exhaustive definition of 'proper commercial considerations', the cases show that certain actions are covered by this phrase. For example, in *Re MC Bacon Ltd* (at 337) it was found that the directors gave the debenture which the liquidator tried to attack in order to ensure that their company might make it through a period of financial embarrassment. In *Re Fairway Magazines Ltd* (at 930) the desire of the directors, in giving a debenture, according to their evidence, was said to keep the company going through a cash injection and this qualified as proper commercial considerations. In these cases, as well as in the case of *Re Ledingham-Smith* ([1993] BCLC 635), the transactions were entered into because of pressure being exerted by creditors. Examples of exerting pressure are threats: to institute ordinary legal proceedings; to initiate winding-up or bankruptcy proceedings; to refuse to continue to supply critical goods or services;[29] to cut off financial support.

It has been a principle of English law since the eighteenth century that preferential transactions entered into because of pressure will not be set aside. The reason why pressure ensures that any transaction is not a preference that can be adjusted is that preference entails an act of free will (*Ex parte Topham* (1885) LR Ch App 614; *Butcher v Stead* (1875) LR 7 HL 839 at 846) and pressure negatives the free will of the debtor. The pressure must be genuine (*Graham v Candy* (1862) 3 F & F 206; 176 ER 93; *Re Greaves* (1881) 45 LT 80; *Re Cooper* (1882) 19 Ch D 580; *Re Allen* (1971) 115 SJ 244) and not fraudulent (*Re Wrigley* (1875) LR 20 Eq 763) and if this is the case then a transaction will not constitute a preference for sections 239 or 340 purposes. It could be said that if there is pressure then the debtor, in granting a preference, could not have been influenced by a desire to benefit the creditor. The result appears to be that creditors should exert pressure on those of their debtors who seem to be in financial difficulty or have continuously reneged on promises to pay debts. It would not be very difficult for most finance providers or traders to ensure that they indulged in genuine pressure. In *Rooney v Das* ([1999] BPIR 404), where the bankrupt, who had paid, before his bankruptcy, four creditors out of the many to whom he owed money, gave evidence that:

> The first, second and third respondents all either in writing or verbally threatened legal proceedings against me which obviously caused me great concern.
>
> The motivation for paying the first, second and third respondents was driven by a desire to avoid legal proceedings and stop the respondents hassling me. This was my only reason for making the payment.
>
> In no way was I wanting to put the respondents in a better position than my other creditors (at 407).

---

[29] For example, see *Leyland DAF v Automotive Products* [1993] BCC 389.

The Cork Committee considered the situation where creditors apply pressure before being paid and a majority decided in favour of retaining pressure as a defence to a preference action.[30] But clearly such a view encourages creditors to exert as much pressure as they can and to grab what is possible before administration, liquidation or bankruptcy eventuates and if any payment is challenged they can point to such pressure to justify the payment. Seemingly this provides advantages for those creditors who are strong or understand the law and the legal system and its rules, usually the wealthier creditors such as banks. These advantages are usually at the expense of the small, less well-informed and less powerful creditors who can ill afford to get little or nothing out of a bankruptcy or winding up. All of this is 'totally antithetical to the purposes behind the enactment of laws preventing preferences, namely to ensure that there is a collective process involving a *pari passu* distribution of the debtor's assets.'[31]

When an insolvent enters into transactions with creditors who are not connected or associated with that insolvent and the transactions can be classified as preferences, then the principal reason is because of commercial considerations. In the main creditors are paid so that they will not pursue threatened winding-up or bankruptcy proceedings, stop lines of credit, or they will continue to supply goods or service. Consequently, if these kinds of transactions are above reproach there are likely to be few or any transactions for an office-holder to challenge. Office-holders will be limited to transactions where the recipient of the preference is a connected person or an associate of the insolvent.

37.3 Court orders[32]

As with sections 238(3) and 339(2), which deal with transactions at an undervalue, sections 239(3) and 340(2) provide that the object of any court order is to restore the position to what it would have been if there had been no preference given. Consequently, it is unnecessary to rehearse the earlier discussion in the context of transactions at an undervalue.

Sections 241(1) and 342(1) apply to claims for preferences, although some of the examples of orders set out there will be more relevant to orders where preferences have been established. For instance, orders that broadly fall within sections 241(1)(d) and 342(1)(d) are likely to be the

---

[30] Para 1256.
[31] A. Keay, *McPherson's Law of Company Liquidation*, at 591.
[32] For a more detailed discussion, see A. Keay, 'The Recovery of Voidable Preferences: Aspects of Recovery' [2000] Cfi LR 1.

most common. These paragraphs provide that any person may be required to pay, in respect of any benefits received from the insolvent, to the office-holder, such sums as the court directs.

Section 241(1)(c) indicates that a court could order the release or discharge of any security[33] given by the company. This was ordered in *Mills v Edict Ltd* ([1999] BPIR 391 at 394) where the judge found that the creation of a charge constituted a preference within section 239 and made an order setting aside the charge.

As with the situation where transactions at an undervalue have been entered into, the law protects certain third parties. Broadly, the exposition in Chapter 36 and given in relation to transactions at an undervalue is applicable here.

---

[33] This is defined in section 248(b)(i) to include 'any mortgage charge lien or other security'.

Chapter 38

Transactions Defrauding Creditors

38.1 Introduction

In Chapters 36 and 37 of this Part, we considered two actions available to office-holders, known as adjustment actions. This chapter focuses on proceedings that are somewhat different, certainly as far as the legislative base is concerned. Sections 423–425 are provisions which provide for the avoidance of transactions designed to defraud creditors. The provisions are descendants of the Statute of Elizabeth in 1571. The sections may be employed against any debtor, corporate or individual, whether or not that debtor is or becomes subject to some formal insolvency administration. Section 424 dictates who may commence proceedings under section 423 for the avoidance of a transaction. A number of people qualify to bring proceedings, namely liquidators, administrators, bankruptcy trustees, the creditors of an insolvent person or company[1] and persons who are litigants in proceedings against the insolvent;[2] these persons may bring proceedings on the basis that they are victims of a transaction entered into by the insolvent. Victims of a transaction[3] may, even where the debtor is subject to an insolvent administration, take action under section 423, provided that they have obtained the leave of the court (section 424(1)(a)). Interestingly the case law that has developed in relation to section 423 is dominated by actions conducted not by insolvency office-holders, but by creditors of debtors.[4]

---

[1] For example, see *Re Ayala Holdings Ltd* [1993] BCLC 256.

[2] For example, *Pinewood Joinery v Starelm Properties Ltd* [1994] 2 BCLC 412 at 418.

[3] They must be victims at the time of the application. They do not have to be victims at the time of the transaction.

[4] For example, see *Arbuthnot Leasing International Ltd v Havelet Leasing Ltd* [1990] BCC 636; *Re Ayala Holdings Ltd* [1993] BCLC 256; *Menzies v National Bank of Kuwait Ltd* [1994] BCC 119; *Pinewood Joinery v Starelm Properties Ltd* [1994] 2 BCLC 412; *Agricultural Mortgage Corp Pty Ltd v Woodward* [1994] BCC 688; *Royscot Spa Leasing Ltd v Lovett* [1995] BCC 502; *Midland Bank plc v Wyatt* [1995] 1 FLR 696; *Dora v Simper* [1999] BCC 836; *Jyske Bank (Gibraltar) Ltd v Spjeldnaes (No2)* [1999] 2 BCLC 101; [1999] BPIR 525; *National Westminster Bank plc v Jones* [2001] 1 BCLC 98; [2000] BPIR 1092 (CA).

The advantage of sections 423–425 is that, unlike many provisions in the Act, there are no time limits specified as to when the transaction which is sought to be challenged must have occurred.

The aim of the provisions is to prevent debtors from disposing of assets so as to frustrate their creditors.

It should be noted that liquidators and trustees in bankruptcy will need, once the Enterprise Act begins to operate, to secure approval from either the liquidation committee or the court in the case of the former and the creditors' committee or the court in the case of the latter before initiating proceedings under section 423 (para 3A of Schedule 4 and para 2A of Schedule 5).

38.2 Transactions at an undervalue

Section 423(1) states that it applies to transactions entered into at an undervalue. The subsection provides that a debtor enters into a transaction at an undervalue if:

- he or she makes a gift or the transaction does not provide the debtor with any consideration;
- the transaction is entered into in consideration of marriage; or
- the transaction is entered into for a consideration the value of which, in money or money's worth, is significantly less than the value, in money or money's worth, of the consideration provided by the debtor.

This essentially replicates that found in section 339(3) (and similar to section 240(3)) in relation to transactions at an undervalue. The last of the instances explaining what constitutes a transaction for these purposes will be the most difficult to establish. This situation involves, as we saw when considering sections 238 and 339, comparing in money or money's worth the consideration given by the debtor and that received by him or her (*Agricultural Mortgage Corp Pty Ltd v Woodward* [1994] BCC 688 at 693). Liquidators, administrators and trustees in bankruptcy may take proceedings against a person on the basis of sections 238 or 339 with a claim under section 423 being used as an alternative basis for the claim. There appears to be in practice a considerable overlap between section 423 on the one hand and sections 238 and 339 on the other. This is illustrated in *Agricultural Mortgage Corp Pty Ltd v Woodward* (a section 423 case) where the comments of Millett J in *Re MC Bacon Ltd* ([1990] BCLC 324 at 340) were relied on in relation to the meaning of undervalue in section 238.[5]

---

[5] The Court of Appeal in *Menzies v National Bank of Kuwait* [1994] BCC 119 at 128–129 said that the analysis of section 238(4)(c) by Millett J applied *mutatis mutandis* to section 423(1)(c).

Interestingly, there have been more reported cases dealing with section 423 compared with cases on sections 238 and 339 combined. This may be explained partly by the fact that most applications have been made by creditors rather than insolvency office-holders and of course only liquidators, administrators and bankruptcy trustees may avail themselves of sections 238 or 339, and partly by the fact that an applicant under section 423, unlike applicants under sections 238 and 339, is not required to prove that the debtor was, at the time of the impugned transaction, insolvent.[6]

Like sections 238 and 339, a claim is not going to succeed unless it can be established that the transaction is entered into for a consideration the value of which, in money or money's worth, is significantly less than the value, in money or money's worth, of the consideration provided by the debtor. The court has to form the view as to the price which the property representing the consideration given by the defendants and that given by the debtor(s) would fetch in the open market, thus providing a 'correct valuation' (*National Westminster Bank plc v Jones* [2001] 1 BCLC 98 at 122; [2000] BPIR 1092 at 1115).

It may be of assistance to an applicant that in considering any claim under section 423 a court will not look at the impugned transaction in isolation; it is necessary that a court looks at a transaction as a whole (*Agricultural Mortgage Corp Pty Ltd*).

38.3 The purpose

In order to be successful under section 423, the critical element which must be proved by the applicant is that the person entering into the impugned transaction (this will be the debtor ordinarily) had the purpose of either putting assets beyond the reach of a person who is making, or who may make at some time, a claim against the debtor or otherwise prejudicing the interests of such a person (a creditor or potential creditor) in relation to the claim. In *Jyske Bank (Gibraltar) Ltd v Spjeldnaes (No2)* ([1999] 2 BCLC 101; [1999] BPIR 525), it was stated that all that an applicant has to do is to prove that the purpose of the debtor was to put the assets beyond the reach of the applicant. It was not necessary to prove that the purpose was specifically designed to defeat the applicant's claim against the debtor. Proving that something was done with a particular purpose in mind, because a subjective assessment must be undertaken, is never easy. Actually obtaining an understanding of the meaning of 'purpose' is not easy. In *Brady v Brady* ([1989] AC 755 at 778) Lord Oliver

---

[6] Insolvency does not have to be proved under section 339 where the transaction occurred within two years of bankruptcy (section 341(2)).

(with whom the other Lords agreed) said 'purpose' can have several shades of meaning. His Lordship opined that the word is of wide content, but the mischief against which the section (in which it is contained) is aimed must be taken into account and 'purpose' must be distinguished from 'reason' (at 779).

As indicated above, in section 423 the legislature has stated that an order is only made if the debtor entered into the impugned transaction for the purpose of putting assets beyond the reach of creditors. Until recently, what an applicant had to prove as far as purpose was concerned was not clear. The preponderance of authority provided that an applicant under section 423 must demonstrate that in entering into the transaction, where the debtor might have a number of purposes in mind, it was the debtor's dominant purpose either to put assets beyond the reach of claimants, or to prejudice claimants.[7] According to Mr Edward Evans-Lombe QC (sitting as a deputy High Court judge) (as he was then) in one of the leading cases, *Chohan v Saggar* ([1992] BCC 306), the purpose of the debtor that falls within section 423(3) must be the 'dominant purpose'; it was recognised that the debtor might well have other valid purposes. The approach gained authoritative support notwithstanding some concern being expressed about it and notwithstanding that this position was not consistent with the courts' approach to section 238.[8] In *Pinewood Joinery v Starelm Properties Ltd* (1994] 2 BCLC 412) Judge Moseley QC (sitting as a High Court judge) doubted, albeit in an *ex tempore* judgment, whether the applicant had to prove a dominant purpose on the part of the debtor. He felt that it was strange that if a debtor had two purposes which are of equal importance in his or her mind, the debtor could not have the requisite purpose as he or she did not have a dominant purpose at all (at 419). In *Barclays Bank Pty Ltd v Eustice* ([1995] BCC 978 at 990), the Court of Appeal had accepted that the dominant purpose approach was fair and accurate. Admittedly, a differently constituted Court of Appeal, in *Royscott Spa Leasing Ltd v Lovett* ([1995] BCC 502), stated that a judge had to be satisfied that it was the debtor's substantial purpose to injure claimants and this test was less strict than the dominant purpose test (at 507),[9] but the Court approved of the general approach adopted in *Chohan v Saggar*. Notwithstanding this, in both *The Law Society v Southall* ([2001] BPIR 303) and *Commissioners of Inland Revenue v Hashmi* ([2002] BPIR 271) Hart J doubted whether any gloss had to be added to the statutory purpose and he would, if the matter was free from uncertainty, have eschewed notions of dominant purpose. It appears that the learned judge would, if the

---

[7] *Chohan v Sagar* [1992] BCC 306; affirmed on appeal ([1994] 1 BCLC 706; [1994] BCC 134) and reiterated by Evans-Lombe J in *Jyske Bank (Gibraltar) Ltd v Spjeldnaes (No2)* [1999] 2 BCLC 101; [1999] BPIR 525.

[8] L. Sealy and D. Milman, *Annotated Guide to the Insolvency Legislation*, 5th edn, Bicester: CCH (1999) at 466.

[9] This was applied by Jonathan Parker J in *Re Brabon* [2001] 1 BCLC 11 at 44–5.

matter was free from authority, hold that provided that one of the purposes of the debtor in entering into the impugned transaction fell within section 423, that would be sufficient for the applicant to succeed. In any event, in the latter case Hart J did find that the debtor had as his dominant purpose the prejudicing of creditors.[10]

But the matter seems to have been resolved to some degree by the decision of yet another differently constituted Court of Appeal, in *Inland Revenue Commissioners v Hashmi* ([2002] 2 BCLC 489; judgment delivered on 3 May 2002), involving an appeal from a decision of Hart J and mentioned above. The Court held that the dominant purpose test was to be rejected. But the decision might not have ended all controversy concerning section 423. Instead of proving a dominant purpose, Arden LJ, in handing down the leading judgment, said that what an applicant must establish is that the debtor had the purpose required in section 423, i.e., he or she intended positively that the assets would be put out of the reach of creditors. Arden LJ said that for something to constitute a purpose it must be a real substantial purpose in contrast with what might be a consequence of what the debtor did. In other words, if the evidence showed that a debtor entered into a transaction for a purpose other than to prejudice his or her creditors, but the consequence of the entering into the transaction was to prejudice creditors, the applicant would not succeed. Laws LJ said that the applicant must establish that the debtor was substantially motivated by one of the aims set out in section 423(3) when entering into the transaction that is challenged. Simon Brown LJ was of the opinion that the issue was whether the court was able to be satisfied that a substantial purpose of the transaction was to permit the debtor to escape his or her liabilities.

It is difficult to determine at this point how much the approach taken in *Inland Revenue Commissioners v Hashmi* will differ from the dominant purpose approach. It is noteworthy that in *Re Brabon* ([2001] 1 BCLC 11 at 45) Jonathan Parker J said that he found it difficult to distinguish between a substantial purpose test and a dominant purpose test. What is also of some concern is that, as indicated above, the three judges, while all rejecting the dominant purpose test, all expressed what an applicant had to establish in different ways. Arden LJ appeared to be the most liberal and Simon Brown LJ the most strict. Where the *Inland Revenue Commissioners v Hashmi* approach may assist an applicant is where a person had two equally important purposes in effecting the transaction impugned, as a court might well say, certainly on the view of Arden LJ in *Inland Revenue Commissioners v Hashmi,* that he or she had a substantial purpose.

According to the judge in *Chohan v Saggar* ([1992] BCC 306), purpose was to be equated with 'intention' (at 321) but result was not to be equated

---

[10] The decision of Hart J in *Southall* was overturned by the Court of Appeal ([2002] BPIR 336) on the basis that the Court did not think that the facts disclosed the necessary section 423 purpose, but no comment was made about Hart J's reservations about the dominant purpose test.

with purpose. Therefore, just because the effect of a transaction was to put assets beyond the reach of creditors, that in itself would not impugn it unless the debtor had the requisite purpose (at 321). This approach was clearly approved of by the Court of Appeal in *Inland Revenue Commissioners v Hashmi*. In establishing a case, the applicant only has to demonstrate that the requisite purpose applies to a single creditor.[11]

In several cases it has been held that a transaction is not saved just because the debtor did not have a dishonest motive or he or she took legal advice to the effect that what was being done was in order, provided that the court is satisfied that the section 423 purpose existed at the time of the transaction (*Arbuthnot Leasing International Ltd v Havelet Leasing Ltd* [1990] BCC 636 at 644; *Midland Bank plc v Wyatt* [1995] 1 FLR 696 at 698; *Re Brabon* [2000] BPIR 537 at 570). The motive or knowledge of the person who enters into the transaction impugned with the debtor is not relevant (*Moon v Franklin* [1996] BPIR 196).

While the existence of debts or claims against the debtor at the time of the transaction may be of assistance in establishing the fact that the debtor had the requisite purpose, that fact alone will not suffice, but may be an important factor in the case.[12]

Finally, on the question of purpose, all judges seem to agree that the requisite purpose does not have to be the sole purpose of the debtor in entering into the transaction under challenge.[13] Clearly, a debtor could have several purposes.

38.4 Fraud and inferences

Unlike with its precursor, there is no need to prove an intent to defraud on the part of the debtor when bringing proceedings under section 423. As no intent to defraud has to be proved now, it might be argued that the courts should be prepared to infer the requisite purpose in certain circumstances. Prior provisions permitted courts to infer purpose, but it is not clear whether courts will take that view with section 423. In *Chohan v Saggar* the Court saw no reason (at 323) for giving a different meaning to section 423 nor taking a different approach than the Court of Appeal in *Lloyd's Bank Ltd v Marcan* ([1973] 1 WLR 1387), when the appellate court considered the immediate ancestor of section 423. The decision in *Moon*

---

[11] Section 423(3)(b). See *National Westminster Bank plc v Jones* [2001] 1 BCLC 98; [2000] BPIR 1092.

[12] G. Miller, 'Transactions Prejudicing Creditors' [1998] Conv. 362 at 373.

[13] For instance, see the Court of Appeal decisions in *Royscott Spa Leasing Ltd v Lovett* ([1995] BCC 502; *Inland Revenue Commissioners v Hashmi* [2002] All ER (D) 7; judgment delivered on 3 May 2002.

v Franklyn ([1996] BPIR 196) also suggests that inferences may be drawn from the circumstances surrounding the case. Recently, Arden LJ, in giving the leading judgment of the Court of Appeal in *Inland Revenue Commissioners v Hashmi* ([2002]; 2 BCLC 489), said that judges can draw inferences. Earlier, in *Royscott Spa Leasing Ltd v Lovett* ([1995] BCC 502) while the Court of Appeal had not specifically denied the right to make inferences, it indicated that one cannot infer purpose from the fact that the debtor made a transfer for no consideration. As indicated earlier, the Court also said that it was not possible to equate result with purpose (at 508), something with which Arden LJ in the Court of Appeal in *Inland Revenue Commissioners v Hashmi* agreed. This approach can be a hindrance to an applicant because the result of a transaction may be a significant element in proving purpose.[14]

38.5 Orders

The object of any court order, where the applicant is successful, is to restore the position to what it would have been if there had been no transaction entered into (section 423(2)). It has been held that the words 'as far as possible' must be added to this requirement.[15] In addition, any order must protect the interests of the persons who are victims of the transaction.[16] The Court of Appeal in *Chohan v Saggar* ([1994] 1 BCLC 706) said that the court must consider what loss has been sustained and then, as far as practicable, restore the loss (at 714).

Examples of the kinds of orders which a court might make to facilitate the restoration of the position that existed prior to the transaction are provided in section 425(1). Generally these paragraphs reflect those found in section 241(1) and discussed earlier in this Part.[17]

There is some protection of third parties who are *bona fide* purchasers in relation to orders made. While an order may affect the property of, or impose an obligation on, any person, whether or not that person was a party to the transaction impugned, an order is not to prejudice any interest in property which was acquired from a person other than the debtor and was acquired in good faith, for value and without notice of the

---

[14] This appears to have been the case in *Barclays Bank Pty Ltd v Eustice* [1995] 1 WLR 1238 at 1248.

[15] *Chohan v Sagar* [1992] BCC 306 (affirmed on appeal by the Court of Appeal [1994] 1 BCLC 706).

[16] See the comments of Neuberger J in *National Westminster Bank plc v Jones* [2001] 1 BCLC 98 at 121; [2000] BPIR 1092 at 1113.

[17] Above at 491–2.

relevant circumstances, or prejudice any interest deriving from such an interest. Also, an order is not to require a person who received a benefit from the transaction in good faith, for value and without notice of the relevant circumstances, to pay any sum unless he or she was a party to the transaction (section 425(2)).

In *National Westminster Bank plc v Jones* ([2001] 1 BCLC 98; [2000] BPIR 1092), the court said that if a court is satisfied that a transaction is within section 423(1) and (3), it has a wide discretion as to what it may order. Unlike with sections 238 and 339, a court does not have to restore the position to what it was before the transaction was entered into, although usually it will do so. But it may actually decide that nothing should be done (at 121; 1113–1114).

If one victim of a transaction brings proceedings under section 423 and succeeds, then the court may make an order which is in effect a form of class relief, providing a benefit to all creditors.[18] This is further indicated by section 424(2) which provides that an application made by a victim of a transaction is treated as an application on the part of every victim of the transaction.

---

[18] See *Moon v Franklin* [1996] BPIR 196; *Dora v Simper* [1999] BCC 836.

Chapter 39

Invalidation of Floating Charges

39.1 Introduction

In liquidation or administration the office-holder will carefully scrutinise charges existing over company property. While company property which has been validly charged with payment of particular debts is not part of the general assets available to satisfy the claims of unsecured creditors in winding up or administration, floating charges may, in certain circumstances, be challenged and subjected to an order of invalidation. A floating charge that was created over the undertaking or property of a company being wound up in insolvency or subject to administration and which was created within a certain period prior to the commencement of winding up or administration (subject to certain exceptions contained in section 245(2))[1] may be declared invalid under section 245.

If a charge can be successfully challenged the chargeholder cannot claim priority as a secured creditor and there will be more assets available for distribution among the general body of unsecured creditors.

Section 245 seeks to prevent companies on their last legs from creating floating charges in favour of certain creditors in order to secure past debts and give them an advantage over other creditors.[2] For example, X, an unsecured creditor of Y Ltd, agrees to continue to provide credit to Y Ltd if the company agrees to give security for the continued credit and the advance by X is used to satisfy or reduce the existing unsecured debt to X. This involves both X's debt being converted from unsecured to secured, effectively giving X a preference, and it leaves the company in no better position financially.[3] So, where a floating charge is created in

---

[1] This area is explicitly made applicable to Scotland as well as England and Wales, by section 245(1).

[2] See in relation to an earlier section, *Re Orleans Motor Co* [1911] 2 Ch 41 at 45.

[3] An example taken from A. Keay, *McPherson's Law of Company Liquidation*, London: Sweet & Maxwell (2001) at 604–5.

the relevant time period by a transaction, not made *bona fide* for the benefit of the company, but made in order to provide certain moneys for the benefit of certain creditors of the company to the prejudice of other creditors of the company, it is invalid (*Re Destone Fabrics Ltd* [1941] Ch 319 at 324).

It should be noted that liquidators will need, when the Enterprise Act begins to operate, to secure approval from either the liquidation committee or the court before initiating proceedings under section 245 (para 3A of Schedule 4).

39.2 The relevant time

As with many of the provisions considered in this Part of the book, the time when the charge was created is critical. Charges are only invalid if they were created within the relevant time (section 245(2)). 'The relevant time' is defined in section 245(3) and provides that any floating charge created within the 12 months preceding the onset of insolvency may be invalid (section 245(3)(b)). 'Onset of insolvency' can mean, where a company is in administration, one of three dates, namely: the date of an administration order (section 245(5)(a)), the date on which the copy of the notice of appointment is filed where administration is initiated out of court by a floating chargeholder or the company (or its directors) (section 245(5)(b)), or, where the administrator is appointed in other ways, the date on which the appointment of an administrator takes effect (section 245(5)(c)). If the company is in liquidation, the date is the commencement of winding up[4] (section 245(5)(d)).

In addition, section 245(3) provides that charges created in favour of a connected person may be invalidated where they were created within the period of two years prior to the onset of winding up (section 245(3)(a)). Finally, if the company was or is in administration, the 12 months or two years mentioned in section 245 are extended to cover the period between the making of the application to the court for an administration order and the making of the order (section 245(3)(c)), or if no administration order was made, the time is extended to cover the period between the filing with the court of a notice of intention to appoint an administrator by a floating chargeholder or the company (or its directors) and the making of the appointment (section 245(3)(d)).

Where a charge is created in the 12 months prior to the periods mentioned in the last paragraph and it favours a person who is not a connected person, the charge is regarded as not being created within

[4] See above at 480–1 for the meaning of 'commencement of winding up'.

the relevant time except where the company is either unable to pay its debts within the meaning of section 123 or became unable to pay its debts (within the meaning of section 123) because of its entering into of the transaction under which the charge is created (section 245(4)).

39.3 Void charges

Floating charges created within the relevant time are, subject to the defence in section 245(4) and certain exceptions under section 245(2), void.

While section 245 fails to indicate that a charge created as a floating charge within the relevant time falls under the provision if it is either converted into a fixed charge at the option of the creditor before the commencement of liquidation or it crystallises before that time, e.g., because of the appointment of a receiver, the definition of 'floating charge' in section 251 provides that 'floating charge' includes a charge that was created as a floating charge. Hence, section 245 would apply where a floating charge covered by the section is converted into a fixed charge.

39.4 Exceptions

A floating charge falling under section 245 may not be totally invalid; it might come within one of the exceptions, applicable whether the charge-holder is a connected person or not. Charges are not invalid to the extent that they secure:

- the value of so much of the consideration for the creation of the charge as consists of money paid, or goods or services supplied, to the company at the same time as, or after, the creation of the charge (section 245(2)(a));
- the value of so much of that consideration as consists of discharge or reduction, at the same time as, or after, the creation of the charge, of any debt of the company (section 245(2)(b)); and
- the amount of such interest (if any) as is payable on the amount falling within either of the above in pursuance of any agreement under which the money was so paid, the goods or services were so supplied or the debt was so discharged or reduced (section 245(2)(c).

Section 245(2)(a) purports to make an exception where funds are extended by the creditor in order to revitalise a failing company. Whether there has, in fact, been money advanced by the chargeholder within this provision will be a question which will depend upon the circumstances of the particular case. In considering the circumstances, the courts will probably examine substance and not form (*Re Matthew Ellis Ltd* [1933] Ch 458). In some cases where it appeared that there was an actual payment of money to the company, but this was really no more than a transparent subterfuge designed to secure a creditor in respect of an existing debt, the charge has been invalidated. In *Re Orleans Motor Co* ([1911] 2 Ch 41) directors who had guaranteed the company's bank overdraft took a floating charge over its assets in return for a payment to the company of £1,500 which was to be applied in reducing its overdraft. It was held that this was not in substance a payment of money to the company: it was, in the view of Romer LJ (*Re Matthew Ellis Ltd* [1933] Ch 458 at 478), no more than a device by which the directors obtained security for themselves as contingent creditors of the company, the company itself simply acting as a 'conduit pipe' through which they reduced their own potential indebtedness to the bank.

Section 245(2)(a) covers not only cash but also goods and services supplied. The inclusion of goods and services in section 245 makes it clear that cash in literal terms is not the only commodity that brings the exception into play. Bank honouring cheques of a company drawn on an overdraft account in favour of the company's creditors were regarded as equivalent to cash under previous legislation (*Re Thomas Mortimer Ltd* (unreported, 17 February 1925, Romer J) noted at [1965] 1 Ch 186; *Re Peruss Pty Ltd* (1980) 5 ACLR 176 at 179) and one would assume that under section 245 a court will see them as equivalent to cash as the intention of Parliament in drafting section 245(2)(a) must surely have been to make clear that anything which adds value to the company can fall within the exception.[5] To come within the exception, the money paid, or the goods or services supplied, must be to the company. In *Re Orleans Motor Co Ltd* ([1911] 2 Ch 41), as the moneys which were paid to secure charges were paid to the company's bank and were never paid to the company and never became part of the assets of the company, Parker J held that the charges were not valid (at 45). In *Re Fairway Magazines Ltd* ([1992] BCC 924), where money was paid into the company's overdrawn bank account, it was held that a charge was invalid in similar circumstances because the money never became available to the company to be used as it liked. It is debatable whether this is fair as the upshot is that the company does benefit from the transaction.

To escape the invalidity of a charge, any money must have been paid, or goods or services supplied, at the same time as, or after, the creation of the charge, so as to prevent a creditor from having the benefit of a charge in relation to previous advances to the company and getting an advantage over other creditors. The phrase 'at the same time as' has

---

[5] A. Keay, *McPherson's Law of Company Liquidation*, at 609.

never been interpreted in such a way as to require strict contemporaneity as far as the creation of the charge and the payment of the money. There is no problem if the advance follows the creation of the charge. The problem arises where an advance was made before creation. It is always a question of fact and degree whether an advance is regarded as being made at the time of the charge's creation (*Re Shoe Lace Ltd* [1993] BCC 609; [1994] 1 BCLC 111). Where there is a delay in execution of the charge, after the payment of the money by the intended chargeholder, it has not been of concern if the delay could be explained adequately (*Re FA Stanton Ltd (No2)* [1929] 1 Ch 180; *M Hoffman Nominees Pty Ltd v Cosmas Fish Processors (International) Pty Ltd (in liq) (in receivership)* (1982) 1 ACLC 528 at 535). If there is a substantial delay in the execution of the charge, the chargeholder may be required to explain the reason for the delay. In *Re FA Stanton Ltd (No. 2)* ([1929] 1 Ch 180), a delay of 54 days between the first payment of cash and creation of the charge was satisfactorily explained. In the Court of Appeal in *Re Shoe Lace Ltd* ([1993] BCC 609 at 620) Sir Christopher Slade said that 'no moneys paid before the execution of the debenture will qualify for exemption . . . unless the interval between payment and execution is so short that it can be regarded as minimal and payment and execution can be regarded as contemporaneous'.

Also, if section 245(2)(a) is to apply, in relation to any advance subsequent to creation of the charge, the chargeholder must show that it was made in consideration of the charge. To do this it is not necessary for the chargeholder to satisfy the strict requirements of the doctrine of consideration as it applies in the law of contract (*Re Yeovil Glove Co Ltd* [1965] Ch. 148 at 178, 185); the words, 'in consideration of' have been said to mean 'by reason of' or 'because of the existence of a charge', so a prior charge can remain intact on the basis of subsequent payments to the company even though, in the strict sense, these payments have been made on account of a consideration which is wholly past.

For the purposes of section 245(2)(a), the value of any goods or services supplied to the company by way of consideration for the charge is the amount in money which at the time of supply could reasonably have been expected to be obtained for supplying the goods or services in the ordinary course of business (section 245(6)). So, a charge is invalid to the extent that it secures an amount in excess of what is a reasonable value for the goods or services. The rationale for this is to ensure that security is not obtained in relation to prior debts owing to the chargeholder by inflating the value of the consideration for the charge.

Charges that secure many different forms of new value, besides cash, provided to the company by the chargeholder are exempt from invalidity.

39.5 The effect of invalidation

If a charge is avoided then the property over which the charge was created is available for distribution among all of the unsecured creditors. The effect for the once-secured creditor is that a security interest is lost and the creditor must then prove as an unsecured creditor in the winding up. In some cases this effect can significantly increase what unsecured creditors receive from an insolvent estate.

Chapter 40

Extortionate Credit Transactions[1]

40.1 Background to the provision

Sections 244(2) and 343(2) of the Act provide that a court may make an order in relation to an extortionate credit transaction entered into within the three years before either the company went into liquidation (or became subject to administration) or the presentation of the petition on which an insolvent person went into bankruptcy. The effect of the provisions is, therefore, to permit a re-opening of the transaction. Sections 244 and 343 were clearly modelled on sections 137–140 of the Consumer Credit Act 1974 and it is likely the courts will have reference to the cases which have been decided under those provisions.[2]

Sections 244 and 343 have, it appears, the goal of ensuring that the rights of unsecured creditors are not prejudiced by reason of the insolvent company or person having entered into a loan arrangement for which the consideration is excessive. The section is not designed to impugn loans which turn out to be bad bargains, but to allow for the challenging of those loans which are grossly unfair, i.e., loans which no reasonable company or person in normal circumstances would enter into in the absence of some underlying reason, such as where there is a sham agreement designed to confer an undue benefit on the lender.[3]

As yet the section has not been the subject of any reported decision and, therefore, we have no clear guides as to how it will apply. The apparent lack of case law suggests that the provision has not been invoked frequently, or at all, by liquidators, trustees and administrators.

---

[1] It would seem that this area applies equally to Scotland as well as England and Wales.
[2] A. Keay, *McPherson's Law of Company Liquidation*, London: Sweet & Maxwell (2001) at 601.
[3] Ibid at 602.

40.2 The scope of the provisions

The provisions can be invoked where the company in liquidation or administration or the insolvent person in bankruptcy is, or has been, a party to a transaction that involves the extension of credit (sections 244(1) and 343(1)). The powers conferred by sections 244 and 343 are exercisable in relation to any transaction concurrently with any powers exercisable under sections 238 and 339 (transaction at an undervalue).

The provision applies in respect of an extortionate credit transaction. While the word 'credit' is not defined, it is likely that the courts would invoke the definition contained in the Consumer Credit Act. In that legislation 'credit' is defined broadly to include 'a cash loan, and any other form of financial accommodation'. Loan has been explained as:

> [A] contract whereby one person lends or agrees to lend a sum of money to another, in consideration of a promise express or implied to repay that sum on demand, or at a fixed determinable future time, or conditionally upon an event which is bound to happen with or without interest.[4]

Probably, in most cases, the issue will be whether the transaction attacked is a loan. 'Financial accommodation' is likely to include:

> . . . not only the common forms of instalment credit transactions with which companies may acquire goods such as hire-purchase, instalment sale and conditional sale, but any agreement under which the time for payment of the purchase price is extended after delivery.[5]

40.3 Extortionate: the critical element

This term is, quite clearly, the critical part of the provision. In sections 244(3) and 343(3) it is stated that it means (having regard to the risk accepted by the one providing credit) either that the transaction prescribed grossly exorbitant payments (whether unconditionally or in certain contingencies) in respect of the provision of credit, or the transaction grossly contravened ordinary principles of fair dealing. Professor Goode[6] and the court in *Wills v Wood* ((1984) CCLR 7; (1984) 128 SJ 222) both suggest that something that is an extortionate transaction must have

---

[4] A.G. Guest, *Chitty on Contracts*, Vol. 2, 26th edn, London: Sweet & Maxwell (1989) at para 3574.

[5] E. Bailey, H. Groves, C. Smith, *Corporate Insolvency Law and Practice*, London: Butterworths (1992) at 373. Also, see I. Snaith in *The Law of Corporate Insolvency*, London: Waterlow Publishers (1990) at 669.

[6] *Principles of Corporate Insolvency Law*, 2nd edn, at 178.

the elements of unfairness and oppression, while in *Davies v Direct Loans Ltd* ([1986] 1 WLR 823 at 831) Mr Edward Nugee QC (sitting as a deputy High Court judge) expressly disagreed, in that he was of the view that unfairness sufficed. Section 138 of the Consumer Credit Act states that in determining whether a bargain is extortionate, regard must be had to a number of specified matters and courts are probably going to have reference to this section in deciding what is extortionate.[7]

The legislation, in the form of sections 244(3) and 343(3), provides office-holders assistance, in that it states that a transaction to which an application under sections 244 and 343 relates is presumed, unless the contrary is proved, to be extortionate.

40.4 Court orders

If an office-holder can establish that a transaction was an extortionate credit transaction then a court, in its discretion, may order the insolvent to be extricated from its responsibilities linked to the transaction and the order may contain any one or more of the following, as the court thinks fit, namely (sections 244(4) and 343(4)):

(a) provision setting aside the whole or part of any obligation created by the transaction;

(b) provision otherwise varying the terms of the transaction or varying the terms on which any security for the purposes of the transaction is held;

(c) provision requiring any person who is or was a party to the transaction to pay to the liquidator [or administrator] any sums paid to that person, by virtue of the transaction, by the company;

(d) provision requiring any person to surrender to the liquidator [or administrator] any property held by him as security for the purposes of the transaction;

(e) provision directing accounts to be taken between the persons.

---

[7] A. Keay, *McPherson's Law of Company Liquidation* at 603.

Chapter 41

Wrongful Trading

41.1 Background

Section 214, which provides for liability for wrongful trading undertaken by company directors, was introduced as a legislative response to the recommendations in the Report of the Insolvency Law Review Committee, *Insolvency Law and Practice* (known as the 'Cork Report').[1] The Cork Committee was concerned that the fraudulent trading provision (discussed in Chapter 42), which only allowed for criminal actions, was ineffective and that a new provision should be introduced to allow for civil actions for unreasonable trading where only the civil burden of proof would apply.

Section 214 was introduced to stop directors from continuing to trade while their companies are on a slide into insolvency. Coupled with this is the notion that section 214 is to:

> [R]ecoup the loss to the company so as to benefit the creditors as a whole. The court has no jurisdiction to direct payment to creditors or to direct that moneys paid to the company should be applied in payment of one class of creditors in preference to another (*Re Purpoint Ltd* [1991] BCLC 491 at 499).

Section 214(8) provides that the section is without prejudice to section 213 (the fraudulent trading provision) and as a result it would appear that proceedings claiming relief under either sections 214 or 213 may be commenced. These proceedings may only be commenced by liquidators.

If a person is found to have been involved in wrongful trading and is liable to make a contribution to the assets of the company then the court may, on application or of its own volition and pursuant to section 10 of the

---

[1] Cmnd 8558, 1982.

Company Directors' Disqualification Act 1986, make a disqualification order thereby disqualifying the person from acting as a director or taking part in the management of a company.[2]

It should be noted that liquidators will need, when the Enterprise Act begins to operate, to secure approval from either the liquidation committee or the court before initiating proceedings under section 214 (para 3A of Schedule 4).

41.2 The section

The section is only available to liquidators in relation to actions against the past and present directors (including shadow directors (section 214(7)) of the company that is now in liquidation. The company must have entered insolvent liquidation (section 214(2)(a)) and under section 214(6) insolvent liquidation occurs where, at the time of winding up, the company's debts and liabilities, together with the expenses of winding up, exceeded its assets. In bringing proceedings a liquidator should specify a date from which he or she maintained the director should have realised that insolvent liquidation was inevitable.

The conduct which will constitute wrongful trading is restricted by section 214(2). The subsection provides, *inter alia*, that a director will only be liable if he or she knew or ought to have concluded that there was no reasonable prospect of the company avoiding going into insolvent liquidation. Notwithstanding this restriction, as the word 'trading' is not expressly mentioned in section 214, there is no reason why activity short of actual trading may be the subject of an action, such as selling assets with a view to winding up the company or failing to collect debts owed.[3]

Claims should be initiated within six years,[4] from the date when the company entered insolvent liquidation as it is the date when the cause of action accrued (*Re Farmizer (Products) Ltd* [1997] 1 BCLC 589; [1997] BCC 655).

---

[2] The maximum period of disqualification is 15 years: section 10(3). See *Re Brian D Pierson (Contractors) Ltd* [1999] BCC 26 for a case where the respondents were found to have been guilty of wrongful trading and were disqualified from acting as directors as a result.

[3] A. Keay, *McPherson's Law of Company Liquidation*, London: Sweet & Maxwell (2001) at 623.

[4] Limitation Act 1980, section 9(1).

41.3 Elements needed for liability

We have already noted that the company must be in insolvent liquidation. The other main elements that have to be established for liability of the person against whom proceedings have been commenced are that:

- at some time prior to the commencement of winding up the person knew or ought to have concluded that there was no reasonable prospect of the company avoiding going into insolvent liquidation; and
- the person was at that time a director of the company.

41.4 The scope of the provision

Section 214 only applies to directors. 'Director' is defined in section 214(7) to include a shadow director. Persons who give advice in a professional capacity or business relationship are not included within the definition of 'shadow director', even though the directors may act on his or her directions or instructions (section 251). Nevertheless, investigating accountants who are appointed by creditors with clout, as well as accountants involved in an informal corporate rescue, must be especially careful that they are not seen as shadow directors on the basis that they are running the company. The approach that these accountants are to take is to advise the board, but ensure that they permit the board to make its own decisions. Besides shadow directors being liable, *de facto* directors may also be liable (*Re Hydrodan (Corby) Ltd* [1994] BCC 161).

Section 214 includes both objective and subjective tests (section 214(4)). The objective test provides that in the course of assessing a claim made against a director courts must consider what a director ought to know or ascertain, the conclusions which ought to be reached and the steps which the director ought to take and evaluate whether the steps the director took were those which a reasonably diligent person would have taken. The reasonably diligent person who is used here is one who has the general knowledge, skill and experience that may reasonably be expected of a person who carries out the same functions as are carried out by the director subject to proceedings. The provision then goes on to introduce the subjective element by referring to things that are specific to the respondent director, namely his or her general knowledge, skill and experience. It must not be thought that these two tests, in any way, lessen the responsibility of a director who is not very experienced and who does not have the knowledge of the reasonable director. Every director must not only meet the standard relevant to his or her experience, but also the standard of a reasonably diligent director. Where persons are given specific, specialised roles, such as the 'sales director' or 'finance director', then special skills must be expected of that person (*Brian D Pierson (Contractors) Ltd* [1999] BCC 26 at 55). The upshot is that a director's efforts, or lack thereof, will be assessed in conjunction with the two tests, and the director has to attain the higher of the standards set by the tests. The consequence is that where directors attain the standard of a reasonable person who undertakes their functions in relation to their companies, but they fail to conduct themselves in such ways as would be expected of persons with their knowledge, skill and experience, they could be held liable under section 214. Likewise, if directors act according to the standards of their knowledge, skill and experience, but they fail to have conducted themselves according to how a reasonable person would have conducted himself or herself, they will be liable.

> Obviously the concern of the legislature would be that neither inexperienced nor incompetent directors are to be protected because of the mere fact that they are inexperienced or incompetent, and those who are experienced are not able to say that while they did not live up to their standards, they did what an average person would have done.[5]

The courts are to consider the kind of company managed by the director, as well as the type of business in which it was involved (*Re Sherborne Associates Ltd* [1995] BCC 40 at 54; *Re Produce Marketing Consortium Ltd* (1989) 5 BCC 569 at 594; *Re Brian D Pierson (Contractors) Ltd* [1999] BCC 26 at 55). Consequently, the courts will not be expecting as much general knowledge, skill and experience of a director of a company which has limited systems and doing a reasonably small amount of business, compared with a director of a company that has extensive and intricate systems and is carrying on a large-scale business (*Re Produce Marketing Consortium Ltd* (1989) 5 BCC 569 at 594–595). Section 214(4) should enable the courts to make some allowances where non-executive and part-time directors are concerned (at 595). Nevertheless, courts will approach cases with the notion that certain minimum standards can be assumed to be attained in whatever the company or its business (at 595).

Ancillary to section 214(4) is section 214(5), as it assists in the interpretation of the former provision. Section 214(5) does this in that it states that the reference in section 214(4) to the functions carried out in relation to the company by the director includes any function that the director does not carry out but were entrusted to him or her. As a result directors are held responsible for failing to carry out those actions and functions that they should have done.

---

[5] A. Keay, *McPherson's Law of Company Liquidation* at 625.

Palmer's Corporate Insolvency Law summarises the position when it states:[6]

> The court is thus required to arrive at a conclusion as to the appropriate conduct and acumen of an hypothetical person assuming him to have possessed in combination the levels of general knowledge, skill and experience which the director in question subjectively did possess and which objectively he ought to have possessed in view of the position held.

When courts come to the point of assessing whether there was no reasonable prospect of a company avoiding insolvent liquidation, they will have regard for a wide range of factors which may be presented in evidence. One author has identified the following factors: pressure from creditors owed debts, the withdrawal of support from banks, the loss of contracts, the fact that other contracts cannot be obtained, and the failure to pay Crown debts.[7]

Before bringing proceedings, it is necessary for the liquidator to settle on a point of time from which it is alleged the director knew or ought to have concluded that there was no reasonable prospect of the company avoiding going into insolvent liquidation. Care must be taken over this, for a liquidator is not entitled, if his or her original date does not hold up in court, to invoke other dates (*Re Sherborne Associates Ltd* [1995] BCC 40 at 42). The court is permitted, it appears, to impose its own starting point for wrongful trading (*Re Purpoint Ltd* [1991] BCC 121 at 128).

41.5 Defences

Directors are only able to avail themselves of a single defence, namely that a court is satisfied that after becoming aware that the company was bound for insolvent liquidation, the director took 'every step with a view to minimising the potential loss to the company's creditors as (assuming him to have known that there was no reasonable prospect that the company would avoid going into insolvent liquidation) ought to have taken' (section 214(3)). Directors have the burden of establishing the elements of a defence. The critical issue is what constitutes 'every step?' It is not possible to formulate a list of steps that can be guaranteed as saving directors from liability. However, seeking and putting into effect the advice of appropriate professionals[8] constitutes a fair approach to take. But it must be emphasised

---

[6] P. Davies *et al.* (eds), Vol. 1, London: Sweet & Maxwell, at 1256.

[7] S. Griffin, *Personal Liability and Disqualification of Company Directors*, Oxford: Hart Publishing (1999) at 66. It is likely that with the abolition of Crown priority by the Enterprise Act 2002, the last instance will no longer apply.

[8] See F. Oditah, 'Wrongful Trading' [1990] LMCLQ 205 at 208 where the learned commentator argues that if a director acts on the informed advice of an auditor a strong case should be able to be mounted against the director being held liable.

that doing this will not necessarily provide a good defence. It will very much depend on the circumstances and the view that a court takes of what has been done. Some of the appropriate things to do might be:[9]

- calling a creditors' meeting in order to advise them of the state of the company;
- liquidating the company;
- suggesting a chargeholder might appoint an administrative receiver;
- appointing an administrator;
- convening regular board meetings to review the position of the company.

Resignation, while appropriate in some cases, might not be in others as it will not be possible, after resignation, for the director to take action to minimise losses for creditors.[10] If a director is unable to gain support from other directors, then he or she cannot even petition for the winding up of the company as a single director is not entitled to take such action (*Re Instrumentation Electrical Services Ltd* (1988) 4 BCC 301), unless he or she is able to do so in some other capacity, such as a creditor. What seems critical is for the director to ensure that a detailed record of all that the director has done to minimise the losses of creditors is retained in some form.[11]

It might be thought that the termination of business is the most prudent thing to do, but in fact that could end up being the most prejudicial action as far as creditors are concerned. Even continuing to trade by paying cash for all supplies and services etc. might not be regarded as sufficient because there will still be an accumulation of overheads, making the overall debt position worse.[12]

In evaluating any defence, a court is required by section 214(4) to consider if the director took the steps which a reasonably diligent person who has the general knowledge, skill and experience that may reasonably be expected of a person who carries out the same functions as are carried out by the respondent director, and the general knowledge, skill and experience that the respondent director has.

Besides relying on section 214(3), a director could argue that there was a reasonable prospect of the company avoiding insolvent liquidation and, consequently, section 214(2) is not fulfilled.

If a director fails under section 214(3) to establish a defence, or is unable to convince a court that the liquidator's case is not made out, he or she is unable to be excused for wrongful trading under section 727 of the Companies Act 1985 on the basis that he or she had acted honestly and

---

[9] A. Keay, *McPherson's Law of Company Liquidation* at 627.
[10] A. Hicks, 'Advising on Wrongful Trading: Part 2' (1993) 14 Co Law 55 at 58.
[11] A. Keay, *McPherson's Law of Company Liquidation* at 628.
[12] F. Oditah, 'Wrongful Trading' [1990] LMCLQ 205 at 214.

reasonably. The reason is that ground in section 727 is incompatible with the objective nature of the test found in section 214 (*Re Produce Marketing Consortium Ltd* [1989] 1 WLR 745; (1989) 5 BCC 399; *Re Brian D Pierson (Contractors) Ltd* [1999] BCC 26).[13]

41.6 Orders

If a liquidator succeeds, the court may, in its complete discretion, order a director to contribute an amount to the assets of the company in liquidation (section 214(1)). The amount to be ordered is at the court's discretion (*Re Produce Marketing Consortium Ltd* (1989) 5 BCC 569 at 597). However, any order must be compensatory and not penal (*Re Produce Marketing Consortium Ltd* (at 597). After saying that, it might be noted that the compensation ordered does not have to be based on the loss suffered by creditors (at 598). The sum that can be the subject of an order is the amount by which it can be discerned that the assets of the company have been depleted by the wrongful trading of the director (*Re Produce Marketing Consortium Ltd* at 598; *Re Purpoint Ltd* [1991] BCLC 491). It has been suggested that courts may take into account in their considerations the fact that a director was culpable in doing what he or she did that constituted the wrongful trading,[14] with the result that courts may treat directors who have been reckless more harshly than those who have acted honestly and perhaps naively (*Produce Marketing* at 598). It is likely that if directors have lied that will be taken into account. No orders may be made in favour of particular creditors, as the aim of section 214 is to assist the liquidator to recoup the loss to the company so as to benefit all of the creditors of the company (*Re Purpoint Ltd* [1991] BCLC 491 at 499).

Section 215(2) allows courts, where they have made declarations against directors, at their discretion, to include further orders in the form of directions to support the declarations. For instance, a court might direct that the amount which it has ordered against the director is to be a charge on any debt or obligation due from the company to the director, or on any mortgagee or charge or any interest in a mortgage or charge on assets of the company held by or vested in the director, or any person on behalf of the director, or any person claiming as assignee from or through the director (section 215(2)(a)). Also, the court may, from time to time, make such further or other order as may be necessary for enforcing any charge imposed under section 215 (section 215(2)(b)).

---

[13] See the comments of Nelson J in *Bairstow v Queens Moat Houses plc* [2000] BCC 1025.

[14] S. Griffin, *Personal Liability and Disqualification of Company Directors* at 83.

The compensatory system provided has been criticised on the basis that the persons who have been the real victims of the wrongful trading, primarily the creditors subsequent to the time when wrongful trading commenced, do not receive all of the compensation; a portion of it will be paid to those who had become creditors prior to the wrongful trading commencing.[15]

On the positive side, relief provided under section 214 does not go to secured creditors who hold charges over company property, but is for the benefit of unsecured creditors (*Re Produce Marketing Consortium Ltd* at 598). This is because a liquidator who proceeds pursuant to section 214 is doing so on behalf of the creditors and contributories of the company, and not on behalf of the company (*Re Oasis Merchandising Ltd* [1997] 1 All ER 1009).[16]

41.7 Some reflections

Shortly after the Act became law, academics and practitioners regarded section 214 enthusiastically and felt that it might be the much-needed protection unsecured creditors seek.[17] Unfortunately, it is debatable whether it can be said that section 214 has improved things for creditors. In more recent times, commentators have been more circumspect and less optimistic about what it has achieved and what it might do in the future. It is probably not stating the point too strongly that section 214 has not fulfilled the hopes of commentators and creditors alike. Notwithstanding the fact that the section has been with us for over 16 years and during a period of a huge number of liquidations (primarily in the early–mid 1990s), there have only been a small number of reported cases. Admittedly some claims might have been either paid on demand by the liquidator or settled after the initiation of proceedings, but prior to hearing,[18] but the general view of practitioners who know what is happening in practice is that section 214 has not been regularly relied upon.[19] One commentator has made the adroit point that there has been an average of 18,000 insolvent liquidations per year since 1986 and all in all one would have

---

[15] A. Hicks, 'Advising on Wrongful Trading: Part 1' (1993) 14 Co Law 16 at 17.

[16] Compare the earlier decision of Knox J in *Re Produce Marketing Consortium Ltd* (1989) 5 BCC 569.

[17] R. Schulte, 'Enforcing wrongful trading as a standard of conduct for directors and a remedy for creditors: the special case of corporate insolvency' (1999) 20 Co Law 80.

[18] See A. Hicks, 'Wrongful Trading – Has it been a failure?' (1993) 8 IL&P at 134.

[19] See the comments of P. Godfrey and S. Nield in this regard: 'The wrongful trading provisions – all bark and no bite' (1995) 11 IL&P 139 at 140.

expected more actions to have been initiated.[20] Another commentator has drawn the rather depressing conclusion that section 214 'is of no interest to a liquidator, no benefit to creditors and for wrongdoers it is the impotent progeny of a fine legal theory'.[21] It is respectfully submitted that the comment is probably fair.

Undoubtedly, one of the things that has held back liquidators is the lack of funding and the uncertainty over the issue of funding by third parties. This issue, in relation to liquidator proceedings, was discussed here in Chapter 26 in detail and we will not repeat that discussion here, save to note that wrongful trading actions are the proceedings that have probably suffered the most from the funding crisis. The defeat of the liquidator in the recent case of *Re Continental Assurance* ([2001] BPIR 733) and the huge costs that it entailed is also likely to have dissuaded many liquidators from taking proceedings except where the case is absolutely watertight.

---

[20] S. Griffin, *Personal Liability and Disqualification of Company Directors* at 97.
[21] R. Schulte, 'Enforcing wrongful trading as a standard of conduct for directors and a remedy for creditors: the special case of corporate insolvency' (1999) 20 Co Law 80 at 88.

Chapter 42

Fraudulent Trading

42.1 Introduction

There have been provisions in company legislation for many years, since 1928, that have made it an offence to carry on a business of a company with an intent to defraud creditors. Such legislation provided that a civil remedy could be sought where fraudulent trading, as it was called, could be proved. But the Report of the Insolvency Law Review Committee, *Insolvency Law and Practice* (known as the 'Cork Report')[1] put forward the opinion that the fraudulent trading provision possessed significant inadequacies in dealing with irresponsible trading, such as the fact that the criminal burden of proof applied to civil actions and, also, applicants were required to establish actual dishonesty and real moral blame (*Re Patrick and Lyon Ltd* [1933] Ch 786). The recommendation of the Cork Committee was that the provision be amended and that criminal liability should apply only in relation to fraudulent trading and a new provision should be introduced to permit the taking of civil actions. The legislature responded by introducing wrongful trading, a civil action,[2] and fraudulent trading was divided into two. First, there was section 213 of the Act, which provided for a civil action. Second, there was section 458 of the Companies Act 1985, providing for a criminal prosecution of fraudulent trading. The two provisions dealing with fraudulent trading are essentially identical, with the primary difference being procedural. Under section 213, the applicant will be the liquidator, while criminal proceedings under section 458 must be initiated by the Crown. Critically, while a criminal prosecution may be initiated whether or not the company is in liquidation, civil actions may only be commenced where the company has entered liquidation.

---

[1] Cmnd 8558, 1982.
[2] See Chapter 41 for a discussion of this provision.

The offence of fraudulent trading is committed by every person who knowingly is a party to the carrying on of a business of a company with intent to defraud creditors of the company or creditors of any other person, or for a fraudulent purpose (section 458). The provision can be invoked even where the intention is to defraud future creditors of the company (*Re Smith* [1996] 2 BCLC 109). We will focus on the civil provision, section 213, as it is that provision which might assist in swelling the asset pool.

Section 213(1) sets out the conduct that constitutes the action of fraudulent trading, i.e., intent to defraud creditors or having a fraudulent purpose. Section 213(2) then states who is liable in civil action and for what they can be liable. The persons who are able to be proceeded against are those who knowingly are parties to the carrying on of a business of a company with intent to defraud creditors. Such persons are liable to make such contributions to the company as the court thinks proper. Commonly, the persons who will be the subject of such actions will be the company's directors. But they are not the only ones who may, theoretically, be sued. In a recent decision, *Re BCCI; Banque Arabe Internationale D'Investissment SA v Morris*,[3] Neuberger J held that section 213(2) was not limited to those who managed or controlled the company that had failed. The learned judge said that a company that was involved in and assisted and benefited from the business of the failed company and did so knowingly, could fall within section 213.

It is likely that while we have seen some fraudulent trading applications under section 213,[4] there will be relatively few. It is generally easier to prove under section 214, as it has a lower threshold of proof.

It should be noted that liquidators will need, when the Enterprise Act begins to operate, to secure approval from either the liquidation committee or the court before initiating proceedings under section 213 (para 3A of Schedule 4).

42.2 Intent to defraud

As one would expect, the notion of fraud is at the centre of section 213. The interpretation given to the meaning of 'fraud' has been of great importance. The meaning of the word has been the main issue that courts have had to address over the years, for fraud is difficult to define at the best of times, as it has different meanings in different contexts.[5] The

---

[3] [2002] BCC 407.

[4] See, for example, the recent cases of *Re BCCI; Morris v State Bank of India* [1999] BCC 943; *Bernasconi v Nicholas Bennett & Co* [2000] BCC 921; [2000] BPIR 8; *Morris v Bank of America* [2000] BPIR 83 (CA).

[5] J. Farrar, 'Fraudulent Trading' [1980] JBL 336 at 339.

meaning of 'carrying on business with intent to defraud', a phrase found in section 213, has never been defined statutorily and certainly when one considers the case law, one can see that there has not been a consistent approach adopted as far as the test that should be applied.

In *Re William C Leitch Bros Ltd* ([1932] 2 Ch 71), Maugham J gave the phrase a wide meaning when he said that:

> If a company continues to carry on business and to incur debts at a time when there is, to the knowledge of the directors, no reasonable prospect of the creditors ever receiving payment of those debts, it is, in general, a proper inference that the company is carrying on business with intent to defraud (at 77).

This case dealt directly with issues that were clearly intended to be covered by section 213's precursor. In this case the governing director of the company had, at a time when the company was, to his knowledge, unable to pay its debts, ordered goods on credit which subsequently became the subject of a floating charge created in favour of the director.[6] Because of this, the proposition enunciated by Maugham J was probably formulated more widely than was strictly necessary for the decision of the case and, significantly, in the subsequent case of *Re Patrick & Lyon Ltd* ([1933] Ch 786), the same judge declined to hold that the director was personally liable even though he had deliberately delayed in despatching notices of intention to wind up voluntarily so that he could protect a charge that he held from invalidity under the precursor of section 245.

In more recent times, the Court of Appeal in *R v Grantham* ([1984] 2 WLR 815; [1984] BCLC 270) adopted a robust approach, either distinguishing or disapproving of earlier decisions and espousing the view that it was not necessary for the applicant to have to establish that there was no reasonable prospect of the creditors of the company ever receiving payment of what was owed to them, for a claim to succeed. The court indicated that if persons have some hope or expectation that ultimately all debts would be paid, they may still be liable, if at the time of getting the credit they are aware that there is no reason for thinking that the debts will be able to be paid when they become due or shortly afterwards. Effectively, the court was requiring some action that was close to recklessness. In *Re L Todd (Swanscombe) Ltd* ([1990] BCC 125), the court said that there is a need for evidence of, in the words of Maugham J: 'actual dishonesty involving, according to current notions of fair trading among commercial men, real moral blame' (*Re Patrick and Lyon Ltd* [1933] Ch 786 at 790).

---

[6] The director was declared personally liable for £6,000, the amount of the debts incurred, which was charged on a debenture held by him.

We find, in *Bernasconi v Nicholas Bennett & Co* ([2000] BCC 921; [2000] BPIR 8), an attempt at trying to reconcile things by saying that for fraudulent trading it was necessary to demonstrate that there was 'intent to defraud or reckless indifference whether or not the creditors were defrauded', but after making that comment Laddie J stated that dishonesty was a critical element in the action (924; 12–13). In fact, the judge said that it was the dishonesty factor that distinguished section 213 from a section 214 action (at 925; 13).

All of this has created uncertainty and probably means that a liquidator would be far more inclined, where possible, to initiate proceedings pursuant to section 214, subject to what we have said in relation to such actions in Chapter 41.

The test for intent to defraud is subjective and not objective, in that the state of the mind of the respondent at the time of the alleged fraudulent trading will be the deciding factor. But, having said that, objective considerations are not irrelevant. The circumstances surrounding alleged fraudulent trading must be taken into account and a respondent may have some difficulty extricating himself or herself from liability if the subjective view held was not reasonable.[7]

For a person to be liable there must be some positive action taken, so if an officer of, or adviser to, the company, such as the company secretary, neglects to inform the directors that the company is insolvent and what the consequences are in continuing to trade, that person is not liable criminally or civilly, as there is a need for some positive conduct for there to be fraud.[8] A person is not liable merely because he or she nominated a person as a director who committed fraudulent trading, or because he or she had the opportunity of influencing the conduct of the affairs of the company. Company officers will not, necessarily, be liable for trading while the company is insolvent. In such a case there may well be no fraud involved and it is likely, in any event, that a liquidator would prefer to proceed against directors under the wrongful trading ground.

Carrying on business is critical to the action and this phrase is interpreted broadly by the courts, as illustrated in *Re Sarflax Ltd* ([1979] 1 All ER 529).

> In that case a company which was engaged merely in collecting and distributing its assets was deemed to be carrying on business within the meaning of that term within a forerunner of section 213. A company had agreed to sell goods to buyers who were in Italy. The buyers asserted that the goods supplied were unsatisfactory and they rescinded the contract. Litigation commenced in England, but was not followed through. However, litigation that had been commenced in Italy was continued and a judgment order was made against

---

[7] See *Re Augustus Barnett & Sons Ltd* (1986) 2 BCC 98, 904.
[8] See *Re Maidstone Buildings Ltd* [1971] 1 WLR 1085. See the criticism of this case by S. Griffin in *Personal Liability and Disqualification of Company Directors*, Oxford: Hart Publishing (1999) at 46.

the company, after the company had ceased trading and entered voluntary liquidation. The liquidator sought a declaration that the business of the company had been carried on with intent to defraud creditors. This application was based on the fact that before the advent of liquidation the company had distributed its assets to some of its creditors, and this included its parent company. The judge held that the company was carrying on business as there was a continuous course of active conduct.

The phrase 'any fraudulent purpose' appears to provide a wide ambit for the provision (*Re Cyona Distributors Ltd* [1967] Ch 889 at 902 per Lord Denning MR) and it has been said that it covers frauds committed against prospective creditors as well as current ones (*Re Seillon* [1982] Crim L R 676; *R v Kemp* [1988] QB 645; (1988) 4 BCC 203; *Re Smith* [1996] 2 BCLC 109). It has been suggested that those most likely to be protected by the phrase 'any fraudulent purpose' are customers of the company.[9]

42.3 Bringing proceedings

Only liquidators are able to apply for an order under section 213[10] and in taking action the liquidator is seeking compensation on behalf of the general body of creditors. The upshot is that courts are unable to direct that specific creditors be compensated for losses that they have suffered as a result of fraudulent trading (*Re Esal (Commodities) Ltd; London and Overseas (Sugar) Co Ltd v Punjab National Bank* [1993] BCLC 872 and affirmed on appeal at [1997] 1 BCLC 705 (CA)).

To keep within the limitation period, proceedings, being for the recovery of a sum of money, must be commenced within six years of either the resolution to wind up, in voluntary liquidation, or the making of a court order, in compulsory winding up (*Re Farmizer (Products) Ltd* [1995] BCC 926).

42.4 Court orders

If the liquidator is successful, a court will be primarily concerned about awarding a sum to the liquidator in order to compensate the creditors for the improper actions of the person subject to the proceedings. No order

---

[9] S. Griffin, *Personal Liability and Disqualification of Company Directors* at 43.

[10] The liquidator may give evidence at the hearing of an application: section 215(1).

will usually provide any amount that exceeds the company's indebtedness during the period identified as to when the fraudulent trading occurred (*Re Cyona Distributors Ltd* [1967] Ch 889 at 902; [1967] 1 All ER 281 at 284 (CA)). However, courts, under precursors of section 213, and in addition to an order for compensation, have been minded to include a punitive element in the order. On the basis that the present section is wider than its forebears, a court might be inclined to include a punitive award if the circumstances are appropriate.[11]

Courts have struggled with determining what should be an appropriate order of compensation. This is demonstrated by the case of *Re L Todd (Swanscombe) Ltd* ([1990] BCC 125).

> In this case the liquidator of a company applied for a declaration that a former director of the company was liable for fraudulent trading. Specifically it was argued that the director was knowingly a party to the carrying on of business with intent to defraud creditors. Before winding up it seems that the director received substantial amounts of cash in relation to transactions involving the sale of company goods, but these transactions were not entered in the books of the company. Her Majesty's Customs and Excise discovered these facts when investigating the company. The precise amount of VAT, interest and penalties due to Customs was not proved before the court. The Court ultimately made a declaration that the director was liable for fraudulent trading and that he was liable for debts, namely the VAT, interest and penalties to the extent of £70,000.

Courts will have regard, in determining whether punitive damages should be ordered, for the following: the length of the duration of the fraudulent trading; whether there were inadequacies in the company's accounting procedures; the excessive nature of directors' remuneration; and the order in which the company endeavoured to discharge its debts.[12]

Where a court makes a declaration, it is, at its discretion and like under section 214, empowered to make further directions to give effect to its declaration (section 215(2)). For instance, a court might direct that the amount which it has ordered against the director be a charge on any debt or obligation due from the company to the respondent, or on any mortgage or charge or any interest in a mortgage or charge on assets of the company held by or vested in the respondent, or any person on behalf of the respondent, or any person claiming as assignee from or through the respondent (section 215(2)(a)). Also, the court may, from time to time, make such further or other order as may be necessary for enforcing any charge imposed under section 215 (section 215(2)(b)).

---

[11] Compare the comments of Knox J in *Re Produce Marketing Consortium Ltd* (1989) 5 BCC 569 at 597, a case dealing with section 214. See Chapter 41.

[12] S. Griffin, *Personal Liability and Disqualification of Company Directors* at 54.

42.5 The proceeds

Like with wrongful trading claims, it would seem that any recoveries are not available to a chargeholder who has a charge over the present and future assets of the company. This is because the liquidator is proceeding in his or her own capacity, for the benefit of creditors and not on the company's behalf (*Re Oasis Merchandising Services Ltd* [1995] BCC 911 and affirmed on appeal by the Court of Appeal at [1997] 1 All ER 1009; [1997] BCC 282).

Chapter 43

Breach of Directors' Duties

43.1 Introduction

When any formal administration procedure in relation to an insolvent company occurs, the office-holder will examine the conduct of the directors of the company and consider if they may be liable for certain activities during the life of the company that involved breaching their duties to their company. If successful, the office-holder will receive money or property that will swell the assets to be distributed to the creditors. Most frequently, any action will be commenced by a liquidator, so our focus will be on the proceedings considered by a liquidator, but it must not be forgotten that other office-holders, such as administrators and administrative receivers, are also entitled to proceed on behalf of the company against directors who are culpable. If any action is initiated for breach, the office-holder will be bringing proceedings in the name of the company, in contrast to actions brought under specific provisions in the Act, such as section 214 for wrongful trading.

This chapter is merely an introduction to the liability of directors for the breach of the duties that they owe to their companies. It is not intended to rehearse much of the law that applies to this area. That is ably done by the many company law texts that are available.

The definition of 'director' in section 251[1] includes any person occupying the position of director, by whatever name called. This will, therefore, cover a person who has been validly appointed pursuant to the legal requirements (a *de jure* director), but also encompasses a person or a company who may be regarded as someone who is usually called a '*de facto* director'[2]

---

[1] The same definition is in section 741(1) of the Companies Act 1985.
[2] See, for example, *Re Kaytech International plc* [1999] BCC 390.

or a 'shadow director'.[3] The former is a person who acts as a director although he or she has not been validly appointed. The latter is someone in accordance with whose directions or instructions the directors of the company are accustomed to act.[4] Professor Goode has distinguished a *de facto* director from a shadow director in the following manner:

> [T]he former [*de facto*] acts himself as if he were a director whereas the latter [shadow director] acts through the *de jure* or *de facto* directors.[5]

Directors may be either executive or non-executive. The former is a person who sits on the board of directors and is employed full-time in some capacity in the management of the company, such as a managing director (or chief executive officer as that person tends to be known as now). Non-executive directors are not employed by the company; they are outsiders. The role of such directors is, *inter alia*, to vet what is proposed by the executive directors and they are paid directors' fees for their efforts.

43.2 Directors' duties

At common law, directors owe important and somewhat onerous duties to their companies. The reason for the existence of these duties is that directors are fiduciaries and the company and its shareholders are in positions of vulnerability as the affairs of the company are often within the almost total control of the directors. A liquidator may be able to recover assets lost by the company resulting from directors' breaches, obtain an account of profits received by directors in breach of their duties, or obtain compensation for the loss suffered by the company, as a result of improper gains made by directors as a consequence of breaches.

The standard by which executive and non-executive directors are judged are the same (*Dorchester Finance Co Ltd v Stebbing* [1989] BCLC 488).

Some Commonwealth countries, such as Australia, Canada and New Zealand, have introduced statutory duties for directors. Thus far, the UK has decided not to do so. However, this is likely to change in the near future. In its Final Report to the Department of Trade and Industry, the Company Law Review Steering Group,[6] established to review core company law in the UK, has recommended that directors' duties be

---

[3] 'Shadow director' is defined in section 251 and section 741(2) of the Companies Act 1985. See *Re Hydrodan (Corby) Ltd* [1994] BCC 161; *Secretary of State for Trade and Industry v Deverell* [2000] 2 BCLC 133; [2000] BCC 1057. In the former case, Millett J contrasted a *de facto* director with a shadow director.

[4] See, for example, *Secretary of State for Trade and Industry v Deverell* [2000] 2 BCLC 133; [2000] BCC 1057.

[5] R. M. Goode, *The Principles of Corporate Insolvency Law*, 2nd edn, 1997, at 445.

[6] *Modern Company Law: For a Competitive Economy*, Vol 1, 2001, Chapter 3.

codified. The government in its White Paper, *Modernising Company Law,*[7] has indicated that it shares the view of the Steering Group.[8]

The duties may be divided into two broad categories: duties of good faith and duties of care and skill.

43.3 Duties of good faith

The duties of good faith have often been defined more specifically as including the following duties:

- to act honestly in the best interests of the company;
- to avoid conflicts between the company's interests and personal interests;[9]
- to exercise powers for the proper purpose;
- to act with an unfettered discretion.

It can be argued that there is only one duty owed and that is to act honestly in the best interests of the company and all the other duties are able to be subsumed under this major duty. Nothing really turns on this point for our purposes. The duties are known as fiduciary duties. The duties are not as strict as those placed on trustees, for directors are not trustees (although they are in trustee-like positions). Nevertheless, the duties placed upon directors are stringent, relatively speaking, and quite strictly enforced by the courts.

The powers of the directors cease on liquidation, but directors are not permitted to take advantage of this and benefit from using company information (*Lord Corporation Pty Ltd v Green* (1991) 9 ACLC 1094 at 1104). In voluntary liquidation the office of the directors continues and so proceedings may be taken by a liquidator against the directors for actions committed in relation to company affairs after the commencement of winding up.

43.4 Duties of care and skill

Directors must exercise reasonable care, skill and diligence in carrying out their responsibilities. While the duties of good faith are owed in equity, duties of care and skill are owed at both common law and equity (*Bristol*

---

[7] Cm 5553–1, Vol 1, July 2002, TSO.
[8] Ibid at para 3.5.
[9] While many company law texts refer to this as a duty, it is submitted that it is debatable whether this constitutes a duty as such.

and West Building Society v Mothew ([1996] 4 All ER 698 (CA)). Historically, it is probably fair to say that duties of care and skill have not been as strictly enforced as the duties of good faith. However, recent years have shown the courts to be more concerned to enforce care and skill responsibilities. One of the main concerns that the courts have articulated in relation to dealing with care and skill is their lack of business acumen and their concomitant reluctance to judge the decisions of directors.

The classic case in this area is *Re City Equitable Fire Insurance Co Ltd* ([1925] Ch 407), which set out the basic principles covering care and skill largely in subjective terms. The case provided, *inter alia*, that directors need not manifest, while undertaking their duties, a greater degree of skill than may be expected of the non-professional reasonable person. Somewhat famously, the court said that directors were not bound to give continuous attention to the affairs of their companies and this has been said to have caused the poor attendance of some directors at board meetings. Also, the court stated that if it is prudent, from a business point of view (and taking into account the constitution), that some duty be left to some other official, then a director, in the absence of grounds for suspicion, is justified in trusting that official to perform such a duty honestly.

It has been said that a director must exhibit the care and skill that may be reasonably expected from a person of his or her knowledge and experience (*Dorchester Finance Co Ltd v Stebbing* [1989] BCLC 498). This, therefore, provides for a variable standard of care which makes it more difficult to establish negligence on the part of a director.

The law has tightened things more in recent times and the indication is that the courts of today will require greater vigilance on the part of directors.[10] The older cases that devised the law did so with the post of non-executive director in mind. It was generally accepted that non-executive directors had no serious role to play within the company.[11] The principles that were formulated are totally inappropriate for executive directors and, of course, the commercial world has changed significantly over time. The subjective tests formulated in *Re City Equitable Fire Insurance Co Ltd* as far as care and skill are concerned have been replaced with an objective test, in the following terms: did the director exhibit such care as an ordinary man might be expected to take on his own behalf? (*Dorchester Finance Co Ltd v Stebbing* [1989] BCLC 498), as well as some subjective criteria.

So, the upshot is that directors will probably not be seen to be fulfilling their duties if they fail (certainly regularly) to attend board meetings or they do not apply their judgement carefully in considering what they are told by company employees and company advisers. The law still permits

---

[10] See *Re Majestic Recording Studies Ltd* (1988) 4 BCC 519. See A. Walters, 'Directors' duties: the impact of the Company Directors' Disqualification Act 1986' (2000) 21 Co Law 110.

[11] P. Davies, *Gower's Principles of Modern Company Law*, 6th edn, London: Sweet & Maxwell (1997) at 641.

directors to rely on others without incurring liability, but only if they had no reason to distrust them (*Norman v Theodore Goddard* [1991] BCLC 1028).

The cases that have the most profound effect on the area are probably *Norman v Theodore Goddard* and *Re D'Jan of London Ltd* ([1993] BCC 646; [1994] 1 BCLC 561), where the courts held that the wrongful trading provision embodies the standard required of a director at common law, in terms of care, skill and diligence. It will be recalled, from Chapter 41, that section 214 provides that a director is liable if he or she 'knew or ought to have concluded that there was no reasonable prospect that the company would avoid going into insolvent liquidation' unless the court is satisfied that the director 'took every step with a view to minimising the potential loss to the company's creditors' as ought to have been taken. The section requires directors to act as a reasonable diligent person having the knowledge, skill and experience that may be reasonably expected of a person performing the same functions, as well as having the knowledge, skill and experience which the director has.

In a very recent case, Jonathan Parker J (in *Re Barings plc (No5)* [1999] 1 BCLC 433) considered the duties of directors in general. As far as duties of care and skill are concerned, his Lordship said (summarising the authorities) that:

(1) Directors have, both collectively and individually, a continuing duty to acquire and maintain a sufficient knowledge and understanding of the company's business to enable them to discharge their duties.

(2) While directors are entitled (subject to the articles of association of the company) to delegate particular functions to those below them in the management chain and to trust their competence and integrity to a reasonable extent, the exercise of the power of delegation does not absolve a director from the duty to supervise the discharge of the delegated functions.

(3) No rule of universal application can be formulated as to the duty referred to in (2) above. The extent of the duty and the question whether it has been discharged, must depend on the facts of each particular case, including the director's role in the management of the company (at 489).

43.5 Statutory developments

Hitherto, we do not have in the UK, unlike some Commonwealth countries, statutory provisions that have codified the duties owed by directors. However, Parliament has included in the Companies Act some provisions that regulate how directors may act and carry out their duties. These are found in Part X of the Act which is headed 'Enforcement of Fair Dealing'.[12] It is not within the scope of this book to deal with them.[13]

43.6 Duties to creditors[14]

The traditional view of directors' duties is that they are owed to the company – so that directors are under a fiduciary obligation to exercise their powers *bona fide* in the interests of the company as a whole. It is trite law that directors owe duties to their companies as a whole but not to any individual members or other persons, such as creditors.[15] However, there is clear authority that in certain cases directors have a duty to consider creditors' interests. According to the predominance of judicial and academic view, the duty is mediated through the company,[16] that is, directors have a duty to their companies to consider creditors' interests, rather than being a duty that directors owe directly to the creditors.[17]

The fact that directors owe a duty to take into account creditors' interests was first established in a formal way by the comments of Mason J

---

[12] See sections 311–347.

[13] See the coverage in P. Davies, *Gower's Principles of Modern Company Law*, 6th edn, London: Sweet & Maxwell (1997) at 623–40.

[14] For a detailed discussion of the topic, see, for example, L. S. Sealy, 'Director's Wider Responsibilities – Problems Conceptual, Practical and Procedural' (1987) 13 Mon U LR 164; C. Riley, 'Directors' duties and the interests of creditors' (1989) 10 Co Law 87; D. Prentice, 'Creditor's Interests and Director's Duties' (1990) 10 OJLS 265 at 275; V. Finch, 'Directors' Duties: Insolvency and the Unsecured Creditor' in A. Clarke (ed.), *Current Issues in Insolvency Law*, London: Stevens (1991) at 87; R. Grantham, 'The Judicial Extension of Directors' Duties to Creditors' [1991] JBL 1; S. Worthington, 'Directors' Duties, Creditors' Rights and Shareholder Intervention' (1991) 18 MULR 121; D. Wishart, 'Models and Theories of Directors' Duties to Creditors' (1991) 14 NZULR 323; A. Keay, 'The Director's Duty to Take into Account the Interests of Company Creditors: When is it Triggered?' (2001) 25 *Melbourne University Law Review* 315; A. Keay, 'The Duty of Directors to Take Into Account Creditors' Interests: Has It Any Role to Play?' [2002] JBL 379.

[15] If authority is necessary, see *Percival v Wright* [1902] 2 Ch 421; *Multinational Gas and Petrochemical Co v Multinational Gas and Petrochemical Services Ltd* [1983] Ch 258; *Peskin v Anderson* [2000] BCC 1110 (and affirmed on appeal by the Court of Appeal (14 December 2000). Also see the comments of the Jenkins Committee, Cmnd 1749 (1962) at para 89.

[16] D. Prentice, 'Creditor's Interests and Director's Duties' (1990) 10 OJLS 265 at 275.

[17] This has the support of the predominance of academic commentators. For example, see D. Prentice, 'Creditor's Interests and Director's Duties' (1990) 10 OJLS 265 at 275; S. Worthington, 'Directors' Duties, Creditors' Rights and Shareholder Intervention' (1991) 18 MULR 121 at 151; L. S. Sealy, 'Personal Liability of Directors and Officers for Debts of Insolvent Corporations: A Jurisdictional Perspective (England)' in J. Ziegel, *Current Developments in International and Comparative Corporate Insolvency Law*, Oxford: Clarendon Press (1994) at 486.

of the Australian High Court in delivering the leading judgment in *Walker v Wimborne* ((1976) 137 CLR 1) where his Honour said:

> In this respect it should be emphasised that the directors of a company in discharging their duty to the company must take into account the interests of its shareholders and its creditors. Any failure by the directors to take into account the interests of creditors will have adverse consequences for the company as well as for them (at 5–6).

While his Honour's statement may have been of a rather casual nature, the impact of the dictum has been far-reaching and it has been either acknowledged or even eagerly taken up by many other courts in the Commonwealth, including those in the UK, with the result that at certain points in the life of a company, its directors may be forced to give consideration to the interests of the creditors. The first indication that a UK court might consider imposing on directors a requirement to consider the interests of creditors was in 1980 in a dictum of Lord Diplock in *Lonrho Ltd v Shell Petroleum Co Ltd* ([1980] 1 WLR 627) when his Lordship said that it is the duty of the board to do what would be in the best interests of the company and that this does not just refer to its shareholders, but may include the interests of its creditors (at 634). Later in the 1980s the idea of directors owing some duty to take into account the interests of creditors had been regarded as providing a real protection for creditors of companies.[18]

The case law had indicated that the duty is only owed in certain circumstances, but it is not clear as to what those circumstance are. The exception to the traditional view that directors do not have to pay attention to creditors is ill-defined; there is a distinct lack of judicial unanimity as to the actual circumstances which will cause directors to have to consider creditors' interests. It has been held that directors owe a duty to take into account creditor interests when their company is insolvent (*Kinsela v Russell Kinsela Pty Ltd* (1986) 4 ACLC 215; (1986) 10 ACLR 395; *Liquidator of West Mercia Safetywear v Dodd* (1988) 4 BCC 30; *Yukong Lines Ltd of Korea v Rendsburg Investments Corporation* [1998] BCC 870), near to, or in the vicinity of insolvency (*Nicholson v Permakraft (NZ) Ltd* (1985) 3 ACLC 453; *Brady v Brady* (1988) 3 BCC 535 (CA)), of doubtful insolvency (*Nicholson v Permakraft (NZ) Ltd* (1985) 3 ACLC 453 at 459, 463, 464; *Brady v Brady* (1988) 3 BCC 535 at 632 (CA)), where there is a risk of insolvency (*Nicholson v Permakraft (NZ) Ltd; Liquidator of West Mercia Safetywear v Dodd*) and even where there is financial instability (*Facia Footwear Ltd (in administration) v Hinchliffe* [1998] 1 BCLC 218). Certainly there needs to be more clarification from the courts as to what might trigger the duty.[19]

---

[18] V. Finch, 'Directors' Duties: Insolvency and the Unsecured Creditor' in A. Clarke (ed.), *Current Issues in Insolvency Law*, London: Stevens (1991) at 91.

[19] See A. Keay, 'The Director's Duty to Take into Account the Interests of Company Creditors: When is it Triggered?' (2001) 25 *Melbourne University Law Review* 315.

There remains the issue of whether the cause of action has any relevance given the advent of wrongful trading and the existence of other actions discussed earlier in this Part. There will be situations where a liquidator or administrator will not be able to pursue successfully a claim for a preference, a transaction at an undervalue, a transaction defrauding creditors, or even for wrongful or fraudulent trading because, *inter alia*, of the matters raised earlier in this Part (such as funding), and proceedings for breach of duty are worthy of consideration.[20] The fact of the matter is that if one excludes the breach of duty action then there have been (and will continue to be) cases[21] where liquidators would not have succeeded and creditors would have been prejudiced.

There is nothing prohibiting a liquidator from coupling a claim against a director for breach of the duty to take into account the interests of creditors with any of the kinds of proceedings mentioned earlier in this Part. There is no need for the liquidator to have to decide whether he or she is going to rely on this duty alone. Coupling a claim for breach of duty with one or more other claims could well be the most prudent course of action to adopt.

In closing, one must note two things. First, there are disadvantages in initiating breach of duty actions, which are discussed immediately below, and these apply to an action taken against a director for failing to take into account the interests of creditors. Second, many of those who take a contractarian approach to corporate law[22] are against imposing a responsibility on directors to consider creditor interests, because to do so would reduce efficiency and in any event creditors are able to invoke protection measures such as taking security or having restrictive provisions inserted in the contract made with the company.

43.7 Disadvantages with actions

The first disadvantage with actions for breach of duty is that courts are permitted to grant relief to the respondent director under section 727 of the Companies Act 1985. This provision permits a court, wholly or in part, to relieve officers from liability in relation to proceedings for negligence, default, breach of duty, or breach of trust.[23] The courts are only allowed to

---

[20] For a detailed discussion, see A. Keay, 'The Duty of Directors to Take Account of Creditors' Interests: Has it Any Role to Play?' [2002] JBL 379.

[21] Such as *Ring v Sutton* (1980) 5 ACLR 546; *Kinsela v Russell Kinsela Pty Ltd* (1986) 4 ACLC 215; (1986) 10 ACLR 395; *Liquidator of West Mercia Safetywear v Dodd* (1988) 4 BCC 30.

[22] The brand of contractarianism that is most vociferous is the law and economics movement.

[23] The defence does not have to be specifically pleaded: *Re Kirby's Coaches Ltd* [1991] BCC 130.

exercise this jurisdiction if they are satisfied that the person who sought relief had acted honestly and reasonably and that, having regard to all the circumstances of the case, he or she ought fairly to be excused (*Re J Franklin & Sons Ltd* [1937] 4 All ER 43).

A second possible disadvantage is that usually it is the liquidator who will initiate proceedings, but he or she will issue the proceedings in the name of the company. It is likely that the respondent director will apply for an order for security of costs pursuant to section 726 of the Companies Act 1985.[24] If the company is insolvent, as it will be in most situations, that may lead a court to making the order requested. It must be added that it cannot be said that there is a presumption that security will be ordered against a company in liquidation.

The third drawback with proceedings for breach of duty is that even if an order is obtained, it has to be enforced. It is quite possible that the director(s) may be impecunious, rendering the proceedings possibly tantamount to useless.

Probably the biggest disadvantage with taking action for breach of duty is the fact that if anything is recovered from the director, it can be taken first by any secured creditor who has a floating charge over all present and future company property and who has not been paid.

---

[24] For an admirable treatment of security for costs in relation to company law, see D. Milman, 'Security for Costs: Principles and Pragmatism in Corporate Litigation' in B.A.K. Rider (ed.), *The Realm of Company Law*, London: Kluwer Law International (1998) at 167.

References

Bailey, E., Groves, H. and Smith, C., *Corporate Insolvency Law and Practice*, 2nd edn, London: Butterworths (2001).

Berry, C., Bailey, E. and Schaw-Miller, S., *Personal Insolvency Law – Law and Practice*, 3rd edn, London: Butterworths (2001).

Conaglen, M., 'Voidable Preferences Under the Companies Act 1993' [1996] *New Zealand Law Review* 197.

Cook, C., 'Wrongful Trading – Is it a Real Threat to Directors or a Paper Tiger?' [1999] *Insolvency Lawyer* 99.

Cooke, T.E. and Hicks, J., 'Wrongful Trading – Predicting Insolvency' [1993] JBL 338.

Davies, P. *et al.* (eds) *Palmer's Corporate Insolvency Law*, Vol. 1, London: Sweet & Maxwell (1986).

Davies, P., *Gower's Principles of Modern Company Law*, 6th edn, London: Sweet & Maxwell (1997).

Doyle, L., 'Ten Years of Wrongful Trading' (1996) 18 *Insolvency Law and Practice* 10.

Farrar, J., 'Fraudulent Trading' [1980] JBL 336.

Farrar, J., 'The Bankruptcy of the Fraudulent Preference' [1983] JBL 390.

Farrar, J., 'The Responsibility of Directors and Shareholders for a Company's Debts' (1989) 4 Canta LR 12.

Finch, V., 'Directors' Duties: Insolvency and the Unsecured Creditor' in A. Clarke (ed.), *Current Issues in Insolvency Law*, London: Stevens (1991).

Finch, V., 'Is Pari Passu Passe?' [2000] *Insolvency Lawyer* 194.

Finch, V., *Corporate Insolvency Law: Perspectives and Principles*, Cambridge: Cambridge University Press (2002).

Finch, V. and Worthington, S., 'The Pari Passu Principle and Ranking Restitutionary Rights' in F. Rose (ed.), *Restitution and Insolvency*, London: LLP (2000).

Fletcher, I.F., 'Voidable Transactions in Bankruptcy: British Perspectives' in J. Ziegel (ed.) *Current Developments in International and Comparative Corporate Insolvency Law*, Oxford: Clarendon Press (1994).

Fletcher, I.F., *The Law of Insolvency*, 3rd edn, London: Sweet & Maxwell (2002).

Godfrey, P. and Nield, S., 'The wrongful trading provisions – all bark and no bite' (1995) 11 *Insolvency Law and Practice* 139.

Goode, R.M., *The Principles of Corporate Insolvency Law*, 2nd edn, London: Sweet & Maxwell (1997).

Griffin, S., *Personal Liability and Disqualification of Company Directors*, Oxford: Hart Publishing (1999).

Grantham, R., 'The Judicial Extension of Directors' Duties to Creditors' [1991] JBL 1.

Hicks, A., 'Advising on Wrongful Trading: Part 1' (1993) 14 Co Law 16.

Hicks, A., 'Advising on Wrongful Trading: Part 2' (1993) 14 Co Law 55.

Hicks, A., 'Wrongful Trading – Has it been a failure?' (1993) 8 *Insolvency Law and Practice* 134.

Keay, A., 'In Pursuit of the Rationale Behind the Avoidance of Pre-Liquidation Transactions' (1996) 18 *Sydney Law Review* 55.

Keay, A., 'Liquidators' Avoidance of Preferences: Issues of Concern and a Proposal for Radical Reform' (1996) 18 *Adelaide Law Review* 159.

Keay, A.R., *Avoidance Provisions in Insolvency Law*, Sydney: LBC Information Services (1997).

Keay, A., 'Preferences in Liquidation Law: A Time for a Change' (1998) 2 *Company Financial and Insolvency Law Review* 198.

Keay, A., 'The Recovery of Voidable Preferences: Aspects of Recovery [2000] *Company Financial and Insolvency Law Review* 1.

Keay, A., 'Transactional Avoidance: Critical Aspects of English and Australian Law' (2000) 8(1) *International Insolvency Review* 1.

Keay Andrew, R., *McPherson's Law of Company Liquidation*, London: Sweet & Maxwell (2001).

Keay, A., 'The Director's Duty to Take into Account the Interests of Company Creditors: When is it Triggered?' (2001) 25 *Melbourne University Law Review* 315.

Keay, A., 'The Duty of Directors to Take Into Account Creditors' Interests: Has It Any Role to Play?' [2002] JBL 379.

Lynch, I., 'Doing Business with the Devil – Insolvency, Commercial Misconduct and the Criminal Law' [1999] *Insolvency Lawyer* 119.

McCoid, J., 'Bankruptcy Preferences and Efficiency: An Expression of Doubt' (1981) 67 *Virginia Law Review* 247.

Miller, G., 'Transactions Prejudicing Creditors' [1998] Conv 362.

Milman, D. and Parry, R., 'Challenging Transactional Integrity on Insolvency: An Evaluation of the New Law' (1997) 48 NILQ 24.

Milman, D., 'Security for Costs: Principles and Pragmatism in Corporate Litigation' in B.A.K. Rider (ed.), *The Realm of Company Law*, London: Kluwer Law International (1998).

Milman, D. and Parry, R., 'A study of the operation of transactional avoidance mechanisms in corporate insolvency practice', Oxford: GTI Specialist Publishers (1998).

Mokal, R., 'Priority as Pathology: The Pari Passu Principle Myth' (2001) 60 CLJ 581.

Mokal, R. and Ho, L., 'Consideration, Characterisation and Evaluation: Transactions at an Undervalue After *Phillips v Brewin Dolphin*' (2001) 1 JCLS 359.

Oditah, F., 'Wrongful Trading' [1990] LMCLQ 205.

O'Donovan, J., 'Corporate Insolvency: Policies, Perspectives and Reform' (1990) 3 *Corporate and Business Law Journal* 1.

Otter, K., 'Influential Desire – Dominant Intention?' (1990) 3 (6) *Insolvency Intelligence* 42.

Parry, R., *Transaction Avoidance in Insolvencies*, Oxford: Oxford University Press (2001).

Pennington, R., *Pennington's Corporate Insolvency Law*, 2nd edn, London: Butterworths (1997).

Prentice, D.D., 'The Effect of Insolvency on Pre-Liquidation Transactions' in B. Pettet (ed), *Company Law in Change: Current Legal Problems*, London: Stevens (1987).

Prentice, D., 'Creditor's Interests and Director's Duties' (1990) 10 OJLS 265.

Prentice, D., 'Directors, Creditors and Shareholders' in E. McKendrick (ed.), *Commercial Aspects of Trusts and Fiduciary Obligations*, Oxford: Oxford University Press (1992).

Prentice, D., 'Corporate Personality, Limited Liability and the Protection of Creditors' in C. Rickett, and R. Grantham, *Corporate Personality in the 20th Century*, Oxford: Hart Publishing (1998).

Riley, C., 'Directors' duties and the interests of creditors' (1989) 10 Co Law 87.

Sappideen, R., 'Fiduciary Obligations to Corporate Creditors' [1991] JBL 365.

Sealy, L.S., 'Director's Wider Responsibilities – Problems Conceptual, Practical and Procedural' (1987) 13 *Monash University Law Review* 164.

Sealy, L.S., 'Personal Liability of Directors and Officers for Debts of Insolvent Corporations: A Jurisdictional Perspective (England)' in J. Ziegel, *Current Developments in International and Comparative Corporate Insolvency Law*, Oxford: Clarendon Press (1994).

Sealy, L.S. and Milman, D., *Annotated Guide to the Insolvency Legislation*, 5th edn, Bicester: CCH (1999).

Schulte, R., 'Enforcing wrongful trading as a standard of conduct for directors and a remedy for creditors: the special case of corporate insolvency' (1999) 20 Co Law 80.

Seligson, C., 'Preferences Under the Bankruptcy Act' (1961) 15 *Vanderbilt Law Review* 115.

Snaith, I., *The Law of Corporate Insolvency*, London: Waterlow Publishers (1990).

Verrill, J., 'Attacking Antecedent Transactions' (1993) 7 JIBL 485.

Walters, A., 'Directors' duties: the impact of the Company Directors' Disqualification Act 1986' (2000) 21 Co Law 110.

Weisberg, R., 'Commercial Morality, the Merchant Character and the History of the Voidable Preference' (1986) 39 *Stanford Law Review* 3.

Wishart, D., 'Models and Theories of Directors' Duties to Creditors' (1991) 14 *New Zealand Universities Law Review* 323.

Worthington, S., 'Directors' Duties, Creditors' Rights and Shareholder Intervention' (1991) 18 *Melbourne University Law Review* 121.

Part IX

Misconduct

It is impossible and, therefore, most unfortunate and regrettable that one cannot write a book on insolvency without mentioning in some detail the issue of misconduct. Unfortunately, insolvency law is littered with instances, some of them very public and major, of the misconduct of persons connected with companies which have failed and bankrupts and their associates. Those most often at fault are the officers of companies, probably because of the fact that they have more opportunity than others to commit wrongs and significant sections of this Part consider the actions of such officers. In the 1990s the misconduct of Robert Maxwell in running his corporate empire came to light. Perhaps the most celebrated instances in recent times have been the claims of misconduct surrounding the problems of the huge American companies, Enron and WorldCom, both of which entered Chapter 11 bankruptcy in the United States.

One of the purposes of most insolvent administrations, particularly liquidations and bankruptcies, is to permit the investigation of the affairs of insolvents.[1] This is necessary as a matter of public interest. The public must be satisfied that there has been no commercial impropriety or commission of fraud by insolvents who have gone bankrupt, or, in relation to companies which have entered liquidation, by their officers or associates.[2] The investigative powers of office-holders in insolvency administrations were extended in the public interest by the Insolvency Act to overcome dishonesty and malpractice (*Bishopsgate Investment Management Ltd v Maxwell* [1992] 2 All ER 856 at 876; *Re Arrows Ltd (No4)* [1994] BCC 641 at 646). There is a public concern over the failure of companies, in particular, and there is a perceived need to safeguard the public from the

---

[1] See *British and Commonwealth Holdings plc (joint administrators) v Spicer & Oppenheim* [1993] BCLC 168 at 172 per Lord Slynn; Report of the Insolvency Law Review Committee, *Insolvency Law & Practice* ('the Cork Report') at para 194.

[2] See Cork Report at para 198(h).

failures of companies, especially large and well-known ones (*Bishopsgate Investment Management Ltd v Maxwell* [1992] 2 All ER 856 at 871).

It is a shame that it is not unusual for office-holders, when investigating the affairs of an insolvent, to discover that the bankrupt or the company's directors acted improperly prior to, or after, the advent of insolvency. The fact that this state of affairs exists has meant that insolvency law provides for criminal and regulatory sanctions which can be applied 'on behalf of society at large against individual debtors, or against the directors or managers of insolvent companies, whose conduct amounts to a violation of, or a sufficiently serious threat to, the norms of acceptable commercial behaviour'.[3]

This Part examines the civil and criminal proceedings which may be available in relation to misconduct, committed either before or after the advent of insolvency and sometimes even after the commencement of a formal insolvency administration. In some ways fraudulent and wrongful trading could have been handled in this Part, as they involve, to a large extent, forms of malpractice, but we felt that it was more appropriate to consider them in Part VIII. This Part is dedicated to a consideration of misfeasance in relation to the affairs of insolvent companies, the disqualification of company directors and the prosecution of offences, particularly in liquidations and bankruptcies. It is possible to regard those against whom bankruptcy restrictions orders have been made as being guilty of misconduct. However, such orders have been discussed in some detail in Part V and the discussion need not be repeated.

Throughout this Part, except where indicated to the contrary, any reference to 'the Act' or to section numbers will be references to the Insolvency Act 1986. Except where indicated to the contrary, any reference to 'the Rules' or rule numbers will be references to the Insolvency Rules 1986 (SI 1986/1925).

---

[3] I.F. Fletcher, 'Juggling with the Norms: the Conflict Between Collective and Individual Rights under Insolvency Law' in R Cranston, *Making Commercial Law*, Oxford: Clarendon Press (1997) at 394.

Chapter 44

Misfeasance[1]

44.1 Introduction

It is an undoubted fact that many cases of misconduct over the years have been committed by persons connected with companies that have entered insolvent liquidation. In order to overcome the problem of costs and delay which applies to the pursuit of legal proceedings against such persons in relation to their defalcations, companies legislation has provided for many years an alternative summary procedure which was designed to facilitate the recovery of assets improperly dealt with and to enable the liquidator to obtain compensation for misconduct which had caused loss to the company (*Re Kingston Cotton Mill Co (No. 2)* [1896] 2 Ch 279 at 283, 288; *Re London & Colonial Finance Co* (1897) 13 TLR 576). The present provision is section 212 of the Act and is known as the misfeasance section.

It must be noted that there is no distinct wrongful act known to the law as misfeasance; section 212 and its ancestors are purely procedural in effect (*Re B Johnson & Co (Builders) Ltd* [1955] Ch 634 at 648).[2] The provision does not create new rights or liabilities, but is simply intended to provide a summary mode of enforcing rights which, apart from the section, could have been enforced by the company[3] prior to liquidation, or which came into existence by virtue of special statutory provisions which apply in winding up (*Re Home & Colonial Insurance Co* [1930] 1 Ch 102 at 132).

---

[1] For further discussion, see F. Oditah, 'Misfeasance proceedings against company directors' [1992] LMCLQ 207; S. Griffin, *Personal Liability and Disqualification of Company Directors*, Oxford: Hart Publishing (1999) at 23–38; A. Keay, *McPherson's Law of Company Liquidation*, London: Sweet & Maxwell (2001) at 822–35.

[2] See *Cavendish-Bentinck v Fenn* (1887) 12 App Cas 652 at 669; *Re City Equitable Fire Insurance Co* [1925] Ch 407 at 527; *Re Buena Vista Motors Pty Ltd* [1971] 1 NSWLR 72 at 74.

[3] Rights personal to a creditor or contributory in an individual capacity could not be enforced: *Re Hill's Waterfall Estate Co* [1896] 1 Ch 947.

The court is entitled under section 212 to examine the conduct of certain persons and, if there has been any misfeasance or breach of fiduciary or other duty in relation to a company in liquidation, it may order the restoration, repayment or accounting of money or property or the contribution of such sum to the company by way of compensation in respect of the misfeasance or breach of duty.

'Misfeasance' is an extremely broad term (*Re B Johnson & Co (Builders) Ltd* [1955] Ch 634). In *Walker v Wimborne* ((1976) 3 ACLR 529) it was said that:

> However, it is well established that 'misfeasance' in this context means 'misfeasance in the nature of a breach of trust, that is to say, it refers to something which the officer . . . has done wrongly by misapplying or retaining in his own hands any moneys of the company or by which the company's property has been wasted, or the company's credit improperly pledged' (at 533).

In addition it is now clear that negligence will be covered by section 212 (*Re B Johnson & Co (Builders) Ltd* [1955] Ch 634; *Re Simmon Box (Diamonds) Ltd* [2002] BCC 82 (CA)), because the section refers not only to misfeasance, but also 'breach of any fiduciary or other duty'.

The conduct that is alleged to constitute misfeasance does not have to occur when the company is insolvent (*Gamble and Mann v Hoffman* (1997) 15 ACLC 1314 at 1326), providing that the company is in liquidation when proceedings for misfeasance are instigated.

44.2 The applicant

The following are permitted to apply for a court examination of conduct: the official receiver, the liquidator, or any creditor or contributory of the company (section 212(3)). Importantly, a contributory is only allowed to apply when leave of the court is secured (section 212(5)).

Most frequently, the liquidator is the applicant. Creditors might apply when a liquidator fails to do so for one reason or another. *Re Westlowe Storage and Distribution Ltd* ([2000] BCC 851; [2000] 2 BCLC 590) represents a recent example of where a creditor brought proceedings and was successful.

44.3 The respondent

Any of the following may be the subject of an application: a past or present officer of the company; a former liquidator of the company; an administrative receiver of the company; and any other person who is or has been concerned, or taken part, in the promotion, formation or management of the company (section 212(1)).

Before proceedings can be taken against a former liquidator,[4] the leave of the court must be obtained (section 212(4)).

> In *Re Centralcrest Engineering Ltd* [2000] BCC 727, a liquidator was found liable for misfeasance. The misfeasance consisted of first allowing the company to continue to trade without securing the sanction of either the court or the liquidation committee and second not terminating trading when it was clear that the liquidator should have terminated trading and sold the assets as quickly as possible.

Commonly the person who is the respondent to proceedings is an officer of the company.

As was discussed in Chapter 7,[5] the Insolvency Act now, as a result of the enactment of the Enterprise Act 2002, provides a dedicated provision, para 75 of Schedule B1, that addresses misconduct of administrators. Under this provision the court may examine the conduct of an administrator on the application of the official receiver and the following who are connected with the company, namely: the administrator; liquidator; a creditor; or a contributory.

The importance of para 75 is that it permits a creditor or guarantor of the company to bring an action directly against the administrator even after the administrator has been discharged, if, for example, he or she had conducted a sale of the company's business at an undervalue or carried on the day-to-day management of the company negligently. Such conduct will have a knock-on effect on the potential realisations of all the creditors.

44.4 The conduct

Respondents may be liable if they have 'misapplied, retained or become accountable for money or property of the company, or guilty of misfeasance or breach of any fiduciary or other duty'. The inclusion of the words 'breach of duty' will enable claims against directors for breach of the duty of care and skill to be the basis for a misfeasance action (*Re D'Jan of London Ltd* [1993] BCC 646; [1994] 1 BCLC 561; *Re Simmon Box (Diamonds) Ltd* [2000] BCC 275), as well as a breach of fiduciary duties, such as in *Re Westlowe Storage and Distribution Ltd* ([2000] BCC 851; [2000] 2 BCLC 590), where a director was held liable for diverting a contract from the company to another company.

---

[4] For a discussion of the liability of these office-holders for negligence under section 212, see K. de Kerloy, 'Assessing a liquidator' or administrator's liability for negligence and proceedings under section 212 of the Insolvency Act 1986' (1999) 15 IL&P 79.

[5] Above at 93.

44.5 Orders

If a case is successfully made out, then an order for repayment or contribution, together with interest, would ordinarily follow as a matter of course. But, a court is not obliged to make an order: it has a discretion (*Re Westlowe Storage and Distribution Ltd*). A court has a discretion to award only part of the compensation sought (*Re Home and Colonial Insurance Co Ltd* [1930] 1 Ch 102). Courts are able to order compensation as they think fit. In claims founded on negligence a court could award compensation provided that the negligence caused loss or damage (*Re Simmon Box (Diamonds) Ltd* [2002] BCC 82 (CA)).

If a court decides to make an order, it may make one of the kinds of orders set out in section 212(3) or, as far as administrators are concerned, in para 75(4) of Schedule B1, such as compelling restoration of property taken from the company. The order will usually provide that the respondent pay the amount of the loss suffered as a result of the misconduct (*Bishopsgate Investment Management Ltd v Maxwell (No2)* [1993] BCLC 814; [1993] BCC 120, affirmed on appeal: [1994] 2 All ER 261; [1993] BCLC 1282 (CA)).

Courts may decide to apportion liability between one or more respondents. Where several officers were charged with responsibility for the same wrongful act, they have usually been made jointly and severally liable (*Cavendish-Bentinck v Fenn* (1887) 12 App Cas 652 at 661; *Re North Australian Territory Co; Archer's Case* [1892] 1 Ch 323 at 341).

If a liquidator has an award in his or her favour and succeeds in recovering money pursuant to the order, he or she will be entitled to deduct the costs of the action and then the money remaining is available to any holders of charges over the present and future property of the company. Unsecured creditors will be allowed to share in what is left (*Re Anglo-Austrian Printing & Publishing Co* [1985] 2 Ch 891). This might entail the unsecured creditors receiving nothing or a reduced dividend from a recovery. As a consequence, a liquidator may be inclined to refrain from taking misfeasance proceedings. Floating chargeholders, as creditors, may themselves bring proceedings under either section 212 or para 75. Of course, they will only do so where a shortfall exists.

44.6 Relief

Courts are permitted to grant relief to a respondent to misfeasance proceedings, under section 727 of the Companies Act 1985. This provision permits a court, wholly or in part, to relieve officers from liability in relation to proceedings for negligence, default, breach of duty, or breach of trust. The defence does not have to be specifically pleaded (*Re Kirby's Coaches Ltd* [1991] BCC 130). The courts are only allowed to exercise this jurisdiction if they are satisfied that the person who sought relief had acted honestly and reasonably and that, having regard to all the circumstances of the case, he or she ought fairly to be excused (*Re J Franklin & Sons Ltd* [1937] 4 All ER 43).

On some occasions the respondent to a misfeasance proceeding has been given relief pursuant to section 727, either wholly or in part, subject to the condition that he or she makes good the full amount for which he or she was liable.[6] This only will occur if it is not detrimental to the interests of creditors and the members themselves had acquiesced to the commission of the wrongful act.

---

[6] See *Re Sunlight Incandescent Gas Lamp Co* (1900) 16 TLR 535; *Re Home & Colonial Insurance Co* [1930] 1 Ch 102. For a recent case where the section was not applied, see *Re Westlowe Storage and Distribution Ltd* [2000] 2 BCLC 590.

Chapter 45

Disqualification of Directors[1]

45.1 Introduction

There have been provisions covering the disqualification of directors since the Companies Act 1929; however, it was not until the advent of the Company Directors' Disqualification Act 1986 ('CDDA') that disqualification became a significant part of the law. This legislation was enacted in response to the recommendations of the Cork Report, which had stated that:

> To provide proper safeguards to the general public, the law must also provide that those whose conduct has shown them to be unfitted to manage the affairs of a company with limited liability shall, for a specified period, be prohibited from doing so.[2]

The aim of disqualification is to protect the public (*Re Migration Services International Ltd* [2000] BCC 1095). The effect of a disqualification order is that the relevant person is not able to act as a director, a liquidator, or administrator of a company, a receiver or manager of a person's property or involved in any way with the promotion, formation or management of a company for a set period without the leave of the court (CDDA, section 1). The disqualification period will depend on what basis the disqualification order was made. For some grounds, such as persistent breaches of companies legislation, the term of disqualification is 5 years maximum (CDDA, section 3(5)), whereas if a court has held that a director is unfit to hold office the term is a minimum of 2 years and a maximum of 15 years (CDDA, section 6(4)).

---

[1] For further discussion, see S. Griffin, *Personal Liability and Disqualification of Company Directors* at 133–223; R.M. Goode, *Principles of Corporate Insolvency Law*, 2nd edn, at 477–93; A. Keay, *McPherson's Law of Company Liquidation*, London: Sweet & Maxwell (2001) at 845–51.

[2] At para 1808.

While the disqualification of directors has not been seen traditionally as part of the insolvency process, it can well occur as a direct result of the insolvency of companies and it is a common occurrence and, therefore, it warrants some consideration.

45.2 The nature of proceedings

Although an order pursuant to an application made under the CDDA will impose a form of penalty on a director, proceedings are classified as regulatory and civil in nature and not criminal proceedings (*Re Westminster Property Management Ltd* [2000] 2 BCLC 396 (CA); *DC, HS and AD v United Kingdom* [2000] BCC 710 (European Court of Human Rights)). Consequently, Articles 6, 8 and 13 of the European Convention for the Protection of Human Rights are not available to the defendant to prevent the use of answers which he or she gave in interviews with the official receiver, in the course of the latter's investigations into the causes behind the collapse of a company in proceedings for disqualification (*DC, HS and AD v United Kingdom* [2000] BCC 710 (European Court of Human Rights); *WGS and MSLS v United Kingdom* [2000] BCC 719 (European Court of Human Rights)).

45.3 The bases for orders

Disqualification may occur in three different ways. First, those who are undischarged bankrupts[3] or (from the time when the bankruptcy provisions of the Enterprise Act take effect) subject to a bankruptcy restriction order are disqualified automatically (CDDA, section 11(1)). This also applies to those who are in default in relation to payment under a county court administration order (and the court revokes the order) (CDDA, section 12). Second, where directors of insolvent companies are found by a court to be unfit to be concerned in the management of a company, the court must disqualify (CDDA, section 6).[4] Section 6 has, in fact, turned out to be

---

[3] For a consideration of the length of disqualification periods, see A. Mithani, 'Determining disqualification periods – what the court should take into account' (1998) 14 IL&P at 318.

[4] During the 2001–2002 year, there were 548 disqualifications under section 6 (DTI's Company Report 2001–2002, p 38). There were also 1,213 directors disqualified by undertaking. This is discussed later.

the most important provision in the CDDA, and is discussed under the next heading in more detail. Third, where a court makes an order as a matter of discretion (CDDA, sections 2–5, 8, 10).[5]

45.4 Directors of insolvent companies found to be unfit

45.4.1 *General*

The primary purpose of section 6 is clearly to be the protection of the public. In *Re Lo-Line Electric Motors Ltd* ([1988] Ch. 477) it was said that the provision was:

> [T]o protect the public against the future conduct of companies by persons whose past records as directors of insolvent companies have shown them to be a danger to creditors and others (at 486).

Also, the court said that the rights of the individual must be protected (at 486). Following these comments, in *Re Sevenoaks Stationers (Retail) Ltd* ([1994] Ch 164) Dillon LJ opined that the section was designed to protect the public and with particular concern for potential creditors of companies (at 176).

Recently, the Court of Appeal (Criminal Division) in *R v Evans* ([2000] BCC 901) emphasised that the aim of director disqualification is the protection of the public. Also, the Court said that the period of disqualification is to reflect the level of risk to the public that a person poses; disqualification is not designed to exact punishment (at 903).

The Secretary of State for Trade and Industry[6] initiates proceedings and will seek a finding from a court under section 6 that a person is unfit for office. For a case to be established it must be proved that the person against whom proceedings have been issued is or has been a director of a company that has at any time become insolvent, and this means that the company went into liquidation and had insufficient assets to pay its debts and other liabilities (including the expenses of winding up (section 6(2)(a)), the company was subject to administration (section 6(2)(b)) or an administrative receiver had been appointed to the company (section 6(2)(c)).

Besides considering the actions of the director in relation to the company that had become insolvent and, perhaps, sparked the proceedings, a court may have regard to the director's conduct in relation to other companies

---

[5] During the 2001–2002 year, there were 152 disqualifications under sections 2–5, 16 under section 8 and 0 under section 10 (DTI's Company Report 2001–2002, p 38).

[6] The Secretary of State may request the official receiver to initiate proceedings: *In re Pantmaenog Timber Company Ltd*, *The Times*, November 14, 2000, Judge Weeks QC (sitting as a High Court judge).

(CDDA, section 6(1)(b)). But a court will only be concerned with evidence of the conduct of the person as a director, including conduct as a shadow or *de facto* director (CDDA, section 6(3)),[7] therefore ruling out any evidence concerning conduct that related to other positions held by the director, or other situations in which he or she found himself or herself

Before a court will hold that a person is not fit to be a director and should be subject to disqualification, the Secretary of State must establish that the person is culpable. Stating what circumstances will lead a person to be regarded as culpable is not easy for there is some divergence in the cases. It has been stated that commercial misjudgment does not constitute culpability, yet a lack of commercial probity and, in extreme cases, gross negligence or total incompetence, would be regarded as culpable conduct (*Re Lo-Line Electric Motors Ltd* [1988] Ch 477 at 486). In other instances courts have said that the one against whom proceedings have been brought must have been involved in serious failures (*Re Bath Glass Ltd* (1988) 4 BCC 130 at 133) or guilty of breaching standards of commercial morality so that the public was in danger if the person continued in office (*Re Dawson Print Group Ltd* (1987) 3 BCC 322 at 324). Conversely, some judges have said that higher standards should be expected and have held that directors are unfit where less than serious conduct has occurred. Some courts have placed emphasis on the risk to which creditors were put rather than concentrating on commercial morality (*Re Stanford Services Ltd* (1987) 3 BCC 326 at 334). An example of unfitness might, according to *Secretary of State for Trade and Industry v McTighe* ([1997] BCC 224 at 231 (CA)), be the adoption of a policy of non-payment of a certain class of creditor. Recently, Lawrence Collins J in *Re Bradcrown Ltd* ([2001] 1 BCLC 547; [2002] BCC 428) made it clear that directors could be disqualified if they just did what they were told and, consequently, abdicated their responsibility. In *Bradcrown*, the director who was disqualified had taken no steps to satisfy himself that the transactions, the subject of the disqualification hearing, were in the interests of his company. This is another indication that courts will no longer tolerate directors pleading passivity, although in *Bradcrown* it was observed that if a director was given professional advice and that failed to draw to his or her attention that transactions were improper, he or she may not be regarded as unfit, or the giving of such advice might lead to a reduction in the disqualification period. It is impossible to lay down a particular set of circumstances or a standard as each case must depend on its own facts.[8] This is probably one of the reasons for the large volume of cases that have gone to the courts.

---

[7] See *Re Richborough Furniture Ltd* [1996] 1 BCLC 507; *Secretary of State for Trade and Industry v Hickling* [1996] Ch 678; *Secretary of State for Trade and Industry v Deverell* [2000] 2 BCLC 133; [2000] BCC 1057.

[8] S. Griffin, *Personal Liability and Disqualification of Company Directors* at 165. The learned author sets out a number of categories of conduct as common examples which may ordinarily lead a court to concluding that a person is unfit (at 167–78).

Whether a person is to be regarded as unfit will depend on the factors contained in Parts 1 and II of Schedule 1 to the CDDA (section 9(1)). The matters that are set out in Part I are to be considered in all cases and Part II matters are to be taken into account where the company was insolvent. Matters in Part I include: the person being guilty of misfeasance; the extent of the person's responsibility for the company's failure to keep accounts in accord with section 221 of the Companies Act 1985; and the extent of the person's responsibility for the failure of the directors to prepare annual accounts. The matters in Part II include: the extent of the person's responsibility for the causes of the company's insolvency; the extent of the person's responsibility for the giving of preferences within section 239;[9] and the person's failure to cooperate (under section 235) with the office-holder appointed because of the insolvency of the respondent's company.[10]

45.4.2 *The length of disqualification*

Where a court comes to the conclusion that a director is unfit, it must impose a term of disqualification. The range that can be considered is from 2 years to not more than 15 years (CDDA, section 6(4)). The courts have a discretion as to what period they will impose, but the discretion is to be exercised in accordance with relevant principles (*Secretary of State for Trade and Industry v McTighe* [1997] BCC 224 (CA)). The following will be taken into account by a court: the seriousness of the conduct; the extent of the conduct; and the role the person played in the company.[11] In *Re Sevenoaks (Retail) Ltd*[12] the Court of Appeal laid down guidelines for the setting of disqualification periods. The Court said that there are three categories.

First, there were particularly serious cases[13] for which a period of in excess of 10 years should be attached. Second, where there were cases which involved serious matters, but which did not warrant the top penalties, a disqualification period of between 6 and 10 years was appropriate.[14] Third, the range of 2 to 5 years was to be applied to cases where the misconduct established was not of a particularly serious kind (at 174). It is

---

[9] See *Re Funtime Ltd* [2000] 1 BCLC 247.

[10] A. Keay, *McPherson's Law of Company Liquidation* at 849.

[11] S. Griffin, *Personal Liability and Disqualification of Company Directors* at 180.

[12] [1991] Ch 164 and approved of on many occasions, e.g., *Secretary of State for Trade and Industry v McTighe* [1997] BCC 224 (CA).

[13] Such as fraudulent trading, cases of dishonesty and persistent contraventions of statutory requirements.

[14] For an example of the invoking of this category, see *Re Migration Services International Ltd* [2000] BCC 1095.

permissible for a court, in coming to a decision, to weigh up the conduct of the person in the section 6 proceedings, the fact that he or she gave false evidence (*R v Morrgate Metals Ltd* [1995] BCLC 503) and the person's failure to cooperate with the official receiver (*Secretary of State for Trade and Industry v McTighe* [1997] BCC 124 (CA)).

45.5 Procedure

There have been attempts to try to reduce the costs and the time involved in obtaining a disqualification. One instance is the use, in the 1990s, of formal undertakings given by directors who were targeted for disqualification proceedings. Directors would give undertakings to the Secretary of State that they would not act as a director for a specified period of time. It was questionable whether undertakings were either effective or in the public interest, in that a decision would be made on a director's disqualification without any consideration by a court of the director's actions and circumstances.[15] But since the advent of the Insolvency Act 2000, undertakings have been given statutory recognition. Section 1A(1) of the CDDA now provides that the Secretary of State may accept an undertaking, which may include an agreement by a person not to act as: a director; a receiver of a company's property; an insolvency practitioner; or in any way take part in the management of a company unless leave of the court is secured. The period in the undertaking must be for at least 2 years and be no more than 15 years (CDDA, section 1A(2)). According to section 1A(4), the Secretary of State may take into account, in deciding whether to accept an undertaking, factors other than criminal convictions notwithstanding the person giving the undertaking may be criminally liable in respect of those matters.

The Secretary of State must, before she may accept an undertaking, judge that the conduct of the director makes him or her unfit to be involved in the management of a company (CDDA sections 7(2A), 8(2A)(a) and 9(1)(a)). Also the Secretary must come to the view that accepting an undertaking is in the public interest (CDDA sections 7(2A), 8(2A)(b)).[16]

It is possible for a court order to vary an undertaking that has been given (CDDA, section 8A(1)).

---

[15] See the comments of Mummery LJ in *Secretary of State for Trade and Industry v Davies* [1998] BCC 11.

[16] During the 2001–2002 year there were 1,213 disqualifications on undertaking under section 6 (DTI's Company Report 2001–2002, p 38).

45.6 Leave to continue

A director who has been found unfit under section 6 of the CDDA, and disqualified, may apply to the court under section 17 of the CDDA to seek the court's leave to continue to act notwithstanding the disqualification order. It is customary for the judge who hears the disqualification application to also hear an application for leave.[17] In considering an application for leave, the courts have an unfettered discretion as to whether they order leave and on what conditions. Before granting leave, they must ensure that there is no danger to the public (*Re Grayan Building Services Ltd* [1995] Ch 241). The decision to grant leave is not taken lightly.

---

[17] See *Re TLL Realisations Ltd* [2000] BCC 998.

Chapter 46

Offences

46.1 Introduction

In undertaking investigations, an office-holder might discover improper or dishonest conduct, on the part of the insolvent company's officers, others associated with the company, the bankrupt or his or her associates or even a former office-holder who administered the insolvent's affairs previously, and it might be felt that this conduct should be the subject of prosecution.

While taking action for offences committed is not at the forefront of office-holders' thinking, because they are primarily focusing on ascertaining what assets the insolvent had and recovering those in the hands of others, office-holders have a public responsibility to report actions that constitute offences. For instance, liquidators in compulsory liquidations are required to report to the official receiver any past or present officer or member of the company who has been guilty of an offence (section 218(3)). In ensuring that potential wrongdoers are deterred, the Cork Report referred to the need to bring properly prepared prosecutions against miscreants and for the application of appropriate sanctions.[1] The offences exist not only to deter, but also to punish and to encourage people to assist the office-holder in discharging his or her duties.

There are a large number of offences that can potentially be committed both before and after the commencement of a formal insolvency administration and some of these have been mentioned at various points elsewhere in this book. While some offences are provided for in the primary statute, the Insolvency Act, others can be found in other legislation, such as the Companies Act 1985[2] or the Theft Acts. It is not possible for us to deal with

---

[1] Cmnd 8558, 1982, Chapter 48.

[2] For a discussion of offences under the Companies Act 1985, see A. Keay, *McPherson's Law of Company Liquidation*, London: Sweet & Maxwell (2001) at 860–1.

all of the offences that might be committed. This is partly because of the volume of offences, but also because of the fact that different offences can be committed in relation to different kinds of insolvency administration. We will focus on those offences that might be regarded as the most common and the most important, and those that are found in the Insolvency Act. Although we will limit our coverage of the number of offences, we will also have to restrict the scope of the discussion. More specialised texts deal with offences in more detail.[3] The offences that are covered can be divided into those that can be committed in relation to bankruptcy and those that can be committed in relation to winding up.

46.2 Procedure

Sections 218 and 350 provide how offences under the Insolvency Act are to be initiated. These sections provide a welcome change to the situation that existed prior to 1986, when the process was fragmented and inefficient.

Section 218 states that if it appears to a court in the course of a compulsory winding up that a former or existing officer of the company has been guilty of an offence for which criminal sanctions apply, the court may direct the liquidator to refer the matter to the prosecuting authority, namely the Director of Public Prosecutions (DPP) (section 218(1)(2)(a)). The court may take this action on its own motion or on the application of a person interested in the winding up, including the liquidator, although as already mentioned, section 218(3) requires a liquidator to report to the official receiver the fact that a former or existing officer of the company has been guilty of an offence. It is probable that the official receiver should refer the matter to the DPP without the need for any reference to the court.[4]

Liquidators in voluntary liquidations must, if the same circumstances exist as in section 218(3), report the matter to the DPP. In addition, the liquidator is to furnish to the DPP such information as the DPP requires and provide access to facilities for inspecting and taking copies of documents under the control of the liquidator (section 218(4)). The court may, where it appears in the course of a voluntary winding up that any past or present officer of the company, or any member of it, have been guilty of criminal conduct and the liquidator has not made the aforementioned

---

[3] For instance, A. Keay, *McPherson's Law of Company Liquidation* at 852–61; I.F. Fletcher, *The Law of Insolvency*, 3rd edn, London: Sweet & Maxwell (2002) at 349–70 and 699–705; E. Bailey, H. Groves, and C. Smith, *Corporate Insolvency Law and Practice*, 2nd edn, London: Butterworths (2001) at 590–6; C. Berry, E. Bailey and S. Schaw-Miller, *Personal Insolvency Law – Law and Practice*, 3rd edn, London: Butterworths (2001) at 627–38.

[4] L. S. Sealy and D. Milman, *Annotated Guide to the Insolvency Legislation*, 5th edn, Bicester: CCH (1999) at 257.

report to the DPP, direct the liquidator to make a report. This action may be taken either on the court's own motion or as a result of an application by a person interested in the winding up (section 218(6)).

If the liquidator does make a report to the DPP, the DPP may refer the matter to the Secretary of State for Trade and Industry for further inquiry and the Secretary of State is to investigate the matter which has been referred as well as any other matters relating to the affairs of the company and which are felt to be in need of investigation (section 218(5)). Where either the DPP or the Secretary of State initiate criminal proceedings following a section 218 report, section 219(3) requires the liquidator and every past and present officer and agent of the company, except any defendant to criminal prosecution, to give to the DPP or Secretary of State all reasonable assistance in connection with the proceedings.

Likewise in bankruptcy, prosecutions may only be instituted by the Secretary of State, or by or with the consent of the DPP (section 350(5)).

46.3 Offences in liquidations

There are many offences of a procedural nature and they are not mentioned here, for example, the failure of a company, whose members passed a resolution to wind up, to give notice of the resolution in the *Gazette* within 14 days of the resolution (section 85(2)). The prosecutions relating to these offences must be heard in a summary fashion.

Like the balance of this chapter, this section is mainly concerned with offences under the Insolvency Act. The Companies Act 1985, for example, provides other offences which may be prosecuted. These offences are detailed in Schedule 24 to the Companies Act. The Schedule sets out the mode of prosecution together with the penalties that may be imposed. Also, a person may be charged with offences relating to the breaches of other legislation, such as section 18 of the Theft Act 1968, which provides that where a company contravenes section 15 of that Act by obtaining property by deception, any director or manager is guilty of an offence if the obtaining of the property was done with the consent or connivance of the director or manager.

The offences that are discussed here are, primarily, those contained in the Insolvency Act and the main focus is on those set out in sections 206–211. Any references to 'officers' in these provisions includes shadow directors.[5]

---

[5] For example, see section 206(3).

46.3.1 *Fraud in anticipation of winding up*

Former or existing officers (including shadow directors (section 206(3))) of the company are deemed to commit offences if, within the 12 months preceding the commencement of winding up, they perform certain fraudulent acts (section 206(1)), including concealing any part of the property of the company to the value of £500 or more (section 206(1)(a)), fraudulently removing company property to the value of £500 or more (section 206(1)(b)) and concealing or destroying company books or papers (section 206(1)(c)). A person is deemed to have committed an offence if, within the 12 months prior to commencement of winding up, or after the commencement of winding up, that person has been or is privy to the actions of officers which involve (section 206(2)):

- concealing, destroying, mutilating or falsifying books or papers affecting or relating to the company's property or affairs;
- making any false entry in any book or paper affecting or relating to the company's property or affairs;
- fraudulently parting with, altering or making omissions in any document affecting or relating to the company's property or affairs.

Furthermore, a person is deemed to have committed an offence if, after the commencement of winding up, the person is privy to the actions of officers which involve any activity of officers mentioned in section 206(1) and that is outlawed (section 206(2)).

Anyone who takes in pawns or pledges, or otherwise receives property of the company where the one pawning, pledging or disposing of the property does so in circumstances which amount to an offence pursuant to section 206(1)(f), commits an offence if he or she (the one receiving the property) knew the property to be pawned, pledged or disposed of in breach of section 206(1)(f) (section 206(5)).

According to section 430 and Schedule 10, the penalties for a breach of section 206(1), sections 206(2) or 206(5) are seven years' imprisonment or a fine or both where the prosecution is brought on indictment. If a prosecution is brought summarily the penalty is six months' imprisonment or the statutory maximum or both.

Defences for those charged with offences under either sections 206(1) or 206(2) are found in section 206(4). Unusually defendants have the burden of proof and their defence must be established on the balance of probabilities (*Morton v Confer* [1963] 1 WLR 763; [1963] 2 All ER 765).

46.3.2 *Transactions in fraud of creditors*

Where a company winds up, an offence is committed by an officer if he or she either has made or caused to be made any gift or transfer of, or charge on, or has caused or connived at the levying of any execution against the company's property, or concealed or removed any part of the company's property since, or within two months before, the date of any unsatisfied judgment or order for the payment of money obtained against the company (section 207(1)).[6] There are two exceptions, namely a person is not guilty of an offence where the conduct referred to in section 207(1)(a) was committed more than five years before the commencement of winding up, or if it is proved that at the time of the allegedly criminal conduct there was no intent to defraud the company's creditors. The section 207 offence is punishable by two years' imprisonment or a fine or both where proceedings have been brought by indictment, and where initiated summarily the penalty is six months' imprisonment or a fine equal to the statutory maximum or both (sections 207(3) and 430, and Schedule 10).[7]

46.3.3 *Misconduct in the course of winding up*

Under section 208(1) former and existing officers commit offences if they:

- fail to disclose to the liquidator all of the company's property and the details surrounding the disposition of company property (except where this took place in the ordinary course of company business);
- fail to deliver up to the liquidator all parts of the property of the company of which they have control and/or custody and are required by law to deliver up;
- fail to deliver up all books and papers belonging to the company and under their control and required by law to deliver up;
- fail to disclose to the liquidator that a false debt has been proved in the winding up; or prevent, after the commencement of winding up, the production of any books and papers affecting the company's property or affairs.

Also, a person commits an offence if there is an attempt, after the commencement of winding up, to account for any part of the company's property by fictitious losses or expenses and the person is deemed to have committed the offence if the attempt was made at any creditors' meeting within the 12 months preceding the commencement of winding up (section 208(2)). A person has a defence to any of the first three offences in section 208(1) if he or she is able to prove that there was no intent to defraud and anyone charged with the last offence mentioned in section

---

[6] See *R v Enver* (unreported, Court of Appeal (Criminal Division), January 20, 2000, Auld LJ, Wright J and Judge Mellor) where the court considered a breach of section 207.
[7] The statutory maximum is £5,000 according to section 32 of the Magistrates' Courts Act 1980 as amended by section 17 of the Criminal Justice Act 1991.

208(1) has a defence if able to prove that there was no intent to conceal the state of affairs of the company or to defeat the law (section 208(4)).[8] Prison sentences have been imposed, such as in *Re Brevis* ([2001] All ER (D) 09) for a breach of section 208. After an appeal a director of a failed company was given a sentence of nine months, for failing to discover all company property to the liquidator.

46.3.4 *Falsification of company books*

An offence is committed by an officer or contributory if, during the course of a winding up, he or she destroys, mutilates, alters or falsifies any books, papers or securities, or makes or is privy to the making of any false or fraudulent entry in any register, book of account or document of the company with intent to defraud or deceive any person (section 209).[9]

46.3.5 *Material omissions from statement relating to company's affairs*

If any past or present officer of the company makes any material omission in any statement relating to the affairs of the company, an offence is committed (section 210(1)). Any person who, before winding up, makes a material omission in any statement is deemed to have committed an offence (section 210(2)). A defence is available if the defendant can prove that there was no intent to defraud (section 210(4)).[10]

46.3.6 *Fraudulent representations to creditors*

An offence is committed by past or present officers if they make false representations or commit any other fraud for the purpose of obtaining the consent of the company's creditors or any of them to an agreement with reference to the company's affairs or to the winding up (section 211(1)(a)). Section 211(1)(b) states that officers are deemed to have committed an offence if, prior to the winding up, they made any false representations or committed any other fraud for that purpose.[11]

---

[8] The same penalty prescribed for section 206 applies for a breach of section 208.
[9] The penalties are the same as for a contravention of section 206.
[10] The penalties are the same as for a contravention of section 206.
[11] The penalties are the same as for a contravention of section 206.

46.3.7 *Restriction on re-use of company name*

It is an offence under section 216 to re-use a company's name, except in limited circumstances, where the company has entered insolvent liquidation.[12] If a person breaches section 216 he or she may be liable to imprisonment or a fine or both (section 216(4)).[13]

46.3.8 *Offence of fraudulent trading*

It is an offence if a company carries on business with intent to defraud its creditors or the creditors of any other person, or for any fraudulent purpose (Companies Act, section 458). In such circumstances any person who is knowingly a party to this activity is liable to a fine or imprisonment or both.[14] The provision is the criminal counterpart to section 213 of the Act, the latter only dealing with civil liability.[15]

46.4 Offences in bankruptcy[16]

Offences in bankruptcy can be broadly divided into conduct that is regarded as criminal *per se* and those that are provided for in relation to breaches of restrictions that are imposed on bankrupts.

While the Cork Committee called for more prosecutions,[17] it is questionable whether we have actually seen more since the advent of the Insolvency Act. Nevertheless, the provision of offences is critical to a robust system and particularly to deter improper activity.

Importantly, a person commits an offence under the Company Directors' Disqualification Act 1986 if he or she acts as a director while an

---

[12] This means that at the time of entering liquidation, the company's assets are insufficient for the payment of its debts and other liabilities and the expense of winding up: section 216(7).

[13] See section 430 and Schedule 10 to the Act. The latter provides that the penalty is two years' imprisonment or a fine or both where the prosecution is on indictment and where the prosecution is initiated summarily then the penalty is six months' imprisonment or a statutory maximum fine (the statutory maximum is £5,000 according to section 32 of the Magistrates' Courts Act 1980 as amended by section 17 of the Criminal Justice Act 1991).

[14] The punishment (see Schedule 24 to the Companies Act 1985) is seven years' imprisonment or a fine or both where the prosecution is brought on indictment. Where the prosecution is brought summarily the punishment is six months' imprisonment or the statutory maximum or both. The statutory maximum is £5,000 according to section 32 of the Magistrates' Courts Act 1980 as amended by section 17 of the Criminal Justice Act 1991.

[15] See Chapter 42.

[16] For a detailed discussion of these offences, see I.F. Fletcher, *The Law of Insolvency*, 3rd edn, at 351–69.

[17] At para 1900.

undischarged bankrupt or (from the time that the bankruptcy provisions in the Enterprise Act 2002 operate) a bankruptcy restrictions order is in force in respect of him or her (section 11) and a bankrupt might be prosecuted under the general criminal law for such a breach.[18]

However, it is with the terms of the Insolvency Act with which we are mainly concerned and this is where the bulk of offences are to be found. A bankrupt can be prosecuted for anything done before bankruptcy and up to the point of discharge (section 350(3)). A prosecution may not be launched against a person whose bankruptcy has been annulled, but if the prosecution was initiated before the annulment, it can proceed (section 350(2)). The primary offences in bankruptcy are found in Chapter VI of Part IX in the Insolvency Act. The provisions that set out the offences allow the prosecution merely to prove the necessary conduct and the burden of proof is placed on the bankrupt as it is up to the bankrupt to establish why he or she should escape liability. Bankrupts are not guilty of certain of the offences in this Chapter of the Act if they can establish, on the balance of probabilities (*R v Carr-Briant* [1943] KB 607), that at the time of the conduct constituting the offence there was no intent to defraud or to conceal their state of affairs (section 352). So, in effect the initial burden of proof as far as fraud or concealment is concerned is shifted from the prosecution to the defendant (*R V Daniel* [2002] BPIR 1193).

It is not intended to consider each of the offences in depth although each will be mentioned. The penalties for the offences discussed below are found in Schedule 10 to the Act.

46.4.1 *Failure to disclose or inform of disposal of property*

Bankrupts commit offences if they do not to the best of their knowledge and belief disclose to their trustees all of the property that comprises their estate (section 353(1)(a)). Similarly, bankrupts are committing offences if they fail to inform their trustee of any property disposal that has taken property from their estate and give details of the disposal (section 353(1)(b)). There is no offence if the disposal is in the ordinary course of business that the bankrupt carries on, or it involves a payment of the ordinary expenses of the bankrupt or his or her family (section 353(2)).

46.4.2 *Concealment of property*

There are, in section 354, several offences that a bankrupt might commit in relation to property forming part of the bankrupt estate. Specifically, a bankrupt is guilty of an offence if he or she engages in any of the following:

---

[18] See I.F. Fletcher, *The Law of Insolvency*, 3rd edn, at 358–60.

- not delivering up possession of property that is part of the bankrupt estate and under his or her control and possession, when required by law to do so (section 354(1)(a));
- concealing either any debt due to or from him or her or property (presently £500 or more)[19] that is required to be delivered up (section 354(1)(b));
- doing something in the 12 months preceding the petition or during the period between the presentation of the bankruptcy petition and the commencement of bankruptcy, that would have been an offence under section 354(1)(b) if a bankruptcy order had been made (section 354(1)(c)).

In addition, a person commits an offence if he or she, during the period between the presentation of the bankruptcy petition and the commencement of bankruptcy, removed any property of the value of £500 or more, the possession of which had been or would be required to be given up (section 354(2)).

Finally, section 354(3) provides that a bankrupt is guilty of an offence where he or she, without reasonable excuse fails, on being required by the official receiver or the court, to account for the loss of a substantial part of his or her property in the 12 months preceding the petition's presentation or during the period between the presentation of the bankruptcy petition and the commencement of bankruptcy. An offence is also committed if the bankrupt is not able to provide a satisfactory explanation for the loss occurring. It has been held that this offence did not offend against the Human Rights Act 1998 (*R v Kearns* [2002] BPIR 1213).

46.4.3 *Improper dealings with records*

A bankrupt might be subject to a number of prosecutions relating to what was done with or to the bankrupt's papers and records. A bankrupt commits an offence if he or she does not deliver up possession of all books, papers and records that are under his or her control and possession when required by law to do so (section 355(1)).

Section 355(2)(3) provide that a bankrupt will be liable for a number of actions in relation to his or her records, including concealing, destroying, mutilating, falsifying or altering them or making any omissions in relation to them. The offence applies to doing this in the 12 months preceding the petition (two years if trading records[20] are concerned – section 355(4)) or during the period between the presentation of the bankruptcy petition and the commencement of bankruptcy.

---

[19] Insolvency Proceedings (Monetary Limits) Order (SI 1986/1996) Article 3, Schedule, Part II.
[20] These are defined in section 355(5).

46.4.4 *False statements*

Bankrupts commit offences if they make any material omissions in relation to any statement made pursuant to the bankruptcy provisions in the Act and covering his or her affairs (section 356(1)). Furthermore offences are committed by bankrupts if they are involved in falsehoods, including making false representations and knowing or believing that false debts have been proved in the bankruptcy (section 356(2)).

46.4.5 *Fraudulent disposal of property*

If a bankrupt makes, or has within the five years before the commencement of bankruptcy made, any gift or transfer, or given any charge on the bankrupt's property, an offence is committed (section 357(1)). This sounds harsh, but there is the defence in section 352 that at the time of the conduct constituting the offence there was no intent to defraud is available. A further offence is committed if the bankrupt conceals or removes any part of his or her property (before bankruptcy commences) or within two months before the date on which a judgment for the payment of money has been made against the bankrupt and the judgment was not satisfied before bankruptcy occurred (section 357(3)).

46.4.6 *Absconding with property*

It is an offence to leave or attempt to leave the jurisdiction with any property worth £500 or more and that had to be delivered up (section 358(a)).

46.4.7 *Dealing with property obtained on credit*

If a bankrupt disposed of property obtained on credit and not paid for, in the 12 months before the filing of a bankruptcy petition, or obtained during the period between the presentation of the bankruptcy petition and the commencement of bankruptcy, he or she commits an offence (section 359(1)). But a disposal in the ordinary course of business is saved by section 359(3).

46.4.8 *Obtaining credit*

A bankrupt is not permitted to obtain credit of £500 or more without disclosing his or her position to the credit provider (section 360(1)(a)). This provision applies to a bankrupt after his or her discharge if a bankruptcy restriction order is in force against that person (section 360(5)). When obtaining credit, a bankrupt against whom a bankruptcy restriction order is in force must disclose this to the credit provider (section 360(6)).

46.4.9 *Engaging in business*

It is an offence for a bankrupt to engage in a business under any name but his or her own and to enter into business transactions without disclosing that he or she was adjudged bankrupt (section 360(1)(b)).

46.4.10 *Failing to keep proper accounts*

If a bankrupt was involved in a business during the two years prior to the filing of the bankruptcy petition, then that bankrupt committed an offence if proper accounting records were not kept throughout the period and any part of the period between the presentation of the bankruptcy petition and the commencement of the bankruptcy period, or records were not retained (section 361(1)). A defence to this is where the bankrupt's unsecured liabilities at the commencement of bankruptcy did not exceed the sum of £20,000, or the bankrupt can prove that his or her omission was honest and excusable (section 361(2)). When the bankruptcy provisions of the Enterprise Act are operational this offence will be repealed as far as bankrupts are concerned, although such action might be taken into account when a court is deciding whether to make a bankruptcy restrictions order against a bankrupt (para 2(1)(a) of Schedule 4A).

46.4.11 *Gambling*

A bankrupt is guilty of an offence if he or she, in the two years prior to the fling of the bankruptcy petition, materially contributed to, or increased the extent of, his or her insolvency by gambling or by rash and hazardous speculations (section 362(1)(a)). The same applies if the bankrupt did this during the period between the presentation of the bankruptcy petition and the commencement of bankruptcy (section 362(1)(b)). The financial standing of the bankrupt at the relevant time will be taken into account in determining whether any speculations were rash and hazardous (section 362(2)).

This offence is one of strict liability notwithstanding the Human Rights Act 1998 and so there is no need to prove *mens rea* (*R v Muhamad, The Times*, August 16, 2002).

As with the previous offence, when the bankruptcy provisions of the Enterprise Act are operational this offence will be repealed as far as bankrupts are concerned, although such action might be taken into account when a court is deciding whether to make a bankruptcy restrictions order against a bankrupt (para 2(1)(j) of Schedule 4A).

46.5 Offences in other administrations

There are other offences that can be committed before or during the course of other forms of formal insolvency administration. Most of these are not as serious as those already considered, many of them imposing liability for the failure to execute some administrative action, such as the failure of an administrative receiver to send, within 14 days of vacation of office (except by death), notice to the Registrar of Companies (section 45(4)(5)).

46.6 The types of proceedings

Some offences can only be prosecuted by way of summary proceedings, while with other offences the DPP has a choice whether to indict or proceed to a summary disposition of the matter. More often than not, if there is a choice the preference will be for summary proceedings. Any information relating to an offence which is triable in a magistrates' court in England and Wales may be tried provided that it is laid at any time within three years after the commission of the offence and within 12 months of the time when evidence, in the opinion of the DPP or the Secretary of State, as the case may be, justifying proceedings comes to his or her knowledge (section 431(2)).

References

Bailey, E., Groves, H. and Smith, C., *Corporate Insolvency Law and Practice*, 2nd edn, London: Butterworths (2001).

Berry, C., Bailey, E. and Schaw-Miller, S., *Personal Insolvency Law – Law and Practice*, 3rd edn, London: Butterworths (2001).

de Kerloy, K., 'Assessing a liquidator's or administrator's liability for negligence and proceedings under section 212 of the Insolvency Act 1986' (1999) 15 *Insolvency Law and Practice* 79.

Finch, V., *Corporate Insolvency Law: Perspectives, and Principles*, Cambridge: Cambridge University Press (2002).

Fletcher, I.F., 'Juggling with the Norms: the Conflict Between Collective and Individual Rights under Insolvency Law' in R. Cranston, *Making Commercial Law*, Oxford: Clarendon Press (1997).

Fletcher, I.F., *The Law of Insolvency*, 3rd edn, London: Sweet & Maxwell (2002).

Goode, R.M., *The Principles of Corporate Insolvency Law*, 2nd edn, London: Sweet & Maxwell (1997).

Griffin, S., *Personal Liability and Disqualification of Company Directors*, Oxford: Hart Publishing (1999).

Keay, Andrew, R., *McPherson's Law of Company Liquidation*, London: Sweet & Maxwell (2001).

Lynch, I., 'Doing Business with the Devil–Insolvency, Commercial Misconduct and the Criminal Law' [1999] *Insolvency Lawyer* 119.

Milman, D., 'Curbing the Phoenix Syndrome' [1997] JBL 224.

Mithani, A. 'Determining disqualification periods – what the court should take into account' (1998) 14 *Insolvency Law and Practice* 318.

Oditah, F., 'Wrongful Trading' [1990] LMCLQ 205.

Oditah, F., 'Misfeasance proceedings against company directors' [1992] LMCLQ 207.

Ong, K., 'Disqualification of directors: a faulty regime?' (1998) 19 Co Law 7.

Sealy, L.S. and Milman, D., *Annotated Guide to the Insolvency Legislation*, 5th edn, Bicester: CCH (1999).

Walters, A., 'Directors' Disqualification' (2000) 21 Co Law 90.

Walters, A., 'Directors' Disqualification after the Insolvency Act 2000: The New Regime' [2001] *Insolvency Lawyer* 86.

Wheeler, S., 'Swelling the Assets for Distribution in Corporate Insolvency' [1993] JBL 256.

Index